From the Cold War
to a New Era

★

From the Cold War to a New Era

The United States and the Soviet Union,
1983–1991

Updated Edition

Don Oberdorfer

★

The Johns Hopkins University Press
Baltimore and London

Originally published in 1991 as *The Turn from the Cold War to a New Era: The United States and the Soviet Union, 1983–1990,* by Poseidon Press.
Johns Hopkins Paperbacks edition, 1998
9 8 7 6 5 4 3

The Johns Hopkins University Press
2715 North Charles Street
Baltimore, Maryland 21218-4363
www.press.jhu.edu

Designed by Liney Li

Library of Congress Cataloging-in-Publication Data

Oberdorfer, Don.
  [Turn]
  From the cold war to a new era : the United States and the Soviet Union, 1983–1991 / Don Oberdorfer. — Updated ed.
    p.   cm.
  Originally published: Turn. New York : Poseidon Press, c1991.
  Includes bibliographical references (p.   ) and index.
  ISBN 0-8018-5922-0 (alk. paper)
    1. United States—Foreign relations—Soviet Union. 2. Soviet Union—Foreign relations—United States. 3. United States—Foreign relations—1981–1989. 4. Soviet Union—Foreign relations—1975–1985. 5. Soviet Union—Foreign relations—1985–1991. I. Title.
E183.8.S65024   1998
327.73047—dc21   97-48386
                                                                      CIP

A catalog record for this book is available from the British Library.

CONTENTS

6

PREFACE TO THE JOHNS HOPKINS EDITION

For most of the second half of the twentieth century, the hostility between the United States and the Soviet Union was the central factor in international life, threatening mass destruction, dominating global politics, and affecting the lives, attitudes, and even nightmares of people everywhere. In the early 1980s, with the advent of a highly ideological U.S. administration, the conflict deepened. Then, with the arrival of a new Soviet leader who sought to reform a moribund system, spirited and often intense negotiations between the leaders of the two nations began to melt the ice between them. Slowly, the antagonism diminished, until eventually neither country felt threatened by the other.

By the dawning of the 1990s, a web of political and personal connections had been created between the leaders, governments, and peoples of the United States and the Soviet Union. When Iraq invaded Kuwait in August 1990, unprecedented cooperation between Washington and Moscow gave rise to hopes for a New World Order in which the two nuclear superpowers would stand together against international troublemakers. But before this could be tested, the Soviet Union collapsed from within.

This is the story of one of history's great turning points, in which two mortal enemies, with enough destructive power in their arsenals to annihilate each other and nearly everyone else, worked their way from hostility to reconciliation in less than a decade. How they did so will forever be regarded with fascination by those who examine our times.

For those of us who lived through those years, often amazed at each day's headlines, the events took place so rapidly and in such unexpected ways that even now the story is difficult to recall or understand. The great turnabout recorded here is a jumble of images and impressions in our minds: evil empire, Star Wars, KAL 007, Geneva, Reykjavik, Malta, the march of Soviet troops out of Afghanistan, the revolution in Eastern Europe, the collapse of the Berlin Wall, the abortive coup in Moscow, the final hauling down of the hammer-and-sickle flag. We can recall presidents, general secretaries, and some of their leading diplomats who played starring or supporting roles. But how did the change take place? What were the discussions and decisions that brought it about? This book is a step-by-step chronicle of what happened as the story unfolded.

As a journalist and student of history, I have long been fascinated with turning points, perhaps because they give meaning and more lasting importance to the rapid flow of daily events. My first book, *Tet!*, was a history of the turning point of the Vietnam War, the dramatic battle of 1968 that changed the way the United States responded to a drawn-out military conflict in Asia. Similarly, the developments between the United States and the Soviet Union in the period covered in these pages seemed to me another unmistakable turn of the hinge of history.

I began working on the book in 1988, at a time when Ronald Reagan and Mikhail Gorbachev had shown by word and deed that a new and more positive relationship was emerging between the powers. I continued my research and reporting into the first year and a half of the administration of George Bush, as communism fell in Eastern and Central Europe and came under heavy pressure in its Soviet homeland. I wrote the bulk of the manuscript for the original edition on a leave of absence from my post as *Washington Post* diplomatic correspondent in the second half of 1990, not knowing that only a year later the Soviet Union and its ruling Communist Party would disappear. Although the book was well received by reviewers, scholars, and the public, it was in a sense unfinished, because the story came to a natural conclusion with the epochal change in Moscow. The Johns Hopkins University Press edition provides an opportunity to extend the narrative to the final eighteen months of the Soviet Union.

As a working journalist, I covered many of the events described in this volume, including most of the ministerial and summit meetings, for the next day's or next weekend's newspapers. As a practitioner of contemporary history, I was able to go back later, for this book, to interview nearly all the key participants in both capitals during a time when events were still fresh in their minds. While underlying trends in the two nations are of basic importance, to a large degree this is a story of remarkable human actors on a mammoth stage and the ways they dealt with and thought about each other. Some of the most important aspects of the story told here do not appear in the records of the White House, the Kremlin, or in any diplomatic archive, for they deal with the personal impressions and subjective judgments underlying decisions and actions. Such ideas are rarely expressed in formal minutes.

On the U.S. side, my efforts were aided by longstanding acquaintance with many of the key American participants, who were willing to speak to me for this book candidly and often extensively. I recognize and gratefully acknowledge the help of each of these people, from presidents to Foreign Service officers, in the Acknowledgments. I wish to express my special gratitude to former Secretary of State George Shultz, now at the Hoover Institution at Stanford University, who took an interest in this project from my first discussion of it with him, and who spent a great deal of time patiently answering my questions in thirteen interviews over a period of sixteen months.

On the Soviet side, my work was greatly enhanced by the policy of *glasnost* which, in the context of improved U.S.-Soviet relations, made possible previously unprecedented access to USSR policymakers, particularly during a six-week visit to Moscow in early 1990, when openness was in full flower. To a greater extent than had earlier been the case with events of the immediate past, I was able to obtain from Soviet participants their description of Moscow's decisions and reactions. Those who assisted me in this respect are recognized in detail in the Acknowledgments. I also wish to express special thanks to the Gorbachev Foundation, Moscow, for making available unpublished transcripts of some of the most important discussions between Gorbachev and Bush in 1990 and 1991.

I have written this book primarily for the use of interested citizens, journalists and students in the United States and abroad. To make this work as useful as possible to scholars and historians as well, I have provided extensive notes at the end of the text identifying the sources on which I have relied, especially for information that was not previously or generally available, except for material given to me in confidence.

This account begins with the events of 1983, because that was a critical year for the two governments and the alliances they led. It was "the Year of the Missile," the deadline imposed by NATO for the United States to place new intermediate-range nuclear missiles on the soil of its Western European allies, an endeavor that took place against massive Soviet opposition. The year 1983 is also well remembered for President Reagan's "evil empire" and "Star Wars" speeches, and for the Soviet Union's shooting down of an unarmed Korean Air Lines jet. It is less well known as the time when some things began quietly to change for the better, despite the sharply rising tension between Washington and Moscow.

As originally written, the narrative ended with the events of the Washington summit meeting of mid-1990. Aside from several minor corrections, I have made no changes in the text of the original edition. Chapter 10, which appears for the first time in this edition, was written in the fall of 1997 and is based, more so than earlier portions, on memoirs of participants, many of which are now available.

As a practitioner of contemporary history, which seeks to transcend journalism but is written only a few years later, I have been inspired by a quotation from Dame C. Veronica Wedgwood, a noted British historian: "History is written backward but lived forward. Those who know the end of the story can never know what it was like at the time." I undertook this early account of one of the great turning points of history even without knowing its end, which came much more quickly than anyone had guessed. What follows is intended to convey what happened and what it was like at the time.

From the Cold War to a New Era

★

1. A Candle in the Cold

The snow began falling Thursday night, about an hour after Secretary of State George Shultz arrived home from a twelve-day trip of twenty-one thousand miles to China, Japan and other Asian nations. Late the next morning, federal government workers were dismissed because of the unrelenting heavy snowfall, and Shultz was warned by Metropolitan Police that if he did not leave the State Department soon he would be snowed in for the night. On Saturday, February 12, 1983, Washington awoke to a rare winter scene of sixteen to twenty inches of snow and flurries all around. As skiers frolicked on Washington streets and snow plows struggled to open two lanes for traffic on Pennsylvania Avenue, President and Mrs. Ronald Reagan canceled their plans to spend the weekend at Camp David, their Catoctin Mountain retreat, and invited George and O'Bie* Shultz to the family quarters of the White House for dinner. On that Saturday night in early 1983, in the wake of one of the most severe blizzards the capital had seen in this century, United States policy toward the Soviet Union began to change.

The first two years of Reagan's administration had concentrated on the domestic economic shifts that were being called the Reagan revolution and the massive military buildup sponsored by

* A nickname derived from her maiden name, Helena O'Brien.

the President. But starting with the intimate dinner with the Shultzes, Reagan would shift more of his attention to making contact with the Soviet Union in a manner that could ease the tension between Washington and Moscow. Although no one—including Reagan himself—could have predicted it at the time, this would be the start of a change for the better in relations between the two leading nations of the world. In the beginning, the shifting of gears would be almost imperceptible, an unseen quickening of presidential interest in ties with the Soviet Union.

In the initial stage, Reagan's desire to engage the Soviet Union in more productive dialogue would not get very far. His administration was not ready and, equally important, the leadership in the Kremlin was in disarray. Eventually there would be a new Soviet leader, Mikhail Gorbachev, who would develop new policies toward the United States and the rest of the world, and after that a successor U.S. president, George Bush, who would take the improved relationship with Moscow into a more openly cooperative phase. In 1989 and 1990 Bush and Gorbachev would work together as the Berlin Wall came down, Germany was reunited and Iraq was forced to end its conquest of Kuwait.

Those dramatic shifts were still unforeseen at dinner in the White House on the snow-covered evening of February 12. Reagan told Shultz that he had been fascinated by the television coverage of the secretary's trip to China, where he had met Deng Xiaoping and other Chinese leaders in the Great Hall of the People in Beijing. The President, encouraged by his wife, Nancy, wondered if it would be possible to arrange his own journeys to the Soviet Union and China, and how this might be done. Shultz replied that such trips would be "a great idea if it comes about in the right way." He explained that to make such top-level visits meaningful, step-by-step improvements in relations would be needed.

Reagan, reflecting on Shultz's point, said that he recognized it would be difficult to move quickly with either communist nation. The path was somewhat blocked, Reagan said, by his National Security Council staff, then headed by his longtime California associate William Clark, by his Department of Defense, headed by Caspar Weinberger, and by his own lifetime of harsh rhetoric about communists, which included the statement at his first press conference as President that the Soviets "reserve unto themselves the right to commit any crime, to lie, to cheat" in order to promote world revolution. In his first two years in the White House, Reagan had become known at home and abroad as the leader of an anti-Soviet crusade of unprecedented intensity. Nevertheless, it was clear to Shultz that the President was interested in undertaking personal negotiations with the Soviet Union and ready to move toward improved relations.

Shultz told Reagan he was scheduled to meet at the State Department three days later, on Tuesday, February 15, with the veteran Soviet ambassador to the United States, Anatoly Dobrynin, as part of an extensive review of U.S.-Soviet relations that they had begun the previous month. "Why don't I just bring him over here?" Shultz suggested.

Reagan was enthusiastic, but he did not want the world to know about his private chat with the Soviet ambassador. Every effort should be made to keep the meeting strictly secret, the President decided. Reagan said he did not intend to get into the details of arms talks or other pending issues but to tell Dobrynin that if Soviet leader Yuri Andropov was ready to do business, he would also be ready.

Precisely at 5:00 P.M. Tuesday, Dobrynin and his two top aides, Oleg Sokolov and Victor Isakov, arrived as scheduled at the diplomatic entrance of the State Department and were escorted to Shultz's seventh-floor office. There, without prior notice to Dobrynin, Shultz told him that the President wanted to see the two of them privately. Dobrynin seemed neither surprised nor the least bit ruffled by this news. As Soviet ambassador in Washington since 1962, he had dealt with John F. Kennedy when the two nations came close to war in the Cuban Missile Crisis while Reagan was still a movie actor known best as the host of *General Electric Theater* and Shultz was dean of the Graduate School of Business at the University of Chicago. Dobrynin had conferred with every president since Kennedy, and was so familiar with the White House that when Mikhail Gorbachev came to call in 1987, the veteran ambassador guided him from the Red Room to the nearest toilet without directions or assistance, to the astonishment of the Americans present.

After informing Dobrynin of the meeting with Reagan, Shultz took him down his private elevator to a waiting White House car in the State Department basement garage. It was a familiar place to Dobrynin, whose limousine had been permitted to take him into the basement and park there in a secluded spot on his frequent confidential visits during the Nixon, Ford and Carter administrations. This practice was stopped by

Secretary of State Alexander Haig early in the Reagan administration
in a symbolic declaration that Moscow's ambassador, even the long-
serving dean of the diplomatic corps, would have no special privileges
but would have to go through the public front door like everyone else.
At Shultz's side in February, however, confidentiality was once more
the order of the day. With even more stealth than the ambassador had
experienced in the past, Shultz and Dobrynin were whisked past the
Southwest Gate of the White House, the most convenient access point
to the West Wing, where the President and his senior staff have their
offices and usually receive visitors. They proceeded to the East Gate on
the far side of the executive mansion, where official visitors to the
President are rarely received. They were then escorted to the family
quarters on the second floor of the White House, where Reagan was
waiting.

Earlier in the day, Shultz had spoken once by telephone with Michael
Deaver, the deputy White House chief of staff and close personal aide
to Reagan, who heartily approved of the meeting with Dobrynin, and
twice with National Security Adviser William Clark, who strongly disapproved. "Judge" Clark, a former California Supreme Court justice,
saw the session as a ploy to engage Reagan in Soviet affairs, in Clark's
view prematurely. He suspected that behind the scenes, perhaps behind
the President's back, the event had been stage-managed by Shultz,
Deaver and Nancy Reagan, all of whom were more interested than Clark
in a warming of U.S.-Soviet relations. Shultz learned that Clark had
urged the President to cancel the meeting with Dobrynin, but that his
objections had been brushed aside.

For all of Reagan's well-known views about the Soviet Union, until
the meeting with Dobrynin he had never had a serious business meeting
with a Soviet official. Reagan had briefly met Leonid Brezhnev at a
reception when the Soviet leader visited President Nixon in California
in June 1973. As President, he had met Dobrynin at diplomatic functions
at the White House and paid a call on him at the Soviet Embassy to
sign the condolence book at the death of Brezhnev in November 1982,
but that was the extent of his personal contact. For Reagan, this first
attempt at face-to-face diplomacy with a representative of the other great
power was of major significance. After his long career in acting, Reagan
seemed to learn best by playing a role in the large or small dramas
taking place around him. In the meeting with Dobrynin, Reagan for the
first time was trying on the part of negotiator with the Soviet Union. He

considered this tryout encounter to be important and had prepared what he wanted to tell Dobrynin.

The meeting in the family quarters took nearly two hours, an unusually long conference for the President, whose attention span was notoriously short. About one-third of the meeting was devoted to the overall relations between Washington and Moscow, with Reagan emphasizing his willingness to be constructive. About a third involved the status of the arms control negotiations aimed at reducing strategic and intermediate-range nuclear weapons. The final third covered human rights.

Reagan devoted special attention to the plight of seven Pentecostal Christians from Siberia who had been living as unwelcome guests in the basement of the U.S. Embassy in Moscow since June 1978. The Pentecostals had pushed their way past surprised guards and taken refuge in the diplomatic building in an effort to obtain permission to leave the country. When Soviet authorities refused their demand to emigrate, the United States had permitted them to stay in the Embassy for humanitarian reasons. Reagan emphasized to Dobrynin that such cases ought to be solved quietly and quickly, and that release and safe passage for the Pentecostals would make it easier for him to take positive steps toward the Soviet Union.

The problem of the Pentecostals in the Embassy was just the sort of human interest story that seized the attention of Reagan, who was often bored with military hardware questions or broad foreign policy issues but was fascinated with the plight of individual people. More than a year earlier, when career diplomat Jack Matlock saw the President at the end of a tour of duty in Moscow, Reagan to his surprise did not ask him about General Secretary Brezhnev, Soviet foreign policy or arms control but about the Pentecostal Christians holed up in the U.S. Embassy basement. "Are we doing enough for them? Why do not the Soviets let them go? What goes on in their minds that they can't let people go? Why is it they won't let them practice their religion?" had been the questions on Reagan's mind. When Vice President George Bush and Shultz visited Moscow for Brezhnev's funeral in November 1982, they had taken time to look in on the Pentecostals in their cramped Embassy refuge because of Reagan's interest in the case.

After the discussion with the President, Shultz and Dobrynin returned to the State Department at 6:59 P.M. to join several aides on each side who had been swapping stories and making small talk while waiting for them. During the review in Shultz's office that followed the White House meeting, Dobrynin referred to the case of the Pentecostals as "the special topic." The canny ambassador knew that this question—unlike many broader issues that had been raised—was something he might be able to do something about in the short run. In the cable he drafted that night on his surprise meeting with Reagan, Dobrynin recommended that arrangements be made to resolve the Pentecostals' plight quickly in view of the President's plea.

Reagan's interest in improved relations could hardly have come at a more difficult time, so far as Moscow was concerned. Andropov, who had been looking for ways to get talks with Washington going again since taking office at the death of Brezhnev, dropped out of sight from the end of January to February 21 for reasons that were not disclosed at the time, but that made a meeting with Reagan increasingly unlikely from that time on. That February, Andropov, who had a long history of kidney disease, suffered kidney failure so serious that for the rest of his life he had to undergo regular hemodialysis, a procedure of mechanical cleansing of the blood to remove the impurities that healthy kidneys would otherwise eliminate. Several times a week Andropov was hooked up to a dialysis machine in his office, in his Moscow apartment or in the special VIP section of the Central Clinical Hospital, and his blood was circulated through the device. When Reagan was initiating his contact through Dobrynin, the collapse of Andropov's kidneys was a state secret.

Dobrynin's cable did not receive an enthusiastic welcome in the Kremlin. The top levels of the Soviet leadership were worried about Andropov's health and furious at a long succession of insults and slights from Reagan as well as apprehensive about the massive U.S. military buildup. It appeared to the Kremlin that Reagan was "speeding up the arms race and making all kinds of nasty statements, and at the same time he's trying to get these people [out] and creating an impression that it will change much in our relations," according to Georgi Kornienko, who was first deputy foreign minister at the time. Nevertheless, it seemed to the professional diplomats in Moscow that it should not be hard to provide exit permits for two families of Siberians if Reagan was so interested in them. The Kremlin leadership agreed that the continuing presence of the Pentecostals in the U.S. Embassy was "a stupid obstacle" to improved relations and Foreign Minister Andrei Gromyko recommended that it be solved, recalled Andrei Aleksandrov-Agentov, the foreign policy assistant to General Secretary Andropov.

On February 28, a few days after Andropov returned to work in the Kremlin, the Soviet Embassy notified the State Department that Moscow would reassess the situation of the Pentecostals in the Embassy, "taking all factors into account"—language that suggested that they would be permitted to leave. By April all the Pentecostals had left the American Embassy, and before the end of June they and other members of their extended families were on their way out of the country.

On July 28, U.S. and Soviet negotiators agreed on a new long-term grain agreement worth $10 billion in sales to U.S. farmers over the next five years. Reagan insisted at the time, and repeated in his memoirs, that this was a concession to the Kremlin in response to the release of the Pentecostal Christians, which he considered "a hope-giving development" in a situation of almost total conflict between the two countries, and "the first time the Soviets had responded to us with a deed instead of words." While Shultz agreed that the release of the Pentecostals was a clear sign of Soviet willingness to work with Reagan, the secretary did not believe that the grain accord was an adequate quid pro quo. The Soviet leaders were well aware of the domestic pressure on the administration from American farmers to sell the grain, making it a less than convincing gesture of reciprocity, Shultz insisted.

• EVIL EMPIRE AND STAR WARS

Ronald Reagan was of two minds about the Soviet Union, and even some of his closest associates disagreed about which one was dominant. Michael Deaver, who had been an aide to Reagan since 1966 and had almost a filial relationship with the older man, was convinced that Reagan saw that he was destined to change the United States relationship with the Soviet Union. In Deaver's view, "He was the last president that we will ever have who had lived through two [world] wars and the depression. He was the most anti-communist president we would have or ever have had. And yet deep down I knew he believed that each of us was chosen for something and that this might be what he could do . . . because of his background, his age, his philosophy." William Clark, who had been an aide to Reagan even longer and who had originally hired Deaver in California, held a very different view of what Reagan believed. As the national security adviser saw it, Reagan was flatly opposed to just about everything the Soviets stood for and was skeptical about moving forward with them until there was a clearcut structure for dialogue, a workable agenda and tangible Soviet moves to justify confidence.

The clash between Reagan's two oldest advisers on the White House staff is suggestive of the dichotomous nature of Reagan's views. On the one hand, he could condemn the Soviet leaders with sincerity and zeal, using the harshest rhetoric ever heard from a U.S. President, and on the other he could express a persistent willingness, even an eagerness, to reach out to them in constructive discussions. To some extent Reagan's duality of mind arose from his formative experiences as president of the Screen Actors Guild in Hollywood, which had left him with two vital convictions. One was a passionate opposition to communists, domestic or foreign; the other was an unbounded confidence in his own ability to convince others of the rightness of his positions in face-to-face encounters. By 1983 Reagan's vociferous opposition to Soviet communism was universally known. Only a few people knew that, at the same time, he was eager for contacts with Moscow. According to Shultz, the President never wavered or hesitated when given the opportunity to engage in dialogues with the Soviets, despite the opposition from close associates in the White House and elsewhere in the administration. Robert Mc-Farlane, who observed Reagan at close range as his deputy national security adviser or national security adviser from 1982 to the end of 1985, ascribed some of his willingness to engage to a "self-confidence that he was an historic figure and that he was terribly effective in persuasion. . . . He had enormous self-confidence in the ability of a single heroic figure to change history."

The paradox of Ronald Reagan was never more pronounced than in early 1983. While seeking to open a working relationship with the Soviet Union along the lines discussed with Dobrynin on February 15, Reagan on March 8 delivered his famous dictum that the Soviet Union was "an evil empire" and "the focus of evil in the modern world." On March 23, he announced the ambitious and controversial Strategic Defense Initiative, fiercely resisted by the Soviets, to neutralize the Soviet military threat to the United States by making ballistic missiles "impotent and obsolete."

Some Reagan partisans would say later that the President portrayed the Soviets as evil and announced the Star Wars program in order to build up his bargaining power for future negotiations with Moscow. The evidence suggests, however, that Reagan, at least, was acting out of longstanding and strong convictions rather than any considerations of strategy. While Reagan later found SDI useful in dealings with the Soviet Union, he was not a Machiavellian or even a Kissingerian figure seeking to manipulate the international environment through his pronouncements. Reagan held to a very broad strategy for dealing with the Soviets, which he had enunciated even before coming to office: build up U.S. military power and then negotiate from a position of strength. But he was not a tactician and was often uninterested in and even uncomprehending of the details of the negotiations themselves. Whatever others might think, Reagan saw no contradiction between speaking his mind against godless communists in Moscow and seeking to establish a working relationship with them, or between starting a new high-technology program that would negate the very basis of Soviet military power and at the same time seeking to persuade Moscow to make large-scale cuts in its nuclear weapons arsenal.

Reagan's denunciation of the Soviet Union as "an evil empire" was probably the most famous bit of oratory that this rhetorically inclined President ever uttered. But while it was cited in praise or condemnation hundreds of times by others, Reagan himself hurled his celebrated epithet at Moscow only once, on March 8, 1983, before the annual convention of the National Association of Evangelicals at Orlando, Florida. Reagan never repudiated the statement, but he also never repeated it. In fact, when asked by *Time* in mid-December 1983 if he felt his comments had been appropriate and if he would say the same thing again, Reagan responded, "No, I would not say things like that again, even after some of the things that have been done recently," a reference to the downing of Korean Air Lines Flight 007 and the Soviet walkout from the arms talks. Much later, at the 1988 Moscow summit, Reagan would say that the Soviet Union was no longer "an evil empire." Asked about his famous remark after he walked through Red Square, Reagan replied, "I was talking about another time, another era."

The words "evil empire" and "focus of evil in the modern world" originated with Reagan's conservative speechwriter Anthony Dolan, in his first draft of the proposed presidential speech to the convention of the Evangelicals, who were part of Reagan's conservative political constituency. Dolan had written the President's powerful anticommunist speech to the British Parliament the previous June and at every turn sought to dramatize Reagan's anticommunism, just as others in the Reagan staff and State Department sought to mute it.

Despite Reagan's interest in the Pentecostal Christians living in the

Moscow Embassy and the encouraging word from the Soviet government he had received a few days before, the President made no mention of this topic to the U.S. Evangelical leaders. Most of the speech concerned religious and sexual morality issues, especially the administration's demand that parents be notified if minor children were to be given birth control devices. Reagan's stand on this issue was so hotly debated within the White House that the President finally wrote this section of the speech in his own hand to silence the dissension. There was less attention in the White House to the briefer remarks on foreign policy, although at one stage a draft was returned to Dolan with the Soviet Union section entirely eliminated with a big "X" drawn across the paper by someone on the White House staff. When the matter was referred to Reagan, he restored the offending section and even strengthened it to some extent.

The main purpose of the international section of the speech was to enlist the Evangelicals in the administration's fight against the nuclear freeze movement, which sought an immediate halt to production of nuclear weapons. The nuclear freeze, which was backed by many American churches, was under intense debate in Congress. Reagan's argument against it was buttressed partly on policy grounds, such as the necessity for "peace through strength," but also in an emotionally charged message of moral judgment:

> Let us pray for the salvation of all of those who live in that totalitarian darkness—pray they will discover the joy of knowing God. But until they do, let us be aware that while they preach the supremacy of the state, declare its omnipotence over individual man, and predict its eventual domination of all peoples on the earth, they are the focus of evil in the modern world. . . .
>
> So, I urge you to speak out against those who would place the United States in a position of military and moral inferiority. . . . In your discussions of the nuclear freeze proposals, I urge you to beware the temptation of pride—the temptation of blithely declaring yourselves above it all and label both sides equally at fault, to ignore the facts of history and the aggressive impulses of an evil empire, to simply call the arms race a giant misunderstanding and thereby remove yourself from the struggle between right and wrong and good and evil.

Toward the end of the address, Reagan turned to a prediction about the future of the Soviet system that seemed merely hyperbolic at the time, but in the light of world events later would appear prophetic: "I believe we shall rise to the challenge. I believe that communism is another sad, bizarre chapter in human history whose last pages even now are being written."

Reagan had made a career of lambasting the Soviet Union from his days as a spokesman for General Electric two decades earlier to his campaigns for the presidency in 1976 and 1980, and thus it was hardly a surprise for him to speak out in vivid and even elemental terms. In this context, no one who read the draft of the Evangelical speech in advance predicted that the words would become a label for Reagan's views long after the occasion was forgotten. However, the catchy phrase "evil empire" seemed to sum up Reagan's early view of the Soviets in a world of black and white. Moreover, it was an allusion to the popular 1977 George Lucas film, *Star Wars*, a futuristic morality play about the struggle to wrest control of a galaxy from a threatening and immoral "empire," and its 1980 sequel, *The Empire Strikes Back*. Reagan's address to the Evangelicals was dubbed by the press the "Darth Vader speech," after the villain in the Lucas films.

Much has been written about the origin of the Strategic Defense Initiative, which quickly became known as the "Star Wars" plan, and which became a central issue in U.S.-Soviet nuclear arms negotiations. The key point in nearly all the accounts is that even before entering the White House, Reagan was uncomfortable with nuclear deterrence based on the principle of mutual assured destruction, in which each side checks the other with the threat of annihilation. He was fascinated with the prospect of a technological breakthrough that would create hardware that could stop incoming missiles. Reagan often called the idea "my dream," which suggests the magical nature of its hold on him. Some of his aides saw SDI as a way to create bargaining leverage with the Soviet Union; others saw it as an obstacle, making serious agreements with the Soviet Union improbable if not impossible. Reagan, though, appears to have been deeply committed to the idea for its own sake. No one was ever able to shake his deep belief that his dream could actually come to fruition and thus change the world for the better.

On July 31, 1979, almost eighteen months before becoming President, Reagan visited the North American Aerospace Defense Command (NORAD), the underground nerve center responsible for defense against nuclear missile attack. There he discovered to his shock and dismay that there was no defense against even a single Soviet missile fired against the United States. According to Martin Anderson, who accompanied Reagan to NORAD and later served on his White House staff, Reagan left the command post shaking his head with dismay and worried that as President he would have only two choices—"to press the button or do nothing"—if there was a nuclear missile attack.

By early 1983, as recounted by Anderson in his book *Revolution*, the concept of creating a defense against ballistic missiles had been endorsed by the Republican party and explored in several high-level meetings in the Reagan White House, in which Anderson participated. Adding to Reagan's strong views were his experiences at periodic dooms-day exercises after becoming President in which he was forced to consider what he would do if informed that missiles had been launched against the United States. Secretary of Defense Caspar Weinberger, who par-ticipated along with Reagan in these periodic exercises, observed that they were "a very unsettling experience" for the President. Weinberger knew from discussions with Reagan going back to their California days that "he had a very deep revulsion to the whole idea of the nuclear weapons" on a philosophical level and that he was even more gripped by "the spectacle of not having any defenses, having these things coming in, and what does he do as president? Does he order retaliation or what? How many minutes have we got? 12 minutes, 9 minutes, all that."

In a highly classified briefing by the Defense Department, Reagan was informed that at least 150 million Americans would be killed in a nuclear war with the Soviet Union, a horrifying prospect. Reagan, who sponsored the most massive peacetime military buildup in U.S. history, was no secret dove. He was, however, deeply opposed to the possession and use of nuclear weapons, despite the fact that they had become the central ingredient in U.S. military power. Reagan stated his anti–nuclear weapons views on many occasions but, strangely enough, it was a shock when they later surfaced in negotiations with the Soviet Union. Most officials of the administration, as well as much of the public, did not take his anti–nuclear weapons statements seriously because they seemed dreamy and impractical for a U.S. president, especially one with Rea-gan's anticommunist policies and hard-edged oratory.

Reagan's abhorrence of the nuclear threat was an important factor in his decision to launch the ballistic missile defense program in a meeting with the uniformed heads of the U.S. military services, the Joint Chiefs of Staff, on February 11, 1983. It was the Friday of the great Washington snowstorm and the day before the cozy dinner of the Reagans and Shultzes. Road conditions were so bad that the chiefs had to use four-wheel-drive vehicles to get to the White House for the noon meeting. Once around the table in the Cabinet Room, the military leaders, partly by prearrangement with McFarlane, then deputy White House national security adviser, reported that the possibility of a space-based defense against incoming missiles was more promising than in the past.

"Wouldn't it be better to protect the American people rather than avenge them?" General John Vessey, chairman of the Joint Chiefs, asked Reagan, in a phrase he had picked up from a preliminary briefing by the chief of naval operations, Admiral James Watkins. When the chiefs finished their report, McFarlane interjected:

> Mr. President, this is very, very important. For 37 years we have relied on offensive deterrence based on the threat of nuclear counterattack with surviving forces because there has been no alternative. But now for the first time in history what we are hearing here is that there might be another way which would enable you to defeat an attack by defending against it and over time relying less on nuclear weapons.

As McFarlane anticipated, Reagan immediately seized on what had been said and insisted that something be done to pursue strategic defense. During the dinner with Shultz the following evening, the President mentioned the possibility of a defensive shield over the United States, but the secretary of state was not aware of the discussion with the Joint Chiefs of Staff and did not realize that Reagan's remarks had any immediate or operational significance.

To the shock of even some of the chiefs and the surprise of all but a very few intimate aides, the President proceeded in rapid fashion to develop the idea the Joint Chiefs had given him. On March 23, only six weeks after the meeting with the military leaders, Reagan announced in a televised address his high-priority program to intercept and destroy incoming missiles:

> Wouldn't it be better to save lives than to avenge them? Are we not capable of demonstrating our peaceful intentions by applying all our abilities and our ingenuity to achieving a truly lasting stability?
>
> I think we are. Indeed, we must. After careful consideration with my advisers including the Joint Chiefs of Staff, I believe

there is a way. Let me share with you a vision of the future which offers hope. It is that we embark on a program to counter the awesome Soviet missile threat with measures that are defensive. Let us turn to the very strengths in technology that spawned our great industrial base, and that have given us the quality of life we enjoy today. . . .

With these considerations firmly in mind, I call upon the scientific community in our country, those who gave us nuclear weapons, to turn their great talents now to the cause of mankind and world peace, to give us the means of rendering these nuclear weapons impotent and obsolete.

If the United States could perfect a defense against ballistic missiles or even make such a defense somewhat effective, the nature and balance of military power in the world, the workings of alliances and much else would be altered fundamentally, as the world was altered by the development of the first atomic bomb or the intercontinental ballistic missile. However, high administration officials, who normally were deeply involved in international decisions, knew nothing of this revolutionary aspiration until the very eve of the announcement. A large number of experienced government professionals thought (and still think) that a space-based shield to stop ballistic missiles was impractical. But whether they were inclined to scoff or to believe, just about everyone had serious qualms about the way the program was launched. Far more than the development of the atomic bomb or the intercontinental ballistic missile, this dramatic development was a bolt from the blue, even to senior officials of the government.

McFarlane, who had helped engineer the surprise decision, was rebuffed when he proposed trying to enlist the support of top congressional leaders of both parties and major U.S. allies before the announcement. Reagan wanted it held strictly secret until it could be announced on his own terms, McFarlane was told. Assistant Secretary of Defense Richard Perle, who later became a leading proponent of strategic defense, was appalled to be handed a copy of Reagan's intended text near midnight in Lisbon, Portugal, where he and Secretary of Defense Weinberger were attending a NATO meeting. "That's no way to surface a new policy," Perle protested. With the approval of Weinberger, who had opposed the Joint Chiefs' original recommendation, Perle initiated a transatlantic blitzkrieg of telephone calls seeking a delay until the matter could be more fully discussed and allies informed. The request was rejected.

Shultz, who also received an "eyes only" draft of the statement just a day or two in advance, was immediately concerned that a sudden and radical change in U.S. strategic doctrine would "hit the allies right between the eyes." The more Shultz looked into it, the more he believed that the program had not been thought through. Shultz detected a confusion in Reagan's mind, which persisted for years to come, about whether the shield would stop all nuclear weapons, including those on bombers and cruise missiles, or only ballistic missiles. To allay Shultz's concern, some changes were made in the speech. But the day before the announcement, Shultz told Reagan in a telephone conversation that he had "great reservations" about the implication that the United States was changing its strategic doctrine.

In Moscow, the SDI announcement brought forth fierce opposition. If ballistic missiles were actually to be rendered "impotent and obsolete," the principal basis of the Soviet Union's claim to be one of two great nuclear powers would be demolished. The creation of an antimissile shield would make it theoretically possible for the United States to plan, threaten or even execute a nuclear strike against the USSR with diminished fear of retaliation. Even more frightening to the Kremlin was the prospect of being forced into an expensive high-technology race with the United States that it could not afford and probably could not win.

The first retort came from Andropov himself on March 26, only three days after the Reagan SDI speech and the day when the Soviet leader resumed his official activities after what was rumored to be several days of kidney treatment. In an interview with *Pravda*, Andropov accused Reagan of telling a "deliberate lie" about Soviet military strength, the harshest personal comment from a Soviet leader against his U.S. counterpart in many years. He charged that the SDI plan was "a bid to disarm the Soviet Union in the face of the U.S. nuclear threat."

Experts at the Soviet Academy of Sciences, stimulated by physicist Yevgeni Velikhov, who had just returned from discussions with American physicists and space scientists at the time of Reagan's announcement, argued that the Star Wars program was impractical and that any partial success it might achieve could be nullified by modest countermeasures. But despite such advice and doubts about its practicality, the Soviet leaders "could not ignore such a position" as that outlined by Reagan on March 23, especially since it was soon to be backed up by many billions of dollars, according to Andropov's foreign policy assistant, Andrei Aleksandrov-Agentov. "So whether it was a practical idea or not, they had to account for the reality—the real factor in the policy of the United States. That's why this Star Wars declaration was a contribution for substantial worsening of our relations without any doubt. And perhaps it was good that the reaction of Andropov was so swift, just to make things clear," said the Kremlin aide.

Reagan could hardly have guessed when he promulgated the SDI program that it would dominate negotiations with the Kremlin for the next four years or that it would be a catalyst for a critical reassessment in Moscow of the place of military power in the security of the Soviet state.

• A GOLDEN ANNIVERSARY

The year 1983 marked the fiftieth anniversary of diplomatic relations between the United States and the Soviet Union, but it was not an auspicious time. The two most powerful nations were unremittingly hostile in their speech and thought about each other, and the powerful buildup of weapons on both sides continued at a rapid pace. George Kennan, who had had longer personal experience in U.S.-Soviet diplomacy than any other American, having arrived in Moscow as a young Foreign Service officer shortly after President Franklin Roosevelt extended diplomatic recognition to the Soviet state, said in May 1983 that U.S.-Soviet relations were in "a dreadful and dangerous condition." A prestigious commentator on Soviet affairs, Kennan declared that the antagonism, suspicion and militarization of thought between Washington and Moscow "are the familiar characteristics, the unfailing characteristics, of a march toward war—that, and nothing else."

Aside from the U.S. purchase of Alaska from the czarist government in 1867 and the brief U.S. intervention in Siberia against the Bolshevik revolution in 1917, the interaction of these two vast and populous continental countries had been limited until the fortunes of war made them allies against Hitler's Germany in World War II. While remarkably different in many respects, Russia and America had been linked from time to time as potentially powerful outsiders that could dominate the Old World. As far back as the 1830s the French historian and political theorist Alexis de Tocqueville, in his classic work, *Democracy in America*, wrote:

> There are at the present time two great nations in the world, which started from different points, but seem to tend towards the same end. I allude to the Russians and the Americans. . . .
>
> All other nations seem to have nearly reached their natural limits, and they have only to maintain their power; but these are still in the act of growth. All the others have stopped, or continue to advance with extreme difficulty; these alone are proceeding with ease and celerity along a path to which no limit can be perceived. The American struggles against the obstacles that nature opposes to him; the adversaries of the Russian are men. The former combats the wilderness and savage life; the latter, civilization with all its arms. . . . The principal instrument of the former is freedom; of the latter, servitude. Their starting-point is different and their courses are not the same; yet each of them seems marked out by the will of Heaven to sway the destinies of half the globe.

De Tocqueville's prophecy seemed to be coming true when the United States and Soviet Union emerged from World War II as the two most powerful states and the leaders of global alliances that dominated the world politically and militarily. With the rapid growth of nuclear weapons programs, Washington and Moscow became the acknowledged leaders of a bipolar world, each holding the other at bay in a potentially suicidal grip described by J. Robert Oppenheimer as "two scorpions in a bottle."

By the mid-1980s, the United States and the Soviet Union, with about 11 percent of the world population, accounted for 23 percent of the world's armed forces, 60 percent of its military expenditures, 80 percent of the weapons research and 97 percent of all nuclear weapons. The world's stockpile of nuclear weapons, which totaled three in 1945 (one was test-fired and the two others destroyed Hiroshima and Nagasaki, Japan), had grown to over sixty thousand by 1983. The nuclear arsenals contained the equivalent of more than 1 million Hiroshimas. They represented 2,700 times the explosive energy released in all the battles of World War II, when 38 million people died.

Despite the Strategic Arms Limitation Treaties (SALT I and II) of 1972 and 1979, which were intended to limit the growth of their weaponry, by 1983 the United States possessed more than ten thousand "strategic" nuclear weapons capable of hitting the Soviet Union on long-range missiles or bombers, and the Soviet Union possessed nearly eight thousand "strategic" weapons deployed to strike the American homeland.

With their two formal alliances, the North Atlantic Treaty Organization (NATO) and the Warsaw Pact, and an extensive network of bilateral arrangements, Washington and Moscow could put military forces almost anywhere on the globe within a matter of days. The United States maintained more than three hundred major installations abroad, covering 2 million acres. The Soviet Union had fewer permanent sites but, since the 1970s, had demonstrated a global reach of impressive proportions. Soviet military aircraft had flown Cuban troops into African wars at short notice. In a direct application of military force, more than one hundred thousand Soviet troops were fighting outside the country's borders in Afghanistan.

Conflict, violence and international tensions had increased in nearly every region of the world, with 45 of the world's 164 nations involved in forty conventional and guerrilla wars in 1983, according to a study by the U.S. Center for Defense Information, a private think tank led by former senior military officers. The United States supplied arms to twenty of the nations at war and the Soviet Union supplied arms to thirteen, but in many cases neither of the great powers could dictate to their clients the course or limits of conflicts that were fueled by religious fundamentalism, national and ethnic discord and struggles over resources.

Reagan had come to power convinced that, for the first time, the Soviet Union had achieved military superiority over the United States, placing the United States in a vulnerable position, and that a massive U.S. military buildup was necessary to rectify this imbalance. The prevailing climate of thinking in the Reagan administration was exemplified by the Defense Department's policy guidance for fiscal year 1983. A document stamped secret and intended to be used for military planning and internal consumption rather than public relations, it described the international strategic environment in dire terms:

> The U.S. faces grave challenges to its national security in the 1980s. Traditional areas of superiority over the Soviet Union have been eroded or reversed because of the massive Soviet buildup of military power that has been inadequately answered

by the U.S. and its Allies. As a result, the Soviets are increasingly disposed to and capable of projecting their power abroad (directly and indirectly through surrogates) and exacerbating existing instabilities. Moreover, Soviet inspired and/or supported "wars of national liberation" will continue. Thus, the Soviets pose a serious threat to the U.S., its Allies and its interests at all levels of conflict and on a global scale.

The response to this threat, as the Reagan administration saw it, was the largest military buildup in U.S. peacetime history. Its purposes were described in the Pentagon's secret policy guidance:

> U.S. forces must be capable of dealing with Soviet aggression in any area—Europe, the Persian Gulf, Northeast Asia, or elsewhere—both by defending in the given area and, if to our advantage, by exploiting Soviet vulnerabilities elsewhere at times and places of our choosing. This ability to act simultaneously in widely separated theaters requires a mix of ready and sustainable forward deployed and U.S.-based forces, prepositioned stocks, U.S. naval superiority, mobility and support structure assets that will allow us to project power and fight at whatever level of intensity is required. This will involve utilizing the combined capability of the U.S., its allies and friends.

The deepening of antagonism reflected, in part, the rise in the United States of the conservative movement that sponsored the election of Reagan, who was the least centrist president of the modern era, and the shattering of the internationalist consensus that had dominated U.S. foreign policy since 1941. The objectives of the U.S. government abroad seemed to many to have shifted from the management of conflicts to more ambitious aims—to "prevail" in any possible war, to roll back what was perceived to have been an advancing tide of communism in the 1970s. In Moscow, the Soviet leaders believed that after herculean efforts they had finally achieved global equality with the United States in the 1970s, and that Washington had accepted this. They responded with bitterness and anger, tinged with a sense of betrayal, to the military buildup and anticommunist activism from Washington. In both camps, black and white thinking seemed to be prevailing over shades of gray.

The United States and the Soviet Union were shaving the tolerance that had averted dangerous confrontations in earlier decades.

The most prominent struggle between Washington and Moscow in 1983 was over influence in Europe, specifically the battle over deployment of the new U.S. intermediate-range missiles in West Germany, Italy and Britain. The Reagan administration had inherited this battle from the Carter administration, under whose leadership NATO vowed in December 1979 to deploy the new weapons within four years unless Moscow agreed to eliminate the threat posed by its own new intermediate-range nuclear deployments. The perception in the West was that the U.S. Pershing II and ground-launched cruise missiles would restore the military balance in Europe by compensating for the Soviet SS-20s that had been deployed in large numbers in the 1970s. But in Moscow, the new U.S. weapons, especially the highly accurate Pershing II, were seen as upsetting an existing balance and posing an ominous threat of surprise attack to the Soviet Union.

Western European peace activists, who saw their countries becoming the front line of nuclear battle between East and West, were marching in massive demonstrations against deployment of the new atomic weapons close to home. As the battle of the Euromissiles raged, it took on a political importance that overshadowed the military interests involved: For the United States to lose the right to deploy the missiles on the soil of its European allies would be a devastating blow to the NATO alliance; for the Soviet Union to lose the fight against those new U.S. weapons would be a powerful blow to its prestige in Europe. The stakes were high on both sides and, after years of negotiations, no compromise solution was in sight.

• MOVING TOWARD A THAW

In January, Shultz had begun his series of extensive discussions with Ambassador Dobrynin after sending Reagan a paper on "U.S.-Soviet Relations in 1983" proposing an intensified dialogue with Moscow and obtaining the President's permission to proceed. A month after the dinner with the Reagans on the snowy February weekend and the subsequent meeting of Reagan and Dobrynin, Shultz sent to the White House a more detailed paper outlining "Next Steps in U.S.-Soviet Relations." Shultz's

March 16 proposals were for a slow but steady opening to the Soviets through discussions across a broad agenda covering arms control, regional conflicts, trade and other bilateral issues and human rights. The last specifically included the case of the Pentecostals, who were then still in the U.S. Embassy in Moscow, and that of Anatoly Shcharansky, the Soviet human rights activist who had been imprisoned since 1978.

Shultz suggested that if things went well, he might travel to Moscow in July to see Foreign Minister Gromyko and General Secretary Andropov, and that in September Gromyko might come to Washington to see Reagan when the Soviet minister made his annual visit to the United Nations General Assembly. All this would help set the stage for a Reagan-Andropov meeting in 1984, a U.S. presidential election year.

Clark was strongly opposed to moving rapidly on relations with Moscow. Clark's deputy, McFarlane, told Shultz that he "couldn't believe the fly specking" of his proposals at the hands of the National Security Council staff. Another White House official said Clark sent his own handwritten message to Reagan, accompanying Shultz's proposals for movement on the Soviet front, expressing a sharp dissent. Vice President Bush told Shultz that "absolutely vicious memos" went to Reagan from the National Security Council staff whenever he sent over a memo from State. Indeed, Shultz seemed out of step with the strongly anti-Soviet tenor of the administration's rhetoric and its military buildup, and especially with the reluctance of Secretary of Defense Caspar Weinberger to contemplate any conciliatory moves toward Moscow. Yet Shultz remained convinced from his private talks with Reagan that the President was ready to move ahead toward more serious engagement with the Soviets.

The situation began to change in the spring when Jack Matlock, a career professional with extensive Soviet experience, was recruited to replace Richard Pipes, a Harvard professor known for his anti-Soviet views, as the chief Soviet policy official on the National Security Council staff. Matlock, who was U.S. ambassador to Czechoslovakia, was summoned home in May. In asking that he take the NSC post, McFarlane told him that "the President had felt that when he came into office we were too weak to negotiate, particularly after the shambles that our defense establishment was in, that his first priorities had to be getting the economy back in shape in terms of inflation and economic growth and getting the defense budget moving up to a more adequate level. And though this had not been totally achieved, he felt that the trends were now sufficiently positive that it was time to move to the next phase of his agenda, which was to engage the Soviets in negotiation now that he had the chips to do it." Matlock took the job.

The restoration of U.S. self-confidence was a theme of Shultz's June 15 testimony to the Senate Foreign Relations Committee, which took a strange journalistic bounce and inadvertently played a role in cementing the administration's policy. The committee had been asking for months for a top-level presentation on Soviet policy, and Shultz's lengthy statement, which took him forty-eight minutes to read, was by far his most extensive since he arrived at Foggy Bottom. "Having begun to rebuild our strength," said Shultz in testimony that had been personally approved by Reagan, "we now seek to engage the Soviet leaders in a constructive dialogue—a dialogue through which we hope to find political solutions to outstanding issues." Shultz set out a very broad four-part agenda for dialogue with the Soviet Union, covering human rights, arms control, regional issues and bilateral questions, that was to shape U.S.-Soviet discussions for the rest of the Reagan administration. At the same time, Shultz outlined an ambitious policy of active opposition to Moscow, declaring that "where it was once our goal to contain the Soviet presence within the limits of its immediate postwar reach, now our goal must be to advance our own objectives, where possible foreclosing and when necessary actively countering Soviet challenges wherever they threaten our interests."*

The following morning, the two leading newspapers that reach the capital had opposite interpretations of Shultz's testimony in their top news positions on page one. *New York Times* reporter Philip Taubman, under the headline "Shultz Testifies Rifts with Soviet Aren't Inevitable," interpreted the testimony as unusually conciliatory and gave little attention to the confrontational aspects. My report in *The Washington Post*, under the headline "Shultz Outlines Policy of Opposing Soviets," accentuated the ambitious strategy of checking the Soviets everywhere and gave less play to his conciliatory statements. Shultz, who had not intended to declare a policy change in either direction, was puzzled by the contradictory newspaper accounts. The State Department bureaucracy was equally perplexed and unsure how to explain Shultz's policy to inquiring journalists and foreign diplomats. After hours of uncertainty,

* Shultz also spoke of forging an American response to the USSR "beyond containment," a phrase that had little resonance in 1983, but would return with a different meaning and greater emphasis in the first year of the Bush administration.

State Department aides were authorized to conduct briefings along the lines of the *Times* version of the testimony. On June 18, Shultz enunciated the emerging consensus in a private meeting with Dobrynin, stressing that the United States had restored its strength and confidence and was ready to talk. "That was a watershed" in U.S. diplomacy, according to Thomas Simons, then the State Department's director of Soviet affairs. From that moment on, State's internal position papers and a growing number of public statements bore down on the theme of a stronger United States and its willingness to negotiate.

By coincidence, as Shultz was testifying in the Senate, Andropov was speaking to the final session of a policymaking plenum of the Communist Party Central Committee. On June 15, his sixty-ninth (and last) birthday, the Soviet leader suggested it was time to take a new look at Soviet foreign policy, declaring that "the threat of a nuclear war overhanging the world makes one appraise in a new way the basic meaning of the activities of the entire communist movement." The evidence is that Kremlin leaders were trying to decide if there indeed was any chance to deal with this strange, exasperating U.S. President, who was strident one day and seemed to be sending feelers for negotiation the next. Some argued the conciliatory line was all a charade, intended to boost Reagan's fortunes past the 1984 election. Others saw a possibility of working with Reagan. Either as diplomatic courtesy or in hopes of improvement, Andropov sent a July 4 message to Reagan, pledging the "unbending commitment of the Soviet leadership and the people of the Soviet Union to the cause of peace, the elimination of the nuclear threat and the development of relations based on mutual benefit and equality with all nations."

Several days after receiving the Independence Day message, Reagan decided to draft his own reply. This was not a new venture for the President, who had sent a letter to General Secretary Brezhnev in April 1981, while recuperating from the attempt to assassinate him. The President liked to write letters and hoped in this way to establish a direct connection with Soviet leaders. In the letter to Andropov, as with the Brezhnev letter, Reagan put his own ideas on paper in longhand and then discussed the missive with his top advisers.

Reagan's draft of his July 11 letter to Andropov reflected his strong antipathy to nuclear weapons. If it had been sent as Reagan originally wrote it, it would have been a historic document that first established his goal of eliminating all nuclear weapons, a goal that the President, almost alone in his administration, ardently sought. Reagan wrote:

> Let me assure you the govt & the people of the United States are dedicated to the cause of peace & the elimination of the nuclear threat. It goes without saying that we seek relations with all nations based on "mutual benefit and equality." Our record since we were allies in W.W. II confirms that.
>
> Mr. Sec. General don't we have the means to achieve these goals in the meetings we are presently holding in Geneva? If we can agree on mutual, verifiable reductions in the number of nuclear weapons we both hold could this not be a first step toward the elimination of all such weapons? What a blessing this would be for the people we both represent. You and I have the ability to bring this about through our negotiators in the arms reduction talks.

Scratched out by Reagan after the last words of his longhand draft was another mention of his goal—"reduction talks that could lead to the total elimination of all such weap."

Reagan handed his draft to Clark the next morning, and the national security adviser in turn consulted some of the foreign policy experts on the White House staff. As was true with few exceptions during the course of the administration, the experts were horrified by the idea of eliminating nuclear weapons, considering this to be impractical and heedless of the nuclear deterrence that had kept the peace since 1945. In a memo to Reagan July 9, Clark recommended that references to nuclear weapons be eliminated "to counter the risk of so emphasizing the importance we attach to arms reductions as to lead the Soviets to up the ante." Reagan accepted his staff's advice and took out the references to reducing or eliminating nuclear weapons. Using the Clark memo as his guide, Reagan recopied the letter in his own handwriting on White House stationery, dated July 11, 1983, with these final paragraphs:

> Mr. General Secretary could we not begin to approach these goals in the meetings now going on in Geneva? We both share an enormous responsibility for the preservation of stability in the world. I believe we can fulfill that mandate, but in order to do so, it will require a more active level of exchange than we have

heretofore been able to establish. There's much to talk about with regard to the situation in Eastern Europe and South Asia and particularly this hemisphere as well as in such areas as arms control, trade between our two countries and other ways in which we can expand East-West contacts.

Historically our predecessors have made better progress when they communicated privately and candidly. If you wish to engage in such communication you will find me ready. I await your reply.

The letter was received with surprise and confusion in Moscow, according to Kornienko, especially because the handwritten missive from Reagan coincided with a standard diplomatic demarche from Shultz giving no hint of potential movement in U.S. interaction with Moscow. The Soviets were puzzled about which U.S. view to accept as authentic and how to respond. After a few days, they solved the problem by sending back two separate replies—a tough Foreign Ministry response to the State Department message and a more positive Andropov letter to Reagan, also drafted in the Foreign Ministry, which was delivered by the Soviet Embassy to the White House August 4 in a sealed envelope. The letter included a brief PS in the Soviet leader's handwriting expressing the hope that Reagan would "give serious consideration to the thoughts I have expressed and that you will be able to respond to them in a constructive spirit." Andropov's handwriting was so shaky that White House aides felt Andropov was either under great tension or suffering from a motor infirmity.

In response to Reagan's suggestion of confidential communication, a procedure that was second nature in the Kremlin, Andropov wrote:

I shall welcome a concrete, businesslike and candid exchange of opinions with you on these and other questions. I agree that the exchange be confidential when the interests of the matter so dictate. For my part I would propose to do this through the Soviet Ambassador in Washington and a person whom you would designate.

Despite Dobrynin's status as dean of the diplomatic corps and his long experience in dealing with Washington officialdom, the Reagan administration was not happy about dealing with Moscow exclusively through him. Dobrynin, a bluff, hearty man who had been an aide to Foreign Minister Vyacheslav Molotov as well as Andrei Gromyko before becoming ambassador to Washington in 1962, was something of an operator, in Washington parlance, and officials were uncertain at times whether the ideas he expressed were his own or those of his government. In addition, Shultz often found that he could not understand what Dobrynin was saying in his accented but rapid-fire English, and the ambassador was much too practiced to use an interpreter. He also rarely took notes and usually was not accompanied by a note-taker, even in important meetings, raising doubts in Washington about the accuracy of what he sent back to Moscow.

Dobrynin, in turn, considered Shultz lacking in flexibility and may have doubted his clout within an administration that was sharply divided on Soviet policy. Dobrynin made a number of efforts to do business directly with the White House, as he had done in the days when Henry Kissinger was running President Nixon's foreign policy from the White House basement as national security adviser, often without the knowledge or participation of the State Department. After telephoning Clark on the occasion of the death of Brezhnev, Dobrynin opened a dialogue with the Reagan national security adviser and on several occasions exchanged confidential written messages between the Kremlin and the White House by sending an Embassy official to Clark's apartment. Shultz knew nothing of these exchanges.

In the summer of 1983 Clark sought to obtain formal responsibility for high-level dialogue with Moscow for himself and McFarlane, arguing to Reagan in a July 9 memorandum that "it's clear that the Russians have never taken any subordinate level seriously" and that the NSC staff (unlike the State Department) had a proven record of keeping secrets. Shultz, whom Clark described as "a solid economist," should perhaps take charge of a Pacific Basin initiative, the NSC adviser proposed to the President.

Clark also volunteered to travel to Moscow to pursue the U.S.-Soviet dialogue, an idea that had been suggested by Dobrynin. The notion that Shultz might go to Moscow in the summer, as the secretary had suggested in the spring, had faded because of the lack of progress in the relationship with the Kremlin. As it turned out, neither Clark nor Shultz went to Moscow in 1983.

• SHOWDOWN FOR SHULTZ

The summer of 1983 was not a good time for Shultz, who had been named secretary of state the previous summer after the ouster of Reagan's first secretary of state, Alexander Haig. Besides the differences of opinion and bureaucratic competition with Clark on Soviet policy, Shultz was engaged in what seemed to be a losing battle for control of policymaking regarding more urgent issues of Lebanon and Central America. Shultz had learned to his dismay in mid-July that McFarlane had gone to Syria and Saudi Arabia on a secret trip related to Lebanon aboard the airplane of the Saudi ambassador to Washington, Prince Bandar. Clark maintained then and later that Shultz had been informed of the NSC deputy director's clandestine visit, but the secretary of state was certain he was neither consulted nor even informed.

Even worse was the infighting over Central America. In the third week of July, Reagan approved a Defense Department plan for a large increase in U.S. air, sea and land operations near Nicaragua, including preparations for a possible U.S. naval blockade. The first Shultz knew of it was when *The New York Times* disclosed it with a splash on Saturday, July 23, in a front-page article by Philip Taubman. There was an immediate uproar in Congress, where Central American policy was under heated debate. When Shultz asked Clark on Monday morning if a new presidential order had been issued on Nicaragua, as reported in the *Times*, Clark was evasive. The NSC staff aide for Central America, Alfonso Sapia-Bosch, had shown a copy of Reagan's order to Shultz's assistant secretary for Latin affairs, Langhorne Motley, but refused to give him a copy and said he would only show it to Shultz if the secretary read it in his presence. The Pentagon plans had not been disclosed in interagency meetings at Motley's level that were supposed to be formulating Central American policy, nor at a National Security Council meeting on Central America that Shultz had attended.

At the White House on Monday morning, Shultz complained to Reagan that he was very concerned about disarray in administration policy. Clark, who was present, said everything was fine. Hearing two opposite opinions from Shultz and Clark, the President had said nothing. At another meeting with Reagan in the afternoon, Clark objected that Shultz's criticism was unfair. However, Shultz learned that the presidential order on Central America, which he had not seen until after the contents were disclosed in the *Times*, had been issued fully a week earlier.

Making all this more humiliating for Shultz was the widespread press and public perception that Clark had become the dominant figure in U.S. foreign policy, as depicted in cover stories about Clark in *Time* and *The New York Times Magazine* and a front-page story by Lou Cannon in *The Washington Post* describing Clark as "the strong man of President Reagan's many-sided policy in Central America." On August 3, NBC's veteran diplomatic correspondent, Marvin Kalb, reported it was unlikely that Shultz would serve in a second Reagan administration, if Reagan were reelected. Shultz complained to an aide, "The unraveling of my image is a problem. If they want to paint me as a hopeless, irrelevant person, it will be hard to correct."

Confronted with this, Shultz boiled over, marching into the Oval Office and telling Reagan he was ready to resign. "Either you want a secretary of state who is sort of an errand boy—and if that's what you want, that's not me—or you want somebody that you can have some confidence in," Shultz exploded. He said he was ready to leave, and nobody need worry about him because "I've got tenure" at Stanford University. In this first of at least four attempts to resign during his six-and-a-half-year stay at the State Department, Shultz gave the President a list of potential successors. Reagan, astonished at the sudden volcanic eruption by this seemingly steady team player and dismayed at the prospect of losing another secretary of state to internecine struggles, mollified Shultz with words of confidence in him and promises of greater authority and regular meetings with the secretary in the Oval Office.

George Pratt Shultz, sixty-three, a former Princeton football player and ex-Marine with a baby-pink complexion, brought to the job long experience in government and an interesting American background. An early ancestor, Peter Shultz, came to the United States from Germany around the time of the American Revolution, possibly as a mercenary to fight for the British, but soon took up the colonists' cause. Later the family settled on farms in western Indiana and became Quakers; nevertheless, the second Peter Shultz, the grandson of the founding immigrant, was not a proper Quaker pacifist but a soldier for the Union army in the Civil War. Birl Shultz, the secretary of state's father, was a history teacher and high-school principal in Indiana before he became one of the first of his family to move East to obtain his Ph.D. at Columbia University. In 1922 he organized the New York Stock Exchange Institute to provide training for employees of the big board. "Doc" Shultz, as he was known, was the author of standard textbooks on the securities market and the respected mentor of a generation of Wall Street stock traders, including Donald Regan of Merrill Lynch, later secretary of the treasury and White House chief of staff. Regan described the elder Shultz as "tweedy, patient, encyclopedic in his knowledge of Wall Street and its workings . . . a worldly Mr. Chips." Margaret Pratt, "Doc" Shultz's wife, was the daughter of a prominent Episcopalian minister. The couple reared their only child, George, as an Episcopalian, but his Quaker heritage may have contributed to his reserved, self-contained way of dealing with others, an attribute that often made his personal views difficult to discern. An official who worked under him in the Nixon administration said that frequently "the only way you could get a clue about what George thought was how high he raised his eyebrow" even in meetings with close aides. Assistant Secretary of Defense Richard Perle, who spent many hours conferring with Shultz on contentious issues, said, "There are substances that absorb radiation and substances that bounce it back, and he's like lithium—he just absorbs enormous quantities of whatever you throw at him and you don't get anything back."

Shultz was an economics major at Princeton, where he acquired a Princeton Tiger tattoo on his rump that would fascinate his children and intrigue the public when its presence was reported in the press decades later. After combat service as a U.S. Marine officer in the Pacific in World War II, Shultz obtained his Ph.D. in industrial economics at Massachusetts Institute of Technology in 1949 and began a career as a professor, with a sideline as a labor-management mediator. By the time he became secretary of state, he had held a wide variety of posts in a multifaceted career combining academia, government and business: professor at MIT; staff economist for the Eisenhower administration's Council of Economic Advisers; dean of the Graduate School of Business at the University of Chicago; secretary of labor, director of the budget and secretary of the treasury in the Nixon administration; and president of Bechtel Corporation, the giant worldwide construction company headquartered in San Francisco. While at Bechtel he kept his hand in his original career by concurrently serving part-time as a professor of management and public policy at Stanford University and living in a faculty house on the Stanford campus. Even on this part-time basis, Shultz was granted tenure on the Stanford faculty, which he retained along with his faculty house in an "on leave" status after resigning from Bechtel to become secretary of state in 1982. By that time, Shultz was a wealthy man from his business career, but he considered the campus his home. When troubled or challenged, he threatened to return to it as he did in the 1983 conversation with Reagan.

Shultz first met Reagan when Reagan, then governor of California, invited him to Sacramento in 1974, shortly after Shultz left the Nixon administration to live in California, and interrogated him relentlessly about the workings of the federal government. It was clear to Shultz that Reagan was planning to run for president and thinking about how to do the job of president if he should be elected in 1976. Later Reagan and Shultz sized each other up again at a dinner at Shultz's house at Stanford. Eventually Shultz served as chairman of Reagan's economic advisory committee in the 1980 campaign and was a spokesman on economic issues.

Flexible on many political issues but absolutely unyielding on questions that struck him as matters of personal or public ethics, Shultz as secretary of the treasury clashed with President Nixon in refusing to order the Internal Revenue Service to investigate the President's political enemies and in refusing to stop an IRS audit of Nixon's income tax returns. Nixon referred to Shultz as a "candy ass" in an Oval Office conversation that was taped and eventually made public in connection with Watergate. According to Reagan biographer Lou Cannon, Nixon wrote Reagan after the November 1980 election that "I do not believe that he [Shultz] has the depth of understanding of world issues generally and the Soviet Union in particular that is needed for this [secretary of state] job." Subsequently there were numerous reports that Shultz was Reagan's first choice as secretary of state but that a misunderstanding in a telephone conversation with Shultz during the transition period led the President-elect to believe Shultz had turned down the job. Shultz is certain that the job was never offered. Cannon, who looked into the incident extensively, concluded that Shultz was the first choice of Reagan's transition committee but that, perhaps because of Nixon's memo, Reagan chose Haig.

Shultz obtained his initial familiarity with the Soviet Union on two official trips to the USSR in 1973 while serving as Nixon's treasury secretary. He conferred with General Secretary Brezhnev, Premier Aleksei Kosygin and other high officials about a U.S.-Soviet trade agreement. As president of Bechtel, Shultz also had experience with Soviet officials, canceling the contract for construction of a proposed Moscow trade center after he came to suspect it could somehow be involved in espionage. Shultz was unimpressed with what he saw in the Soviet Union, which he described before becoming secretary of state as "a failure in economic terms" and "appalling as a system in human terms." While he was deeply conservative and skeptical about Moscow, Shultz's experiences also left him believing it was by no means impossible to deal constructively with the Soviet leadership. In 1983, Shultz was one of the few top officials in the foreign policy ranks of the Reagan administration who thought so, and the only one who had any practical experience in dealing with Soviet leaders.

Shultz was a very different figure from the secretaries of state who had preceded him over the previous decade. Henry Kissinger was a professorial conceptualizer of international affairs, a strategist who had a sophisticated European view of the flow of power among nations, but who was saddled with the task of ending an unsuccessful war and presiding over the ebbing of American endurance and international prestige. Cyrus Vance was a lawyer who took on the world, case by case, with great energy and integrity until sheer fatigue and accelerating conflict in Iran and Afghanistan shattered the chances for rational mediation. He resigned on principle over President Carter's unsuccessful hostage raid in 1980. Edmund Muskie, who served briefly after Vance's resignation, was a political figure of great prestige and communications skills who did not have time enough to make an impact in the job. Alexander Haig, Reagan's original secretary of state, was a career military officer turned politician, with a broad view of global strategy but also a transparent ambition for the presidency that poisoned his relations with Reagan's protective phalanx at the White House.

As an economist and a professor, Shultz brought to the job a patience for long-term enterprises and objectives that was unusual. His extensive labor-mediating experience gave him confidence in the utility of personal negotiations and a stolid equanimity when everything seemed on the verge of falling apart. On a bureaucratic level his four cabinet posts— more than any other American in history, except for Elliot Richardson, who tied the record—provided Shultz with a sure sense of how the Washington game was played. On the other hand, he was a newcomer to many international political and military issues that were familiar to those around him, seeming at the start, for example, to be surprisingly naive about the Middle East, and he was a novice on arms control questions, many of which have highly technical aspects. As a correspondent covering U.S. diplomacy, I often found Shultz difficult to fathom, almost mysterious at times, because he so rarely gave a clue to what he was thinking or advocating in the inner circles. Much of what is in this book about Shultz's attitudes and especially his relations with Reagan was unknown to me and other journalists at the time because "the Sphinx," as we sometimes called him, would not tell us.

One thing stood out. Shultz was renowned in governmental circles as a man of integrity and good judgment. Kissinger, who later became critical of Shultz's plodding pace and lack of grand strategy as secretary of state, wrote in awe of his qualities in his memoir, *Years of Upheaval*, which was published just about the time Shultz was named secretary of state in 1982. "If I could choose one American to whom I would entrust the nation's fate in a crisis, it would be George Shultz," Kissinger wrote. By 1983, however, Shultz was facing a crisis of his own inside the Reagan administration.

By the time Reagan went to his ranch in California for his summer vacation in mid-August, the administration's inner struggle had abated temporarily and Shultz had decided to stay on. Moreover, Washington and Moscow had begun to take some modest steps toward improving relations. The Siberian Pentecostals who had been living in the U.S. Embassy had left the USSR for new homes in the United States, and a KGB official indicated to a U.S. diplomat that the celebrated dissident Anatoly Shcharansky might be released from prison early the following year. The Soviets had agreed to talks on upgrading the emergency "hot line" communications link with Washington and to separate discussions on the consular and cultural agreements that Shultz had proposed. More reasonable Soviet positions were noticed in the Madrid talks on European security and human rights issues, and on some minor aspects of the Geneva arms talks. The arrangements for the new Long Term Grain Agreement had been agreed to by negotiators on both sides. And on August 20, in a gesture recommended by Shultz, Reagan ended U.S. controls on the sale of gas pipeline equipment to the Soviet Union.

From California on August 24, Reagan sent a new letter to Andropov, which like the first one was not made public. This one was much less personal, being largely written by the White House staff, and in the main was a statement of the U.S. position in the Euromissiles dispute in response to arguments advanced by Andropov in his August 4 letter. But in a broader dimension, Reagan observed in the first paragraph of his letter that he could see from Andropov's earlier letter "that we both recognize the awesome responsibility history has placed on our shoulders to guide the two most powerful countries in the world in this difficult and dangerous period." Reagan went on to say, in a passage that reflected his desire for dialogue:

> You have asked me to try to understand Moscow's view of some of the critical issues, and I can assure you that I do try. Could I ask in return that you take a look at the world as it appears from Washington? As Commander-in-Chief, I have not a single military unit on combat status. If all national leaders could say the same we would be on our way to a safer world. If each of us determined we would not resort to war as a solution to any problem, arms reduction would be simply and easily achieved. If on the other hand we approach the issue holding to a belief that war is somehow inevitable, then we are doomed to failure. I think that we must find a way either to discuss these problems frankly, or at the very least, to give greater weight to the attitudes of the other party when making fateful decisions. In the end, it really makes no difference whether we reduce these problems by specific understandings or by simply acting so that they are reduced. The essential point is that they must be reduced if we are to give the other important items on our agenda a fair chance of success.

Within a week of Reagan's letter, a serious new problem, unforeseen by either the President or the General Secretary, was to bring a crisis in their relations, beginning with a burst of rocket fire against a civilian airliner high above Soviet Asia.

2. The Ebb Tide

The telephone rang at 6:30 A.M. on Thursday, September 1, 1983, in George Shultz's bedroom on a tree-lined street in suburban Bethesda, Maryland. Two aides were on the line reporting that a Korean Air Lines 747 had disappeared from the skies the night before near the Soviet Far East, and that it seemed increasingly certain that the Soviet Union had shot it down. The 269 people aboard, including many Americans, were presumed dead.

The secretary of state was horrified to hear that a civilian airliner had been shot down by a Soviet military plane, which apparently had been tracking it for a long period of time. He hurriedly dressed and had breakfast with two house guests from California. As the gravity of the news began to sink in, Shultz told his guests that the future relations of the United States and the Soviet Union would depend in part on whether the Soviets accepted blame for "a terrible mistake" or "whether they try to defend it."

Shultz arrived at his office at 7:53 A.M that Thursday and plunged into the crisis five minutes later with an intelligence briefing, followed by a meeting with four senior aides, headed by Under Secretary of State Lawrence Eagleburger. With his aides standing by at his elbow, Shultz placed a call on a secure government line to William Clark, the President's national security adviser, who was in California with the vacationing Reagan. It was only

5:22 A.M. on the West Coast but for eighteen minutes, Shultz and Clark discussed the intelligence reports received from Asia. A secret U.S.-Japanese listening post in northern Japan had intercepted radio transmissions from a Soviet pilot as he visually inspected the plane, fired his missiles and reported to his headquarters in Russian, "The target is destroyed."

After negotiations with U.S. intelligence agencies and Japanese officials about use of the highly classified intercepts, Shultz convened a press conference at the State Department at 10:45 A.M. and made public the shocking news of the shootdown. Shultz's statement was a deliberately spare, methodical rendition of the actions of Soviet fighter planes, based on the intercepts, as they pursued and destroyed Korean Air Lines Flight 007. With that prelude, the final sentences from the usually impassive Shultz carried a powerful emotional wallop: "The United States reacts with revulsion to this attack. Loss of life appears to be heavy. We can see no excuse whatsoever for this appalling act."

Shultz's announcement and the outcry that followed would plunge the already strained relations of the two leading nations to new depths of enmity. The Soviet Union, just as Shultz had feared, would at first seek to deny all knowledge and responsibility for the downing of the civilian airliner, despite convincing evidence to the contrary. A week later, Shultz and Soviet Foreign Minister Andrei Gromyko would clash bitterly in Madrid at probably the most acrimonious meeting the two nations' leading officials ever held. Before the end of September General Secretary Yuri Andropov was to issue a written statement—which, unknown to the Soviet or American public, emanated from the hospital room where he was living out his final months—that seemed to write off any possibility of improved relations with the government of Ronald Reagan. By the end of the year, a war scare in Moscow and the walkout of Soviet negotiators from the Geneva arms talks would bring the relations of the United States and the Soviet Union to a dangerous low point and cause a shudder of apprehension throughout the world.

• THE KAL 007 CRISIS

The KAL 007 crisis began in the early hours of September 1 in the Far East—midday on August 31, Washington time—when the Korean airliner flying from Alaska to Seoul strayed three hundred miles off course and penetrated Soviet air space, for reasons that probably will never be conclusively established.* Soviet fighter pilot Lieutenant Colonel Gennadi Osipovich, then thirty-nine years old, was on duty at his base in the Soviet Far East when he received an order to intercept an intruding aircraft: "Invader has violated state border. Destroy target." After firing bursts of warning shots from his Su-15 jet fighter, which Osipovich said later his target probably could not see, he received a final order to "Destroy invader" just as the aircraft was about to fly out of Soviet air space. He recalled later, "I fired two missiles and brought down the target." He had attacked a large aircraft with its lights and flashers on, unlike any reconnaissance plane he had ever seen, but he insisted that he "never thought for a moment" that it was a civilian airliner. "The trouble for all Soviet pilots is that we do not study civilian aircraft belonging to foreign companies," said Osipovich years later.

The fatal missiles struck KAL 007 on Wednesday, August 31, at 3:26 A.M. Tokyo time, or 2:26 P.M. Washington time. All radio transmissions suddenly ceased from the airliner as parts of the jumbo jet were blown apart and the rest of the ship and its passengers and crew spiraled thirty-five thousand feet in a final twelve-minute plunge into the Sea of Japan.

The disappearance from the skies of the civilian airliner at first confounded air controllers and government agencies in the Far East. But within hours, U.S. intelligence agencies began assembling the pieces of the puzzle based on fragments of the radio intercepts. By 10:30 P.M. Wednesday, the night before Shultz was informed of the shootdown, CIA Director William Casey informed White House national security adviser

---

* Reagan, giving credence to the most well-accepted U.S. theory in the wake of the disaster, wrote in his 1990 memoir, *An American Life*, that "we determined, based on the circumstances of the incident, that the crew of Flight 007 . . . apparently set the computer on the plane's automatic pilot system incorrectly, allowing it to stray north into Soviet airspace instead of flying toward Japan." He did not say how this was "determined" or by whom.

Clark by telephone of "unconfirmed" reports that a Korean airliner was down and "it may have been forced down or shot down by the Soviets." Clark, who was in Santa Barbara, telephoned Reagan at his secluded ranch with the news.

Although he was caricatured internationally as a cowboy with his finger on the trigger, the President's immediate reaction was cautious. "Bill, let's pray that it's not true," he told Clark. But if it is true, Reagan went on, "at this particular time we've got to be very careful that we don't overreact." After a second report from Casey through Clark three hours later that the likelihood was growing that the Soviets had downed the plane, Reagan went to bed for the night. Shultz's staff, which also had concluded sometime after midnight that the Soviets probably had shot down the airliner, decided not to wake the secretary of state.

As Reagan had noted, the shootdown came at a very sensitive time, domestically and overseas. Over the summer Reagan's political aides had begun the start of planning for his 1984 reelection campaign. The President's pollster, Richard Wirthlin, had told him that the popular fear of his leading the United States into an unnecessary war was his most serious political vulnerability. Overseas, U.S.-Soviet relations and the international environment generally were still extremely tense despite the feelers that Reagan and Shultz had begun putting out earlier in the year. Looming just ahead was what had been forecast to be the "hot autumn" of 1983, the time when U.S. intermediate-range missiles with nuclear warheads were to be deployed in Western Europe in the face of intense opposition from Moscow and European peace activists.

Because the KAL crisis broke the week before Labor Day, much of the top rank of the U.S. government, like Reagan, was on vacation. This provided the opportunity for Shultz and the State Department to take the lead in the initial stages without challenge from other elements of the divided and quarrelsome administration. The nearly immediate decision in Shultz's seventh-floor office at the State Department that Thursday morning was to get the word out quickly of what had really happened in the Pacific the night before. One important reason, in Shultz's view, was "to let the Soviets know that we knew what happened. They shouldn't think that they could in some manner deny it. And while we were outraged, at the same time, we felt well, if they know that we know and we have this thing all clear, maybe there's some way there can be a sensible response." Shultz's last aim suggested that the unwritten code of conduct between the two nations had come a long way since May 1960, when Soviet leader Nikita Khrushchev announced that Soviet defenders had shot down an intruding U.S. spy plane but, to trap the Americans into false denials, deliberately withheld the crucial news that U-2 pilot Francis Gary Powers was alive and in custody.

Shultz's senior deputy on KAL 007 was Under Secretary Lawrence Eagleburger, a former Henry Kissinger aide at the White House and State Department with much experience in the top ranks of government. A shrewd and sometimes astringent observer of the Washington scene, Eagleburger had remarked early in the Reagan administration that it was in reality "a coalition government" made up of two kinds of conservative officials: one group intent primarily on pursuing its ideology after decades in the political wilderness and the other group primarily concerned with the practical job of governing the country. The chain-smoking, tough-talking Eagleburger was among the pragmatists, but he was worried about the ideologists. It was important, he felt, to get ahead of events and in control of the news flow. "I had the firm view that the more you did publicly and the more you did it in a firm way, tough way, the less likely you were to be charged with being a wimp and the less likely you were to have a lot of sanctions, either from the [Capitol] Hill or from the right within the administration."

Another member of the team gathered in Shultz's office that morning was his executive assistant, Raymond Seitz, who urged the secretary to break the news to the public in person. He later conceded he had an ulterior motive: to demonstrate that the beleaguered Shultz was in charge.

When Shultz read the U.S. account of the shootdown in the State Department briefing room, reporters could hear his voice occasionally rising in anger as he described the attack on the unarmed civilian airliner, an attack that had snuffed out more lives than any other U.S.-Soviet incident since the beginning of the Cold War. Among the sixty-three Americans on the plane, all presumed dead, was Representative Larry McDonald of Georgia, the chairman of the John Birch Society. Aware of the international repercussions of the act and its aftermath, Shultz was calm but his emotions showed. NBC News correspondent Roger Mudd, commenting on the live press conference, called Shultz's reaction "controlled fury." Assistant Secretary of State Richard Burt, who played a major role in the handling of KAL 007, observed the secretary's suppressed passions. "He really has it in his eyes," Burt said as he watched Shultz announce the startling news of the Soviet Union's use of deadly force.

• MOSCOW REACTS

There is no indication that Soviet leader Yuri Andropov or the other Politburo members were consulted as fighter planes stalked and destroyed KAL 007. Marshal Nikolai Ogarkov, then chief of staff of the Soviet armed forces, said at an extraordinary press conference nine days after the fact that the decision to shoot down the intruding aircraft had been taken by a local air defense commander. While it may be literally true that this commander gave the order to open fire, the prevailing evidence today is that a higher military headquarters in Moscow was queried on the night of August 31 and instructed the local commander in the Far East to follow existing procedures, which called for an intruding plane to be stopped at all costs, violently if necessary. Marshal Sergei Akhromeyev, who was Ogarkov's deputy at the time and later his successor as chief of staff of the Soviet armed forces, told me that the shooting down "was decided by Moscow," though he declined to say who in the capital was consulted. Georgi Kornienko, then first deputy foreign minister and longtime associate of Foreign Minister Andrei Gromyko, said he was informed that the decision was made in the Ministry of Defense, which did not take the matter to the Politburo but told the local commander, "Try to make the plane land. If not, act according to regulations."

Whatever the reports from its own military channels, the Soviet leadership heard about the disappearance of KAL 007 quickly from the State Department. Around midnight August 31 in Washington, less than ten hours after the fatal attack, Assistant Secretary of State Burt awakened Oleg Sokolov, the Soviet Embassy's ranking diplomat in the absence of Ambassador Anatoly Dobrynin. Sokolov was told by telephone that the plane had disappeared near the Soviet border, that a U.S. congressman and many others were on board and that information was urgently requested from Moscow. Shortly thereafter the U.S. Embassy in Moscow made a similar appeal to the Foreign Ministry. The following morning, amid mounting evidence that a Soviet fighter had destroyed the plane, Sokolov was called to the State Department, where he was presented with a renewed demand for information.

There is little doubt that the Soviet military believed at the time it was shooting down an intruding aircraft engaged in military reconnaissance, in the popular parlance, a "spy plane." For years, the U.S. military had been flying intelligence missions right along the Soviet border in the Far East, and one such mission was in the air shortly before KAL 007 was shot down. The immediate Soviet justification for destroying a civilian airliner that flew across its border and over militarily sensitive areas was that KAL 007 was pursuing a covert espionage mission, and to a startling degree that has remained the view of senior Soviet officers, despite the lack of evidence for this hypothesis. The Soviet defense minister, Dmitri Yazov, appeared convinced of the espionage thesis five years after the shootdown, in August 1988, when he brought up the matter with Secretary of Defense Frank Carlucci, his guest in the Crimea during an official trip. Riding in the privacy of an official limousine, Yazov asked Carlucci in the most confidential of tones, "Tell me, why did you Americans use that Korean airliner as a spy plane?" Carlucci, a former deputy director of the CIA, was taken aback by the question but quickly rebutted the charge. "Don't be silly. We didn't use it as a spy plane. If we want to get information from you, we've got all the satellites in the world. We don't need a spy plane," Carlucci responded. To which Yazov persisted, "Yes, that's right. That's why I wondered why you used it as a spy plane." Akhromeyev and others continue to insist, without producing any evidence, that "KAL 007 purposefully changed its route and flew over Soviet air space," for what purpose and at whose order, the marshal said recently, he does not know.

For Russia, which has often been invaded by hostile armies, and especially for the communist regime, which has perceived itself to be surrounded by enemies since 1917, tight control of its borders has been an obsession bordering on paranoia. In an earlier Korean Air Lines incident, in 1978, a KAL 747 was forced down in European Russia by Soviet jet fighters after it mistakenly flew over the heavily fortified Kola Peninsula. Two passengers were killed. According to a later investigation by Seymour Hersh, the Soviet pilot stubbornly ignored orders from a superior officer to shoot down the plane, which was easily identifiable as a civilian airliner in the daylight incident. After that, Soviet air defense was further tightened.

This time, the order to shoot was obeyed unquestioningly, with heavy loss of life. It was quickly apparent to officials in Moscow that the international consequences would be severe. Those with experience in the West realized the claim that the plane had been spying would not save Moscow from strong condemnation for killing innocent passengers. It was one of those moments when the often well-prepared Soviet security system faced the unexpected—and in this case, failed the test. While the world listened expectantly for a Soviet explanation of what had happened, Moscow for five days denied responsibility for the attack despite the extensive evidence made public in the United States, thus making its problems much worse. It has long been a mystery why the Soviet Union chose to handle the aftermath of the shootdown in such a damaging fashion. But according to Georgi Kornienko, then first deputy minister of foreign affairs and a participant in the discussion, the decision to deny responsibility was made personally by Soviet leader Yuri Andropov almost on the spur of the moment on the recommendation of Defense Minister Dmitri Ustinov. Kornienko's account provides a case study of the highly personal and sometimes disastrous way in which the higher officials of the Soviet Union operated at the time.

Kornienko, who was Gromyko's closest aide at the Foreign Ministry and had had lengthy experience in U.S. affairs, became concerned after receiving the U.S. inquiries through the Soviet Embassy in Washington and the U.S. Embassy in Moscow. Learning that a Soviet fighter had shot down the airliner, Kornienko recommended that the Soviet Union accept responsibility and go on to say that, even though the plane appeared to be on an espionage mission, Moscow regretted the loss of life, which was not intended. In a recent interview Kornienko said that Gromyko agreed with him but, as sometimes happened, the foreign minister was reluctant to take a stand on an issue likely to be controversial among other senior members of the Politburo. In a number of such cases, including this one, Gromyko made clear to Kornienko that he would not object if he wished to argue the case with higher authorities.

Kornienko had had a good relationship for many years with Andropov and decided to telephone him directly. When he reached the ailing Andropov at the VIP hospital at Kuntsevo, the General Secretary heard him out and then placed a call on another line to Defense Minister Ustinov, who was a powerful figure politically and personally close to Andropov and whose support had been essential in Andropov's election ten months earlier. With Kornienko listening to Andropov's side of the conversation, Ustinov strongly objected to any statement implying that the Soviet armed forces had erred, arguing that nobody would ever know or be able to prove that the Soviet Union had shot down the airliner. Kornienko considered this a ridiculous argument in an era of long-range radars and eavesdropping devices, and he felt sure that Ustinov's own military experts would have told him so if he had chosen to consult them rather than give his own emotional reaction.

Surprisingly, despite Andropov's sophistication and his fifteen years as chief of the KGB intelligence apparatus, the leader accepted Ustinov's view and ordered that the Soviet Union make no admission that it had downed the airliner or statement of regret about the loss of life. Asked how Andropov could make such a bizarre decision in view of the predictable consequences of worldwide consternation, Kornienko said, "He was really not in good shape in those days."

As Shultz was issuing his statement at the State Department detailing the Soviet fighters' pursuit and destruction of KAL 007, the Soviet news agency Tass was preparing to issue a very different account at the direction of the Soviet leadership: a statement that an "unidentified plane" had been warned by Soviet fighters and had flown away in the direction of the Sea of Japan.

As the international reaction to the shocking deed and deceptive words began to roll in, the editors of the Soviet government newspaper *Izvestia* assigned one of its most senior writers, Aleksandr Bovin, to interpret the situation. Bovin, a former judge and senior Communist Party member who was among his country's most independent journalists, refused to write anything until the Soviet Union issued an apology for shooting down the airplane. Bovin had worked for Andropov at the Central Committee of the Communist Party before Andropov moved to the KGB in 1967 and was on good terms with the party leader. He tried in vain to telephone Andropov but was told he was leaving on vacation. Bovin then took his urgent concern to the next ranking Soviet official on duty, Politburo member Mikhail Gorbachev, who was living through one of his first international crises. In what Bovin would later describe as a "rather harsh talk," Gorbachev seemed unsympathetic to Bovin's complaints that the Soviet public response to the air disaster was woefully inadequate and told the journalist not to be so agitated. "I am nervous," Bovin told Gorbachev, "because I see this flood of propaganda that is being leveled against us."

• MEETING IN MADRID

It was clear from its first moments that the meeting of Secretary Shultz and Foreign Minister Gromyko in Madrid on September 8, one week after the KAL 007 shootdown, was going to be a tense and difficult one. The atmosphere was strained and the diplomatic amenities barely observed. Shultz declined to meet Gromyko at the front door of the U.S. ambassador's residence in Madrid as expected, and the dining-room table set aside for the meeting—which originally had been planned as a luncheon—was bare, without even the usual carafes of water or soft drinks, pads and pencils.

Later Shultz called it "a rock-and-sock meeting" and quoted his veteran State Department interpreter, William Krimer, as saying he had never seen anything remotely like it in nearly two decades of participating in high-level U.S.-Soviet exchanges. Gromyko's view was much the same: He said it was "probably the sharpest exchange I ever had with an American secretary of state, and I have had talks with 14 of them."

The original U.S. plan had been to use this session, the first such top-level meeting with the Soviets in nearly a year, to give impetus to a broad improvement in relations, including an invitation for Gromyko to visit the White House in the fall and the exploration of a possible Reagan-Andropov summit meeting in the spring of 1984. But then KAL 007 and its bitter aftermath made the original plan impractical and raised strong doubts about whether the Shultz-Gromyko meeting would be held at all.

The very first question asked by reporters of Shultz after he announced the shooting down of the Korean airliner was whether his planned meeting with Gromyko would take place. "I certainly will want to meet with Foreign Minister Gromyko and hear what he says about this," responded Shultz, anticipating that he would obtain authority from Reagan to go ahead with the meeting. Later he did so, but only after a battle at the White House with Secretary of Defense Caspar Weinberger and others. Weinberger argued that calling off this and other planned meetings would dramatize the message that "this kind of action was intolerable" and should carry "a very high penalty" for the Soviets. Shultz countered that it was more important than ever to see Gromyko to "tell him straight out our views of this" and that "refusing to meet with people is not the way to do it." The compromise reached in the National Security Council session with Reagan on Friday evening, September 2, was that Shultz would meet Gromyko as scheduled—but that the planned luncheon would be canceled and Shultz's agenda would be limited to KAL 007, human rights in the Soviet Union and U.S. complaints of Soviet noncompliance with arms control agreements. All those topics were certain to be anathema to Gromyko. The game plan guaranteed an explosive meeting.

The U.S. strategy in the KAL 007 crisis was to keep the Soviet Union on the defensive with strong rhetoric and international condemnation, especially after Moscow fanned the global fire by refusing to accept responsibility. At the same time, Reagan accepted the Shultz position that U.S. sanctions or other retaliatory actions be kept to a minimum, lest sanctions become a divisive issue between Washington and its allies. The administration should not permit the Soviets to portray the crisis as a U.S.-Soviet political issue when it really was a moral question of the Soviet Union against the world, Shultz argued.

It was a surprise to some at the September 2 National Security Council meeting that Reagan endorsed this policy rather than accept proposals for stronger action against the Soviets from Treasury Secretary Donald Regan and other advisers. However, it was in keeping with the caution Reagan had initially expressed to Clark and at times to others. In many respects, it was the perfect strategy for Reagan, who performed best when declaiming powerful words and sweeping verities but was uncomfortable with ordering drastic action. In a televised speech to the nation from the Oval Office on September 5, which Reagan rewrote himself from staff members' less rhetorical drafts, the President described the shootdown as a "massacre" six times and also called it an "atrocity" and a "crime against humanity." Reagan declared that "there is no way a pilot could mistake this for anything other than a civilian airliner" although within the administration it had been well accepted by September 2 that the shooting was indeed a case of mistaken identity. On the action side, however, Reagan merely asked Congress to pass a joint resolution condemning the Soviet attack on the airliner, canceled the planned renewal of a U.S.-Soviet transportation accord and asked for an international investigation of the shootdown. Moreover, Reagan rejected a proposal by Weinberger that arms control negotiations with the Soviet Union be called off until there was a resolution of the KAL shootdown, and sent U.S. negotiators Paul Nitze and Edward Rowny back to Geneva in a public White House ceremony. In view of all this, New Right fund raiser Richard Viguerie accused Reagan of being "Teddy Roosevelt in reverse: he speaks loudly but carries a small twig."

As Shultz was flying to Madrid September 6, Tass published a new Soviet government statement admitting for the first time that, after warnings were unavailing, a Soviet fighter plane "fulfilled the order of the command post to stop the flight," that is, to shoot it down. The statement continued to charge that the airliner was on a spy mission concocted by the U.S. government, and depicted the Soviet Union as blameless. Gromyko took the same tack the following day in his address to the closing session of the three-year-old Madrid conference of the thirty-five-nation Conference on Security and Cooperation in Europe (CSCE), which was the occasion for the meeting with Shultz. "Soviet territory, the borders of the Soviet Union are sacred," declared Gromyko in condemning the "criminal act" of the intruding flight. Shultz took the unusual step of summoning television cameras to issue an immediate attack on Gromyko's callousness toward human life and his "continued falsehood" even before hearing the Soviet minister's private explanation the following day.

Gromyko arrived at the agreed meeting place, the U.S. ambassador's residence on a hillside overlooking Madrid, in a black sedan with curtained windows in the back. An aide, not the secretary, met him at the door. Close to two hundred reporters and photographers were milling around on the lawn outside, having been admitted to the heavily guarded and walled compound after being searched by U.S. security.

Shultz and Gromyko began their meeting with a one-on-one confidential session, with interpreters also present, in the library of the residence. Shultz immediately broached the KAL 007 shootdown and the status of the Soviet dissident Anatoly Shcharansky, who continued to languish in a labor camp. Gromyko did not want to discuss either subject and in a few minutes the two ministers emerged red in the face and both obviously very angry. After they joined the other members of the two delegations around the unadorned dining table, Shultz raised the question of Soviet responsibility for KAL 007. Gromyko broke in to say he had already made clear in the private session that he would not discuss the subject, and if Shultz was determined to persist there was no reason to continue the conversation. Gromyko then gathered his papers and stood up as if to leave. To the anxiety of some in his party, Shultz stood up, too, but made no effort to dissuade Gromyko. If you want to leave, "fine, go," Shultz said sharply. Some of Shultz's aides braced themselves for the bust-up of the meeting in its early minutes, which would have quickly escalated the already high level of worldwide tension.

Gromyko, however, kept talking as he stood in the dining room, occasionally pacing but not walking out. After a minute or two, it became clear he was reluctant to end the meeting prematurely, though he and Shultz were exchanging caustic words about what subjects were to be discussed. Shultz declared that he would not try to dictate what Gromyko would talk about, and Gromyko should not dictate what Shultz would say. Each would make his points as he wished. Finally Gromyko sat down to begin a presentation on the arms race and nuclear war. "The world situation is now slipping toward a very dangerous precipice," the Soviet minister said near the start of his remarks. "It is plain that the great responsibility for not allowing a nuclear catastrophe to occur must be borne by the U.S.S.R. and the U.S.A. together. In our opinion, the U.S.A. should reevaluate its policies, and the President and his administration should look at international affairs in a new way." Shultz, bound by his tight instructions, ignored Gromyko's remarks about U.S. policy.

After two hours, Gromyko emerged, waved aside the impatient press corps and left with nothing to say. A few minutes later, a grim, unsmiling Shultz emerged with notes in his hand. Citing "the unprovoked Soviet destruction of a defenseless, unarmed Korean airliner" and "the preposterous explanation" that only compounded the problem, Shultz declared flatly that "Foreign Minister Gromyko's response to me today was even more unsatisfactory than the response he gave in public yesterday. I find it totally unacceptable."

Shultz's indignant denunciation of Gromyko within two or three minutes of his departure was human and admirable at one level, but chilling at another level, in its implications for the fabric of dialogue between the superpowers. It seemed unlikely that the meetings with Gromyko in the White House that had been planned in connection with his September trip to the United Nations would go forward now. And the icy chill between the two leading nations could be dangerous, especially at a time when there were struggles in many areas and, it seemed, a confrontation-minded administration in Washington.

Reflecting the spreading sense of apprehension, Pope John Paul II warned three days later that the world might be moving from the postwar era to "a new prewar phase." A week after that, on September 17, Gromyko canceled his annual visit to the United Nations General Assembly after the governors of New York and New Jersey, reacting to popular sentiment against the shooting down of KAL 007 and encouraged by a National Security Council staff member, refused to permit landing rights for Gromyko's special Aeroflot jet. The same day, Reagan, in his

Saturday radio address, weighed in once more against the "crime and cover-up" of the Soviet Union. "We may not be able to change the Soviets' ways, but we can change our attitude toward them," said Reagan. In a passage that seemed to consign the Soviets to outer darkness, the President added: "We can stop pretending they share the same dreams and aspirations we do. We can start preparing ourselves for what John F. Kennedy called a long twilight struggle."

• MOSCOW'S SEASON OF GLOOM

The autumn of 1983 was a time of sadness and worry for the leaders of the Soviet Union.

A year earlier, in November 1982, they had buried Leonid Brezhnev at the Kremlin wall after an agonizing half-decade of failing health, ending what would later be known as "the years of stagnation." His successor as general secretary, Yuri Andropov, was seen as decisive and sophisticated—a welcome change. Vice President George Bush, the official U.S. representative at the Brezhnev funeral, found Andropov "more communicative and more open" in an initial meeting that had a more "friendly and jocular ambiance" than he had expected, possibly because both Andropov and Bush were former chiefs of their respective intelligence agencies. Shultz, who accompanied the vice president, came away with the view that Andropov was "a man of real ability, powerful . . . a formidable adversary." But this widespread impression of a full-time, functioning leader was seriously degraded within only a few months.

After Andropov's kidneys failed in February 1983, he slowed his activities and had difficulty walking, though foreign visitors reported that his mind was sharp. During the visit of Finnish President Mauno Koivisto in June, Soviet protocol was changed so that the General Secretary no longer met high-ranking visitors at the airport; at the Kremlin banquet for the Finnish leader, Andropov delivered his speech sitting down, and two men had to assist him to rise for the toasts. In July, West German Chancellor Helmut Kohl found that although Andropov was hardly permitted to walk at all, he was clear and vigorous in his arguments. Nonetheless, a West German photographer, who studied the Soviet leader through his camera's magnifying lens during a photo session with Kohl, confided that Andropov "is a man with the mark of death on his face."

The General Secretary's health took a sharp turn for the worse in late September or early October 1983, when he went from vacation to permanent residence in a specially prepared VIP suite in the Kremlin's Kuntsevo Hospital. Sometime in the fall, one kidney was reported to have been removed. Andropov continued to try to run the country via telephone and memoranda with the help of a small group of trusted associates, including his Politburo protégé, Mikhail Gorbachev. But the combination of disabling kidney disease, diabetes and heart trouble made Andropov immobile and invisible in the final months of his life, restarting the succession struggle within the Politburo.

In retrospect, the short fifteen-month reign of Yuri Andropov prepared the ground for the dramatic changes later introduced by Gorbachev. Andropov was Gorbachev's sponsor and patron in the Politburo, without whom Gorbachev would never have risen to the top. "We owe everything to him," Raisa Gorbachev remarked in Washington in 1987 when she spotted a photograph of the tall, gaunt, bespectacled former leader. Andropov recognized—as Brezhnev had not—that Soviet society and the Soviet state were in trouble, and that far-reaching changes would have to be made. It was in 1983, during the Andropov era, when a variety of serious studies were authorized—Gorbachev later said there were 110—to investigate major problems, most of which were economic, facing the country. The ideas generated in these and other frank discussions later formed the intellectual basis for Gorbachev's *perestroika* reform program.

Andropov was no iconoclast and he was not ready for radical change. A tough, austere and self-confident party man who had served fifteen years as head of the KGB secret police and intelligence agency under Brezhnev, he was a firm believer in discipline. But his KGB experience and his earlier service as Soviet ambassador in Hungary (where he is thought to have played a role in arranging the 1956 invasion) gave him a greater knowledge of the outside world than any of his predecessors since Lenin. For years before becoming general secretary, Andropov as KGB chairman along with Foreign Minister Andrei Gromyko and Defense Minister Dmitri Ustinov composed a virtual executive board of the Brezhnev Politburo regarding foreign policy issues. They presided over the development and use of the global reach of Soviet military power in the 1970s. And it was they, with Brezhnev's blessing, who made the fateful

1979 decision to send Soviet troops into Afghanistan. Almost immediately after taking power, however, Andropov began to suggest the need to shift the Soviet Union's priority from foreign activities to domestic economic growth.

The most pressing foreign policy crisis that Andropov inherited was the struggle with the West over deployment of the new U.S. intermediate-range missiles in Western Europe, which was coming to a head that fall. In this context Andropov on September 28 issued an unusual statement dealing at length with the "dangerous, inhuman policies" of the Reagan administration, especially the U.S. military buildup and the "militarist course that poses a grave threat to peace." In a declaration that appeared to write off any chance for improved relations during the Reagan era, Andropov declared that "even if someone had any illusions about the possible evolution for the better in the policy of the present U.S. administration, the latest developments have finally dispelled them."

Andropov's statement and nearly all others from Moscow at the time emphasized the growing danger of war. To a degree, this appears to have been a tactic intended to mobilize antiwar sentiment, especially in Western Europe. But the campaign also reflected growing worry in the Soviet leadership about both the intentions and the capabilities of Reagan, who in his first term was the most outspokenly anticommunist president the United States had ever had and who was presiding over the greatest peacetime military program in U.S. history.

In October 1983 the Soviet leadership began a serious effort to prepare its domestic population for a crisis with the United States. The 18 million members of the Communist Party were told in a series of closed meetings that there was no chance for agreement at the Geneva arms talks, and that the country and its economy must be prepared for a deterioration in relations after Washington deployed new missiles in Europe that would threaten the USSR. A documentary film produced in the Defense Ministry and broadcast on Soviet television portrayed the United States as a dangerous militaristic power bent on world domination. The film showed U.S. nuclear explosions and various U.S. missiles, interspersed with scenes of war victims, Soviet war memorials and words of Moscow's peaceful intentions. After the U.S. invasion of Grenada on October 25, which turned out to be the high-water mark in the Reagan administration's use of military force overseas, Soviet Vice President Vasily Kuznetsov said the U.S. leadership was "making delirious plans for world domination," which were "pushing mankind to the brink of disaster." Personal attacks on Reagan in the Soviet press reached a peak, with the U.S. President depicted as a "madman" and compared to Adolf Hitler.

November 1983, two months after the downing of KAL 007, was probably the high point of military tension between Moscow and Washington in the 1980s. Unknown to the public in either nation and to all but a few officials, it was more than just talk.

From November 2 to 11 the United States and its NATO allies conducted Exercise Able Archer, a "nuclear release exercise," in order to test the communications and command procedures for the use of nuclear weapons in case of war. The secret exercise did not involve the movement of troops or nuclear weapons, but it did involve the simulation of the orders that would have to be given to employ those weapons in war. The U.S. nuclear war plan, or Single Integrated Operational Plan (SIOP), on the Pentagon books at the time under orders signed by Reagan, called for the United States in a full-scale war to use its nuclear arsenal against 50,000 Soviet targets, including 25,000 military targets, 15,000 industrial or economic targets and 5,000 targets associated with the Soviet leadership. If the Soviets fired back, as they were certain to do, it would be virtually a doomsday scenario. After being briefed on the war plan, Reagan considered it "a scenario for a sequence of events that could lead to the end of civilization as we knew it."

Exercise Able Archer was a regular command post exercise that had been carried out repeatedly in previous years, but the 1983 exercise was more extensive than ever before. The original plan for the 1983 exercise called for Weinberger, members of the Joint Chiefs of Staff, the supreme commander of NATO and, in its very first discussion stages, even Reagan and Bush, to participate in this sophisticated test of nuclear attack procedures. According to Robert McFarlane, who had succeeded William Clark two weeks earlier as the White House national security adviser, this part of the "war game" was scaled down and most of the top-ranking civilian and military officials were taken out of the exercise because of concern about the high state of Soviet nervousness. Nevertheless, the exercise was still more realistic than in the past.

In a nuclear era cat-and-mouse drill, the Soviet Union and its Warsaw Pact allies monitored such exercises through their electronic listening posts, with the United States and NATO in turn monitoring the Pact responses. This time an unusually sharp increase in the volume and urgency of the Warsaw Pact traffic was noted. More ominously, Moscow placed on higher alert status about a dozen nuclear-capable Soviet fighter aircraft stationed in forward bases in East Germany and Poland, evidently in response to what it perceived as the heightened threat arising from what it could detect of Able Archer.

A report from Oleg Gordievsky, then the deputy KGB "resident" or intelligence chief in the Soviet Embassy in London, who was secretly working for British intelligence, indicated that some KGB units were telling Moscow that NATO was moving troops (which did not happen, according to U.S. officials) to prepare for a real attack on the Soviet Union. In the tense atmosphere of crisis, some in KGB headquarters in Moscow appeared to have concluded that U.S. forces had been placed on a real alert, and that the countdown to nuclear war might already have begun. On the night of November 8–9, according to Gordievsky, Moscow sent flash telegrams to its KGB stations in Western Europe to gather all possible information on the highest-priority basis of U.S. preparations for a surprise nuclear missile attack against the Soviet Union.

Gordievsky was a second-generation intelligence veteran with extensive experience in Moscow and abroad who had been secretly recruited by the British as a double agent in 1975. Gordievsky reported that a series of special nuclear war alerts—*Raketno Yadernoye Napadenie*, or Surprise Nuclear Missile Attack alerts—had been instituted in Moscow two years earlier, in 1981, by Andropov while he was chairman of the KGB on grounds that a nuclear first strike had become a serious possibility under the Reagan administration. To many sophisticated officers in Soviet intelligence, such a surprise attack on the USSR seemed unlikely, Gordievsky reported. Nevertheless, he explained to a CIA official, "A closed political system dominated by men of weak intellect, with little understanding of the world and ideological blinders, is prone to self-indoctrination."

Within a few weeks after the end of Able Archer 83, the London CIA station reported, presumably on the basis of information obtained by the British from Gordievsky, that the Soviets had been alarmed about the real possibility that the United States was preparing a nuclear attack against them. A similar report came from a well-connected American who had heard it from senior officials in an Eastern European country closely allied to Moscow. McFarlane, who received the reports at the White House, initially discounted them as Soviet scare tactics rather than evidence of real concern about American intentions, and told Reagan of his view in presenting them to the President. But a more extensive survey of Soviet attitudes sent to the White House early in 1984 by CIA Director William Casey, based in part on reports from the double agent Gordievsky, had a more sobering effect. Reagan seemed uncharacteristically grave after reading the report and asked McFarlane, "Do you suppose they really believe that?" The national security aide said he did not think the highest Soviet leaders could put credence in a completely nonexistent U.S. intention to attack. "I don't see how they could believe that—but it's something to think about," Reagan replied.* In a meeting with his senior White House advisers the same day, Reagan spoke about the biblical prophecy of Armageddon, a final world-ending battle between good and evil, a topic that fascinated the President. McFarlane thought it was not coincidental that Armageddon was on Reagan's mind.

Without reference to Able Archer or the Gordievsky reports, Reagan wrote in his memoirs that by late 1983 he had learned to his surprise that "many people at the top of the Soviet hierarchy were genuinely afraid of America and Americans" and that "many Soviet officials feared us not only as adversaries but as potential aggressors who might hurl nuclear weapons at them in a first strike." This being the case, Reagan recalled, "I was even more anxious to get a top Soviet leader in a room alone and try to convince him we had no designs on the Soviet Union and the Russians had nothing to fear from us."

Even after the end of Exercise Able Archer on November 11, tension between Washington and Moscow remained extremely high because of the imminent deployment of the U.S. intermediate-range missiles. The

---

* Two U.S. Special National Intelligence Estimates (SNIEs) in May and August of 1984, the latter made after extensive information was received in Washington from Gordievsky, concluded that the war scare was part of a Soviet campaign to intimidate the United States and its allies and that it may also have reflected an internal Soviet power struggle at the time. "They seem to have wanted to convey to us a higher pucker factor than normal," said a U.S. intelligence official who accepted the conclusions of the 1984 studies, and who pointed out that the Soviets were not observed to have taken other mobilization steps to prepare for war. But nearly six years later an extensive restudy of the evidence by the President's Foreign Intelligence Advisory Board concluded that the earlier estimates had been remiss in dismissing the possibility that the Soviet leadership actually believed the United States was planning a nuclear first strike. The newer study, sent to the White House in February 1990, said the Soviet leaders believed the correlation, or balance, of forces in the world was turning toward the United States in 1983 and were convinced Washington was seeking military superiority. Therefore, the study said, Soviet leaders may have taken seriously the possibility of a U.S. nuclear strike against the Soviet Union.

first U.S. ground-launched cruise missiles scheduled for NATO deployment arrived in Britain on November 14. Before the end of the month, the Italian and German parliaments voted to accept the U.S. missiles, which were quickly deployed, and Soviet negotiators walked out of the Geneva arms talks.

A statement by Andropov on November 24 confirmed the Soviet pullout from the talks and announced military countermeasures, including the deployment of even more Soviet missiles in East Germany and Czechoslovakia and redeployment of Soviet nuclear-armed submarines closer to the coasts of the United States. But after all the talk of dire consequences and threats of war, the countermeasures did not shock the West, as had been expected. It was clear the Soviets had suffered a massive political defeat in Europe. Moscow's withdrawal from the arms talks suggested that the Kremlin leaders were sulking in their tent.

Inside the Soviet Union, the talk of an impending war was having a more powerful effect. Visitors reported that Muscovites seemed sincerely worried that the world was on the brink of nuclear catastrophe. At the end of the year, the White House began receiving stacks of letters solicited by Soviet authorities from their citizens calling for Reagan to stop the drift toward war. Most of the letters were generated by the Soviet youth newspaper, *Komsomolskaya Pravda*, which printed a form letter to Reagan saying, "We vote for peace," and suggested it be sent by schools and other institutions to the American President. But a large number had personal inserts that were genuine and heartfelt, in the opinion of State Department Soviet experts called to the White House to decipher the avalanche of Russian-language mail. One letter read, "Mr. President, why are you promoting nuclear war? Don't you realize what war is? We, the grandmothers, appeal to you."

Looking back on this period in an article for the scholarly journal *Foreign Affairs*, American historian Walter Laqueur was reminded of a letter written by a Russian poet and diplomat, Fyodor Tiutchev, to his wife two centuries earlier. "What is bewildering," the Russian wrote, "is the conviction—and it is becoming more and more general—that in all the perils that confront us, the direction of affairs is given over to a way of thinking that has no longer any understanding of itself. It is like being in a carriage, descending an increasingly precipitous slope, and suddenly realizing that there is no coachman in the box."

• IVAN AND ANYA MEET JIM AND SALLY

It was my practice to meet privately every few months with Ambassador Anatoly Dobrynin at the Soviet Embassy, just as I kept in touch with senior American officials. In one of these periodic meetings late in 1983, the veteran diplomat said he was seriously concerned by a growing "hatred" toward his country on the part of the American people. It was a strong word, deliberately chosen, Dobrynin said. In some respects, he felt the current American attitude was worse than that of the 1950s, because in those days anti-Soviet feeling was mostly generated by hysteria about Soviet espionage, which was an internal U.S. issue, while the current antipathy was directed against the Soviet Union itself. The ambassador, who was a member of the Communist Party Central Committee and made periodic trips home, felt that a parallel deterioration was taking place in Soviet public opinion. The Soviet public at large had not been anti-American despite the differences and occasional crises between the two nations. But according to Dobrynin, the Soviet public for the first time was beginning to think of America as the enemy.

It was a worrisome period in both Moscow and Washington but, in both places, there was a strong sense that emotions should not be allowed to get out of hand. It was as if the leading nations, having absorbed the realities of life and death in the nuclear age, had developed a biological mechanism of some kind for self-preservation that would not allow passions free rein.

The first signal that Moscow was calling off the war fever came from Defense Minister Dmitri Ustinov, addressing a meeting of Soviet veterans on December 14: "As you can see, comrades, the situation in the world is very tense." Then he added:

> But no matter how complicated the military and political situation, there is no point in dramatizing it. Soberly appraising the full seriousness of the current situation, we must see that imperialism is far from omnipotent and we are not frightened by its threats. The Soviet people have strong nerves. We people of the older generation have experienced much more difficult times than now.

Suddenly the barrage of fearsome predictions in Moscow about the imminent danger of war trailed off. The Soviet Union was still unhappy about the U.S. missile deployment in Europe and other developments, but it was no longer apocalyptic in its declarations.

In the United States the move toward a thaw that had begun earlier in the year, but had been interrupted by the downing of KAL 007 and the Euromissile deployment, got underway again. Now even more than in the summer, senior figures of the administration were confident that the United States was in a strong position to negotiate effectively with the Soviets and were eager to demonstrate this. The successful U.S. invasion of Grenada in late October had boosted Reagan's self-confidence and popularity, especially coming immediately on the heels of the disastrous terrorist attack on U.S. Marine headquarters in Beirut. The deployment of the U.S. missiles in Europe in late November was considered a major success for U.S. policy and NATO solidarity, and the Soviet walkout from the arms talks, which was widely disapproved in the West, seemed only to underscore Soviet isolation.

The political context of these developments was the approach of the 1984 presidential campaign, in which foreign policy issues were shaping up as Reagan's most notable area of political vulnerability. The President's pollster, Richard Wirthlin, had been at work since late June 1983 developing an overall campaign plan for dealing with the issues, objectives, constituencies, target states and likely Democratic opponents. Wirthlin reported informally to Reagan in September 1983 and presented his findings in a thick written report the following month. Reagan was told in Wirthlin's campaign plan that in the past six presidential elections, war and peace issues were consistently of greater concern to voters than bread and butter issues. In the American system, the president alone has his finger on the nuclear button and therefore is considered responsible for the conduct of foreign affairs to a far greater degree than any other officeholder. With the economy rebounding dramatically by the fall of 1983, foreign policy stuck out as Reagan's most serious problem. Wirthlin reported that in early September, shortly after the downing of KAL 007, his private polls showed 51 percent of the public disapproving of Reagan's handling of foreign affairs and 43 percent approving. The public was just about evenly split on the question of whether Reagan's handling of the Soviet Union was increasing (43 percent) or decreasing (42 percent) the chances for war. Either Walter Mondale or John Glenn, who seemed at that point the most likely Democratic presidential nominees, could be expected to attack Reagan vigorously on the peace issue. The campaign plan pointed out that "a year from now the claim that the Reagan administration has maintained the peace would be fortified if we could show some progress in negotiating an arms settlement."

Mindful of public opinion and concerned about the high state of tension with Moscow, Reagan's advisers were telling him late in 1983 that it was time to send the Kremlin new signals of willingness to improve relations. McFarlane, who had succeeded William Clark as presidential national security adviser in mid-October, told Reagan in a long conversation aboard Air Force One during the President's trip to Japan in November that the massive increases in the U.S. defense budget were not likely to last, that the earlier Soviet perception of U.S. weakness was being reversed and that it was time to consider a framework for translating the improved U.S. position into permanent gains through negotiations with Moscow.

After the Soviets broke off the arms talks in late November, Assistant Secretary of State Richard Burt drew up a plan to adopt a more conciliatory U.S. stance. Burt's memorandum was the basis for a presentation by Shultz to the President on December 16. A central aim of U.S. policy, Shultz said, should be to demonstrate that the administration was steady and open to dialogue "even if the Soviets are not." To pursue this aim, Shultz recommended that Reagan make a major speech on U.S.-Soviet relations "not to change our policy but to stress our determination to pursue a dialogue and to achieve positive results." Shultz said the administration should be particularly careful in its rhetoric about the Soviets in order to appear "serious and steady." He also suggested that a letter be sent to Andropov to suggest ways to restart the arms dialogue, especially the strategic arms negotiations. The letter to Andropov was sent by Reagan on December 24.

With Reagan on his usual year-end holiday in California, Shultz flew on December 31 from his home in Stanford to the estate of former U.S. Ambassador Walter Annenberg in Palm Springs, where the President was staying. After a round of golf in late morning, Shultz sat down with Reagan in the early afternoon to discuss plans and prospects for 1984. By now, drafts for a major presidential speech on Soviet policy were circulating in the White House and State Department, and Shultz discussed the basic ideas with Reagan and McFarlane, who was also present.

From the administration perspective, the January 16, 1984, speech, which was delivered in the White House and beamed live to Western Europe, was a turning point in the U.S. attitude toward Moscow, offering an olive branch from Reagan rather than the harsh accusations of the past. Instead of blasting the "evil empire" or the Soviet "crime against humanity" in the skies over the Far East, Reagan spoke hopefully of the chances for renewed dialogue, declaring that "1984 is a year of opportunities for peace." (Domestic commentators on the address noted that it also was a year of a presidential election.) The guiding principles in dealing with the Soviet Union, Reagan announced, would be "realism, strength and dialogue." Though Reagan spoke broadly of differences between the two nations, "communism" or "communists" were never mentioned. Twice in one passage Reagan spoke of the goal of "compromise" with the Soviet Union, a concept that had been shunned in administration pronouncements until that time. And Reagan declared, as he had stated for the first time before the Japanese Diet on November 11, that "my dream is to see the day when nuclear weapons will be banished from the face of the Earth."

Unlike most high-profile Reagan speeches, this one was drafted principally by Soviet policy experts, especially Jack Matlock of the National Security Council staff, rather than the more conservative wordsmiths of the White House speechwriting team. But the most vivid part of the speech, and the only part to be long remembered, was the peroration, which Reagan had drafted himself:

> Just suppose with me for a moment that an Ivan and Anya could find themselves, say, in a waiting room or sharing a shelter from the rain with Jim and Sally, and there was no language barrier to keep them from getting acquainted. Would they then debate the differences between their respective governments? Or would they find themselves comparing notes about their children and what each other did for a living?
>
> Before they parted company they would probably have touched on ambitions and hobbies and what they wanted for their children and the problems of making ends meet. And as they went their separate ways, maybe Anya would be saying to Ivan, "Wasn't she nice, she also teaches music." Maybe Jim would be telling Sally what Ivan did or didn't like about his boss. They

might even have decided that they were all going to get together for dinner some evening soon.

Above all, they would have proven that people don't make wars. People want to raise their children in a world without fear and without war. They want to have some of the good things over and above bare subsistence that make life worth living. They want to work at some craft, trade or profession that gives them satisfaction and a sense of worth. Their common interests cross all borders.

If the Soviet government wants peace, then there will be peace. Together we can strengthen peace, reduce the level of arms, and know in doing so we have helped fulfill the hopes and dreams of those we represent and, indeed, of peoples everywhere. Let us begin now.

The Soviet leadership was not impressed with Reagan's change in tone—at least not immediately. The Soviet press denounced the speech as an election-year exercise, and *Pravda* carried the satirical news that "Jim" is usually unemployed, that he and "Sally" would have to take "Ivan and Anya" to a soup kitchen for dinner and that the two Americans are afraid of FBI surveillance of their chance encounter with the Russians. Foreign Minister Gromyko denounced the speech as a "hackneyed ploy" motivated by presidential politics.

On January 18, two days after Reagan's address, Gromyko along with other foreign ministers appeared in Stockholm at a thirty-five-nation meeting on European security and disarmament. The Soviet foreign minister delivered one of his vitriolic attacks on the "aggressive foreign policy" of the United States and seemed to scoff at Reagan's revised rhetoric.

The blame for disrupting the Soviet-U.S. dialogue on limiting nuclear arms in Europe lies with the U.S. administration. Rather than pursue negotiations and display a desire to seek agreements, the U.S. administration has set out to upset the existing correlation of forces. Its aim is to acquire military superiority over the Soviet Union, superiority of NATO countries over Warsaw Treaty countries through a massive buildup of its nuclear armaments. This, in the thinking of U.S. strategists, might supposedly win them a nuclear war. . . .

New missiles, bombers and aircraft carriers are being churned out in some kind of pathological obsession. New means of mass destruction are being experimented with. In short, the present U.S. administration is an administration thinking in terms of war and acting accordingly. . . .

It is deeds that are needed, not verbal exercises which have been resorted to especially often in Washington in the last few days. They are clearly a tribute to the considerations of the moment and people know only too well the real meaning of such ploys. However agile the deception—whether crude or sophisticated—the real state of affairs does not change. What is required is a substantial turn in policy: from the policy of militarism and aggression to one of peace and international cooperation.

Following the address, Shultz and Gromyko met for five hours at the Soviet Embassy in an atmosphere notably different from that set by the Soviet minister in public. Though the session was not highly productive, the two men went through their briefs calmly and without rancor. In a total reversal of the limited agenda of their Madrid meeting in the wake of the downing of KAL 007, Shultz was ready to discuss anything and everything with Gromyko this time—especially the subject of arms control negotiations. For the first time, Gromyko himself introduced the subject of human rights—if only to go on quickly to "more serious" things, but still it was a recognition that the topic was discussible. It was also agreed, but not immediately announced, that the East-West negotiations on reducing conventional forces in Europe be restarted. As the session ended, Shultz asked the Soviet foreign minister how they should describe it to the press waiting outside. "It was a necessary meeting," said Gromyko. Shultz agreed and later told his aides that as a result of the meeting, "the ice was cracked."

• THE DEATH OF ANDROPOV

The period following the Reagan speech and the Stockholm conference was a time of mixed signals and mysterious portents in Moscow. Unlike many Soviet puzzles, this one was solved soon enough. Yuri Andropov was finally at the end of his long struggle.

On January 24, six days after Gromyko's harsh denunciation of U.S. policy, *Pravda* printed a written "interview" on the same topics with Soviet leader Andropov. The entire text was read by the announcer on the main Soviet evening news program in thirteen minutes of heavily nuanced abstraction that must have been almost incomprehensible to the average Soviet citizen. The positions attributed to Andropov were the same as those of Gromyko but the tone was completely different. Andropov's remarks were made more in sorrow than in anger, with none of the slashing rhetoric used by Gromyko, and they suggested a much greater willingness to talk things over with the United States.

I was in Moscow at the time, having flown to the Soviet capital after the Stockholm conference. The discrepancy in tone seemed very strange to me. I wondered if this discrepancy meant that Gromyko was being subtly repudiated by others in the Soviet leadership. Senior Soviet officials denied that any gap existed between the Kremlin and the Foreign Ministry but they gave no satisfactory explanation for the difference in tone. Much later I learned from Soviet sources that Gromyko had already prepared and circulated his Stockholm speech to Soviet leaders before the Reagan address and did not wish to make major changes at the last moment without Politburo approval. Gromyko reconsidered his posture after his return to Moscow, especially in the light of the businesslike meeting he had held with Shultz. According to Kornienko, then Gromyko's deputy, it was Gromyko and his Foreign Ministry that initiated Andropov's written "interview" to signal a willingness to restart a serious dialogue with Washington. Unknown to me or the public, Andropov sent a new letter to Reagan on January 28, which, while unyielding on arms control and other issues, signified a desire to communicate.

For the most part, though, the reaction I found in the Soviet capital toward the United States and, in particular, the Reagan administration in January 1984 was a combination of dismay and despair. The Soviet hierarchy had hoped that Ronald Reagan would be another Richard Nixon, an anticommunist conservative who would be willing to work with Moscow out of *realpolitik*, if not conviction. Instead, Reagan to that point had seemed to Moscow implacably hostile. Moreover, his military buildup and especially the new high-technology Star Wars program seemed to Moscow intended to threaten its security and to deny it the position of strategic parity with the United States that it had won in the 1970s. Rubbing salt on the wounds, Reagan on January 23, one week after the Ivan and Anya speech, accused the Soviet Union of violating the arms control treaties it had previously signed with the United States.

"People wonder, *why* can't we live with the Americans," exclaimed Radomir Bogdanov, deputy director of the U.S.A. and Canada Institute and, it was well known, formerly a senior official of the KGB. "You are trying to destroy our economy, to interfere with our trade, to overwhelm and make us inferior in the strategic field. . . . All the trust and confidence have been destroyed. We must have *deeds!*" he said, slapping his hand on the small table between us in his office. Not just words, "*deeds!*" Again, "*deeds!*" Bogdanov, who was notably franker than any other party or government official I saw during my visit, said "nobody is taking seriously" the supposed Reagan change of heart evidenced by the January 16 speech. *Izvestia* commentator Valentin Falin, a former (and future) official of the Communist Party Central Committee, said Reagan's conciliatory words about Soviet policy reminded him of a joke about a shop whose front window was filled with clocks and watches. When a potential customer brought in his watch for repair, the attendant announced that the business there was circumcisions rather than time-pieces. Asked why the window was filled with clocks and watches, the attendant sweetly responded, "What do you expect us to put in the window?" Reagan's business is "the circumcision of socialism," said Falin. His recent speech was merely an attempt to choose "softer words for the same policy."

It was fascinating to me that, for all this ferment, the preoccupation in Moscow was not with the United States, the Euromissiles or any other aspect of international affairs. When I asked what were the most important questions facing the country, nearly all of the twelve Soviet officials or journalists whom I met, including a senior Central Committee official and a general, named the internal management or economy of the USSR. I was surprised to hear not a word from anyone on the subject of their leadership of the international communist movement. It simply did not come up.

The hole in the doughnut of every conversation, I reported in a *Washington Post* op-ed piece on my discussions in Moscow, was the subject of Andropov's health. This was on everyone's mind, but hardly anyone had any information, at least none he was willing to share. I questioned everyone I met about the long-absent leader, and found only one person who stated clearly that he had had actual contact with Andropov in recent months. This was the journalist Aleksandr Bovin, a former member of Andropov's staff at the Central Committee, who said he had spoken to the leader on the telephone December 20, almost a month before my visit. Asked what was wrong with Andropov, Bovin gave the standard official reply, "I am not a doctor." I was solemnly assured by Vadim Zagladin, first deputy chief of the International Department of the Central Committee, that Andropov was on the mend and "he will appear, I promise you." I have no doubt he ardently hoped this would be the case.

The last months of his life must have been as excruciating for Andropov as they were depressing to those in Moscow who had counted on him for the strong leadership that had so long been lacking in those troubled times. He had finally reached the top of this very hierarchical system at age sixty-eight, only to suffer a dramatic physical setback within three months, which sharply limited his activity and would lead to his death a year later. He knew at an early date what was in store, but there is no report of self-pity or remorse. "I don't have much time, but I think it's my duty to do everything I can during that time," Andropov told his foreign policy assistant, Andrei Aleksandrov-Agentov. When the aide paid what was to be a final visit to his boss in early January, about a month before his death, Andropov was in a wheelchair moving about the hospital suite, which had been decorated to resemble a Moscow apartment. "He knew that he was dying but he did not lose hope, and hoped for the best," Aleksandr Bovin told me much later. Even as the end neared, according to the journalist, Andropov was making preparations for his speech to his constituency in connection with the local elections to be held a few weeks later, and there was talk of his appearing before a television camera in his hospital room to make his political appeal.

Toward the end of January, according to the official medical report issued later, his condition deteriorated as one after another of his internal organs failed. Yuri Andropov died in his hospital room at 4:50 P.M., Moscow time, on February 9, 1984.

3. The Chernenko Interlude

The 390-day reign of Konstantin Chernenko, who succeeded Yuri Andropov as leader of the Soviet Union, was almost entirely lacking in bold ideas or dramatic initiatives. It also was a time of frustration and uncertainty in Moscow. Nonetheless, the period between February 1984 and March 1985 would be important to the great turn in U.S.-Soviet relations in several respects. During this period, Washington and Moscow would get back to business, resuming arms negotiations. Foreign Minister Andrei Gromyko would visit the White House, thereby advancing the diplomatic dialogue to a higher level than at any previous time in Ronald Reagan's presidency. The U.S. President would be reelected, clearing the way for the pursuit of improved relations with Moscow in his second term. In all these ways and in unseen internal maneuvers in Moscow, the unsteady interlude of Konstantin Chernenko would pave the way for dramatic change between Moscow and Washington under his successor, Mikhail Gorbachev.

Yuri Andropov's long illness had been hidden from most of the Soviet public, covered up by clever propaganda and a profusion of statements issued in his name. His death was a surprise to the great majority of Soviet citizens. But there was no hiding the physical condition of Chernenko, who was seventy-two years old when he took office and was suffering from such an advanced stage of emphysema that he faltered during his televised inaugural speech from a podium atop Lenin's Tomb, running out of breath in the middle of sentences. He was unable to hold a salute to the military parade as it passed before him in Red Square. Two weeks later, in his second televised address from the Kremlin, Chernenko stumbled over his text and again ran out of breath. At one point he lost his place for nearly half a minute to the embarrassment of the Politburo members seated behind him and, when he finally resumed, skipped an entire page of his text.

In many respects, the Politburo's selection of Chernenko suggested the restoration of the era of Leonid Brezhnev, whom Chernenko had served as loyal lieutenant for more than thirty years. The two men had met in 1950 in Moldavia, where Brezhnev was party secretary and Chernenko his aide for propaganda and agitation. After Brezhnev moved to Moscow, he brought along his friend and sponsored him in the national party apparatus, using Chernenko as his chief of staff and most trusted assistant in the Central Committee and eventually the Politburo. At the Vienna summit with President Jimmy Carter in 1979, Foreign Minister Andrei Gromyko and Defense Minister Dmitri Ustinov carried most of the spontaneous discussion for the infirm and large unfocused General Secretary Brezhnev. But American officials noticed that when things became physically difficult for Brezhnev, he turned to Chernenko for assistance. The white-haired Siberian native, who came from hardy peasant stock, never differed with Brezhnev in public nor, as far as is known, in private.

Brezhnev sought to promote Chernenko as his successor but when he died late in 1982 the job of General Secretary went to Andropov. There is no official record of how the votes were cast or why, but one credible theory is that Gromyko and Ustinov, both powerful Politburo insiders who worked intimately with Andropov for years in the Brezhnev era, considered Andropov well-prepared but did not consider Chernenko strong enough to lead the country amid growing problems. Why Chernenko was selected to succeed Andropov in early 1984 is also a matter of speculation. It appears that a majority of the Politburo was not yet ready to name its youngest member, Mikhail Gorbachev, who was twenty years younger than Chernenko and whose election would certainly have meant an extensive generational change in the leadership. The decision to pick Chernenko may have been made easier by the knowledge that his reign was almost certain to be a brief one in view of his health and by an implicit understanding that Gorbachev would be next.

To the extent Chernenko had any views on foreign affairs, they seemed to emerge from the Brezhnev era. He signaled soon after becoming General Secretary that he sought to return to the early 1970s period of Soviet-American détente if he could do so without shifting established Soviet positions. In this sense he was less confrontational than Andropov and less inclined to portray the international situation in dire terms. For the most part, though, Chernenko as General Secretary ceded foreign policy leadership to Gromyko. "He was a very sick man, so probably it would be more correct to speak of a Gromyko foreign policy," according to Andrei Aleksandrov-Agentov, who continued as national security assistant in the General Secretary's office under Chernenko. Gromyko's relationship with Chernenko was suggested by an incident during the Andropov funeral. As the Politburo stood at attention during the ceremony, Gromyko turned to Chernenko and instructed him in a whisper—loudly enough for a microphone to pick up—"Don't take off your hat." U.S. Ambassador to the Soviet Union Arthur Hartman, who accompanied Vice President Bush to a meeting with Chernenko following the funeral, noticed that Gromyko seemed to go out of his way to interrupt the leader and dominate the discussion, in contrast to the great deference shown by Gromyko and everyone else to Andropov a year earlier. "It was quite clear that this guy was not a world class leader," said Hartman.

Chernenko became General Secretary on February 14. Nine days later, he sent a letter to Reagan reiterating the Kremlin's strong opposition to the U.S. missile deployment in Western Europe but also calling for "a dialogue that would be aimed at searching for common ground, at finding concrete and mutually acceptable solutions in those areas where it proves realistically possible."

Some of the same ideas were percolating in Washington, where Secretary of State Shultz and National Security Adviser McFarlane were preparing a top-level review of U.S. policy now that Moscow had a new leader. Chernenko's suggestion "may provide an opportunity to put our relations on more positive track," McFarlane stated in a policy memorandum for the President on February 24, written in preparation for a meeting with Reagan and the senior members of the National Security Council on March 1 in the residential quarters of the White House. While McFarlane urged that any moves be quiet so as not to raise public expectations, he suggested intensified personal exchanges across a broad range of issues between Shultz and Soviet Ambassador Anatoly Dobrynin in Washington, and between Gromyko and Ambassador Hartman in Moscow, with the possibility of another Shultz-Gromyko meeting "if there's sufficient movement." The President wanted to go farther. He made it clear he was interested in a summit meeting with Chernenko, perhaps in the summer if it could be arranged.

One of the topics of the March 1 meeting was the forthcoming visit to Moscow by retired Lieutenant General Brent Scowcroft, who had been national security adviser to President Ford and was well regarded by just about everyone at the top of the Reagan administration. McFarlane, who had worked at the Ford NSC staff under Scowcroft, believed the Soviets would respond positively to confidential messages sent outside of the normal diplomatic channels through an authoritative outsider. Shultz was not enthusiastic, but went along. Scowcroft had arranged to go to Moscow March 8 as a member of the Dartmouth Group of private foreign policy experts, and he was given a personal letter from Reagan to Chernenko and authorized to make additional comments in discussions with top Soviet officials. To give official standing to the unusual mission, Shultz discussed the Scowcroft trip with Dobrynin, and Hartman took it up with the Soviet Foreign Ministry. When Scowcroft got to Moscow, however, the Soviets declined to arrange an appointment for him with Chernenko or any other top official. "If they've got something to tell us, why don't they tell us officially?" Hartman was asked by a skeptical Soviet official. On several other occasions in the years that followed, the Reagan administration proposed to use special confidential channels or emissaries for high-level negotiations with Moscow. The Soviets were never interested.

Despite the failure of the Scowcroft mission, official letters between Reagan and Chernenko went back and forth with great intensity early in 1984, covering a long list of subjects including strategic arms, chemical weapons, nuclear testing and bilateral issues. On March 7, Shultz handed Dobrynin a lengthy presidential reply to Chernenko's initial letter and took ninety minutes to discuss it. In an effort to appeal to the Soviet leader, Reagan thanked the Kremlin anew for releasing the Pentecostal Christians from the U.S. Embassy the previous year and added a handwritten postscript referring sympathetically to the millions of Soviet citizens killed in World War II.

The Soviet leader responded with a second letter on March 19.

Another Reagan letter was presented by Shultz to Dobrynin on April 16. For the most part, the proposals, suggestions and responses on the U.S. side were unexciting products of the government bureaucracy. The Chernenko letters and the other aspects of the dialogue were initiated and managed by Gromyko's Foreign Ministry with no particular direction from the Soviet leader, according to Georgi Kornienko, who was first deputy foreign minister. The flurry of communications did not result in any substantial agreements. Nevertheless, the belief among those officials in Washington who knew of the letters was that they were beginning to defuse the severe tensions of 1983 and move the relationship into more constructive channels.

The optimism was soon shattered with the May 8 announcement that the Soviet Union would boycott the Summer Olympic Games at Los Angeles. This was a disappointment in view of preliminary indications that the Soviets would participate despite the U.S. boycott of the 1980 Moscow Olympics in protest against the invasion of Afghanistan. Moreover, Moscow's boycott of the Los Angeles Olympics came amid a number of lesser steps that suggested a reversal of Chernenko's gradual opening to the Reagan administration. American officials suspected that the sudden cooling of relations reflected a power struggle within the Soviet leadership. By the time of the Olympics decision, the U.S. Embassy in Moscow was hearing disparaging comments about Chernenko's competence as well as his health from well-placed Soviets. The Embassy concluded from the circumstances that the KGB must have inspired or at least tolerated the negative remarks to foreigners about the Soviet leader, which suggested an unusual degree of infighting and even instability at the top. Another factor in the Soviet decision not to participate in the Olympic Games may have been a desire not to cooperate with the United States in any way that could be used by the White House to further Reagan's campaign for reelection.

• THE SUMMER OF REENGAGEMENT

By midsummer, the Kremlin had recovered its readiness to move ahead with U.S. relations. On June 6, Dobrynin brought Shultz a letter to Reagan from Chernenko, the first in two and a half months, promising to provide answers to U.S. proposals on several small bilateral issues and to resume discussions of Middle East and southern Africa issues. In another meeting seven days later, Dobrynin urged Shultz to move ahead on bilateral issues, which the ambassador said should be easy to do, and also to tackle the more difficult arms control and security problems. Dobrynin said that even though 1984 was a presidential election year, "We are not afraid to be seen negotiating with this administration." Chernenko's letter and Dobrynin's statements to Shultz were followed by other indications that the Kremlin had lifted a ban on negotiations with the Americans before the U.S. election. A few weeks later a Soviet official in Belgrade told an American diplomat that Moscow had decided in June to "unfreeze" U.S.-Soviet relations. About the same time, a Hungarian Politburo member quoted Chernenko as having told Warsaw Pact leaders in late June that U.S.-Soviet relations were back on track and should improve "shortly," either before or after the November election.

The Kremlin's shift may have reflected its grudging acceptance of the increasingly likely prospect that Reagan would be reelected. On May 31, the Gallup poll reported that Reagan was far ahead of either Walter Mondale or Gary Hart, his two most prominent Democratic opponents, and there was increasing belief in world capitals that the challengers would not be able to catch up to the President by election day.

Ever since it had pulled out of the Geneva arms talks the previous winter after the deployment of new U.S. nuclear missiles in Europe, the Kremlin had been on the defensive internationally for refusing to negotiate. In speeches, statements and even offhand quips, Reagan hammered on the Soviet Union to return to bargaining, and effectively countered criticism of U.S. positions by pointing out that the Soviets weren't even at the table. Moscow, however, had sworn not to return to bargaining until the United States withdrew its new missiles from Europe. Some senior Soviet diplomats felt this was a serious tactical mistake. The absence of negotiations was hurting Moscow more than it was hurting Washington, and the Soviet stance seemed to lessen, rather than heighten, the public pressure on Washington to change its position.

Late in June, after more than six months on the defensive, the Kremlin finally came up with a way to take the initiative by emphasizing the need to negotiate about weapons in space, an issue increasingly important to Moscow because of Reagan's Star Wars program. At 9:00 A.M. on June 29, Dobrynin delivered to Shultz a proposal to begin U.S.-Soviet talks in Vienna in September—even before the U.S. presidential election—for the sole purpose of preventing "the militarization of outer space." Two hours later, the Soviet Union publicly announced the offer with great fanfare, suggesting that Moscow had its eye on a propaganda advantage.

It was widely anticipated that Washington would reject the offer because of its unwillingness to negotiate any restrictions on Reagan's cherished SDI program. But surprisingly, McFarlane convened the Senior Arms Control Policy Group (SACPG), the senior interagency committee on the subject, which went by the infelicitous acronymic name of "Sackpig," and won immediate agreement to call the Soviets' bluff. McFarlane announced the same night U.S. acceptance of the Soviet offer to meet in September, with a condition—the new talks should lead also to resumption of negotiations on offensive arms, which Moscow continued to boycott. The Soviets, as anticipated in Washington, backed off immediately, denouncing the U.S. counteroffer and standing by its own plan. In addition to the public dialogue, Reagan and Chernenko exchanged letters on the subject inconclusively.

Late in July the diplomatic tennis game resumed with a new public offer from Moscow on the twenty-first for talks on banning space weapons, a counteroffer on offensive arms from Washington on the twenty-fourth, a Soviet rejection of the U.S. plan on the twenty-seventh, an amended counteroffer from Washington on the twenty-eighth and a final Soviet rejection on August 1. Though nothing was agreed, the meaning of all these volleys was that the Soviet Union and the United States were maneuvering publicly and intensively about resuming the arms talks for the first time since the Soviet walkout the previous winter. And the two sides were edging toward including the space issue in the resumed negotiations, although the conditions were still at issue.

The highly visible exchanges with Moscow were helpful to Reagan's defense against the Democratic charge that his anti-Soviet ideological stance and military buildup were increasing the danger of war. Since his "Ivan and Anya" speech on January 16, Reagan had avoided strident rhetoric against the Soviet Union and in three subsequent speeches emphasized his willingness to work with the Kremlin. On Saturday morning, August 11, however, Reagan was warming up for his weekly radio address, this one from his California ranch, when he ad-libbed a voice check into a microphone in the presence of radio technicians from the White House press corps: "My fellow Americans, I am pleased to tell you today that I've signed legislation that will outlaw Russia forever. We begin bombing in five minutes."

Even more than public statements he had made, Reagan's offhand

and, he thought, off-the-record comment seemed to many to confirm his passionate antipathy for the Soviet Union, as well as a dangerous tendency to think in terms of military confrontation. Several people who knew Reagan well said he often joked in a freewheeling manner in such microphone checks, but this did not still the outrage in the United States and abroad. In Moscow, the leadership issued a formal statement through the Soviet news agency calling Reagan's words an "eye-opener" about his real intentions.

Tass is authorized to state that the Soviet Union deplores the U.S. President's invective, unprecedentedly hostile toward the U.S.S.R. and dangerous to the cause of peace. This conduct is incompatible with the high responsibility borne by leaders of states, particularly nuclear powers, for the destinies of their own peoples and for the destinies of mankind.

The State Department countered that "the Soviet Union is blowing this subject way out of proportion for propaganda purposes." Nonetheless, Reagan was embarrassed and some of his aides were appalled by his careless words, which were spoken midway between the Democratic National Convention that nominated Walter Mondale as its presidential candidate and the Republican National Convention, which would nominate Reagan for his second term.

It was in this context, on August 13, two days after the "bombing Russia" gaffe, that Shultz flew to Los Angeles to participate with Reagan in a meeting with Italian Foreign Minister Giulio Andreotti and asked for a private session with the President. Over a working lunch at the Century Plaza Hotel before the Andreotti meeting, Shultz reported that unofficial hints had been received about Foreign Minister Gromyko's interest in coming to Washington to meet Reagan when he made his annual trip to New York in September to participate in the general debate of the United Nations General Assembly. Shultz pointed out that such a Gromyko visit to the White House had not taken place since the Soviet invasion of Afghanistan late in 1979 and that "we would be reinstituting something without a change in Afghanistan." On the other hand, he remarked, "if we could get something going [with Moscow] that would be a little more constructive, that would be helpful. This is a way to do it."

Shultz made it clear he was not recommending such a visit, but merely broaching the possibility. "You may want to think this over" and decide later, the secretary suggested. Reagan, who was more anxious than ever to have a meeting with a senior Soviet official, jumped at the chance to see Gromyko. "No, I don't have to think it over. I think we should definitely do it." Shultz repeated, "You don't have to decide now." But Reagan responded, "I know what I think." Within a day or two, Moscow was discreetly informed that if Gromyko was interested in coming to Washington, he would be welcome.

• GROMYKO VISITS THE WHITE HOUSE

When Andrei A. Gromyko arrived in New York in September 1984, he was seventy-five years old, nine years older than the Soviet Union itself, and had been a senior diplomat for forty-five years, since being sent to Washington by personal order of Joseph Stalin in 1939. In a record unequaled by any diplomat of a major nation in modern times, Gromyko had been foreign minister for twenty-seven years. He accompanied Stalin to the Yalta Conference with Franklin D. Roosevelt and Winston Churchill, was the Soviet representative at the founding of the United Nations, and sat scowling beside Nikita Khrushchev when the colorful Soviet leader banged his UN desk. He met President John F. Kennedy in the White House after U.S. intelligence had spotted Soviet missiles being installed in Cuba in 1962 but, keeping his poker face, did not reveal anything about the military deployment that would bring the two nations to the brink of war.

Khrushchev at times ridiculed his foreign minister, once telling a group of Americans in Gromyko's presence, "When I tell Gromyko to take off his pants and sit on a cake of ice, he does it. And he keeps sitting there until I tell him to get up." Gromyko had greater status under Leonid Brezhnev, Yuri Andropov and Konstantin Chernenko, for whom he was nearly indispensable as the implementer—and sometimes architect—of Soviet foreign policy. The faithful servant was made a member of the Politburo in 1973 by Brezhnev and took on increasing responsibility for policymaking. From about 1975, when Brezhnev began to lose his grasp of events, to Gromyko's retirement as foreign minister in 1985, "The foreign policy of the Soviet Union was developing under the sign of Gromyko and a Gromyko trademark could be attached and labeled to every item," said Valentin Falin, who watched the process at close range as a Soviet ambassador and senior Communist Party official.

The son of peasants from a family of former serfs, Gromyko was a diligent student, with what one of his coworkers called "an elephant memory" and a cautious demeanor in his relations with political leaders in the Kremlin. According to Georgi Kornienko, who worked with Gromyko for more than thirty years and was his deputy for twenty years, Gromyko preferred to share responsibility for major decisions with other senior members of the Politburo, especially Yuri Andropov and Dmitri Ustinov. In the late 1970s and early 1980s, when Andropov was KGB chairman and Ustinov minister of defense, the three were the principal members of working groups on various foreign and military issues within the Politburo, which were set up to compensate for Brezhnev's infirmity. Often the three would meet alone to determine the essential outline of what was to be done. Although Gromyko was by far the most experienced of the three in foreign affairs, Gromyko "would never try to press very hard" to get his way if the others did not share his view of the matter at hand, according to Kornienko. On some questions, such as what to say about the downing of KAL 007, Gromyko permitted Kornienko to take a controversial recommendation forcefully to the leadership even though the foreign minister was reluctant to make the argument himself. But once a Politburo decision was reached on an issue, Kornienko said, Gromyko "acted as if it was his deep conviction" and gave no hint of hesitation or dissent even if he had privately disagreed.

Shultz's invitation to Gromyko to come to the White House reached Moscow at a time of stress in the Soviet inner circle. Chernenko had gone on vacation in mid-July but caught a cold in damp, inhospitable weather. When he did not get better, he was secretly flown back to Moscow in early August and placed in a hospital near the Kremlin where doctors could keep a close eye on his emphysema. Chernenko did not emerge until September 5, by which time Gromyko had accepted the invitation. Despite the strain of Chernenko's hospitalization and rumors of renewed power struggles over the succession, the decision to send Gromyko to Washington was a collective one made by the Politburo, with no objection voiced from any quarter, according to foreign affairs adviser Aleksandrov-Agentov. Quite probably, Mikhail Gorbachev had a strong hand in the decision, since it was later revealed that he had presided over the Politburo while Chernenko was ill.

Gromyko's personal reaction to the invitation is unclear. The foreign minister's comments about Reagan foreign policy had been caustic and unrelenting. On July 27 Gromyko told former Senator George McGovern during a three-hour conversation at Yalta, where Gromyko was on his summer holiday, that he expected Reagan to be reelected but that in this case he did not expect "productive" U.S.-Soviet relations in the next four years. Rather than make progress toward negotiating arms reductions and other agreements, Gromyko told McGovern, Reagan and his aides "want to cause trouble. They want to weaken the Soviet system. They want to bring it down." At the same time, an opportunity to meet Reagan face to face could not be ignored. Among other things, a Gromyko visit to the White House would be a return to the familiar procedures of the pre-Afghanistan past and thus perhaps set a precedent for the future if Reagan was reelected. In his memoirs, Gromyko suggested that the 1984 invitation stemmed primarily from Reagan's domestic political requirements, and he was well aware that a high-profile visit to the White House just weeks before the election would undercut the Democratic argument that Reagan's policies were increasing the danger of war. But Gromyko explained to Democratic presidential nominee Walter Mondale, whom he saw the day before meeting Reagan, that he had been invited to the White House many times by U.S. presidents and had always accepted their invitations.

In a three-hour meeting with Shultz at the U.S. Mission to the United Nations before flying to Washington, Gromyko was sharply critical of U.S. policy, especially in the field of nuclear armaments. When Gromyko declared that the objective must be eventually to eliminate completely the vast arsenals of nuclear weapons that were piling up, Shultz encouraged him to discuss that objective at the White House. "If you're serious, you should talk to the President about that, because he feels the same way," said Shultz, mindful of his leader's strong personal aversion to nuclear arms.

Reagan prepared with unusual intensity for his meeting with Gromyko. Finally he would be face to face with a senior Soviet leader in the White House, with the whole world waiting for the outcome. In preparation for the meeting, the State Department sent the President several sets of proposed "talking points" that could be the basis for his presentation to Gromyko on current issues of U.S. policy and Soviet-American relations. Before the meeting, however, Reagan informed Shultz he had written his own "talking points," which he showed the secretary.

From the days of Lenin to those of Chernenko, Reagan declared in opening the discussion in the Oval Office, Soviet policy has been to promote world revolution. In U.S. eyes, he said, the Soviet Union is an expansionist state, giving rise to American concern. Nevertheless, he continued, the United States respects the Soviet Union's status as a "superpower" and has no wish to change its social system. The United States does not seek military superiority over the Soviet Union, but wants to deal with Moscow as an equal. The United States wants to resume arms control bargaining and will be flexible in its positions if the Soviet Union will return to the negotiating table, Reagan declared; regular high-level exchanges between the two sides would also help.

Gromyko, in response, took exception to the President's characterization of Soviet objectives. "Certainly we take the view that the capitalist order will be replaced by the socialist order," said the foreign minister, who began his career as an economist and who as a senior diplomat had published three monographs on American capitalism under the pseudonym G. Andreyev. Gromyko went on to say that "we believe this in the way people believe the sun will rise tomorrow morning—but this process will occur quite naturally, as a result of historical development. We do not believe in political or military intimidation, and nobody should accuse us of trying to change America's social structure by force, nor that of any other country. We have no such plans and never have had."

It quickly became apparent that Gromyko had not come to Washington to negotiate the details of agreements but to size up Reagan for the Soviet leadership and to discuss the relationship on a philosophical level, which the Soviets call the "level of principle." Gromyko focused on what he termed "the question of questions"—the broad issue of peace or war in the nuclear age. And he hammered away at the dangers of the "mountain of nuclear weapons" possessed by the United States and the Soviet Union. "We keep inventing new ones. The mountain is growing. One wonders, what happens next?"

Reagan was most comfortable at precisely this level of broad generality: the fundamental reasons for the West's belief that it was threatened by the Soviet Union's ideology and actions, the deep sense that this mistrust was at the heart of the conflict and, above all, Reagan's abhorrence of nuclear weapons and his belief they must never be used. Reagan presented Gromyko with an account of basic beliefs rarely discussed by leaders of the two nations in their more practical and issue-related discourse. In a line that Reagan would later repeat to Mikhail Gorbachev, he told Gromyko: "We can't accomplish anything talking about each other. We have to talk to each other."

But all did not go completely as planned. To put across an arms control position being pressed with particular intensity by the United States at the time, Reagan agreed to make the point personally and directly in a carefully arranged interlude between the morning discussions in the Oval Office and the luncheon in the State Dining Room. When the morning talks were over, the President dismissed everyone else and asked Gromyko to remain behind. The two men could be seen talking head to head briefly through the windows facing the Rose Garden in what Gromyko called "a standing conversation." But after the day was over, State Department inquiries to Soviet officials about the key arms control position drew a blank, casting doubt on whether Gromyko had received the message Reagan was supposed to convey. Deputy Assistant Secretary of State Mark Palmer later checked with the White House staff to find out what had happened. He learned that a security aide keeping an eye on Reagan through a hidden peephole had seen the seventy-three-year-old U.S. President ask the seventy-five-year-old Soviet foreign minister if he would like to use the private toilet adjoining the Oval Office. Gromyko went into the bathroom and then emerged, after which Reagan excused himself and did the same. Then the two men proceeded briskly to the luncheon.

Waiting in the State Dining Room was Nancy Reagan, who was enthusiastic about the meeting with Gromyko, as she was about any sign of a thaw in the chilly relations with Moscow. Nearly everyone who was close to presidential decision making in the Reagan years observed that the First Lady was an important factor in Soviet affairs. Although she was reluctant to acknowledge her views or her influence while still in the White House, she wrote in her 1989 memoir, *My Turn*, that she encouraged her husband to tone down the harsh rhetoric toward the Soviet Union, to consider a more conciliatory relationship with Moscow and to undertake talks with Soviet leaders. "With the world so dangerous, I felt it was ridiculous for these two heavily armed superpowers to be sitting there and not talking to each other," Mrs. Reagan wrote. Michael Deaver, then White House deputy chief of staff, said that she persistently asked him in 1983, "What are we doing about the Soviet thing?" and that she initiated the invitation for Shultz and his wife come to the White House for dinner on the snowy February night in 1983 when Reagan began to consider moving toward improved relations with Moscow. In the intense infighting within the administration, especially on Soviet affairs, the First Lady was considered a consistent backer of Shultz, whom she admired and trusted. Shultz's aides noticed that he was unusually attentive to Mrs. Reagan and very careful to maintain a good relationship with her.

At the preluncheon reception for Gromyko, the First Lady was a vivacious and even slightly flirtatious hostess. Gromyko, who rarely drank alcohol, took a glass of cranberry juice from a waiter and proposed to toast Mrs. Reagan, who was drinking soda water. In a famous exchange, Gromyko urged that Mrs. Reagan should "whisper peace in the President's ear every night." She replied, with a quip that Gromyko would repeat with great amusement, "Oh sure—but I'll whisper it in yours, too."

Gromyko chose to interpret what he heard from the President at the White House as substantial agreement on the "level of principle." At the same time, he challenged Reagan to translate his conciliatory aims into more cooperative U.S. positions in the many outstanding conflicts between the two nations. Gromyko found little give from Reagan on specifics, whether it was the arms talks or regional conflicts. Yet according to Kornienko, who attended the White House talks, "the impression of Gromyko was rather positive in the sense that maybe here is the time to go ahead" with early resumption of the arms talks even without concrete compromises from the United States, because of the "very line of Reagan in favor of doing something."

When he returned to the Soviet Embassy after the three-and-a-half-hour White House visit, Gromyko personally drafted a statement on the meeting to be released in his name by Tass. I interpreted it at the time as almost wholly negative, providing a useful corrective to the rosy view being spun out to reporters by the White House and especially by its political advisers. But a careful reading indicates that the Soviet foreign minister was moving away from the vituperation of his previous declarations on U.S. policy, including some that had been issued just a day or two earlier, and that in his convoluted language Gromyko suggested a surprising amount of room for a future improvement in relations.

> The discussions with President Reagan during which both sides set out the basic lines of policy of the Soviet Union and the United States do not, unfortunately, warrant a conclusion about practical positive changes in the U.S. administration's foreign policy course. There were no visible signs of it being ready to take realistic positions on the substance of acute problems of war and peace without whose mutually acceptable so-

lution a turn for the better is impossible either in Soviet-American relations or in the international situation.

The President spoke in favour of more frequent meetings between representatives of the two sides—at a high, middle or other levels.

As such, if combined with the necessary content of negotiations and if, as well, constructive goals are set, namely, an end to the arms race, the reduction of nuclear arms, so as to ultimately bring about its complete elimination, and removal of dangerous international tensions, all this would certainly help to straighten out the state of affairs both in the world as a whole and in the field of bilateral relations between the two powers.

But this in [sic] not the case. The Soviet Union will continue to judge the real intentions of the American side by its practical deeds. The future will show whether or not Washington is going to correct its line of policy.

On a personal level, Gromyko was impressed with Reagan's courtesy and lack of frostiness despite the many harsh things he had said about the Soviet Union. As Gromyko was preparing to leave Washington the day after the meeting, a Soviet Embassy aide telephoned me at *The Washington Post* to request a copy of a photograph that had been printed in that morning's paper. Gromyko, he said, would like to take it back to Moscow as a souvenir. I arranged to send the picture to the Soviet Embassy, which is located right behind the newspaper on the next street. The photo Gromyko wanted depicted Reagan with both hands on Gromyko's arms in a gesture of intimacy. Though nobody knew it then, the symbolic laying on of hands was a significant moment for both men. It would be the first of many business meetings between Ronald Reagan and a top Soviet official. For Andrei Gromyko, forty-five years after he first came to Washington, it would be his final trip to the White House.

• IN SEARCH OF THE BEAR

The third week in October, just before the second televised debate between Reagan and his Democratic challenger, Walter Mondale, millions of Americans came face to face with an allegorical version of their views and emotions about the Soviet Union. A thirty-second commercial paid for by the Reagan campaign depicted a large, menacing brown bear crashing through a forest. To the thump-thump of a heartbeat in the background, the narrator intoned:

> There is a bear in the woods. For some people, the bear is easy to see. Others don't see it at all. Some people say the bear is tame. Others say it's vicious, and dangerous. Since no one can really be sure who's right, isn't it smart to be as strong as the bear—if there is a bear?

As the bear reached the top of the hill at the end of the commercial, viewers saw the figure of a lone hunter with a rifle slung over his shoulder keeping watch. Some viewers thought it might be Ronald Reagan. There was no doubt in anyone's mind about the identity of the menacing bear—the Soviet Union.

The "bear ad," which was among the few memorable episodes of the 1984 presidential campaign, was the creation of Hal Riney, a San Francisco advertising man who was responsible for colorful commercials for Bartles & Jaymes wine coolers, Gallo wines and many others. Riney, who had never produced political commercials before, had been recruited early in the year by Reagan's campaign and asked to suggest some ads on issues as well as on Reagan's general appeal. In response, he came up with the "Morning Again in America" commercials of soft-focus depiction of patriotism and national well-being, as well as the bear ad about the menace of the Soviet Union.

Riney, who was fifty-two, described himself as a Republican, and "more of a hawk than a dove," though essentially unpolitical when it came to foreign affairs. He conceived the bear ad while sitting in a local bar, his favorite spot for inspirations. To produce it, he hired a trained bear in the Olympic peninsula of his native state of Washington and narrated the voice-over message himself. At once very simple and yet sophisticated in its ambiguity, the bear ad was an immediate favorite of the Reagan political managers and of the President himself. Test audiences gave it higher rates of approval and recall than any other political ad in the Reagan inventory that year. Though it was prepared in the spring, the campaign saved this powerful television tool for saturation viewing at a critical moment in the campaign. That time came after Reagan was battered by Mondale in the first televised debate October

7, and just before the next and final televised debate, centering on foreign policy, on October 21. Most commentators said Reagan "won" the last debate. He thereby ended any serious challenge from Mondale.

By 1984, the United States had had four decades of important and kaleidoscopic interaction with the Soviet Union, ranging from World War II alliance to Cold War antagonism, and then from confrontation to détente and back to wary antagonism. By the 1980s, as the bear ad suggested, there was a great deal of ambiguity as well as animosity in American public attitudes about the USSR.

Public opinion sampling in 1984 indicated that half of Americans (49 percent) saw the Soviet Union as an "enemy" and nearly all the rest saw it as an unfriendly country that was not a full-blown enemy. About two-thirds of the public (63 percent) agreed with Reagan's early view that "the Soviets lie, cheat and steal—they'll do anything to advance the cause of communism." It was the overwhelming sentiment (84 percent) that "the Soviets are constantly testing us, probing for weakness, and they're quick to take advantage whenever they find any."

At the same time, a strong note of caution had emerged in American attitudes, primarily because of sharply increased public consciousness of the dangers of nuclear war. A nearly unanimous 96 percent of Americans polled agreed that "picking a fight with the Soviet Union is too dangerous in a nuclear world," and almost as large a number (85 percent) said the two nations must *never* resort to war to settle their differences. While three-fourths (74 percent) of the public said the Soviets can't be "trusted" to abide by a nuclear arms control agreement, half the public (51 percent) believed that, nevertheless, Reagan should increase his efforts to limit the buildup of U.S. and Soviet nuclear weapons. The public had adopted a "live-and-let-live" pragmatism about Moscow and expressed a strong desire for improved relations. In the words of Reagan's personal pollster, Richard Wirthlin, the public wanted its leader to stand up to the Russians, but also to talk with them.

The ambivalence of public attitudes and official policies toward the Soviet Union weighed on Shultz, whose tendency from his days in academia was to try to find and to articulate a theory of what he was seeking to do. In September, he had spoken from notes at an off-the-record meeting of the Council on Foreign Relations in New York of the need for a clearer policy to reconcile the sharp differences and common interests of the United States and Soviet Union. On October 18, Shultz addressed the subject publicly and at length in a speech in Los Angeles:

We are left with two inescapable truths: in the nuclear age we need to maintain a relationship with the Soviet Union. Yet we know that they have acted in ways that violate our standards of human conduct and rule by law and that are repugnant to us— and they will likely continue to do so in the future. What kind of relationship can we reasonably expect to have in these circumstances? How can we manage U.S.-Soviet relations in a way that can endure over a long period?

The U.S.-Soviet relationship, of course, is a global one. We impinge on each other's interests in many regions of the world and in many fields of endeavor. A sustained and sound relationship, therefore, will confront the fact that the Soviets can be expected periodically to do something abhorrent to us or threaten our interests.

This raises the question of linkage. Should we refuse to conclude agreements with the Soviets in one area when they do some thing outrageous in some other area? Would such an approach give us greater leverage over Moscow's conduct? Or would it place us on the defensive? Would it confirm our dedication to fundamental principles of international relations? Or would it make our diplomacy seem inconsistent? Clearly, linkage is not merely "a fact of life" but a complex question of policy.

Shultz's conclusion was that "linkage is a tactical question" but that, in general, sudden shifts in U.S. policy in disapproval of Soviet actions were not the way to pursue U.S. interests. Harking back to the lessons of the KAL 007 shootdown, he praised Reagan's decision to send the U.S. arms negotiators back to Geneva even while condemning the Soviet attack on the airliner, a fundamental break with the "linkage" idea. To replace what Shultz condemned while out of office as "light switch diplomacy" of quick policy changes, he called for development of a long-term strategy to deal with the Soviet Union.

"The way is wide open to more sustained progress in U.S.-Soviet relations than we have known in the past," Shultz declared. But with the third leader in three years in the Kremlin, he said, "We cannot confidently fathom, much less predict, the direction of Soviet policy."

• COMING OF THE ARMS TALKS

On November 6, 1984, Ronald Reagan was elected to his second term as President by a landslide, sweeping forty-nine of the fifty states and winning a huge majority of the popular vote. The following day Ambassador Arthur Hartman took a message to the Soviet Foreign Ministry from Reagan to Chernenko. Taking a leaf out of Gromyko's book and the previous correspondence, the President said that with some agreement having been reached on overall principles, it was time to move forward to specific accords. Reagan, in an interview with *Time*, emphasized the need to resume negotiations with the Soviet Union to reduce nuclear arms.

> I just happen to believe that we cannot go into another generation with the world living under the threat of those weapons and knowing that some madman can push the button some place. . . . My hope has been, and my dream, that we can get the Soviet Union to join us in starting verifiable reductions of the weapons. Once you start down that road, they've got to see how much better off we would both be if we got rid of them entirely.

At 3:00 P.M. on Saturday, November 17, the weekend before Thanksgiving, a Soviet Embassy official brought Moscow's answer to Reagan to a nearly empty State Department. The Kremlin proposed new U.S.-Soviet negotiations on nuclear and outer space arms, with the specific objectives in such talks to be settled at a meeting of Shultz and Gromyko in early January. After dickering between the two capitals over the wording, a meeting of the two foreign ministers was announced for January 7–8 in Geneva. The Thanksgiving Day announcement came just one day short of a year after Soviet negotiators had broken off the Geneva talks on intermediate-range nuclear weapons.

For George Shultz, the end of Reagan's first term and the coming of the new arms talks was a period of growth and change. By the fall of 1984 he had been secretary of state for more than two years and was gaining in command of foreign policy issues and confidence in his ability to deal with them. From Shultz's point of view, the replacement of William Clark by Robert McFarlane as White House national security adviser late in 1983 created a much more comfortable situation. McFarlane was less inclined to initiate end runs around the secretary of state, and his views about Soviet policy were much closer to those of Shultz. The son of a Texas congressman, McFarlane was a former staff member of the National Security Council under Brent Scowcroft and the Senate Armed Services Committee under John Tower. Unlike Clark, who lived on a ranch and who came to town with Reagan as an outrider from California, McFarlane was a Washington insider with middle-of-the-road views on most policy issues.

In contrast to his improving relationship with the White House, Shultz was in deepening philosophical and operational conflict with his opposite number at the Pentagon, Caspar Weinberger. The Shultz-Weinberger conflict had surfaced in dramatic fashion over the use of U.S. military force in Lebanon, which Shultz favored and Weinberger opposed. Shultz strongly urged keeping the U.S. Marines in Beirut even after the terrorist truck bomb attack that took the lives of 241 servicemen in October 1983, but Weinberger along with the White House political staff successfully urged that the troubled mission be terminated. February 7, 1984, the day when Weinberger teamed up with Vice President George Bush and White House Chief of Staff James Baker to order the pullout of the Marines while Shultz was out of the country on a diplomatic trip, was close to the low point of Shultz's tenure as secretary of state. By the fall of 1984 Shultz and Weinberger were at odds on a list of issues ranging from arms talks to air strikes, and their disputes were becoming the talk of Washington. Starting with a speech by Shultz at a New York synagogue in late October advocating the use of military force against terrorism, the two leading cabinet officers engaged in an unseemly public debate about some of the most basic issues of U.S. policy. Reagan, who valued his relations with both men and who was passive or unable to make up his own mind on many of the issues at hand, did not intervene.

After the November election, Shultz met with the President in the Oval Office and suggested that in the second term, either he or Weinberger should go home. "We have to have a unified posture here," Shultz told Reagan, "and you have to do something about it. I think I'm right and Weinberger's wrong about these things, but you're better off to have a unified picture. And I'm glad to go. It's a good time to go. I've been here now a certain amount of time. I'll go out and do something else." But as in the past, Reagan refused to choose between the two strong-willed cabinet officers. He told Shultz he would "think about it," which in his lexicon meant that nothing was likely to be done, but that he definitely wanted Shultz to stay. In a later conversation Reagan told McFarlane, "If I were to fire George and put Cap over at State, I would get bad policy. So I'm not going to do that. George is the man I want there. But I'm not going to fire Cap. He's my friend." Reagan said he was looking to McFarlane to "make it work."

Shultz and Weinberger had a long history together going back to 1970 when Shultz was secretary of labor in the Nixon cabinet and Weinberger chairman of the Federal Trade Commission. Nixon, impressed by both men, proposed to name Shultz director of the Office of Management and Budget and Weinberger deputy director. Shultz barely knew Weinberger, so he invited him to his office at the Labor Department for what amounted to a job interview. "We talked and we got along just fine, and I therefore reported to the President, 'Great. We're able to work together. It won't be a problem,' " Shultz recalled. Weinberger worked as Shultz's deputy for two years at OMB, which is among the most powerful agencies of the inner government, and he became OMB director after Shultz moved on to be secretary of the treasury in 1972. Later, after Shultz became president of Bechtel Corporation in 1975, Weinberger was hired as Bechtel's general counsel and they worked together again until Weinberger left to join the Reagan cabinet in January 1981.

Both Shultz and Weinberger say today that they got along agreeably during most of their many associations, but a number of others who saw them at close range have a distinctly different view. Former officials of the Office of Management and Budget said Weinberger smoldered with resentment because of Shultz's dominance there. It is clear that at Bechtel the two men had opposing views on some issues. Weinberger was essentially a litigator and fighter, and Shultz tended to negotiate in case of differences. Both were strong personalities who wanted to run their own show but again, Shultz was in the dominant position in the organization. As cabinet officers in the Reagan administration, they were for the first time no longer in a superior/subordinate position with Shultz in the lead, but in parallel posts. Weinberger was closer to Reagan personally than was Shultz, and the defense secretary was closer politically on most issues to Reagan's core supporters among conservatives. But on foreign policy questions, Reagan had a tremendous—and increasing—regard for Shultz and his judgment, which was often poles apart from that of Weinberger. Admiral William Crowe, who worked with both men on policy issues as chairman of the Joint Chiefs of Staff, recalled that "as long as Weinberger and Shultz were arguing, there wasn't a consensus on anything. The President never, as far as I could tell, arbitrated any of those disputes. He just let the water seek its own level, which seemed to me a funny way to run a railroad."

The impending resumption of the arms negotiations required the United States to have one position, not two positions. There was a growing sense that, perhaps for the first time, both Washington and Moscow were serious about trying to hammer out agreements rather than simply posturing for public opinion in Europe and this country. But imposing organization and order on this uncoordinated and often fractured administration was a serious problem.

Reagan, buoyed by his election triumph and his soaring hope to do something important to reduce nuclear weapons, participated more extensively than previously in the discussions of arms control issues in preparation for the January 7–8 meeting of Shultz and Gromyko in Geneva. Starting with a National Security Council meeting on November 30, Reagan took part in five full-scale meetings with his top cabinet and arms advisers leading up to the negotiations. This was an unusual amount of time and attention for a president who was so uninvolved several years earlier that he did not even seem to know that the Soviets relied primarily on land-based missiles for their nuclear clout.

As the reopening of the arms talks approached late in 1984, McFarlane suggested that Paul Nitze, who had been the U.S. negotiator in the suspended Euromissiles talks and who had had an illustrious career in government dating back to 1940, become the "czar" of arms control based in the White House. However, partly to keep the bureaucratic action under his own control but also because he sorely needed help from an old pro, Shultz arranged to install Nitze in an office on the seventh floor of the State Department just around the corner from his own, with the title of special adviser to both the President and secretary of state. A man of great experience, wealth and culture, Nitze at age seventy-seven was a person Shultz could easily relate to and trust. Nitze and James Timbie, a much younger career expert whom Shultz quickly came to respect, put on a crash course in arms control for Shultz that December, spending hours with him going over issue after issue and preparing thick briefing books for Shultz to study. Shultz was determined "he was not going to be out-matched, out-historied, out-knowledged by Gromyko and that he would not concede Gromyko anything," according to Timbie. "He was going to sit down and hold his own, and he did."

Before the negotiations with the Soviets could possibly succeed, the negotiations within the administration had to produce U.S. positions with broad support. Since consensus and discipline were not going to be imposed by Reagan, Shultz set out to build his own. Instead of keeping the negotiating delegation small and secretive, as some recommended, Shultz brought all the key arms control players from all the agencies into his delegation and made them partly responsible for the results.

First Shultz asked McFarlane to be a senior member of his delegation to the coming Geneva talks. This would send a message of White House support to the Soviets, Shultz believed, and also help create the consensus he was seeking. McFarlane jumped at the chance to participate and Reagan agreed.

Next Shultz invited the entire membership of the Senior Arms Control Policy Group to accompany him to Geneva. This group, chaired by McFarlane, included Assistant Secretary of Defense Richard Perle, who had been a roadblock in many earlier episodes and was constantly battling his State Department counterpart, Assistant Secretary Richard Burt. Another official who often disagreed with Shultz was Kenneth Adelman, director of the Arms Control and Disarmament Agency. After being asked by Shultz to accompany him to Geneva, Adelman argued that it was unbecoming for a secretary of state to lead "a traveling road show" of arms control experts and that it would merely play into the hands of critics who said the administration was unable to get its act together. Shultz insisted, making the disarming argument—which had never occurred to Adelman—that the experts might actually be needed in the negotiations with Gromyko in Geneva.

The central issue in the internal deliberations was what to say and do in Geneva about the SDI program, which Reagan sought to protect at all costs and the Soviet Union sought to curb above all else. The administration discussion was affected by a visit shortly before Christmas from British Prime Minister Margaret Thatcher, the European leader that the President most admired and was most inclined to accommodate. Thatcher was concerned about the implications of SDI for the Atlantic alliance and impressed with the passionate Soviet opposition she had heard in a London visit by Moscow's then second-ranking leader, Mikhail Gorbachev. In a meeting at Camp David with the participation of Shultz and McFarlane but not of Weinberger, who had become an ardent SDI advocate, Thatcher and Reagan agreed on a four-point statement of international reassurance on the aims of SDI. Point two was that SDI-related deployments would "have to be a matter of negotiations" with the Soviet Union in view of the 1972 Anti-Ballistic Missiles (ABM) Treaty which seemed to ban such defenses.

Weinberger was furious that he had been excluded from the discussions, and now all the more suspicious that Shultz would trade away part of Reagan's "dream"—and the Defense Department's fastest growing program—to Gromyko at Geneva. With the negotiating instructions for the Geneva meeting still undecided, Weinberger insisted on participating in a meeting with Reagan, Shultz and McFarlane on the subject during the President's annual New Year's holiday at the Annenberg Estate in Palm Springs, California.

The meeting took place under a huge impressionist painting of irises in the sumptuous sitting room of the wealthy publisher's mansion on the afternoon of December 31, several hours before the dinner and New Year's Eve party given in Reagan's honor. McFarlane, sitting next to Reagan on a white sofa, presented the draft of the presidential instructions he had drawn up in Washington. Shultz and Weinberger, sitting in overstuffed chairs at either end of the sofa, with a long coffee table dividing them, faced each other symbolically and substantively. Weinberger had a long list of objections to the proposed instructions and a thick loose-leaf book of arguments, but his basic point was that Shultz should not talk at all about the SDI program with Gromyko at the Geneva meetings, so that nothing could be given or traded away. Reagan was sympathetic to this point of view, but he was also impressed with Shultz's argument that space defense was the primary topic of interest to Moscow and that it was unrealistic to refuse to discuss it. Finally, Reagan came down on Shultz's side. "Cap, we can't know where it all will come out, but we are going to engage [with the Soviets]," the President said. "So George, go over there and get it started without giving up anything."

• NEGOTIATIONS IN GENEVA

Secretary Shultz's U.S. Air Force Boeing 707, called by reporters the "Ship of Feuds" because it contained so many warring elements of the administration, took off for Geneva from Andrews Air Force Base near Washington at 6:10 P.M. on January 5, 1985. Because of the unusual number of senior government officials, staff and bodyguards along, the press corps aboard the plane was limited to six seats, less than half the usual contingent. Through the luck of the draw of names from a hat, I was one of the six. I had often traveled abroad on flights with the secretary of state since I began covering the State Department full-time in 1976, but this trip was unlike the others. The idea that such a diverse group would travel together was new, and everyone seemed to be cautious and restrained, almost walking on eggs. All seemed absorbed in their briefing books, or the one copy of Shultz's prepared "talking points" for the meeting with Gromyko that was available to members of the delegation. There was little of the normal banter among officials and virtually no drinking. There was so much interest in who was seated where that the on-board press corps drew up a seating diagram as an indication of the pecking order of officialdom. With the meeting billed as the most important one between the United States and the Soviet Union since the invasion of Afghanistan five years earlier, there was enormous interest in just about everything. In Geneva a massive press corps of eight hundred journalists and technicians was waiting for us, including the anchors of all three major U.S. television networks.

One reason for the unusual air of reticence by the officials on the plane, we learned later, was that before leaving Washington Shultz had ordered all members of his delegation, except for spokesman Bernard Kalb, to say nothing to reporters until the meetings with Gromyko were over. Nonetheless, I stood for a long time in the darkened aisle of the airplane over the North Atlantic talking with the "Prince of Darkness," as Richard Perle had been dubbed in the press corps. The following morning in Geneva, Perle was summoned to the secretary's suite where Shultz and McFarlane chewed him out for speaking to me in violation of the rules. Perle responded that we had not been talking about the substance of the negotiations, and that he did not understand the rule to preclude social conversation with an old acquaintance. The two senior officials were not amused, and threatened to send Perle home if he did not keep strictly away from reporters.

Nobody knew it at the time, but the Shultz-Gromyko negotiations created patterns and set precedents that would become a part of U.S.-Soviet negotiations for years to come. From then on, Shultz and James Baker after him were accompanied by experts from myriad agencies of the government when meeting the Soviets for ministerial-level negotiations. In most cases the President's national security adviser or his deputy accompanied the secretary of state. Eventually the Soviets followed suit, bringing a variety of diplomatic and military experts of their own to deal with their American counterparts. A news blackout lasting from the start of substantive discussions until the announcement that they were over, which Shultz enforced at Geneva, was also a feature of many of the summit meetings and high-level negotiations to come.

The Geneva discussions themselves took place over two days of the most numbing cold wave that the lakeside Swiss city had seen for years. The atmosphere across the bargaining table was not much warmer, observed Nitze, who participated in the inner core of the negotiations. The Soviets demanded a clear statement that one of the objectives of the new negotiations was to "prevent an arms race in space"—their price for returning to the talks on offensive weapons. Shultz resisted but finally went along.

The most contentious issue, though, was the relationship between the three subjects that would be under negotiation in the new talks: strategic weapons, intermediate-range weapons primarily based in Europe, and the newer, more controversial area of weapons in space. Gromyko insisted that a definite relationship should be established among the three, implying that the two traditional negotiating arenas would be used as leverage for concessions on space. Shultz did not dispute that the three were related, but insisted that progress in one area should not be held back by lack of movement in others. "Round and round we went, both within the U.S. delegation and between the U.S. and U.S.S.R. delegations," observed Kenneth Adelman. Gromyko's argument reminded the irreverent Arms Control and Disarmament Agency director of a rhyme he had learned in grammar school, "All things related are, such that when one touches a flower, one disturbs the furthest star." Finally, late on the last day, more than two hours after the scheduled completion of the talks, as the hordes of journalists waited and the world seemed almost to hold its breath, a compromise was reached.

> The sides agree that the subject of the negotiations will be a complex of questions concerning space and nuclear arms, both strategic and intermediate range, with all the questions considered and resolved in their interrelationship. The objective of the negotiations will be to work out effective agreements aimed at preventing an arms race in space and terminating it on Earth,

at limiting and reducing nuclear arms, and at strengthening strategic stability.

Nobody could quite explain what the words meant in theory or practice, but both Washington and Moscow were satisfied they could live with the declaration. It was in the interest of both sides, as they saw it, to get back to arms control negotiations.

Within a few days after the agreement in Geneva, Konstantin Chernenko suffered an undisclosed physical setback that was the beginning of the end for him. On January 18, a State Department official traveling in Eastern Europe was told at the Foreign Ministry of a Soviet ally that Chernenko had had a stroke and lost the use of his arm. The Soviet leader disappeared from view and was unable to attend a Kremlin pre-election rally on February 22, when the Soviet people were informed for the first time that he was ill. Chernenko, obviously weak and failing, reappeared twice more on Soviet television in ceremonial roles, but he seemed to have been propped up before the camera.

Through diplomatic exchanges, meanwhile, Washington and Moscow agreed to send their negotiators to Geneva March 12 to inaugurate their new arms negotiations and thus begin a new chapter in their troubled relations. Almost on the eve of that event, at 7:20 P.M. on March 10, Chernenko died at age seventy-three. Less than twenty-four hours later, a special session of the Communist Party Central Committee elected a much younger and more vigorous man, Mikhail Sergeyevich Gorbachev, fifty-four, as the new General Secretary and thus the leader of the USSR.

4. Gorbachev Takes Command

Neither the Soviet Union nor the outside world could have foreseen the historic consequences that would flow from the election of Mikhail Gorbachev on March 11, 1985, but it was clear within days that this was a major development in world affairs. Gorbachev, who had just celebrated his fifty-fourth birthday in robust health, was a stark and welcome contrast to the three aged and failing general secretaries of the Communist Party who had led the USSR since Leonid Brezhnev began slipping physically a decade before.

Since Richard Nixon's first summit meeting with Brezhnev in Moscow in 1972, there had never been a time when a politically strong U.S. president and a physically strong Soviet general secretary had been in office at the same time. By 1973, Nixon had been hobbled by the Watergate scandal, and he was followed by the unelected (and ultimately unelectable) Gerald Ford. By the time Jimmy Carter came to office, Brezhnev was slipping physically and mentally. He was followed by Yuri Andropov and Konstantin Chernenko, both of whom enjoyed only brief periods of tolerable health. Finally in 1985, the stars were in alignment for the first time in a long time. In Washington, the newly reelected President was riding a wave of popularity and political strength at the start of his second term, eager to meet the new General

Secretary, who quickly showed his mettle as an impressive leader. Moreover, both Reagan and Gorbachev and the nations they headed were ready for a broad improvement in relations after a long period of high tension that had increased military expenditures beyond what either nation could afford and heightened popular as well as leadership concern about the possibility of nuclear war.

It would take most of 1985 to arrange the first Reagan-Gorbachev summit, which in many respects would be a meeting of opposites. But by the end of the Geneva summit, the President and the General Secretary would have taken each other's measure and reengaged their two countries in serious negotiations on the most difficult problems between them.

In a generational leap, Gorbachev was 19 years younger than Chernenko and 13 years younger than the average age of the ten surviving and full voting members of the Politburo. Among world leaders, Gorbachev was 20 years younger than Reagan (74) and much younger than François Mitterrand (68), Yasuhiro Nakasone (66) and Margaret Thatcher (59). The world leader closest to him in age was Helmut Kohl, who was 32 days younger.

After Gorbachev had made his mark in the world, George Kennan told a television interviewer that he was mystified how the Soviet system had produced such a leader. "Numbers of us who have known that country for a long time simply stand without explanation as to how a man with these qualities could have emerged from a provincial party apparatus in the North Caucasus," said the U.S. scholar.

Gorbachev, despite his village origin, was no innocent provincial, having experienced both the dark and the brighter side of Soviet life. The young Gorbachev had learned much about the brutal heritage from the experiences of his own family: One of his grandfathers was sent to Siberia for failing to fulfill his sowing plan in a year of famine, even though half his family had died of hunger; his other grandfather, a collective farm organizer, was unjustly imprisoned for fourteen months as an "enemy of the people" during the Stalinist purges of the late 1930s. Despite this background, the award-winning young farm worker was given a place at the country's most prestigious educational institution, Moscow State University. Gorbachev became the first Soviet leader since Lenin to have a university education, in his case, a law degree.

Gorbachev and his wife, Raisa, also a Moscow State University graduate, also learned much in the school of real life by traveling widely and independently as vacationing tourists through cities and small towns of France and Italy in 1966 and 1967, a rare exposure to the West for a Soviet couple at that time. Accompanied by Raisa wherever possible, Gorbachev had also traveled on official trips to East Germany in the 1960s, Belgium, Bulgaria, Czechoslovakia, France and West Germany in the 1970s and Canada, Great Britain, Italy, Mongolia and Vietnam in the 1980s.

With his education, energy and political skills, Gorbachev rose steadily and rapidly through the Communist Party system. In thirty years as a full-time Communist official, he had been the leader of the youth organization and then of the Communist Party apparatus in his native Stavropol, the national party secretary in charge of agriculture and, since 1980, the youngest voting member of the ruling Politburo.

As the protégé and close ally of Yuri Andropov, Gorbachev was among the few to have had daily personal contact with the dying leader in the last five months of his life, relaying orders and taking an increasingly important role in managing the Soviet party and government. From at least mid-1984 Gorbachev had frequently presided over Politburo meetings in the absence of the failing Chernenko and is believed to have been the dominant figure in many key decisions. "He performs like a person who has been in charge for a while, not like a person who is just taking charge," Secretary of State George Shultz observed to an aide after he met General Secretary Gorbachev for the first time at the Chernenko funeral. "A person who just got there simply cannot have that much command of information and self-confidence."

Reagan had been awakened at 4:00 A.M. on March 11 by his national security adviser, Robert McFarlane, with the news of Chernenko's death, and he began considering more seriously than before whether to attend a Moscow funeral to meet the new leader. By midmorning Reagan had decided it would be "a grandstand play" of little value for him to go to Moscow but that Vice President George Bush and Shultz, who would represent him, would take a personal letter expressing his desire for improved relations and inviting Gorbachev to visit the United States.

Following Chernenko's funeral and the traditional military parade in Red Square, Gorbachev held a reception for foreign visitors in the Krem-

lin, the commanding castle on a hill where Russia had been ruled for
hundreds of years by the czars and for nearly seventy years by the
Communists. The reception was in St. George's Hall, a vast white armorylike room dedicated to the Order of St. George, the highest military
award of Imperial Russia, and decorated with the names of units and
individuals who were presented the order for valor by the czars. Later
Gorbachev met individually with important foreign delegations in St.
Catherine's Hall, a former throne room of the czarinas, one of the most
richly decorated in the Grand Kremlin Palace. The room, which was to
become familiar to Shultz in meetings with Gorbachev in the next three
years, is a stunning reminder of past grandeur, with three gilded bronze
chandeliers, green malachite columns from the Ural Mountains and
replicas of the emblem of the Order of St. Catherine, which was established by Peter the Great in honor of his wife, Catherine I. Set into the
top of the columns around the room is a large scripted "E" (for Ekaterina,
or Catherine) with the numeral "1" drawn through it. Russian legend
has it that Peter established the order after Catherine gave away her own
jewels to purchase the freedom of men from prison.

In the meeting, which lasted an hour and twenty-five minutes, Gorbachev declared that the Soviet Union was not interested in confrontations with the United States, and he challenged the Americans to
negotiate seriously in the forthcoming Geneva arms negotiations. Bush
sensed "something different" in the new Soviet leader. In contrast to his
meetings under similar circumstances with Andropov and Chernenko,
Bush found Gorbachev at ease and informal in "a very smooth performance," using body language to joke with the U.S. vice president as
the Soviet interpreter delivered the English translations. Shultz, who
was able to observe Gorbachev carefully because Bush, as the senior
figure, carried the conversation, briefed State Department aides privately
about his impressions. An aide's notes on Shultz's briefing read:

> G. comfortable with self. Confident but not overbearing. Can
> decide things. Businesslike and bright. Sense of humor. Can be
> provoked but keeps control. . . . Human rights brought up and
> he was provoked. Seemed in control without making a point of
> it.
> Gorbachev will be good at atmospherics. Not just an empty
> guy but full of content. Very different kind of person from others.
> . . . Potential for very strong person.

Shultz was even more emphatic in a conversation in Moscow with Canadian Prime Minister Brian Mulroney, who also met Gorbachev on the occasion of the Chernenko funeral. Mulroney asked Shultz, in light of his discussion with the new leader, when he thought "serious change" might begin in the Soviet Union. Shultz answered with one word: "today."

There was debate from the start about whether the arrival of a more capable and vigorous Soviet leader was ultimately a good thing or a bad thing for the West. Bush had little hesitation on this score after meeting Gorbachev, saying that it seemed to him "a good thing" for the Soviet Union to be coming out of its long time of troubles. "It's up to us to meet the challenge," said the man who would later negotiate on his own with the new Soviet leader.

• A CAUTIOUS BEGINNING

Addressing American intellectuals and movie stars at the Soviet Embassy in Washington five years later, Gorbachev said that in his earliest hours in office "having understood our country and history, the first conclusion we drew for ourselves was that we could not go on living like that. This was said on 11 March, at night." His wife, Raisa, boldly interrupted her husband to add, "The 10th!" In meetings with Communist Party officials a few weeks after taking office, Gorbachev began to articulate a belief he had long held but rarely voiced before, that the Soviet Union was verging on a state of crisis.

For the most part, though, Gorbachev began cautiously in both domestic and foreign affairs, even while conveying in speech and manner that he was in charge and committed to change. Gorbachev initially had a precarious majority in the Politburo and faced skepticism bordering on opposition from Old Guard members of the *nomenklatura* bureaucracy and elements of the Central Committee. Various accounts of his election suggest there was major opposition in the Politburo, and in some accounts a tie vote was broken in his favor by Gromyko, who made a passionate and unscripted appeal in Gorbachev's favor in the Central Committee session that formally elected the new leader. Still other versions indicate that Gorbachev was assured of the top job even before Chernenko's death. Whatever the case in March, Gorbachev was able to add three allies as full voting members to the Politburo in late April,* giving him a clear working majority, and in July he ousted former Leningrad Communist Party leader Gregori Romanov, who was considered to have been among his chief rivals in the Politburo for the post of general secretary.

In his address to the Central Committee the day he was elected, Gorbachev gave top priority to his allies in the Warsaw Pact, declaring that in foreign affairs:

> [The] first precept of the Party and State is to preserve and strengthen in every way fraternal friendship with our closest friends and allies, the countries of the great socialist community. We will do everything dependent on us to expand cooperation with socialist states, to enhance the role and influence of socialism in world affairs.

In pursuit of this aim, Gorbachev made a point of receiving all six Warsaw Pact leaders together when they were in Moscow for Chernenko's funeral. Six weeks later, on April 26, he presided at a summit of Warsaw Pact leaders in the Polish capital, at which the Soviet-dominated security organization for Eastern Europe, then thirty years old, was renewed for another twenty years, even though some of the allies favored shorter commitments.

Despite the bow to the Eastern European empire, Gorbachev came to office with underlying beliefs in foreign affairs that suggested major changes ahead, according to Andrei Aleksandrov-Agentov, who continued as national security assistant in the General Secretary's office through Gorbachev's first year. "He had the feeling that our foreign policy had become too cast iron, too inflexible, too concentrated upon a number of positions that seemed to be impossible to change." According to his aide, Gorbachev was saying such things privately even before he came to power.

Gorbachev made no immediate changes but began by ordering a number of studies. In domestic affairs, Gorbachev had the benefit of more than one hundred studies of various economic and social problems that had been authorized when his mentor, Andropov, was general sec-

---

* They were Yegor Ligachev, KGB Chairman Viktor Chebrikov and Nikolai Ryzhkov. Ironically, the first two would become critics after a few months, and Gorbachev eventually ousted them from their Politburo posts. Ryzhkov was a loyal supporter as prime minister until 1991.

retary. However, in foreign affairs, few such critical examinations existed. Gorbachev as General Secretary requested studies from the Foreign Ministry, Defense Ministry and KGB as well as the Institute of World Economy and International Relations (then headed by Aleksandr Yakovlev), Georgi Arbatov's U.S.A. and Canada Institute, and other elements of the USSR Academy of Sciences, according to Valentin Falin, a senior Soviet figure, who later became chief of the International Department of the Communist Party Central Committee. Gorbachev "was not an expert in foreign policy at all," said Falin, but he was unusually willing to listen to what others had to say. Unlike his predecessors, he was comfortable with experts and sought their advice directly. Oleg Grinevsky, a senior diplomat who was chief Soviet negotiator at the Stockholm talks on Confidence and Security Building Measures, was among a number of Soviet negotiators summoned by Gorbachev to one-on-one meetings with the General Secretary in his private office. "Nobody [else] is listening," said Gorbachev, who insisted on being given Grinevsky's personal opinion, outside normal bureaucratic channels, of the future of the negotiation he was conducting, the problems involved and possible options for the Soviet Union.

As he settled into the job, Gorbachev began sending signals to key institutions of his general inclination. In mid-May, in his first major tour out of Moscow, he spoke bluntly about the unsatisfactory state of the economy to Leningrad party activists at Smolny Institute, the girls' school that had served as Lenin's headquarters during the 1917 revolution. Speaking in direct terms rarely if ever heard from a general secretary before that time, Gorbachev declared there was no alternative to making major economic changes. "Try to get your apartment repaired. You will definitely have to find a moonlighter [a private contractor operating semi-illegally] to do it for you. He will steal the materials he needs from a construction site."

In July Gorbachev took his message to the military in a rare general meeting of the entire top command of the Soviet armed forces in Minsk. It was the first such meeting with a general secretary since a famous encounter between Leonid Brezhnev and the military in October 1982, just weeks before his death. Neither the text nor even a summary of the Minsk meeting has ever been published, but Marshal Sergei Akhromeyev, who was chief of staff of the armed forces at the time, said Gorbachev expressed two principal ideas: "that the foreign policy of the Soviet Union should be conducted in such a way that military tension in the world would be reduced and, at the same time, the security of the nation should be guaranteed." At the same time, Akhromeyev said, Gorbachev "called on the military to modify their methods." The armed forces chief said this was the beginning of extensive discussions that led eventually to dramatic changes in Soviet military doctrine and major cutbacks in USSR armed forces.

• STUMBLING TOWARD THE SUMMIT

Gorbachev did not reply immediately to the invitation from Reagan, which had been presented by Bush March 13 at the Chernenko funeral, to participate in a summit meeting in the United States. But on March 24, the new Soviet leader sent the first of many private letters to Reagan taking "a positive attitude" toward a meeting and saying that the time and place should be decided later. In a reference to the apparent contradiction between Reagan's tough anti-Soviet rhetoric and the conciliatory tone of some of his letters to Kremlin leaders, Gorbachev cautioned that creating an atmosphere of trust from the existing confrontation was a delicate task.

> Trust is a specially sensitive thing, keenly receptive to both deeds and words. It will not be enhanced if, for example, one were to talk as if in two languages: one for private contacts, and the other as they say, for the audience.

As if to show Reagan he was speaking with a single voice, Gorbachev on Easter Sunday, April 7, made his first major international declaration, a *Pravda* interview in which he spoke about his correspondence with Reagan and used the precise words of his letter, saying that both sides had "a positive attitude" toward a summit meeting. "We regard the improvement of Soviet-American relations not only as extremely necessary but also as a possible matter. . . . I am convinced that a serious impulse should be given to Soviet-American relations at a high political level," Gorbachev said.

At the same time, Gorbachev announced the first of many international initiatives that would take the global limelight: a freeze on the deployment of Soviet intermediate-range missiles in Europe until November, which could be extended to a permanent halt to the deployment if Washington would do the same. The freeze was immediately rejected by the White House as leaving a 10–1 Soviet advantage in Europe and being "nothing new." Gorbachev also proposed a freeze on strategic offensive arms and on the research, testing and deployment of space weapons for the duration of the Geneva arms talks. The White House wasn't interested. But it was clear less than one month after Gorbachev took power that the Kremlin had a new star performing on the world stage, one that Washington would have to take extremely seriously.

Even before Gorbachev's *Pravda* interview, Shultz had agreed to meet Foreign Minister Andrei Gromyko in Vienna in mid-May when the thirtieth anniversary of the Austrian State Treaty was to be celebrated. The Soviets made it clear to the State Department in advance that they considered the meeting a preparation for the proposed summit. Reagan was eager to meet Gorbachev, but as a matter of tactics Shultz was determined not to be the one to press for a summit meeting. He instructed his delegation to say nothing to their Soviet counterparts about the subject, and he vowed not to raise it with Gromyko. Shultz felt "the ball was in their court" after Reagan's invitation. He noted that Gromyko tended to seek concessions for attending meetings of interest to the United States, and he could imagine that Gromyko expected him "to come on bended knee begging for a summit." Besides, the atmosphere had been complicated by the March 24 killing of an American liaison officer in East Germany, Major Arthur D. Nicholson, Jr., and resulting recriminations about Soviet responsibility. Secretary of Defense Caspar Weinberger was particularly adamant in demanding a formal Soviet apology and compensation, which Moscow refused to grant.

Gromyko, like Shultz, was aware that his boss was very interested in "a meeting at the highest level," which is the Soviet term for what is known as a summit in the West. And like Shultz, Gromyko had decided in advance to play it cool. When his chief aide for U.S. affairs, Aleksandr Bessmertnykh, stopped by to see Gromyko at the Soviet Embassy in Vienna shortly before Shultz was to arrive for the talks, the veteran foreign minister was absorbed in reading a detective story rather than in last-minute studying of his brief.

When the U.S. delegation walked into the big room on the second floor of the Soviet Embassy at 2:00 P.M. on May 14, U.S. arms control adviser Paul Nitze realized this was the place in which he had spent many hours negotiating the SALT I agreements in the early 1970s. The room was unchanged and so was the Soviet foreign minister. After some opening remarks by Shultz on the Nicholson murder, Soviet human rights practices and allied access to Berlin, Gromyko interrupted to say the important issue was arms control and that he would now address it. He then launched into a mind-numbing recitation of more than two hours on arms control subjects and a variety of peripheral questions—not including the Reagan-Gorbachev summit.

While Gromyko talked in Russian (though he could speak English well) and his interpreter droned on, Shultz resolved that if Gromyko was going to go through that kind of stuff, then damnit, he had a whole barrelful of it too. The secretary began pulling out of his briefcase various position papers on subjects Gromyko had mentioned. By the time Gromyko finished, Shultz had accumulated a stack of rebuttal papers several inches high. Despite the fact that the expected three-hour duration of the meeting was already over, Shultz launched into his point-by-point presentation, leisurely and completely. As the clock neared the six-hour mark nearly everyone in the two delegations except for Shultz and Gromyko had left the table at one time or another to go to the toilet, but the two ministers were still locked in their verbal marathon. After Shultz finished, Gromyko commenced a counter-rebuttal, and it seemed to Shultz he was deliberately prolonging it. Finally, about 8:15 P.M., the Soviet minister noted dourly that it was past time to leave for the gala reception that was being given by the Austrians in commemoration of their State Treaty.

However, as the two delegations gathered their papers and moved toward the door, Gromyko invited the secretary to a private conference in a corner of the room. "Do you have anything more you want to say to me?" the Soviet minister asked in a whisper, this time in English without interpreters or other aides present.

"No, we've covered everything," Shultz replied.

"What about the summit?" demanded Gromyko.

"What about it?" countered Shultz.

Gromyko said he thought there should be some discussion of the time and place, and that it was out of the question for Gorbachev to come to Washington as Reagan had proposed. "You should come to Moscow."

"You know that is impossible," Shultz responded. "No way the President would come to Moscow. If there's going to be a summit, it ought to be in Washington."

"Perhaps some neutral place," Gromyko suggested in a predictable compromise.

Shultz replied that Reagan would not go to Moscow and that Washington would be best. "And I don't have any authority to talk about anything other than that."

Gromyko then suggested that the meeting be held sometime in late November. This was very close to the mid-November timetable that Reagan had privately discussed with Shultz.

Shultz ended the brief but intense conversation, which had lasted only two or three minutes in contrast to the six hours of roundabout talk preceding it, by saying he would take Gromyko's suggestions back to Reagan and be in touch.

The following day at the Austrian palace near the end of the festivities, Gromyko asked to see Shultz privately again. Perhaps mindful of the downing of the U-2 spy plane in 1960, which had destroyed the Paris summit between Khrushchev and Eisenhower, or of other tense times as summit meetings neared, the Soviet minister cautioned, "We're going to have this summit meeting and it's very important that things not take place that make it impossible. And you have to exercise care and restraint."

"That's not the problem. The problem is what you do," responded Shultz bluntly. Referring to the killing of the American officer in East Germany, he added, "It's things like Major Nicholson and so on. That's what makes it hard to hold a summit. So don't tell me that we need to exercise restraint."

The Soviet spokesman, Vladimir Lomeiko, said in a news briefing only that both sides had expressed "a certain interest" in a summit meeting. Shultz said on Austrian television that "there's nothing to add to what's already known" about plans for a summit. Questioned by the traveling press corps on his Air Force plane on the flight home, the secretary was no more revealing. Neither he nor any member of his official party referred to the whispered conversation with Gromyko or its followup. "I have nothing further to say on the subject" of the summit meeting, Shultz told the reporters gathered round him in the front cabin of his plane. "I just have to leave it there."

A few days later I met Soviet Ambassador Anatoly Dobrynin, who was seeking to nail down the time and place for the summit through his contacts with Shultz. Dobrynin said it was very important for the two leaders to meet face to face as a way of breaking the extreme tension between the two countries. The Soviet-American situation resembled a war, Dobrynin said, but more like World War I, with opposing forces glaring at each other from fixed trenches, than like World War II, with its great mobility. Dobrynin said he was encouraging the Soviet government to go ahead with the Gorbachev-Reagan meeting because, in the existing situation, it might be "a last resort" to change the pattern of relations. Yes, things had improved since the worst days of 1983. In Dobrynin's view Soviet-American relations were now back to "business as usual," but, he added, "Not very good business."

After several exchanges, Dobrynin on July 1 brought Shultz a message from Moscow agreeing that the summit meeting would be held November 19–20 in Geneva. The following day came a major change in Soviet diplomacy that would affect the summit and all that followed. After twenty-eight years, Andrei Gromyko stepped down from the helm of the Foreign Ministry and moved, with Gorbachev's sponsorship, to the largely ceremonial post of chairman of the Soviet Presidium, or President of the Soviet Union. His surprise successor was Eduard Shevardnadze, who was nearly unknown outside the USSR.

The Americans who had been present on the long afternoon in Vienna wondered if the summit announcement and Gromyko's departure were somehow connected. Had Gromyko known in mid-May that he was soon to be kicked upstairs? Had he been trying for one last achievement as foreign minister by arranging the summit on Gorbachev's terms? Or had he been trying to save his job?

• ENTER SHEVARDNADZE

Eduard Amvrosievich Shevardnadze had been first secretary of the communist party of his native southern Soviet republic of Georgia for thirteen years when Mikhail Gorbachev telephoned him in Tbilisi, the Georgian capital, at the end of June with a surprising request. Gorbachev said he had been thinking about a change in the post of foreign minister and had decided that Shevardnadze should do the job. The political leadership was to meet in Moscow the following day, and Gorbachev's plan was to present this idea for approval.

The two men had known each other for nearly twenty-five years, since they were Komsomol (Young Communist League) leaders in nearby areas. They had visited each other's homes and occasionally vacationed together. In late 1979 they had been on vacation together in Georgia, both having recently been appointed candidate (nonvoting) members of the ruling Communist Party Politburo, when they learned about the Soviet invasion of Afghanistan. Although this was an action of profound national and international importance, Gorbachev told Reagan at the Geneva summit that he and Shevardnadze heard about the invasion when it was announced on a radio broadcast and that neither one of them had been involved or even informed of the decision in advance.

While they had talked about many things over the years, including the stagnation of the country in the later Brezhnev years and the difficult problems facing the Soviet Union at home and abroad, Gorbachev had never broached the idea of Shevardnadze's becoming foreign minister. Shevardnadze told me in an interview for this book that Gorbachev's proposal was "the greatest surprise of my life." He had his doubts, "a very big doubt," that he was the man for the job. Although he had been abroad almost a dozen times on official delegations since becoming the leader in Georgia, he knew little about international diplomacy and felt somewhat awed by diplomats. If he met a Soviet diplomat of minister or counselor rank (lower than ambassador) he tended to feel that they were big people who knew things he could not fathom. To meet the ambassador of another country seemed to him even more beyond his limits. Shevardnadze's first reaction was to ask Gorbachev to reconsider. However, all arguments were swept aside by his determined friend, including his trump card: "But I am non-Russian," Shevardnadze exclaimed, assuming that the foreign minister of the USSR should be from the dominant nationality of the country. "You are Soviet," Gorbachev replied. Shevardnadze took the job.

Years later, after he became a celebrated international figure and accepted as a respected colleague among Western foreign ministers in a manner that Gromyko had never been, Shevardnadze said he had never been informed just why Gorbachev had picked him. However, Gorbachev told his foreign policy assistant, Andrei Aleksandrov-Agentov, that he had known Shevardnadze for many years and believed they were quite compatible, and that Shevardnadze had a flexible and creative mind, giving him the potential to be an excellent foreign minister. He might also have said—but apparently did not—that Shevardnadze possessed unusual qualities of courage and determination and that, like Gorbachev, he had seemingly natural and extraordinary political ability.

Shevardnadze was born in 1928, three years before Gorbachev, in the village of Mamati in Georgia, a southern Soviet Republic that has a long history and tradition as an independent state and is known for its quick-witted, practical people. His father was a country schoolteacher and headmaster—remarkably similar to the job that Shultz's father had had in Indiana in his twenties—and the young Shevardnadze received his higher education as a historian in an educational institute. He was also a very active and successful member of the Young Communist League, rising by 1957 to be first secretary of the organization for Georgia. From 1965 to 1972, Shevardnadze was minister of interior, or chief law enforcement officer, of Georgia, which was then famous for rampant black marketeering and corruption. Unofficial publications by dissident groups charged that as minister of interior he condoned, if not actively encouraged, the use of torture in Georgian prisons, but that has not been proved. What is clear is that his investigations led to the ouster of Georgia's communist party boss, Vasili Mzhavanadze, and Shevardnadze's appointment to the job. An often-told story in Georgia is that the new party chief asked officials in an early meeting to vote by raising their left hands. "Keep them up a minute," Shevardnadze said as he roamed the room inspecting the many expensive foreign watches. The first secretary, who wore a modest Russian-made model, ordered the officials to "donate" their fancy timepieces to the state. Shevardnadze also made his mark in economic reforms, especially in the successful use of incentives to boost production in both the agricultural and the industrial fields in enterprise-minded Georgia. Gorbachev paid him three visits as national party secretary for agriculture and issued a glowing endorsement of Shevardnadze's experiments in 1984.

Despite his domestic experience and prestige at home, Shevardnadze felt nearly overwhelmed when he was unexpectedly made foreign minister in July 1985, and he went about learning the job in sixteen- and eighteen-hour workdays, losing twenty-five pounds in the first several months. Instead of summoning Foreign Ministry officials en masse to instruct them on his policies, he met his deputies and division chiefs one by one in personal conferences in which they did most of the talking and he asked questions and made copious notes, a highly unusual procedure for a Soviet official of ministerial rank.

When he met Aleksandr Bessmertnykh, who was in charge of the Foreign Ministry's U.S.A. Department, Shevardnadze learned he had only about ten days to prepare for a scheduled meeting with Shultz, which was to take place in Helsinki on the occasion of the tenth anniversary of the 1975 Helsinki accords. "What are we going to discuss?" the new foreign minister asked. When Bessmertnykh told him that strategic arms negotiations would be the top priority, Shevardnadze plunged into the bewildering details of numbers, ranges and types of nuclear weapons and the often arcane positions of the two parties, which seemed to Shevardnadze like "higher mathematics." Until they left for Helsinki, he and Bessmertnykh met nearly every day in a cram course on U.S.-Soviet issues.

Shultz, too, was preparing for his new counterpart from Moscow, and looking forward to almost any change from the dour and inflexible Gromyko. "Isn't there something better I can do with my life than meet with that son of a bitch?" Shultz said from time to time to Arthur Hartman, the U.S. ambassador to Moscow. Hartman felt it was even more damning that Shultz, as a shrewd negotiator, had come to view Gromyko as a man who didn't know his own interests, who could be rigid beyond the point of rational purpose. Shultz mused to reporters after Gromyko was named president that he had reached an "odd rapport" with his antagonist through the ups and downs of their many meetings. But in the main Shultz looked forward to a more satisfying relationship with the new Soviet foreign minister. Learning that Mrs. Shevardnadze was to accompany her husband to Helsinki, Shultz and his wife, O'Bie, vowed to do all they could to get to know them as individuals and to have "a decent human relationship" with the Shevardnadzes, whatever the political problems might be.

Finlandia Hall in Helsinki on July 30 was crowded with delegations from the thirty-five nations that had signed the Helsinki accords in the presence of General Secretary Leonid Brezhnev and President Gerald Ford a decade earlier. Seated by the French alphabet, the United States was in the front row and the Soviet Union almost at the back. As they entered the hall, Shultz and Rozanne Ridgway, who had just replaced Richard Burt as assistant secretary of state for European and Canadian affairs, thought it would be a good idea to take the initiative to greet Shevardnadze. Ridgway went with Shultz along the front row and up the steps to the back where the Soviet delegation was sitting. "Everybody could begin to see him moving in that direction and up these steps. It just got quieter and quieter as everybody saw what was happening. We watched the Soviet delegation sort of alert Shevardnadze to the fact that Shultz was on his way toward him. When the two men met in that aisle, there was just this explosion of flashbulbs." When the conference began, Shultz delivered a detailed indictment of the Soviet human rights record, mentioning by name two dozen persons as victims of arbitrary arrest. Shevardnadze, who read an address notable for the blandness of both its tone and its delivery, asked the secretary later, "Did you have to give such a speech?" Shultz replied he was required to tell the truth, and the subject was dropped.

Throughout the receptions and informal gatherings in the rest of the conference, Shultz felt it was almost a conspiracy of the crowd to bring the U.S. and Soviet ministers together, often with their wives on hand as well, to encourage their interaction. And while their husbands were exchanging official positions, Nanuli Shevardnadze, who had been a magazine writer in Georgia before her recent move to Moscow, toured Helsinki with O'Bie Shultz, who had been an Army nurse in Hawaii when she met her husband in World War II.

The first business meeting of Shultz and Shevardnadze took place at the colonial-style U.S. ambassador's residence overlooking Helsinki harbor on July 31, a beautiful summer day. Shultz had obtained Shevardnadze's agreement in their brief encounter the day before to experiment with simultaneous translation, using translator's booths and earphones, to reduce the time consumed by cumbersome consecutive translations. This method proved to be so successful that it was employed in nearly all U.S.-Soviet ministerial meetings from then on.

In spite of his crash course in the issues at hand, Shevardnadze felt ill-prepared for his first world-class diplomatic encounter. The Foreign Ministry staff had prepared a thick briefing book and detailed talking points for Shevardnadze, but the minister insisted on making extensive notes in his own hand in preparation for presenting things to Shultz in his own way. At the last minute, he was overwhelmed by the gravity of the issues and his insubstantial grasp of them, and decided to use the ministry's prepared material. Before launching into his presentation, Shevardnadze told Shultz with the disarming openness that, even then, typified his style that he did not understand everything he would be reading. He felt Shultz was "very patient without interrupting me" as he read prepared positions from the papers. The three-hour meeting was the first in a series to prepare for the November summit. And it was the only time in thirty full-scale meetings with Shultz that Shevardnadze felt forced to stick to written talking points.

Shevardnadze's fellow foreign ministers had not yet seen a shift in the substance of Soviet foreign policy, but they quickly pronounced the newcomer's performance at Helsinki a welcome change in tone. Gromyko had often fended off personal inquiries by responding, "My personality does not interest me." In one famous incident Gromyko had been asked by a Western diplomat at the start of a round of talks if he had had a good breakfast and had replied, after an uncomfortable pause, "Perhaps." But his successor, with a three-piece suit and thinning white hair, was a smiling political animal. "We found Mr. Shevardnadze rather *sympathique*," concluded French Foreign Minister Roland Dumas. "It is manifest," said British Foreign Secretary Geoffrey Howe, "that Mr. Shevardnadze is not Mr. Gromyko." Shultz reported to Reagan that he was impressed with the new foreign minister. He was tough, but quite a different person from Gromyko.

• REINTERPRETING THE ABM TREATY

On July 25, shortly before Shultz and Shevardnadze met in Helsinki, Donald A. Hicks, a former senior vice president of Northrop Corporation, a major defense contractor, appeared before the Senate Armed Services Committee for the confirmation hearing on his appointment as under secretary of defense for research and development. That morning Senator Carl Levin, a Michigan Democrat, brought in a sheaf of questions for Hicks on how Reagan's Strategic Defense Initiative could be pursued without violating the legal restrictions of the 1972 Anti-Ballistic Missiles Treaty between the United States and the Soviet Union. Levin let it be known he wanted answers before voting to approve Hicks's nomination to the high-level Pentagon job.

This unspectacular exchange, which got little attention at the time, touched off a political and legal struggle within the Reagan administration and a diplomatic struggle between Washington and Moscow. Surprisingly, the argument, which has not been settled to this day, was about the interpretation of a treaty that both sides had signed and ratified thirteen years earlier. On the surface, the argument was over fine points of historical interpretation and legal precedent. Beneath the surface, the dispute was about the future of the SDI program, a subject of intense interest to Reagan, the Pentagon, conservatives within and outside the administration and (on the other side) most congressional Democrats and the arms control community. The battle over what could or could not be done to pursue SDI was also of deep concern to Moscow, which viewed the SDI program with alarm.

Ever since work had begun in earnest to implement Reagan's "dream" of a space-based shield to stop incoming ballistic missiles, many of its advocates had been uncomfortable with the provisions of the 1972 treaty. One of those provisions seemed to say starkly and clearly that *development* or *testing* of such a system, to say nothing of its eventual *deployment*, was illegal under the treaty and therefore banned under the supreme law of the land. The provision, article V, paragraph I, of the treaty, states:

> Each Party undertakes not to develop, test or deploy ABM systems or components which are sea-based, air-based, space-based or mobile land-based.

If SDI was to go forward very far, it seemed to its backers that that restriction on the space-based system would have to be neutralized or that U.S. adherence to the treaty as a whole would have to be abrogated. In early 1985 an internal Defense Department study sponsored by Deputy Under Secretary T. K. Jones, an ardent SDI backer, argued for a much looser interpretation of the treaty requirements than the one that had been commonly accepted. A similar argument was made in a Heritage Foundation report written by an anonymous government attorney.*

Senator Levin's questions about Star Wars activity and the ABM Treaty were sent to an interagency committee chaired by Assistant Secretary of Defense Richard Perle. When the committee met, nearly every person at the conference table had a different idea of just what was permitted or prohibited by the treaty. Many of the differences were technical in nature. Perle then arranged for a new Pentagon attorney, Philip Kunsberg, to study the negotiating history of the treaty, much of which was still secret, and provide him with an opinion. Kunsberg, thirty-five, had previously worked at the Central Intelligence Agency's

---

* The author, it was later disclosed, was Bretton G. Sciaroni, who later came to public attention for rendering the controversial opinion permitting the National Security Council staff to assist the Nicaraguan Contra rebels after Congress had passed a law prohibiting such aid. The Iran-Contra investigating committee was not impressed with this ruling, and even less so after learning that Sciaroni, a political appointee, had failed the bar exams four times in his native California and the District of Columbia before passing in Pennsylvania, where he did not live.

legal counsel's office, but he had little experience in arms control. Much of his legal activity had been as an assistant district attorney in New York, where he had prosecuted Mafia and pornography cases.

With less than a week of study of the secret record and no contact with members of the U.S. team that had negotiated the treaty, Kunsberg wrote a nineteen-page report concluding that the Soviet Union had never accepted restrictions on space-based ABM systems if they employed "new physical principles" such as laser beams, directed energy weapons and other exotic technology of arms control. This conclusion relied on ambiguous language in a statement attached to the treaty by both sides and was highly controversial within the small circle of government officials who learned of it. Career government attorneys at the Defense Department and the Arms Control and Disarmament Agency, who were intimately familiar with the ABM Treaty, disputed it.

In view of the disagreement within the government, Shultz asked his new State Department legal adviser, Abraham Sofaer, a former federal judge from New York, to study the question. After several all-night bouts of study, Sofaer reached a conclusion similar to—but not as broad as—that of Kunsberg. Sofaer had the benefit of several conversations with Paul Nitze, Shultz's senior adviser for arms control, who had been a member of the U.S. team that negotiated the ABM Treaty in the early 1970s. Nitze had previously backed the generally accepted "restrictive interpretation" of the treaty on several occasions, but after talking to Sofaer he reversed himself and argued that a permissive or "broad interpretation" was justified.

The issue came to a head on Friday, October 4, in a meeting of the interagency Senior Arms Control Policy Group chaired by Robert McFarlane, the White House national security adviser. Richard Perle and Fred Ikle, the under secretary of defense for policy, made the case for a very permissive interpretation of the treaty, including a right to deploy space-based ABM systems. Nitze argued for what became known as the "broad interpretation," which permitted development and testing, but not deployment, of Star Wars components under the treaty. Nobody argued for the long-existing "restrictive interpretation" of the treaty language, which would ban many Star Wars tests. McFarlane said he agreed with Nitze's view. In adjourning the meeting, he also said the group would return to the subject the following Tuesday.

Before that could happen, however, the national security adviser was the guest on *Meet the Press*, NBC Television's Sunday talk show.

When he walked into the studio, McFarlane did not intend to discuss the consensus-in-the-making within the administration. But when asked a skeptical question by Robert Kaiser of *The Washington Post* about how SDI could go forward without violating the ABM Treaty, McFarlane answered by asserting the new "broad interpretation" that had been put forward in the government committee two days earlier.

The reaction among journalists and experts who had been following the SDI-ABM issue but were not privy to the government discussions was that McFarlane had misspoken. However, it soon became clear that this was no slip of tongue but a whole new theory of what the ABM Treaty said. Weinberger, Perle and administration conservatives were euphoric. They considered the ABM Treaty an ill-considered and out-dated document in conflict with the high-priority Reagan objective of protecting the United States against ballistic missiles. Under the new interpretation, the treaty was not much of a problem until the day SDI was ready for full-scale deployment—probably many years in the future.

Nitze, despite his advocacy of the new interpretation, quickly realized that such a startling reversal of the requirements of an important treaty would have explosive impact in Congress, where the opposite interpretation had previously been advanced by the executive branch, including the Reagan administration. Nitze was also worried about the reaction of the European allies, for whom SDI was already a controversial subject. Nitze expressed his concern to Shultz, who was angry that McFarlane had announced an important government policy without a complete discussion within the administration and without a presidential decision. "You didn't get elected to anything. When it comes to matters of this kind, that's for the President to decide, not for you or me or anybody else," Shultz told McFarlane.

In a meeting with Reagan on Friday, Shultz and McFarlane recommended that the new interpretation of the ABM Treaty be accepted as "fully justified" from a legal standpoint, but that Shultz be authorized to state that the SDI program would continue to be conducted in accordance with the traditional "restrictive interpretation." Reagan accepted the idea, which was announced by Shultz in a speech in San Francisco on Monday. Critics pointed out that this split-level decision left Reagan the option to change his position again whenever he chose (though he never did so as President). Ultimately Congress voted to deny funds for any SDI tests that exceeded the "restrictive interpretation" of the treaty, and after struggles with the lawmakers Reagan reluctantly went along.

The treaty reinterpretation saga made a more immediate impact in Washington than in Moscow. This was because the Soviets had already concluded that Reagan was driving all-out to pursue his SDI program, in Soviet terms to place weapons in space, and that he was cynically sweeping away all obstacles in his path. Making the U.S.-Soviet treaty a dead letter by denying its original meaning was a trick, a "Catch 22," in the eyes of Deputy Foreign Minister Viktor Karpov. Like Nitze and Gerard Smith, Karpov was among those who had negotiated the ABM Treaty in 1972, and he had worked on some of the very phrases that were being reinterpreted by the U.S. administration thirteen years later. Karpov was certain the new interpretation was simply intended to assert some legal basis for otherwise-illegal testing of SDI components. "That's the only meaning of that interpretation and we understood that," he recalled later.

• OFFENSE AND DEFENSE

The principal U.S. interest in negotiating with the Soviet Union about nuclear arms was to reduce the huge arsenal of globe-girdling offensive weapons that was a physical threat to the United States unparalleled in its history. The country was blessed with vast oceans on either side and essentially friendly neighbors north and south. Until the combination of nuclear weapons and intercontinental missiles came along, the threat to American territory from foreign enemies was minimal.

The vast pileup of nuclear offensive arms was unsettling to the Soviet Union as well. American nuclear forces were structured to threaten the existence of the Soviet leadership and their state, as Moscow well knew. Moreover, Gorbachev and his new team were more conscious than their predecessors of the economic troubles of the country, induced in large part by massive military spending.

Both Reagan and Gorbachev, as their public statements and private letters testified, were strongly committed to reducing the threat posed to their nations and to humankind by long-range offensive nuclear arms. At the same time, both men presided over military programs that produced ever more powerful, sophisticated and accurate nuclear weaponry. Since March 1983, the emergence of Reagan's SDI program had become a major new factor. Suddenly the defensive side of the equation—which had been relatively stable since the signing of the 1972 Anti-Ballistic

Missiles Treaty—was subject to unpredictable change. If the Star Wars program could actually succeed in creating an effective shield against a substantial number of Soviet intercontinental weapons, the balance of power between the two nations would be dramatically changed.

Beginning with the new Geneva negotiations authorized by Shultz and Gromyko in January 1985, both the offensive and defensive sides of the nuclear arms equation were in play. The Soviet Union used offensive arms as a "bargaining chip," offering unprecedented cutbacks in its long-range nuclear arsenals *if* the United States would eliminate the potential defensive threat from the SDI program. The United States advocated massive cuts in U.S. and Soviet long-range offensive arms as well, but there was sharp and enduring disagreement within the administration about its defensive "bargaining chip"—that is, whether to offer some restraints on the SDI program to obtain the offensive arms cuts the Soviets were dangling.

On August 28, shortly after returning from his summer vacation, Gorbachev invited top editors of *Time* to his office for his first interview with Western journalists since taking office. "The situation in the world today is highly complex, very tense. I would even go so far as to say it is explosive," Gorbachev declared in words that were blazoned in big type across his forehead on the cover of the magazine's next issue. The central problem, as he explained it, was that "the development of science and technology has reached a level where the broad-scale introduction of new achievements, particularly in the military field, can lead to an entirely new phase in the arms race." He was talking about SDI, he made plain. An agreement to prevent an arms race in space was possible and verifiable. He added:

> Without such an agreement it will not be possible to reach an agreement on the limitation and reduction of nuclear weapons either. The interrelationship between defensive and offensive arms is so obvious as to require no proof. Thus, if the present U.S. position on space weapons is its last word, the Geneva negotiations will lose all sense.

The idea of restraints of some sort on the SDI program in return for offensive arms cuts was under discussion within the administration in Washington. Nearly everyone was talking about such a deal, it seemed, except for the chief sponsor of SDI, who was single-minded in his determination to press ahead. On September 17, in his first formal news conference since his cancer surgery two months earlier, Reagan seemed to rule out any bargain involving SDI.

> Q. As you head toward the summit, one of the big questions is whether you would be willing to explore the possibility of a tradeoff on the space weapons for big cuts in the Soviet arsenal.
>
> Reagan: . . . Rather than that kind of negotiation, I think at this summit meeting what we should take up is the matter of turning toward defensive weapons as an alternative to this just plain naked nuclear threat of each side saying we can blow up the other. I would hope that if such a weapon proves practical, that we can realistically eliminate these horrible offensive weapons, nuclear weapons, entirely.

Asked if as a good negotiator he might be keeping his cards hidden regarding a deal on SDI, Reagan responded:

> I don't mind saying here, and normally I don't talk about, as you said, what's going to be your strategy in negotiations, but in this, this is too important to the world to have us be willing to trade that off for a different number of nuclear missiles when there are already more than enough to blow both countries out of the world.

The tradeoff Reagan rejected became more tangible ten days later when Shevardnadze, on his first trip to Washington, presented the President with a lengthy letter from Gorbachev outlining a new Soviet negotiating offer. For the first time, the Soviets offered to cut the long-range nuclear arsenals of the two countries by 50 percent. This figure had first been mentioned in a Washington speech by George Kennan in 1981, at a time when acceptance of such a cut by either side seemed fantastic. When proposed by Moscow four years later, it was a huge and headline-grabbing cut, which quickly became the official target for both sides, even though the fine print of what was to be covered meant that the actual reductions were much smaller. One problem with the September 27 proposal from the U.S. standpoint was the definition of strategic arms, which was disadvantageous to Washington. An even more serious problem was the central condition in Gorbachev's offer: it would be good only if Reagan agreed to "a complete ban on space attack weapons," which was how the Soviet Union described SDI.

• MEETING IN MOSCOW

Moscow was decked out with red bunting and hammer-and-sickle flags for the November 7 anniversary of the 1917 revolution when Shultz and his party arrived on Monday morning, November 4, for an important set of meetings with Gorbachev and Shevardnadze two weeks before the Geneva summit.

It had begun snowing heavily when Shultz's plane was on the tarmac at Helsinki, where the U.S. party had spent the night to break the trip from Washington. The plane took off in the snowstorm, heading east into Russia above the clouds. There was no snow on the ground in Moscow as Shevardnadze greeted Shultz warmly at the airport. The sun was out, and it was a beautiful clear, crisp November day. Shultz and Shevardnadze met for six hours that day, including lunch, at the Foreign Ministry's elaborate turn-of-the-century guest house on Alexei Tolstoy Street, going over in detail the state of play on each major subject under discussion.

The following morning at ten, Shultz met Gorbachev in the General Secretary's working office at Central Committee headquarters. Gorbachev had asked that his first negotiating session with a U.S. secretary of state be kept very small. The participants were, for the Soviet Union, Gorbachev, Shevardnadze and Ambassador Dobrynin, plus an interpreter, and for the United States, Shultz, McFarlane and Ambassador Hartman plus an interpreter. They posed for pictures briefly, after which the press was shooed out. Then the meeting began.

A feisty Mikhail Gorbachev, who had a sheaf of notes before him that he rarely consulted, began by remarking in challenging fashion that there was so much "disinformation" about the Soviet Union in the United States that it seemed impossible to build a healthy relationship.

Shultz, trying to set a positive tone, quoted Reagan as saying, as the President often did, that "the United States and the Soviet Union should be talking to each other rather than talking about each other."

Gorbachev was not reassured. He wanted Shultz to understand he knew all about people in the United States. He knew, for example, that

Shultz and Weinberger had worked together in the same company before coming to Reagan's cabinet. He did not explain what he thought the significance of this to be.

"Look, the person to focus on is President Reagan," responded Shultz. "He's the boss. Reagan has popularity. He speaks with authority. If he makes an agreement, he's able to get support for the agreement. This is what is important in any negotiation, to know that somebody can deliver."

Gorbachev quickly picked up Shultz's reference to the SALT II strategic arms treaty of 1979, which was signed by Carter and Brezhnev but never ratified by the U.S. Senate. Without mentioning names, Gorbachev criticized those who signed treaties but never brought them to fruition.

Shultz wanted Gorbachev to understand that SALT II had been withdrawn from Senate confirmation because of the Soviet invasion of Afghanistan—not because of a basic U.S. policy reversal.

Before the translation could be completed, an agitated Gorbachev interrupted: "Leave arguments like that for the press. We are not uninstructed on these issues." SALT II was "dead and buried" even before the invasion of Afghanistan, said Gorbachev, who had been a candidate member of the Politburo at the time.*

The United States got out of the SALT II treaty because it did not want to be constrained by it, Gorbachev charged. "You wanted to carry out your own programs" of increased military expenditures and curtailed social programs, he said. "Don't come in and use arguments with me about SALT II. It shows you don't respect us."

As for linking arms control to regional issues such as Afghanistan, Gorbachev continued with a rush of words, "You ought to put that one in mothballs. It's old hat. I don't want to play games, but if the American administration doesn't want to make a change then we'll go on forever [as before]. We Soviets will lose interest if you keep arguing the way you just have. In fact, we can just go read each other's newspapers— we don't have to have a meeting." Gorbachev did not seem to recognize that Shultz, privately and publicly, was a leading opponent of the "linkage" between arms control and regional issues.

Hardly pausing for the consecutive translation, Gorbachev moved

* Shultz, who was at Bechtel Corporation in 1979 and had never really examined the issue before, later came to believe that Gorbachev was right—that Afghanistan was an excuse to withdraw a treaty already in deep trouble.

on to criticize U.S. attitudes toward the Soviet Union. In a complaint that seemed to reveal Moscow's insecurity, he said, "We need courage and struggle and honesty [to make things better]. Somehow you set it up so I can't win. We sincerely want to change for the better, but you say this just shows that we are weak. And then when we don't show an interest in improving relations, you say we are intransigent."

Venturing into U.S. domestic politics, Gorbachev went on to say, "The Republicans, if they want to stay in power, it might be worthwhile to see if they can do anything in U.S.-Soviet relations." Another recommendation: "The administration should not be so tied to the military-industrial complex, which just chews up money and programs by the billions."

As for the arms negotiations, Gorbachev struck a theme he would repeat often. "Does the United States think that its present policies of exercising pressure and strength, that these policies have brought the Soviet Union back to the negotiating table? If that is the kind of thinking that motivates those around the President, then no success is possible." On the other hand, he said, "I hope the United States will consider it to be in its national interest to improve relations with the Soviet Union."

He had been speaking with great candor, Gorbachev reminded the Americans. He was offering some advice, and it was free. Dobrynin had told him that Henry Kissinger was earning $150,000 per year for advice. Gorbachev noted wryly that it seemed as though Kissinger was making more for advice on the outside than he had been making as U.S. secretary of state.

The reference to Kissinger's pay gave Shultz the chance to interrupt this startling monologue to say he, too, had been earning more money on the outside than as secretary of state. Keeping the floor, Shultz presented two letters from Reagan, one about a new U.S. arms control position just tabled at Geneva, and the other about future channels for confidential dialogue between the two nations. (No special channel was ever worked out, despite repeated U.S. efforts.)

There were many things in Gorbachev's presentation he could not agree with, said Shultz, but rather than dwell on these he preferred to discuss the meeting at Geneva and the U.S. approach to the state of relations. Shultz continued, "I have not the slightest doubt the President has a great desire to see a more constructive relationship between the two countries which would enable us to deal with one another in a realistic and pragmatic way. Realistic in that each side should know that we operate under two very different systems. You think yours is better; we think ours is better. But there is a responsibility on these two great powers which is tremendous and which leads to the conclusion that both must work for a more constructive relationship. We know the present state of our relationship is unsatisfactory. The reason for the coming meeting is to do better. That is the way the President wishes to approach in a very serious manner the upcoming meeting in Geneva."

Gorbachev, warming to this approach but impatient, interrupted the translation to say, "If that is so, maybe we can succeed."

Shultz went on to say that negative reasons for the meeting, such as the avoidance of war, especially nuclear war, were important. But there were positive reasons as well. "What sort of a world do we want to build for the future? This sort of reason weighs very heavily with the President. The world is changing very rapidly. You want to see progress and so do we. . . . The United States and Soviet Union will be interacting all over the world as it changes, sometimes in volatile situations which may not even be created by the two great powers but could affect them. We need to see how these could be managed."

At this point the secretary broached a subject of special interest to himself and, he believed, the Soviet leaders, although it was a topic completely different from what they were accustomed to hearing from American officials. It was a brief professorial and analytical discourse on global trends. "We may in fact be reaching the end of the industrial age and moving into what we might think of as the information age, where we will have to think about new ways of working, how people behave, possibly relocating populations. . . . Society is beginning to organize itself in profound ways. All of this creates opportunities to work together," Shultz said. Although U.S. intelligence and most of the State Department's own Sovietologists were dubious, he had believed from an early point that Gorbachev was an agent of change in the Soviet Union and should be encouraged to understand that rapid change was underway throughout the developed world. Shultz would return to this topic in greater detail, and with greater effect, in his later meetings with Gorbachev.

Shultz then moved to the immediate business at hand, arms control issues at the looming Geneva summit. He began to explain the U.S. view that the strategic situation had changed since the signing of SALT I and the ABM Treaty in 1972, when the premise had been that if strategic defenses were constrained, offensive forces would be significantly reduced. Clearly this had not happened. As a result there were more missiles and warheads than ever, generating the interest of both nations in radical reductions of atomic arms. At the same time, the assumption of deep constraints on defense was not as strong as it had been in 1972. Moreover, many new developments in science and technology, such as the development of ballistic missiles with extraordinary accuracies, MIRVs (independently targetable multiple-warhead missiles) and mobile missiles had created new situations.

"Are you saying that the ABM Treaty is obsolete because of the quality of weapons? Just what are you suggesting?" Gorbachev demanded.

Shultz said, no, the ABM Treaty was "of tremendous importance," and he noted that Reagan had ordered that all U.S. work remain within the "narrow definition" of the treaty. But the issue now was how to manage a transition to increased dependence on defense, he said.

Before that could be fully translated, Gorbachev interrupted to object vociferously to the new interpretation of the ABM Treaty and display his familiarity with affairs in Washington. Turning to McFarlane, who had presided over and announced the ABM Treaty reinterpretation, Gorbachev, the first law school graduate at the head of the Soviet Communist Party, exclaimed, "I'm amazed that you would base your judgment on the advice of a lawyer who previously only had experience prosecuting drug and porno cases!"*

Gorbachev was adamant on the subject of SDI, calling it an attempt to justify an ABM system, which would otherwise be banned by treaty, through "unworthy means." He went on, "We're smart people and we know what's going on and we know why you're doing this and you're inspired by illusions. You think you're ahead of us in information, you think you're ahead of us in technology and that you can use these things to gain superiority over the Soviet Union. But this is an illusion. Other people have recognized this." The Soviet leader declared solemnly that, "You can rest assured that we will not help the United States get out of its ABM Treaty obligations. We will not assist you with the politics of it or in technical ways so that you can take the arms race into space."

* Gorbachev almost certainly was referring to my page-one story in *The Washington Post* two weeks earlier reconstructing the ABM Treaty reinterpretation and making the point in the second paragraph that the background of lead Pentagon attorney Philip Kunsberg "includes battles against pornographers and the Mafia but no arms control experience."

"We'll figure out ourselves what our policy is on defense," Shultz responded. "In fact, yours is the same," he charged, alluding to U.S. allegations of a massive Soviet space defense research program. "We don't see anything wrong with defending ourselves."

With the exchanges hot and heavy across the table, Gorbachev listed crippling "illusions" on the part of the United States: that the Soviet Union was weaker economically and therefore would be weakened more by an arms race; that the United States was stronger technologically and thus could gain superiority in weapons through SDI; that the Soviet Union was more interested in the Geneva negotiations than the United States; that the Soviet Union only thought of damaging U.S. interests in regional conflicts around the world; that it would be wrong to trade with the Soviet Union because this would just raise its capability. "These are all illusions" in which the United States was failing to draw lessons from history. "The Soviet Union knows how to meet its challenges," Gorbachev declared.

The big question was whether the United States was interested in improving relations. It had a big budget, largely due to military expenditures. It was financed 80 percent by borrowing money, producing high interest rates, Gorbachev declared. He was informed that 18 million Americans were employed in the military-industrial complex. "Perhaps the Soviet Union could place orders in the United States and relieve the U.S. economy of having to be dependent on arms. Maybe the U.S. administration has lost its way in trying to find a policy toward the Soviet Union. Even the signals that we send to you are distorted by you."

Shultz by now was pointedly trying to interrupt. As an economist he could say that U.S. society was nowhere near as dependent on military orders as Gorbachev seemed to think. Yes, there were some programs important to some industries, but "even in its glory days" military procurement was no more than about 3 percent of GNP. Shultz turned to McFarlane, a career military man, who told Gorbachev it was "just not so" that decision making was heavily influenced by the military in the United States. "If you look at the Cabinet and prior Cabinets, you find that they are not militarily dominated."

Gorbachev did not seem to be buying it. "Dobrynin tells me that people in the United States are still listening to those who think in terms of illusions" about the USSR, the General Secretary taunted. "Are you afraid you'd lose your jobs if you admitted this?"

"I've got news for you," Shultz fired back, in language similar to that of his attempted resignation in the Oval Office two years earlier. "I've got a tenured position in a university. So I don't worry about those things."

This remarkable conversation continued more deeply into the issues of arms control, with McFarlane, taking the lead on the American side of the table, declaring, "We've needed to have this occasion to talk to each other for more than five years." McFarlane spoke of the growth in ballistic missile accuracy with its potential for enhancing a first nuclear strike, and about the growth of the Soviet Union's attempts to expand its influence in distant areas. Neither trend was healthy, he said. Moreover, new Soviet programs, such as the production of mobile missiles, were creating new problems. "We've relied in the past on the strategy of damaging the other side, but you don't like being the target of missiles and neither do we." Alluding to SDI, McFarlane said, "We want to begin today to see how defensive systems might be introduced for greater stability and a safer relationship. But we need a concept so the dangers aren't increased."

Gorbachev sharply disputed McFarlane's view of SDI. "I hope this is not your last word," because, if so, "nothing will result from the negotiation" on arms reductions in Geneva, the General Secretary declared. Weighing his words carefully, Gorbachev summarized the Soviet position: "There will be no 50 percent reductions. You are operating from a different logic. If you want superiority through your SDI, we will not help you. We will let you bankrupt yourselves. But also we will not reduce our offensive missiles. We will engage in a buildup that will break your shield. We don't want war, but neither are we going to allow unilateral advantage. Therefore, we will increase nuclear arms. But we are patient, and we still have hope."

As for the forthcoming meeting with Reagan in Geneva, Gorbachev took the view that "using it as a get-acquainted meeting is too restrictive, and so too is just setting an agenda for the future." He realized that all the difficulties that had piled up could not be solved in one meeting, but it would be a disappointment to the Soviet and American people and the world if the leaders did no more than just meet. "So what we should be thinking about is the interests of the world and how they can be served by moves that would lead to a major political impetus to get a drastic improvement in our relations. We need policies that meet the preoccupation with world problems. The great question is war or peace. That's what preoccupies people everywhere. We should have as our intent the development of a dialogue to reduce confrontation, encourage détente and peaceful coexistence. That is what the world wants."

Then Gorbachev, in a precursor of statements and negotiations to come, said he would be willing to reduce nuclear forces to zero on condition that the two sides prevent the militarization of space. Shultz did not comment on this surprising statement.

As the meeting wound up, Gorbachev said he was also prepared to discuss with Reagan at Geneva regional, bilateral and other problems. At an earlier point he alluded to the possibility of cooperation even in the field of human rights.

Shultz thanked Gorbachev for his time. He conceded that "we certainly see things in a different light. We've never really discussed how to solve these problems. . . . We think the meeting in Geneva can be successful. And that we ought to keep negotiating in the Geneva arms talks."

After the exhausting four-hour meeting, the Americans tried to assess what they had seen and heard from this headstrong and newly minted international figure. There was a good deal of criticism of Dobrynin, who was nodding vigorously at times, egging Gorbachev on, when the Americans thought he should have known better. They wondered about the quality of the reports and advice Dobrynin had been supplying from Washington for twenty-three years.

To McFarlane, Gorbachev had been "curious, vigorous, active, articulate, argumentative, self-assured [and] occasionally impulsive." Though McFarlane was unhappy about Gorbachev's misinformation about the United States, he was impressed that he seemed to listen to the rebuttals in a way that suggested he might be open to changing his mind. This would be a first for a Soviet leader, McFarlane thought. Hartman, recalling Gorbachev's grasp of Soviet arms control positions, wondered what would happen in the Geneva conversations with a Ronald Reagan who was given to the broadest generalizations.

Shultz seemed glacially calm and pleased with himself in the aftermath of the meeting. If Gorbachev had thought he would win concessions through pressure tactics on the eve of the summit, it must be clear to him now that he was wrong. Shultz was happy that he had gone head to head with Gorbachev and stood his ground, that he had answered seriously and candidly without getting bogged down in dozens of contentious statements. Shultz sensed that Gorbachev's disjointed remarks had a cathartic quality, as if these things had been on his mind and it was important to get them out. The secretary felt sure the Geneva summit would not be a repeat of what he had just heard. Such a replay would bring about a failed summit, and the Soviets didn't want that any more than the White House did. Shultz was reinforced in this view by a conversation with Shevardnadze to tie up loose ends, which occurred after the meeting with Gorbachev. The Soviet foreign minister said both sides would have to work hard in the remaining two weeks "to make certain that the [summit] meeting would be a success."

Looking back years later, Shevardnadze felt this initial Gorbachev-Shultz business meeting had been very important. True, it was contentious, but the Soviet foreign minister also thought it helped to identify the positions of the two sides in a very honest way, to make it possible to engage later. Even the dramatic moments helped. "This sense of drama in Moscow in some way facilitated eventual success at Geneva," Shevardnadze said later. "Because in the wake of the Moscow meeting we concluded and the Americans concluded that we have at all costs to try to find a compromise."

Before leaving Moscow on Tuesday night, Shultz held a news conference at Spaso House, the classic prerevolutionary mansion that has been the residence of the U.S. ambassador since diplomatic relations were established in 1933. "There was nothing surprising" in his discussions, Shultz reported to the press. "We anticipated a frank and thorough review of the issues; that's what we had." Shultz said bluntly that "there are deep differences remaining" after the talks, and that "there was no narrowing" of the gaps on the key arms control issues. Asked by Bernard Gwertzman of *The New York Times* if it seemed at all realistic to expect even a face-saving agreement in principle on arms issues at the summit, Shultz responded, "I wouldn't bet *The New York Times* on it."

Like most others in the press corps, I found Shultz's report almost startling for the absence of any reportable progress. The correspondents accompanying had little confidence that Reagan and Gorbachev could accomplish anything of importance at the summit that had not been worked out in advance. We viewed Shultz's eleventh-hour trip to the Soviet capital as the final chance to engineer a deal before the summit. No deal had been made and from the tone of Shultz's remarks and a few hints from his aides, we surmised that the meeting with Gorbachev had been more confrontational than conciliatory. With Gorbachev continuing to insist that restraining SDI was essential for a successful summit, it seemed to me that the likelihood of a sharp clash between the two leaders at Geneva was now very high.*

As I wrote my story on a laptop computer in the Spaso House dining room, which had been converted to a temporary filing room for the secretary's traveling press, I thought what a disaster the Geneva summit was likely to be and guessed that Shultz, who had been so unyielding and, it seemed to me, so bleak in the press conference, must be privately distraught. But while I was composing a deeply pessimistic news story to convey my sense of impending doom, Shultz appeared a few feet away at the door of the dining room with a drink in his hand, smiling and appearing unusually relaxed. He had time to kill because he had agreed to delay his departure an hour so that the reporters could file or broadcast their stories. I looked down at my story about the failure of the presummit meeting in Moscow, then I looked up at the relaxed and happy Shultz. It reminded me of a comic strip feature I had known in my youth, What is wrong with this picture? I did not understand why Shultz was smiling, and under the protocol between officials and reporters I could not get up from my seat to go over and ask him; that would have started an avalanche by other reporters. Following my journalistic instincts I toned down the pessimism in my story for reasons I did not understand.

On the airplane after leaving Moscow, Shultz walked to the back of the plane where the press corps was seated to chat off the record. He had taken off his suit jacket and tie and was wearing his favorite blue sweater with a Department of State seal. He seemed supremely confident that, despite everything he had heard from Gorbachev in his office, the Geneva meeting would not be a failure. He did not disclose his conviction that Gorbachev would blink.

• MOMENTS OF TRUTH AT THE GENEVA SUMMIT

President Reagan, his wife, Nancy, Shultz and the other senior members of the presidential entourage landed at Geneva in Air Force One at 10:25 P.M. on Saturday, November 16, to prepare to meet Mikhail Gorbachev

---

* Reagan seems to have drawn the same conclusion. He wrote in his diary after a telephone report from Shultz on the meeting in Moscow, "Gorbachev is adamant we must cave in on SDI. Well, this will be a case of an irresistible force meeting an immovable object."

the following Tuesday. Reagan wore a heavy coat and scarf but looked cold and tired as he greeted the Swiss president and delivered a short statement in the subfreezing chill of the heavily guarded tarmac. His rich actor's voice sounded tremulous as he set the stage for the meetings to come. There were "deep differences" between the United States and the Soviet Union, he declared. But he hoped fervently for a "fresh start" in Geneva.

Those two concepts, deep differences and a fresh start, sum up in a few words the essence of the Geneva summit. In intensely personal fashion that few had anticipated, the two leaders grappled with intractable differences in policy, especially over Reagan's antimissile defense plan. Although those differences were not resolved, Reagan and Gorbachev found common ground on a personal level and, most importantly in the long run, started a process of interaction that had lasting impact on themselves, their nations and the global scene. Writing about the meeting with Reagan at Geneva two years later in his book *Perestroika*, Gorbachev called the summit "necessary and useful." He added, "In the most difficult periods of history, moments of truth are needed like air."

Geneva 1985 was the fourteenth summit meeting involving U.S. and Soviet leaders since Franklin D. Roosevelt, Joseph Stalin and Winston Churchill had met in Tehran in November 1943 to plan wartime strategy. Some of the summit meetings had been of great historical importance, including the Big Three meeting in Yalta (1945), the Kennedy-Khrushchev meeting in Vienna (1961) and the first Nixon-Brezhnev meeting in Moscow (1972). Public fascination with the meetings of world leaders and their possibilities for diminishing or increasing international tension had grown steadily, along with the media coverage. As Reagan prepared to leave Washington on Saturday, two hundred members of the White House press corps, forty White House press aides, fifteen Secret Service agents assigned to press control duties and about ten tons of television equipment took off ahead of him in a chartered Pan American 747 jumbo jet. The giant press plane towered over the diminutive Air Force One on the tarmac at Andrews Air Force Base. A total of 3,614 journalists, a large number of them television technicians, registered at summit headquarters in Geneva. It seemed odd that the press corps was so enormous for a meeting so small that, for more than half the time, only two men and two interpreters were involved. During most of the summit, the press knew little or nothing of what was actually going on because no one was telling. The two sides had agreed on the first day to impose a news blackout until the announcement of the final results.

Reagan, at seventy-four, was nearing the end of his career in politics. Since early in his presidency, he had been hoping to meet a reigning Soviet leader, full of confidence that through force of personality he could persuade the rival chieftain to change his nation's course. For two years, Reagan had been frustrated by the failing health of Moscow's leaders, who "kept dying on me," in the President's phrase. Now a younger man had come to power, one who was both more vigorous and more open-minded than his predecessors, and Reagan was ready. Robert McFarlane, the White House national security adviser, believed the President saw himself as a heroic figure on the order of one of his more dramatic motion picture roles, destined to change history by rescuing mankind from the deadly threat of nuclear weapons and ballistic missiles. Shultz looked at his boss's ambitions in less theatrical terms, but the secretary of state noted that Reagan delighted in the role of negotiator and that he was good at this task, despite his legendary inattention to detail. Reagan had been reelected the previous November by a huge margin, and as the summit approached his popularity soared. The moment was at hand for the veteran anticommunist to try his hand at making peace, on his own terms, with the world's ranking communist leader.

Gorbachev, at fifty-four, was in the early months of his leadership of the USSR and feeling his way toward historic changes in the life of his nation. Having improved his political position at home, Gorbachev on the eve of the Geneva summit began to explore major innovations in foreign affairs. On his first trip to the West as General Secretary, to Paris October 2–5, Gorbachev spoke for the first time of "reasonable sufficiency" in armaments as a Soviet goal. This was a fundamental downgrading from the Brezhnev goal of "equal security," which had meant that the Soviet Union should be as strong as all its potential opponents taken together. Gorbachev also began to define the Soviet aspiration of "peaceful coexistence" in a new way, not as a temporary respite in the ideological struggle between East and West but as a tenet of a global society that was increasingly interconnected and interdependent, and thus had little room for class struggle. The new leader of the Soviet Union was hinting of changes in some of the most basic Soviet foreign policy concepts and policies of the past. But these early expressions of Gorbachev's "new thinking" did not make much impact in 1985.

They were not spelled out in detail, and the world was not ready to believe that Gorbachev was serious.

The Soviet leader had been exchanging letters with Reagan since March and paying careful attention to Embassy and press reports from Washington describing the President's policies and character. Although self-confidence is one of his strongest traits, Gorbachev was nervous going into his first encounter with Reagan, according to a member of his Geneva team. The General Secretary had been informed by diplomatic protocol that he and Reagan would have only fifteen minutes together before joining their teams for the rest of the summit. Gorbachev saw this brief period as his main opportunity to persuade the President that he really was different and determined to make a change from the dealings of the former general secretaries. After arriving in Geneva on Monday morning, Gorbachev spent some time rehearsing what he would say to Reagan in those crucial fifteen minutes. He told his aides he had decided from the start to recognize that the President was an older man and give him that consideration. He had also stocked up on items of special interest to Reagan, including some of Moscow's latest anti-establishment jokes and a Soviet scientific prediction of a severe earthquake in California of at least 7.0 on the Richter scale within three years.*

Reagan, too, was intensely curious about his opposite number and determined to engage him face to face for far more than the announced fifteen minutes. The President had a full report from Shultz about the tumultuous conversation in Moscow two weeks earlier. For many weeks before that, the President had been receiving special briefings and policy papers in preparation for Geneva, so many that he became bored with the long buildup. The National Security Council and State Department had drawn up extensive "talking points" for Reagan to use with Gorbachev on each subject and occasion. As with his meeting with Gromyko in the White House, the President tossed out most of the officially supplied remarks and wrote his own more personal ones.

One briefer who did not bore Reagan was Suzanne Massie, the voluble author of *Land of the Firebird: The Beauty of Old Russia*, who had met the President in January 1984 and who introduced him to Russian history and the positive virtues of the Russian people in a total

---

* An earthquake did occur in San Francisco, 7.1 on the Richter scale, in October 1989, three years and eleven months after Geneva.

of eighteen meetings throughout the Reagan presidency. Massie counseled Reagan before Geneva, "You're older, wiser and with more experience than Gorbachev. Nobody in your cabinet is trying to knife you. So you are stronger." For his part, Reagan was reading *Firebird* with great attention, as his advisers learned at a preparatory session with the President in Geneva the day before the summit. While Paul Nitze was reviewing nuclear negotiations issues one last time, Reagan's eyes glazed over and there was a long silence. Finally, the President announced, "I'm in the year 1830," an incongruous remark that stunned Shultz, White House Chief of Staff Donald Regan and the others. Reagan went on to ask, "What happened to all these small shopkeepers in St. Petersburg in the year 1830 and to all that entrepreneurial talent in Russia? How can it have just disappeared?" Deputy Assistant Secretary of State Mark Palmer, who realized that Reagan had been reading about Old Russia, responded that small business instincts hadn't disappeared, but were active just below the surface of the official economy.

In its extensive preparations, the State Department had even drawn up "talking points" for Nancy Reagan to use in her contacts with Raisa Gorbachev. But it seemed as though the First Lady didn't need the suggestions. "From the moment we met, she talked and talked and *talked*—so much that I could barely get a word in, edgewise or otherwise," according to Mrs. Reagan. As this suggests, the former actress from Hollywood and the doctor of philosophical science from Moscow State University did not enjoy each other's company.

The President was the official host for the first day of the talks, Tuesday, November 19, at Château Fleur d'Eau, a nineteenth-century villa on the western shore of Lake Geneva. Awaiting Gorbachev's arrival in the foyer of the villa, the President made his first spot decision of the meeting—to take off the heavy coat and scarf he was wearing and greet Gorbachev in the wintry weather outside without them. Gorbachev, who arrived bundled up and whose thinning hair was turning gray, appeared older than the U.S. President, twenty years his senior, in the initial photographs. The contrast was particularly fascinating to viewers in the Soviet Union, who had heard of Reagan as an elderly Cold Warrior but had not seen much of him on their home screens before Geneva. As they shook hands for the first time, Reagan decided there was something likeable about Gorbachev—a warmth in his face and his style, not the coldness he had come to expect from Soviet leaders.

With a half-dozen advisers on each side waiting for them in a conference room, Reagan took Gorbachev and their two interpreters to a smaller, more comfortable room with a crackling fire in the fireplace. "You and I were born in small towns about which nobody's ever heard and no one ever expected anything of either of us," the President began. "There are all these people sitting in the next room. They have given us 15 minutes to meet in this one-on-one and we can do that and we can go out there and spend the next three days doing what they have written for us to do. They've programmed us—they've written your talking points, they've written my talking points. We can do that, or we can stay here as long as we want and get to know each other and we can create history and do some things that the world will remember in a positive way." Reagan also told Gorbachev in this or another early meeting, "Here we are, two men in a room together, and probably the only two in the world who could start World War III, or perhaps make peace and avoid a war."

In a remark that may have startled Gorbachev, the President also pointed out that their task in working together would be much easier "if there was a threat to this world from some other species, from another planet, outside in the universe." In that case, Reagan continued, "We'd forget all the little local differences that we have between our countries, and we would find out once and for all that we really are all human beings here on this Earth together."* The initial private meeting of the two leaders lasted just over an hour rather than the planned fifteen minutes.

The two leaders recessed for lunch with their respective staffs, and then got down to work intensively on arms control Tuesday afternoon.† Just before ending the morning session, Reagan had made his case for the SDI shield to protect humanity from nuclear missiles. Gorbachev responded with a declaration very similar to the one he had presented

---

* The invasion from outer space stuck in Gorbachev's mind. He referred to Reagan's comment in belittling fashion in his speech to the Twenty-seventh Communist Party Congress on February 26, 1986, and again at the Forum for a Nuclear-Free World in Moscow on February 16, 1987. "Isn't a nuclear disaster a more tangible danger than the landing of unknown extraterrestrials?" he asked at the Party Congress. "Isn't the ecological threat big enough? Don't all countries have a common stake in finding a sensible and fair solution to the problems of the developing states and peoples? Lastly, isn't all the experience accumulated by mankind enough to draw perfectly justified practical conclusions today, rather than wait until some other crisis breaks out? What does the U.S.A. hope to win in the long term by putting forward doctrines which can no longer fit U.S. security into the modest dimensions of our planet?"
† During the luncheon break in Geneva, McFarlane briefed Reagan, Shultz and Regan on the first clandestine shipment of U.S. missiles to Iran, which was later to become a central issue in the investigations of the arms sales scandal.

to Shultz in the Kremlin: The Soviet Union would not cooperate in a
U.S. plan to gain military superiority. If the United States persisted with
SDI, there would be no reduction in offensive weapons and the Soviet
Union would respond to the U.S. program in its own way.

During an earlier trip to Geneva, a White House advance man had
inspected the summerhouse near the swimming pool at Château Fleur
d'Eau and suggested that with its good camera angles and fireplace it
would be an ideal place for a Reagan-Gorbachev tête-à-tête. The President and First Lady had inspected the summerhouse on Sunday and
agreed. Tuesday afternoon, a fire was going in the fireplace and White
House stewards were in place with coffee and tea, along with several
photographers. About an hour into the afternoon session, Reagan turned
to Gorbachev at the conference table and suggested the two of them go
for a walk in the fresh air. Gorbachev quickly agreed. With interpreters
by their side, they strolled about one hundred yards down a winding
gravel walkway toward the lake and the waiting summerhouse. Here
Reagan pulled out a manila envelope containing a short document, in
Russian and English versions, proposing an arms control deal between
the two nations. He handed a copy to Gorbachev as they sat on overstuffed
chairs before the fire. The General Secretary took out his reading glasses
and began to study the Russian version.

The proposal, which had originated in Washington with arms adviser
Paul Nitze, was in the form of "guidelines" or joint instructions to be
issued to negotiators at the Geneva arms talks.* The first point was
acceptance of 50 percent reductions in strategic offensive arms. The
second point was an interim agreement on intermediate-range missiles
in Europe leading to eventual elimination of these weapons. The third
point, which was the most contentious, dealt with strategic defense.
Point four called for effective verification of any agreements that might
be reached.

Regarding the 50 percent cut in offensive arms, said Gorbachev,
"That's acceptable." He said he was prepared to discuss details of what
the 50 percent would encompass.

On the second point, he had questions about the INF (Intermediate-
range Nuclear Forces) accord, especially about the status of British and
French missiles and about air-launched weapons.

The third point, though, was the sticker. "The sides should provide

---

* Eleven months later, Gorbachev would surprise Reagan with his own set of proposals,
in a similar form, at the summit in Reykjavik.

assurances that their strategic defense programs shall be conducted as permitted by, and in full compliance with, the ABM Treaty." It went on to say: "The sides should agree to begin exploring immediately means by which a cooperative transition to greater reliance on defensive systems, should such systems prove feasible, could be accomplished." The first sentence evaded the question of what "full compliance" with the treaty would mean, under the various interpretations of the document. The second sentence said, rather explicitly, that the Soviets should accept and cooperate with SDI.

Gorbachev reminded Reagan that it had been agreed in the Shultz-Gromyko meeting in January that there must be an "interrelationship" between the cuts on offensive arms and halting weapons in space. Where was this relationship in the paper that Reagan had handed to him?

The President said he didn't see that the two subjects were linked. SDI could help get rid of nuclear weapons, and he was prepared to share the technologies and answers with the Soviet Union.

Gorbachev said he wouldn't comment on that for the moment, but he wanted to know which interpretation of the ABM Treaty Reagan had in mind in his idea of "full compliance."

Reagan acknowledged there was more than one version of what was required by the treaty. Suggesting that he was going for the "broad interpretation," the President said, "The laboratory theory of the ABM Treaty simply isn't enough." Then, in a declaration that he hoped would win Gorbachev over to his way of thinking, he told the Soviet leader that if the SDI research program was successful, the United States would share the results of its work with the Soviet Union so that they could enjoy security together.

"Why should I believe what you have to say about sharing the results of research?" Gorbachev demanded. He may have been aware that many U.S. officials were scornful of Reagan's insistence that the United States should or would share expensive and highly classified Star Wars technology with the USSR. The suggestion had come under sharp criticism since Reagan broached it publicly in a 1984 campaign debate with Walter Mondale. Six months before Geneva, U.S. officials acknowledged they might not even share all the technological secrets of SDI with America's major allies. But Reagan never backed away from the concept of sharing and told Gorbachev it should resolve his problems. In the summerhouse meeting, he proposed that U.S. and Soviet negotiators draw up "a specific agreement" on the sharing of space research, which he and Gorbachev could sign.

"Why don't we just announce that both sides have agreed to renounce research, development and testing of space weapons?" Gorbachev countered.

"I don't know why you keep talking about space weapons," Reagan responded. "We don't really know what the nature of these weapons would be, but we certainly don't have any intention of putting something into space that would threaten people on Earth. But what we're talking about now is a shield that would protect our country" if threatened by nuclear missiles from any quarter.

"We have read everything you've ever said and considered everything you've ever said with regard to SDI," Gorbachev said as they sat face to face before the fire. "I think I can understand you at the human level," he added. He could understand that strategic defense had captured the President's imagination. But as a political leader, Gorbachev said, he simply could not agree with Reagan on the concept. There was no way Reagan could sell it to him. Instead, he asked the President to join him in finding a way to formulate guidelines to their negotiators that would stop SDI.

"People want defense and they look at the sky and think what might happen if missiles suddenly appear and blow up everything in our country," Reagan said in rejoinder. "And people don't want that."

Gorbachev responded, "The missiles are not yet flying, and whether they would fly depends on how we conduct our respective policies. But if SDI is implemented, only God himself would know where it would lead." The Soviet Union wanted to stop it before it started, he declared in closing the discussion.

After sixty-five minutes of deadlock in the summerhouse, the two men stood up, put on their overcoats and began walking back up the path to the château. As they did, they engaged in friendly and almost casual conversation, which produced one of the most important results of the Geneva summit. Despite almost unanimous advice from his advisers not to broach the matter first, Reagan raised the point that Gorbachev had never visited the United States and asked, "Why don't we have the next summit meeting next year in the United States?"

"I accept," said Gorbachev without hesitation. "But you've never seen the Soviet Union. . . . Let's have the next one after this one in the following year in the Soviet Union."

Reagan accepted, and a few minutes later, after Gorbachev and his party had departed, the President gleefully informed the U.S. team that the next two summit meetings were already agreed upon. The advisers could hardly believe it. Agreement on a follow-on summit was among the top-priority U.S. objectives in Geneva. Gorbachev's approval of two summits to come meant Geneva could be described as a success in public relations terms, no matter what else happened.

At 11:30 A.M. Wednesday at the Soviet Mission, the dispute over Star Wars reached its high point for the Geneva summit. Six top officials, led by Shultz and Shevardnadze, accompanied each leader at the long conference table. Simultaneous translation with interpreters and earphones was being used. Thus, Reagan and Gorbachev had eye contact and their body language was easy to read as each responded to the other's argument. The accompanying high officials seemed to fade into the background, becoming mere fascinated spectators, as the two world leaders spoke with a passion that is rare in summit dialogue, and that some of those watching said they would never forget.

After a private discussion on human rights, Reagan and Gorbachev joined their aides and began where they left off in the summerhouse the previous day, with general agreement on 50 percent cuts in offensive strategic arms but complete disagreement on strategic defense.

"I don't know what's at the bottom of the U.S. position" on SDI, complained the Soviet leader. Maybe it was fueled by the "illusion" that the United States was ahead in the technology and information transfer systems on which SDI was based, or maybe on the "illusion" that the United States could employ SDI to forge military superiority over the Soviet Union. "I just don't see any reason why you should be committed to SDI," said Gorbachev. It would mean $600 billion to $1 trillion in new expenditures in the United States for the military-industrial complex—"maybe that is the reason." Speaking with mounting urgency, Gorbachev said he was reluctant to inject tension into this discussion, but that "everything is coming to a halt if we can't find a way to prevent the arms race in space."

Reagan described Gorbachev's cost estimates as "fantasy," and went on to defend his plan. Ignoring his prepared notes, Reagan sought to set the Soviet leader straight. "SDI isn't to conduct war in space. There are nuclear missiles which, if used, would kill millions on both sides. Never before in history has the prospect of a war that would bring about the end of civilization been out there. Even if everybody reduces [offensive missiles] by 50 percent, it's still too many weapons. So SDI gets around that and the United States is building a defensive system. It's not an offensive system. I'm talking about a shield, not a spear."

"I hear your arguments, but I'm not convinced," Gorbachev shot back. "It's emotional . . . part of one man's dream." He was not suggesting that Reagan did not want peace, but the reality was that SDI would open a new arms race. "I don't think you see me as a bloodthirsty person who wants to drag his country into conflict," said Gorbachev, speaking earnestly and very forcefully. "I want to reduce the number of weapons, but SDI is threatening a new arms race."

"We are at the point where the two sides are going to have to get beyond suspicions," countered Reagan. The Soviet Union had missiles it could use against the United States. In this situation, mere words wouldn't reduce the threat from either side. "We're trying—the United States—to see if there is a way to end the world's nightmare about nuclear weapons—"

Frustrated, Gorbachev interrupted: "Why don't you believe me when I say the Soviet Union will never attack?"

Before Reagan could answer, Gorbachev pressed him again: "Please answer me, Mr. President. What is your answer?"

And again, as Reagan tried to respond. "I want an answer from you. Why won't you believe me?" demanded Gorbachev.

The electricity was in the air as Reagan finally was able to reply. "Look, no individual can say to the American people that they should rely on personal faith rather than sound defense."

Shifting his ground, Gorbachev declared: "Why should I accept your sincerity on your willingness to share SDI research when you don't even share your advanced technology with your allies? Let's be more realistic. We're prepared to compromise. We've said we'll agree to a separate INF agreement. We'll talk about deep cuts in START (the strategic offensive weapons). But SDI has got to come to an end."

There was a long silence.

"Mr. President, I don't agree with you, but I can see you really mean it," said Gorbachev.

Then, all passion spent, Gorbachev said, "Maybe this has all grown a little bit heated. I was just trying to convey to you the depth of our concern on SDI."

The discussion continued, but the Americans present sensed that a crucial point had been registered. Shultz felt it was "like a coin dropping" to see Gorbachev's reaction, the acceptance at some deep personal level of the inevitability of SDI research. Until this point, Shultz believed the General Secretary was seriously determined to stop the SDI program in its tracks. But now, confronted with the unyielding depth of Reagan's conviction, Gorbachev seemed to realize that, as Shultz saw it, "there was no way in any negotiation he was going to talk the President out of that research program."

McFarlane had a similar reaction, though with more sympathy for the Soviet leader's predicament. The White House national security adviser was himself frustrated by the President's combination of stubbornness on some issues and indecisiveness on others. McFarlane had already decided a month earlier, and had so informed Shultz, that he would resign after the Geneva summit because of his frustration with Reagan's style of management. As he watched Gorbachev across the table attempting to deal with a Reagan who on this subject was adamant and unyielding, McFarlane could imagine the Soviet leader saying to himself, " 'I'm talking to a man who is not hearing me intellectually. He's dismissing my kind of sensible criticisms of his program and he keeps coming back to me with this rather romantic image of a future that is disconnected from reality. But I, Gorbachev, have to deal with the fact that this guy is supported by allies and people and Congress. What the hell am I going to do with this guy?' "

• WRAPPING UP THE SUMMIT

At the end of the first full meeting of the leaders and their aides on Tuesday morning, Reagan, after prodding by Gorbachev, had agreed to authorize a working group of lower-level officials to begin drafting a joint statement to be issued at the end of the summit. The diplomats began meeting at 9:00 P.M. Tuesday but, with their bosses at loggerheads, they made little progress in finding acceptable language on the contentious arms control issues. By midday Wednesday, with the end of the summit coming into view, the two leaders themselves were beginning to discuss what they would say to the world. Near the close of the climactic meeting where they had clashed on SDI, Reagan told Gorbachev, "We'll have to tell people that the possibility of reducing nuclear weapons by 50 percent has been destroyed by the suspicion of ulterior motives." The Soviet leader made it clear he would put the blame elsewhere. "Strategic defense is your idea. It's the United States that's determined to develop and introduce weapons into space."

The joint statement would prove to be important because, with the leaders' imprimatur, it would serve as a charter and authorizing document for the bureaucracies of the two governments to use in expanding U.S.-Soviet relations across the board in a period of improving ties.

The statement had a long and bizarre history. The State Department had been considering ideas for the statement since the summer, and during most of the fall had been quietly discussing with the Soviet Embassy agreements and declarations that might be reached and announced in a variety of areas. In October, Shultz brought a draft summit communiqué to Reagan, explained each point orally and obtained the President's approval. Shultz gave a copy of the draft to Shevardnadze as the basis for discussion in New York on October 25, when the Soviet minister was at the United Nations for the special meeting commemorating the world body's fortieth anniversary.

Up to this point, the State Department and National Security Council staff had been careful not to bring the Defense Department into the drafting process out of bureaucratic rivalry and fear of trouble. Shultz had already complained to Reagan that it appeared the Defense Department was going to throw up roadblocks to progress at the summit.*

Weinberger, who had not been invited to attend the Geneva meeting, learned about the draft communiqué through Washington leaks *after* the Soviets had already been given a copy. Not surprisingly, he was furious. He began to nitpick the text, for example claiming that it was a violation of administration policy to say that "serious differences can only be overcome by sustained dialogue." In his view, they could only be overcome by the Soviet Union changing its aggressive ways. After hearing from his defense secretary in private, Reagan decided he did not favor a prenegotiated communiqué at all, because such a document would be the work of bureaucrats, not himself and Gorbachev.

On November 11, Veterans Day, the second in command at the Soviet Embassy, Oleg Sokolov, came to an empty State Department to work on the joint statement with State Department aides. But when Ambassador Dobrynin called on Shultz several days later to finalize the summit communiqué that his deputy had worked out, Shultz told him the U.S. side was not in a position to agree to anything in writing. The President felt that to have a prearranged communiqué would detract from

---

* On the eve of Geneva, Weinberger wrote a letter to Reagan urging him not to give in on the several arms issues, a letter that dominated early news accounts from Geneva when it was leaked to *The Washington Post* and *The New York Times.*

the meeting, and it would be better to work on the statement in Geneva, "even though this appears a little chancy," Shultz said. Dobrynin was taken aback.

At lower levels, the diplomats kept working, no matter what their bosses said. Not surprisingly, the discussion was particularly intense on arms control issues, the same subjects that were causing heated arguments between the leaders. Gorbachev wanted to deal with the subject of nuclear war, initially proposing a joint summit statement that nuclear war was not inevitable. He had also noticed Reagan's declarations to the UN General Assembly and the Japanese Diet in 1983 that "a nuclear war cannot be won and must never be fought," and he agreed completely. As early as September, Gorbachev had suggested to Reagan that such statements could be the basis for an understanding between them at Geneva. It was logical for both leaders to endorse this broad pronouncement, which became the cornerstone of their joint statement. Agreement on any aspect of the current arms negotiations, however, was much more difficult.

Late Wednesday afternoon, Shultz and Shevardnadze reported to their leaders about the deadlocked discussions in the working group. On the spot, Gorbachev dictated several decisions that he thought should facilitate agreement—including acceptance in the joint statement of 50 percent cuts in strategic arms and acceleration of the pace of the U.S.-Soviet arms negotiations. The General Secretary told Reagan that he would like a joint statement to be issued to climax the summit.

The Soviets had previously announced that Gorbachev would give a news conference at the conclusion of the summit. Shultz, after checking out his idea privately with Reagan, told the two leaders late Wednesday that there should be a final ceremony Thursday morning and added, "You have to get up and make statements, each one of you." They didn't need to be long or complex, the secretary said, but "we can't go away from this meeting without people hearing from you personally. We'll work on this communiqué, but that's not enough. That's just something that people get issued. They want to see you people get up and say something in each other's presence." Reagan and Gorbachev agreed.

Even after Gorbachev's instructions, the working group again bogged down Wednesday evening on several points of the joint statement to be issued Thursday morning. It took the personal intervention of Shultz with Gorbachev around ten o'clock that night, including a personal attack on the inflexibility of Deputy Foreign Minister Georgi Kornienko, to break the deadlock. The Soviet drafters received new instructions after midnight that made possible the final compromises on the document at 4:30 A.M., only a few hours before the ceremony at 10:00 A.M., where it was to be issued. To deal with the space issue, the U.S. team agreed to fall back on the language issued by Shultz and Gromyko in January. As completed and published, the joint statement did not mention SDI or the ABM Treaty.

> The sides, having discussed key security issues, and conscious of the special responsibility of the U.S.S.R. and the U.S. for maintaining peace, have agreed that a nuclear war cannot be won and must never be fought. Recognizing that any conflict between the U.S.S.R. and the U.S. could have catastrophic consequences, they emphasized the importance of preventing any war between them, whether nuclear or conventional. They will not seek to achieve military superiority.
>
> The President and the General Secretary discussed the negotiations on nuclear and space arms.
>
> They agreed to accelerate the work at these negotiations, with a view to accomplishing the tasks set down in the Joint U.S.-Soviet Agreement of January 8, 1985, namely to prevent an arms race in space and terminate it on earth, to limit and reduce nuclear arms and enhance strategic stability.

For the first time, the Soviet Union in the Geneva joint statement accepted the principle of discussions with the United States on human rights, which had been the subject of some tough private talk between Reagan and Gorbachev during their meetings. At Soviet insistence, the statement referred cautiously to "resolving humanitarian cases in the spirit of cooperation." Soviet negotiators in the working group insisted there were no words in the Russian language for "human rights."

The regional conflicts that had also engaged Reagan and Gorbachev during their talks were not mentioned in the joint statement except in very vague fashion. But Shultz, especially, thought he had heard a slight change in the way Gorbachev discussed Afghanistan, and told others in the U.S. delegation that Moscow might be reevaluating its stance there. This was among the first hints of a major policy change to come.

There were differing views among Gorbachev's advisers of the unusual political figure who was President of the United States. Aleksandr

Yakovlev, who accompanied Gorbachev to all except the one-on-one meetings and who would be an increasingly close adviser in the years to come, was as skeptical of Reagan at the end of the Geneva summit as he had been at the beginning. "It seemed to me that everything looked like theatre, and that in this theatre was a professional actor." The Kremlin security adviser, Andrei Aleksandrov-Agentov, was amused at the index cards the President pulled out in several meetings to quote Lenin and Stalin in ways that the Soviet officials believed were fallacious. The cards reminded Aleksandrov-Agentov of the reminders he and others used to prepare for the ailing Brezhnev, though Reagan was obviously much more vigorous.

Reagan's initial interest in Gorbachev had been stimulated by British Prime Minister Margaret Thatcher, the President's closest friend among foreign leaders, who said after her discussions with Gorbachev just before he became General Secretary, "I like Mr. Gorbachev. We can do business together." There was no doubt in Reagan's mind after Geneva that Gorbachev was "completely different" from all previous Soviet leaders and that he could also do business with the Soviet leader, though he could not know then how far the interaction would take their two nations.

As for the Soviet side, according to Shevardnadze's account of Geneva, "We saw that Reagan was a person you could deal with, although it was very hard to win him over, to persuade him of the other point of view. But we had the impression that this is a man who keeps his word and that he's someone you can deal with and negotiate with and reach accord."

5. High Stakes at Reykjavik

The year 1986 would be pivotal for Mikhail Gorbachev's foreign policy. Early in the new year, the General Secretary would begin actively transforming it, first with a set of lofty goals for elimination of nuclear weapons and then with a revision of national policy and ideological doctrine presented to the Twenty-seventh Communist Party Congress, the supreme assembly of the Soviet Union, which convened every five years. For decades Moscow's positions had seemed utterly inflexible, set in concrete. Gorbachev would set out to change all that. In 1986 he would be a man in motion, managing to a remarkable degree to take the initiative in world affairs as no Soviet leader had done before him.

Gorbachev had taken the measure of Ronald Reagan at Geneva late in 1985 and found that they had much common ground on a personal level, but there was also an intractable disagreement over SDI. Frustrated by his inability to persuade Reagan to give up or even restrain pursuit of his "dream" of a space-based defense, Gorbachev would stall for six months on setting a date for the next summit meeting while seeking a guarantee that he would not come away empty-handed. At the end of the summer the impatient Soviet leader would propose a "preliminary meeting" with Reagan on neutral ground, gambling that he and the President, if left to their

own devices, could reach agreement on a sweeping deal involving
offensive arms and space defense.

   The meeting at Reykjavik would be full of surprises, including
a sudden ending startling to both sides. The mid-October weekend,
which was described by Secretary Shultz in its immediate after-
math as "the highest-stakes poker game ever played," remains
even today the subject of speculation and dispute. Though it ap-
peared to end in stalemate, Reykjavik paradoxically would be a
turning point in the relations between the two nations. It may have
been the most fascinating meeting of U.S. and Soviet leaders ever
held.

• GORBACHEV'S NEW PROGRAM

On the morning of January 15, 1986, Soviet Ambassador Anatoly Dobrynin telephoned Secretary of State Shultz to inform him that an important
announcement was about to be made in Moscow. Shortly before the
phone call came, the Soviet Embassy had sent over a letter from Gorbachev to Reagan, and a State Department translator was hard at work
on it. The letter and the Soviet announcement contained a Gorbachev
proposal to eliminate all nuclear weapons worldwide by the year 2000.
As soon as the substance was known, Shultz summoned his special arms
control adviser, Paul Nitze, Assistant Secretary of State Rozanne Ridgway and several other aides, and later called in Assistant Secretary of
Defense Richard Perle to join the discussion about how to respond.

  · The January 15 plan, which presaged the high bidding at Reykjavik
ten months later, was a bold idea of the sort that appealed to Gorbachev.
Because of the sweeping nature of the objective, it appeared at first
blush to be a return to the "General and Complete Disarmament" proposals, advanced mostly for propaganda effect, of the Khrushchev era.
However, the Gorbachev plan for eliminating nuclear weapons was set
forth in phases, and in the first phase, the U.S. officials noted with
fascination, all U.S. and Soviet intermediate-range missiles would be
eliminated from Europe, with no requirement that British or French
nuclear missiles be scrapped or that Moscow be entitled to retain a
European nuclear force equal to that of London and Paris. This was a
major shift, and seemed to go a long way toward accepting Reagan's
1981 "zero option" proposal for eliminating all intermediate-range mis-

siles from Europe, a proposal that had been ridiculed by many in the West as well as the East as one-sided and unnegotiable. There was one major hitch: all reductions were conditional on a halt to "development, testing and deployment" of Reagan's Star Wars program. Interestingly, Gorbachev did not mention "research."

Shultz and Nitze went to the White House to see Reagan at 2:00 P.M. the same day to suggest a positive U.S. response to Gorbachev. The National Security Council staff, now under Admiral John Poindexter, suggested that the United States welcome the Soviet initiative. Inside the Oval Office, the officials found Reagan eager to endorse Gorbachev's messianic proposal for denuclearizing the world in the next fourteen years. Reagan's comment was startling: "Why wait until the year 2000 to eliminate all nuclear weapons?" Before the day was out, the White House had issued a statement in Reagan's name welcoming the Gorbachev proposals, especially its plan for abolishing nuclear weapons, and promising that the United States would give it "careful study."

Reagan was looking forward with keen anticipation to his next summit meeting with Gorbachev. In a series of private letters beginning shortly after returning home from Geneva, Reagan sought to persuade Gorbachev that his Star Wars antimissile shield would not be a threat to the Soviet Union or its strategic position. The Soviet leader was unconvinced, and he was wary of Reagan's references to another summit at which the same set of issues discussed at Geneva could be aired again inconclusively.

The Geneva summit had been a public relations coup for both Reagan and Gorbachev, demonstrating that both were statesmen of stature aiming to reduce tensions between themselves and between their governments. But while Reagan achieved this at no cost to his position within his political system, for Gorbachev it was a different story. He had approached the summit proclaiming that the Star Wars program was a dire threat to peace and international stability, but at Geneva he had been unable to persuade Reagan to stop or even slow his multi-billion-dollar effort. After he returned, Politburo member Vladimir Shcherbitsky, an Old Guard figure from the Ukraine, spoke skeptically of the results of the summit. More ominously, public statements by Marshal Sergei Akhromeyev, chief of staff of the Soviet armed forces, sounded doubts about the achievements at Geneva, which was one of the first times the Soviet military had suggested a dissent from the Gorbachev position. Skepticism about the success of the summit also surfaced in the Soviet press.

Late in December, less than a month after Geneva, Reagan had formally proposed through Shultz that their second summit be in Washington in late June 1986. Gorbachev did not respond immediately to the President's invitation. Informally Ambassador Dobrynin was telling American officials that June seemed too early, because time was needed to work out substantial agreements to justify such a meeting, and that September might be better. The maneuvering over summit dates, which went on through the spring and summer, worried White House political advisers. They were concerned that Gorbachev would maneuver to delay the summit to late September or October—as he eventually did—and that this would place Reagan under undue political pressure to produce results on the eve of the November 4 congressional elections.

While fending off Reagan early in the year, Gorbachev was moving toward a fundamental reordering at home. Almost unnoticed in the text of his January 15 arms offers was a phrase that was to become his watchword in foreign affairs—"new political thinking." The phrase would be Gorbachev's way of summing up the revolutionary changes he would seek in Soviet foreign policy in the last half of the 1980s—from militarization to demilitarization, from orthodoxy to flexibility, from secrecy to openness, among others. The changes had their roots in ideas germinating below the surface long before Gorbachev's accession to power, some of them stretching back for a decade or even more. They had been discussed privately and informally and then had gradually come to the surface in the work of scholars and journalists. In 1986, Gorbachev made the ideas his own. Like so much of what Gorbachev sponsored and brought about in foreign affairs, at first the changes seemed to be matters of nuance or rhetoric and were widely discounted in the West. The dramatic proof that they were real came later.

Gorbachev had concentrated in his first year on cementing his power and authority domestically and making connections internationally with Reagan and European leaders. Beginning in early 1986, Gorbachev began to address more intensively the policies and mechanisms that would transform Soviet foreign policy. In his book, *Perestroika*, Gorbachev identified the Twenty-seventh Congress of the Soviet Communist Party, which took place between February 25 and March 6, 1986, as the most important landmark in his move to "new political thinking." The Party Congress, which meets every five years, has the authority to set the party rules and elect a new Central Committee. In theory, it is the supreme body of the Soviet ruling party, and its meeting is regarded as a major historical event. The previous Congress had been presided over by Leonid Brezhnev in February 1981.

Gorbachev's January 15 nuclear disarmament program, which was announced six weeks before the Party Congress, was the sort of big idea that is expected of Soviet leaders on such an occasion. According to Valentin Falin, a senior Communist Party official, the nuclear disarmament program was originally drawn up after extensive discussion in the Politburo, with the intention of making it a central feature of the Party Congress. However, Falin said Gorbachev decided to make the ambitious program public ahead of the Party Congress so that it would not be discounted as a "party political move" but seen as "a practical suggestion of the Soviet Union as a nation."

In the first minutes of the Twenty-seventh Party Congress, Gorbachev served notice that Soviet foreign policy was in transition:

> A turning point has arisen not only in internal but in external affairs. The changes in the development of the contemporary world are so profound and significant that they require a rethinking and comprehensive analysis of all its factors. The situation created by nuclear confrontation calls for new approaches, methods and forms of relations between the different social systems, states and regions.

The vast and ever-growing array of nuclear weapons amassed by the United States and the Soviet Union was threatening physical annihilation on a hair-trigger basis. This state of affairs was increasingly viewed in the new Soviet leadership as fundamentally untenable. According to Yevgeni Primakov, then an adviser to Gorbachev and later a Politburo member and member of Gorbachev's Presidential Council, the new General Secretary quickly realized that "we had approached the limit beyond which it would mean the destruction of human civilization. And this movement was from both sides. The question arose immediately whether we can break this tendency."

If there was ever a single moment at which the priorities of Soviet foreign policy changed from advancing communism to living with the noncommunist world, it was the Political Report of Gorbachev to the Twenty-seventh Party Congress, in effect his keynote address. Gorbachev listed "principled considerations" that he said had been adopted from the beginning of his administration. Almost all of these considerations represented important shifts from previous Soviet policy or doctrine.

First, "the nature of today's weapons leaves no state the hope of defending itself by technical military means alone—let us say, with the creation of defenses, even the most powerful. The insuring of security is taking the form more and more of a political task and can be solved only by political means."

Second, "security when one speaks of relations between the U.S.S.R. and the U.S.A. can only be mutual. . . . The highest wisdom is not in worrying only about oneself, or, all the more, about damaging the other side; it is necessary for all to feel that they are equally secure."

Third, "the U.S.A. and its military-industrial machine, which so far does not intend to slow its pace, remains the locomotive of militarism. . . . But we understand very well that the interests and goals of the military-industrial complex are not at all the same as the interests and goals of the American people and the real national interests of that great country."

Fourth, "the present day world has become too small and fragile for wars and policies of force. . . . This means realizing that it is in fact impossible to win the arms race, just as it is impossible to win a nuclear war itself. . . . Therefore it is essential above all to considerably reduce the level of military confrontation. In our time genuine equal security is guaranteed not by the highest possible, but by the lowest possible level of the strategic balance, from which it is essential to exclude entirely nuclear and other types of weapons of mass destruction."

Finally, Gorbachev declared that "in the present situation there is no alternative to cooperation and interaction between all states. Thus objective, and I stress objective, conditions have arisen in which the confrontation between capitalism and socialism can take place only and exclusively in the forms of peaceful competition and peaceful rivalry."

Closely linked to this final point was Gorbachev's discussion in the report of "global problems affecting all humanity" that cannot be solved by one state or even a group of states such as the socialist countries. This requires "ever more insistently that there should be constructive and creative interaction between states and peoples on the scale of the entire world," declared Gorbachev. To avoid nuclear catastrophe and deal with other global problems, he went on, it is essential to resolve things "jointly in the interest of all concerned"—that is, by neither the socialist world nor the capitalist world alone.

Gorbachev's view that policy must be based on interaction with one world of shared dangers and objectives rather than two worlds with different aims grew out of the concept of "common security" most prominently espoused in the early 1980s by the international commission led by Swedish Prime Minister Olof Palme, and fashionable among Western Europe's Social Democrats. For the Soviet Union, though, it was something of an ideological bombshell. The Communist Party had been founded and nurtured on belief in the class struggle and irreconcilable conflict in which socialism would triumph over capitalism. Now that great division of the world was being shunted to the background in the emphasis on dealing with universal problems.

According to Eduard Shevardnadze, who participated in the Politburo and Central Committee debates preceding the Party Congress as well as the big meeting itself, it was very difficult for many communists to accept the idea that the battle with capitalism was no longer the decisive factor in shaping international relations. "Our underlying basic, fundamental position was the position of class and class values and this is how we were brought up—all of us," Shevardnadze told me. He added that Gorbachev's conclusion to the contrary "gave rise to a very stormy reaction" in debates at the Foreign Ministry and elsewhere even after the Party Congress was over.

For the Soviet military, the shift had profound implications, which were to develop in detail in the months that followed. The most fundamental change, according to Marshal Akhromeyev, was "the conclusion that these global dangers should come to the foreground of policies, and we should shift the military confrontation which was in the foreground to the background." Reflecting on the change in thinking, Akhromeyev said, "For me personally, to rethink all these things and to view the situation from a different angle was very painful. . . . Most of my life I've thought in a different manner."

"Peaceful coexistence" of capitalism and socialism had been the slogan of the Soviet Union since the days of Nikita Khrushchev, but in Soviet doctrine, as enshrined in the program adopted by earlier party congresses, peaceful coexistence was to be merely a temporary respite in the eternal battle, a "specific form of class struggle." That statement was dropped from the party program by the Twenty-seventh Party Congress at Gorbachev's urging. Also expunged from the Communist Party program was another classical statement of the existing ideology: "Should the imperialist aggressors nevertheless venture to start a new world war, the peoples will no longer tolerate a system which drags them into devastating wars. They will sweep imperialism away and bury it."

Gorbachev was well aware that it was one thing to declare new policies and quite another to implement them. In international relations, he was aided in implementation by Eduard Shevardnadze, who had become an increasingly important ally within the Politburo on a broad range of domestic and foreign policy questions. Moreover, Shevardnadze by the spring of 1986 had begun to shake up the Ministry of Foreign Affairs, whose former spirit was symbolized by the giant medieval-looking Stalin-era skyscraper on Smolenskaya Square where Vyacheslav Molotov and Andrei Gromyko had long held sway. To energize the cautious Soviet diplomats and put a new stamp on the policy, Shevardnadze persuaded Gorbachev to come in person to the Foreign Ministry to enunciate the new thinking in international relations. In keeping with the importance of the occasion, Shevardnadze summoned home Soviet ambassadors from all over the world. On May 23, these diplomats joined the senior staff of the Foreign Ministry and foreign aid and trade officials to fill all six hundred seats in the second-floor Foreign Ministry auditorium. So far as anyone could remember, it was the first time in history that a General Secretary had come to the Foreign Ministry to address its assembled leadership.

Gorbachev got quickly to his central point: Soviet diplomacy "must contribute to the domestic development of the country." It was not something disconnected from domestic policy but rather integral to it. Gorbachev declared that his highest foreign policy was to "create the best possible external conditions" for social and economic development at home. This meant maintaining peace, "without which everything else is pointless." On the other side of the coin, Gorbachev quoted a conclusion of the Twenty-seventh Party Congress that "without an acceleration of the country's economic and social development, it will be impossible to maintain our positions on the international scene."

The primacy of the country's domestic needs, especially the need for external calm in order to pursue internal growth, might seem pedestrian or commonplace. In fact, it was a substantial break, at least in theory, with the past ethos in which the Soviet Union had zealously pursued its "internationalist duty" as leader of world socialism, at massive costs in military spending and political prestige. The change meant that to a far greater degree than in the past, the Soviet Union would define its interests in much the same way as other nations, without the distorting prism of Marxist ideology.

In a detailed speech lasting two and a quarter hours, which was barely mentioned in the press at the time, and which never has been published in full, Gorbachev spoke to the assembled diplomats of the "overriding importance for the new thinking to prevail in diplomacy" in order to keep up with the times, with no hesitation about discarding stereotypes and clichés of the past. To an assemblage accustomed to maintaining fixed Soviet positions for years and even decades, the General Secretary spoke of the necessity for realism and pragmatism to prevail in negotiations and of the need to meet one's negotiating partners halfway. In a passage that seemed to be a direct slap at the previous era, Gorbachev went on to say that "it would be inadmissible if our persistence in defending this or that position grew into senseless stubbornness, if Soviet representatives were called Mr. Nyet"—a term often applied to Molotov and Gromyko.

Departing again from the traditional stand, Gorbachev declared that the Soviet approach to humanitarian issues required fundamental reassessment. "Some of our diplomats shrink instinctively when they hear the words human rights. Some ambassadors even ask for instructions as to how they should act in this field," said the General Secretary scornfully. He declared that the 1917 revolution gave "real rights" to people and that protection of those rights is "a basic function of the socialist state." Soviet diplomats "can and must discuss this subject freely with the West, for what is being done in this country to provide respect for human rights is really impressive. This is no propaganda, this is an objective reality," Gorbachev maintained.

On the directions of policy Gorbachev stressed, as he had in his initial declaration in March 1985, that "Soviet foreign policy should give priority to relations with socialist countries." But here there was a new requirement, scarcely ever mentioned by his predecessors as they crushed Eastern European deviations with Soviet tanks, for "respecting those countries' experience and dignity [and] understanding their national peculiarities." Gorbachev declared, in words he would repeat as Eastern and Central Europe approached revolutionary change, "We should never suppose that we may lecture others. No one has given us that right. On the contrary, being the most powerful state in the socialist community, we must be modest."

Though it was not published at the time or even included in the summary of his Foreign Ministry speech that was released more than a year afterward, Gorbachev also revealed a shift in military policy that would have major implications for the Soviet defense system and for arms negotiations with the West. The idea that the Soviet Union could be as strong as any possible coalition of states opposing it—a central military precept of the Brezhnev era—"is absolutely untenable," Gorbachev told the Foreign Ministry audience. "To follow this tenet means patently to act contrary to the nation's interest," Gorbachev said.

Several weeks before Gorbachev's appearance, Shevardnadze had begun his own restructuring of Soviet diplomacy, reorganizing departments and bureaus and naming new deputies and ambassadors in what would become an extensive turnover. By May 1987, one year after Gorbachev's appearance at the Foreign Ministry, seven of the nine deputy foreign ministers were new in the Gorbachev era, as well as seven of the ten Soviet ambassadors-at-large. Moreover, eight of the sixteen chiefs of regional departments of the Foreign Ministry had been changed, as well as 68 of Moscow's 115 ambassadors posted overseas. After decades in which the personnel as well as the policies of Soviet diplomacy changed very little, the transition was dramatic.

From the standpoint of American affairs, the most prominent shift was the reassignment of Anatoly Dobrynin to a senior post in Moscow as chief of the International Department of the Central Committee of the Communist Party. In his twenty-four years as ambassador to the United States, *Time* columnist Hugh Sidey noted, Dobrynin "ambled through the streets of Washington like a Russian bear who resembled your Uncle Ralph." For decades, Dobrynin had dealt with just about everybody who was anybody in official Washington. "I have known six presidents and nine secretaries of state," he reminisced at his farewell party. "Should I go back and write, it would probably fill the Library of Congress." At the time of his departure there was speculation that in his new post, with an office close to that of Gorbachev in Communist Party headquarters, he would eclipse the newcomer, Shevardnadze, in the leadership of Soviet foreign policy much as Henry Kissinger and Zbigniew Brzezinski often seemed to have had more influence from their White House offices than the secretary of state. It did not turn out that way in Moscow. Although Dobrynin continued to be a vocal advocate of new political thinking and to appear at Gorbachev's side in top-level meetings with Americans, it became increasingly clear that the close relationship of Gorbachev and Shevardnadze was the dominant axis of Soviet diplomacy.

Dobrynin's replacement in Washington was Yuri Dubinin, who had started his diplomatic career in Paris and had been ambassador to Spain but who spoke little English when he arrived in the U.S. capital in June 1986. Dubinin was a quick learner of the language and of Washington ways, but he never developed the clout that his predecessor had amassed in his long years in the ornate mansion on Sixteenth Street, only a few blocks from the White House.

Another key figure in U.S. affairs was Aleksandr Bessmertnykh, who was named a deputy foreign minister just before Gorbachev's appearance at the Foreign Ministry in 1986 and who eventually replaced Dubinin as ambassador to the United States in 1990 and, in 1991, replaced Shevardnadze as foreign minister. Bessmertnykh had spent nearly his entire career either in the United States—at the Soviet Embassy in Washington or at the United Nations in New York—or in charge of dealing with the United States at the Foreign Ministry in Moscow. Fluent in English and knowledgeable about the United States from long experience, Bessmertnykh had been considered one of the most pragmatic of Soviet diplomats even before the "new thinking" became fashionable.

• A CASE OF THE BLAHS

While Moscow was inaugurating new thinking and new diplomatic personnel, developments in Washington in the spring and early summer of 1986 were adding to the difficulties of U.S.-Soviet relations and threatening to reverse the momentum that had seemed so promising when the two leaders met at Geneva. In the absence of high-level personal dialogue or preparations for another summit meeting—both of which were conspicuously missing in first half of 1986—Washington, especially, seemed to have reverted to its pre-Geneva hard line. Soviet officialdom, which had expected greater consideration and a smoother ride after the first meeting of Reagan and Gorbachev, was reacting indignantly.

On March 7, the day after the end of the Twenty-seventh Party Congress, the United States ordered the Soviet Union to reduce sharply its diplomatic Mission to the United Nations in New York from about 270 diplomats to 170 in four stages of 25 each over the coming year. The cutback was due to "wrongful" acts, including espionage. The Soviets angrily protested the "arbitrary" and "utterly illegitimate" order and said it would do direct damage to Soviet-American relations and preparations for the next summit. According to State Department officials, the action had been authorized by Reagan six months earlier because of espionage directed from the Soviet Mission, by far the largest of any country at the United Nations. Implementation of the cuts had been put off several times to avoid repercussions as the Geneva summit approached, and then to avoid embarrassing Gorbachev on the eve of the Party Congress.

Less than a week later, on March 13, two U.S. warships loaded with sophisticated electronic gear sailed six miles inside the Soviet Union's twelve-mile territorial limit in the Black Sea, very close to the coast of the Crimea. Under the justification that naval vessels were entitled to "innocent passage" between points at sea, the Navy had been sailing into Soviet territorial waters for years, and provocatively close to the Soviet coast since early in the Reagan administration. Such missions were cleared in advance with the State Department, which rarely objected but sometimes asked for delay. This mission, apparently the first since the Geneva summit, drew a bitter public blast from Moscow, which warned that any repetition could lead to "serious consequences."*

By late March, it was evident that U.S.-Soviet relations were suffering from a case of the blahs. Despite the meeting in Geneva and Gorbachev's bold words early in the year, almost everything seemed bogged down in the usual suspicions and discord. Gorbachev's dramatic January arms proposals had not led to new flexibility on intermediate-range missiles at the Geneva bargaining table, and recent U.S. proposals were equally disappointing to the Soviets. On another front, Moscow was still campaigning vigorously for a total ban on underground nuclear tests; Gorbachev even proposed a summit meeting with Reagan somewhere in Europe exclusively on that subject. Washington was not interested in that or any other means of curbing the tests, which the Defense Department insisted were essential for keeping the nuclear stockpile up to date. The administration considered underground testing a phony issue, being put forward essentially for propaganda purposes. U.S. policymakers were also irritated that Shevardnadze had ignored or passed up invitations to begin discussing the next Reagan-Gorbachev summit.

Gorbachev wasn't happy with the situation, either. On April 2, he wrote to Reagan:

* Two years later, during a similar mission by the same two warships in the Black Sea, a Soviet frigate deliberately rammed one of the U.S. ships. But after this incident and a personal plea by Marshal Akhromeyev to the Joint Chiefs of Staff during a visit to the Pentagon, the Navy ceased the practice of penetrating Soviet territorial waters, according to Admiral William Crowe, at the time chairman of the Joint Chiefs.

More than four months have passed since the Geneva meeting. We ask ourselves: what is the reason for things not going the way they, it would seem, should have gone? Where is the real turn for the better?

As Gorbachev saw it, the Soviet Union had made "new approaches" in arms negotiations only to find little reciprocity from the United States. And outside the negotiating arenas, he wrote:

We hear increasingly vehement philippics addressed to the U.S.S.R. and are also witnessing quite a few actions directly aimed against our interest, and to put it frankly, against our relations becoming more stable. All this builds suspicion as regards to the U.S. policy and surely creates no favorable backdrop for the summit meeting.

Delivering Gorbachev's letter during a good-bye call on the President, the departing Ambassador Dobrynin said he did not believe the time was right to set a date for the promised summit meeting in Washington. Nevertheless, an official visit by Shevardnadze to the U.S. capital was scheduled for mid-May to resume the high-level dialogue and discuss summit plans. But on April 15, when the United States bombed Libya in retaliation for a Libyan-sponsored terrorist attack in Europe, the Kremlin vehemently protested the U.S. military action and canceled the Shevardnadze trip.

From late April to mid-May, the Soviet Union was distracted by a crisis of its own—the explosion of the nuclear reactor at Chernobyl in the Ukraine, the world's worst nuclear accident. The Soviet leadership was notified within a few hours of the accident early on April 26. Soaring radiation levels from the accident began to be picked up in Sweden, Finland and other parts of Europe two days later. But for eight days the Soviet authorities were silent except for a single bland and unenlightening statement, until the Ukrainian health minister finally advised the local public to take measures against the radioactivity. Eventually 200,000 people were evacuated and 600,000 workers were mobilized to try to clean up the radioactive mess. For all his talk of *glasnost*, Gorbachev had nothing to say about the disaster until May 14. Then, eighteen days after the explosion, he went on Soviet television looking somber and exhausted, to give the first detailed explanation and to condemn Western "lies" about the severity of the accident. Many in the Soviet Union as well as in the West were outraged by the long silence from the Kremlin while radioactivity from Chernobyl threatened Soviet citizens and drifted over twenty other countries as well.

It was in this atmosphere in late April and May that a fierce argument raged within the top ranks of the Reagan administration about SALT II, the arms control treaty signed by President Carter and General Secretary Brezhnev in 1979 but never ratified by the Senate. Reagan had opposed SALT II as a presidential candidate but after becoming President agreed to observe its numerical limits despite his distaste for the treaty. The uniformed military and the State Department argued it would be self-defeating to exceed the limits because Moscow was in a better position to add more strategic weapons quickly if the treaty were abandoned. Conservatives led by Secretary of Defense Caspar Weinberger and his allies on Capitol Hill denied that the Soviet Union would benefit and argued that it was already cheating on the SALT II and ABM treaties. Beyond the practical arguments, SALT II was a symbolic issue to both sides—a symbol either of modest accomplishment and hope through arms agreements or of the futility of arms accords.

In June 1985 Reagan had announced after an intra-administration battle that despite misgivings he would "go the extra mile" to stay within the SALT II limits. The most compelling reason for the President's decision was the approach of a U.S.-Soviet summit meeting. "Do we want the allies and Congress dumping all over the President just as he's about to meet Gorbachev?" asked a White House official at a crucial point in the policy debate.

In the spring of 1986, the battle resumed at a time when U.S.-Soviet relations were sagging and there was no summit in sight. After several rounds of full-scale guerrilla war on SALT II between Shultz and Weinberger and their various supporters, Reagan on May 27 announced that he would no longer live by the SALT II limits. Congress, the allies and the Soviet Union were all sharply critical. Weinberger, however, was jubilant that "we are no longer bound by that flawed agreement." Shultz, although he had argued in private against the decision, supported it publicly.

• ZERO BALLISTIC MISSILES

At 2:00 P.M. on June 12, an intimate meeting was convened in the White House Situation Room, the basement conference room where highly secret matters, including classified intelligence and U.S. military operations, are often discussed with the President. The subject of the meeting was the next step in the arms negotiations but, unlike most such planning sessions in the past, none of the government arms experts or negotiators were present—only the President and a handful of his very top officials.

On this occasion Weinberger, who was usually unenthusiastic about new U.S. arms offers, presented one more radical than anything that had come from Washington until that time. At the beginning of the year Gorbachev had proposed eliminating all nuclear weapons, a proposal that nearly everyone in official Washington—except Reagan—thought was outlandish. So in response, said Weinberger, why not propose to the Soviets a plan to eliminate all ballistic missiles?

Intercontinental ballistic missiles, which could travel across thousands of miles in a matter of minutes with a deadly nuclear cargo, were the main threat to the United States from the Soviet Union and also the most important threat to the Soviet Union from the United States. The idea of eliminating these powerful and dangerous weapons had strong appeal to the visionary and romantic side of Ronald Reagan. As was the case with his proposed antimissile shield over the United States, eradicating ballistic missiles would be another way to turn back the clock to the way things used to be in the more civilized and simpler times of his boyhood in Dixon, Illinois. In those days, wars were fought among combatants in far-off trenches and the United States was in no danger of annihilation from afar.

The concept of completely eliminating U.S. and Soviet missiles had come up before in general terms in earlier discussions between Reagan and Gorbachev. In a one-on-one meeting in Geneva, the Soviet leader had made the point that if nuclear missiles were destroyed, there would be no need for a Star Wars defense against them. Reagan had agreed with him, according to the interpreter's notes that were read with surprise by Shultz and McFarlane. In a letter to Gorbachev in February 1986, three months later, Reagan repeated in writing to the Soviet leader what he had said at Geneva: "If there were no nuclear missiles, then there might also be no need for defenses against them."

At first glance a utopian proposal by a secretary of defense to eliminate his most potent weapon would seem highly improbable, especially in a world in which ballistic missile technology was thirty years old and in which France, China and Israel and a number of other nations in addition to the Soviet Union possessed their own ballistic missiles. (According to a Library of Congress report in the spring of 1986, at least a dozen Third World countries in the Middle East, Asia and South America had also developed or were developing ballistic missiles.) Practical or not, the idea of eliminating ballistic missiles had a considerable hidden history in the E Ring of the Pentagon, the headquarters of the Defense Department's political echelon.

The originator of Zero Ballistic Missiles as a U.S. negotiating proposal was Fred Ikle, the Swiss-born defense intellectual and former professor who had been director of the Arms Control and Disarmament Agency in the Nixon and Ford administrations and who during most of the Reagan administration was under secretary of defense for policy, the number-three official at the Pentagon. Ikle had long considered the incredible speed of intercontinental missiles—and the resulting threat of surprise attack—the most dangerous attribute of the Cold War. Shortly before joining the Nixon administration in 1973, Ikle suggested in the scholarly journal *Foreign Affairs* that the United States and the Soviet Union "could jointly decide to replace the doomsday catapults invented in the 1950s with arms that are incapable of being launched swiftly. If the strategic order could be transformed in this way, the dominant fear of surprise attack which drives our arms competition would loosen its grip."

The distinction between dangerous "fast-flying" ballistic missiles that threatened a nuclear surprise attack (and in which the Soviets had a numerical advantage) and less dangerous "slow-flying" bombers and cruise missiles (in which the United States had an advantage) was a central tenet of Reagan administration arms control. The idea was to get rid of the "fast-flyers" to the greatest degree possible.

In late December of 1985, Ikle met over lunch in the Executive Office Building in the White House compound with Donald Fortier, who recently had become deputy national security adviser when Poindexter moved up from the deputy's job to replace Robert McFarlane. Fortier was interested in new ideas, especially for the next U.S.-Soviet summit.

Among those Ikle suggested was a "zero missiles initiative." According to Ikle's notes of the lunch, he said this could be a historic proposition on the order of the 1946 "Baruch plan" under which the United States proposed to place control of atomic energy in the United Nations (but which was blocked by the Soviet Union). Ikle expected that the idea of eliminating ballistic missiles would be attacked as impractical, but he told Fortier it was "not more infeasible" than the 50 percent reduction in strategic arms that had been endorsed at the Geneva summit. With Gorbachev beginning to capture the world's imagination, there would be important public relations advantages to such a bold proposal. In another set of Ikle notes about the same time, he listed "zero ballistic missiles" under the heading of public relations when classifying various suggestions as "comprehensive," "marginal" or "PR."

There is no indication that Fortier, who became critically ill several months later and died of cancer in August 1986, acted on the suggestion. But meanwhile, in the spring, the idea came up in a luncheon conversation of Ikle and Max Kampelman, who was the chief U.S. arms negotiator at the Geneva talks. Kampelman, a prodefense Democrat who had once been a staff aide to Senator Hubert Humphrey, knew how to get things done in Washington. The two officials, who had known each other for many years, were searching for a U.S. proposal dramatic enough to compete with Gorbachev's January 15 plan for a nuclear-weapons-free world. When Ikle introduced the Zero Ballistic Missiles concept into the discussion, Kampelman enthusiastically agreed it was an important idea. He urged Ikle to discuss it with the Joint Chiefs of Staff, who often had a notion of military feasibility different from those of Weinberger and the political echelon at Defense. In another luncheon a few weeks later, Ikle told Kampelman he had informally broached the idea to the chiefs and that he had also taken it to Richard Perle, the conservative activist on arms negotiations issues who was nominally Ikle's subordinate at the Pentagon. After initial reluctance, Perle liked the proposal for his own reasons, including the belief that an offer to eliminate ballistic missiles would put the Soviets on the defensive. As Perle saw it, a U.S. offer to give up its means for offensive missile operations would destroy the theoretical basis for Soviet objections to SDI.

At their second meeting, Ikle said he planned to take his Zero Ballistic Missiles idea next to Weinberger, and Kampelman agreed to discuss it with Shultz. Ikle and Kampelman then followed through with their respective cabinet heavyweights, with positive results all around. Thus, the ground was prepared in classic Washington style for consideration of a potentially revolutionary proposal without the knowledge of the government bureaucracy with its legions of experts, or the press, which is close to that bureaucracy.

Ikle was not present at the intimate White House meeting when Weinberger raised the idea, nor had he been informed in advance that this would be done. Shultz had no advance notice, either, but he had been primed for the subject by his discussion with Kampelman. Moreover, Shultz had been concerned by the increasingly accurate and harder-to-destroy ballistic missiles in the hands of the Soviet Union while the administration's drive for a new mobile U.S. intercontinental missile, the M-X, was still stuck in Congress because of controversy about how and where it was to be based. Well before Weinberger made his ballistic missiles proposal, Shultz recalled, he had made a little speech on the subject in a small meeting with the President.

> You know the Soviet Union is not in our class economically or in terms of human values. There's only one thing the Soviet Union can do better than we can for sure. Maybe there are some things they can produce like ballet dancers but in these big matters, there's only one thing they do better than we do and that is to produce ballistic missiles. And that's not because we don't know anything about engineering. It's because our political system has a hard time with it, and particularly land-based missiles. . . .
>
> Furthermore, it's the ballistic missile that is the threat to the security of the United States directly. Not since we got rid of the British at the time of our revolution has anything threatened our land like the ballistic missile does.

A growing deadlock in the politics of arms control was also a factor in consideration of the Zero Ballistic Missiles proposal. Shultz was anxious to get back to serious bargaining with the Soviets, but he seemed blocked at nearly every turn by the intransigence of Weinberger, who opposed changes in the U.S. positions on offensive arms and argued for stonewalling against all efforts to negotiate limits on SDI. Moreover, the departure of McFarlane from the White House had eliminated a frequent Shultz ally and replaced him with Poindexter, a technocratic figure who usually remained neutral in policy disputes and who was giving Weinberger more frequent access to Reagan than he had had before.

All this was in the background when Weinberger put the proposal to eliminate all ballistic missiles on the table in the June 12 "principals only" meeting of the National Security Planning Group, the innermost circle of the President and his senior national security team. Shultz felt it was "pretty far out," but at least it seemed to be a break in Weinberger's adamant opposition to shifts in U.S. negotiating positions on strategic arms. Shultz immediately said he thought Weinberger's proposal was a good idea that ought to be seriously pursued. Poindexter, who was surprised to see Weinberger and Shultz in rare agreement, informed Shultz that he was going to work with Weinberger to attempt to prepare a proposal for formal consideration. Shultz did not object.

In the last ten days of June, Shultz was in Southeast Asia on his annual summertime trip to the foreign ministers' meeting of the Association of Southeast Asian Nations when he received a secret cable transmitting a draft of the Zero Ballistic Missiles proposal that had been worked up by Poindexter and Weinberger directly with Reagan. Rather than deal with the substance of such an important issue from thousands of miles away without his key advisers, Shultz telephoned Paul Nitze and Jim Timbie to apprise them of what had been going on and ask them to consider the proposal, which he retransmitted through secure channels. Nitze's initial reaction on hearing of the proposal shortly after it was offered was to tell a White House staffer it was "ridiculous." But with the President and his heavyweights involved, Nitze had to take it seriously.

Around this time, Colonel Robert Linhard, Poindexter's arms control chief on the National Security Council staff, was authorized to work with the administration's senior arms control advisers to refine Weinberger's idea. As Linhard and some of his NSC staff aides saw it, a clear-cut proposal to eliminate all U.S. and Soviet ballistic missiles would have been shocking to the public and military community and might have been rejected out of hand, but some less stark version of the idea might have merit as part of an offer to the Soviets. Poindexter, too, felt that in mid-1986 the timing was not right for a big new U.S. arms cut proposal. Moreover, the British and French governments, which had been confidentially contacted, wanted no part of a plan that might impinge on their ballistic missiles. As reworked by the arms control experts, Weinberger's bold idea of banning all ballistic missiles was watered down and complicated so that only the germ of the proposal survived.

The muted version of the Zero Ballistic Missiles plan was approved by Reagan and his top advisers and dispatched to Gorbachev in a letter dated July 25. The letter proposed that (1) the United States would not withdraw from the ABM Treaty for at least five years (Moscow was asking for a fifteen- to twenty-year nonwithdrawal commitment), and (2) if either side wished to deploy strategic defenses after that, it would be required to submit a plan for sharing the benefits of strategic defense and for eliminating all ballistic missiles.

There was never a formal meeting of the National Security Council at which the letter was subjected to a full-scale review. Instead it was handled in what Admiral William Crowe, chairman of the Joint Chiefs of Staff, described as "a screwy manner" and others described as a highly unusual "top-down" procedure, basically being negotiated by Poindexter with the other principals. When Crowe finally saw a draft of the letter in the late stages of its consideration, he was informed that Weinberger and Shultz had both approved and was told, "Jesus, don't rock the boat. It's the only thing they've agreed on in years." Besides, it seemed to Crowe and others that the Soviets were likely to reject the proposal anyway, since ballistic missiles were even more vital to the Soviet arsenal than they were to that of the United States.

And so they did. When Gorbachev finally got around to replying to the July 25 proposals on September 15, seven weeks later, he described the U.S. proposals on space as a step backward rather than forward. Gorbachev did not even mention the Zero Ballistic Missiles aspect.

A few of the top officials were disappointed, but others in the select circle who knew about the proposal were relieved, considering it a harebrained scheme of a mischievous nature. Zero Ballistic Missiles seemed dead and buried as a topic for discussion between the United States and the Soviet Union any time in the next few years. But it would rise from its grave—with dramatic impact—when Ronald Reagan and Mikhail Gorbachev sat down to negotiate at Reykjavik.

• THE DANILOFF CASE

On August 23, a thirty-nine-year-old Soviet physicist named Gennadi Zakharov stepped onto a subway platform in Queens, New York City, to meet a Guyanan of several years' acquaintance, who was working for a U.S. defense contractor. As the Guyanan handed over some secret documents that had been supplied for the occasion by the FBI, an embracing couple dressed as joggers broke off their caress and pounced on Zakharov. After a fight, the two FBI agents handcuffed and arrested Zakharov on charges of espionage.

Had Zakharov worked for the Soviet Embassy in Washington or the Soviet Mission to the United Nations, he would have had diplomatic immunity from prosecution and would have been quickly expelled from the United States. As an employee of the United Nations, however, he had no such immunity. He was interrogated, booked and jailed in the Metropolitan Correctional Center in Manhattan awaiting trial. A request from the Soviet Embassy that Zakharov be released to the custody of the ambassador was denied by the New York court.

Seven days after Zakharov's arrest, *U.S. News & World Report* correspondent Nicholas Daniloff was lured to a meeting along the Moscow River in the Soviet capital, handed an envelope containing secrets by a Soviet acquaintance and immediately seized by KGB agents in an operation that seemed deliberately arranged to parallel the earlier arrest. As a private U.S. citizen, Daniloff did not possess diplomatic immunity. He was taken to Moscow's notorious Lefortovo Prison, charged with espionage and denied release in the custody of the U.S. ambassador.

From Daniloff's arrest on August 30 until his flight home from Moscow September 29 and Zakharov's flight home from New York September 30, the intertwined fate of the U.S. journalist and the Soviet physicist engaged the two governments in a highly publicized test of wills. Ronald Reagan and Mikhail Gorbachev became personally and at times deeply involved. In the end their two chief diplomats, George Shultz and Eduard Shevardnadze, worked out the nearly simultaneous releases in eleven hours of personal diplomacy, and did so in way that cemented an unprecedented relationship of trust and confidence between a U.S. secretary of state and a Soviet foreign minister. This relationship affected all that followed during the Reagan administration and set the stage for similarly close ties between Shevardnadze and James Baker, Shultz's successor in the administration of President Bush, in 1989 and 1990.

The arrest of Zakharov did not come out of the blue. The FBI had been watching him for three years as he recruited and cultivated potential agents, mainly students he met on college campuses. In May 1986, he had obtained a written espionage "contract" from Leakh Bhoge, the young Guyanan, who had become an FBI double agent. Before arresting

Zakharov, the FBI circulated a summary of its case and a request for approval of the arrest to the White House, State Department, Defense Department and Central Intelligence Agency.

The U.S. agency that might have been expected to have the greatest concern about the consequences of Zakharov's arrest, the State Department, responded to the FBI on August 21 that it had "no foreign policy objection." This decision was made at a time when Shultz, his assistant secretary for European affairs, the chief of the Soviet desk and the chief of the Soviet desk's bilateral affairs branch were all on vacation. Later some State Department officials in this chain of command said the decision was a mistake, in view of a long history of retaliation against private Americans in Moscow for the jailing of Soviet agents inside the United States. Had all the experts been on hand, one of them said later, there would have been a serious proposal advanced to tell the Soviets quietly to send Zakharov home to avoid an all-but-certain crisis. Others in the chain of command at State, however, said there was no way to avert the arrest, although the department knew that the consequences would be serious. "We felt we had the goods on Zakharov," said the senior State Department Sovietologist, Deputy Assistant Secretary Thomas Simons. "We decided to approve [the arrest] because it was what used to be called the right thing. In U.S.-Soviet relations you don't stop doing the right thing in order to sweeten the pot for other elements in the relationship."

The news of Zakharov's arrest and the denial of his bail reached Moscow at a time of unease about the Reagan administration. Two high ranking Communist Party officials told Dimitri Simes, a well-connected U.S. Sovietologist, that the Kremlin interpreted the arrest as showing contemptuous disregard for Soviet interests at a time when Moscow was already angry about Washington's attitudes and actions. Simes was told that Aleksandr Yakovlev, the former Soviet ambassador to Canada and a close Gorbachev confidant, and Anatoly Dobrynin, the former Soviet ambassador to the United States, were among those urging a tough response, and that Gorbachev personally approved this policy. From the U.S. point of view, the Kremlin had broken the unwritten rules of the espionage game by sending a man without diplomatic immunity to "run agents" from a United Nations job. But from the Kremlin point of view, the United States had violated the rules of the game by jailing a Soviet citizen and denying him bail, rather than sending him home.

There was no indication that Yakovlev, Dobrynin or Gorbachev himself selected Daniloff as the target of retaliation. Daniloff is believed to have been the choice of the KGB, which had long kept a close watch on the knowledgeable U.S. journalist, who was of Russian descent. The KGB had built up a record of Daniloff's contacts with Soviet citizens, including at least two who appear to have been placed in Daniloff's path by the secret police authorities.

One of those two was "Father Roman," a man claiming to be a Russian Orthodox priest, who had first contacted Daniloff in December 1984 and a month later had left an envelope in Daniloff's mailbox containing a sealed letter addressed to U.S. Ambassador Arthur Hartman. With considerable misgivings, Daniloff had handed over the letter to the U.S. Embassy. It turned out to be an offer of information about Soviet rockets, which the CIA station in the Embassy sought to follow up. Unknown to Daniloff, a CIA officer in the Embassy used Daniloff's name in contacting "Roman" in a telephone call taped by the KGB and even referred to Daniloff in a letter to "Roman" that was intercepted and placed on file at the KGB. With this evidence on hand, the KGB was prepared to spring a trap on Daniloff any time it chose.

The retaliatory arrest of a respected American journalist on spy charges in Moscow was big news in the United States and, as Daniloff's confinement stretched on, public indignation mounted. After an initial silence while he tried in vain to obtain Daniloff's release through private correspondence with Gorbachev, Reagan declared the arrest "an outrage" and warned it could become a "major obstacle" in U.S.-Soviet relations. "There will be no trade," Reagan announced in Denver on September 8. Shultz, in an address at Harvard three days earlier, had expressed "outrage" and said, "Let there be no talk of a trade for Daniloff. We and Nick himself have ruled that out."

On September 10, the Soviets offered to release Daniloff to the custody of the U.S. ambassador in Moscow if the United States would make a parallel arrangement for Zakharov. On September 12, Reagan approved the move, while writing in his diary that "this does not mean a trade. This we will not do. Their man is a spy caught red handed and Daniloff is a hostage."

As administration critics were quick to notice, the simultaneous release of Daniloff and Zakharov to ambassadorial custody was the beginning of an arrangement that closely resembled a swap, which was politically unacceptable under the circumstances. The official discussion of a swap-style settlement did not end there. Shortly before the two men were let out of their respective cells, Washington had secretly proposed that Daniloff be permitted to leave the USSR, while Zakharov would be exchanged for a dissident or dissidents whose release was desired by the West. For the moment, the Soviets did not accept or reject this face-saving plan, the effect of which would have been to return Zakharov as Moscow desired. They just let it sit.

The reason for the surprising shift toward compromise in the U.S. capital was a confidential study of the case against Daniloff by State and Justice Department lawyers. State Department Legal Adviser Abraham Sofaer reported to Shultz after studying details of the case quietly supplied by the Soviet government that the journalist was in deep trouble. Although Daniloff was not a spy and had not been engaging in espionage, Sofaer concluded that the evidence the KGB had amassed against him, including the secret package he was handed just before his arrest, the letter he delivered from "Father Roman" and the telephone call and follow-up letter by the CIA operative, would be sufficient to convict Daniloff in a Soviet court. The shocker was Sofaer's additional judgment, backed up by that of the assistant attorney general in charge of the Justice Department Criminal Division, Stephen Trott, that the same evidence against a Russian would be sufficient to convict him as a spy in U.S. courts. Sofaer and Trott told Shultz, "This man is in trouble because of us."

Shultz took his findings to Reagan, arguing that "we owe Daniloff something" because of CIA culpability in the case against him. Shortly thereafter, he brought Sofaer to brief the President. Reagan showed a compassionate interest in Daniloff's welfare, but he was skeptical of Sofaer's conclusion. The President kept going back to the clear and simple point that Daniloff was an innocent person. The State Department legal adviser, who had been a federal prosecutor and judge in New York earlier in his career, responded that "innocent people sometimes get convicted." He told Reagan that the legal standard to judge the case was not guilt or innocence, but the question of evidence, "and the evidence here could convict Daniloff in a federal court in the United States." In Shultz's view the fact that Daniloff had been badly compromised by U.S. government mistakes put his case in a completely different light. As Sofaer described it to Shultz and Reagan, the United States would not be trading a criminal for a hostage, which was how they had publicly described the case, but trading a criminal for a hostage who could be convicted as a criminal in court. Under the circumstances, according to Sofaer, it was "more in the nature of a legitimate trade due to their [the Soviets'] skillful manipulation and our dumb actions."

All this was beneath the surface (in fact, never made public) when Shevardnadze and a Soviet Foreign Ministry delegation arrived in Washington September 18 for two days of meetings with Shultz that had been scheduled before Daniloff's arrest. This was Shevardnadze's first trip to Washington in a year and the first Shultz-Shevardnadze meeting since the Geneva summit. The purpose of the talks was to discuss the full range of issues between the United States and the Soviet Union with an eye toward setting up the next summit meeting.

Suddenly the Zakharov-Daniloff cases stood in the way. The day Shevardnadze arrived, Gorbachev publicly called Daniloff a "spy who was caught in the act." Anger about the case was at a high pitch in the United States. Conservatives in Congress, led by Representative Jack Kemp, demanded that Shultz refuse to meet Shevardnadze until Daniloff was free. Shultz ignored the demand, as he consistently did when asked not to confer with the Soviets, but he knew that the intense emotion and high stakes involved would make the negotiations with Shevardnadze unusually difficult.

At 9:00 A.M. on September 19, Shultz waited for Shevardnadze to arrive for their first meeting at the State Department. Standing in a foyer outside his office, Shultz watched with a sense of empathy as the Soviet foreign minister was escorted down the long corridor for the official greeting and the start of their meetings. Shevardnadze looked ashen and uneasy, Shultz thought. Out of consideration for his counterpart, Shultz suggested that they begin by meeting alone. Accompanied only by their two interpreters, he and Shevardnadze walked through his spacious ceremonial office with its big fireplace to the small back office, which he and his predecessors often used for meetings with their inner circle. As soon as Shevardnadze was seated, Shultz told him, "You and I have a very hard problem to wrestle with. We have tried to work together as human beings and I want you to know that however strained and difficult this may be, you will be treated with decency and respect by me." That said, Shultz delved into the substance of the problem, including the bluntly stated U.S. view of Soviet conduct in the Daniloff case. Shevardnadze was just as blunt in saying that he knew that Daniloff was an intelligence agent, either for the United States or for one of its allies. The one-on-one meeting in the inner office went on for two and one-half hours while other members of the delegations waited in suspense.

Shevardnadze had a letter from Gorbachev he wanted to deliver in person to Reagan, so Shultz telephoned the White House and arranged an immediate visit. As with Ambassador Dobrynin in early 1983, Shultz took Shevardnadze through the East Gate to avoid reporters and photographers. This time, by prearrangement with Shultz, the President's role was not the conciliatory one Shevardnadze had seen in Geneva, but that of a wronged and angry man, his cheeks flushed, as he denounced the Daniloff arrest. Reagan told his Soviet visitor that he resented the accusation that Daniloff was a spy after he had given his word to Gorbachev personally that this was not the case. "I enjoyed being angry," Reagan wrote in his diary afterward.

Not realizing that he would be going directly from the State Department to the White House, Shevardnadze had left Gorbachev's letter at the Soviet Embassy. While aides sent for it, the Soviet foreign minister told Reagan of its most important and surprising element—a proposal by Gorbachev to meet Reagan in October in either London or Iceland to explore holding a full-fledged summit meeting later. Reagan opted for Iceland, but said he would not respond officially to Gorbachev's proposal until Daniloff was free. Reagan, Shultz and the few other aides who knew of the offer kept it strictly secret while the Daniloff controversy was played out.

The official talks of the U.S. and Soviet delegations got underway around a long conference table at the State Department several hours after Shevardnadze's meeting with Reagan. The controversy surrounding the Daniloff case overshadowed the other discussions in the public eye, but the diplomats tried to put it aside as they dealt with the difficult issues of arms control, regional conflicts, human rights and bilateral accords. A second plenary meeting of the two delegations was held the following morning at the State Department. In formal exchanges and side discussions, the two delegations were chipping away ever so slowly at the glacial mass of the issues between them. One result of the conferences, barely noticed at the time but eventually significant, was the final compromise on notification of major troop movements and other confidence-building measures under negotiation in a three-year-old Conference on Disarmament in Europe at Stockholm. Even in the midst of the Daniloff dispute, Shultz and Shevardnadze agreed on separate messages to their delegations, which made possible the thirty-five-nation agreement announced in Stockholm September 21.

After the meetings in Washington, the two foreign ministers traveled to New York for the annual round of speeches and diplomatic conferences in the opening weeks of the United Nations General Assembly session. There in four meetings in a variety of secluded settings over five days— a United Nations conference room, the Soviet Mission and the office of the U.S. ambassador to the United Nations—Shultz and Shevardnadze worked out the swap. It was a complex arrangement under which Daniloff would be permitted to leave for home first without a court appearance and Zakharov would be freed the next day after pleading *nolo contendere* ("no contest") to espionage charges in federal court. A leading Soviet dissident, Yuri Orlov, would also be brought from a Siberian labor camp to the United States as part of the deal. Shevardnadze also promised to work for the release of a half-dozen other prominent dissidents on a list provided by Shultz. Eventually nearly all of these came out, without public reference by either side to the Daniloff case.

Like their most important Washington discussions, the New York negotiations were very private, with each minister accompanied by only one senior aide, usually Assistant Secretary of State Rozanne Ridgway with Shultz and Deputy Foreign Minister Aleksandr Bessmertnykh with Shevardnadze and one interpreter on each side. Before each session, Shultz carefully went over the positions to be taken with Reagan or Poindexter, and he reported directly to the White House by telephone or in person after the discussion. On some of the most sensitive issues, Shultz kept his personal views so close to his vest that he refused to tell his own aides working with him on the negotiation what he was advising Reagan.

Except for the list of the dissidents whom Washington desired released, no paper was passed between the two ministers. "The two sides never wrote anything down," according to Ridgway. "We worked and we talked and said, 'Now this is what we understand.' Then that might not be correct, and they'd object. At the end, when both sides were able to repeat orally to the other precisely what was going to happen, the two men shook hands and went back to their respective missions." Both Shultz and Shevardnadze were relying entirely on the word and the authority of the other in a high-profile crisis involving the prestige of the two governments and the sensitivities of their police and intelligence agencies. At this stage, the leadership echelons of the two governments had little confidence in one another. Nevertheless, Shultz relied on Shevardnadze's word that he could deliver Daniloff from the KGB prison and Orlov from a Siberian labor camp. Shevardnadze relied on Shultz's word that he could bring Zakharov through the U.S. court system and out of the United States.

Shortly after Daniloff left Moscow, and before Zakharov was to appear in court in the first step toward his release, Bessmertnykh telephoned Ridgway in great alarm. Neither the Soviet Embassy nor its attorneys had been contacted by U.S. legal authorities, and there were suggestions that problems had arisen on the U.S. side. "The minister has placed his trust in what Secretary Shultz has said would happen as Daniloff moves to leave the Soviet Union, and yet we see nothing happening," Bessmertnykh said. "We have become concerned."

"Sasha [Bessmertnykh's nickname], the secretary of state is a man of his word," Ridgway responded.

"Yes, my minister believes that Secretary Shultz is a man of honor," Bessmertnykh agreed.

"That is correct, and the U.S. side of this will be honored," Ridgway assured the Soviet diplomat.

Alerted by Ridgway, Shultz went to work with the White House and Attorney General Edwin Meese to resolve the complications. The carefully choreographed federal court appearance of Zakharov went off as scheduled, and he was put on the next Aeroflot flight for home.

"If you ask me, it was in that moment when Shultz and Shevardnadze realized that for certain kinds of issues, they were going to have to deal with them personally, and each placed confidence in the word of the other and the ability of the other to deliver what he said he could deliver," observed Ridgway. Shultz had never had that sort of relationship with Gromyko, nor had any U.S. secretary of state developed that sort of relationship with a Soviet foreign minister. In the disputes and deadlocks to come, this personal trust proved to be of vital importance at several key points.

On the morning of September 30, while Daniloff was flying home to a joyous welcome in Washington, Shultz appeared in the White House briefing room to announce the release of Zakharov and the impending release of Orlov. Before the press could pepper him with skeptical questions about the arrangement, the President entered the room and took over the podium. Reagan then announced that he had accepted a proposal by Gorbachev to meet October 11 and 12 in Reykjavik, Iceland, "in the context of preparations" for a full-scale summit to take place later in Washington.

• REYKJAVIK: HOW IT HAPPENED

The most spectacular summit meeting of the 1980s was also the least planned. During the high-stakes weekend at Reykjavik, Ronald Reagan and Mikhail Gorbachev would bargain seriously about eliminating within ten years all of the offensive ballistic missiles in their arsenals, the most destructive weapons ever assembled and the underpinnings of their global military power. Going beyond even this, the leaders of the United States and the Soviet Union would discuss eliminating their entire stocks of nuclear weapons, whether they were in the form of missile warheads, gravity bombs or even artillery shells. Had the two leaders ended their meeting in agreement on any of these proposals and been able to follow through, the Reykjavik summit would have marked the most radical reduction in military capacity ever brought about by negotiations. It would have changed the course of history overnight.

As it was, the most personal and least predictable of all the recent summits broke down in its final hour in disagreement over limits on Reagan's cherished SDI program. Reagan and Gorbachev and the two aides who sat with them during their bargaining—George Shultz and Eduard Shevardnadze—would leave the summit meeting either angry or dazed at the sudden collapse of the exhilarating bargaining. However, profound relief that it did not succeed would be the predominant emotion among astonished military strategists and leaders of Western European nations when they learned what had been afoot. The potentially historic deals had been undertaken without serious study of the consequences and without consultation with Congress or the allies whose security was also at stake. Former U.S. Secretary of Defense James Schlesinger wrote that "Reykjavik represented a near disaster from which we were fortunate to escape." Former President Richard Nixon wrote, "No summit since Yalta has threatened Western interests so much as the two days at Reykjavik."

The historical irony is that while Reykjavik appeared to be a failure at the moment the meeting ended, in the long run it would be a success of major importance. The discussions between Reagan and Gorbachev in the Icelandic capital would place the leaders of the United States and the Soviet Union on a path of nuclear arms reduction and political accommodation that was to have tremendous significance. "Reykjavik marked a turning point in world history," Gorbachev wrote a year later in his book, *Perestroika*. "It tangibly demonstrated that the world situation could be improved. . . . At Reykjavik we became convinced that our course was correct and that a new and constructive way of political thinking was essential." Reagan, in his memoirs published in 1990, called Reykjavik "a major turning point in the quest for a safe and secure world."

The Reykjavik summit was born of frustration mixed with boldness on the part of Gorbachev. On the first day of the Geneva summit in November 1985, Gorbachev had unhesitatingly and unconditionally agreed to meet Reagan again in Washington in 1986 and Moscow in 1987. But the very next day, his hopes for a deal on arms issues had been dashed by Reagan's stubborn insistence on pursuing his Star Wars defense program. Gorbachev believed the Geneva summit was the beginning of a vitally important change in the relationship between the United States and the Soviet Union, but the months since then had produced little movement in the active correspondence between the two leaders or in the bargaining between the teams of diplomats who represented them at the Nuclear and Space Talks in Geneva.

Since early in 1986, Gorbachev had made it increasingly plain that, despite his earlier commitment, he would not go to a full-scale summit meeting in the United States without assurances that tangible accords would come out of it. Gorbachev had told the Twenty-seventh Party Congress in February that the next summit should deliver "practical results" on arms issues rather than being the occasion for "idle conversation." In March, he had proposed a one-issue summit limited to nuclear testing, an idea Washington had flatly rejected because it had no intention of providing comfort or compromise on that issue. In April, he had complained to Reagan in a letter that U.S. actions had created "no favorable backdrop" for the next summit meeting, which he said should be "truly meaningful and substantial" in its results. Gorbachev had agreed to send Shevardnadze to Washington in May to begin discussing the next summit, but he had canceled the trip when the United States bombed Libya. Reagan had then proposed that Shultz and Shevardnadze meet in midsummer to begin the summit preparation process. Gorbachev had rejected that in a letter to the President on June 19, suggesting instead that the two sides move ahead in "all natural channels" across the range of issues, and that the two ministers review the progress in September.

Gorbachev said explicitly at several points that he was not establishing any "precondition" for the next summit, yet he was maneuvering in every way possible to insist on a crucial condition: that it be a guaranteed success in substantive terms, rather than simply a public relations exercise. Turning to the process of diplomacy as a way to protect himself, Gorbachev had sent Deputy Foreign Minister Aleksandr Bessmertnykh to Washington in late July with a proposal for a U.S.-Soviet "work program" of intensive consultation on all pending issues. This would prepare for the Shultz-Shevardnadze meeting in mid-September, which in turn would decide whether the basis existed for scheduling the summit. Reagan and Shultz had immediately accepted the idea, realizing that it was Gorbachev's way of testing the waters. Teams of U.S. and Soviet senior arms control officials had met in Moscow August 11–12 and in Washington September 5–6 to discuss every issue in their field, but there were few notable shifts in position on either side. On August 27–28 teams of experts on regional conflicts headed by Under Secretary of State Michael Armacost and Deputy Foreign Minister Anatoly Adamishin met in Washington to go over the positions on Afghanistan, Angola, Central America and other areas, again without notable shifts. "We are not interested in an empty summit," Adamishin told reporters as the meeting concluded. "We have to decide yet whether the summit should take place, because it has to be productive. It has to have some results—concrete results."

It seemed to Shevardnadze toward the end of the summer that there was "no movement at all—endless discussion and debate, mutual recriminations and accusations with actually no progress." At this point Gorbachev, who had been on his summer vacation at the Black Sea since August 19, surprised his foreign minister. Without previous discussion or warning, he telephoned Shevardnadze to suggest a preliminary meeting with Reagan in a third country "to try and get some breakthrough." What was needed, according to Gorbachev, was a "highest level political decision" to move the process. This might be done, he thought, in a very personal set of meetings with Reagan, without teams of advisers sitting in to second-guess or restrain them. The September 15 letter including the invitation to Reagan was drafted by Shevardnadze and Deputy Foreign Minister Bessmertnykh and flown to Gorbachev's Black Sea villa for signature. Shevardnadze took the letter with him to Washington and presented it to the President September 19 at the height of the Daniloff case. It said in part:

> In almost a year since Geneva, there has been no movement on these [nuclear arms] issues. Upon reflection and after having given thought to your last [July 25] letter, I have come to the conclusion that the negotiations need a major impulse; otherwise, they would continue to mark time while creating only the appearance of preparations for our meeting on American soil.
>
> They will lead nowhere unless you and I intervene personally. I am convinced that we shall be able to find solutions, and I am prepared to discuss with you in a substantive way all possible approaches to them and identify such steps as would make it possible—after prompt follow up by appropriate government agencies—to make my visit to the United States a really productive and fruitful one. This is exactly what the entire world is expecting from a second meeting between the leaders of the Soviet Union and the United States.

Once the proposal for a preliminary meeting was made, a major planning exercise began in Moscow under the supervision of Shevardnadze and Gorbachev's increasingly close Communist Party adviser, Aleksandr Yakovlev. These preparations, which were very secret at the time, involved teams of officials from what was known in Moscow as the "group of five": the Foreign Ministry, the Central Committee of the Communist Party, the KGB intelligence and secret police agency, the General Staff of the armed forces, and representatives of the defense industry. While experts were involved in the details, the crucial discussions were in a closed circle at the top. "Gorbachev wanted a breakthrough" and could not rely on the usual cumbersome procedures, according to Bessmertnykh. A key figure in this planning, Chief of the General Staff Marshal Akhromeyev, was assigned to accompany Gorbachev to Reykjavik as his chief arms negotiating aide.

The basic Soviet strategy at Reykjavik was to advance a disarmament package of historic importance with one big string attached: the cuts would happen only if Reagan reined in the SDI program. The curbing of SDI was an essential part of the plan. According to Yakovlev, "We understood that it was a new stage, a new turn of the armaments race." If SDI were not stopped, Yakovlev said, "We would have to start our own program, which would be tremendously expensive and unnecessary. And this [would bring] the further exhaustion of the country." If Reagan refused to negotiate SDI limits, Gorbachev calculated, it would be clear to everyone that he valued his "dream" over the massive cuts in offensive arms that the Soviet Union could offer. The Soviet leader later conceded that "in advancing that package, we wanted to show to the world that SDI is the main obstacle to an agreement on nuclear disarmament."

While extensive preparations were underway in Moscow, the Americans were given the impression that the discussions would focus primarily on the less fundamental issues of Euromissiles and nuclear testing. "Secrecy was very important in presenting his plans to the Americans," said a Soviet official who accompanied Gorbachev to Reykjavik. "He felt that secrecy was half the battle." When I asked Yakovlev three years later if it had been the intention of the Soviet side to catch Reagan off-balance by presenting him at Reykjavik with much more important choices than expected, he replied simply, "I think it was a surprise for him." Akhromeyev told me, "It was very hard to guess what the results of Reykjavik would be, because the problems that we wanted to discuss there were not discussed beforehand with the American side." Asked why there was no advance notification as is normal in high-level negotiations, Akhromeyev replied, "It's simply that we did not have enough trust between our two sides."

So far as can be determined, there was only one leak suggesting that Gorbachev was planning something much bigger than a preliminary discussion. Just a day or two before the meeting, the State Department received a report from an Indian official that former Ambassador Dobrynin, then one of the senior secretaries of the Communist Party Central Committee, had said that Gorbachev was planning to come to Reykjavik with major new proposals and then trap the United States into refusing to meet him halfway. Arms adviser Paul Nitze, one of the few in Washington who paid any attention to the report, felt this was a positive omen rather than a cause for concern. The more Gorbachev was willing to compromise, the better, Nitze calculated. He was confident that Reagan would stand firm against going further than he intended to go, while simply pocketing Gorbachev's concessions.

In Washington, the preparations for the meeting were much less extensive than preparations had been for the Geneva summit or would be for the summits to come. No agenda was agreed in advance with the Soviet Union, and the two sides did not even exchange lists of who would accompany the leaders. There was precious little time for preparations on the U.S. side. The paragraph containing Gorbachev's invitation to Reagan in the September 15 letter was deleted from the copy that was made available to the U.S. arms control and Soviet affairs bureaucracy; only a few top officials were apprised of it in strictest secrecy before the meeting was announced by the President at the windup of the Zakharov-Daniloff case on September 30. Not until then did the U.S. preparations go into high gear for the October 11–12 meeting. The senior arms control team, headed by Nitze, had just completed extensive meetings with their Soviet counterparts in August and September with no hint of major new Soviet moves to come, and therefore they assumed that there would be little that was new in Soviet positions in Reykjavik. Reagan, Shultz and the top officials of the administration had participated personally in drafting the positions in the July 25 letter to Gorbachev, and expected to rely on that as the mainstay of the U.S. stance.

The "concept paper" drawn up at the State Department and used by the White House staff in preparation for Reykjavik said that the discussions would be "working meetings to prepare for Gorbachev's visit to the United States." The meetings were not expected to produce agreements but to lay the groundwork for subsequent agreements, the paper said. "The Soviets were not coming to Reyjkavik to engage in tough negotiations. That we knew," recalled Kenneth Adelman, director of the Arms Control and Disarmament Agency, who expected from Gorbachev "the usual platitudes, without effect but without harm either." On the eve of his departure, Reagan was complacent, telling Hugh Sidey of *Time* that "I am curious about what brought this flat-out invitation to meet now."

Adelman was present in the main White House planning meeting on the eve of Reykjavik with Reagan and his top advisers when various suggestions for changes in existing U.S. positions were discussed and discarded. In retrospect, the meeting was memorable for two things. One was a statement by Shultz that Gorbachev would be interested in the aspect of the July 25 letter that alluded to a ban on ballistic missiles, and would want to know if the President was really serious about this or if it was merely a bureaucratic ploy. The other was Reagan's eagerness to return to face-to-face discussions with Gorbachev and his confidence that he could work things out with the Soviet leader informally and in private. As he did on a number of occasions, Reagan that day told the story of how, as president of the Screen Actors Guild in Hollywood, he had paved the way for a deal. The negotiating breakthrough came as Reagan engaged his management counterpart in private discussion while standing next to him at urinals during a recess in the talks. "Everyone was delighted with the outcome of this 'urinal diplomacy,' " said Adelman, who was especially struck with Reagan's enthusiasm. "If only he could get into a situation like that at Reykjavik . . . then he and Gorbachev could make a real settlement."

• THE REYKJAVIK SUMMIT

One morning in late September, U.S. Ambassador to Iceland Nicholas Ruwe received an urgent call from the office of the country's prime minister, Steingrimur Hermannsson, asking Ruwe to drop whatever he was doing and come over right away. Hermannsson had just been visited by the Soviet ambassador, Yevgeny Kosarev, who asked that the Icelandic capital of Reykjavik, whose eighty-seven thousand population is about the same as that of Sioux City, Iowa, play host to the leaders of the United States and Soviet Union in a meeting being secretly prepared for mid-October. Hermannsson was amazed and also dubious. Iceland was a member of the NATO alliance and on better terms with Washington than Moscow, but he had heard nothing of this surprising plan from U.S. authorities. Ruwe, a former campaign assistant and personal aide to Richard Nixon, was also taken aback and agreed to check. This did not take long. Immediately after returning to the rented apartments that served as both the modest Embassy and the ambassador's residence, Ruwe learned that the State Department had been trying to reach him frantically on his rarely used secure telephone, which had not been in working order for months. On an open line to Washington, he asked guardedly, "Are a couple of fellows coming my way pretty soon to have a talk?" His superiors back home, who were surprised that he knew, told him that he and the Soviet ambassador were supposed to broach the plan together to the Icelanders. The Soviet ambassador had jumped the gun.

The meeting in Reykjavik was that kind of improvised affair from start to finish. First Lady Nancy Reagan did not come because she had been told it was to be a working meeting, with no social activities, but Raisa Gorbachev was there in a three-quarter-length silver fox coat, attracting extensive coverage from world media while the leaders were closeted in the talks under a porous news blackout. The Icelandic government proposed that the talks be held in the leading hotel but the security chiefs of the two sides settled on Hofdi House, an isolated two-story house with a seaside view, which was more easily protected. They apparently did not know, or perhaps did not care, that Hofdi House was widely reputed to be haunted. The British government had sold the house in 1952 after its ambassador, who resided there at the time, complained of noises in the night, doors that opened by themselves and pictures that kept falling off walls. As late as the 1970s, according to a former British Embassy aide who kept track of the exploits of the house, a picture in the first-floor dining room, where Reagan and Gorbachev met for two days, one day fell off its hook for no apparent reason.

The first session opened on Saturday, October 11, at 10:30 A.M., with just the two leaders and their interpreters around the small dining-room table. Gorbachev announced in the opening minutes that he had proposals to make in every area of the arms relationship. After some general discussion about the state of relations between the two nations, Gorbachev suggested they call in Shultz and Shevardnadze while he presented the initiatives he had brought. When the foreign ministers had taken their seats, Gorbachev opened a file folder at his right hand and began reading and explaining the weighty Soviet proposal, a task that took an hour. Perhaps inspired by the proposed "guidelines" for negotiators that Reagan had presented to him in the summerhouse on the first day of their meeting in Geneva, Gorbachev's proposals were in the form of an elaborate set of "instructions" to be issued by the two leaders to their two chief diplomatic aides as the basis for the forthcoming Washington summit. After reading it, Gorbachev handed over an English translation of the document to Reagan.

DIRECTIVES

To the Foreign Ministers of the USSR and the USA Concerning the Drafting of Agreements on Nuclear Disarmament

Mikhail Gorbachev, General Secretary of the CPSU Central Committee, and US President Ronald Reagan, having considered the situation in the field of nuclear arms and having brought the position of the two countries considerably closer together at their working meeting at Reykjavik, Iceland, agreed to issue directives to their countries' foreign ministers to prepare the texts of accords and agreements to be signed in Washington during the General

Secretary's official visit to the United States on (date of visit), which are to be based on the following key provisions.*

Gorbachev's proposals covered the three main arms negotiating areas—strategic weapons, intermediate-range forces in Europe and space weapons—plus nuclear testing. Included in the paper he handed Reagan or in his explanatory remarks were a number of significant shifts in Soviet policy.

On strategic weapons, Gorbachev agreed to make 50 percent cuts across the board in all categories of strategic arms, and for the first time accepted major cuts in the big Soviet heavy missiles, for which there was no U.S. counterpart. Gorbachev told Reagan the cuts in heavy missiles would be "substantial," and later agreed to 50 percent. Slashing these giant weapons, which posed the most worrisome threat to the United States, had long been one of the most important U.S. objectives. Moreover, Gorbachev told Reagan he would redraw the definition of strategic weapons in a way acceptable to the United States, previously a major sticking point in the negotiations.

On intermediate-range missiles, Gorbachev stated more clearly than before that Moscow had dropped its longstanding demand that British and French weapons be taken into account, and now dropped even his previous demand that these weapons be frozen at their existing levels. Gorbachev also promised later negotiations on the U.S. demand for restrictions on Soviet deployment in Asia.

On the ABM Treaty and space weapons, Gorbachev proposed a mandatory ten-year period of nonwithdrawal from the ABM Treaty. Earlier in the year the Soviets had demanded a fifteen- to twenty-year period, and in September "up to 15 years." Gorbachev was no longer demanding that SDI research be banned, but he insisted it be confined to the laboratory. This eventually became the most contentious issue at Reykjavik.

"He's brought a whole lot of proposals, but I'm afraid he's going after SDI," Reagan told his senior aides when they met in the U.S. Embassy's secure soundproof room, or "bubble," just after the morning meeting. Shultz was surprised at how substantive and sweeping Gorbachev's proposals were, "really coming our way." Paul Nitze was "ex-

* The full texts of Gorbachev's initial proposal and the others exchanged by him and Reagan at Reykjavik are printed in the Appendix.

cited," calling Gorbachev's opening bid the best Soviet proposal he had ever seen. Others were more skeptical of what it meant. As the meeting ended, U.S. aides began redrafting Reagan's presentation for the afternoon session to take account of Gorbachev's sweeping proposals.

When the talks resumed at 2:00 P.M., the foreign ministers rejoined the leaders, as they did for the remaining day and a half of the summit. Reagan and Gorbachev sat facing each other at the ends of the dining-room table, with Shultz and Shevardnadze facing each other on the two sides. Interpreters sat at two corners of the table, with two note-takers sitting slightly behind.

Upstairs on the second floor the remaining officials milled around in two separate suites and a common social room, where some of the most interesting discussions of the summit took place in very informal fashion. Suddenly high-ranking members of the Soviet hierarchy, whom it was almost impossible for Americans to see in Moscow, were accessible for hours at a time for coffee and conversation, with introductions if needed by former Ambassador Anatoly Dobrynin. In one corner Aleksandr Yakovlev reminisced about his student days at Columbia University and described the origins of *perestroika*. On a sofa in another corner, Marshal Sergei Akhromeyev had an ice-breaking discussion for nearly an hour with Admiral John Poindexter, the presidential national security adviser. Even through a Soviet interpreter, it was quickly apparent to Poindexter that Akhromeyev was a straightforward and probably sincere military man, whose words were to be given great weight. "I got the distinct impression from him that they really did want to reduce their forces, but they were genuinely concerned about the United States," Poindexter said later. "I told him in all honesty, we were concerned about them. We didn't see any signs of reductions. They had very large conventional forces and were building elaborate strategic forces. He had to look at it from our point of view, that we had to be very suspicious of what their motives were."

U.S. diplomat Charles Hill, who was executive assistant to Shultz and had dealt with communist governments for years, was struck by a sea-change in Soviet demeanor in the Reykjavik coffee breaks. In the past, it seemed to him, conversations with Soviet diplomats stayed close to the party line. "You knew you were talking to someone who wasn't a real human being. You were talking to a programmed mind of someone doing something for some reason other than what an individual human being would do on his own hook. And suddenly somebody at the top said, 'It's okay to be a human being again.' And their officials from top to bottom changed. Their personalities changed, their approach changed, their scathing wit changed. . . . Suddenly the lid was off and you could be yourself to a certain extent."

Beyond the heavily protected walls of the small house, about two thousand members of the world press were gathered behind barriers or waiting at several press centers that had been set up in the little town. And around the globe, millions of people in every continent turned their ears and eyes to Reykjavik.

Reagan, reading at length from his note cards, began the afternoon meeting by outlining U.S. positions on the arms issues that Gorbachev had raised. The President welcomed some of the proposals, asked for more details on others and expressed objections to still others. Most of the positions Reagan presented were based on his July 25 letter and on U.S. stands recently taken in the Geneva negotiations. An irritated Gorbachev called them "a set of moth-balled proposals that are already choking the Geneva talks."

Though Gorbachev was frustrated at what Reagan had brought, it was agreed at the afternoon session that a group of arms experts would meet that night to try to reconcile the details of the two plans that had been put forward, and that another working group of experts on the non-arms issues would also be convened. Reagan and Gorbachev did not meet that evening. The President was taking pills, Shultz was told, which made his participation in an evening session inadvisable.*

When the U.S. arms control team walked up the steps of Hofdi House at 8:00 P.M., they had no inkling that they were to sit down with Akhromeyev, a Soviet negotiator with more authority and self-confidence than any they had ever met before. Until they arrived in Reykjavik, the Americans did not know Akhromeyev would be present; even then, the betting among the U.S. participants was that he would stay aloof from face-to-face negotiations about specific issues.

A slender man with light blue eyes and a calm, businesslike manner, the Soviet Union's most prestigious active-duty military officer had been a professional since he enlisted in 1940 at age seventeen and was sent to the Soviet military and naval academy at Leningrad. He was a deputy platoon leader at the start of the war, was wounded in the siege of

---

* When I interviewed him in 1990, Reagan said the medication was of no consequence, and may have been pills to combat his occasional allergies.

Leningrad, fought the Germans at Stalingrad and then in the Ukraine. He ended World War II as a major and commander of a tank battalion. After three decades of service in command and staff positions, Akhromeyev was named chief of staff of the Soviet armed forces and first deputy minister of defense by Konstantin Chernenko in September 1984, when Marshal Nikolai Ogarkov was abruptly removed from those positions. Akhromeyev called himself "the last of the Mohicans," being, at age sixty-three, one of the last senior Soviet officers on active duty who had fought in World War II. He used the phrase because, like many Russians of his generation, he had read in translation the James Fenimore Cooper novel of the American Indians as a young man. Akhromeyev had come to admire Gorbachev and support his drive for national reform and, by the time of Reykjavik, was working closely with the new General Secretary. The Soviet marshal told Shultz at a dinner in 1987 that of all the things that had happened in his long career, the desperate defense of Leningrad, when he had almost starved and frozen to death in the trenches, had been, until his work with Gorbachev, "the proudest days of my life." But now, he added, "I can see that I am once again, in a way, fighting for my country."

Across the table from Akhromeyev, as head of the American delegation, was Paul Nitze, whom the Russians referred to respectfully as *starik*, "the old man." Nitze was then seventy-nine years old, with a keen and active mind, and his career in the U.S. government went back to World War II and included authorship in 1950 of NSC-68, the basic blueprint for U.S. policy in the Cold War. Nitze was a member of the U.S. team that had negotiated the SALT I strategic arms treaty and the ABM Treaty with Moscow in the early 1970s, and he had won fame for his daring though unsuccessful attempt to work out a deal on intermediate-range missiles in 1982 in a "walk in the woods" in Geneva with his Soviet counterpart, Yuli Kvitsinsky.

Others on the U.S. side of the working-group negotiations at Reykjavik included Max Kampelman, Edward Rowny, Kenneth Adelman, Richard Perle, Robert Linhart and James Timbie, all arms negotiators or experts. The Soviet side included Viktor Karpov, a longtime arms negotiator and deputy foreign minister; Yevgeni Velikhov, a physicist and Gorbachev adviser; and Georgi Arbatov and Valentin Falin, whom the Americans considered propagandists rather than arms experts despite their high positions.

There was no doubt from the first who was in charge of the Soviet team. Akhromeyev introduced himself to the Americans with the disclaimer that he was "no diplomat" and "no negotiator" but a career military man. "So let's not repeat all the familiar arguments. Let's see how much progress we can make tonight." When Karpov launched into a standard recitation of Soviet views, Akhromeyev placed his hand on his colleague's arm and halted him without embarrassment. To the surprise of the U.S. team, Akhromeyev seemed able to make some important decisions on the spot. "If you can persuade him," said Shultz adviser James Timbie, recalling that night, "that's it. He just says, 'Da.' He doesn't say he has to go back and check with his minister or 'We'll take it home and think about it.' He's incredibly sure of himself."

The teams worked all night until 6:30 A.M. with a break for consultations with superiors from 1:45 A.M. to 3:00 A.M. After the break, Akhromeyev abruptly shifted some elements of the Soviet approach on strategic arms cuts to meet U.S. objections. With the Soviet marshal in the lead on his side of the table, the two teams made more progress in one night toward a strategic arms treaty than U.S. and Soviet negotiators in Geneva had made in years.

Less progress was made on the Euromissiles. The key breakthrough on that subject came Sunday morning, when Gorbachev and Reagan agreed to eliminate all intermediate-range missiles in Europe—the President's famous "zero option"—and to limit Soviet INF forces in Asia to one hundred warheads, with the United States having the right to deploy an equal number on U.S. territory. Gorbachev, who seemed to doubt that Reagan would actually agree to eliminate all INF missiles in Europe, took Reagan's assent to this as an important sign of the President's seriousness. At this point the U.S. team was so confident of a Euromissiles agreement that Assistant Secretary of State Ridgway began hastily informing Britain, Belgium, Italy, the Netherlands and West Germany, the Western European countries where the U.S. INF missiles were based, in most cases over very heavy political opposition, that a U.S.-Soviet deal was being reached to eliminate them from their countries.

Sunday morning, Reagan was euphoric at what was happening, taking the view that "literally a miracle was taking place, that they were expressing agreement on all these various things and there was a complete in-depth discussion of every aspect." But then, using a term from his sports announcer days in radio, he said that Gorbachev "threw the curve." The General Secretary emphasized, even more than on the previous day, that no cutbacks on offensive arms could proceed without agreement on the stalemated issue of defensive weapons, namely SDI. It was all a package, because the Soviet Union would not reduce its offensive weapons under the shadow of a major new defensive weapon, Gorbachev insisted. Therefore to obtain the strategic and intermediate-range cuts, Reagan would have to compromise on SDI. By this stage, the discussions had gone far beyond the original idea of a "directive" to the foreign ministers; both leaders were negotiating for an actual deal.

Reagan proposed that the two teams work out language to describe their progress on strategic and intermediate-range forces in the past two days and turn over the disagreements on space issues to the negotiators at Geneva. Gorbachev was having none of it. He knew the Geneva negotiators would have no authority to compromise. At one point he muttered, "*Kasha* forever," meaning, "We could be eating this porridge forever."

The deadlock deepened as Gorbachev rejected Reagan's effort to put aside the space issue. "No, let's go home. We've accomplished nothing," Gorbachev said, as if to terminate the summit. It had been scheduled to end at noon on October 12, and by now it was close to 1:30 P.M. At the last minute, both sides agreed to recess over lunch and try again for agreement on space weapons in the afternoon. In the meantime Shultz and Shevardnadze, who had a better track record of forging agreements than their bosses, were to try to resolve the differences.

As the leaders and their motorcades left for lunch, Shultz summoned five senior members of the U.S. team to remain behind: Nitze, National Security Adviser Poindexter, Arms Negotiator Kampelman, NSC Arms Control Chief Linhard and Assistant Secretary of Defense Perle. "We're at a very serious impasse," said the secretary, explaining that the two sides were at loggerheads on SDI.

Before the discussion could get very far, Shevardnadze and several aides arrived. The two teams sat down at a conference table facing each other, and Shultz began to speak of some of the smaller issues left over from the night before.

Shevardnadze cut him off cold. "There's one issue before us—whether or not the President is prepared to agree on a period of time, 10 years, when there will be no withdrawal from the ABM Treaty and strict adherence to its terms." If this could be agreed, Shevardnadze said, other issues can be solved. But if not, "there'll be no agreement on anything." Gorbachev feels this "very strongly," the foreign minister insisted. Turning to Kampelman, he said imploringly, "You are a creative person—can't you think of something?" Then to Nitze: "You are so experienced, can't you come up with something?"

Sitting at one end of the table was Air Force Colonel Robert Linhard. A scholarly and imaginative officer, he had been on the National Security Council staff since 1981 and its chief arms control expert since January 1986. At the time of Reykjavik he was a few months short of forty years old. Now, consulting with Richard Perle, who was sitting next to him, Linhard began formulating a possible solution to the problem. As Linhard saw it, there were a number of "tools" at hand. He believed from his knowledge of internal discussions that Reagan was ready as a compromise to accept Gorbachev's demand for a ten-year period of nonwithdrawal from the ABM Treaty. The two sides had agreed in principle in the Akhromeyev-Nitze bargaining the night before on 50 percent cuts in strategic nuclear arms, including missiles and bombers, over five years. That left the question of what would take place in the second five years of the ten-year nonwithdrawal period that seemed to be shaping up. As Linhard saw it, the second five years could be the time to apply the Zero Ballistic Missiles idea, which had been offered in vague form in the July 25 letter with the assent of the U.S. military. With Perle assisting him, Linhard began writing in a firm, clear hand on a yellow legal pad. After a minute or two, they passed their handiwork to Poindexter, who read it with astonishment.

The national security adviser was surprised by the proposal, because he knew something the others at the table, except for Shultz, were not aware of. Over dinner with the President, Shultz and White House Chief of Staff Donald Regan the previous evening at the U.S. ambassador's residence in Reykjavik, Poindexter had suggested that it was time to consider resurrecting Weinberger's Zero Ballistic Missiles proposal and putting it on the table in Reykjavik. Unless the United States could suggest something dramatic, Poindexter argued, it could be placed in the very difficult position of having been offered large-scale Soviet concessions and having no response other than to reject them due to the SDI conditions. While no formal decision was taken, it was clear to Poindexter after the dinner discussion that, if a dramatic U.S. proposal was needed, Reagan was "on board" the Zero Ballistic Missiles idea. Now, as Shultz and his team sat across the table from Shevardnadze, Poindexter had leaned over to the secretary of state, who was sitting next to him, and whispered that "we ought to consider what we talked about last night," namely the proposal to eliminate ballistic missiles. Then, without prompting from him, Linhard had composed a version of the same idea and passed it up the table on the page of lined paper. Poindexter heartily approved, and he passed it along to Shultz. The secretary paused, read it carefully and, in a whispered conversation, gave it to Nitze and Kampelman for their opinion. Nobody objected.

"You've seen some writing at this end of the table," Shultz announced to the Soviet team, which was watching this maneuvering. "This is an effort by some of us here to see if we can't break the impasse." Shultz went on to say he did not have permission from Reagan to present the idea they were working on, "and when he hears of this, he may hit my head against the wall," but he was prepared to discuss it with the understanding it was not an official U.S. proposal.

Shultz then read the scrap of paper:

Both sides would agree to confine itself to research, development and testing which is permitted by the ABM Treaty, for a period of 5 years, through 1991, during which time a 50% reduction of strategic nuclear arsenals would be achieved. This being done, both sides will continue the pace of reductions with respect to the remaining ballistic missiles, with the goal of the total elimination of all offensive ballistic missiles by the end of the second 5-year period. As long as these reductions continue at the appropriate pace, the same restrictions will continue to apply. At the end of the 10-year period, with all offensive ballistic missiles eliminated, either side would be free to deploy defenses.

While all the elements had been considered before, this proposal marked a profound change in the handling of the Zero Ballistic Missiles idea. No longer was this a concept to be the subject of a murky "plan" to be submitted after five years, as in the July 25 letter Reagan had sent to Gorbachev. As written at the conference table at Reykjavik, it was now a real proposal with a timetable and a deadline. If agreed, it committed the United States and the Soviet Union to eliminate their entire inventories of ballistic missiles, their most powerful weapons, within ten years. In the U.S. case, this would mean scrapping about 1,650 missiles capable of carrying 7,800 nuclear warheads, roughly three-fourths of them aboard missile-firing submarines and the rest on land-based missiles. For the Soviet Union, it would mean scrapping about 2,300 missiles capable of carrying 9,200 warheads, by U.S. figures, roughly two-thirds of them land-based and the rest on missile-firing submarines. While the two sides had agreed on Saturday night to reduce their forces to 6,000 strategic missile warheads on each side over five years, including those on air-launched cruise missiles, this new plan would go much further, down to zero for ballistic missiles. It was vastly more ambitious.

Shevardnadze discussed the U.S. idea in Russian with several aides on his side of the table. He expressed doubt that Gorbachev would accept it, especially because of the last sentence permitting either side to deploy space-based strategic defenses after ten years. But he said it was worth considering.

As the U.S. team was filing out of the conference room, Reagan arrived back at Hofdi House to prepare for the afternoon meeting. The President and his aides moved upstairs, where Shultz and Poindexter presented him with the proposal they had just presented on a conditional basis to Shevardnadze.

Reagan asked Shultz if he understood correctly that within ten years all the Soviet SS-18 "heavy missiles" as well as other Soviet land-based and sea-based missiles would have to be eliminated. He was told that was correct.

In that case, the nature of the threat to the United States would have changed, Reagan observed, which suggested a reason for extension of the ABM Treaty nonwithdrawal clause to ten years. The President seemed pleased, saying the proposal struck him as imaginative. "He gets his precious ABM Treaty, and we get all his ballistic missiles. And after that we can deploy SDI in space. Then it's a whole new ball game."

Reagan, ordinarily the last person to bring up operational questions, paused to ask if elimination of all ballistic missiles over ten years would be practical. Turning to Perle, the Pentagon's renowned skeptic about arms control, Reagan wondered if the United States could eliminate its ballistic missiles that fast. "I think we can," responded Perle, adding that another two years or so might make the operation easier. He also noted that other weapons in the works, which would not be covered by this drastic cutback, could protect U.S. security, referring to cruise missiles and the new defense-penetrating Stealth bomber. Under further questioning by Reagan, Perle said he supported the plan.

The President then turned to Lieutenant General John Moellering, the Joint Chiefs of Staff representative at Reykjavik, and asked if the uniformed chiefs would support the proposal. Moellering, who had not taken part in the lunchtime meeting and had no instructions from the chiefs, was noncommittal.

At the end of the conversation of less than thirty minutes with his aides, Reagan seemed intrigued with what he later called "the most sweeping and important arms reduction proposal in the history of the world," which had been born on a yellow pad that afternoon at Hofdi House. He did not say, however, whether he was going to submit it formally because at this point Gorbachev arrived.

As tension continued to mount, and the international press waited expectantly outside, the afternoon session finally began at 3:25 P.M. Reagan was carrying the new U.S. proposal on the same piece of paper on which it had been handwritten earlier. The President sent it out to be typed so it could be handed over to Gorbachev officially.

The Soviet leader, however, had been briefed on the U.S. plan by Shevardnadze and had drafted a counterproposal that made three crucial changes in the U.S. plan: First, Gorbachev tightened the restrictions on SDI that would be imposed under the ABM Treaty, specifically confining it to the laboratory as in his Saturday morning proposal. Then, he wanted to eliminate all strategic nuclear arms, including cruise missiles and manned bombers, rather than just ballistic missiles, in the second five-year period. Finally, he said that after the ten-year nonwithdrawal period from the ABM Treaty was over, the two sides should make "mutually acceptable decisions" about what to do regarding space defenses. This implied a Soviet right of veto.

Reagan responded, "We obviously have a different interpretation of the ABM Treaty and we have for a long time. Let's just say we will take this up again in Washington when you come to Washington for the summit."

"No, then there will be no package," Gorbachev said bluntly.

As the deadlock deepened, Shultz jumped in to suggest that the two sides try to work something out. "Let's make sure what the differences are."

At 4:30 P.M. the leaders recessed for an hour once more to seek to bridge the gap. By this time the careful preparations in Moscow and the casual preparations in Washington had all been left far behind; the bargaining between Reagan and Gorbachev had taken flight into a stratospheric realm.

In a side room, Reagan and his aides decided to redraft their yellow-pad proposal using some of Gorbachev's wording but keeping the key U.S. concepts. Linhard and Perle, who were sent off to do the redrafting, could find no unoccupied room in Hofdi House, so they put a board over a bathtub and worked out the new text on this makeshift desk.

Gorbachev, accompanied by Shevardnadze, came out of the meeting with Reagan very excited. Conferring with Akhromeyev and Bessmertnykh, the Soviet leader could not stay still. He sat down, leaped up, went to a window, sat down again and moved around some more. "Everything could be decided right now," he said.

Like the coaches in a prize fight between rounds, members of the U.S. team sought to prepare their standard-bearer for the final battle. According to Kenneth Adelman, who was in the meeting, "We tried to explain to the President and those around him, the differences on the offensive side between scrapping all ballistic missiles (as we proposed) and all strategic arms (as they wished)" in the final five years. The Soviets were much more dependent on ballistic missiles, since they did not have as many nuclear-armed manned bombers or subballistic cruise missile drones, which would not be included in this category. But if all nuclear weapons were eliminated, the Soviet Union would be left with a much larger conventional army, and no nuclear counterweight in the U.S. arsenals. However, Reagan often used the terms "nuclear missiles" and "nuclear weapons" interchangeably in private as well as in public, and never seemed to fully appreciate the important difference between them. The crucial thing to him was that they were all nuclear.

Just before the final session started, Chief of Staff Regan suggested it might be necessary to stay in Reykjavik for another night. Reagan grimaced. "No, we just can't do that," he said wearily. Some of those present thought he was tired of Gorbachev, and was thinking of a late dinner in Washington with Nancy. Then he added, in the understatement of the day, "Hell. He doesn't want to set up a summit. He wants to have a summit. Right here."

Reagan and Gorbachev, Shultz and Shevardnadze, returned to the meeting room. Everyone was battered and weary, but the pressure was tremendous. By now it was 5:30 P.M. on the second day of a meeting that had been scheduled to end at noon, and the world was waiting impatiently.

"Look, here's what we're prepared to do," said Reagan, and read the text of the cosmetically redrafted U.S. proposal.

Gorbachev immediately noticed that his requirement for the "laboratory testing" limit under the ABM Treaty was not included, and wanted to know if it had been omitted on purpose.

Yes it had been, Reagan responded.

Gorbachev then returned to what he had described as a discrepancy in the U.S. proposal. In the first five years, 50 percent of all "strategic offensive arms" would be eliminated, but in the second five years only "offensive ballistic missiles." Why this difference?

"I thought you were interested in missiles," Reagan responded.

"No, we're interested in weapons," said Gorbachev. Mindful of the U.S. advantage in manned bombers, he wanted to know where they would be reduced under the Reagan proposal.

"We've proposed reducing all ballistic missiles on land and sea," said Reagan. But he added he was ready to include all the nuclear weapons that he could.

"We ought to reduce the whole triad,"* Gorbachev proposed.

"If you're going to do that, you'd better take out the word, strategic. That way we would also be eliminating all ballistic missiles," Reagan replied.

Shultz interjected, "We have to be careful, when it comes to eliminating all strategic offensive arms, that we look out for the short-range ballistic missiles because they're being dealt with in another place. In fact, maybe here is the place to deal with it decisively."

Gorbachev agreed. "We could deal with them. We could say here that we are going to freeze them, [referring to the battlefield nuclear weapons so contentious in Europe] and then start talks about how to destroy them."

Several times Gorbachev returned to the question of the difference between the two five-year periods, the first during which all strategic weapons of any type would be cut 50 percent, and the second during which only offensive ballistic missiles would be eliminated, leaving bombers and cruise missiles.

"I don't think there has to be this contradistinction," said Gorbachev, referring to the enormous practical differences in the two radical cutback plans. "Maybe we can sort this out."

"Yes, we can sort it out," said the President helpfully.

Finally Reagan said across the small dining-room table to the Soviet leader, "It would be fine with me if we eliminated all nuclear weapons."

Gorbachev responded, "We can do that. Let's eliminate them. We can eliminate them."

---

* The three-part strategic nuclear arsenal of land-based ballistic missiles, submarine-based ballistic missiles and heavy bombers.

Reagan repeated that he really thought Gorbachev was mainly interested in ballistic missiles, but added that if all nuclear weapons were to be eliminated, "We can turn it all over to the Geneva people and they can draft the agreement and you could come to the United States and sign it."

Shultz, who was looking on, said nothing. Later other officials blamed him for not stepping in to stop Reagan from offering to give up the U.S. nuclear arsenal as the bargaining took flight. Looking back, Shultz said, "I really felt that he's the President. He got elected twice. He has made no secret of his view on nuclear weapons. So who am I to stop him from saying what he believes and what he's campaigned on?"

As for the Zero Ballistic Missiles proposal, in retrospect Shultz has said he faults himself for permitting it to be brought up in the form it was at Reykjavik. Though Shultz personally was convinced that elimination of ballistic missiles would be to U.S. advantage and create a safer world, he came to believe it was "too big a step," proposed too quickly, for the European allies and the rest of the world to accept. Reagan, though, had no second thoughts. When I asked him in 1990 what he thought would have happened if he and Gorbachev had emerged from Hofdi House announcing an agreement to give up all their nuclear weapons or even all their ballistic missiles, Reagan replied with a characteristic shake of his head, "I thought the world would have greeted it with great joy."

As it happened, the conversation between Reagan and Gorbachev on the last afternoon at Reykjavik took a different turn. After the common rhetorical resolve to eliminate all nuclear weapons, Gorbachev returned to the ABM Treaty and his demand that research, development and testing be confined to the laboratory. "The Soviet side is for strict observance of the treaty and only laboratory testing. I cannot do without the word, laboratory," he told Reagan.

"I have promised the American people I will not give up SDI," declared Reagan, referring to the dream he had conceived and nurtured since early 1983. "You're asking me to give up SDI." The President continued, "In the agreement we're looking at, you have 10 years [nonwithdrawal from the ABM Treaty]. We have an agreement we can be very proud of," and now he was asking Gorbachev for "just this one thing."

"It's not a trivial thing—it is everything," responded Gorbachev. Suggesting that he had political constraints too, Gorbachev said, "I cannot carry back to Moscow an agreement that gives up this limitation of research and testing to the laboratory."

Reagan promised again, as he had in Geneva, to "share the benefits" of SDI. "I have made a personal commitment. We will have a treaty which involves sharing. What more can you ask?"

Gorbachev ridiculed the idea, as he had in Geneva. The United States would not even share milking machines for cows with the Soviet Union—so why would it share the secrets of its antimissile defense?

"We have the chance for developing the greatest relationship that any U.S. and Soviet leader have ever had," said Reagan. "We have a good personal relationship. It's just one thing."

Gorbachev reiterated that from his standpoint, SDI-related work could only be done in laboratories. "If you agree, we could write that down and sign it now."

Reagan said he would not destroy the possibility of proceeding with SDI. He could not confine work to the laboratory.

"Do I understand this is your final position—you will not confine work to the laboratory?" Gorbachev asked.

"Yes," replied Reagan. He would stay within the limits of the treaty, but there is disagreement about what the treaty proscribes. "I cannot give in."

"Is this your last word?" demanded Gorbachev.

"Yes," responded Reagan.

The agreement must include strict observance of the ABM Treaty and confinement of research and testing to the laboratory, Gorbachev reiterated. "If this is not possible, then we can say good-bye and forget everything we have discussed."

They went back and forth on the same points. Gorbachev, in frustration, said, "You're using one word to frustrate a meeting that had promised to be historic."

The Soviet leader said once more that he was being asked to permit the United States to develop a space-based system that could destroy his country's nuclear weapons potential, at a time when the two sides were proceeding to deep reductions and elimination of nuclear weapons. The President would not like it if the Soviet Union had asked that of him. It was not an acceptable request. It could not be met.

Reagan said that if Gorbachev believed the United States wanted some military advantage, he should not worry.

"I can't do it," said Gorbachev.

By now it was nearly 7:00 P.M. For nearly an hour, the leaders of the two greatest military powers had been facing each other across the table, locked in dispute in the most intense and urgent way over an issue of central importance to both of them. The dispute over SDI had narrowed down to a single concept, even a single word—"laboratory." They had tried appeals to logic, to political imperatives and personal consideration. In the end there seemed no way out.

Finally Gorbachev said gravely that he would like to move everywhere he could, and that he had tried to do so. He said his conscience was clear before the President and his people. What had depended on him, he had done.

The words hung in the air.

Reagan closed his briefing book and stood up. Gorbachev stood. Both leaders gathered up their papers and left the room.

As they stood together before parting, Gorbachev asked the President to pass on his regards to Nancy Reagan. To a U.S. aide who was listening, it seemed that Gorbachev once more was trying in a small way to close the gap between himself and an angry Ronald Reagan.

As they proceeded to their cars, the irate look on Reagan's face conveyed his emotions.

"I don't know what else I could have done," said Gorbachev.

"I do. You could have said yes," the President replied.

• THE AFTERMATH OF REYKJAVIK

As they left Hofdi House for the last time, the U.S. and Soviet leaders were both visibly angry after having soared so far toward historic agreements and a common vision of a demilitarized future, only to plummet to earth in the final hour.

Gorbachev and Shevardnadze got into their limousine, and for a long time they sat as if in a daze without saying a word, each lost in his own thoughts. They were driven to the Soviet cruise ship anchored at the Reykjavik dock that was being used as a floating hotel and headquarters, and had a few minutes to gather their thoughts. Gorbachev was still "boiling, very angry," when he arrived at the ship, a Soviet participant said. On the way to the theater where Gorbachev was to give a news conference, Shevardnadze, who had left the meeting shaken and depressed, guessed that Gorbachev would tell the world press what had happened, and draw the lesson that "one can't deal with that U.S. administration." The theater that had been taken over for the press conference was jammed with journalists, most of them looking grave.

Gorbachev spoke in detail of the Soviet positions that had been offered and of the failure to reach agreement due to SDI. But in the end, Gorbachev declared, "The United States remains a reality, and the Soviet Union remains a reality. . . . I think that the U.S. President and I should reflect on the entire situation that ultimately evolved here at the meeting, and make another attempt to step over the things that divide us." He said the Soviet Union "will be waiting, without withdrawing the proposals that we have made public."

As he left the press conference hall, Gorbachev told Shevardnadze that he had decided what tack to take only as he searched the faces of the pale and worried people before him: "I looked at the audience and this is what I decided: That I have to talk constructive, be constructive." Shevardnadze thought the change in Gorbachev's mood was surprising and striking. Later analysis reaffirmed the generally positive Soviet view of the outcome.

Reagan, Shultz and the American team went from Hofdi House to the U.S. ambassador's residence. Reagan, who was very tired from the long and tense day, headed to his room to rest. On the way he encountered Richard Perle coming up the stairs of the residential apartment. "We sure tried," said Reagan, shaking his head with disappointment. Perle suddenly felt disappointed, too, although until that moment he had felt the summit had turned out well.

Gathered around the dining-room table in the residence, Shultz briefed the others on the final meeting. Gorbachev wanted to gut SDI, he said; Reagan wouldn't give in. Shultz praised Reagan in emotional terms, saying he had never been prouder to work for this President. At that point someone reported that Gorbachev was about to give a news conference on the summit results, and Shultz hurriedly left for the press center to get the U.S. story out.

Shultz's words at the news conference were balanced between "extremely important potential achievements" and a "deeply disappointed" U.S. President, but his appearance told a less complex, and to most journalists, more honest story. "No one who attended the summit, or watched the secretary's televised news conference at its end, is likely ever to forget the sense almost of grief etched across Shultz's usually expressionless face," wrote David Ottaway of *The Washington Post*. But by the end of the day, the administration had decided that Reykjavik was a great success. "No, it's not a bust. We got very far. It's like going 99 yards and not scoring on the last yard," Chief of Staff Donald Regan told reporters as he boarded Air Force One for Washington. Over the coming days, Reagan, Shultz and just about every official who was present at Reykjavik went into a high-gear public relations effort to blunt the accusation that Reagan's obsession with his Star Wars plan had sunk the summit. Charges and countercharges were hurled between Washington and Moscow, and between the administration and its critics at home, over what had been said and done at Reykjavik. The European allies were furious that Reagan had been willing to negotiate radical arms cutbacks with Gorbachev without any consultation and, apparently, with little consideration of their security.

Two weeks after Reykjavik, on October 27, Reagan and his senior foreign policy and defense team met in the White House Situation Room to discuss new instructions to the U.S. negotiating team at Geneva. Around the table, there seemed to be general satisfaction with what had happened at Reykjavik until Arms Control Director Kenneth Adelman proposed that the Zero Ballistic Missiles proposal be withdrawn from the U.S. negotiating position as neither feasible nor wise. After some discussion, Admiral Crowe spoke up, reading slowly and deliberately in his Oklahoma drawl from a paper he had drawn up for the occasion. Crowe and the other members of the Joint Chiefs of Staff had been stewing about Reagan's offer to eliminate all ballistic missiles within ten years, which they had never had a chance to study in advance of its presentation and which they considered totally unsatisfactory. With great trepidation, the JCS chairman had informed Secretary Weinberger in advance that he would vigorously oppose the President's proposal at the meeting. Crowe thought it might well be his last day in the job.

Speaking for the uniformed chiefs, who had been represented by a staff officer in Reykjavik while Akhromeyev, the Soviet armed forces chief of staff, was playing a key role, Crowe wanted to remind the President of the value of the strategic triad of land-based ballistic missiles, submarine-based ballistic missiles and manned bombers, all carrying nuclear weapons. The chiefs were having a difficult time keeping the triad modern and effective, and believed it would be extremely costly, and probably impractical, to replace it with lesser weaponry. "Mr. President," Crowe said in the summary of his presentation, "we have concluded that the proposal to eliminate all ballistic missiles within 10 years time would pose high risks to the security of the nation." On hearing this extraordinary pronouncement from the chairman of the Joint Chiefs of Staff, Reagan changed the subject, and told the admiral how much he liked the military. "It was the most incredible thing in my life," said Crowe later.

At the same meeting, Shultz rebutted criticism of the Zero Ballistic Missiles proposal by saying that the American people would gladly pay whatever it took to maintain a valid conventional deterrent if nuclear weapons could be eliminated. Shultz estimated that such a nonnuclear defense could be obtained for $400 billion to $450 billion per year, a giant jump of up to 50 percent above the existing military budget of just under $300 billion. Shultz meant to be encouraging, but some of the officials in the room found his ideas appalling. The administration was in no position to advocate a massive boost in the military budget in the name of arms reduction, and in the face of an already enormous budgetary deficit and a President adamantly opposed to tax increases.

In Moscow, Gorbachev, after returning empty-handed from his second face-to-face meeting with Reagan, encountered political problems in the Soviet capital. Letters began turning up in *Pravda* and other newspapers questioning Gorbachev's negotiations with the Americans, especially after Washington expelled fifty-five Soviet diplomats as part of a tit-for-tat series of expulsions by the two sides. Gorbachev on October 22 felt it necessary to go on Soviet television for the third time since the summit to defend his actions, which suggested to American experts that despite his great self-confidence, the Soviet leader was still having political problems at home.

Shultz and Shevardnadze met in Vienna November 5–6 in what was probably the most unsatisfactory set of meetings they ever held. Shultz brought his full array of senior U.S. arms advisers, hoping to advance the strategic and INF positions that had been worked out at Reykjavik. Shevardnadze brought only Viktor Karpov as an arms expert, and Karpov got into a shouting match with Nitze over what had been decided in the all-night working group at Reykjavik, to the point that Nitze called Karpov "a liar." Shevardnadze compared Washington's post-Reykjavik positions to a "political theater of the absurd," and the two sides seemed at a complete standoff.

For all the backbiting and backsliding, something fundamental had changed in the Soviet perception of Reagan. "Some initial feelings came that it's possible to talk with him, possible to convince him of something," said Gorbachev's close adviser, Aleksandr Yakovlev, who accompanied him to the Icelandic capital. "In Reykjavik I first saw [Reagan's] human hesitation about what decision to make, and it seemed to me he wasn't acting. I saw his internal hesitation, his batting back and forth in his mind what to do. On the one hand, as it seemed to me, he was interested in the idea of universal nuclear disarmament, on the other hand sticking to the idea of such a funny toy as SDI. . . . In this man I saw that his professional ability to put on an act somehow wavered. He could be seen from a different angle as a human being and as a politician."

As Marshal Akhromeyev saw it, Reykjavik was a major event eclipsing all the discussions that had gone before. It would have been hard to imagine in the past that the United States would propose to eliminate all ballistic missiles on land and sea within ten years, and the Soviet Union propose to get rid of all strategic offensive arms. "You can understand that this is not simply a group of people or a newspaper proposing such an initiative. I am an eyewitness to the fact that all these proposals were made in all seriousness. This was a great moral breakthrough in our relations, when the sides were able to look far into the future. But in the end they did not reach a common solution and went their own ways," Akhromeyev said.

Three weeks after the Reykjavik meeting, the Republican party lost control of the Senate in the U.S. congressional elections, changing the Washington political environment for Reagan's final two years. Neither U.S.-Soviet relations nor Reykjavik was a significant factor in the campaign. On the day of the election, an Iranian-backed magazine in Beirut revealed that the White House had been trading arms for U.S. hostages in secret bargaining in Tehran. That revelation and the ones that followed led to sweeping changes in White House personnel. Admiral Poindexter resigned under fire as the presidential national security adviser, and was succeeded by former Deputy Defense Secretary and Deputy CIA Director Frank Carlucci, a more politically experienced official who was ready to deal with the Soviet Union on the basis of pragmatism and mutual interest and who did not share Reagan's interest in radical shifts in nuclear weaponry. The Reykjavik proposals for elimination of all ballistic missiles or all nuclear weapons were quietly abandoned. But the bargaining on the strategic and intermediate-range weapons issues discussed at Reykjavik continued on a more serious basis than ever before.

6. To the Washington Summit

On New Year's Day 1987, President Reagan and General Secretary Gorbachev did not exchange televised greetings to each other's nation as they had the year before in the afterglow of the Geneva summit. Late in December, the Soviet Foreign Ministry had rejected Reagan's offer, declaring that "we have no basis for an exchange of New Year's messages." In light of the disputes about what had been said and done at Reykjavik and other differences between Moscow and Washington, said spokesman Gennadi Gerasimov, "Why should we create any illusions about our relations?"

The events of 1985 and 1986 had broken the ice and improved the atmosphere between the United States and the Soviet Union, without producing tangible agreements. The discussions at Reykjavik, however, had made impressive strides in the direction of a historic deal to reduce nuclear arsenals before the bargaining broke down over the SDI issue. In the spring of 1987, the momentum toward offensive arms accords would resume, especially the drive for a U.S.-Soviet treaty to eliminate their intermediate-range nuclear forces in Europe and elsewhere. After lengthy and complex negotiations, Gorbachev would come to Washington in December to sign the INF Treaty with Reagan in the East Room of the White House, providing tangible proof that the two powers could accomplish things of great importance working together. At

*the same time, the Soviet Union was preparing for a memorable
step of its own that would have a powerful effect on East-West
relations: the withdrawal of its military forces from Afghanistan.*

• MARKING TIME

The early months of 1987 were difficult ones both in Washington and
in Moscow.

Since the 1986 election day revelation of U.S. arms dealings with
Iran and especially since November 25, when the diversion of Iran arms
profits to the Nicaraguan Contra rebels was revealed, the Reagan administration had been battered day after day by new disclosures of double-
dealing or incompetence. The public reservoir of goodwill toward Reagan, which had been so high throughout the first six years, was being
drained rapidly. As in the case of the Watergate scandal more than a
decade earlier, the Iran-Contra scandal, as it came to be known, gripped
political Washington like a fever.

Some of the internal disarray since November had resembled a shoot-
out between warring potentates inside the administration. Secretary
Shultz, who objected strenuously to a false statement about arms sales
being prepared for submission to Congress, had put his job on the line
in a tense showdown over the matter with Reagan. CIA Director William
Casey, who was on the other side of the argument, asked the President
to fire Shultz. National Security Adviser John Poindexter was forced to
resign and was replaced by Frank Carlucci. Colonel Oliver North, the
Iran-Contra operator in the NSC, was fired. Casey had a brain seizure,
resigned and died a few months later of brain cancer. White House
Chief of Staff Donald Regan was forced to resign and was replaced by
former Senate Republican Leader Howard Baker.

Shultz and Weinberger, both of whom remained in place, had opposed the arms sales to Iran, but their agreement on the Iran issue did
nothing to mute their other differences. At a National Security Council
meeting on February 3, after priming Reagan with glowing reports on
the research progress of SDI, Weinberger asked for immediate presidential approval to start deployment of some elements of the antimissile
system, which previously had been considered a decade or so away.
Shultz and Joint Chiefs of Staff Chairman Admiral William Crowe, know-

ing that such a move would have dire consequences for relations with Moscow, objected that such a decision was neither necessary nor wise. The minutes of the secret meeting were leaked to an SDI enthusiast and appeared within forty-eight hours in *The Washington Times*, including a remark from Reagan that the United States should not dither about whether a deployment decision would be in compliance with the ABM Treaty as the Kremlin interpreted it. "Don't ask the Soviets—tell them," the President was quoted as saying. The news of what was afoot touched off an uproar in Congress and strong objections from the allies. Weinberger's proposal was shelved.

In Moscow, this was a time of disillusion and frustration. Gorbachev had been in power nearly two years, and the expectations he had raised were not being met. Since the previous summer, Gorbachev had turned sharply critical of the Communist Party bureaucracy, being convinced that the political power centers of the existing system were standing in the way of essential economic and social reform. But Gorbachev was having a difficult time convincing the Communist Party leadership and bureaucracy even to consider diluting their entrenched power and prerogatives. Starting the previous July, Gorbachev had made known his intention to hold a plenary meeting of the Central Committee to deal with political reform within the party. It was planned and postponed three times in the fall and winter, and finally scheduled for late January. As the meeting approached, Gorbachev summoned nearly all the three hundred members of the Central Committee, one by one, to his dacha outside Moscow in an extraordinary and intense personal lobbying campaign for political reforms. Gorbachev was quoted later as threatening to resign if the party plenum rejected his plans to move ahead.

In mid-1986, Gorbachev had told a group of Moscow writers that "Soviet society is ripe for change." In fact, change in many aspects of society had been taking place at a dramatic pace for decades. By 1987, the beginning of Gorbachev's third year as General Secretary, the Soviet Union was in some respects a fundamentally different nation—or group of nations—than it had been before the Great Patriotic War, as World War II was known there. In 1939, the vast country spanning eleven time zones from Western Europe to the Sea of Japan was two-thirds rural and a country of barely literate peasants ruled by an urban political class that had participated in the 1917 Bolshevik revolution. On the eve of the war, only 10 percent of the people of school age or older had had an eighth-grade education. By 1987, the population of the USSR was two-thirds urban, about the same as other advanced Western nations, and 71 percent of those school age or older had an eighth-grade education. Many had high-school or even university degrees. Even though the quality of the educational experience was poor in many cases, the exposure to the tools of modern life contributed to a growing independence of thought and an erosion of blind faith in the authorities, which made Gorbachev's rhetoric and promises of reform intensely popular while hope for fundamental change was high. No longer were the horizons of Soviet citizens limited to their home villages or provincial cities. By 1987, the country's 281 million citizens had access to 87 million television sets across the country, along with 83 million radios. Even though the broadcasts and the newspapers were under the control of the party and the state, an increasingly sophisticated populace had learned to read between the lines about politically sensitive subjects. And with the beginning of Gorbachev's policy of *glasnost* in the mid-1980s, the people were exposed for the first time to much more realistic news about their country's condition, news that admitted and even dramatized troubles and failures of Soviet society that they knew only too well from personal experience.

Since World War II, the Soviet Union had been building and maintaining powerful military forces. By the 1970s it had achieved strategic parity in nuclear weapons with the United States and an impressive global reach, but at an unprecedentedly high economic cost. Currently, the consensus of Soviet economists is that nearly 25 percent of the Soviet Union's goods and services (GNP) has been devoted to the military in recent decades, far greater than even the highest official estimates in the West. By contrast, about 3 percent of GNP has been devoted to health, which a noted Soviet economist, Abel Aganegyan, said is the smallest share of any developed country. In the mid-1980s, infant mortality of 26 out of 1,000 live births put the Soviet Union fiftieth in the world. Life expectancy at birth for Soviet men was 63 years, about the same as Mexico or Brazil. In 1987, the Soviet Union had 1,500 cases of diphtheria, the United States, one; the Soviet Union had 860,000 cases of hepatitis, the United States, 56,000.

The Soviet economy, based on the Stalinist model with the emphasis on central controls, had performed effectively in the early postwar years. But in the late 1970s Soviet economic growth had slowed, and military spending was soaking up an increasing share of national output. By the early 1980s, it was clear to Soviet scholars that the economy had become stagnant, and this in the face of a quickening revolution in computers and other technology that was rapidly changing the economies of industrialized East Asia and the West.

This sense of falling behind was clearly felt by many of those around Yuri Andropov and gave impetus to the first moves in many years toward economic reform. I recall vividly a conversation in Moscow in January 1984 with Fyodor Burlatsky, a former Central Committee staff member under Andropov and a commentator for *Literaturnaya Gazeta*. "Do you know what country bothers us most? And it isn't you [the United States]," Burlatsky asked. The surprising answer was Japan. "They're in the forefront of the Third Industrial Revolution and we are nowhere," Burlatsky complained. By 1987, it was estimated that the Soviet Union possessed about two hundred thousand microcomputers, most of them very unsophisticated compared to the personal computers in the West. The United States had over 25 million. For reasons such as these, an impatient Gorbachev and those around him realized more clearly than most outside observers that the Soviet Union had to make drastic improvements in its economic structure or be a third-rate power economically and ultimately militarily.

At the Central Committee plenum that convened in the Kremlin January 27, Gorbachev for the first time used the word "crisis" to describe the country's social and economic predicament. "At some point the country began to lose momentum, difficulties and unresolved problems started to pile up, and there appeared elements of stagnation and other phenomena alien to socialism. All this seriously affected the economy and the social and spiritual spheres," Gorbachev declared.

The Twenty-seventh Party Congress a year earlier had begun the task of restructuring, but now Gorbachev reported, "We see that change for the better is taking place slowly, and that the business of reorganization is more difficult, and that the problems that have built up in society are more deeply rooted than we first thought." He listed some of the failures of the system: lack of concern for ordinary citizens, waste, corruption, growing cynicism, loss of enthusiasm for work, decline of patriotism, alcoholism, drug abuse and rising crime. In the economy, he said, "most plan targets have not been met since the early 1970s" and the system seemed impervious to change.

Having failed in 1986 to persuade the party apparatus to support sweeping changes, Gorbachev at the January plenum shifted to democratization as a way to turn the bureaucrats around or turn them out. He proposed to introduce multiple candidacies and secret ballot voting for local government officials and party officials, including party secretaries, up through the level of Union republics (just below the national level). In his closing address to the plenum, Gorbachev declared, "We need democracy like air." But the Central Committee, to the leader's growing irritation, was having little of it. Its resolution only vaguely endorsed democratization and said nothing about multiple candidacies or secret ballots for party elections.

In foreign policy, Gorbachev and his aides had to decide how and when to pick up the threads of negotiation with the United States following the Reykjavik summit. A Soviet effort to resume negotiations aimed at eliminating all nuclear weapons, as Gorbachev and Reagan had discussed on the last afternoon at Reykjavik, had gotten nowhere with Shultz and a U.S. team when Foreign Minister Shevardnadze met them a month later in Vienna. Moreover, the Soviet strategy of blaming SDI for the lack of final agreement at Reykjavik had fallen flat. The most influential circles in the West, rather than condemning SDI, seemed grateful to the space-defense program for blocking radical U.S.-Soviet agreements at Reykjavik that in their eyes could have been disastrous.

In the face of all this, one Soviet option was simply to stand pat, with all potential arms cutbacks linked to the SDI issue as they had been during and since Reykjavik. However, Gorbachev could see from his experience in Iceland that Reagan would not abandon his SDI position and that even the chance of a modest compromise to slow it down was not great. For Moscow to continue to make SDI its arms control touchstone would mean a stalemate in the remaining two years of the Reagan presidency, with no guarantee that Reagan's successor would have different views. In the meantime, international tensions could mount and crises could erupt between Washington and Moscow, at a time when Gorbachev needed both the international prestige and international calm to help him attempt the increasingly difficult changes at home.

Under the supervision of Shevardnadze, a major review of Soviet policy toward the United States took place in Moscow late in 1986 and early in 1987 to assess the merits and disadvantages of continuing to do business with Reagan. The inevitable conclusion was that Moscow had no alternative to moving ahead, despite its disappointment at the final results of Reykjavik and the battering that the U.S. administration was taking in the Iran-Contra scandal. Just after the breakup of the negotiations at Reykjavik, Nikolai Shishlin of the Central Committee had predicted to an American, "There will be a period of blackness, then things will become lighter again." On February 28, the day after Reagan named the well-regarded former Senate Republican leader, Howard Baker, as his new White House chief of staff, the dawn broke with a Gorbachev announcement untying the tightly bound package of arms issues as presented in Iceland. The Soviet Union had "singled out" the problem of medium-range missiles in Europe from the package, Gorbachev announced, and proposed that "a separate agreement be concluded on it, and without delay." No longer was a deal on SDI a condition of an agreement on the Euromissiles. The main reason for the change, Deputy Foreign Minister Bessmertnykh told me a few weeks later, was that an INF treaty seemed obtainable during the Reagan presidency, and that even a modest arms treaty with Reagan would pave the way for more important treaties and a better relationship under Reagan's successor. About the same time, former Ambassador Dobrynin, now a senior Central Committee aide to Gorbachev, told an American visitor that the leadership believed an INF Treaty could be signed at a summit meeting in the fall.

The day after Gorbachev's announcement decoupling the Euromissiles accord from the other arms issues, the State Department advised Reagan this meant that Gorbachev wanted another summit meeting before the end of the year and was willing to finesse the SDI issue to get it. Two days after that, Reagan appeared in person in the White House Press Room to welcome Gorbachev's statement. It was Reagan's first appearance there since the announcement of the diversion of Iran arms sales funds to the Nicaraguan Contras three months earlier. The possibility of doing business with Moscow was widely viewed by Washington political commentators as a lifesaver for Reagan, who was being besieged from all sides in the most serious political crisis of his administration. On March 6, the White House announced that Shultz would travel to Moscow in mid-April to "maintain the momentum" toward a medium-range missiles accord and a possible summit meeting of Reagan and Gorbachev later in the year.

• SHULTZ IN MOSCOW: THE SECOND ZERO

At a Christmas party at the U.S. ambassador's residence in Vienna the previous December, Marine Sergeant Clayton Lonetree had walked up to the CIA chief of station. "I'm in something over my head. I need to

218

talk to you about it," the Marine security guard said to the intelligence veteran. Lonetree, a twenty-five-year-old American Indian, confessed that he had given information to KGB agents in Moscow, where he had previously been stationed, as well as in Vienna. As part of the widening investigation that followed, a second former Marine security guard from Moscow, Corporal Arnold Bracy, confessed on March 20 to conspiring with Lonetree to bring Soviet agents on midnight forays into the communications center and other top-secret areas of the Moscow Embassy. Bracy made his confession under heavy pressure from the Naval Investigative Service.

Bracy's confession that KGB agents had roamed the most secret parts of the Moscow Embassy threw the U.S. government into a near panic. Believing that virtually everything in its most sensitive diplomatic post had been compromised, the State Department ordered the Moscow Embassy to shut down processing of all classified information on computer terminals, electric typewriters and even manual typewriters for fear they might have been programmed by nocturnal KGB visitors to emit telltale electronic pulses. Embassy officials spoke to one another in whispers and wrote messages to Washington in longhand to be taken out of the country in the diplomatic pouch. As the investigation mushroomed, the entire twenty-eight-man Marine security guard detachment in Moscow was sent home and replaced. A specially equipped communications van resembling a campers' Winnebago was flown to Moscow to facilitate Shultz's reports to Washington during his April mission. There was an uproar in Congress and the press. The cover of *Time* portrayed a handsome U.S. Marine in full dress uniform with a blackened eye.

The KGB-in-the-Embassy scare followed a hemorrhage of U.S. intelligence secrets resulting from Soviet recruitment of a variety of Americans in sensitive posts: an FBI agent, Richard Miller; a former National Security Agency official, Ronald Pelton; a former CIA trainee for operations in Moscow, Edward Lee Howard; and a Navy family, John Walker, his brother and son. The arrest of Marine guards from the Moscow Embassy touched off new revelations about highly sophisticated listening devices that had been planted by the Soviets in the superstructure of the new U.S. Embassy chancery building being erected to replace the antiquated structure long in use on Tchaikovsky Street. The sophisticated bugs had been discovered years before; construction had been halted because of them in August 1985.

Shultz had scheduled meetings on April 13–14 in the Soviet capital to advance the arms negotiations and other issues. Shortly before he was to leave Washington, the Senate passed a resolution demanding that he cancel his talks on security grounds. The secretary refused, but announced he would register a sharp protest about the KGB penetration while in the Soviet capital. "They invaded our sovereign territory and we're damned upset about it," Shultz told a news conference.

When Shultz took the matter up with Foreign Minister Shevardnadze on the first day of the talks, there was a disappointing lack of sympathy from his counterpart, who had looked into the charges from the Soviet side. "Mr. Secretary, you are being deceived," Shevardnadze said bluntly. At the Kremlin conference table in St. Catherine's Hall the following day, Gorbachev told Shultz he was satisfied there had been no physical penetration by KGB agents into the Embassy or break-in of the U.S. ambassador's office. "Can I tell the President that it's against your policy and rules to allow intelligence agencies to physically penetrate our embassy building?" Shultz asked. "Yes, this is precisely so," Gorbachev replied.

Shultz was impressed with the top-level denials but nearly everyone in the State Department and Marine Corps continued to assume the worst—until the Embassy spy scare fizzled out seven months later the same way it had begun, with admissions from Lonetree. In November, after being courtmartialed on charges of passing information to the Soviets, Lonetree underwent voluntary and intensive "damage-assessment" interrogations by security officials as part of a deal with the government. In these carefully monitored interviews Lonetree convinced even the Naval Investigative Service that, while he provided some information about the Embassy to the KGB, he never brought Soviets into the Embassy building and never helped others to do so. By this time, the espionage charges leveled against Bracy had been dropped for lack of evidence. Bracy had repudiated his original statement immediately after signing it, saying he had been pressured by NIS investigators into signing without even being permitted to read it. When investigators examined the log books kept by the Marines on their shifts at the Moscow Embassy, they discovered that Lonetree and Bracy never worked together at night at the two duty stations described in Bracy's statement during the period of their alleged conspiracy. Moreover, highly sophisticated electronic devices that monitored the Embassy's communications center indicated there had been no unauthorized or unreported entries. But all this did not become known until months after the initial revelations rocked Washington. Like so many other Washington sensations, it just went away. No action was taken against the NIS investigators who had obtained the Bracy "confession" or against higher-ups who had failed to examine it critically. The security officials who had panicked and the members of Congress who had been so indignant shrugged and said they had been reacting to a worst-case scenario that was plausible at the time. U.S. Ambassador Jack Matlock told a visitor that the KGB penetration of his Embassy building had been "a nonoccurring event."

When the Embassy spying scandal erupted on the eve of Shultz's trip, Soviet officials saw it as one more sinister effort to disrupt any possible improvement in U.S.-Soviet relations. "It has become a routine operation for your people to have the kettle of emotions on the fire, to raise these problems, whenever something looks as though it is improving between us," said Georgi Arbatov, director of the U.S.A. and Canada Institute and a member of the Communist Party Central Committee. Arbatov cited the U.S. discovery of a "Soviet combat brigade" in Cuba, later shown to be a unit that had existed there for nearly two decades, as the Senate was preparing to take up ratification of the SALT II treaty in 1979; the U.S. charges of a deliberate "massacre" in 1983 after the Soviet Union had mistakenly shot down Korean Air Lines Flight 007; the charge on the eve of the 1985 Geneva summit that cancer-causing "spy dust" (later shown to be noncancerous) had been used to track U.S. personnel in Moscow; and the arrest of Gennadi Zakharov and the refusal to release him on bail as the two nations were maneuvering toward what became the Reykjavik summit in 1986. "It is absolutely obvious that there are rather influential people, groups, maybe institutions, that are against any normalization of relations between the United States and the Soviet Union," Arbatov charged. Deputy Foreign Minister Bessmert-nykh, who was also suspicious but less prosecutorial, said the State Department seemed to have a rule in its handbook of diplomatic practice always to create a tense atmosphere in order to improve the U.S. bargaining position at key meetings.

The spy scandal did not help Shultz's position when he went to Moscow in April 1987 in a difficult negotiating posture. In White House deliberations before his departure, Weinberger objected to holding the meeting in the Soviet capital because of the lack of Embassy security. Shultz won that point with Reagan but he lost on nearly every other point in head-to-head arguments with Weinberger on the nature of his instructions. Consequently, Shultz took with him new administration positions on space arms issues that moved away from some of the U.S. concessions given to Gorbachev at Reykjavik—for example, the United States would agree to only a seven-year nonwithdrawal period from the ABM Treaty, rather than ten years. Shultz was given hardly any flexibility on the increasingly pressing issues of intermediate-range missiles.

Gorbachev viewed the Shultz mission as the acid test of U.S. willingness to make a deal on the Euromissiles, and he was preparing a new maneuver for the secretary. In Prague on April 10, shortly before Shultz's arrival in Moscow, Gorbachev announced that he was willing to freeze the number of Soviet shorter-range missiles in Europe, those with a range of five hundred to one thousand kilometers. He proposed new U.S.-Soviet negotiations with the aim of "deep cuts in and ultimate elimination of" these weapons. In discussions with Shultz, he went even further. *

The Soviet Union had two nuclear weapons systems, the SS-12 and the SS-23, in the five-hundred- to one-thousand-kilometer Shorter-Range Intermediate Nuclear Forces (SRINF) band; the United States had none. Because these Soviet weapons were so closely linked to the next-longer range of weapons, NATO had insisted that any INF treaty involve reductions in both shorter- and longer-range categories. Moreover, the United States insisted on the right to build up its forces in the SRINF band to match any SRINF missiles that the Soviet Union chose to retain in a treaty agreement.

In their meeting in St. Catherine's Hall in the Kremlin on April 14, Shultz reiterated to Gorbachev the U.S. position that whatever number of SRINF missiles Moscow chose to retain, the United States must have "the right to match." Gorbachev, however, was strongly opposed to a deal in which the United States would be building up its weapons in

---

* The shorter-range missiles, called SRINF (Shorter-Range Intermediate Nuclear Force), had a peculiar status in the arsenals of East and West. The United States and Soviet Union each had many hundreds of strategic missiles with very long ranges that could reach across the globe. In the next-lower band were the Longer-Range Intermediate Nuclear Force (LRINF) missiles with ranges from 1,000 to 5,500 kilometers. Here the Soviets had a distinct advantage in numbers, but were eager to trade off their SS-20s and other weapons for the U.S. Pershing II and ground-launched cruise missiles that had been deployed to Europe starting in 1983. Just below this category in range were the Shorter-Range Intermediate Nuclear Force (SRINF) weapons, which could reach 500 to 1,000 kilometers. These weapons were distinct from the under-500-kilometer-range battlefield weapons—short-range rockets, nuclear field artillery, nuclear land mines and the like—which NATO was very reluctant to give up in the face of the Soviet Union's massive land army.

any category while the Soviet Union was making the lion's share of the reductions. He told Shultz that the number of SRINF the Soviet Union proposed to retain would be zero, thereby making moot the U.S. right to match, and that Moscow proposed to carry out this total elimination of shorter-range nuclear weapons "in a short period of time," later defined as one year. The destruction of all longer-range INF weapons as originally advocated by Reagan had been known as the "zero option" or the "first zero." The elimination of all SRINF weapons as advocated by Gorbachev quickly became known as the "second zero."

By his bold decision, Gorbachev sidestepped what was likely to be a long and contentious negotiation on SRINF. It was dramatic evidence that Gorbachev was eager to achieve a quick Euromissiles agreement with the Reagan administration. But the faster Gorbachev moved, the more unsettling his actions were to conservative political leaders, defense strategists and military commanders in the West, who were already alarmed at the anti–nuclear-weapons drift that had emerged from Reykjavik. Acceptance of the second zero would leave only battlefield nuclear weapons of the two powers dedicated to the defense of Europe. Those who feared the "denuclearization" of Western defenses in Europe, while the might of powerful Soviet ground forces remained, saw the second zero as a dangerous step along an anti–nuclear-weapons road they did not wish to travel.

Gorbachev pressed Shultz for an immediate answer to his proposal, but the secretary refused, saying it was necessary to consult the NATO allies. Gorbachev responded that it was ridiculous to claim that the U.S. administration could not make and impose a decision if it wished to do so. "What are you afraid of?" Gorbachev taunted. Shevardnadze joined in, saying that "it's amazing that the United States is objecting to unilateral Soviet elimination" of this class of missiles.

Shultz held his ground on what he knew was a delicate question in the alliance. Although the refusal to respond to Gorbachev's second-zero offer made for a sticky afternoon in the Kremlin, Shultz privately considered the situation a godsend. The more the Soviets attacked him for deferring to the NATO allies, the more this reassured the nervous Europeans that the alliance mattered.

After dealing with the Euromissiles issues, there was a recess in the talks for twenty-five minutes to await the arrival of Marshal Akhromeyev, whom Gorbachev had summoned to participate in the discussion of strategic and space arms. Shultz, who had hoped such a hiatus would come, guided Gorbachev and an interpreter to one end of the blond wood table for an informal seminar on how the world was changing economically, one of the favorite subjects of the economics professor turned diplomat. Shultz had broached the subject to Gorbachev at their meeting in November 1985, shortly before the Geneva summit. At Geneva, Gorbachev had followed up by discussing economics with Shultz briefly while the two of them were awaiting the arrival of Reagan on the second afternoon.

In the April 1987 meeting, Shultz gave Gorbachev a more extensive exposure to what he called the Information Age. Many extremely important things going on had little to do with the East-West confrontation, but would go far to determine the future of every country, Shultz said. Ideas and information had become the key to scientific and economic progress; a society that restricted the flow of information and failed to give its people the room for creativity would not be able to keep up, he said, in a soft-sell plea for human rights. Moreover, no society that walled itself off from this global flow could prosper, just as no society could prosper in the long run without access to global markets. The amount of money that changed hands in world financial markets in a single day was more than $1 trillion—more than the entire budget of the U.S. government for a year, he pointed out. Many of these transactions and much of the world's business flowed out of computer terminals in a constant data stream that respected few borders, though the Soviet Union did not participate and most of its telephone lines could not handle data traffic.

Shultz pulled out four-color graphs and pie charts of global trends that he had brought along for the Soviet leader. According to these, the Soviet Union accounted for 15 percent of world production of goods and services (compared to 28 percent for the United States) but only 2 percent of world trade. The charts showed that the shares of both the U.S. and Soviet economies in world manufactured exports were slipping, while Japan and East Asia were coming up fast, having mastered the Third Industrial Revolution of high technology, which had scarcely a toehold in the Soviet economy outside the military sector. There was a single global economy to a greater degree than ever before, but the Soviet Union was hardly a part of it. Shultz showed Gorbachev a photograph of the shipping label for some integrated circuits used in manufacturing by an American firm. The label read: "Made in one or more of the following countries: Korea, Hong Kong, Malaysia, Singapore, Taiwan, Mauritius,

Thailand, Indonesia, Mexico, Philippines. The exact country of origin is unknown."

Assistant Secretary of State Rozanne Ridgway, who watched Shultz outlining the facts of modern economic life to Gorbachev, felt that the secretary was "trying to get inside of Gorbachev's mind," to get him to see the world differently. As a professional academic, Shultz firmly believed that planting ideas in people's minds could make a big difference. From his first meeting with Gorbachev at the Chernenko funeral he had been impressed with the Soviet leader's appreciation that the world was changing rapidly and his receptivity to new ways of understanding that change. In his economic discussions with Gorbachev, Shultz was playing the economist's long game in investing, in this case intellectually, for an eventual payoff. Gorbachev appeared to be fascinated, and some of the concepts seemed to stick. In his book *Perestroika*, written five months later, Gorbachev described the current international scene as "a world of fundamental social shifts, of an all-embracing scientific and technological revolution, of worsening global problems— problems concerning ecology, natural resources, etc.—and of radical changes in information technology." On the eve of Gorbachev's arrival for the Washington summit in December 1987, Shultz arranged to make a full-scale address on the Information Age to the World Affairs Council in the capital. As a diplomatic correspondent, I could not understand why Shultz would pick such an abstract subject while the press was eager to learn his views on the burning questions of the forthcoming summit. I told my editors there was no news in the Shultz speech, and hardly anyone else covered it either. We did not know that Shultz, with an audience of one in mind, had made arrangements to have his address immediately translated into Russian, so that he could give copies to the arriving Soviet leader and his party.

In St. Catherine's Hall in April, Shultz's economic discussion with Gorbachev ended with the arrival of Marshal Akhromeyev for the discussion of strategic and space arms. The dialogue turned out to be Reykjavik revisited, with many of the same arguments exchanged. If the United States began to deploy antimissile systems in space, Gorbachev said, there would be no agreement on cutting strategic offensive arms. The Soviet Union would never recognize the spread of the arms race to space as something natural. This would permit no trust of any kind between the two great powers, he said. Gorbachev insisted, "Your administration has painted itself into a corner. The orders have been placed, industries have been engaged, and it expects a technological break-through with computers and information systems. President Johnson had said, 'He who rules space rules the world.' "

Nonetheless, Gorbachev announced he was willing to make one last effort. The Soviet side, he confided, was thinking of an expanded inter-pretation of "laboratory testing" that would cover ground-based research in various scientific centers, so long as no object was launched into outer space. And even there, he said, he was willing to negotiate with the United States on which objects would be specifically banned from space. Gorbachev must have known from reading the American press that this very approach, to negotiate a list of what was permitted and what was prohibited from space, had been recommended by Paul Nitze and Shultz in the White House deliberations just before the secretary's departure for Moscow, but that it had been rejected by Reagan.

"U.S. policy is one of extorting more and more concessions," Gor-bachev complained bitterly when Shultz did not pick up his offer. "Two great powers should not treat each other like this."

Shultz, who by now had had extensive exposure to Gorbachev in Moscow, Geneva and Reykjavik and was not inclined to hide his feelings, responded sarcastically, "I'm weeping for you."

Finally Gorbachev addressed the subject of the next summit meeting. In addition to signing an INF Treaty, he would like to work out "key provisions" for the settlement of strategic offensive arms, space issues and nuclear testing—something Shultz would hear much more about six months later. "I am ready to meet the President of the United States in order to reach agreement on these 'key provisions' and conclude a treaty on medium-range missiles," Gorbachev said.

After the General Secretary had covered all the items on his list, he invited Shultz to bring up his concerns. The first item on Shultz's list was human rights.

Despite Gorbachev's prickly reactions in previous conversations with Reagan and Shultz, the "new thinking" had brought about positive de-velopments in this field. Anatoly Shcharansky had been freed in a prisoner exchange with the West the previous February on the eve of the Twenty-seventh Party Congress, and Yuri Orlov had been sent to the United States in October as part of the Daniloff exchange. Two months later, in December, Gorbachev had telephoned the Soviet Union's most celebrated dissident, Andrei Sakharov, the famed Soviet physicist and Nobel Prize winner, and invited him and his wife, Yelena Bonner, to return to Moscow, ending nearly six years of internal exile in the closed city of Gorky. This momentous action had convinced many skeptics in the West that Gorbachev was serious about internal reform.

Following advice that had been given to Reagan by Richard Nixon before the Geneva summit, the U.S. administration had been taking a low profile on human rights issues, pressing them in private but saying little in public. But over the months, Shultz had become increasingly passionate in his private views as a result of firsthand encounters with Soviet dissidents, their families and supporters in the United States. At Spaso House, the U.S. ambassador's residence, the night before meeting Gorbachev on the April trip to Moscow, Shultz had attended the annual Passover seder for Jewish activists, including many *refusniks* who had been denied permission to emigrate. Wearing a yarmulke, the Episcopalian secretary of state made the rounds of tables and delivered an emotional speech that was covered by the American press and television. "You are on our minds, you are in our hearts," declared Shultz. "We never give up, we never stop trying, and in the end some good things do happen. But never give up, never give up. And please note that there are people all over the world, not just in the United States, who think about you and wish you well and are on your side." With his attendance at the seder, Shultz confronted the Soviet leaders for the first time with a dramatic demonstration of high-level U.S. views on Soviet turf.*

At the conference table in the Kremlin, Gorbachev objected to Shultz's activities at the seder, saying that the secretary was ignoring the millions of Soviet Jews who had no wish to emigrate and was only meeting with "all the rotten people." Shultz seemed to be stimulating Soviet Jews to complain and apply for emigration, it seemed to Gorbachev. This would be interference with Soviet internal affairs, and would not be accepted.

Shultz was ready with an answer. "I've got a deal for you. I've got a great big airplane. If you don't want [the *refusniks*], there isn't a person

* All the prominent Jews at the 1987 seder had been released by Passover the following year. Shultz, asked by *Washington Post* editors and reporters as he finished his six and one-half years as secretary of state what he would like to be remembered for, answered, "Ida Nudel." The Jewish fifty-six-year-old *refusnik*, who had attended the seder, was permitted to emigrate to Israel in October 1987 as an official gesture to Shultz after seventeen years of harassment. The secretary received Nudel's personal thanks in a moving telephone call immediately after she arrived in Israel and later met her in Jerusalem during a Middle East negotiating trip.

in my party, including the reporters, that wouldn't give up his seat for those people. And you can just put them all on and get rid of them if you don't want them. We'll take them."

After some further testy exchanges, the discussion turned to regional issues, especially Afghanistan. Gorbachev said he had hoped after the Geneva summit that the United States would cooperate in seeking a solution. Referring to reports that Washington had decided to supply more Stinger antiaircraft missiles and other weapons to the Afghan resistance, Gorbachev charged that "U.S. policy now is to put sticks in the spokes."

His irritation rising, Gorbachev declared that "it is not Soviet policy to pick a fight with the United States, but rather to take legitimate U.S. interests in the world into account. The Soviet Union expects the same from the United States. It is not true that the cause of tension is the two systems. Until 1917 there had only been one system—the capitalist system—and there had been the First World War, not to speak of all the other wars. In World War II we had a coalition of states with different systems. What does exist is each country's national interest; it is not just the United States that has a national interest. Seeking a balance of such interests is the art of foreign policy." What was needed, Gorbachev told Shultz as the meeting came to a close, was for the United States and Soviet Union to work together.

At this stage in 1987, Shultz and his aides were skeptical that the Soviet Union intended to get out of Afghanistan as it proclaimed it would do. The view in Washington was that the only way to bring about a Soviet withdrawal was to increase the military pressure against Soviet troops and the Kabul regime they were supporting. The day after the Kremlin meeting, in a new test of *glasnost*, Shultz was interviewed on Soviet television with the understanding his remarks would not be censored. The secretary presented the harshest assessment of the war that Soviet television viewers had heard to that time: "You have come into conflict with the people of Afghanistan. The Afghan people want you to leave their country; they do not want your armed forces to be in their country. How many soldiers do you keep there— 120,000?"

At this point, Shultz apparently overstepped even the expanding limits of tolerance on the part of the Soviet television. According to monitors, the following two sentences were not translated into Russian: "It is a very devastating war, and they do not want you there.

They want peace with you, but they do not want you occupying their country."

Shultz and his Soviet hosts had agreed, or so the Americans thought, to say nothing about the results of the secretary's Moscow mission until after the last of the talks were finished on April 15. Shultz had scheduled a late afternoon press conference that day before flying to Brussels to brief the NATO allies.

After a very uninformative U.S. briefing several hours after the end of the April 14 Shultz meeting with Gorbachev in the Kremlin, I was back at *The Washington Post* Moscow bureau putting together a thin account of the day's activities when, about 1:00 A.M., Tass began transmitting a lengthy account of the Gorbachev-Shultz discussion. The Tass dispatch included a variety of bitter charges and caustic remarks about U.S. positions, but it also disclosed Gorbachev's proposal to eliminate the second zero within a short time. When someone asked Shevardnadze the following day about the postmidnight release, he quipped, "This is *glasnost*. This is the way we do things here."

After Shultz's news conference, he flew on to Brussels. On the plane, Shultz was optimistic about the allies' reaction to Gorbachev's offer, which required the Soviet Union to eliminate another class of weapons—the shorter-range or SRINF missiles—and required the West (so far as we knew then) to eliminate none. In view of the sensitivity of the second zero inside the Atlantic alliance, Shultz was careful not to take a public position, but he told us, not for quotation, that the offer was so one-sided in favor of the West that he was not sure the Soviet leaders would be able to sell it if there were a democratic legislature in Moscow.

• OPPORTUNITY LANDS IN RED SQUARE

May 28 was a balmy spring evening in Red Square, a national holiday in honor of Soviet border guards, and Muscovites and tourists were strolling near Lenin's tomb in the broad space outside the Kremlin wall. About 6:00 P.M. a small white single-engine airplane came in from the south, circling so low that many of the strollers ducked as it narrowly missed the famous mausoleum on one side and a tower of the GUM department store on the other side of the square. Finally the small plane skimmed to a landing on the cobblestones just south of the celebrated onion domes of St. Basil's Cathedral. A Soviet painter who had a stand near the cathedral thought the landing might be some kind of sports event, especially when the pilot stepped out of the little craft wearing a red aviator suit and a motorcyclist's helmet. A foreign tourist in the square guessed it must be the private plane of Soviet leader Mikhail Gorbachev, whose office was just across the Kremlin wall. Security men in the square, which is well guarded at ground level, took no immediate action on the assumption that the landing was perhaps a scene from a movie about which they had mistakenly not been notified.

Stepping out of the plane, which was marked with the black-red-and-yellow flag of West Germany, was Mathias Rust, a nineteen-year-old amateur aviator from Hamburg, who had taken off that morning in Helsinki, Finland, and flown all day by sight at low altitude, without radar or radio contact, across four hundred miles of Soviet air space to the symbolic center of Soviet national life. Witnesses said the young pilot told the gathering crowd he had come on "a mission of peace" to bring Gorbachev a twenty-page plan for a nuclear-weapons-free world. The young man signed autographs and accepted bread as a gift from the friendly crowd that gathered around him. After about an hour of confusion, police took him away to the KGB's Lefortovo Prison, where U.S. journalist Nicholas Daniloff had been incarcerated nearly a year earlier.

The bizarre flight of Mathias Rust was deeply embarrassing to the Soviet military. Marshal Akhromeyev, chief of staff of the Soviet armed forces, knew nothing about the day-long flight across his nation's territory until he was informed by telephone that a foreign plane had landed in Red Square. Chief Air Marshal Aleksandr Koldunov, who had headed the air defense forces since 1978, had gone home from his office for the night without having heard that anything was amiss. According to Akhromeyev, a Soviet interceptor aircraft had spotted Rust's Cessna when it crossed the Soviet-Finnish border, and had radioed the news to his headquarters. "And it was not even necessary to shoot him down," said Akhromeyev, who added that the Soviet jet would only have had to fly close to the little single-engine Cessna to bring it down, apparently referring to a standard military maneuver that would have trained the fighter's fiery jet exhaust at the smaller plane, causing it to crash. However, the commanding officer of the air defense unit on the ground did not trust the interceptor pilot or believe his report, Akhromeyev said, and did not even report the intrusion up the line. To the chagrin of the chief of staff, "This flight was not registered, monitored in any way."

When the Cessna landed, Gorbachev and the senior members of the Politburo, along with Defense Minister Sergei Sokolov, were in East Berlin at a Warsaw Pact summit meeting coinciding with the 750th anniversary of Berlin's founding. After hearing the news from Red Square, the Soviet leaders cut short their visit, flew back to Moscow and convened an emergency Politburo meeting. Sokolov was summarily retired as defense minister and air defense chief Koldunov was fired. Sokolov, whose removal had been rumored for weeks in Moscow, was the first defense minister to be ousted since Nikita Khrushchev's firing of Marshal Georgi Zhukov in 1957 for meddling in party affairs. In Sokolov's stead, Gorbachev's surprise choice as the new defense minister was General Dmitri Yazov, who was leapfrogged over twelve more senior members of the Soviet high command. Yazov was a newcomer to Moscow military leadership circles, having been transferred to the capital only four months earlier from the command of the Far Eastern Military District. He was known as an outspoken advocate of *perestroika* in the military.

The humiliation in Red Square gave Gorbachev the opportunity to seize the initiative and shake up the Soviet military establishment. In what became known as the "Rust massacre," the General Secretary asserted his political authority over the military in bold and spectacular fashion. Now he had his own man as defense minister and a close working relationship with the armed forces chief of staff. One senior official joked that for his services, Rust should be awarded the Order of Lenin. Instead, however, the young German was jailed for fourteen months before being released to return home.

Up to this point, Gorbachev's relations with the career military had been tenuous. He had forged a close relationship with Akhromeyev, who was the most illustrious soldier still on active duty, but other members of the military high command had been slow to back the General Secretary's policies. Gorbachev would say later—and Akhromeyev would confirm—that some military leaders had warned him he was moving too fast to change the strategic concepts of the USSR.

Indeed, the changes were extensive, beginning with the Twenty-seventh Party Congress in February 1986, when Gorbachev began shifting the emphasis from military power to political accords as the basis for Soviet security. According to Akhromeyev, who played a key role as chief of the General Staff, from early 1986 to the beginning of 1987, "We held a series of discussions, conferences, in which the leadership of the Ministry of Defense took an active part, in which we discussed military theory and military practice, as a result of which we came to the understanding and elaborated the new military doctrine." He added that revision of the Soviet military doctrine was also discussed on a number of occasions in meetings of the Defense Council, the top political-military institution in the country, which was headed by Gorbachev. Akhromeyev is believed to have been its secretary.

By mid-1987, Gorbachev had imposed or announced a number of policies that cut across the grain of traditional Soviet military thinking. The first to come to public notice was the unilateral moratorium on nuclear testing that Gorbachev imposed on the Soviet nuclear weapons program beginning in August 1985 and extended in stages to the increasing discomfort of the Soviet military until February 1987, while the United States continued to test its nuclear weapons. Another new policy, less tangible at first but more important in the long run, was the concept of "reasonable sufficiency" or "sufficient defense," according to which armaments should be reduced to the level necessary for strictly defensive purposes. Moreover, Gorbachev said publicly that the side with the greatest number of weapons—which usually was the Soviet Union—should make asymmetrical reductions to achieve meaningful cutbacks.

The Warsaw Pact meeting that Gorbachev, Defense Minister Sokolov and other members of the Soviet leadership were attending when Rust landed in Red Square in May 1987 enshrined many of the new concepts in official policy. For the first time, the Soviet Union and its Eastern European allies issued a public declaration on their military doctrine:

> The military doctrine of the Warsaw Pact, just as of each of its members, is subordinated to the task of preventing war, nuclear and conventional. . . .
>
> The military doctrine of the Warsaw Treaty member states is strictly a defensive one. It proceeds from the view that the use of the military road for resolving any disputed question is intolerable in the present conditions. Its essence is that:
>
> • The Warsaw Treaty member states will never, under any circumstances, start hostilities against any country or any alliance

of countries unless they become the target of a military attack themselves.

- They will never be the first to use nuclear weapons.

- They have no territorial claims to any state either in Europe or outside it.

- They do not view any state as their enemy.

These were enormous changes in the expression of Soviet military views. In 1971, by contrast, the Soviet minister of defense, Marshal Andrei Grechko, had declared that "military doctrine is a system of scientifically founded and officially endorsed views on questions of *the preparation and the victorious waging of war* in defense of the interests of the Soviet Union and the countries of the social commonwealth."

Another important break with tradition was Soviet acceptance of on-site inspections and other intrusive means of verifying compliance with arms agreements. Traditionally, the Soviet Union had opposed practical commitments of this sort, considering them little more than attempts at legalized espionage to uncover Moscow's military secrets. Abandoning this traditional mania for secrecy was crucial to reducing distrust of Moscow and providing the West with a high degree of confidence that the Soviet Union would keep its word on cutbacks in arms. Without this shift toward openness, it is unlikely that the INF Treaty could have won such widespread approval in the West.

The first indication that Gorbachev was moving toward openness in security matters came in private discussions with his aides at the 1985 Geneva summit, according to several participants. Yevgeni Primakov, who later became a Politburo member and a member of Gorbachev's Presidential Council, recalled sitting at a table with Gorbachev and other advisers during the summit when the General Secretary asked unexpectedly, "What do you think about this idea to open our laboratories?" Gorbachev's question was in response to Reagan's proposal, submitted several weeks before the summit, for a reciprocal opening of laboratories to monitor space-defense research. The U.S. proposal was made in part because nobody in Washington expected that the Soviets would agree to allow their research facilities to be inspected.

In the discussion among the Soviet advisers, the point was made that the Soviets needed such "control" (the Soviet word for inspection) more than the United States did, to check up on what was going on, according to Primakov. "From the psychological point of view, it was very difficult for me, because all of a sudden he proposed this idea." Fyodor Burlatsky, who was also present at Geneva, said it was Gorbachev's view that the United States was ahead of the Soviet Union in many aspects of military technology and therefore, "It is maybe more dangerous for them than for us" to have extensive inspections.

An important breakthrough over military objections came in 1986 in connection with the thirty-five-nation Conference on Disarmament in Europe (CDE). As the three-year-old negotiation on confidence-building measures neared its end, it became clear that no agreement was possible unless Moscow was willing to permit on-site and aerial inspection of its ground and air forces in Europe. The chief Soviet negotiator, career diplomat Oleg Grinevsky, discussed the situation with Gorbachev in a one-on-one conversation initiated by the General Secretary, and thereafter was summoned to a Politburo meeting where the question of opening Soviet territory to inspection was debated. According to Grinevsky, "Some around the table were concerned that inspection would be used against our security interests. It was hard to get used to the idea of foreigners being able to see all parts of the Soviet Union." The counterargument, though, was that "we would get the same access to the territory and forces of NATO countries. We could receive the same amount of information. Without this information and verification, we would have no assurance that the information provided by NATO on their forces was correct. If we had really decided to change from military to political bases for our security, to base our security on political relationships, then this assurance and information were even more important to us."

After at least two discussions of the subject in the Politburo, it was decided to accept one or two on-site challenge inspections per year of Soviet forces, which could also demand inspections of Western forces. This unexpected shift in Moscow's position was the crucial factor in the successful completion of the CDE negotiations. Although the Soviet General Staff was opposed to this reversal of policy, an official said, the Politburo decided to send Akhromeyev to Stockholm to announce the new position in August 1986, to give it stature and clout, and also to hold the line against further concessions. Grinevsky told his U.S. counterpart, Stockholm negotiator Robert Barry, "You watch, we're going to end up more in favor of [on-site] inspections than you are." During the discussions at Reykjavik, Gorbachev had told Reagan, with a twinkle in his eye, that if they could get the questions of principle resolved, "you will be *astounded*" at how much verification the Soviet Union could accept.

Soviet academics and some officials had been thinking for years that extreme secrecy in military matters, a tradition going far back in Russian history, damaged national security more than it helped. The rest of the world reacted with suspicion and fear of what the Soviet military was up to, creating fertile conditions for exaggerated fears and "worst-case" estimates of Soviet power that fueled military programs in the West. In many cases, what the secrecy hid was weakness rather than strength. Aleksandr Yakovlev, who participated in the confrontation with the military over openness, told the story of his attempt while serving as Soviet ambassador to Canada to open up the polar regions of the USSR to reciprocal visits of Soviet and Canadian Eskimos. After the idea was rejected in Moscow, Yakovlev traced the problem to the General Staff of the armed forces. When Yakovlev pressed the point with a high-ranking officer, demanding to know what kind of military installations this rigid secrecy was protecting, the general replied, "We don't want to let them in *not* because they might see something there. We don't want to let them in because they would see that there's *nothing* there."

After the mid-1987 military shakeup, the Soviet Union produced increasingly promising proposals for on-site inspections of missile installations and missile manufacturing plants that made the INF Treaty much easier for the United States to accept. As Grinevsky had predicted, by late 1987 U.S. officials began to resist some of these proposals from Moscow when they realized the extent of Soviet access to U.S. military sites and U.S. defense industry that would be required.

• AFGHANISTAN: TOWARD THE EXIT

In mid-September, Foreign Minister Shevardnadze came to Washington for a round of talks that was expected to focus primarily on unresolved aspects of the INF Treaty and a Reagan-Gorbachev summit. On the second day of talks, however, Shevardnadze asked for a private meeting with Shultz. In the secretary's small inner sanctum where they had begun their discussions of the Daniloff case a year earlier, Shevardnadze unveiled a surprise. He said that all Soviet troops were going to get out of

Afghanistan, probably by the end of the Reagan administration. He wanted American help to make it happen.

Soviet officials, including Gorbachev and Shevardnadze, had been saying for months that a decision had been made in principle to withdraw Soviet military forces. In the absence of any decline in the fighting, which reached its high point in 1987, or other tangible move toward withdrawal, these statements had been greeted with skepticism in Washington. Nevertheless, the earnestness of Shevardnadze's confidential disclosure, the timetable he described and the increasingly close relationship between the two ministers convinced Shultz that this was something very important. Shortly after their private discussion, the ministers participated in a much larger meeting of their two delegations to consider regional problems, including Afghanistan. It seemed to Shultz like "rerunning an old movie," with Soviet officials repeating the same fruitless arguments as in the past about the Afghan situation, as if there had been no fundamental change. "I'm sitting there saying to myself, 'Why are we having this discussion?' " Shultz recalled. "And I looked over to Shevardnadze once and I could see he was having the same thought, but it was going on and we just sort of let it go on." In deference to Shevardnadze's wish for confidentiality, Shultz said nothing publicly about his disclosure and discussed it with only a few of the most senior U.S. officials. However, it colored his view of what was happening from that point on.

The Soviet invasion of Afghanistan in December 1979 had been a world-changing event and, as it turned out, the high-water mark of Soviet military intervention abroad since World War II. The sudden advance of Soviet troops, tanks and warplanes into a neighboring country demolished what was left of the détente that had developed between Washington and Moscow in the 1970s. It drastically affected the international climate of the 1980s, deepening fears that the Soviet Union was embarked on a course of expansion through force of arms. But as the years went on, the loosely organized resistance forces of the Afghan guerrillas, aided by arms and supplies from the United States, China and Islamic countries, fought the Soviet army to a standstill. Like the United States in Vietnam in an earlier era, the Soviet Union found itself waist deep in the big muddy. To remain in would be to sink further into the quagmire; to get out would risk the collapse of the Soviet position in a neighboring country and a dangerous erosion of the Soviet geopolitical position in Eastern Europe and worldwide.

Moscow's decision to withdraw from Afghanistan was among its most important of the Gorbachev era, with powerful impact on its relations with the United States. The decision also had major repercussions within the Soviet Union, where the bloody war was increasingly traumatic for both the army and the people.

By the time Shevardnadze imparted his news to Shultz in September 1987, the decision to get out within a relatively short time had been in place for at least nine months. The Afghan communists knew it, but the United States did not.

Exactly who participated in the Politburo decision to get out of Afghanistan is still unknown, although many details of the Soviet discussions with the communist regime in Kabul and others can now be reported. In the recent past, new light has also been thrown on a related question—how the Soviets decided to put their troops into Afghanistan in the first place. It is a strange story.

An official investigation by a committee of the Supreme Soviet in 1989 reported that the decision to invade in 1979 had been made by "a small group of individuals" who did not even consult the entire Politburo, to say nothing of the Central Committee of the Communist Party or the Supreme Soviet legislature. The report named General Secretary Leonid Brezhnev, Defense Minister Dmitri Ustinov, KGB Chairman Yuri Andropov and Foreign Minister Andrei Gromyko as the decision-makers. Senior Soviet officials said at least one other major figure, Politburo member and ideology chief Mikhail Suslov, was directly involved.

According to the account of a well-placed Soviet expert, the decision to intervene was made in late November or early December 1979, in a conference in Brezhnev's office. For the first part of the meeting, the deteriorating situation in Afghanistan was discussed by other top officials in the absence of Brezhnev. Although intervention had been debated from time to time for many months, a crisis point was reached in September when the Afghan communist leader closest to Moscow, Nur Mohammed Taraki, was overthrown and later killed by his deputy, Hafizullah Amin, whom Moscow had been plotting to get rid of. As relations between Moscow and Kabul worsened following Taraki's death, there were rumors, which have never been substantiated, that Amin, who had studied at Columbia University during two periods in the 1950s and 1960s, had CIA connections and might turn to the Americans for help.

In Moscow, there had been debates for months about what to do.

On the crucial day, after about forty minutes of discussion, consisting mostly of bitter condemnation of Amin, the door opened and Brezhnev shuffled in. According to the Soviet source, who had access to an eyewitness account, the doddering General Secretary, with Gromyko holding his elbow to assist him, shook hands with and kissed all his colleagues. In a whisper loud enough to be heard by others in the room, Gromyko summarized the situation and told Brezhnev that Amin was a terrible man. According to this account, Brezhnev got to his feet, placing his palms on the table in front of him, and said only two words, *neporyadichnii chelovek*, meaning, "indecent person." Spoken in this Mafialike manner, Brezhnev's words about Amin were taken as an order to eliminate him. On December 24, 85,000 Soviet troops began pouring into the country, and three days later Amin was overthrown and killed. Soviet forces, which were later increased to about 120,000, installed a regime headed by Babrak Karmal, which was more to Moscow's liking. In the face of the widespread opposition to Soviet intervention within the country and in the outside world, Moscow's troops became increasingly bogged down in a bloody occupation.

By the time Gorbachev came to power in 1985, it had long been clear that Afghanistan was a costly stalemate. Unlike Brezhnev and Andropov, Gorbachev had no personal responsibility for the war. He and Shevardnadze heard the news of the Soviet invasion on the radio and had no part in the decision to intervene. In 1983, Gorbachev bluntly told one of his hosts on his visit to Canada that the Afghan war was "a mistake."

Though it was not announced at the time, Gorbachev said later that his policy shift began in April 1985, only a month after he took power, when "the Politburo conducted a hard and impartial analysis of the position [in Afghanistan] and started even at that time to seek a way out of the situation." In retrospect, it is clear that Gorbachev came to power determined to liquidate the war on the best terms possible. In a geopolitical sense, the retreat from Afghanistan was a part of his broader effort to calm the periphery of the Soviet Union and improve its international standing in order to shift its priorities and resources from military to civilian pursuits. Another part of the same effort was Gorbachev's rapprochement with his most powerful neighbor, the People's Republic of China. After offering olive branches to China in a speech in Vladivostok in July 1986, Gorbachev received a private message from Chinese leader Deng Xiaoping, sent through the Romanians. While Deng would be interested in a summit meeting to end the quarrel of the two giants of international communism, he persisted in demanding Soviet action to remove China's "three obstacles" to normalized relations. One of the obstacles was the Soviet occupation of Afghanistan.

Like the United States in Vietnam earlier, Gorbachev tried a wide variety of methods to bring an end to his national "mistake," including diplomatic approaches and threats intended to neutralize the U.S.-led coalition that backed the Afghan rebel forces, attempts to shore up the client regime in Kabul politically and the use of massive firepower in the war zone in an effort to improve the military situation on the ground. So long as Moscow's troops remained, all these efforts were fruitless.

Shortly after Gorbachev took office, Moscow began encouraging the UN mediation efforts of a determined Ecuadorean diplomat, Diego Cordovez, who had been convening meetings in Geneva and shuttling between major capitals since 1982 seeking a negotiated solution. "From the time Gorbachev came in, things began to change," said Cordovez. "It was immediate and very significant. In May, only two months after he took over, they came up with a number of ideas on how the negotiations should move forward." At the same time, Gorbachev began exerting heavy pressure on Pakistan to stop serving as the conduit for U.S., Chinese and Saudi weapons and supplies for the Afghan *mujaheddin*. And at midyear he assigned General Mikhail Zaitsev, one of the Red Army's most illustrious commanders, to turn the tide of battle militarily, giving him a charter to step up the war (but no more troops) and giving him a year, at the most two years, to start winning.

According to a report presented by Shevardnadze to the Supreme Soviet in 1989, the "political decision of principle" to withdraw was made in December 1985. The first outward sign came in Gorbachev's prominent statement at the Twenty-seventh Communist Party Congress in February 1986 that "counterrevolution and imperialism have turned Afghanistan into a bleeding wound." The remark implied that the "bleeding" must stop one way or another. He also said the USSR wanted to bring home its troops "in the nearest future" and that agreement had been reached with the Kabul regime on a "phased withdrawal" of the troops when there was a political settlement ending the war and barring "foreign armed interference."

Deputy Foreign Minister Yuli Vorontsov said Afghan leader Babrak Karmal had been told several times that Soviet troops were going to leave at some unspecified point and that he must broaden the basis of his regime to survive without them. Karmal did not take these statements seriously, at one point telling Gorbachev, "If you leave now, you'll have to send in a million soldiers next time." Karmal also did little to seek reconciliation domestically, as Moscow was urging. In May 1986 Karmal, the man the Soviets had installed during the 1979 invasion, was removed as head of the People's Democratic Party of Afghanistan (PDPA), the local version of the communist party. He was replaced by Mohammad Najibullah, former head of the Afghan secret police, who had better relations with Moscow and was considered by the Soviets to be more flexible.

Meanwhile, in a decision that would dramatically affect the course of the war, Reagan in April ended a debate of several years' duration among U.S. agencies by ordering the CIA to provide the Afghan resistance with Stinger antiaircraft missiles for the first time. The shoulder-fired high-technology weapons began showing up by late summer, and in September they destroyed three Soviet helicopter gunships in the first of many successful attacks. The impact on the military balance of power in Afghanistan was immediate. Soviet forces, already stretched thin protecting cities, main roads and outposts scattered through the rugged terrain of Afghanistan, no longer had mastery of the air. Close air support from the Soviet and Afghan air forces became sparse. Vital air supply flights were grounded. In this new situation, the Kremlin would either have to increase its fighting force sharply or see its effectiveness decline relative to the *mujaheddin*.

Gorbachev decided not to up the ante. In November 1986, after what is believed to have been a decisive Politburo meeting, the Soviet attitude toward continuing the Afghan war changed dramatically. A senior adviser to Gorbachev, who previously had expressed confidence in success in Afghanistan, told a visiting delegation of Americans from the unofficial Dartmouth U.S.-Soviet discussion group, "We know we have to get out, but we don't know how to get out. Please help us." At the beginning of December, Pakistan's permanent foreign secretary, Abdul Sattar, was invited to Moscow by Deputy Foreign Minister Vorontsov, who had been given the responsibility for Afghan negotiations and who had been a fellow ambassador of Sattar in India years before. According to a Pakistani official, Vorontsov was very candid, speaking of the Afghan "bleeding wound" and saying in no uncertain terms, "We are leaving." The Soviet diplomat asked Pakistani help in working out a political solution and averting a possible bloodbath following a Soviet withdrawal.

In mid-December, Najibullah and the top members of his Afghan Politburo—but not the noncommunist members of his government—were invited to Moscow on an "official friendly visit," the first such high-visibility visit by the Afghan leadership in six years. On December 12, they filed into St. Catherine's Hall in the Great Kremlin Palace, the elegant room with the green malachite columns where Gorbachev met Shultz and other foreign delegations. Across the conference table were Gorbachev, Shevardnadze, Prime Minister Nikolai Ryzhkov, Defense Minister Sergei Sokolov, KGB Chief Viktor Chebrikov, Central Committee Secretary Anatoly Dobrynin and other top Soviet leaders. With all these officials looking on, Gorbachev delivered the hard message his visitors had been summoned to hear: Soviet troops would be withdrawn from Afghan territory within one and a half to two years—thus at the latest by the end of 1988.

"We understand that. You cannot fight for us indefinitely. We must do it ourselves," said the Afghan leader, according to Vorontsov, who was present. Najibullah, while not very happy about the idea, seemed to accept it. Vorontsov observed, however, that some of the other Afghans did not take Gorbachev's declaration to be final.

Shortly after returning to Kabul, Najibullah convened a meeting of the Central Committee of the PDPA. In a secret report, the Afghan leader revealed that Gorbachev had told him the Soviet Union was planning to remove its troops by mid-1988. The PDPA would be given "its chance, with full support" from Moscow, Gorbachev was quoted as saying, but this would be done only for a limited time. After that, "We have to survive by ourselves," Najibullah informed his party. A high-level PDPA staff member who was present for Najibullah's report was so shaken that he fled the country through the French Embassy a few weeks later and revealed what had happened.

All this time, the UN-sponsored mediation effort under Diego Cordovez continued at Geneva and in side meetings by Cordovez with officials in Moscow, Washington, Kabul and Islamabad. At the beginning of 1987, the formal offer on the table from Moscow and Kabul was for Soviet troops to withdraw over forty-two months after the pullout began, if guarantees of nonintervention and other conditions were met. In March, this was reduced to twenty-two months and then to eighteen months in intense negotiations. Pakistan was holding out for a Soviet withdrawal period no longer than seven months. The obvious compromise was twelve months. Gorbachev had indicated privately in the meeting with Najibullah the previous December that he was prepared eventually to accept a twelve-month pullout. But throughout most of 1987 the Soviets—and a reluctant Afghan leadership—did not do so.

The leading hypothesis of Cordovez and many retrospective analysts was that Gorbachev and the Soviet political leadership were eager to get out of Afghanistan, but that the Soviet military was unwilling to accept a military defeat. When Defense Minister Sokolov, who had supervised the invasion in 1979, was fired on May 30 after Mathias Rust's plane landed in Red Square, for example, Cordovez was told by his principal Soviet contact, "This is good for you." However, senior Soviet military and diplomatic officials say today that this analysis of the military's position was a misreading of the situation. Marshal Akhromeyev said he as deputy chief of staff and Marshal Nikolai Ogarkov, then chief of staff of the Soviet armed forces, had advised the political leadership in 1979 against sending Soviet forces to Afghanistan in the first place. "It was absolutely clear to us that in such a country as Afghanistan, in a country which has many deserts and mountains and has an area of 1.5 million square kilometers, that troops numbering 100,000 men could not solve the problem by military means," according to Akhromeyev. But he said the answer from the Kremlin was, "We have heard your opinion. Now follow the orders." The military command followed orders to get in and to fight but was never reluctant to get out, the senior Soviet officer said. Vorontsov, the chief Foreign Ministry negotiator on Afghanistan, was even more emphatic that despite the widespread perception to the contrary, Soviet military officers were "the main proponents of getting out." In the internal discussions, according to Vorontsov, the military's watchword was, "The army cannot fight against the people. We must get out." Nonetheless, American experts on the war believe some elements of the Soviet military dragged their feet on the withdrawal, and held out for terms that would minimize the chances a postwithdrawal collapse in Kabul.

The growing antiwar sentiment in the Soviet Union weighed heavily on the military, as it did on Gorbachev and the country's political leadership. The war was increasingly unpopular and was being blamed for a rise in draft dodging, drug addiction and other ills among youth. As was the case with the American war in Vietnam, the growing number of bodies coming back played a significant role in shaping public attitudes, which could not be ignored even in a mostly authoritarian state. In most cases, the headstones of young men in Soviet cemeteries made no reference to how or where they died, but everyone knew. An American diplomat who made a practice of visiting cemeteries in the mid-1980s was struck by the number of new graves of military-age men. By 1987 about one person in six in an officially sponsored public opinion poll in Moscow said the use of Soviet troops in Afghanistan was wrong and unjustifiable by any internal developments there, a surprising number in view of the survey's sponsorship and the understandable caution among the public about criticizing official policy. The same year, a survey of more than one thousand Soviet citizens traveling in the West—and thus freer to express their views—reported that 45 percent disapproved of official policy in Afghanistan, and only 24 percent approved. This reflected a steady increase in disapproval from similar surveys in 1986 and 1984. "Our poor boys are dying for nothing in Afghanistan," said a Russian blue-collar worker traveling in the West.

The forecast of what would happen after Soviet troops withdrew was a complex issue. Moscow was making a bet, against greater or lesser odds depending on one's assessment, that the Kabul regime that had been so ineffective since 1979 would rally after Soviet withdrawal, and that the increasingly powerful *mujaheddin* forces would begin to weaken. Vorontsov said he and some other Soviet officials expected the situation to change completely after Moscow's troops went home, depriving the rebels of an infidel foe. But there is little evidence that this confidence was widely shared either in Moscow or in Kabul. While Najibullah's morale remained high, said an Afghan government insider, most of the others in the Kabul leadership were "very afraid."

On July 20, 1987, Najibullah and members of his team were summoned to the Kremlin for another meeting with Gorbachev. Once more, Gorbachev spelled out his intention to withdraw Soviet military forces within a limited time. Dobrynin later told a high-level visitor from an Islamic country that because of mixed signals being received in Kabul, it was necessary for Gorbachev to look the Afghan leader in the eye and tell him, "I hope you're ready in 12 months because we will be going, whether you are or not." Vorontsov, who attended the meeting, said Najibullah was under no illusions about Soviet intentions, though some of those around him found them difficult to accept.

Two days after meeting Najibullah, Gorbachev told the Indonesian newspaper *Merdeka*, "In principle, Soviet troop withdrawal from Afghanistan has been decided upon." The Soviet leader added, "We favor a short time-frame for the withdrawal. However, interference in the internal affairs of Afghanistan must be stopped and its non-resumption guaranteed." Soviet diplomats abroad were told they could use this statement as the basis for saying, from that point on, that the "political decision" had been made to withdraw.

Even without knowledge of the substance of the discussions between Moscow and Kabul, which were secret at the time, it was increasingly evident to close Western observers that there had been substantial movement in the Soviet position during the Gorbachev era and especially in 1987. Still, the inner sanctum statement by Shevardnadze to Shultz on September 15 was a revelation to the secretary of state. Even after hearing Shultz's report, other senior officials of the Reagan administration were skeptical that the Soviets would withdraw their troops by the end of the Reagan administration, as Shevardnadze had said. It seemed too good to be true, and too much of a risk for even Gorbachev to take. But over the months to come, the doubters would be proven wrong. Lieutenant General Boris Gromov, the commander of the Soviet combat force in Afghanistan, would complete the withdrawal by walking back across the steel bridge at the Soviet border point at Termez on 11:55 A.M. on February 15, 1989, twenty-six days after Reagan's term of office was up.

• A TREATY TAKES SHAPE

Under the political battering of the Iran-Contra scandal early in 1987, Reagan had dismissed White House Chief of Staff Donald Regan and on February 27 named former Senate Republican Leader Howard Baker as his successor. Baker, a flexible and experienced politician from Tennessee, initially set for himself the objective of trying to reinforce what he perceived to be Reagan's basic desire to have an accommodation with the Soviet Union on nuclear missiles—the medium-range ones in Europe and, if possible, the long-range ones as well. Baker was convinced on the basis of his private conversations with the President from his Senate days that "Reagan deep down inside had always felt that his tough talk, his commitment to the renovation and modernization of the armed forces were all preliminary to and prelude to the capstone of his foreign policy career, which would be, as he put it, to make the world safer from nuclear weapons or to abolish nuclear weapons. That remark in Iceland was not a throwaway. That was his fundamental commitment."

Nevertheless, the preoccupation in the White House in the early months of 1987 was political survival, not nuclear survival. In the first days of March, just after Baker's arrival at the White House, Reagan's pollster, Richard Wirthlin, recorded the all-time low point of public confidence in the Reagan presidency. Wirthlin reported to Reagan that 52 percent of those polled disapproved of the way he was doing his job, compared to 47 percent who approved. Not since January 1983 had Reagan's approval rating as reported to the White House by Wirthlin been less than 50 percent.

In the spring, after Shultz returned from Moscow with Gorbachev's offer of the "second zero" on shorter-range INF missiles, criticism of the prospective deal erupted. Richard Nixon, Henry Kissinger and Brent Scowcroft expressed worry about potential "denuclearization" of Western Europe. Leaders of the French and British governments were unhappy with the idea and the West German government was divided. At this point senior NATO military commanders were inclined to resist the second zero and try instead to deploy new shorter-range U.S. missiles to match a residual number of Soviet missiles because of their fear of denuclearization of Europe. Some European leaders feared that Reagan was pursuing a foreign policy triumph with the Soviet Union at the expense of their security and that, as columnist Jim Hoagland reported from Brussels, "the runaway horses set loose at Reykjavik are on the gallop again." After a late spring meeting where new problems were discussed, Reagan turned in frustration to his new chief of staff when only the two of them were left in the Oval Office. "Howard, I think I'm the only person left in this government who wants to try to see the completion of an INF Treaty with the Soviets," Reagan complained. Baker said his boss was wrong, that "many people" wanted the treaty, and urged him to hang tough.

In Britain, Italy and West Germany, the key countries where U.S. missiles were based, public opinion polls reported greater trust and confidence in Mikhail Gorbachev than in Ronald Reagan, a startling turnaround in European public views of the leaders of the two alliances. As the political muddle in Europe persisted, West Germany's conservative government headed by Chancellor Helmut Kohl marked time until June 4, before approving the "second zero" plan that Shultz had brought from Moscow nearly two months earlier. A week later NATO gave formal approval to the elimination of the shorter-range INF missiles at a meeting of NATO foreign ministers at Reykjavik June 12.

In the negotiations in Geneva, the United States and the Soviet Union had presented differing but overlapping drafts of the proposed INF Treaty, and diplomats had begun working long hours to finish the treaty by the fall or winter. On July 23, Gorbachev made their job easier with another headline-making concession. Instead of insisting on the right to retain one hundred medium-range warheads in the Asian part of the Soviet Union, theoretically to balance U.S. nuclear weapons deployments in Asia and the Pacific, Gorbachev agreed to eliminate these weapons as well. Washington quickly agreed to drop its counterdemand for one hundred medium-range missiles to be deployed on U.S. soil. Now the two sides were heading for what was called "global double zero," no more U.S. or Soviet medium-range missiles to be deployed anywhere in the world, and no more short-range INF missiles anywhere as well.

Suddenly, however, a new complication came to the fore. Although Moscow had agreed to exclude British and French medium-range nuclear missiles from the U.S.-Soviet treaty, a position that was distinctly unpopular with the Soviet military, the Soviet Union now began to demand the elimination of West German Pershing IA missiles, shorter-range (SRINF) weapons that belonged to the Germans but were equipped with U.S. nuclear warheads that remained under U.S. control. From the U.S. point of view these were German weapons that could not be included in a U.S.-Soviet pact, but from Moscow's point of view they were U.S. weapons. After behind-the-scenes communications between Washington and Bonn, including a secret appeal from Reagan, Chancellor Kohl made a surprise announcement August 26 that Germany would dismantle the missiles in question after the U.S.-Soviet treaty was signed and implemented. In that case, Washington agreed, it would destroy the nuclear warheads.

After all of this maneuvering—and much detailed negotiating at Geneva on verification and other aspects of the treaty—Shevardnadze came to Washington in mid-September. This was the occasion when the Soviet foreign minister informed Shultz in confidence of the impending pullout from Afghanistan. Virtually all the press and public interest focused on the negotiations to complete the INF Treaty and prepare for the U.S.-Soviet summit, where it would be signed. After three days of talks, the two sides announced they had reached "agreement in principle to conclude a treaty" eliminating all INF missiles. Little progress was made on the more complex issues of a strategic arms treaty and space agreement. To sign the INF Treaty and "to cover the full range of issues in the relationship between the two countries," a joint statement declared, Reagan and Gorbachev would meet in Washington in the fall. The "exact dates" for the third Reagan-Gorbachev summit meeting would be set during a trip by Shultz to Moscow in October, the announcement said.

• GORBACHEV BALKS

A special train carrying Secretary Shultz, National Security Adviser Frank Carlucci, their aides, bodyguards and thirty-five members of the American press rolled out of the Helsinki station bound for Moscow at 7:15 P.M. on October 21. The train ride, which had been arranged at the last minute with the Finnish and Soviet governments, was a surprise. It would not be the last or the biggest surprise of a memorable visit.

Shultz had spent five days in Israel, Egypt and Saudi Arabia—his first trip to the Middle East in twenty-nine months—before flying to Helsinki. Shultz liked the Finnish capital and found it a useful place to rest for a night or two and confer with his traveling party of officials before flying into Moscow. When Shultz arrived in Helsinki this time, however, Moscow airports had been fogged in for two days. As hope dwindled that the severe fog would lift to permit Shultz's U.S. Air Force plane to land on the third day, the State Department's resourceful travel chief, Executive Director Patrick Kennedy, arranged the special train.

The atmosphere was festive as the six modern Finnish railroad cars rolled along in the direction of the USSR. Shultz was something of a train buff and often operated an elaborate model train in the upstairs study of his Stanford home for his own delight and that of his grandchildren. The secretary was all smiles as he and O'Bie strolled through the press car, where the reporters had pulled out the bottles of whiskey, beer and soft drinks they had brought on board. Carlucci and his wife, Marsha, also walked through and stopped to chat. Despite a long career in government as a Foreign Service officer, ambassador, deputy CIA director and deputy secretary of defense, Carlucci had never been to the Soviet Union. His keen anticipation was obvious.

The roadbed became quite rough after the train passed the Soviet border, where a Soviet engine took over and a special dining car and a car filled with Soviet security agents were added. It was very bumpy as the train rolled on in the foggy morning light to Moscow, where one of the city's main railroad stations had been draped with Soviet and American flags in honor of Shultz's arrival.

Shevardnadze greeted Shultz warmly at the familiar Foreign Ministry guest house on Alexei Tolstoy Street, where most of the discussions were to take place, and Shultz seemed genuinely glad to see him. The rapport between the two men was evident and growing. Assistant Secretary of State Rozanne Ridgway remarked that the Soviet foreign minister had turned out to be "rather sweet." Everyone seemed confidently to expect that more details of the INF Treaty, perhaps the last outstanding details, would be wrapped up in the next two days and dates would be set for the Reagan-Gorbachev summit, as promised in the joint statement that had been issued in Washington a month earlier. It was the Soviet side that had suggested that line in the joint statement.

The first strange note was from Gary Lee, *The Washington Post* Moscow correspondent, who learned that U.S.A. Institute officials and other usual sources for the Moscow press had been told in a directive to say nothing about the approaching summit meeting. Usually accessible Soviets were lying low. On the afternoon of the first day, U.S. officials said later, a meeting of U.S. and Soviet arms control experts called to work on INF Treaty details was "totally unproductive." The Soviet side did not even show up for a scheduled second meeting.

On the morning of the second day, I joined other members of the U.S. press pool at the Spassky (Savior) Gate, which opens onto Red Square in the East Wall of the Kremlin near St. Basil's Cathedral, just a few yards from where Mathias Rust's airplane had landed five months earlier. The plaque on Spassky Tower said it had been built in 1491, one year before Columbus discovered America, and had been used by the czars and their retinues. Black official cars and an occasional long black Zil limousine with security cars front and back whizzed at high speeds in and out of the Kremlin through the gate under the watchful eyes of uniformed guards. A Soviet Foreign Ministry official in charge of press contacts met us at the gate, which is closed to the public, and walked with us into the business side of the Kremlin, where tourists are not permitted. The bustling sounds suddenly fell away, and I could hear birds chirp and see a great expanse of grass and some white birches near the classical Presidium building where Gorbachev had one of his offices. It reminded me of the sudden calm, amid the noisy city, of the Imperial Palace in Tokyo. Our Foreign Ministry guide seemed as optimistic as everyone else, telling us we would have "some good news to report" before the day was over.

Gorbachev met Shultz in St. Catherine's Hall precisely at 11:00 A.M. The Soviet leader posed for pictures with Shultz and the U.S. team and, through his interpreter, fielded shouted questions from the U.S. press pool. Standing next to Shultz, he seemed to me a surprisingly ordinary-looking person, a very human figure rather than a man of destiny who radiated power or command. He seemed at ease and didn't hesitate to answer questions, but he did not ham it up for the cameras or try to be clever as was often the case with U.S. politicians. Responding to a shouted question from our ranks about a trip to the United States, Gorbachev said, "I think it's going to happen." That seemed the final signal, if one were needed, that the agreement on the summit dates was in the bag.

After the reporters and photographers were escorted out, Gorbachev turned to Shultz and said, "How should we proceed?"

The secretary said his instructions were to complete the INF Treaty or to move the discussion to the point where it would be possible to complete the INF Treaty before the Washington summit. As for strategic arms, "it should be possible for you and the President to have an in-depth discussion" during the Washington visit, laying the groundwork for completing the treaty in the spring of 1988, the final year of the Reagan administration.

After Shultz and Shevardnadze reported on the status of their nearly completed work on INF, the talk turned once again to the SDI question, which Gorbachev called "this central problem." The Soviet Union had been flexible on the issue, Gorbachev said, but the United States had been "locked in concrete." He wanted to reiterate what he had said in a speech a few days earlier in Prague: Strategic offensive arms and space were "the root problem . . . the most important issues for the United States and the Soviet Union." Gorbachev complained to Shultz, "You've never mentioned space. You're still not talking about space. And if that isn't addressed, then movement in other areas makes no sense."

As Gorbachev saw it, the problem came down to two issues: strict observance of the 1972 Anti-Ballistic Missiles Treaty and the "optimum correlation of the elements of both sides' strategic forces." At this point Gorbachev began dangling a package deal, which became more explicit during the course of the discussion: U.S. agreement to a ten-year period of strict compliance with the ABM Treaty "as we both interpreted it and observed it before 1983," in return for Soviet agreement to establish reduced limits on strategic offensive arms. In essence, it was the Reykjavik package revisited.

From this point on, the discussion began to take on a surrealistic quality. Gorbachev was well aware from the meetings at Geneva and Reykjavik that Reagan was adamantly opposed to limitations on his cherished SDI program, yet he was insisting on confining U.S. activities in space within the strict or narrow interpretation of the ABM Treaty. Reagan had repeatedly opposed such limitations, even though he was abiding by them for the time being on the advice of Shultz and because of congressional insistence. The President had said time and again if the choice was between reducing offensive weapons and pursuing his "dream" of a shield against missiles in space, he would hold fast to his dream. Gorbachev, Shultz and Shevardnadze had all been witnesses to the stalemate and breakup in the final hours of Reykjavik one year earlier on this very issue.

Gorbachev, however, refused to give up. If he could not obtain an explicit deal at present, he would insist that a "key provisions agreement" be worked out that would cover the main ideas of limitations on strategic arms and space arms in a START (strategic arms) Treaty. The negotiators at Geneva should be working on this, he declared. "Such an agreement must be completed in time for a summit, for signature by myself and the President," said Gorbachev. He seemed to be saying this was a condition for his attendance at the Washington summit.

Shultz responded that such big issues would have to be decided by Gorbachev and the President themselves and could not be decided in advance of the summit by lower-level negotiators at Geneva.

"We just can't get together in Washington for an extemporaneous discussion. It's not going to be possible to have a second Reykjavik," countered Gorbachev. "The Soviet Union wants to improve relations with the United States. It's the United States that's lagging behind."

At this point Gorbachev reached into his papers and pulled out an eighty-nine-page U.S. State Department document with blue letters on a white cover: *Soviet Influence Activities: A Report on Active Measures and Propaganda, 1986–87,* which had been given to him by Dobrynin. Also on the cover was a reprinted cartoon from the October 31, 1986, issue of *Pravda* showing a broadly smiling U.S. military officer giving dollars to a grinning white-jacketed medical researcher in return for a big beaker of germs, labeled "Virus AIDS." The caption said in Russian that "The AIDS virus, a terrible disease for which up to now no known cure has been found, was, in the opinion of some Western researchers, created in the laboratories of the Pentagon."

Waving the document in the air, Gorbachev began a remarkable exchange by noting that the report criticized the "Mississippi peace cruise," an eight-day steamboat cruise in 1986 involving U.S. and Soviet participants. The report called it a Soviet-front activity concocted in the Kremlin. Gorbachev recalled that during the discussion of people-to-people exchanges at Geneva, he had praised the peace cruise as the sort of activity that was good. "Did you guys pick this [cruise] out on purpose just to show that I tried to deceive the president?" Gorbachev demanded.

Shultz could not remember ever seeing the document Gorbachev was displaying, even though it had been issued to the press by the Department of State earlier in the month. For the most part, it was the product of the CIA and other U.S. intelligence agencies in response to a 1985 Act of Congress requiring an annual report on anti-U.S. propaganda. "I'm not familiar with this document. Can I have it?" he asked Gorbachev.

"No, this is my only copy," the Soviet leader replied. "But I raise it because can't the United States live without portraying the Soviet Union as the enemy?" It seemed to him that some people in America were worried about a more positive public attitude toward the Soviet Union, that they were trying to portray two years of expanding people-to-people exchanges as a KGB penetration.

"Wait a minute," responded Shultz, trying to make the point that skepticism about the Soviet Union in the United States had a serious basis in Moscow's past actions. "Let me tell you some of the things that bother Americans. Take a look at Jimmy Carter. He is a man of good will, and he suddenly learned the lesson when the Soviet Union went into Afghanistan. KAL is another episode. These are the kinds of things that, in fact, bother Americans. And that's legitimate."

"Why don't you look into Gary Powers and the U-2 incident?" shot back Gorbachev.

Shultz was even sterner as he returned to the KAL episode. "Look, the problem in terms of impressions is that Gromyko sat in Madrid with all the other foreign ministers and said, 'Yes, we did it, and we'll do it again if we have to.' You know, a chill went through that whole room."

"How much did you pay in an insurance program for the pension of the pilot who flew the KAL?" demanded Gorbachev. "The guy was a spy and you needed to pay his pension."

"I'm not going to dignify that kind of innuendo with a comment," responded Shultz.

Gorbachev replied, "I'm going to ignore your answer too."

"Read Gromyko's speech. Everybody was appalled by it," said

Shultz, returning to the fray. And he kept going: "Look at what you're doing now about the spread of rumors that the United States had invented AIDS and was trying to spread it. And we were very happy when the Soviet authorities told us you were going to stop that campaign."

"Then why are you raising it?" Gorbachev demanded to know.

Those who had accompanied Shultz in his two previous meetings with Gorbachev had noticed that the Soviet leader seemed at some point in each meeting to show his temper about some aspect of U.S. policy or action. There was nothing to do but to stand firm and ride it out.

"Let me tell you what my own attitude is toward this relationship, and Dobrynin can verify this, because my attitude has remained constant since the 1970s," said Shultz, seeking to broaden the discussion. "The improvement of relations between the United States and the Soviet Union is the most important endeavor in international affairs; there is no more important task. But it's a difficult task, because our societies are different."

Gorbachev interrupted: "The Soviet Union didn't tell the United States how to change, what it should do."

Shultz responded: "We're not telling you how to change. You've got your own system and you're trying to change the system. We're fascinated by the process that you're going through as you try to change your system. And we'd like to know more about it. But it's a Soviet problem. It's not our problem."

Gorbachev, picking up *Soviet Influence Activities* again, asked, "If that's your attitude, that it's our problem and not your problem, then how can a document like this come to be?"

Shultz replied he had not seen it before, but that he suspected it wasn't as bad as Gorbachev had said.

Gorbachev continued, "It's a throwback to the old approach. What good did a document like this do? If the Secretary ever went around the Soviet Union, he wouldn't find people portraying Americans as enemies or ready to precipitate a bloodbath the way Soviet citizens are portrayed in the United States. President Reagan likes to say that everything is possible in this relationship once trust is established. Documents like this don't produce confidence or trust. There's been an improvement. We welcome it. The United States seems to be afraid of it." The General Secretary said he wanted to end this exchange by emphasizing that the Soviet Union wanted to improve relations. "The desire is [there] on the Soviet side, and the United States should think about it."

"I agree," said Shultz. "Both sides desire to improve relations."

"Okay, let's forget it," Gorbachev said, changing the subject.

The discussion went back to the unresolved question of dates for the Washington summit. "The President for his part is still hoping that you can come to the United States. He's prepared to receive you with respect and dignity and friendship," said Shultz, who added that late November would be the most convenient time from Reagan's standpoint.

"What kind of an agenda do you expect to have, in light of what we've just been saying here?" Gorbachev wanted to know. Especially, "What would be prepared for the meeting on strategic arms and space?"

Shultz said it would be a broad agenda reflecting all aspects of the relationship. He had made it clear in earlier remarks that Reagan would want to discuss human rights and regional issues such as Afghanistan and Southern Africa, as well as arms issues. Certainly there would be an INF Treaty to sign. As for strategic arms, "I can only tell you what I would like to see come out of it and that is a result which would enable us, given a push by you and the President, to complete work on a treaty by next spring." But, Shultz added, he could not guarantee this.

For the first time in the meeting, Shultz turned to Carlucci and asked him to comment on the prospects for a START (strategic arms) Treaty. The prospects were good and the President would like to move ahead, said the national security adviser. But Carlucci, a short, feisty former Princeton wrestler, told Gorbachev bluntly, "I am troubled by what you are doing when you place all this emphasis on linking the narrow interpretation of the ABM Treaty to START." He said Reagan would not be willing to accept "artificial restraints" on SDI. Carlucci said what was needed was a way to assure the Soviet Union of greater predictability about SDI without trying to restrain it through the ABM Treaty.

According to one participant on the U.S. side, Gorbachev threw his pencil down on the table after Carlucci's comment and expressed even greater concern about the coming summit. The agenda that he wanted—an INF Treaty, an agreement on "key provisions" on strategic arms and space, and progress on halting nuclear tests—"really hasn't emerged," said the General Secretary. "In that circumstance, I've got to wonder about the meaning of the summit. Would the leaders gain or lose in the eyes of their own countries and the world if there were a summit?" He went on to say, "I don't think they're going to understand if Reagan and I keep meeting and we have nothing to show for it, especially since in public both sides are saying that strategic arms are key."

At this point the confidence, almost certainty, that Gorbachev would agree to dates for the coming summit suddenly evaporated. There was surprise on the American side of the table. Shultz felt that Reagan would be disappointed. But rather than raising a bid to meet Gorbachev's new price, Shultz called his bluff by accepting the possibility that there would be no third summit meeting: "Well, if you feel that way about it, then maybe we'd better find a different way to wind up the INF Treaty. It's virtually complete. It should be signed. It should be ratified. It should be put into effect. It would carry more weight if the President and General Secretary signed it, but it could also be signed by the negotiators in Geneva. If there's not going to be a meeting of Reagan and Gorbachev, we'll have to give serious thought to some other way to sign the treaty."

"When I asked about the agenda for the Washington meeting, I didn't mean I wasn't going to come," said Gorbachev, seeming to backtrack momentarily. He said he wanted to visit the United States, but repeated that this could only happen if there were substantive results to justify it.

Shultz cautioned that there was not a great deal of time if the summit was to take place in 1987 as planned. The meeting could be delayed until 1988, but then there would be less time available for the Reagan administration to seek ratification of the INF Treaty or accomplish anything else in the relationship.

"Everything is a lot clearer after my talk with you," said Gorbachev. (Some of those on the other side of the table felt that everything was a great deal murkier.) "Both sides need to do some thinking. Clarify what should be done." He said that he would report to the Soviet leadership—a rare and, in retrospect, significant reminder that he was not a free agent—and that Shultz should report to the President.

Trying again to put the summit back on track, Shultz said, "There is merit to the proposition that meetings of the two superpowers should be able to take place without the world shaking. There is a lot to discuss. It isn't necessary that every central issue be resolved."

Gorbachev agreed with that, but said he felt the summit should be conducted in the manner he had described.

As the four-hour meeting drew toward its close, Shultz warned that Gorbachev should weigh carefully the advisability of tying the entire relationship with the United States to SDI.

Dobrynin then jumped in for the first time to say that the situation "seems headed for catastrophe" because of lack of movement on SDI.

So why not "rethink the matter" and use the remaining six weeks before early December to achieve progress?

"I don't have any objection to that kind of approach, but it's not realistic," said Shultz. He explained that Reagan believes it is "absolutely inappropriate" to link strategic arms reductions to space.

"This seems to indicate that everything that could be said has been said," Gorbachev observed. He said he would write a letter to Reagan expressing his views. "There is still time to reach an agreement on key provisions" regarding strategic arms and space, he insisted.

Shultz repeated it was unlikely that that kind of agreement could be reached.

"We can't just walk away from these problems," said Gorbachev finally. As he said that, the Soviet leader stood up and began to walk to the other side of the table, shaking hands with the Americans as the meeting broke up.

Shultz, Carlucci and their delegation—arms adviser Paul Nitze, Assistant Secretary of State Rozanne Ridgway, Ambassador Jack Matlock and their note-taker, State Department Director of Soviet Affairs Mark Parris—left the Kremlin blinking with surprise at what they had just witnessed.

Shultz, who had long experience in observing people in negotiating situations, thought he had detected something different about Gorbachev's demeanor from the start of the meeting. Recalling a line from Carl Sandburg's poem "Chicago," Shultz previously had viewed Gorbachev as cocksure, "laughing even as an ignorant fighter laughs who has never lost a battle." But on this occasion, Shultz told his team in the postmortem session, he no longer saw "a boxer who had never been hit." The secretary did not know what had happened or when, but he could sense that "this boxer's been hit."

Shultz's instinct was amazingly accurate. Ambassador Matlock had told him in Helsinki of some rumbles, which he could not verify, of trouble in the Soviet leadership, and it was known that an unusual session of the Central Committee had met on October 21, the day the special train left the Finnish capital for Moscow. However, it was only on October 30, a week after the meeting in St. Catherine's Hall, that news leaked out that Gorbachev had been openly and sharply criticized for the first time in the Central Committee session. The critic was Gorbachev's former ally Boris Yeltsin, who boldly charged that perestroika was losing momentum and the confidence of the people, and that a "cult of personality" was growing up around Gorbachev in the Politburo.

Gorbachev indeed had been nicked politically. Since the summer, Yegor Ligachev had been emerging as the standard-bearer within the Politburo of a conservative faction unhappy with Gorbachev's reform program. At the same time, Yeltsin was coming to the fore from the opposite direction, in the first of what would be many frontal challenges. Gorbachev's leadership was increasingly under political challenge within the party, and openly so. It was Gorbachev's new awareness of his own vulnerability that Shultz had sensed across the conference table.

Starting with the October 21 Central Committee plenum and the meeting with Shultz two days later, Gorbachev began exercising greater caution, which was notable in his much-awaited address on the occasion of the seventieth anniversary of the Bolshevik revolution in early November. In retrospect, it was a crucial change in the Soviet leader. Given the herculean task Gorbachev had set for himself in fundamental reform of Soviet society, economy and political life, hesitation was dangerous. The question arose whether a leader who did not throw caution to the winds could possibly do the job.

The Shultz team's postmortem immediately after Gorbachev balked also considered several other factors, personal and political, as explanations for his performance.

Shevardnadze, who was sitting on Gorbachev's right, looked unhappy during the Kremlin meeting, those on the American side of the table thought. Shultz found it unusually difficult to get eye contact with his opposite number. On the other hand Dobrynin, who was seated on Gorbachev's left, displayed no such concern and seemed to play more of a role than usual. There was speculation among the American officials, several of whom distrusted Dobrynin, that he was responsible for the setback. Perhaps the former ambassador believed that Reagan would be susceptible to pressure, especially in view of such vulnerabilities as the continuing Iran-Contra investigations and the sudden October 19 plunge in the U.S. stock market, more than five hundred points in a single day, which made a summit meeting with Gorbachev more politically attractive than ever to the U.S. President.

Another theory was that Gorbachev had sought once again to exert all the bargaining power at hand to force compromises on SDI and had overplayed his cards. *Washington Post* Moscow correspondent Celestine Bohlen, thinking back to the sudden stalemate on the SDI issue at the Reykjavik summit the previous October, began her news analysis of the surprising meeting in the Kremlin: "The same thing happened this time last year."

Shultz played down the unexpected roadblock. In reporting to Reagan by telephone after the meeting, Shultz explained that he had deliberately refused to offer concessions to obtain the summit meeting but that he could reverse himself before leaving Moscow if Reagan so desired. Shultz advised, and Reagan accepted, that "I think we should just pass. We shouldn't push for this." At the same time, Shultz avoided anything that smacked of a counterattack and said as little as possible in public about Gorbachev's refusal to arrange the summit dates. At his press conference before leaving Moscow, Shultz went through a long account of "constructive" and "most worthwhile" discussions before revealing the sensational news near the very end of his report. Asked by a reporter on his plane flying out of Moscow to describe his feelings as he realized that Gorbachev would not agree to the expected summit, the taciturn secretary replied, "You aren't trained in psychiatry, so I won't."

Gorbachev's balk was an enormous story in the American and European press, generating a torrent of speculation about what was going on in Moscow. But on October 26, only three days after Shultz's departure, the Soviet Foreign Ministry suddenly asked for visas so that Shevardnadze and senior aides could visit Washington to discuss the summit meeting. "The Soviets blinked," Reagan wrote in his diary after hearing the news from Shultz. The sudden turnaround in Soviet diplomacy, coming after decades in which positions changed only glacially if at all, did nothing to dampen the curiosity about what had happened inside the Kremlin.

Shevardnadze arrived in Washington on the early morning of October 30 with a conciliatory letter from Gorbachev to Reagan proposing that the summit begin on December 7. The letter said the two leaders should sign the INF Treaty and try to achieve a breakthrough toward a strategic arms treaty that could be signed during a visit by Reagan to Moscow during the first half of 1988. Gorbachev's terms for agreement on SDI included a ten-year period of nonwithdrawal from the ABM Treaty, but there was a slight shift in his language. Instead of insisting that the treaty be "strengthened," Gorbachev now said it must be strictly "observed." His demand for an agreement on "key provisions" as a condition of the summit had been dropped.

At 2:00 P.M., Washington time, the two governments made a simultaneous joint announcement:

Building on progress in U.S.-Soviet relations, including high-level exchanges and the discussions between Foreign Minister

Shevardnadze and Secretary of State Shultz in Washington on October 30, as well as their talks in Moscow, President Reagan and General Secretary Gorbachev have agreed to meet in the United States beginning on December 7, 1987.

Reagan made the announcement in the White House Press Room flanked by Shultz and Shevardnadze. Before the foreign minister could depart, a reporter asked if Gorbachev had "flip-flopped" on the summit. "There was no flip-flop," replied Shevardnadze through his interpreter. "Everything is going on according to plans."

• THE WASHINGTON SUMMIT

As dusk was falling on Monday, December 7, Mikhail and Raisa Gorbachev descended from their blue-and-white Aeroflot jet onto a red carpet laid down on the chilly tarmac at Andrews Air Force Base, just outside Washington. It was the third visit in history by the Soviet Union's senior leader to the capital of the United States. Nikita Khrushchev, full of peasantlike bluster about overtaking and surpassing the United States in economic might, inaugurated the series in 1959, arriving on the same Andrews tarmac for a visit to President Eisenhower and a coast-to-coast tour. Leonid Brezhnev was next in 1973, visiting President Nixon in Washington, Camp David and San Clemente, California, at the height of détente. After another fourteen-year interval, it was Gorbachev's turn to make his mark on Soviet-American history and on the consciousness of the American people.

The summit meeting in Washington in 1987 would be notably different from the earlier meetings of Gorbachev and Reagan. Geneva inaugurated face-to-face communications between the leaders and brought the first intense grappling with their differences, especially on Reagan's antimissile defense plan. Reykjavik was the high point of their personal interaction, in which they sat at the bargaining table in a small room for two days and swapped plans for nuclear disarmament, only to fall back in the end. By the time Gorbachev arrived in Washington, he had left behind most of the demands for curbing Reagan's Star Wars plans that he had insisted on with the President in Geneva and Reykjavik and presented to Shultz in the October meeting in the Kremlin. With rare exceptions, mostly on the prickly subject of human rights, Gorbachev sought to minimize his differences with Reagan for the purposes of the summit. Gorbachev had specified a businesslike summit, declining Reagan's offers of a trip around the United States or even a visit to Camp David. But once in Washington, the Soviet leader took his case to the American people in every way he could.

Unlike meetings in third countries, a summit in the U.S. or Soviet capital is a ceremonial occasion of the first magnitude, dressed up in the pageantry and symbolism of a state visit. The signing of the INF Treaty, the centerpiece of the Washington summit, added a special air of celebration, especially when presided over by the most outspokenly anticommunist president the United States had ever had, and the most articulate and exciting Soviet leader ever to visit the West. For the most part it was a spectacular public performance, broadcast live around the world, and overshadowing the private discussions between the two men. Both leaders had been buffeted by harsh domestic winds since they last met, and both had much at stake in obtaining the political boost that a highly visible and successful meeting could bring. Reagan and Gorbachev spoke to each other—and to the domestic and global audiences—with words, deeds and body language that dramatized the easy familiarity that they had developed in two years. The easing of tension between them and the nations they headed was on display. Like the Khrushchev and Brezhnev visits to Washington, Gorbachev's visit was a political event of historic importance.

The streets of Washington were decorated with red hammer-and-sickle Soviet flags as well as the Stars and Stripes when Gorbachev and his wife arrived at the White House in a black bulletproof Soviet Zil at 10:00 A.M. on Tuesday, December 8. After a trumpet fanfare, a twenty-one-gun salute and brief speeches on the South Lawn, the President led the General Secretary into the Oval Office for their first meeting.

Reagan opened with a discussion of the American dedication to human rights. As a nation of immigrants, he said, Americans valued highly the right of people to travel and to live where they wished. While the recent relaxation of Soviet restrictions on Jewish emigration was welcome, the President said, many more should be permitted to leave. Why establish quotas, Reagan asked; why not just let them go?

Gorbachev, who interpreted Reagan's initial remarks as an effort to put him on the defensive, responded heatedly. "Mr. President, you're not a prosecutor, and I'm not an accused. Let's have a conversation on an equal footing; otherwise, there will be no success in our conversations." He went on to attack the United States for its immigration quotas, for its armed patrols at the Mexican border and the currently discussed plans to build a fortified fence there, which was in Gorbachev's opinion as bad as anything the Soviet Union had ever done.

Reagan responded that the fence was to stop illegal entry by people who wanted to join American society because of its opportunities, not to stop people from abandoning a system they wanted to leave. "There's a big difference between wanting out and wanting in," the President said. Not surprisingly, the debate produced little.

After lunch at the Soviet Embassy, Gorbachev returned to the White House for the signing of the INF Treaty at 1:45 P.M. From the start of summit planning weeks in advance, the White House staff had seemed to be completely inflexible in its demand that this ceremonial high point of the visit be at that precise time on December 8, the first day of the summit. "Do you have any idea why the White House is so fixed on this hour for the signing of the INF Treaty?" asked a bewildered Shultz of his equally bewildered chief of protocol, Selwa Roosevelt. Only later did they realize that the U.S. President, the Soviet leader and the two most important governments on earth had unsuspectingly been doing the bidding of Nancy Reagan's California astrologer, who had picked that date and hour from her charts as most auspicious.

Auspicious or not, it was a close call whether the negotiators would finally complete their work on the highly detailed and complex treaty in time for the signing. The treaty had been repeatedly heralded: The joint statement on September 18 at the end of the Shevardnadze visit to Washington had announced "agreement in principle to conclude a treaty," and on October 23 in Moscow, after the Kremlin meeting with Gorbachev, Shultz announced that "we are virtually there" so far as the INF Treaty was concerned. Furthermore, the joint announcement of October 30, when Shevardnadze flew to Washington and set the summit dates, promised that the INF Treaty would be ready for signing at the summit, and Shultz declared, "If it doesn't get done, Mr. Shevardnadze and I are going to get kicked in the rear end very hard by our leaders."

Nevertheless, last-minute issues persisted, requiring Shultz and Shevardnadze to meet again in Geneva for two days of talks November 23–24 with their negotiators and experts. "We have now completed agreement on all outstanding INF issues," Shultz announced. But lo and behold, more problems cropped up, many of them having to do with the extensive on-site inspection of missile production facilities and missile destruction sites required by the treaty. The U.S. and Soviet negotiators in Geneva worked nearly around the clock until December 7, when they hastily took off together for Washington in a U.S. Air Force military cargo plane, assembling, checking and initialing the forty-one-page treaty and thick stack of associated documents, page by page, as they flew across the Atlantic. Gorbachev's Soviet airliner, coming from a stopover in London, passed the U.S. jet in the air. The INF plane carrying the treaty and its negotiators circled Andrews Air Force Base waiting to land until the welcoming ceremonies for Gorbachev were over.

After arrival in Washington, however, it was discovered that the Soviets had not handed over a required photograph of an SS-20 missile, claiming that no photographs existed of the missile outside the canister from which it is fired. There was consternation among the Americans, and Shultz was ready to recommend that Reagan refuse to sign the treaty unless a photograph could be obtained. Suddenly the photo that did not exist was received from Moscow and presented to the American negotiators at 7:30 A.M. on the day the treaty was to be signed.

The White House was festive as Gorbachev arrived, with the U.S. Marine Band playing spirited American and Soviet marches in the foyer. Congressional leaders, members of the U.S. Joint Chiefs of Staff, the chief of staff of the Soviet armed forces and other members of Gorbachev's party were gathered expectantly in the historic East Room, where Reagan held most of his news conferences and where the assassinated Abraham Lincoln and John Kennedy had lain in state. At a signal, Reagan and Gorbachev marched side by side down a red-carpeted hallway into the room as an announcer intoned, "Ladies and gentlemen, the President of the United States and the General Secretary of the Communist Party of the Soviet Union." Television viewers had goosebumps and the East Room guests responded with a long and loud standing ovation. Then Reagan spoke first:

Thank you all very much. Welcome to the White House.

This ceremony and the treaty we are signing today are both excellent examples of the rewards of patience. It was over six years ago, November 18, 1981, that I first proposed what could come to be called the zero option. It was a simple proposal, one might say disarmingly simple. (Laughter.)

Unlike treaties of the past, it didn't simply codify the status quo or a new arms buildup. It didn't simply talk of controlling an arms race. For the first time in history, the language of "arms control" was replaced by "arms reduction"—in this case, the complete elimination of an entire class of U.S. and Soviet nuclear missiles. . . .

We can only hope that this history-making agreement will not be an end in itself, but the beginning of a working relationship that will enable us to tackle the other issues, urgent issues, before us: strategic offensive nuclear weapons, the balance of conventional forces in Europe, the destructive and tragic regional conflicts that beset so many parts of our globe, and respect for the human and natural rights that God has granted to all men.

As he warmed to his subject, Reagan quoted what he called "an old Russian maxim" that he had been given by the American writer Suzanne Massie and had used in his discussions with Gorbachev, and frequently in public speeches, since the Geneva summit: "*doveryai, no proveryai—*trust, but verify."

Gorbachev interrupted with a good-natured protest, "You repeat that at every meeting."

When the laughter in the East Room died down, the old Hollywood trouper grinned, gave Gorbachev a little bow and replied, "I like it." The room erupted with even more laughter and delight at the comfortable familiarity of the two leaders.

Then it was Gorbachev's turn to speak:

Mr. President, ladies and gentlemen, comrades.

Succeeding generations will hand down their verdict on the importance of the event which we are about to witness, but I will venture to say that what we are going to do, the signing of the first ever agreement eliminating nuclear weapons, has a universal significance for mankind, both from the standpoint of world politics and from the standpoint of humanism.

For everyone, and above all for our two great powers, the treaty whose text is on this table offers a big chance, at last, to get onto the road leading away from the threat of catastrophe.

It is our duty to take full advantage of that chance, and move together toward a nuclear-free world, which holds out for our children and grandchildren, and for their children and grandchildren, the promise of a fulfilling and happy life, without fear and without a senseless waste of resources on weapons of destruction. . . .

May December 8, 1987, become a date that will be inscribed in the history books—a date that will mark the watershed separating the era of a mounting risk of nuclear war from the era of a demilitarization of human life.

Reagan and Gorbachev sat down at a table once used by Abraham Lincoln and signed the "Treaty between the United States of America and the Union of Soviet Socialist Republics on the Elimination of their Intermediate-Range and Shorter-Range Missiles" in two copies, one bound in slate-blue leather for the United States and one in burgundy-red leather for the Soviet Union. The documents required the destruction of 1,846 Soviet nuclear weapons and 846 U.S. weapons within three years, each under close inspection of the other side—about 4 percent of U.S. and Soviet nuclear arsenals. Then the two leaders walked back up the red-carpeted hallway to the State Dining Room where, outfitted with earpieces for simultaneous translation, they took turns speaking to their nations and the world at large via television. *Washington Post* television critic Tom Shales called the afternoon's public events "Christmas, Hanukah, the Fourth of July and your most fondly remembered birthday party all rolled into one."

When the celebration was over and the guests had departed, the two leaders and many of their aides crowded into the Cabinet Room for a business session on other issues. At one point thirty-four people were in the room and Chief of Protocol Selwa Roosevelt was admitting people "like a traffic cop," according to a U.S. aide. Gorbachev almost immediately took the initiative, saying he wanted to talk about what was going on in the Soviet Union. He spoke for fifteen minutes on the progress being made in *perestroika* from handwritten notes in red, green and black ink in a notebook he carried. Reagan, after being on an emotional high all day, had difficulty focusing on the business at hand or on much of anything else. Finally, to get into the conversation, Reagan told one of his famous anti-Soviet anecdotes, this one completely inappropriate to what Gorbachev had been saying. The Soviet leader colored with irritation but otherwise ignored the President's remarks.* When the discussion moved on to conventional arms issues, Reagan seemed unable to remember or relate the U.S. position. Shultz took over the conversation with Gorbachev. The President sat by in embarrassed silence while the Soviet leader and secretary of state talked business.

Reagan's senior aides were appalled. Chief of Staff Howard Baker said to Shultz, "We can't do this any more, to let Gorbachev almost get away with the thing." In the Oval Office, Shultz told Reagan that the meeting in the Cabinet Room had been "a terrible performance." Reagan appeared stricken. He knew Shultz was right, and abjectly asked what he should do about it. Supported by Baker, Shultz suggested there be no more big meetings with Gorbachev before an audience at the cabinet table. From now on, Reagan would perform on the intimate stage of the Oval Office or his small study nearby. The President also would be provided by his aides with succinct talking points on specific issues, in addition to the personal notes he had prepared for himself on the broad principles that interested him.

On returning to the Soviet Embassy, Gorbachev spoke volubly without notes to an eclectic assemblage of American authors, statesmen, actors, activists, clerics and academics, ranging from Henry Kissinger to Yoko Ono, in the first of a series of free-wheeling conversations that would help him dominate the U.S. news media as long as he remained in the country. During the summit Gorbachev spent five and one-half hours in business meetings with Reagan. But he spent seven hours in official dinners and other ceremonial events, and another seven hours meeting unofficial Americans or members of Congress at the Soviet Embassy. Soviet officials permitted much of this to be broadcast live by Cable News Network.

In a meeting with American publishers Gorbachev reacted sharply after being criticized about human rights. For the most part, though, Gorbachev was the apostle of change, speaking with an effortless super-

---

* Reagan tells the story in his memoir, *An American Life*, without reference to the conversation with Gorbachev. "An American scholar, on his way to the airport before a flight to the Soviet Union, got into a conversation with his cab driver, a young man who said that he was still finishing his education. The scholar asked, 'When you finish your schooling, what do you want to do?' The young man answered, 'I haven't decided yet.' After the scholar arrived at the airport in Moscow, his cab driver was also a young man who happened to mention he was still getting his education, and the scholar, who spoke Russian, asked, 'When you finish your schooling, what do you want to be, what do you want to do?' The young man answered, 'They haven't told me yet.' "

articulateness reminiscent of Senator Hubert Humphrey in his Washington heyday. Gorbachev told his audience that first afternoon, in a message that he would repeat in many different ways:

> I feel that something very serious is afoot, something very profound, something that embraces broad sections of the people both in the United States and the Soviet Union—an awareness that we cannot go on as we are, we cannot leave our relations as they are. . . .
>
> In this act there is more of a political symbol, more of a psychological turn. I would call this really a turning point. So let's think about how we should act from now on—where do we go from here? We are by no means in favor of any adventurism. We are against exploiting international relations or the international economic ties. You have to agree that there are so many problems that have arisen today that they cannot be put off any longer.

The response was electric. "The things he said were almost too good to be true; it's as if he came from another planet," said author Joyce Carol Oates, who was also amazed that Raisa Gorbachev said she had read her novel *Angel of Light*. Gorbachev preached a "beautiful picture of the world in which we are all brothers," said evangelist Billy Graham, another invited guest. "He's a very gifted performer," said actor Paul Newman of the Soviet leader. "He'd make a good actor because he's loose and you don't see the machinery of that looseness. He's not working to be loose and easy. He is."

On these occasions, Raisa was always present, and the Americans could see and feel how important she was to her husband. "What was most interesting to me was when the General Secretary was speaking he would always look over toward her, as if to check, 'how am I doing,' " said Wendy Luers, the wife of the president of the Metropolitan Museum of Art. Gorbachev, in an interview with NBC anchor Tom Brokaw just before the summit, said that he and Raisa "discuss everything," including Soviet affairs at the highest level. That was a sensitive point at home. The directors of Soviet television deleted the reference to highest-level policies when the interview was broadcast in the USSR.

Raisa was a strong-willed woman with influence on her husband, as was her Washington hostess, Nancy Reagan. As at Geneva, the two did not get along. The First Lady, who had enjoyed her own career in motion pictures before marrying Reagan, found her Soviet counterpart rude and condescending. When the two women met at the White House, Raisa began, "We missed you at Reykjavik." To which Nancy, taken aback, replied, "I was told women weren't invited." Mrs. Reagan was pained that, although they saw each other several times at the summit, Raisa never mentioned the First Lady's breast cancer operation or the death of her mother, both of which had taken place less than two months earlier.

Traveling from the Soviet Embassy to the White House for the final business meeting with the President on the third and last morning of the summit, Gorbachev demonstrated his popular appeal in the United States. Sitting in the back seat of his Zil with Vice President Bush after a breakfast together at the Embassy, Gorbachev was waving to the cheerful crowds held back by police lines. "It's too bad you can't stop and go in some of these stores, because I think you'd find warm greetings from the American people," said Bush as the heavily fortified car, which Gorbachev called his "bunker," rolled down the street surrounded by police motorcyclists and Secret Service. Suddenly Gorbachev ordered his driver to stop at Connecticut Avenue and L Street, one of Washington's busiest intersections. As the motorcade screeched to a halt and some apprehensive security agents emerged from their cars with their guns drawn, the beaming Gorbachev jumped out of his car, with a surprised Bush trailing behind, and began waving and shaking hands. Bush could see the adrenaline pumping in the Soviet politician. Usually blasé Washingtonians screamed with delight at the visitor who had taken the city by storm. A young woman in the crowd was shown on the evening news proclaiming, "That guy is a PR genius!"

The main business of the summit, beyond the celebration and symbolism, was the discussion of strategic and space arms, just as it had been in Geneva and Reykjavik. Since then, however, there had been major changes on both sides.

In Washington, a new national security team was in place. Caspar Weinberger had resigned on November 5, shortly after the announcement of the date for the December summit, and Reagan had named Frank Carlucci, a much more pragmatic figure, secretary of defense. Replacing Carlucci as presidential national security adviser was his deputy, Lieutenant General Colin Powell, a politically adroit career officer who shunned ideology. Richard Perle had returned to private life several months earlier. With Weinberger gone and the new team in place, the administration for the first time had a group of foreign and defense officials at the top that could work together on most issues. Shultz, Carlucci and Powell began a series of daily 7:00 A.M. meetings over coffee in Powell's office at the White House, with no staff, no formal agenda, no notes and no substitutes. While they did not always see eye to eye, the three men managed to work out the fundamental points of administration positions in the foreign and defense fields in those early morning meetings, before most of the government had even left home for work.

All three advisers were considerably less enthusiastic about SDI than Weinberger had been. But whatever their private views, they were well aware that the man they served, the President, was as dedicated as ever to his dream. The Friday before the summit, with the concurrence of the new security team, Reagan issued a directive setting out seemingly impossible negotiating goals on SDI with Gorbachev: explicit Soviet approval of SDI tests in space, and Soviet approval of U.S. deployment of strategic defenses after the end of an agreed period of nonwithdrawal from the ABM Treaty. Gorbachev had strongly rejected both these positions in earlier meetings.

The Soviet leader, however, had changed his tactics if not his basic posture on SDI since Geneva and Reykjavik and even since the Kremlin meeting with Shultz in late October. Approaching the Washington summit, Gorbachev appeared to have found merit in the view that vehement Soviet opposition actually was shoring up the dwindling support for SDI in Congress, where the President pointed to Moscow's bitter opposition as proof of the program's value and importance. Congress also played a part in Gorbachev's tactical retreat by tying Reagan's hands on SDI. On November 19, less than three weeks before Gorbachev's arrival, the lawmakers completed the defense bill that cut Reagan's budget request for SDI by one-third and barred the administration from executing tests in space that exceeded the narrow interpretation of the ABM Treaty for nearly all the rest of Reagan's term in office. The President reluctantly signed it into law December 4, three days before Gorbachev's arrival.

Reagan raised the subject of SDI with Gorbachev in their meeting in the Oval Office Wednesday morning, their only business session of the summit's second day. "We are going forward with the research and development to see if this is a workable concept and if it is, we are going to deploy it," the President said.

Surprisingly, given all his vehement objections in the past, Gorbachev reacted calmly. "Mr. President, do what you think you have to do. And if in the end you think you have a system you want to deploy, go ahead and deploy. Who am I to tell you what to do? I think you're wasting money. I don't think it will work. But if that's what you want to do, go ahead." Then he added, "We are moving in another direction, and we preserve our option to do what we think is necessary and in our own national interest at that time. And we think we can do it less expensively and with greater effectiveness." Gorbachev's unexpected statement suggested that the Soviet Union would no longer object as a matter of treaty law or principle to eventual U.S. deployment of SDI, but would act in its own national interest to counter SDI if and when the system was ready for operation.

A joint arms control working group under arms adviser Paul Nitze and Marshal Sergei Akhromeyev had been formed Tuesday and worked until midnight Wednesday in an effort to advance the strategic arms and space questions. The working group had made progress on some aspects of the proposed strategic arms treaty, which Reagan and Gorbachev hoped to sign when the President visited Moscow in mid-1988, but the experts were deadlocked as usual on space defense questions.

The most serious issue was that of U.S. testing in space, the very question that had brought about the breakup of the Reykjavik summit. At the Washington summit, Gorbachev no longer insisted that Reagan agree to confine SDI work to "laboratory testing," as he had in Reykjavik. The Soviet leader was more flexible—up to a point. In the first expression of a policy that would become clearer and more important in the Bush administration, Gorbachev also said the Soviet Union would let the United States proceed as it wished with SDI testing, but that the Soviet Union would feel free to withdraw from an offensive arms reduction treaty—thus being able to begin adding again to its strategic arms arsenal—if Moscow judged that the U.S. tests in space went beyond what was permitted by the Anti-Ballistic Missiles Treaty.

After several hours of intense bargaining among Shultz, Shevardnadze and the arms advisers on this and related issues in the White House Cabinet Room, the two sides agreed to an ambiguous statement committing each side to "observe the ABM Treaty, as signed in 1972, while conducting their research, development, and testing as required, which are permitted by the ABM Treaty, and not to withdraw from the ABM Treaty for a specified period of time."

Arguments erupted in the wake of the summit about just what that convoluted language meant. One thing, however, was clear: Gorbachev had decided not to see another summit meeting, especially one with all the ceremony and fanfare of a state visit, collapse in a fruitless argument with Reagan over the future of SDI. Arms adviser Max Kampelman summed up the accommodation on SDI reached by the two powers: "They kicked the can down the road."

While the foreign ministers and arms control advisers were still thrashing out details of the strategic and space arms statements, Reagan and Gorbachev took a ten-minute walk on the grounds of the White House, where photographers had been positioned. The walk had been planned by White House publicists as a way to photograph the two men in intimate discourse outside an office setting, symbolizing a successful summit. Reagan told aides he had an additional purpose in mind: to speak to Gorbachev bluntly and personally about Nicaragua, knowing that the Soviet leader probably would counter with discussion of Afghanistan.

The strolling conversation between an American President who spoke no Russian and a Soviet leader who spoke no English made for wonderful pictures, but it was difficult for their interpreters, who had to stay out of camera range, and confusing to government policymakers, who later obtained only very imprecise reports of what was said. There were no note-takers along, and even the interpreters had a hard time reporting on the dialogue. Reagan said in his memoirs that he told Gorbachev it would "go a long way toward improving U.S.-Soviet relations" if Moscow would stop supplying Soviet weapons to Nicaragua, and that "Gorbachev told me he would do that." When the President brought up the matter at the working luncheon in the Family Dining Room immediately after the walk, however, Gorbachev's answer was much more complex.

Why don't we say in our joint statement that the Soviet Union will not supply arms to Nicaragua? Reagan suggested.

Gorbachev had a counterproposal: Why not say that the two sides accept and support the Contadora accords and Guatemala accords (two Central American peace proposals that Reagan had only reluctantly accepted) and that we agree to practical measures to implement the accords? And in the process of working together, said Gorbachev, the two nations would agree to stop supplying arms to Nicaragua, except for police-type weapons.

When U.S. diplomats followed up this murky comment, Soviet diplomats said Moscow was willing to terminate its supply of weapons to the Sandinista government of Nicaragua if the United States would terminate its supply of weapons to the Nicaraguan Contra rebels, and also terminate arms supplies to U.S. allies in El Salvador, Guatemala and perhaps other Central American governments. Those were not terms that the Reagan administration would accept. But eighteen months later, after Reagan was out of office and George Bush agreed to terminate U.S. aid to the Contras, Gorbachev would tell Bush in a private letter that the Soviet Union had stopped supplying weapons to the Sandinistas.

On Afghanistan, the U.S. objective at the Washington summit was to push Gorbachev for a specific date on which the long-promised withdrawal of Soviet troops would begin. Gorbachev refused to set such a date, although he did confirm to Reagan that the duration of the Soviet pullout would be twelve months or even less. The Soviet leader, however, was clear about one condition: Soviet withdrawal would require a halt in U.S. aid to the Afghan *mujaheddin*.

On this point, the most important statement of the summit came from Reagan rather than from Gorbachev. The United States had committed itself as early as December 1985 to stop its arms aid to the Afghan resistance if the Soviets withdrew from Afghanistan. However, Reagan had not specifically approved that position before it was presented by the State Department to the United Nations and nobody had paid much attention to it at the time. As Soviet withdrawal became an increasingly serious possibility, Reagan and other conservatives were unhappy with this U.S. posture. Shortly before Gorbachev arrived in Washington, Reagan told network anchors in a broadcast interview that the United States would not agree to stop its arms flow because that would leave the "freedom fighters" at a disadvantage. He also made an emphatic statement along the same lines in his private discussion with Gorbachev.

Following the summit, Shevardnadze sent a message to Shultz asking pointedly who was speaking for the United States—the State Department, which was adhering to the 1985 cutoff pledge, or the President, who was insisting that there be no such cutoff of U.S. aid? After discussions that began over the Christmas holidays and culminated in mid-January in a meeting of Reagan, Shultz, Powell and Howard Baker, the United States said it would stop supplying aid to the *mujaheddin* only if the Soviet Union stopped its aid to the Kabul government, in effect abandoning the earlier U.S. pledge. This was to become a heated issue between Moscow and Washington as the endgame approached in Afghanistan.

The Reagan-Gorbachev working luncheon with their top advisers in the Family Dining Room, at which the regional issues were discussed on the final day of the summit, deteriorated into casual conversation between the two leaders as Shultz, Carlucci, Powell and Shevardnadze excused themselves to work on the still-unfinished details of the joint statement. As the delay dragged on, the military honor guards were assembling for the departure ceremony outside and the U.S. Marine Band was preparing to start playing the anthems it had prepared for the occasion. "I hope the band knows a lot of tunes," said an arms control official who knew that the negotiations over the summit statement were still underway.

After a few minutes, though, agreement was reached between the two teams. Reagan went into the White House Library, where Shultz and Powell showed him the proposed text of the communiqué. Shultz explained that both nations agreed they could pursue the testing of their missile defense programs "as required." Reagan looked questioningly to Powell. "Mr. President, I think we're fully protected," said the national security adviser.

Across the hall in the White House Map Room, Gorbachev was huddling over the same text with his advisers, Shevardnadze and Akhromeyev. They explained their interpretation of the arcane words that would be the temporary settlement of the space defense dispute. "All right," said Gorbachev, "we'll go with it."

Outside it was beginning to rain, first a few drops and then steadily. White House ushers produced umbrellas for the Reagans and the Gorbachevs as they said their public good-byes in front of the cameras and reporters on the South Lawn.

Reagan spoke first, calling the summit "a clear success" and comparing its promise of hope with the star atop the national Christmas tree, which the President had lit the evening of Gorbachev's arrival in Washington.

Gorbachev, in turn, declared that "a good deal has been accomplished." Neither he nor Reagan referred to the SDI language, which was too new to be reflected in their prepared remarks. The General Secretary spoke of his impression, which he said had been confirmed by his visit, that "there is a growing desire in American society for improved Soviet-American relations" matching that which was prevalent in the Soviet Union. He ended, as the sudden squall erupted with full force:

> I believe that what we have accomplished during the meeting and discussion will, with time, help considerably to improve the atmosphere in the world at large, and in America itself, in terms of its more correct and tolerant perception of my country, the Soviet Union.
>
> Today, the Soviet Union and the United States are closer to the common goals of strengthening international security. But this goal is yet to be reached. There is still much work to be done, and we must get down to it without delay.
>
> Mr. President, esteemed citizens of the United States. We are grateful for your hospitality, and we wish success, well-being and peace to all Americans. Thank you and goodbye.

7. Reagan in Red Square

The final year of Ronald Reagan's term, 1988, would demonstrate that both the United States and the Soviet Union had decisively entered a new age.

During Reagan's final year the Soviet Union would begin— and nearly complete—the withdrawal of its troops from Afghanistan, the most convincing evidence yet that the expansionism of the 1970s had ended and geopolitical retreat was underway. At midyear, in a retrenchment of another sort, the two nations would complete preparations to destroy the intermediate-range nuclear weapons they had deployed in Europe and elsewhere, about 4 percent of their arsenals, when the U.S. Senate and the Supreme Soviet ratified the Intermediate-range Nuclear Forces Treaty. The Senate action would come as Reagan was on his way to Moscow for a highly symbolic visit that would sum up how far U.S.-Soviet relations and Reagan personally had come since the days of the "Evil Empire" speech and the deep chill of 1983.

It was evident by the time of Reagan's visit that the Strategic Arms Reduction Treaty, mandating deep cuts in the nuclear arsenals of the two nations, was not likely to be completed during Reagan's term of office. As the administration wound down, its ability to make shifts in other policies toward the Soviet Union would also diminish. An undaunted Gorbachev, although increas-

ingly buffeted at home by political opposition and economic set-backs, would fly to New York in December to announce his most dramatic international initiative from the rostrum of the United Nations General Assembly: the unilateral reduction of Soviet military forces by half a million men and large amounts of modern military equipment, much of which was to be removed from the soil of Eastern European countries. On the same visit, he would travel to Governors Island in New York harbor to say good-bye to Reagan in the shadow of the Statue of Liberty and to prepare a working relationship with President-elect George Bush.

• ENDGAME IN AFGHANISTAN

In the early weeks of 1988, I went to see Under Secretary of State Michael Armacost, the number-three official of the State Department, who had special responsibility for policy regarding Afghanistan and other regional disputes involving the Soviet Union. Since a meeting in Geneva in November with his Soviet opposite number, Deputy Foreign Minister Yuli Vorontsov, Armacost had become increasingly convinced that the Soviets were preparing to withdraw from Afghanistan. It seemed to him, he told me, that the Soviet Union was in much the same situation as the United States early in the 1970s in Vietnam: It had fully recognized the high cost of continuing to send its young men to die and had decided to withdraw, but had not made the tough decision about how and when to do it.

Armacost's view was considered much too optimistic by many in official Washington, especially in the CIA and Pentagon, who believed that the talk of withdrawal was a Soviet political deception and not to be taken seriously. The Soviet Union had never withdrawn troops under fire from a foreign occupation since the end of World War II; there was great skepticism that they would do so in Afghanistan. The CIA, which had previously been divided about Soviet intentions in Afghanistan, was now taking a clearer stand that Moscow was *not* getting out. Deputy CIA Director Robert Gates bet Armacost twenty-five dollars that the Soviets would not leave Afghanistan, and Fritz Ermarth, the CIA national intelligence officer for the Soviet Union, bet him fifty dollars that the unthinkable would not happen.

A visiting delegation of Soviet journalists, who came to *The Washington Post* on February 1, provided an insight into Soviet impatience with the war. Among the visitors was Vitaly Kobysh, who had been a staff member of the Communist Party Central Committee until his recent move to the government newspaper *Izvestia* as a political observer, the highest rung in Soviet journalism. When the talk turned to Afghanistan, Kobysh became passionate and agitated, almost shouting across the luncheon table, "We are going to leave Afghanistan in 1988, no matter what! And we need your help!"

On the evening of February 8, Gorbachev went a long way toward settling the issue. When Soviet citizens tuned in *Vremya*, the main television evening news program, they saw and heard an announcer read a lengthy statement in the name of Gorbachev, setting a date—May 15— for the start of the Soviet withdrawal and declaring that all the troops would be out by the following March 15, ten months from the start of the pullout.* The Gorbachev statement set some conditions, notably the signing of the U.N.-sponsored Geneva accords on Afghanistan that were nearly complete and the cessation of outside "interference" in Afghanistan's affairs. What was notable, though, was that this announcement was addressed to the Soviet public, which was weary of the war. It represented a virtual promise from the Soviet leadership to bring the boys home, making it very difficult for Gorbachev to bargain with the Americans about the issue.

Less than two weeks after Gorbachev's announcement, Shultz flew to Moscow for previously scheduled meetings with Shevardnadze and Gorbachev to begin planning the Moscow summit. However, the principal subject on the mind of everyone, including the accompanying press corps, was the negotiations over Afghanistan. Having been a correspondent in Washington and Vietnam during the painful and prolonged U.S. extrication from that war, I was fascinated by how the Soviet Union was trying to handle its retreat. On my first day in Moscow, I saw Radomir Bogdanov, a deputy director of the U.S.A. and Canada Institute, an unusually candid and well-informed person. "This is an event of tremendous significance. It is the beginning of a post-Afghanistan world for us, bringing a different situation externally and at home," Bogdanov said with remarkable prescience, in view of the striking impact of the Afghan pullout on Soviet willingness to use military force and on the

* This was later reduced to nine months, with a February 15, 1989, end-date.

calculations of governments and their challengers in Eastern Europe. "Since World War II, every other major power has lost a war: the British lost east of Suez, the French lost in Algeria, and the United States lost in Vietnam. Until now it hadn't happened to us, but now we will be like everyone else."

Bogdanov's plea, like that of Shevardnadze in the private talks he was having with Shultz, was for U.S. assistance in making the withdrawal as painless as possible. The shape of the post-Afghanistan foreign policy of the Soviet Union was at stake in how the pullout proceeded, Bogdanov said, suggesting that Gorbachev's leadership was on the line. He argued that the future foreign policy of the Soviet Union was far more important to the United States than the future of Afghanistan.

On that first day, Shultz and Shevardnadze talked well past midnight on the subject of regional issues, especially the hardening differences on Afghanistan. Since the Washington summit, Reagan and his senior aides had become increasingly determined that the United States not terminate its military aid to the Afghan resistance unless the Soviet Union stopped its military aid to the Kabul government. Shevardnadze argued that this was a new condition being imposed by Washington in violation of earlier understandings—which was essentially true—and that aid to a legitimate government, recognized by the United Nations and the world community, was a different matter from aid to rebel forces seeking that government's overthrow. Besides, the Soviet Union had agreements with Afghanistan dating back to 1921 "and we intend to live up to them," Shevardnadze told the secretary. In that case, Shultz responded in a statement of the new U.S. policy since the turn of the year, the United States would feel free to continue its aid to the resistance against a regime that was illegally installed by Soviet troops and lacked the support of the Afghan people. The two ministers went round and round the same points, with no compromise in sight.

In St. Catherine's Hall the following morning, February 22, Shultz and his team found an impatient Mikhail Gorbachev. In the photo session preceding the meeting, I noticed a change in Gorbachev's mood from the Washington summit and from earlier meetings with Shultz in the same ornate Kremlin room. No longer was Gorbachev interested in banter with the press. He was plainly irritated by the need for even this brief delay of the business at hand. Gorbachev had become a man in a hurry.

By this time, the Soviet leader had met Shultz three times in Moscow, and he had met Reagan and Shultz three times at summit meetings in

Geneva, Reykjavik and Washington. For all of their differences and sometimes heated debates, Gorbachev had become comfortable with his U.S. interlocutors. After the press was ushered out, Gorbachev expressed his concern about the time less than a year away when he would have to deal with a new group of U.S. officials. Gorbachev told the Americans, "I wish that we could sort of postpone all of this for three or four years so that we could keep working in a quiet setting." For the first time in the Gorbachev-Shultz discussions the Soviet leader had no surprises and no pyrotechnic displays of temper. Deputy Assistant Secretary of State Thomas Simons, who was at the Kremlin table on this and earlier occasions, said he found Gorbachev "subdued."

While arms issues, especially strategic arms, were covered, a much greater proportion of the discussion than usual dealt with regional conflicts in the Persian Gulf, the Middle East and, especially, Afghanistan. Gorbachev expressed dissatisfaction with what Reagan had said about Afghanistan at the Washington summit, when the President had first begun to insist that U.S. military aid to the *mujaheddin* would continue even after Soviet soldiers left. "The United States had said all along that it wanted the Soviet side to declare it would withdraw and set a date," Gorbachev noted. And now he had done this, but it didn't seem to settle anything. There were even those who were "impudent" enough to claim that he had made his declaration to the Soviet people just for propaganda, Gorbachev complained.

"That doesn't include the American side. We're taking what you said at face value," responded Shultz, ignoring the doubts of many in the U.S. capital. The secretary recalled that Shevardnadze had told him the previous September that Soviet troops were getting out. The United States had been confident ever since that this is what the Soviet Union was planning to do, Shultz added.

Gorbachev declared it was "nonsense" that the Soviet Union had ever had any intention of using Afghanistan as a bridgehead, base or road to the warm seas as had been often suspected in the West. "The Soviet Union never had such plans and doesn't now," he said. Gorbachev had only one request of Shultz: that the United States work for the early signing of the Geneva agreements and for their implementation so that there could be a neutral, nonaligned and independent Afghanistan.

Shultz then brought up a troublesome point, the issue of an interim coalition government. For a long time Moscow had insisted that such a government be formed before its soldiers began to leave. At the urging of Washington, Gorbachev had reversed himself the previous winter. But now Pakistan, Washington's ally, having second thoughts about the Geneva agreements, was saying that a political settlement should come before the international accords. Shultz had agreed to take Pakistan's case to Gorbachev, even though the U.S. administration wasn't happy with it.

Gorbachev interrupted Shultz's presentation. "That [Afghan] government is not going to be formed in Moscow or Washington, much less in Pakistan," the General Secretary said. "In fact, we are now finding out how many contacts there are among the Afghan groups themselves that we were unaware of. It's not all that simple. Let's be realistic." Gorbachev was scornful of the shifts in position that were taking place, saying that "the Soviet Union can't dance to the changing moods of the parties there. The matter is too important and we can't be dancing a polka with any of them."

Shevardnadze flew to Washington in late March for another full-scale ministerial meeting in preparation for the Moscow summit. It was the fourth round of meetings between Shultz and Shevardnadze and their diplomatic teams in six months, and the twenty-third set of meetings they had had in the thirty-three months since Shevardnadze had succeeded Andrei Gromyko as Soviet foreign minister. The ministerial meetings, which usually lasted two days, had settled into a useful pattern that was later continued by the Bush administration: The two ministers would meet privately or with only a few aides to set the agenda; second-level officials and experts would go off in working groups on arms control, regional issues, human rights, bilateral questions (and, under Bush, transnational issues), while the ministers dealt with the most important of the subjects at a higher political level; the working groups would report their progress and problems to the ministers, who would try to compromise on some outstanding points; and after most or all of this work had been done, the foreign ministers would report in person to the President, if the meeting was in Washington, or Gorbachev, if it was in Moscow. In this way, the bureaucracies and experts as well as the leaderships were involved, across a wide range of foreign policy business.

Before the March meetings Shultz, hoping that Nanuli Shevardnadze would accompany her husband, had made arrangements for the two couples to go together to a U.S.-Soviet arts festival being held in Boston, where he also planned to show the Shevardnadzes some historical American sights. At the last minute the Soviet minister turned down the invitation. After he walked into Shultz's office at the State Department on the first day of talks, it became evident why a touristic side trip and an open display of personal friendship with the U.S. secretary of state were out of the question at the moment. Shevardnadze was all business, and the business at the top of his list was Afghanistan.

Shevardnadze, as chairman of the special Politburo commission on Afghanistan, had taken a key role in the Kremlin in the decision to withdraw, believing, as he later said, that it was "not a just war." But he also believed that the Soviet Union could not doom or abandon the regime it had put in place in Kabul, and he pleaded with Shultz in often emotional terms for the United States to halt its supply of arms to the Afghan resistance. Shevardnadze argued that Moscow had done nearly everything that Washington had asked: It had taken the political decision to withdraw its troops and set a date for the withdrawal to begin; it had established a short timetable for the pullout, ten months, which had now been reduced to nine months and could even be reduced by another month or two if Washington would cooperate; and it had agreed to "front load" the pullout, as Washington had asked, by removing half of all the Soviet troops in the first ninety days. In short, the Soviets had made all the concessions and arrangements to prepare the Geneva agreements that would place an international imprimatur on its historic withdrawal from Afghanistan. It was all ready, Shevardnadze said, except "this one last piece," and the United States was refusing to cooperate.

Shultz was having none of it. From the U.S. viewpoint, the Soviet Union had gotten itself into this mess by its unjustifiable 1979 invasion and its brutal war and occupation; and it was not up to the United States to make concessions to help the Soviets get out—especially if those concessions would come at the expense of the guerrillas who had fought the vaunted Soviet armed forces to a stalemate. Knowing that the *mujaheddin* had a large stockpile of arms, Washington was willing to reduce or even terminate its future arms shipments—but only in a symmetrical arrangement in which Moscow did the same with its client government in Kabul. To make a reciprocal cutoff easier to swallow, Shultz suggested a three-month temporary halt, or moratorium, on weapons transfers to either side. Shevardnadze wouldn't buy it.

At midday on March 23, the final day of the meetings, the two sides announced the dates for the Moscow summit, May 29 through June 2, but otherwise were able to show little progress toward agreement on any front. Late that afternoon, in a meeting that went three hours overtime,

Shevardnadze demanded a clear-cut "yes or no" answer about the U.S. arms cutoff in Afghanistan. Shultz caucused with Armacost and Lieutenant General Colin Powell, the presidential national security adviser, and responded with his previously fixed position—"yes, if," that is, *if* the Soviets would also cut off arms aid to their clients. "This has been tough going," Shultz told reporters after the meetings ended. Assistant Secretary of State Rozanne Ridgway accompanied a dejected Shevardnadze to his Aeroflot plane at Andrews Air Force Base at 11:00 P.M. to begin the long flight home to Moscow. "He seemed like a very lonely man" going up the ramp to his plane, Ridgway said the following day.

In the wake of the Washington meetings, both sides consulted their clients and assessed whether to go ahead with the signing of the UN-negotiated Geneva accords. Afghanistan and Pakistan were the two principal parties to the proposed agreements, with the Soviet Union and United States signing on as "guarantors."

Pakistan had a serious problem. The agreement it was preparing to sign with Afghanistan committed it "to prevent within its territory the training, equipping, financing and recruiting of mercenaries from whatever origin for the purpose of hostile activities against the other High Contracting Party," when in fact the training, equipping, financing and recruiting of the Afghan insurgents was based in Pakistan and, by agreement with the United States and Islamic countries, these activities were planned to continue after signing of the agreement.

If Pakistan refused to sign the Geneva agreements after having previously accepted virtually every paragraph during six years of UN negotiations, it would risk world condemnation, especially if the Soviets were to use Pakistan's refusal as a reason to postpone or cancel the withdrawal. Pakistan's leaders, especially the civilian prime minister, Mohammed Khan Junejo, did not wish to run this risk. In a telephone call to Shultz on March 30, Junejo said Pakistan wanted to sign the Geneva agreements and hoped the United States would also sign as a guarantor. He assured Shultz he understood that, notwithstanding its pledge in the international documents, Pakistan would continue to be the base and conduit for arms of the *mujaheddin*. To confirm the arrangements with the real power in Pakistan, President Mohammed Zia ul-Haq, it was arranged for Zia to telephone Reagan the same day. About the arms supply to the Afghan resistance, Zia told Reagan, "We'll just lie about it. That's what we've been doing for eight years." He added, "Muslims have the right to lie in a good cause."

The Soviet discussions with its Afghan allies were more complicated, because it was a life-or-death situation for that regime and its adherents. Few officials in either Moscow or Washington believed that President Najibullah's Kabul government could stand alone for more than a few months after the Soviet forces left, even without continuing U.S. aid to the *mujaheddin* rebels. With the United States insisting that it would continue arming the resistance, the odds against the survival of his regime seemed even longer.

On April 3, Shevardnadze flew to Kabul to obtain Najibullah's consent to move ahead with the Geneva agreement despite the U.S. position. He had tough sledding. Najibullah was among the few people in the Kabul leadership who thought his regime had a real chance to survive the Soviet withdrawal. "We are not going to collapse," Najibullah kept repeating, but even he was alarmed by the idea of "symmetry" in the arms supplies of the two great powers. According to Yuli Vorontsov, who was the Soviet Foreign Ministry's leading expert on Afghanistan, the Afghans considered "totally and absolutely unacceptable" any idea that Moscow would limit or stop its arms supplies. Najibullah was also bitterly opposed to the continuation of U.S. military aid to the *mujaheddin* and threatened not to sign the Geveva accords. After three days of difficult discussions, Najibullah accompanied Shevardnadze to Tashkent, two hundred miles inside the Soviet Union. Gorbachev flew from Moscow to meet them. The following day, the two governments announced that all remaining obstacles to the signing of the Geneva accords and the pullout of Soviet troops had been removed.

Shultz, Shevardnadze and the Afghan and Pakistani foreign ministers signed the agreements in Geneva on April 14. But as he signed for the United States as a guarantor of "noninterference," Shultz made an oral declaration to the contrary, reflecting a side agreement that Moscow had reluctantly accepted:

> It is our hope that the Soviet Union will contribute to this process by ending the flow of arms to its client regime in Kabul. But we have made clear to Soviet leaders that, consistent with our obligations as guarantor, it is our right to provide military aid to the resistance. We are ready to exercise that right, but we are prepared to meet restraint with restraint.

When Shevardnadze signed the agreement on behalf of the Soviet Union, he was flooded by mixed emotions, he recounted two years later:

It might have seemed that I should have been happy: There would be an end to the caskets arriving in the country. The account of deaths and expenditure, which had reached 60 billion rubles, would be closed. But, despite this, I felt profoundly depressed. When my comrades asked me what the matter was, I did not conceal what was on my mind: It was hard for me to see myself as a foreign minister who had signed by no means a victory agreement. Such had not been a frequent occurrence in the history of Russia and the Soviet Union. And I was further troubled by the thought of people whom we ourselves had nursed and roused to revolution and whom we were now leaving one-on-one with a deadly enemy.

What is true patriotism: satisfying the arrogance of statehood by sending others' children to die in a foreign country, or the courage to recognize mistakes and prevent new ones, spare young men and restore the country's good name? We live in a world of realities and a world of emotions. Realities dictate one line of conduct, feelings rise up against it.

As the Soviet forces prepared to begin their withdrawal on May 15, Shevardnadze and Soviet KGB Chief Vladimir Kryuchkov visited Najibullah at his home in Kabul. In the course of the conversation, they delicately suggested that while the fighting continued, the Afghan leader's wife and three daughters be evacuated to the Soviet Union for their safety. "We're not leaving our home to go anywhere; we're all staying together," said Najibullah's wife, Fatana, turning down the offer to flee.

• APRIL IN MOSCOW: RHETORIC AND REALISM

On April 21, one week after signing the Geneva agreements, Shultz flew to Moscow for another round of ministerial meetings to prepare for President Reagan's forthcoming trip to Moscow. For the first time in months, Afghanistan did not dominate the discussions.

Even on a spring morning, the sheer drabness of the Soviet capital was a depressing sight to the arriving U.S. party. The dingy buildings and the old smoke-belching cars contributed to the impression of a moldering city that didn't work. Few Americans ever arrived in Moscow without pondering how this could be the capital of "the other super-power."* The reason for the Soviet Union's global standing was its outsized military power, giving rise to a description of the country as "a pygmy with a powerful right arm." Now that Gorbachev was shifting the Soviet emphasis away from military might and preparing to bring Soviet troops out of Afghanistan, the world's fear of Moscow's powerful right arm was diminishing.

The question being insistently asked in Washington was when to begin dismantling the apparatus of the Cold War. For all the talk of a defensive military doctrine and reasonable sufficiency, these policy pronouncements had not yet been backed up with tangible action. The pullout from Afghanistan, which was to start in mid-May, was expected to be the first truly impressive, clear-cut evidence of change.

In the meantime, Gorbachev's policies were under attack and, to some degree, in retreat in the partly democratic, partly authoritarian political system of the Soviet Union. On March 13, politically aware Soviets had been shaken by the publication of a ringing antireform manifesto in *Sovietskaya Rossiya*, the newspaper of the Russian Republic's government. The declaration, titled "I Cannot Betray My Principles," was written by Nina Andreyeva, a Leningrad chemistry teacher, and seized upon by conservatives in the Soviet leadership. It was given wide official circulation and was the talk of Moscow. It took three weeks and a major struggle in the Politburo for Gorbachev to strike back with a full-page *Pravda* article on April 5 rebutting Andreyeva; in the meantime his authority had hung in the balance.

Gorbachev reflected on some of his problems, as well as a spirited defense of the transition that he had begun in Soviet policy, in his meeting with Shultz in St. Catherine's Hall on the morning of April 22. It was something of a valedictory occasion—the last time that a U.S. delegation headed by Shultz would meet the Soviet leader in this former throne room of the czarinas, with its nineteenth-century standing lamps of gold and crystal from St. Petersburg, gilded wooden doors encrusted with semiprecious stones, green malachite columns and other reminders

---

* CIA estimates said the Soviet economy in the mid-1980s was about half the size of the American economy, but to visitors the Soviet Union seemed far behind the West. Independent Soviet economists and Anders Aslund, a Swedish economist who lived in Moscow, have said that the true figure was one-third or less of the U.S. economy. After the recent severe Soviet economic setbacks a World Bank–International Monetary Fund study said Soviet economic output (GNP) in 1989 was only one-tenth that of the United States.

of the grand imperial past. Gorbachev was in the mood to engage in a broad, deep and at times philosophical discussion with his American visitors. But first, he had a sharp protest to register.

As soon as the reporters and photographers left, Gorbachev picked up a folder from the table in front of him. "Here are my notes," he said, displaying the completely empty folder. There were handwritten jottings all over it, down the sides, through the middle and at angles, written in heavy black script by a felt-tipped pen.

"Maybe the Soviet Union has exaggerated the possibilities for our relationship, maybe we haven't always been realistic enough in our assessment of what is possible in terms of reaching a new stage in our relations," Gorbachev began on a foreboding note, which made the Americans stiffen and wonder what was coming next.

"In recent years, bricks have been put into the structure of new Soviet-American relationships," Gorbachev continued. "The progress the two sides have been able to make was the result, first of all, of our more realistic approach to each other. Maybe the two sides are beginning to find a way out of the prison of old stereotypes, away from imposing our own approaches and views on each other and from stressing only our own interests. Because these are the things that in the past have stood in the way of improving relations."

Gorbachev then focused on the sore point that prompted his philosophical discourse—"recent U.S. speeches," especially the most recent speech of Reagan, which had been delivered two days earlier to the World Affairs Council in Springfield, Massachusetts. The full texts of this and other Reagan speeches, most of which were reported at modest length or less in the U.S. press, were routinely obtained by the Soviet Embassy in Washington and propelled by the latest electronic means to the desks of Politburo members only a few hours after they were made. The Springfield speech seemed to show, said Gorbachev, that "the U.S. administration is not abandoning stereotypes, not abandoning reliance on force, not taking account of the political realities and the interests of others, the balance of interests.

"This is an attempt to preach to us, to teach us . . . to characterize Soviet foreign policy as exclusively negative and American foreign policy as exclusively positive," Gorbachev went on, his anger rising. "How am I supposed to explain this? Is it the election campaign? Is it the old policy affections of the President? Has the administration exhausted some limits? Those are domestic questions for you. But there does seem to be a reversal. Maybe both sides have built their policies on illusions. The Soviet side has abandoned its illusions."

Shultz had not seen the Springfield speech, which had not been considered a significant U.S. policy declaration until Gorbachev brought it up. A copy had been sent to the State Department for review a few hours before it was delivered, after Shultz had already left for Moscow. The speech draft was read by lower-level diplomats, who considered it a rather typical product of the presidential speechwriting team, which was among the most conservative groups in the White House. State had made a few suggestions for changes, some of which had been accepted. The U.S. press, which was accustomed to Reagan's anticommunist rhetoric, found nothing surprising in it. Nonetheless, there was much in the speech for Gorbachev to criticize, especially when his major worry became evident: that Reagan would bring the same sort of red-bashing oratory to the Moscow summit, where it would embarrass the Soviet leader on his home ground. Even at this stage there were strong doubts among Soviet conservatives about Reagan's commitment to a new relationship, and there was controversy in party circles about inviting him to the capital of the communist world. If Reagan were to embarrass Gorbachev at the summit, the timing would magnify the damage; the Nineteenth Communist Party Conference, an important event, was scheduled to begin in late June, less than a month after the President's visit.

The Reagan speech to which Gorbachev objected made a point of extolling the virtues of speaking bluntly about the moral superiority of the West, ridiculing the warnings by unidentified "experts" that "this kind of candor was dangerous, that it would lead to a worsening of Soviet-American relations." Reagan suggested that his harsh language actually had been beneficial: "This candor made clear to the Soviets the resilience and strength of the West; it made them understand the lack of illusions on our part about them or their system." Moreover, he added, "We learned long ago that the Soviets get down to serious negotiations only after they are convinced that their counterparts are determined to stand firm. We knew the least indication of weakened resolve on our part would lead the Soviets to stop the serious bargaining, stall diplomatic progress, and attempt to exploit this perceived weakness."

In a passage that won applause and furnished the lead for the stories in *The Washington Post* and *Los Angeles Times*, Reagan also tipped his hat to Moscow, saying that "Soviet-American relations have taken a dramatic turn—into a period of realistic engagement." The Moscow summit, his fourth with Gorbachev, was only a month away, he noted, and "negotiations are underway between our governments on an unparalleled number of issues." On everyone's mind, he said, was "this single, startling fact—that the Soviets have pledged that next month they will begin withdrawing from Afghanistan."

Still, Reagan and his speechwriters could not resist exulting about Afghanistan, where "the Soviets have said they've had enough" and where "the will for freedom has defeated the will for power." Reagan declared "we don't know" if the Soviets have given up their ambitions "to prop up their discredited, doomed puppet regime" in Kabul and proclaimed that "as long as they're aiding their friends in Kabul, we will continue to supply the *mujaheddin* by whatever means necessary."

Looking across the table at the U.S. delegation in the Kremlin, Gorbachev said progress in the Soviet-American relationship had been difficult but necessary. "We value the contributions of the President, of the Secretary, of Mrs. Ridgway, of Matlock, of Nitze and now Powell, who has come on the job, and of Simons," mentioning the name of each American in front of him. "Why should we fritter away the capital that has been built up over so many months? The Soviet Union has to ask if this is the political base on which the President would build his visit to the Soviet Union. Is that the approach he is going to be bringing? We cannot allow such attacks to go unanswered. Are we supposed to bury all the achievements? Who does this serve?" Gorbachev said the first reaction of the Soviet leaders had been to publish Reagan's Springfield speech in full, but that this would have provoked an angry reaction that such a portrayal was "unacceptable from a leader coming to the Soviet Union in a month's time." He added, a little later, "We do not accept the approach we have seen in the recent statements of the President."

After this extraordinary opening blast, Shultz took the floor, extending without any touch of irony or sarcasm Reagan's "warm regards" to the General Secretary. The President was looking forward to visiting Moscow, Shultz said, and appreciated the "thoughtful and constructive" suggestions Gorbachev had sent to him about his activities in the Soviet capital, especially the personal touch of an intimate dinner with the Gorbachevs at their dacha, or country residence.

Shultz said it was evident that "a new page in our relations dated from the first summit" between Gorbachev and Reagan at Geneva. He then summed up the progress that had been achieved in each of the four major areas: human rights, bilateral relations, arms control and regional issues. "Some of these things would have been out of the question four or five years ago. They would have been considered impossible," Shultz said. As for the summit meeting in Moscow, it should be "an occasion for summarizing what had taken place, on the one hand, and on the other, for projecting an image of the future we wish to attain." There should be "the right combination of business-like and substantive activities to go with the public activities, which are important since they would set the tone." Shultz assured Gorbachev that "the President's emphasis would certainly be the outlook to the future."

"That outlook has to be realistic," responded Gorbachev. As he saw it, there were various ways to think about the future. "If there were no place in it for socialism, for the Soviet Union, if [the President] insists that the Soviet Union has to earn the confidence of the United States for there to be progress in relations, then we're headed back to the past.

"I have to say it seems to me that the Soviet Union has already graduated from the primary school of politics," Gorbachev continued. "There has already been progress and it shouldn't be pushed back. But literacy means taking U.S.-Soviet realities into account. The world is very diverse. There are many new countries. Our two countries can live without each other, but it would be better for both to cooperate. Nuclear war is inconceivable. These are the kinds of things that I have in mind."

Shultz interjected, "I recall at Geneva that you and the President agreed that any kind of war between us is to be excluded."

"I have just been making a brief inventory of realities," Gorbachev went on. "If the United States is now coming to revise the achievements and return to a position of force, imposing things on the Soviet Union and the world, an empire-like approach," in that case, the General Secretary reiterated, that would be a return to the patterns of the past.

"The Soviet Union does not pretend to have the final truth," said Gorbachev, in a remark that abandoned decades of Soviet pretensions to infallibility on the basis of "scientific" socialism. He went on to say, in another startling departure from the record of the past, "We do not impose our way of life on other peoples." The General Secretary told Shultz, "We've told you we want to cooperate, we want dialogue, we want to find answers together with the United States."

Gorbachev said he wanted to observe, not in a mean way but in a friendly way, that the pragmatism that was typical of American policy was not working beneficially in this case. "The United States needs a more philosophical approach. The inertia that is inherent in pragmatism makes the United States look only to its own advantage. It needs to look at things more broadly. Unless it does, the two sides would fail on the specifics: there will be a dead end on specific issues."

The General Secretary recalled the time in that very room—it had been just twelve months earlier—when he had looked at the diagrams Shultz had brought of the changes in the world economy. Gorbachev said he had welcomed that talk, thought about it a lot, and consulted experts on what Shultz had told him. "If this continues, then it follows our two countries do have to cooperate."

"I welcome what you've said," replied Shultz. "I believe profoundly that the near future will be quite different from five or ten years before. We need to study it together." The problem, he continued, was that there never seemed to be time to discuss these broader trends and topics with Gorbachev. They were "always crowded out" by the pressure of immediate events.

Gorbachev suggested that once the two of them were out of office and free from day-to-day activity, they would have time for intellectual discussions. He wanted to tell Shultz confidentially—and hoped he would not disclose it publicly—that he was planning to ask the forthcoming Communist Party Conference to impose a limit to the time that party and government officials could serve in their offices.

Shultz countered that the problem was for those who were in office and in charge—not those who had retired—"to get a sense of the trends and build them into their thinking, so that they could be shaping what is done, because the more we can adjust to the trends, the more we could change the balance of problems and opportunities in the direction of the opportunities."

Gorbachev replied that whether he left office or not, the political leadership in both countries was undergoing a generational change that would make it easier to reflect the trends taking place in the world. He was pleased that in the past three years, the Soviet and U.S. leaders had been able to respond better than in the past. "If Vice President Bush is elected, he will be one of us," Gorbachev said, although he guessed that "we will have to continue to prove that to each other." While Bush was campaigning, Gorbachev understood that he was "trying to display some muscles." A change in viewpoint usually goes with a change in positions, the General Secretary observed, quoting a Soviet provincial leader as saying, "Every dog barks up its own tree." Shultz added that the U.S. rule (known as Miles's law, after Rufus Miles, once chief civil servant of the Department of Health, Education and Welfare) was, "Where you stand is where you sit."

The discussion turned to the issues to be taken up by Gorbachev and Reagan when the President arrived in just five weeks. The first was the Strategic Arms Reduction Treaty (START). The two leaders had pledged at the Washington summit the previous December to make all efforts possible to sign the strategic arms treaty at their next meeting. But as the Moscow summit approached, the hopes had faded.

Starting early in the year, Shultz had begun an intensive set of meetings within the administration in a push to complete the START Treaty by the spring. Frank Carlucci, who had succeeded Caspar Weinberger as secretary of defense, was willing to permit Shultz to meet directly with the Joint Chiefs of Staff to discuss military issues, something Weinberger had resisted in every way possible. Shultz began meeting weekly, sometimes twice a week, with the U.S. military leadership in the Pentagon on strategic arms. In time, however, both Carlucci and the uniformed chiefs became concerned about being pushed too quickly into making too many difficult decisions. Arms control skeptics in Congress were dragging out the ratification of the INF Treaty, raising arguments that were designed to warn the administration of rough sledding if it pushed ahead with the much more ambitious START Treaty. Conservatives in and out of government were complaining publicly about what they feared was "a rush to disarm."

Faced with division among his senior advisers, Reagan in mid-February decreed that the administration should "go for the gold," in parlance he borrowed from the Calgary Olympics then underway, and try by all means to finish the START Treaty in time for signing in Moscow. But on February 25, after a briefing by National Security Adviser Colin Powell about the status of the complex bargaining, Reagan told *Washington Post* White House correspondent Lou Cannon that "the time is too limited" to complete the treaty by the time of the Moscow summit. Shultz and Nitze, his arms control adviser, were dismayed by Reagan's shift. They continued to work on the START issues, but without dramatic success.

At the conference table in the Kremlin, Gorbachev told Shultz that he wanted to make progress on START at the summit. But in contrast to his intense pressure for a deal before the Geneva and Washington summits and the high hopes he had harbored before Reykjavik, Gorbachev seemed to realize that the chances for a breakthrough at the Moscow summit were slight. He told Shultz he hoped, at least, for a statement spelling out the progress the two sides had made toward eventual agreement. "Both the United States and the Soviet Union want a good START Treaty, and we'll sign it when we have it," Gorbachev said.

On the related issue of reductions in land armies in Europe, Gorbachev complained about remarks that Nitze and Ridgway had made in a closed and highly classified meeting at NATO headquarters in Brussels. Listening to this across the table, Nitze had the impression that Gorbachev was showing off, boasting to the Americans that the NATO meeting had been penetrated by Soviet intelligence. Both sides agreed, after some banter, that it was important to move ahead toward reducing land armies in Europe.

At this point Gorbachev turned to human rights, the question that had touched off heated protests from him in earlier meetings with both Reagan and Shultz. This time the Soviet leader asked whether the United States would agree to a new approach, starting with the President's visit. "The Soviet approach is that each nation has the right to choose its own way, and that there be no attempt to pressure the other side," said Gorbachev. But if this was unacceptable to the United States, Moscow would emulate the more confrontational U.S. methods, making public its concerns and demanding explanations about human rights issues in the United States. It would be hard to improve the atmosphere if this road was taken, but he said that, nonetheless, it could be done, starting with Reagan's visit. Then there took place the following remarkable exchange about the two systems—an exchange more penetrating than anything said by U.S. and Soviet leading figures to one another up to that time.

Gorbachev: "The United States does not understand that we have different values. The United States values private initiative, private property. Its media, its philosophy, its politicians all protect that. That's the choice of the United States. Whereas in the Soviet Union, we're just beginning to develop new forms of cooperation and individual work. People are asking if that does not mean a return to private property, to capitalism, to the exploitation of the working class. . . . The authorities have to work hard now to prove that these new forms are consistent with socialism. Values are different. We don't impose our values, and you tried to impose your values. This only results in aggravation and a bad atmosphere."

★ *New General Secretary Yuri Andropov meets Vice President Bush, head of the U.S. delegation to the Brezhnev funeral, in St. Catherine's Hall, the Kremlin, November 1982. Others (from left) moving toward them are Gromyko, interpreter Sukhodrev, Shultz, interpreter Krimer (obscured), and Hartman. Early in 1983, President Reagan began secret discussions with Soviet Ambassador Dobrynin, shown here at a White House social event with Caspar Weinberger and Richard Pipes (left), two skeptics, looking on.*

Lucian Perkins/*The Washington Post*

The Reagan Library

★ *The Soviet downing of Korean Air Lines Flight 007 on September 1, 1983, prompted widespread indignation, including this demonstration near the Soviet Embassy in Washington. Amid high tension over missile deployments that fall, KGB official Oleg Gordievsky, who was secretly working for British intelligence, reported that the Soviet leadership feared a surprise U.S. attack.*

★ *Reagan's Strategic Defense Initiative to create an ambitious antimissile shield, which began in a 1983 meeting with his Joint Chiefs of Staff (above), created great concern in Moscow. Below, Bush and his delegation meet new Soviet leader Konstantin Chernenko and Foreign Minister Gromyko in St. Catherine's Hall in February 1984 after Andropov's funeral.*

★ *The Gromyko visit to the White House in September 1984 was a major event in improving ties. Left, the photo Gromyko wanted to take home as a souvenir. Below, the toast in which he suggested Nancy Reagan should whisper "peace" in her husband's ear. Gromyko's trip and the GOP's menacing "bear ad" (above) neutralized the Soviet policy issue in the 1984 presidential campaign.*

Tass

★ *George Shultz's first meeting with Gromyko's successor, Eduard Shevardnadze, in Helsinki in July 1985 was the start of a vitally important relationship. Shown in the middle is Finnish Foreign Minister Paavo Vayrynen. Shultz's first business meeting with Mikhail Gorbachev in Moscow, November 1985 (above), was replete with Soviet pyrotechnics after the press was ushered out.*

AP/Wide World Photos

Terry Arthur/The Reagan Library

★ *Reagan and Gorbachev, plus interpreters and security men,
take a walk to the summerhouse of the U.S. villa at the Geneva
summit, November 1985. On the walk back they agree to future
summit meetings.*

★ *Shevardnadze and Shultz
sign agreements at the Geneva
summit, while their bosses
enjoy each other's company.*

Margaret Thomas/*The Washington Post*

AD RCF

Both sides would agree to confine itself to
research devel and testing which is permitted
by the ABM Treaty. for a period of 5 years,
through 1991, during which time a 50%
reductions of nur strategic nuclear arsenals
would be achieved. This being done, both
sides will continue the pace of reductions
with respect to the remaining ballistic missiles with
the goal of the total elimination of
all offensive ballistic missiles by
the end of a second 5-year period
As long as these reductions continue at
the appropriate pace, the same
restrictions will continue to apply
At the end of the 10 year period,
with all offensive ballistic missiles
eliminated, either side would be
free to deploy whatever defenses

exercise its rights under the
ABM Treaty

★ Gorbachev and Reagan (above) with Soviet and U.S. interpreters Uspensky and Zarechnak at the small table at Hofdi House in Reykjavik, Iceland, where in October 1986 they bargained over eliminating their nuclear arsenals. At left is the original copy of the U.S. offer drafted at the bargaining table by Linhard and Perle to eliminate all ballistic missiles within ten years.

★ Reagan and his advisors (counterclockwise) Regan, Linhard, Shultz, Perle (back to camera), Adelman and Poindexter (obscured by Adelman) agreed on making the unexpected offer.

★ *Reagan's anger at Gorbachev in the final moments of the*
Reykjavik summit, captured in two photographs,
suggested that U.S.-Soviet relations were in deep trouble.

James K.W. Atherton/*The Washington Post*

★ *Mathias Rust, a West German teenager, flew his small plane unchallenged across the Soviet Union and landed in Red Square in May 1987, prompting Gorbachev to retire his defense minister and shake up the Soviet military. Marshal Sergei Akhromeyev (left) worked closely with Gorbachev on military and arms negotiations issues.*

Archive Photos/Reuters

Frank Johnston/*The Washington Post*

★ *Gorbachev was a hero to most Americans by the December
1987 Washington summit, as demonstrated by his reception at
an impromptu motorcade stop in the capital. Raisa Gorbachev
and Nancy Reagan, however, had a strained relationship.*

★ *White House Chief of Staff Howard Baker, an amateur photographer, captured a startled Gorbachev.*

Howard Baker

Bill Fitz-Patrick/The Reagan Library

★ *Washington summit discussions were moved into the Oval Office after Reagan failed to perform well in a larger group. In the circle, clockwise from Gorbachev, are Shevardnadze, Yakovlev, Dobrynin, Carlucci, Baker, Powell, Bush, and Shultz. Participants are wearing earphones for simultaneous interpretation.*

★ *Soviet troops began leaving Afghanistan in May 1988, in a great reversal of the geopolitical tide. In June 1988, Reagan took the message of political and economic freedom to Moscow State University, under the statue of Lenin.*

★ *The walk in Red Square was a highlight of the Moscow summit.*
Talk of an "evil empire," said Reagan, was in "another time, another era."
Gorbachev told a Russian child, "Shake hands with Grandfather Reagan."

★ *At Governor's Island in December 1988, Reagan toasts U.S.-Soviet accomplishments—and their future under Bush. Future Soviet Ambassador and Foreign Minister Bessmertnykh is at end of table, facing camera. National Security Adviser Colin Powell is on his right.*

*The passing of the torch—
under the torch
of Lady Liberty.*

★ *Gorbachev and Shevardnadze meet the Bush-Baker team for the first time at the Malta summit in December 1989 amid the collapse of communism in Eastern Europe, symbolized by the opening of the Berlin Wall. In a high point of good feeling, Gorbachev, his wife, and top aides meet informally with the Bushes and their top aides at Camp David in June 1990.*

★ *In an intimate interlude of their final official meeting, Bush and Gorbachev relax on the porch at the presidential dacha near Moscow in July 1991. Pavel Palazchenko, the familiar Soviet interpreter, is between them. Three weeks later, Gorbachev was the victim of an abortive right-wing coup while vacationing at the Black Sea. Gorbachev, followed by Raisa and a granddaughter, returns to Moscow (below) in a weakened position after the coup unexpectedly empowered the democratic forces. Four months later, at the end of 1991, the Soviet Union was dissolved.*

Shultz: "We accept that there's diversity in governmental arrangements in the world. Countries have to balance the needs for efficiency and the needs for equity, for social justice in society. Everyone has to make that choice, but if you go too far either way, it does not work. Discussion on how to organize, we regard as healthy. There's nothing wrong with it. We have learned from criticism."

Gorbachev: "I'd be interested in what you have to say about U.S. society, whether there is any self-criticism on human rights."

Shultz: "We're worried about our problems. Drugs are a problem. Crime is a problem. They'll be big issues in the upcoming election campaign. Our standard of living is on the whole high, the market is working well, but there are problems. At the lower end of the income scale, especially in inner cities, [living conditions] were undesirable. We worked hard on it; sometimes we were successful, sometimes not. There had been a tremendous struggle on civil rights. In the 1960s and 1970s that had been intense. I was engaged in it. So we took the point seriously. There was no lack of criticism, and on the whole I think we benefited from it." And in his view, Shultz said, it was healthy to discuss human rights in the other country.

Gorbachev: "There's one flaw in your initial position. The United States thinks human rights are violated in the Soviet Union but not in the United States. This approach is visible also in U.S. foreign policy. It says the Soviet Union is all negative and the United States is all good. Its economic system is all beautiful, encouraging initiative in enterprise and the Soviet Union does not. But people choose their own systems. The flaw is that your approach is not self-critical. It's interesting to compare: in the Soviet Union, making propaganda for war is punishable under the law; in the United States, anti-war activists are punished by prison."

Shultz: "They're not. They're punished only if—"

Gorbachev (interrupting): "I've seen the U.S. laws and codes and they are formulated in such a way that anyone who disagrees with the authorities can be accused of anything. They can even be turned against democratic people. What kind of a society is it where one can be followed and monitored, where computer files are kept on millions of people? What kind of laws were the 1950s laws that the State Department referred to to keep Soviet trade unionists from visits? Were they going to undermine the U.S. social system?"

After this intense debate, Gorbachev sat back and said he was going to stop, though he had only mentioned 1 percent of the information he had about the workings of the United States. The two countries were different, he said, and the right approach was to cooperate, not to remodel the other side. Besides, "The United States is not some kind of super government to teach the Soviet Union. It can't even tell Panama what to do."*

Finally, said Gorbachev, "The United States has learned not to notice racism, hunger or poverty in certain countries if it was not in the interests of the U.S. side." Afghanistan was an example: Despite its opposition to Islamic fundamentalism in Iran, the United States was supporting Islamic fundamentalism among the *mujaheddin.*

"So in short," Gorbachev said, peering across the table behind his metal-rimmed glasses, "when is George Shultz right?"

"I'm almost always right," Shultz responded immediately.

Gorbachev joined in the general laughter that filled St. Catherine's Hall.

As they rose from the table for the last time, Gorbachev shook hands with Shultz and each member of his team, and said he was "pleased to meet again with old friends." The Soviet leader added, "I hope nobody will be able to wipe out what we have done together over three years to improve relations."

• THE MOSCOW SUMMIT

Just before 2:00 P.M. on Sunday, May 29, Air Force One landed at Moscow's Vnukovo II Airport, which is used for ceremonial visits and official travel. President and Mrs. Ronald Reagan, waving their right hands in unison like a pair of old troupers, stepped out of the plane into the bright sunlight of a magical Moscow. The streets had been cleaned, the trashy residue of the Russian winter had been hauled away, and nearly every place on the official program had been painted or refurbished. The drab, ugly city I had seen in April had become, for a few days at least, a beautiful and gleaming capital.

* Two months earlier, the U.S.-backed president, Eric Arturo Delvalle, tried to remove General Manuel Antonio Noriega as head of the defense forces and was ousted by Noriega instead, precipitating a crisis. The United States had mounted full-scale economic pressure against the Noriega regime and sent additional troops to the Panama Canal zone, to no effect.

Reagan's first three summit meetings with Gorbachev had been in winter: the icy blasts of Geneva in November, the frigid gusts of Iceland in October, the short days and chilly nights of Washington in December. This time, as Reagan noted in his arrival remarks at the Kremlin, it was almost summer and "some of the seeds are beginning to bear fruit" from the earlier encounters. Reagan referred especially to the INF Treaty, which had finally been approved by the Senate by the lopsided vote of ninety-three to five two days earlier, while Reagan was en route to the Soviet capital. The Senate action made it possible for the U.S. and Soviet leaders to exchange the instruments of ratification in Moscow, placing the treaty officially in force. This was a political deed of great importance, because the previous three U.S.-Soviet treaties—the nuclear testing accords of 1974 and 1976 and the SALT II strategic arms treaty of 1979, signed by Leonid Brezhnev with Richard Nixon, Gerald Ford and Jimmy Carter, respectively—had been stopped in the Senate and never ratified by the United States.

It had been fourteen years since an American president had visited Moscow and that was a weakened Nixon, only five weeks before he was forced to resign because of the Watergate scandal. Reagan, in contrast, had handily survived the Iran-Contra scandal. With a boost from the improved relationship with Gorbachev that had been displayed in Washington the previous December, Reagan was riding high in domestic popularity as he approached the end of eight years in the White House.

To a greater degree than even the 1987 Washington summit, Reagan's visit to Moscow was more symbolic than substantive. Although pending business was discussed in meetings between Reagan and Gorbachev and in working group sessions of lesser officials, the approaching end of the President's term robbed the discussions of much of their intensity. "For all practical purposes, the Reagan administration is over for us," a Soviet official told me on Reagan's first day in Moscow. With a single exception—a forceful effort to convince Reagan to endorse a policy declaration of sweeping principles—Gorbachev chose not to do battle with the President in private or public. His indignant words to Shultz in April about Reagan's hard-edged rhetoric had produced results, namely a collaboration between the State Department and the White House in advance of Reagan's trip that produced some of the most literate and memorable speeches of his presidency.

"The human features of the other nation are now more clearly visible," Gorbachev said, accenting the personal dimension of the summit in his ceremonial welcome to Reagan Sunday afternoon in St. George's

Hall in the Kremlin. He also cited a Russian proverb, "It is better to see once than to hear a hundred times," which aptly summed up both Reagan's receptivity to learning through personal experience and the powerful impact of the visit as disseminated by the new world of global television. Reagan's voyage to the center of international communism was attended, recorded and transmitted, often live, by some five thousand of the world's press, and the sights and sounds were fascinating.

Because of his long career as an anticommunist speaker and his famous stubbornness and scorn for the communist world, Reagan had been the personification of Cold War attitudes toward the USSR. But American public attitudes, like those of the President himself, had been changing, especially since Mikhail Gorbachev began to make an impression unlike that of any of his predecessors. In mid-1986 about half (51 percent) of Americans questioned in a Harris poll had "a favorable impression" of the Soviet leader; on the eve of Reagan's trip this had risen to 72 percent and after the trip Gorbachev's favorable rating soared to 83 percent. Americans had overwhelmingly favored a policy of "getting tougher" with the Soviets in the aftermath of the invasion of Afghanistan at the start of the decade. By late 1987, however, they believed in overwhelming numbers that the United States should "try harder to reduce tensions" with the Soviet Union. At a more fundamental level, U.S. perceptions of the Soviet Union were no longer dominated by a sense of mutual antipathy: In November 1984, when Reagan was elected to his second term, more than half (54 percent) of Americans polled said the Soviet Union was "an enemy"; by late May 1988, a few days before Reagan's trip, only 30 percent still held this view.

Reagan's trip to Moscow crystallized and validated the growing national view that the Soviet Union was rapidly changing from the "evil empire" of his 1983 image—a description Reagan explicitly rejected during his trip to the Soviet capital—to an acceptable partner in something close to a normal international relationship. If Reagan could sit with Gorbachev in the Kremlin, talk with Soviet citizens in Red Square and give a speech to Soviet students in front of a giant bust of Lenin at Moscow State University, who could deny that the Soviet Union had a legitimate place in the world? For Americans, the essence of the Moscow summit was the true normalization of U.S.-Soviet relations, not in the technical sense of the formal diplomatic ties that had been in place since 1933, but in the sense of accepting the Soviet Union as a "non-enemy" nation. For the Soviet people, who had been told that Reagan was a mere cowboy actor mouthing anti-Soviet curses and, at the extreme, another Adolf Hitler, the close-up view revealed instead a sympathetic and even eloquent American gentleman of an older generation. More than any other summit, Reagan's trip to Moscow was a public production that transformed impressions and perceptions. Reagan later compared the occasion to a Cecil B. de Mille motion picture epic, saying he felt as if he had "dropped into a grand historical moment."

Following the arrival ceremony in St. George's Hall, a cavernous armorylike room dedicated by the czars to Russian military valor, Gorbachev led Reagan through the White Corridor, used by society ladies at the czars' court, through several richly decorated chambers to St. Catherine's Hall, where most of Gorbachev's meetings with Shultz had taken place. There the two leaders sat down at a coffee table with interpreters and note-takers for a private talk that lasted seventy minutes.

As he did on several occasions throughout the summit, Gorbachev wanted to discuss the possibilities for U.S.-Soviet trade, the expansion of which was impaired by the Jackson-Vanik amendment tying U.S. "most favored nation" trade benefits to Soviet freedom of emigration. This gave Reagan the opening to bring up human rights, which was a central theme of his during the Moscow summit. The President gave Gorbachev the names of fourteen emigration cases of particular interest to the United States, and suggested that if the Soviet Union relaxed its strictures against religious observances by Jews, not so many Russians would wish to emigrate. Reagan took the occasion to suggest privately, as he had demanded in a highly publicized speech at the Brandenburg Gate the previous June, that the Berlin Wall be torn down. Its removal, said Reagan, would be a symbolic gesture that the Soviet Union was ready to join the broader community of nations. Gorbachev did not accept the President's views, but he displayed little of the feistiness that had been evident in the arguments with Shultz in the same room five weeks earlier.

The Reagans had originally made plans to go, after the Kremlin meeting, to the apartment of Yuri and Tatayana Zieman, Jewish *refusniks* who had been waiting to emigrate since 1977, to show sympathy for their cause. When Soviet authorities learned of the plan, the Ziemans' apartment building was repainted and the street outside repaved. While the President was in Helsinki en route to Moscow, however, Deputy

Foreign Minister Aleksandr Bessmertnykh flew to the Finnish capital for the express purpose of discussing the Ziemans' case. The Foreign Ministry was doing all it could to arrange their emigration, Bessmertnykh told Rozanne Ridgway, and was confident that they would be successful if the issue was not forced. The Soviet diplomat warned, however, that "others," which Ridgway took to be a reference to the KGB, were taking a very tough position. If the Reagans visited the Ziemans, Bessmertnykh said, they might *never* be permitted to leave. The President reluctantly called off the visit to the couple's apartment, although he did see the Ziemans the following day at a U.S. Embassy reception for dissidents and *refusniks.* *

With nothing on the calendar for the late afternoon, the Reagans decided to walk along the Arbat, an old Moscow street that had been restored by the city authorities as a pedestrian mall, a haven for artists, musicians and street life. The Reagans had been intrigued by an earlier suggestion from their son, Ron, that they make an unscheduled visit to the Arbat as a way to see the Soviet people. On that Sunday afternoon, however, the Secret Service objected on security grounds and because of concern that an impromptu walk would violate an agreement to give the KGB security police at least several hours' notice of any presidential movement. Reagan rarely overruled Secret Service objections, but he did so in this case. With only a few minutes' notice to Soviet security, the U.S. party arrived at the Arbat, which was filled with casually dressed Muscovites out for a Sunday stroll. The delighted Russians applauded and cheered the Reagans, who shook hands and waved. When the uncontrolled but friendly crowd surged toward the American visitors, however, the KGB turned nasty, forming a tight wedge around the President and First Lady and punching, kicking or elbowing those who were in the way, including the traveling pool of American reporters and photographers. A White House press aide, Mark Weinberg, screamed at the Soviet police, "Leave them alone! These are Americans! These are our press!" The Reagans themselves pulled the White House press corps dean, Helen Thomas of UPI, inside the protective cordon to shield her from harm, but several American journalists as well as Soviet citizens were beaten in the melee. Reagan wrote in his diary, "I've never seen such brutal manhandling as they did on their own people who were in

* Two months later, after Reagan telephoned Ambassador Yuri Dubinin with a reminder that he had canceled the visit to the Ziemans out of consideration for official Soviet views, the couple was permitted to leave. They now live in Boston.

no way getting out of hand." It was a demonstration to him that "*perestroika* or not, some things hadn't changed." For the rest of the summit Reagan spoke often to aides about the curiosity and friendliness on the faces of the Soviet people, and the brutality of the Soviet police.

Monday morning in St. Catherine's Hall, Reagan and Gorbachev were joined by their senior advisers for a wide-ranging but inconclusive discussion of arms issues. Sitting at the table for the first time since the Carter-Brezhnev summit in 1979 were the U.S. and Soviet defense ministers, Secretary of Defense Frank Carlucci and Marshal Dmitri Yazov. Due to his relentless conflict with Shultz and his opposition to many diplomatic moves, Caspar Weinberger had not been invited to participate in the Geneva and Reykjavik summits. Yazov had not come with Gorbachev to Washington. In March 1988, however, Carlucci and Yazov had met in Bern, Switzerland, to inaugurate a series of military-to-military conversations at high levels, which continued following the Moscow summit.

On Monday afternoon at Spaso House, the prerevolutionary mansion that is the residence of the U.S. ambassador, Reagan was host to human rights activists and *refusniks* in one of the most moving episodes of the summit. At elegantly set round tables, their places marked with White House cards embossed with gold presidential seals, were ninety-eight of the Kremlin's least favorite people, some of whom had only recently been released from prison and others of whom had spent years trying to leave the country. Three of the guests spoke of their dismal experiences and their hopes for the future, and Reagan spoke of the unshakeable American commitment to individual freedom and human rights. He acknowledged the positive changes Gorbachev had made but in the end quoted Pushkin in asking for more: "It's time my friend, it's time. The heart begs for peace, the days fly past. It's time my friend, it's time."

Except for the nearly disastrous walkabout on the Arbat, all the events had been carefully choreographed by the White House staff working with Soviet officialdom. On Tuesday, the third day, a combination of meticulous preparation and last-minute improvisation contributed to the most memorable images of the five-day visit.

Reagan's staff had proposed and the Soviets had accepted nearly all the events that were on his planned schedule. One event that the President's aides had shunned, however, was a Reagan visit to Red Square, where Soviet armed forces passed in review every November 7 in commemoration of the Bolshevik revolution. Shultz, who had made impromptu visits to Red Square several times during his trips to Moscow, argued that it was an appropriate and beautiful sight, which long predated communist rule in Russia. Shultz felt so strongly that during the Helsinki stopover en route to Moscow, he discussed his view with Reagan and gave the President a card on which a proposed suggestion to Gorbachev had been typed: "Mr. General Secretary, I understand that Red Square is quite a sight to see, and some time during the course of this visit, I'd like to see it." Reagan followed through during his Kremlin meeting with Gorbachev on Monday, and it was agreed that Tuesday morning, following another scheduled talk between the two leaders, the Red Square visit would take place.

A few minutes after 11:00 A.M., Gorbachev led Reagan and a small group of aides on foot from the General Secretary's office in the Council of Ministers Building through the ancient Spassky Gate into Red Square opposite the onion domes of St. Basil's Cathedral. It was a bright, warm day close to eighty degrees, and the vast square had been cleared except for the perpetual line of people waiting to enter Lenin's tomb and eight groups of about twenty-five people each who had been positioned by Soviet authorities in scattered locations. As Gorbachev explained the history of the square, the cathedral and other sights, the two leaders stopped to chat with three of the groups of Soviet citizens.

The President told the first group, "I'm glad to be here." A citizen responded, "We are glad your meetings are going well." Reagan said: "We share a view. We want friendship between our countries."

At another group, mostly of Soviet women, Reagan said, "I have great admiration for the women of Russia. You are so courageous and contribute so much to Soviet society."*

The third group included a mother with a small child wearing a blue-and-white playsuit and a white cap. Gorbachev took the boy from the woman's arms and cradled him in the crook of his right elbow. "Shake hands with Grandfather Reagan," Gorbachev said to the child to the delight of the President. At another point Reagan turned to the General Secretary and told the knot of people, "We decided to talk to each other instead of about each other. It's working just fine."

* The stress on the role of women, which was rarely heard from Soviet officials, was appreciated by many surprised Soviet women. It had been suggested by writer Suzanne Massie in a White House meeting with Reagan before the summit, and tried out by Reagan in a predeparture interview with Soviet television. His statement in Red Square about women was prominently cited on the front page of the Communist Party newspaper *Pravda*.

After watching this scene via satellite from five thousand miles away, *Washington Post* television critic Tom Shales wrote, "Shots of politicians cuddling babies are not usually hot stuff. But when the politicians are Mikhail Gorbachev and Ronald Reagan and they are cuddling the toddler in the middle of Red Square, the picture takes on a genial, symbolic momentousness. It's not just two men and a baby anymore."

Back inside the Kremlin grounds, a reporter asked Reagan what had become of the "evil empire" he had warned about in 1983. "I was talking about another time, another era," the President replied, in a remark that was heard and cited proudly by Gorbachev. Another journalist asked the two leaders, "After all these meetings, are you now old friends?" "*Da, da,*" said the General Secretary without hesitation. "Yes," declared the President.

Reagan's most important speech of the summit was Tuesday afternoon at Moscow State University, Gorbachev's alma mater and the most prestigious university in the Soviet Union. There on a stage beneath a giant bust of Lenin and a banner emblazoned with the Soviet hammer-and-sickle, Reagan delivered a stirring tribute to the glories of economic and political freedom, diversity and limited government. Widely acclaimed as one of Reagan's best speeches, it was studded, as was the case in nearly all his Moscow speeches, with quotations from famous Russians, in this case Mikhail Lomonosov, the founder of the university, Boris Pasternak in *Doctor Zhivago* and Nikolai Gogol in *Dead Souls.* * At its climax, Reagan declared:

> Your generation is living in one of the most exciting, hopeful times in Soviet history. It is a time when the first breath of freedom stirs the air and the heart beats to the accelerated rhythm of hope, when the accumulated spiritual energies of a long silence yearn to break free.
>
> I am reminded of the famous passage near the end of Gogol's *Dead Souls*. Comparing his nation to a speeding troika, Gogol asks what will be its destination. But he writes, "There was no answer save the bell pouring forth marvelous sound."
>
> We do not know what the conclusion will be of this journey, but we're hopeful that the promise of reform will be fulfilled. In

---

* The Soviet public was impressed and even moved by Reagan's use of Russian quotations and proverbs. More than any other aspect of the summit, this was mentioned by Russians long after it was over.

this Moscow spring, this May 1988, we may be allowed that hope—that freedom, like the fresh green sapling planted over Tolstoy's grave, will blossom forth at last in the rich fertile soil of your people and culture. We may be allowed to hope that the marvelous sound of a new openness will keep rising through, ringing through, leading to a new world of reconciliation, friendship and peace.

In the question-and-answer period, Reagan became visibly relaxed, placing his arms casually over the top of the lectern bearing the U.S. presidential seal after being asked to compare today's student generation with that of his youth. "I should tell you that when you get to be my age," said the seventy-seven-year-old President in one of his most affecting answers, "you're going to be surprised how much you recall the feelings you had in these days here, and how easy it is to understand the young people because of your own having been young once. You know an awful lot more about being young than you do about being old."

Judging by their repeated and lengthy applause, standing ovation and comments afterward, the students felt surprisingly comfortable with the President and his message. "It was not the Reagan that we expected," said Andrei Fronin, a twenty-five-year-old political science major who had anticipated rhetoric filled with anti-Soviet antagonism. "There was nothing old-fashioned or stale about him. He seemed to be so lively, active and thinking. This was a pleasant surprise." Mikhail Vasyanin, a twenty-year-old student, said, "What I have read a lot about Reagan is that he is a fervent anti-communist. But if an anti-communist could speak so eloquently about principles that are important to us, too, that's impressive." The reaction beyond the campus was difficult to gauge. Reagan's speech was broadcast in full in the United States, but little of it was shown on Soviet television and it received only minimal coverage in the Moscow press.

While their husbands were getting along better every hour, the two first ladies continued their skirmishes before the American press. Wednesday morning at the Tretyakov Gallery, one of Moscow's most famous, the press was gathered to see Raisa Gorbachev give a private tour of the gallery, which was otherwise closed for repairs, to Nancy Reagan. Mrs. Gorbachev, arriving first and announcing that her guest was late, began a discourse on icons, such as those on display, and the Russian soul. When Mrs. Reagan arrived, right on time according to her staff, and started to chat with reporters, Mrs. Gorbachev sought to cut off her discussion, saying it had been decided there would be "no interviews." The tour degenerated into a debate between the two over whether the icons had religious significance, with the American saying yes and the Russian saying no. "There's no feud, but the two are from different worlds," said Mrs. Reagan's press secretary, Elaine Crispen, in a vain effort to soften the social page headlines about the "gloves-off" encounter at the art gallery.

The final business meeting between the Soviet and U.S. leaders late Wednesday morning in St. Catherine's Hall saw the only flash of passion at the summit from Gorbachev, who made a last-minute personal appeal to the President for approval of a broad statement of principles to govern U.S.-Soviet relations. Such sweeping declarations were important to the Soviet leaders, who believed, as Gorbachev had told Shultz in their April meeting, that agreements on overarching principle should have priority over the pragmatic, case-by-case approach favored by the United States. At Soviet urging, Brezhnev and Nixon had issued a statement of "Basic Principles of Relations" in their 1972 Moscow summit and a broad "Agreement on the Prevention of Nuclear War" in their 1973 summit in the United States. Without advance notice to the U.S. side, Gorbachev had proposed such a joint declaration of principles to Reagan in their initial one-on-one meeting Sunday, the first day of the summit. The Soviet leader handed the President the one-paragraph statement he had drawn up:

Proceeding from their understanding of the realities that have taken shape in the world today, the two leaders believe that no problem in dispute can be resolved, nor should it be resolved, by military means. They regard peaceful coexistence as a universal principle of international relations. Equality of all states, noninterference in internal affairs, and freedom of sociopolitical choice must be recognized as the inalienable and mandatory standards of international relations.

Reagan said agreeably that it looked fine to him, but that he would discuss the matter with his advisers. When he did so, they were strongly opposed. As Shultz and the others saw it, Reagan would be signing on to a dubious declaration that could be interpreted by Moscow as it wished, as had been done with the 1970s principles. Moreover, U.S. experts warned of endorsing "peaceful coexistence," which in past decades had been a Soviet code word for a mere truce between governments while class warfare continued, or the inalienable "freedom of sociopolitical choice," which seemed to the experts to suggest that once a nation had "chosen" communism, no criticism or obstruction could be tolerated. Colin Powell thought the "noninterference" commitment might be aimed at undermining U.S. support for the Afghan resistance. The State Department's senior Soviet affairs expert, Thomas Simons, said the proposed statement read as if it might have been written by Andrei Gromyko, who at that point was still the figurehead President of the USSR as well as a Politburo member. In fact, Simons said, "it probably *was* written by Gromyko."

Assistant Secretary of State Ridgway was assigned to work with Deputy Foreign Minister Bessmertnykh on a declaration that could be accepted by the U.S. side, and they did so as part of time-consuming negotiations on a lengthy summit joint statement covering the standard four areas of arms control, regional conflicts, human rights and bilateral issues. As redrafted in these negotiations, the declaration to be issued by the two leaders harked back to the statement made by Reagan and Gorbachev at Geneva that a nuclear war must never be fought. It went on to hope for improved U.S.-Soviet relations through a constructive political dialogue—a process, rather than a set of principles—based on "realism" and "concrete results."

Close to noon on Wednesday, as the last business meeting with Reagan was coming to an end in the Kremlin and the ceremonial exchange of INF Treaty documents was scheduled to begin, Gorbachev abruptly changed the tone of his remarks. With Gromyko sitting on his immediate right, the General Secretary moved forward in his chair in the middle of the long conference table in St. Catherine's Hall, his eyes flashing and his chin out, in body language that reminded an American participant of a prizefighter getting ready for a big punch. "Why is 'peaceful coexistence' a bad term? Why are you against it? What are you against here?" Gorbachev demanded of Reagan. "You told me last Sunday you were for it," he added insistently, handing across the table a sheet of paper containing the original Soviet-drafted paragraph.

Reagan, for whom the argument over theoretical language seemed distant and abstract, shrugged his shoulders and indicated he had no strong objection. At that point, Carlucci on one side of Reagan slipped a note to the President, and Shultz on the other side, prompted by

Ridgway, did the same. Shultz volunteered, "This is no time to start writing" the joint statement. Officials and the press were waiting in a nearby room for the INF Treaty ceremony, and the summit-ending document had been typed and duplicated for release shortly after that. Seeing the note passing, whispering and confusion on the other side of the table, Gorbachev suggested that each side caucus on its side of the long room.

After hearing his aides' objections, Reagan said he understood them and agreed. He walked over to Gorbachev and said, "I'm very reluctant to put this in. I don't want to do it."

The two men stood toe to toe for a few moments. The issue was clearly important to Gorbachev. Perhaps, some of the Americans thought, he had promised Gromyko or others in the Politburo that he would make one last try to obtain from Reagan the kind of statement that the Soviet leadership wanted.

"Well, Mr. President, I don't understand why you're not for peace," protested Gorbachev sharply.

Reagan repeated that he could not accept the language that Gorbachev had suggested.

Gorbachev was silent momentarily. Then, as if to concede his inability to win the day, he brightened. "Mr. President, we had a great time," he said of their fourth summit meeting. He put his arm around Reagan and turned with him to walk through the corridors to St. Vladimir's Hall, one of the most historic in the Kremlin, to exchange the papers putting the INF Treaty into force.

At a table on the steps of St. Vladimir's Hall, the former terrace of the boyars, or aristocrats, at the czars' court, Reagan and Gorbachev sat side by side, flanked by U.S. and Soviet flags. Each put his signature on his own country's INF Treaty ratification documents and handed the other the documents he had signed.*

Gorbachev spoke first:

The exchange a few minutes ago of the Instruments of Ratification means that the era of nuclear disarmament has begun.

---

* The previous day, Shultz and Shevardnadze had signed two lesser arms control accords, an agreement to notify each other before test launches of long-range ballistic missiles and guidelines for a joint experiment to measure the yields of each other's underground nuclear tests. In addition, various officials had signed seven U.S.-Soviet agreements outside the arms control field on cultural exchanges, fishing rights, search and rescue operations at sea, long-range radio navigation, peaceful uses of atomic energy, cooperation in the exploration of outer space and transportation research.

Assessing the work done over these past few days, we can say that what has been happening these days is big politics, politics that affect the interests of millions and millions of people. . . .

Such politics also needs a great idea. Humankind has conceived that idea in the pangs of wars and disasters, tragedies and calamities, strivings and discoveries of the 20th century. This, in our view, is the idea of a nuclear-free and non-violent world. It is that idea that is inscribed in the mandate which the Soviet people give to their representatives at the start of any negotiations. This particularly applies to our negotiations with the United States of America.

Addressing the Soviet people and the Americans, addressing all nations from these hallowed steps of the Moscow Kremlin, I hereby declare we have been working honestly and with perseverance, and we shall continue to do so, to fulfill that historic mandate.

Then Reagan took the rostrum:

Mr. General Secretary, these are historic moments. As we exchange these documents, the instruments of ratification, this treaty, the terms of which we formally agreed to last December in Washington, enters into force.

Mr. General Secretary, you know that our way here has not been easy. At crucial moments your personal intervention was needed and proved decisive, and for this we are grateful. So too, Mr. General Secretary, you are aware of how important the objective, not just of arms control, but of arms reduction, has been to my own thinking, and to the policy of my administration since its outset. . . .

For the first time in history, an entire class of U.S.-Soviet nuclear missiles is eliminated. In addition, this treaty provides for the most stringent verification in history. And for the first time, inspection teams are actually in residence in our respective countries.

And while this treaty makes possible a new dimension of cooperation between us, much remains on our agenda. We must not stop here, Mr. General Secretary; there is much more to be done.

Less than an hour after the ceremony, Gorbachev gave his first press conference ever in Moscow, broadcast live on Soviet television, for correspondents covering the summit. It was my best chance to see the Soviet leader in action, and it proved to be an enlightening experience.

The previously dingy auditorium of the Foreign Ministry Press Center had been modernized with attractive and comfortable seats, and a new simultaneous translation system for the summit had been built into the armrests. Before Gorbachev arrived, various senior officials from the Foreign Ministry, the scholarly institutes and the Soviet press took their seats in the front rows on the lefthand side. They gave the impression of a Soviet College of Cardinals, important people with big offices, cars and reputations. As they sat awaiting Gorbachev, though, their demeanor changed. Suddenly they appeared meek and subservient.

When Gorbachev arrived, he took his seat at the center of the raised dais looking down at the journalists below, with three high officials on each side of him. Gorbachev began by saying that, in accordance with tradition, he would say "a few words" about the results of the meeting. Thereupon he spoke for close to an hour, hardly ever looking at a note, appraising the just-completed summit as "a major event" capping the summits with Reagan, which had been "a unique process in postwar history." He praised the "realism" of U.S. policy, which made important accomplishments possible, and at the same time expressed disappointment with "missed chances" such as the U.S. refusal to accept the political declaration he had proposed.

With the Communist Party Conference just three weeks away and Moscow alive with rumors about internal disagreements, the press conference really became interesting when British correspondent Martin Walker of *The Guardian* rose to ask a question. Walker noted that Boris Yeltsin, the dismissed Moscow Communist Party chief, had given interviews to the Western press, charging that Yegor Ligachev, a conservative senior member of the Politburo, was "slowing down" the reform process and ought to be fired. What was Gorbachev's opinion? While it was unprecedented for an officially disgraced political figure such as Yeltsin to go public with internal Communist Party business, it was equally unprecedented for the General Secretary to be put on the spot about it, live and on camera. Ten days earlier, Gorbachev had declined to speak about divisions in the Politburo when asked by the editors of *The Washington Post* and *Newsweek*, and the issue was considered so sensitive that even the mention of Ligachev's name in an editor's question had been deleted from the interview, which was otherwise published in full by the Soviet press.

I watched with fascination as the blood seemed to drain out of all the faces of the supposedly top officials on the dais facing us. Except for Shevardnadze, who managed an amused smile as the question was translated, the others were frozen-faced, unable or unwilling to commit themselves to any hint of a reaction without knowing what the leader would say or do. I wondered whether the more relaxed reaction of Shevardnadze was caused by his confidence in his relationship with Gorbachev, or whether he reacted as he did because he was a Georgian, a different ethnic group from the dominant Russians.

Gorbachev toyed for a long time with the question, saying he had not seen the texts of Yeltsin's interviews and so on. I felt as if I could almost see the wheels of his brain turning, trying for the right combination of words and attitudes to address the question. Finally, he seemed resolved and went at Yeltsin with sudden ferocity: Yeltsin had spoken up the previous October with his criticism of the leadership organs and his views were found to be "politically erroneous." If he now had more to say, perhaps the Central Committee should summon him and "demand that he explain his position and what he's out for." (I could imagine the baleful drum roll for Yeltsin in the Party meeting.) As to the ouster of Ligachev, "The problem simply is nonexistent, and that's all."

For me, it was one of those rare moments of illumination that come from firsthand observation of events. For all the *glasnost* and talk of democracy and political reform, the leadership politics of Moscow was still in the grip of the autocracy, secrecy and Byzantine tendencies that arose from czarist Russia and the Stalinist era. Despite everyone's efforts, it seemed to me, the gulf between the U.S. and Soviet leaderships was still very great, and there were huge glaciers and icebergs partially hidden beneath the surface.

The political gap was not evident the following morning in the Kremlin when Gorbachev said good-bye to Reagan, declaring that the United States and the Soviet Union "have now taken a really good look in each other's eyes and have a keener sense of the need to live together on this beautiful planet Earth."

Reagan, too, spoke in warm and intimate terms:

If I might just conclude on a personal note, earlier this week at Moscow State University, I mentioned to the young people there that they appeared to my eyes exactly as would any group of students in my country, or anywhere in the world. So, too, did Nancy and I find the faces, young and old, here on the streets of Moscow. At first, more than anything else, they were curious faces, but as the time went on, the smiles began, and then the waves. And I don't have to tell you, Nancy and I smiled back and waved just as hard.

Mr. General Secretary, I think you understand that we're not just grateful to you and Mrs. Gorbachev, but want you to know we think of you as friends. And in that spirit, we would ask one further favor of you. Tell the people of the Soviet Union of the deep feelings of friendship felt by us and by the people of our country toward them.

Tell them, too, Nancy and I are grateful for their coming out to see us, grateful for their waves and smiles, and tell them we will remember all of our days their faces—the faces of hope—hope for a new era in human history, an era of peace between our nations and our peoples.

Thank you and God bless you.

Reagan was escorted to Air Force One at Vnukovo II Airport by Andrei Gromyko in his capacity as President of the USSR. As had been the case in Washington the previous December, it began to rain at the farewell ceremony, which was held under umbrellas. Despite the turn in the weather, it was obvious that Reagan left for home with much warmer feelings than the ones he had landed with four days before.

• PRESIDENT GORBACHEV

A little less than four weeks after Reagan left Moscow, Gorbachev convened a general conference of the Communist Party, the first such special meeting of its kind since 1941. The first Party Conference had been convened when Russia was reeling from a democratic revolution in 1905 and the outcast Bolshevik party, the predecessor of today's Soviet Communist Party, was debating its future. That session marked the first appearance of a Georgian Communist named Joseph Djugashvili (who took the name of Stalin) at a national party meeting, and his first face-to-face meeting with the party's leader, Vladimir Ilyich Ulyanov, or Lenin. Eighteen conferences had been held until the forum fell into disuse under Stalin, and until the Gorbachev era the Party Conference had been forgotten.

The supreme governing body of the Communist Party is the Party Congress, which is held at five-year intervals. Gorbachev had presided over the Twenty-seventh Party Congress in February 1986, less than a year after coming to power, and had laid down guiding principles for his ambitious efforts at change. With the economy still stagnant and his *perestroika* program running into strong bureaucratic resistance, Gorbachev could not wait five years to take his case to the next full-scale national party meeting. Early in 1987, he had proposed convening a Party Conference to make important decisions in the interim. The Nineteenth Party Conference, which convened in the Kremlin on June 28, 1988, was the high-water mark of Gorbachev's effort to use traditional Communist Party mechanisms to transform the Soviet Union.

To a large degree, the disappointing result was determined before the Conference ever met. Despite the best efforts of reformers, party *apparatchiks* from Moscow and across the country dominated the selection process for the nearly five thousand delegates who took their places in the enormous Palace of Congresses just inside the Kremlin wall. There was no applause but an ominous silence during the first sixty minutes of Gorbachev's three-and-a-half-hour keynote speech. The scattered clapping began only when Gorbachev struck a conservative note as a sop to the party regulars.

The Party Conference, whose proceedings were televised to a greater degree than any previous meeting and published nearly verbatim in *Pravda* and *Izvestia*, let the Soviet public and the outside world observe the open clash between progressives and conservatives. In this sense it was "four days that shook the world," as it was described by a fascinated member of the Politburo of the Polish communist party, Jozef Czyrek.

The major substantive result was to reform the system for electing the Supreme Soviet, the national legislature that had previously been a rubber stamp for the Communist Party leadership, and to add power and authority to the ceremonial position of Supreme Soviet Chairman, or President. The post was then held by the seventy-nine-year-old Andrei Gromyko, but it was obvious to all that the new presidency was being tailored for Gorbachev.

Foreign policy played little part in the Party Conference, although Gorbachev in his lengthy keynote address called for the democratization of foreign policymaking. Gorbachev sharply criticized the way important decisions—evidently referring to the Afghanistan invasion, among others—were previously adopted "by a narrow circle of persons, without a collective and all-round study and analysis."

The General Secretary claimed credit for a "new dynamism in Soviet foreign policy," which had given rise to major initiatives with the United States and other powers. "We can give the following answer to the principal question that worries the Soviet people most of all and on which they would like to hear the appraisal of the work in the past three years— whether it became possible to push back the threat of war: yes, undoubtedly so."

Starting with Gorbachev's appearance at the Foreign Ministry after the Party Congress in 1986, it had become Shevardnadze's practice to follow up and embellish upon major Communist Party meetings to give new impetus to foreign policy. In this pursuit, Shevardnadze convened a Foreign Ministry "Scientific and Practical Conference" on July 25, three weeks after the end of the Nineteenth Communist Party Conference, to sum up and advance the foreign policy experiences of the Gorbachev era. Shevardnadze opened the meeting to several hundred people from the top ranks of the Communist Party and government hierarchy, senior military and KGB figures, academic experts and journalists as well as Foreign Ministry officials. It was his effort to breathe a more modern and democratic spirit into Soviet diplomacy.

Since becoming foreign minister in July 1985, Shevardnadze had proven himself a dynamic and imaginative leader, close to Gorbachev politically and in some respects ahead of Gorbachev in intellectual daring and commitment to democracy. Though completely without diplomatic experience at the beginning, the former communist boss of Georgia had also proved to be a quick study and surprisingly open-minded in his attitude toward foreign policy positions. He began meeting regularly in his seventh-floor office suite with his deputies and other key aides in brainstorming sessions and always made it clear that he was interested in hearing new ideas and even blunt criticism of existing policies. From the beginning he asked his subordinates, "Why are you defending this?" according to Deputy Foreign Minister Yuli Vorontsov. "He was always asking why."

Once a week, usually for several hours on Friday afternoon, Shevardnadze moved across the hall to a long baize-covered conference table in a big room dominated by a large painting of Lenin in the snow outside the Kremlin and decorated in old-fashioned European style by a former Soviet ambassador to Italy. This was the meeting place of the twenty-nine-member Foreign Ministry Collegium, which was made up of the deputy foreign ministers, chiefs of main departments and other senior diplomats. This group usually considered one major topic at each sitting, with one official making a presentation and the rest joining in a free-flowing discussion. Sometimes Shevardnadze named an in-house "dissident" to challenge accepted views and sharpen the debates.

The Foreign Ministry's Scientific and Practical Conference in July 1988 gave Shevardnadze the opportunity to push ahead with new directions for Soviet foreign policy, beginning with a remarkable three-hour opening address. Shevardnadze declared that the recent Nineteenth Communist Party Conference had confirmed the overriding priority of Soviet foreign policy: "ensuring through political means peaceful and totally favorable conditions for carrying out transformations within the country." He went on to outline three tasks for Soviet diplomacy: first, the opening up of policymaking and abandonment of elitism; next, the shift from military to political means of dealing with international issues; finally, the importance of public confidence in Soviet diplomacy abroad as well as at home. Each of these tasks represented changes in direction from the past.

First, Shevardnadze called for democratization and the opening of policymaking to wider discussion and public accountability. In the past, he said, the elitism and lack of democracy had given rise to a pernicious "silent zone" around the Foreign Ministry.

> The caste-like exclusiveness of some of its workers, false defensiveness and excessive secrecy, the complete absence of information about its inner life and the artificially implanted assumption of infallibility have contributed greatly during the years of stagnation to the alienating of people from foreign policy and foreign policy from people.
>
> Soviet diplomacy, where the main idea of its activity is the good of the people, must explain itself to the people. It must plan its work in accord with the people's expectations, hopes and aspirations. Without fail, it must be answerable to them for its actions and steps. In the state of law which we are building, this is an obligatory norm for us.

Shevardnadze was particularly critical of provocative statements of the past for their part in creating the image of the Soviet Union as an international enemy, mentioning especially "we will bury you," the famous challenge of Nikita Khrushchev to the West. In a reference to Andrei Gromyko's celebrated walkouts from the United Nations, Shevardnadze condemned "the habit of door slamming that established itself in the 1950s."

On the issue of accountability, Shevardnadze endorsed the suggestion that the newly enhanced Supreme Soviet hold open hearings on foreign policy issues and be permitted to question the foreign minister and other officials, though he would later be angered at some of the parliamentarians' criticisms. He lamented that a constitutionally empowered mechanism for adopting foreign policy was being gained only after "the painful experience of Afghanistan, a drop in the living standards and the damage done to the good name and organic ideals of socialism."

Second, Shevardnadze called for a continuing shift of emphasis from military means to political methods of solving international problems, a position that would bring him into increasing conflict with Soviet military officers.

> There have been a host of small wars in the 40-odd years since World War II. However, none of them has given the side that used force any solid political or other results. Quite the contrary, all of them and each one individually only served to complicate the problems around which the conflicts had arisen and to create new ones. Even if the map of the world has changed, it has been only in minor details. These changes have not been formalized politically or juridically. And in all these instances the existence of nuclear weapons and even their presence in the arsenal of one of the belligerents failed to affect the situation.
>
> It can thus be asserted that war and armed conflicts in the nuclear and space age are objectively losing the functions of instruments of rational policy. Only in very rare instances do such threats lead to any changes in the conduct of a state against which a threat is applied.

In the new circumstances, said Shevardnadze, it was in the general interest, including that of the Soviet Union, to limit the military activities of all states to their own national territory. He cited the withdrawal from

Afghanistan and partial troop withdrawal from Mongolia as "persuasive examples" that this goal was serious. For the Soviet Union to withdraw its troops and weaponry from beyond its borders generally, as it would begin to do from Eastern Europe in 1989, would have enormous global repercussions. The forward presence and outward thrust of Soviet military force since World War II was at the root of the Cold War.*

Finally, Shevardnadze spoke of the vital importance of restoring the Soviet Union's name before its own citizens and the world.

> Today our country is appearing before the world in a completely new light. Humanity is viewing its image differently. We have a host of problems; we have inherited a difficult legacy and it will not be soon before we deal with it, but it is truly impressive how quickly our country's good name is restored.
>
> Also impressive and gratifying is the enormous advance of trust and support which world public opinion is prepared to give—and is giving—to our *perestroika*. There is no prophet in his own land, however.
>
> Sometimes one hears the view that we pay too much attention to what the outside world will say about us. In this connection, I would like to stress the following: In separating wheat from chaff we cannot exhibit indifference to what others are saying and thinking about us, for our self-respect, our well being, our position in the world hinge largely on the attitude of others towards us as well.

Three days of small-group discussions of every aspect of Soviet foreign policy followed the foreign minister's opening address. On July 27, Shevardnadze summed up the results in a closing speech that observed that "critical tones predominated" in the analysis of Soviet foreign policy. "We did not expect anything else, nor did we want it." At the end, he felt it necessary to return to the still controversial decision of the Twenty-seventh Party Congress, subordinating the traditional class-struggle mainspring of Soviet diplomacy to the newer emphasis on universal human values. The "supreme class interest," declared Shevard-

---

* At the United Nations General Assembly in September 1989, Shevardnadze declared that "our fundamental goal is not to have a single Soviet soldier outside the country" and the following month told the Supreme Soviet that the USSR was prepared to liquidate all foreign bases and pull back within its national borders by the year 2000.

nadze, is "the creation of decent, truly human material and spiritual living conditions for all nations, as the primary duty to our own people, the ensuring of our planet's habitability, and a thrifty attitude towards resources. The strength of this class interest, and it is growing, lies in its full concurrence with universal interests."

Nine days later, on August 7, the Politburo conservative leader and ideology chief, Yegor Ligachev, fired a shot across Shevardnadze's bow in a speech in Gorky. Ligachev rejected peaceful cooperation with the capitalist countries and declared, "We proceed from the class nature of international relations. Any other formulation of the issue only introduces confusion into the thinking of Soviet people and our friends abroad."

Politburo reformer Aleksandr Yakovlev then issued a point-by-point rebuttal of Ligachev's views, without naming him, in a speech in Vilnius. Marxism, declared Yakovlev, "is the interpretation of the interests of mankind as a whole from the viewpoint of the history and the development of prospects of all mankind, and not just of individual countries or classes, peoples, or social groups that form part of it."

This ideological dispute—which foreshadowed later disagreements over Soviet policy in Eastern Europe and Germany—was unresolved when Shevardnadze in September flew to the United States. His purpose was to conduct a final round of ministerial meetings with Shultz—the twenty-eighth set of meetings since the two had first met in Helsinki three years earlier—and to participate in the annual round of meetings with the world's senior diplomats at the opening of the United Nations General Assembly in New York.

It was clear by the time Shevardnadze arrived in Washington September 21 that it would be impossible for the two sides to solve the many outstanding issues in the waning months of the Reagan administration. The joint statement issued at the end of the talks September 23 had a valedictory ring to it. "The record of achievement since the November 1985 summit attests to this: goals that have seemed impossible have been reached, and other important goals have been brought within sight," the statement said. At a farewell luncheon at the State Department, Shultz quoted from Shevardnadze's speech to the Scientic and Practical Conference in Moscow, and called his opposite number "one of the thoughtful men of our time."

Shevardnadze responded that he and Shultz had been "good builders of bridges between our two countries." The accomplishments of three years were based on conscious choices made by Gorbachev and Reagan, "by the will of reason and not by the force of circumstances," the Soviet minister declared.

> If we were to rely only on providence and destiny, we could not have had four summit meetings, could not have signed and implemented one of the most complex treaties ever known to human history, or have concluded dozens of other agreements and have begun the preparation of many more very important agreements. We can speak of destiny only in the sense that it has made our countries very close, indeed so close that a movement of the hand can be either an invitation to shake hands or a painful blow. An exchange of blows is not what our countries or the world needs; shaking hands is better.

Shevardnadze was in the midst of his extensive meetings at the United Nations the following week when he was summoned back to Moscow for an emergency meeting of the Central Committee, to be followed immediately by a special session of the Supreme Soviet. In a lightning maneuver, Gorbachev shook up the organization and personnel of the Soviet leadership and ousted Ligachev from the position of Kremlin ideology chief. Moreover, Gorbachev placed Yakovlev, whose ideas were in tune with those of Shevardnadze, in charge of a new Central Committee commission to supervise foreign policy. That seemed to settle the argument over class struggle in foreign affairs for the time being, at least at the Kremlin leadership level.

Gorbachev's shakeup also retired Andrei Gromyko from the presidency of the Soviet Union and from active political life. Gromyko wrote in his memoirs that he had made his decision several weeks earlier while on vacation on the Black Sea and had notified Gorbachev of his intention. Although the methods and many tenets of his foreign policy were under increasing criticism, the old diplomatic warhorse was given a dignified exit by Gorbachev, perhaps in recognition of the part the older man had played in his election in 1985. Just before the vote in the Supreme Soviet was taken for the new president, Gromyko rose to say farewell to public life almost fifty years after Stalin and Molotov had sent him to Washington in 1939 as their emissary to President Franklin D. Roosevelt. There had been "disruptions" in the history of the state since the Bolshevik revolution, the long-time foreign minister conceded. "But the star of socialism has never stopped shining since October 1917. It was ignited so as never to grow dim in the Land of the Soviets." Gromyko died nine months later, on the eve of his eightieth birthday.

Gorbachev's lightning putsch had been an old-style Kremlin maneuver to eliminate political opposition to his policies at home and abroad and add to his already extensive powers. There was nothing democratic about it. The vote to elect Gorbachev chairman of the Supreme Soviet, or president of the USSR, was in the old style, unanimous.

• IN THE SHADOW OF LADY LIBERTY

On November 8, George Bush was elected President over Michael Dukakis after a campaign in which policy toward Moscow played only a minor role, since both candidates applauded the highly popular developments in the U.S.-Soviet relationship. The following Sunday, Soviet Ambassador Yuri Dubinin requested an urgent, immediate and private meeting with Secretary Shultz. When he arrived at the deserted State Department late in the day, Dubinin said Gorbachev had decided to come to the United Nations to make an important speech in early December, and wanted to know if arrangements could be made for a meeting with Reagan. Shultz quickly informed Ridgway and Nitze, and put in a call for Colin Powell, who turned out to be just across the street at the Great Hall of the National Academy of Sciences preparing to sit down at a candlelight dinner for Andrei Sakharov.

Shultz, Powell and the others had the same first reaction, which was irritation that Gorbachev was forcing himself on the U.S. administration in its waning days. After the shock wore off, the officials realized that there was no way to stop Gorbachev from coming to the United Nations, where he had not been since taking power nearly four years earlier, and that an essentially social meeting with Reagan in New York would be a gracious climax to their official relationship. Dubinin had made it clear Gorbachev also wanted to use the occasion to see President-elect Bush. Gorbachev and Bush had met at the Chernenko funeral and the Washington summit, but then Bush had been vice president and not in position to speak or act on his own.

Unlike his advisers, Reagan was delighted from the first that Gorbachev was coming, and quickly approved a December 7 luncheon meeting in New York with the Soviet leader. Bush also agreed to participate, though he insisted on attending as vice president of the Reagan administration rather than as President-elect and would not bring his newly named secretary of state, James Baker, or in any other way suggest that the meeting with Gorbachev would be the first act of his incoming administration.

As the site for the year's most illustrious power lunch, the White House team picked the U.S. Coast Guard station on Governors Island in New York harbor, where tight security was easily established and where there is an ideal view of a classic photographic backdrop, the Statue of Liberty. "This will be our last such meeting," Reagan said in his Saturday radio address before Gorbachev's arrival, "and I must admit that I would not have predicted after first taking office that someday I would be waxing nostalgic about my meetings with Soviet leaders. But here we are, for the fifth time, Mr. Gorbachev and I, together in the hope of further peace."

New York City was decked out with Christmas lights and holiday wreaths. On the eve of Gorbachev's arrival, Soviet officials hinted that he would provide something additional to celebrate. Central Committee staff member Nikolai Shishlin, a spokesman and adviser to Gorbachev, said on *Meet the Press* that Gorbachev was bringing "a Christmas gift to the American people and to mankind." He would not elaborate, but there were hints that Gorbachev was planning a major announcement.

Gorbachev's speech to the United Nations on the morning of December 7 was the first by the leader of the Soviet Union since Nikita Khrushchev's boorish performance in 1960, in the wake of the U-2 affair, when he denounced the UN Security Council as a "spittoon" and called the United States a "disgrace to civilization." This time, the message from Moscow could hardly have been more different.

Gorbachev began by sketching the outline of the new world in which the Soviet Union and all other nations found themselves, "a very different place from what it was at the beginning of this century, and even in the middle of it." The new world was one of global mass communications. "Today, the preservation of any kind of 'closed' society is hardly possible," said Gorbachev, a statement made more credible by the complete cessation of Soviet jamming of foreign broadcasts several weeks earlier. The world economy was becoming a single organism, he said, "and no state, whatever its social system or economic status, can normally develop outside it." In view of these shifts "a new world is emerging," said Gorbachev, which surmounts the lessons of the French revolution of 1789 and the Russian revolution of 1917, which he depicted as historically important but remote.

The new stage, Gorbachev declared, harking back to his statements at the Twenty-seventh Party Congress in 1986 and Shevardnadze's repeated declarations, is "an era when progress will be shaped by universal human interests." Therefore, it requires "the freeing of international relations from ideology." Not that the Soviet Union, or others, would give up its convictions or philosophy, "but it mustn't spread into the sphere of relations between states."

In this new world, Gorbachev went on, it is evident that "the use or threat of force no longer can or must be an instrument of foreign policy." This applied to nonnuclear force as well as nuclear weapons, he said.

In what was immediately interpreted as a message to the world about Soviet intentions in Eastern Europe, Gorbachev declared that "all of us, and first of all the strongest of us, have to practice self-restraint and totally rule out any outward-oriented use of force." He went on to say that "the principle of freedom of choice is a must" for all nations, a universal principle that "knows no exceptions." In this and other respects, the ideas advanced by Gorbachev were an expanded version of the one-paragraph statement of principles he had advanced—and Reagan had rejected—at the Moscow summit.

After forty-five minutes ranging over general precepts, outstanding world problems and a description of *perestroika*, including an explicit commitment to freer emigration and human rights, Gorbachev unveiled the announcement he had come to New York to make.

Today I can report to you that the Soviet Union has taken a decision to reduce its armed forces. Within the next two years their numerical strength will be reduced by 500,000 men. The numbers of conventional armaments will also be substantially reduced. This will be done *unilaterally*, without relation to the talks on the mandate of the Vienna meeting.

By agreement with our Warsaw Treaty allies, we have decided to withdraw by 1991 six tank divisions from the German Democratic Republic, Czechoslovakia and Hungary, and to disband them. In addition, assault-landing troops and several other formations and units, including assault-crossing support units with their weapons and combat equipment, will be withdrawn from the groups of Soviet forces stationed in these countries. Soviet forces stationed in these countries will be reduced by 50,000 men and their armaments, by 5,000 tanks.

All Soviet divisions still remaining in the territory of our allies are being reorganized. Their structure will be different from what it is now; after a major cutback of their tanks it will become clearly defensive.

At the same time, we shall reduce the numerical strength of the armed forces and the numbers of armaments stationed in the European part of the U.S.S.R. In total, Soviet armed forces in this part of our country and in the territories of our European allies will be reduced by 10,000 tanks, 8,500 artillery systems and 800 combat aircraft.

Over these two years we intend to reduce significantly our armed forces in the Asian part of our country, too. By agreement with the Mongolian People's Republic a major portion of Soviet troops temporarily stationed there will return home.

Gorbachev had been expressing some of these ideas about the way he saw the world for several years, but he had never stated them so clearly and forcefully to the global audience from a platform that commanded such attention and respect. Moreover, the dramatic announcement of the massive unilateral military cuts, which amounted to about 10 percent of the Soviet armed forces in U.S. calculations, about 12 percent by Soviet reckoning, and much higher percentages of the most threatening Soviet forces in Eastern Europe, underscored and gave credibility to Gorbachev's message that the Soviet Union had fundamentally changed its way of looking at and dealing with the world.

Soviet foreign policy had been shifting and turning for nearly all the forty-five months that Gorbachev had been in power, but many millions of people in the West were still wary, disbelieving or not paying attention. Gorbachev's appearance at the United Nations, and especially the unilateral military cuts, was a dramatic moment of validation that the changes in Moscow's policy were vitally important and that they were real. Like the Soviet withdrawal from Afghanistan, which had surprised the world and which by December 1988 was more than half-completed, the unilateral military cutbacks were surprising, tangible and mind changing.

"Perhaps not since Woodrow Wilson presented his Fourteen Points in 1918 or since Franklin Roosevelt and Winston Churchill promulgated the Atlantic Charter in 1941 has a world figure demonstrated the vision Mikhail Gorbachev displayed yesterday at the United Nations," declared the lead editorial of *The New York Times*. Retired General Andrew Goodpaster, a former NATO supreme commander and the respected head of a leading NATO support organization, called the unilateral cuts announced by Gorbachev "the most significant step since NATO was founded" and said they opened the way to broad military reductions on both sides. *Newsweek*, taking a less visionary view, said Gorbachev's military cutback "was surely a move forced by his economic woes, but it was also a brilliant way to play a losing hand."

The unilateral cuts Gorbachev announced had been under discussion in Moscow for more than a year between Gorbachev and his military establishment. Starting in late 1987, according to Soviet civilian experts on defense, studies were inaugurated on large-scale reductions of conventional forces, including the controversial question of unilateral moves.

Gorbachev had said in September 1987, in his book *Perestroika*, that while he was sincerely prepared for disarmament, "bearing in mind the bitter lessons of the past, we cannot take major unilateral steps." Statements by a number of high-ranking Soviet officers insisted that reductions in Soviet forces should be balanced against those in the West. In February 1988 a public debate about unilateral reduction involving military officers and civilian experts flared briefly, condemning or praising the controversial unilateral cutback carried out by Nikita Khrushchev in the late 1950s.

At a Warsaw Pact summit meeting in July 1988, Gorbachev had proposed a unilateral cutback of seventy thousand men in East Germany, Czechoslovakia and Hungary, but the proposal ran into opposition among the Soviet allies and was not adopted. In the same month in Moscow, the Soviet General Staff was instructed to begin work on a bigger cutback. Public statements and private comments indicate that the Foreign Ministry, especially Shevardnadze himself, took a leading role in advocating the reductions against considerable military resistance. A senior Foreign Ministry official involved in the discussions said that the unilateral cutbacks were the most difficult issue the diplomats had ever faced with the military, even more touchy than the problems of nuclear arms reductions. For many senior officers, this official said, "nuclear war was really foreign, and they accepted the logic of cuts. But tanks were something very real, and that was different."

Several factors were involved in making the cutbacks possible. First, Gorbachev won over Marshal Akhromeyev, who had been one of the most influential voices in opposition to the idea. In extensive discussions, Gorbachev convinced the chief of staff, who was concurrently first deputy minister of defense, of the political necessity of making the reductions, without which there was little chance for negotiating broader reciprocal reductions with the West. There are also indications that a worsening of the Soviet economy, especially a sharp rise in the budgetary deficit, as well as the September shakeup in the Politburo, in which the influence of Ligachev and other conservatives was reduced, played a role in the decision to move ahead.

Akhromeyev's retirement as first deputy defense minister and chief of staff became known as Gorbachev arrived in New York to address the United Nations, giving rise to speculation that he had quit, or been forced out, because he still disagreed with the unilateral cuts. Akhromeyev consistently denied that this was so and portrayed his retirement as a normal military rotation. There were strong indications later that his retirement was indeed related to the unilateral cuts, but for a reason opposite to the Western line of speculation. A Soviet official close to the situation said that after reversing his position to assist Gorbachev in putting through the cutbacks, Akhromeyev found it difficult to work effectively with other military officials who continued to be strongly opposed. Adding credence to this report is the fact that Akhromeyev continued to have a prominent role as Gorbachev's personal military adviser in 1989 and 1990, even after leaving active duty. In the spring of 1990, some of arms control compromises that he negotiated with the Americans, under the auspices of Gorbachev and Shevardnadze, would be repudiated by the active-duty military.

After the speech at the United Nations, Gorbachev was driven downtown through lower Manhattan and over the ferry to Governors Island in New York harbor. It was an almost cloudless, sunny day. Quarters One, the Coast Guard commandant's residence, was decorated with Christmas wreaths, poinsettias and the Soviet and American flags as Gorbachev's black Zil pulled up with a screeching of brakes at 1:00 P.M. Reagan greeted the Soviet leader and the two began bantering with reporters. Bush, who had remained inside during Gorbachev's arrival, sauntered out of the house almost unnoticed to join the other two. Gorbachev greeted him effusively, taking Bush's hand in both of his.

Gorbachev's main purpose, it became clear, was to draw Bush into the relationship that he and Reagan had developed and to obtain the maximum commitment from the President-elect to continuity after In-auguration Day. Bush said as little as possible, almost the minimum. When reporters and photographers were briefly ushered into the dining room as the luncheon was about to begin, Reagan was asked to comment on Gorbachev's troop-cut announcement. "I heartily approve," said the President. When the reporters turned to Bush for his view, he appeared ill at ease and replied, "I support what the President said." Reagan beamed and patted Bush's arm. Gorbachev interjected, "That's one of the best answers of the year."

Over the elegantly set luncheon table, Gorbachev directed some of his remarks specifically at Bush. "I know what people are telling you now that you've won the election: you've got to go slow, you've got to be careful, you've got to review. That you can't trust us, that we're doing all this for show." But Gorbachev went on, in remarks that some of the Americans at the table would remember vividly for a long time, "You'll see soon enough that I'm not doing this for show and I'm not doing this to undermine you or to surprise you or to take advantage of you. I'm playing real politics. I'm doing this because I need to. I'm doing this because there's a revolution taking place in my country. I started it. And they all applauded me when I started it in 1986 and now they don't like it so much, but it's going to be a revolution, nonetheless."

Shultz, observing the discussion, felt Bush was "a reluctant pres-ence" who did not seem ready to engage Gorbachev. However, at one point in the conversation, Bush responded to Gorbachev's description of the status of *perestroika* by saying American investors would want to know what the reforms would produce in the Soviet Union three to five years in the future. "Even Jesus Christ couldn't answer that question," the Soviet leader replied.

National Security Adviser Colin Powell had informed the Soviet Embassy well in advance that the White House wanted no surprises or attempts by Gorbachev to turn the luncheon meeting into a serious negotiating session. Although there was some discussion of chemical weapons and other East-West questions, in the main it was more like a comfortable dining-room conversation than a meeting of the leaders of the two major blocs. Reagan presented Gorbachev with a framed pho-tograph of their stroll to the summerhouse at their first meeting in Geneva, inscribed, "We have walked a long way together to clear a path for peace." At the end of the luncheon the President lifted a glass of California Chardonnay to the Soviet leader. "This is my last meeting. I'd like to raise a toast to what we have accomplished, what we together have accomplished and what you and the Vice President after January 20 will accomplish together." Gorbachev raised his glass, then lowered it and turned to Bush, saying, "This is our first agreement." As the luncheon broke up, Bush took Gorbachev aside and told him, without being specific, that he looked forward very much to working with him "at the appropriate time."

After the luncheon, Reagan, Bush and Gorbachev posed together on a platform overlooking the Statue of Liberty. That night, Reagan wrote in his diary: "The meeting was a tremendous success. A better attitude than at any of our previous meetings. Gorbachev sounded as if he saw us as partners making a better world."

The day did not end as well for Gorbachev. Since morning, he had been receiving reports of an earthquake in Soviet Armenia, and while on the ferry to Governors Island he had received a telephone call in his car from Prime Minister Nikolai Ryzhkov in Moscow with a preliminary report on the devastation. By late night New York time, as dawn broke in Armenia, it became clear that the quake was a tremendous disaster, and Gorbachev decided to return home without delay. Cutting short his visit to New York and canceling visits to Havana and London, Gorbachev left Kennedy Airport on the morning of December 8 to deal with a natural calamity that left twenty-five thousand dead and close to a half-million people homeless.

In retrospect, Gorbachev's dramatic appearance at the United Nations General Assembly was probably the high point of his forceful leadership on the world stage, and his sudden return home to deal with a domestic crisis a symbolic forerunner of the problems that would preoccupy him thereafter. At the UN, Gorbachev had announced to the world an impressive cut in Soviet armed forces, without having breathed a word of it to the legislature or people of his own country, an act that would seem inconceivable a year or two later. He had gone about as far as he could afford to go in gaining the global initiative and world acclaim by beginning to dismantle unilaterally the Soviet Union's oversize military forces. After the end of 1988 difficulties at home would increasingly narrow his maneuvering room and stay his hand in international affairs. His most dramatic contribution in the world arena in the months to come would be the essentially passive one of declining to interfere as Moscow's Eastern European allies broke loose from their communist allegiance and reoriented themselves to the West. The revolution of 1989 was based in large measure on what Gorbachev had said and done earlier, culminating in the United Nations address of December 1988.

• THE END OF THE REAGAN ADMINISTRATION

Gorbachev's appearance at the United Nations and the announcement of the unilateral cuts in the Soviet military had a powerful effect in the United States. A national public opinion survey a week later reported that a clear majority (54 percent) of those polled believed that the Soviet Union was either "no threat" or only a "minor threat" to the United States. This was a startling change from the Cold War consensus and a shift of fifteen percentage points from the answer to the same question just six months earlier. In addition, two-thirds (65 percent) of those polled said the Soviet Union was primarily concerned with protecting its own national security, while only 28 percent believed Moscow was intent on world domination. Three years earlier, before the first Gorbachev-Reagan summit meeting at Geneva, the assessment of the American people had been just about the opposite.

In a televised message to the American people on New Year's Day, Gorbachev declared, "Americans seem to be rediscovering the Soviet Union—and we are rediscovering America. Fears and suspicions are gradually giving way to trust and feelings of mutual liking." Reagan said in his message to the Soviet people that due to U.S.-Soviet cooperation, the world was safer than it had been a year before, "and I pray it will be safer still a year from now." Thus Reagan, who had come to office calling on Americans to awaken to danger from Moscow, was preparing to leave office having come full circle. After nearly four years of dealing with Gorbachev, Reagan, like most of the American public, was convinced that the threat from Moscow had greatly diminished.

The final weeks of the Reagan administration saw developments that bolstered the optimism about the Soviet Union's new course.

On December 22 at the United Nations, Angola, South Africa and Cuba signed agreements providing for the withdrawal of Cuban troops from Angola and independence for South African–ruled Namibia. The agreements were the product of eight years of persistent negotiation by Assistant Secretary of State Chester Crocker, aided immensely in the

Gorbachev era by the cooperative efforts of Deputy Foreign Minister Anatoly Adamishin and Soviet pressure on Cuba and Angola. Shultz, Crocker and Adamishin were on hand for the signing.

Also with a helping hand from Moscow, the situation was changing in Cambodia, another Third World conflict area. Vietnam had announced in May that it was withdrawing fifty thousand of its occupation troops from Cambodia. Under continuing economic and political pressure from the Soviet Union, Vietnam agreed in early January 1989 to withdraw all its forces by September if a peace settlement in the civil war could be reached by then. (In fact, there was no settlement but the troops were withdrawn anyway.) The moves toward defusing the war in Cambodia contributed to a growing rapprochement between the Soviet Union and China, which had begun negotiating openly and directly about Cambodia. Before the end of 1988, the rival giants of the international communist movement made it known that they were planning a Sino-Soviet summit meeting in mid-1989.

In the Persian Gulf, a point of potentially dangerous U.S.-Soviet confrontation had been defused in July 1988, when Iran unexpectedly agreed to a cease fire in the eight-year war with Iraq. A United Nations Security Council resolution, made possible by the agreement of Washington and Moscow, had helped prod Iran in the direction of stopping the war. Two years later, when Iraq, an old Soviet ally, touched off a new crisis in the Gulf by invading Kuwait, the Soviet Union would join the United States in opposition to the Iraqi invasion, making possible unified international action under the aegis of the United Nations Security Council.

In early January, Shultz and Shevardnadze met for the last time at the Paris conference on chemical weapons, where nearly 150 nations reaffirmed their commitment not to use poison gas and urged swift completion of a worldwide ban on the production or possession of chemical weapons. Reagan had proposed such an international conference in his speech to the United Nations the previous September. On the first day of the Paris meeting, Shevardnadze announced that the Soviet Union would begin destroying its stockpiled poison gas even before the hoped-for treaty was completed.

The weekend before leaving office, Shultz flew to Europe one last time to participate in the closing session of the two-year-old Vienna meetings of the Conference on Security and Cooperation in Europe (CSCE), best known as the Helsinki process. After much controversy involving the Soviet insistence on hosting a CSCE human rights conference in 1991, Shultz persuaded Reagan to accept the Soviet demand and approve the Vienna Declaration. In the Austrian capital on July 17, Shultz accepted the completed CSCE accord for the United States, in recognition of the great advances in human rights in the Soviet Union and Eastern Europe. In his speech, the secretary also spoke of the need for further improvement, reciting a slightly amended version of a poem by Robert Frost:

> The woods are lovely, dark and deep,
> But we have promises to keep,
> And miles to go before we sleep,
> And miles to go before we sleep.

On the morning of January 20, Ronald Reagan received his final national security briefing in the Oval Office from General Colin Powell, who was retiring as national security adviser but would return in the Bush administration as chairman of the Joint Chiefs of Staff. Reagan tried to give Powell the white laminated card containing the codes the President would use to authorize the launching of U.S. nuclear weapons, a card that symbolized all that Reagan feared and loathed. Powell wouldn't accept it, but said that someone would collect the card after Bush had taken the oath of office at the Capitol at noon. As the Reagan administration wound down, it seemed far less likely than at any time since the dawn of the Cold War that the nuclear launch codes would ever be used. The U.S.-Soviet relationship had changed fundamentally. "The world is quiet today, Mr. President," said Powell in his final briefing.

In the brief time left in office after his return from Vienna, Shultz was honored repeatedly for his six-and-a-half years at the helm of U.S. diplomacy, the longest tenure of any secretary of state in the post–World War II era except for Dean Rusk. The Senate under the sponsorship of Republican Richard Lugar and Democrat Ted Kennedy gave a bipartisan luncheon in Shultz's honor, with speeches and toasts. On January 19, Reagan presented Shultz with the Presidential Medal of Freedom, the highest civilian award of the U.S. government, recognizing citizens "who have performed exemplary deeds of service for their country or their fellow citizens." The same day, many hundreds of State Department officials and staff members jammed the diplomatic lobby of the building for a thunderous surprise sendoff to the retiring secretary.

The Shultzes had sold their Washington house, and the moving van came on the morning of January 20. After they had packed their suitcases, George and O'Bie Shultz went down to their basement, to the area that had been used as the office of their State Department security agents, who had watched over them twenty-four hours a day and were still on duty. The guards' basement room had the only functioning television set in the empty house, and there the Shultzes watched along with millions of other Americans as George Bush was sworn in at the Capitol a few miles away. The outgoing secretary of state and his wife had not been invited to the ceremony or to any inaugural events. At 5:00 P.M., no longer an official of the United States at the helm of U.S. foreign relations, Shultz, with his wife, boarded a commercial airline flight for the trip home to their house on the Stanford University campus in California.

8. The Revolution of 1989

The beginning of 1989 brought to office a new U.S. President with a new foreign affairs team that was initially far more cautious in its attitudes and actions toward the Soviet Union than the outgoing Reagan administration. It would take George Bush and his associates most of the year to restore the momentum in U.S.-Soviet relations that had been such a notable feature of the Reagan administration's last years and to blaze a trail into a fundamentally new relationship.

The dramatic developments in Eastern Europe, beginning early in the year and escalating rapidly in the summer and fall, would convince Bush and his secretary of state, James Baker, that the time for waiting was over. The end of the hegemony of the USSR over its former European buffer zone would transform the international landscape and create an urgent requirement for Moscow and Washington to work together.

In July, after visits to Poland and Hungary as those countries prepared to break away from Soviet domination, Bush would secretly invite Mikhail Gorbachev to an informal summit meeting. The Soviet leader was willing, but it would take months to work out the details. By the time they met in the storm-tossed atmosphere of Malta in early December, the Iron Curtain that had divided Europe for a generation had begun to crash down. Inside as well

*as outside the Soviet Union, Gorbachev was losing the political
initiative. At Malta, Bush would volunteer U.S. initiatives openly
intended to shore up the Soviet President. As the 1980s ended,
Bush and Gorbachev would hold a joint press conference—the first
ever held by the U.S. and Soviet leaders—and speak hopefully of
a new relationship between themselves and their countries to sup-
plant the hostility with which the decade had begun.*

• EARLY BUSH: A CAUTIOUS CONSENSUS

On January 23, his first full work day as President, Bush telephoned
Gorbachev and spoke to him for eighteen minutes. It was the first time
in history that the U.S. President and the leader of the Soviet Union
had spoken in an overseas telephone call. Bush told Gorbachev that his
desire for an internal review of U.S. policy was not intended to be "foot
dragging" but to examine the positions Washington would take in the
negotiations on strategic and conventional arms, chemical weapons and
other issues. He also thanked Gorbachev for the warm reception accorded
his son, Jeb, and twelve-year-old grandson, George, during their Christmas visit to the earthquake-ravaged area of Soviet Armenia.

Right from the start, it was clear that Gorbachev was dealing with
a very different person from the last occupant of the Oval Office. Bush
was thirteen years younger than Reagan, a product of old money, Yale
and the Eastern establishment rather than of rural Illinois and Hollywood.
Bush was a cautious pragmatist, not an ideological crusader or dreamer
about a world without nuclear weapons. Reagan had had two terms as
governor of California, no experience in Washington and hardly any
abroad before becoming President; Bush had one of the longest national
office résumés anywhere. The son of a U.S. senator from Connecticut,
Bush had been a U.S. representative from Texas, U.S. ambassador to
the United Nations, chairman of the Republican National Committee,
chief U.S. diplomatic representative to China, director of the Central
Intelligence Agency and, for eight years, Reagan's vice president. As
vice president, Bush had visited seventy-two countries in every continent
and corner of the globe and met the leaders of nearly all important
foreign countries. He had successfully established his personal relationships with many of them.

Out of his interest and exposure, Bush had become something of a foreign affairs buff. Given the choice between spending an hour on domestic issues or spending it on foreign affairs, he would invariably choose the latter. He was not, however, a geopolitical strategist as the last internationally oriented president, Richard Nixon, had sought to be. Bush put forward no grand designs and harbored no stirring passion for changes in the world. Brent Scowcroft, who had long been an unofficial adviser to Bush, described him during the 1988 campaign as "a Rockefeller Republican in foreign policy: tough, hardheaded, sort of power politics oriented—but with a relatively low ideological content compared to the present administration."

As vice president, Bush had been uncomfortable with the harsh anti-Soviet policies and pronouncements of the early Reagan administration and, according to Robert McFarlane, had used his influence where he could in 1982 and 1983 to foster lines of communication to Moscow. Later he felt that Reagan had gone too far in conciliation. Bush was privately appalled at the high-stakes bargaining at Reykjavik in 1986. In an interview after becoming President, Bush told me it would have been "unrealistic" to think of eliminating nuclear weapons as Reagan and Gorbachev discussed in the Icelandic capital. And in mid-1988 while Reagan was basking in the glow of world acclaim with Gorbachev in the Kremlin and Red Square, Bush was notably unenthusiastic as he watched on television from his summer home in Kennebunkport, Maine. When reporters asked his reaction to the Moscow summit, Bush replied, "The Cold War isn't over." His chief of staff, Craig Fuller, felt obliged to warn the vice president that his dour comments would clash noticeably with White House jubilation. "I know," Bush replied. "That's okay."

Bush's attitude during the Moscow summit, as he was gearing up for the fall presidential campaign, was a rare public expression of unhappiness with Reagan policy. For the most part, Bush as vice president was extremely careful to keep his views to himself or to voice them only in his private conversations with Reagan. His penchant for secrecy carried over to his first serious conversation with Shevardnadze when the Soviet foreign minister visited Washington in September 1988 as the Reagan administration was winding down. In a very private breakfast meeting, Bush told Shevardnadze that he hoped for continuity in the U.S.-Soviet relationship forged in the Reagan administration and that, in his view, the more that could be settled between the two countries while Reagan was still in office, the better he would like it. Bush went to unusual lengths to keep his conversation with Shevardnadze from becoming known while he was in the midst of his fall campaign for president. At his request, the only other participants in the meeting were Shultz and a State Department interpreter, and Shevardnadze with a single aide and an interpreter. After the meeting, Bush asked for the U.S. interpreter's notes and requested that no copies be retained at the State Department. Shultz agreed and furnished Bush with the only U.S. record of what was said.

In his presidential campaign against Governor Michael Dukakis, Bush was notably cautious on the subject of policy toward the Soviet Union. While conceding that "Soviet society today is clearly in the midst of dramatic change," candidate Bush declared, "We must maintain the pressure on Moscow to change." Specifically, he said that "this is no time to reduce our leverage" by cutting the U.S. military budget or abandoning SDI research. Dennis Ross, a former National Security Council staff aide who was foreign policy issues director for the Bush campaign, characterized the candidate in midcampaign as "hopeful but also cautious" about developments in Moscow. "He feels that they are significant, they are remarkable, but he also feels that at this point, we don't know where they are going to lead." Along these lines, Bush said in the first televised debate with Dukakis on September 25 in Winston-Salem, North Carolina, that "I think the jury is still out on the Soviet experiment." He added, with remarkable prescience, that "the interesting place, one of the things that fascinates me about this *perestroika* and *glasnost* is what's going to happen in Eastern Europe. You see the turmoil in Poland today." Bush had visited Poland in September 1987, met General Wojciech Jaruzelski and Solidarity leader Lech Walesa, and maintained a steady interest in what was happening there.

Only in the final week of the campaign, in a major address on November 1 at Notre Dame University, was Bush at all specific about the nature or pace of the diplomatic efforts with the Soviets that he had in mind:

> I will pursue more progress with the Soviet Union. We're at a very sensitive stage in the development of superpower relations. Much is changing, much progress has been made, but, if we're to build on that progress, we must size each other up correctly. This is no time for either misplaced hopes or misplaced fears or total inexperience. We must be realistic and informed.

I will therefore instruct my secretary of state to meet with his NATO counterparts as soon as possible and thereafter seek an early meeting with the Soviet foreign minister, Mr. Shevard-nadze, to explore the full range of issues with the Soviet Union. And I will ask him to make clear to the Soviet Union that I am prepared to meet with General Secretary Gorbachev at the earliest time that would serve the interests of world peace. My purpose in such a meeting would not be to achieve any grand break-through, but to engage in a serious and direct examination of where we are and how we can best go forward toward further arms reductions, a decrease in regional tensions and further adherence to human rights and thus toward a sure peace.

Participating in the conception and drafting of that unusual opera-tional passage was Bush's national campaign manager, James Baker, whom Bush named his secretary of state the day after his election victory. Hardly anyone was surprised. Bush and Baker had been close friends for thirty years and had helped each other climb the ladder of the American political system—Bush to the vice presidency and presidency through elective office and Baker to the appointed posts of White House chief of staff and Treasury secretary. On November 23, in another widely expected announcement, Bush named Scowcroft his White House na-tional security adviser. But Bush was not able to complete his foreign affairs–defense policy team until March 10, when he named Wyoming Representative Dick Cheney to be secretary of defense after the Senate rejected Bush's first nominee, John Tower.

All four men were cautious, middle-of-the-road Washington insiders who knew each other well. They had worked closely and harmoniously together at the end of the Ford administration, when Bush was CIA director, Scowcroft was presidential national security adviser and Cheney was White House chief of staff. Baker at the time was under secretary of commerce with Bush's patronage, and in mid-1976 became Ford's chief Republican delegate hunter and later general election campaign chairman. Bush and Baker were each other's closest friends in politics. Cheney was a personal friend of Baker's—they had vacationed together in Wyoming—and was recommended by Baker for the Pentagon post.

At the same time, Scowcroft was a bit apart. As a career military officer, a professor of Russian history at West Point and the Air Force Academy, an assistant to Henry Kissinger at the National Security Council and chief national security adviser to President Ford, the retired Air Force lieutenant general was a foreign policy professional, not an interested amateur. Although he was aware that Baker could have any job in the Bush administration that he wanted, Scowcroft initially considered Baker to be too much a tactical political maneuverer and too lacking in foreign policy depth to be successful as secretary of state.

The policymaking model for foreign affairs of the new administration was fundamentally different from what Washington had known in recent decades. In dramatic contrast to the detached, chairmanlike Reagan, Bush was knowledgeable and very interested in foreign policy and both willing and able to be at the center of discussions on that topic. The close links and consensus of the main actors minimized the personal and bureaucratic struggles that had characterized foreign policymaking since the late 1960s: Henry Kissinger at the NSC versus William Rogers at State; Zbigniew Brzezinski at the NSC versus Cyrus Vance at State; George Shultz at State versus Caspar Weinberger at Defense. Only in the Ford administration or in the final year of Reagan, with Weinberger gone and Colin Powell and Frank Carlucci at the NSC and Defense, was there close coordination among the President's men rather than the familiar "battle for the President's mind." Under Bush, the circle was so tight that people were concerned about the lack of diversity and absence of challenging voices to the policy consensus.

The consensus in this case was skepticism of Gorbachev and criticism of the pace and tone of the Reagan administration's latter-day improvement of U.S.-Soviet ties. In discussions among Bush, Baker and Scowcroft there was agreement to take a close and unhurried assessment of policy toward the Soviet Union, especially toward the major arms negotiations. Scowcroft had more of a conceptual grasp of foreign affairs than Bush, Baker or (when he joined them) Cheney, and he had been outspokenly upset in the latter years of the Reagan administration by the incoherence of its arms policies, especially by Reagan's anti–nuclear weapons tendencies. Scowcroft had made no secret of his lack of enthusiasm for the Intermediate-range Nuclear Forces Treaty, in his view a mistake in the absence of major cuts in conventional land armies first.

As he was announcing his choice of Scowcroft as national security adviser on November 23, Bush also announced that the incoming administration would undertake a "thorough review and analysis" of its international policies, especially those toward the Soviet Union. Despite this early resolve, hardly anything was done to prepare for the study during the preinaugural period and the review was not even launched until weeks after January 20. Eventually the review ballooned to studies of virtually all the problems of the world, carried out by hundreds of senior bureaucrats throughout the government, most of whom were holdovers from the Reagan administration. "If we had any better ideas than the ones we had, we would have used them," said one of the holdovers to Robert Blackwill, National Security Council staff director for Europe, who was in charge of assembling the Soviet-related reviews. The studies were slow: The first substantive reports were not presented to Bush until April, and others were not finished for a month or more after that.

Not surprisingly, the studies recommended few new U.S. policies to cope with radical change. The report on the Soviet Union said U.S. policy should not be designed either to help or to hurt Gorbachev, whom the authors credited with a better-than-even chance of surviving despite his domestic problems. The study took no position on the controversial question of U.S. economic benefits for the Soviet Union, which some officials had proposed as a way of undergirding Soviet reforms.

The report on U.S. defense strategy said:

> Our review concludes that an historic success may now be in the making: present Soviet leaders appear to doubt whether past Soviet political-military strategy is economically supportable or politically or militarily promising. . . . There is broad agreement within the U.S. intelligence community that the Gorbachev leadership has decided to reverse a 20-year pattern of growth in Soviet military spending and force structure in order to boost the civil economy and Soviet foreign policy.

The study also estimated that those new policies in Moscow would last at least five to seven more years. This part of the review, which was drafted in the Pentagon, made no clear-cut recommendation for cuts or even major changes in U.S. military forces. Although the secret review clearly said otherwise, Defense Department officials and even, on occasion, Bush continued until late in 1989 to say publicly that Soviet military spending was still rising.

Scowcroft eventually concluded that the review was "a big disappointment" and that it probably had been a mistake to have expected the bureaucracy to come up with imaginative suggestions. Almost everybody at the top of the new administration agreed that the government had labored and brought forth a mouse. But some in the White House, including Scowcroft's deputy, Robert Gates, found the review helpful in justifying "a conscious pause" in policymaking for several months while the administration got organized.

In the early months of 1989, there was a strange contrast between the caution in Washington and the gathering storm in Moscow. After a burst of diplomacy in the late Reagan years, Washington was ready to do less business than usual under the new administration. But in the Soviet Union, Mikhail Gorbachev was a man in a hurry, and notably impatient. Meeting Margaret Thatcher in London on April 6, Gorbachev said the new American administration's hesitation in developing its policy toward the Soviet Union could imperil the momentum that had been built up in the latter years of the Reagan administration. "Time has its limits," said Soviet spokesman Gennadi Gerasimov, explaining Gorbachev's stand. Asked about the Soviet President's complaint at a White House news conference, Bush replied: "We're making a prudent review, and I will be ready to discuss that with the Soviets when we are ready. . . . We'll be ready to react when we feel like reacting."

• THE GREENING OF BAKER

In early May, James Baker flew to Moscow to resume full-scale diplomacy between the two nations. The first hundred days of the new administration had come and gone, and the section of the strategic review dealing with arms negotiating positions would not be completed for another month. For this reason, Baker planned to use his first mission to Moscow to concentrate on other matters, especially the contentious question of Soviet aid to Nicaragua.

Although Baker had traveled to seventeen countries around the globe as Treasury secretary in Reagan's last term, he had never set foot in the Soviet Union and had had few dealings with Soviet officials. Baker was shocked by his first impressions of "the other superpower." Moscow seemed to him as backward and dingy as his recollection of Mexico City in 1938, where he had gone as a child with his parents from his home town of Houston. When a reporter who had covered Baker at Treasury asked if the Soviet economy reminded him of some of the Third World countries he had dealt with in his former job, Baker said no—this was worse.

James Addison Baker III was a most unusual secretary of state, with a most unusual relationship to the President whom he served. Baker was more political in his interests and experience than any of his predecessors since World War II, with the exception of two former U.S. senators, Jimmy Byrnes and Edmund Muskie, neither of whom stayed in the post very long or made much of a mark. As White House chief of staff for Reagan in his first term, Baker had dazzled official Washington with his political acumen and his keen sense of public relations, including his close relationships with influential members of the White House press corps. Baker was considered only slightly less successful at the Treasury, and that because he was held partly responsible for the disastrous swap with Donald Regan that put the politically inept former Treasury secretary in the post of White House chief of staff. Where Baker really shone was in national politics, especially as presidential campaign manager for Gerald Ford in 1976 and for George Bush in 1980 and 1988.

Jim Baker inherited social status, wealth and great confidence from one of the premier families of Houston, and gained depth and polish in the East at Hill (prep) School and Princeton University. Baker was ten years behind George Shultz at Princeton and a classmate of mine. I remember him as a somewhat serious history major with a well-developed social side. Back in Texas after graduation and service in the Marines, Baker developed an extraordinary competitiveness and deal-making ability. Bush, as an oil entrepreneur then living in Houston, became his close friend in the late 1950s. In 1970, when Baker entered the political arena for the first time as Houston campaign manager for Bush's unsuccessful U.S. Senate campaign, Baker discovered he had both a talent and a thirst for the managerial side of politics. As manager of Bush's campaign for the Republican presidential nomination in 1980, Baker was credited with insisting that Bush drop out of the race as soon as Ronald Reagan had won enough delegates to assure him of the nomination. Had Baker not forced Bush out—before Bush was psychologically ready—Reagan would not have picked him as his vice presidential running mate. There is little doubt that Bush would never have become President without Baker and that Baker would never have come to national prominence without Bush, who sponsored him in Washington jobs.

The close personal and political relationship of Bush and Baker was the cornerstone of the secretary of state's power and standing within the administration. It was virtually certain that Baker would never experience the damaging and demeaning treatment at the hands of the White House staff or rival factions within the administration that Shultz and many of his predecessors had suffered. Baker did not always have his way in foreign policy decisions, for Bush had his own strong ideas about some issues, but he always had a say. In some respects the relationship of Bush and Baker was the reverse of the traditional one for a president and his secretary of state; in this case, the President was an expert on diplomacy and his chief diplomat was an expert on politics. Baker was known in Washington as a hard worker, a quick study and a skillful negotiator, but initially he lacked experience with or historical perspective about large areas of U.S. foreign relations.

About an hour after he arrived in Moscow on May 10, 1989, Baker in a blue suit and his favorite green tie arrived at the turn-of-the-century Foreign Ministry guest house on Alexei Tolstoy Street, where Shevardnadze welcomed him to the Soviet capital. The two men had become acquainted in a two-hour meeting in early March in Vienna on the occasion of the opening of the new East-West talks on conventional forces in Europe. In Moscow they seemed at ease with each other. Shevardnadze had invited Baker and his wife, Susan, to his private apartment for dinner with himself and his wife, Nanuli, something he had never done with the Shultzes, even though at this point the chemistry between Shevardnadze and Baker was not as strong or striking as that which had developed between Shevardnadze and Shultz.

After posing for photographers in the lobby of the Foreign Ministry guest house, the two ministers and their interpreters went into a side room of the richly decorated former mansion for an initial private conversation that was supposed to last twenty-five minutes. They emerged after forty-five minutes into a white marble conference room with gold trim and crystal chandeliers to join their two delegations at a long conference table.

The issues of the day were Afghanistan and Nicaragua, the former the top priority for the Soviet Union, the latter the most urgent question for the United States. "They will say they aren't linked, and we'll say they aren't linked," Baker told me in discussing the two regional disputes shortly before leaving for Moscow. However, he added with a big smile, "one is close to us, the other is close to them."

The last Soviet troops had left Afghanistan on February 15 as promised, despite several pauses in the withdrawal process and persistent Soviet protests about the continuing flow of U.S. weapons to the Afghan *mujaheddin*. According to conservative estimates, about 1 million of Afghanistan's 12.5 million people had been killed by the time the Soviet troops departed, and about 5 million had fled as refugees to neighboring Pakistan or Iran. At least another 1 million had been displaced from their homes within the country. Most of the deaths were civilian, but close to 100,000 resistance fighters were also among the dead. The official Soviet Defense Ministry figure for Soviet military deaths was 13,831, but that included only those who were killed in action; a more comprehensive estimate of Soviet war deaths from all causes is 36,000. By 1989, it was estimated that three-fourths of Afghanistan's villages had been severely damaged or destroyed, in addition to large sections of the country's few major cities.

The Reagan administration had refused to stop the arms supply unless the Soviets stopped their arms aid to the Kabul government, a deal Moscow had rejected. However, Soviet officials continued to argue that the U.S. aid violated the April 1988 Geneva agreements. On a political basis, they thought that the United States should help Moscow free itself with honor from the long war in the interest of stabilizing U.S.-Soviet relations and setting a healthy precedent for Soviet cooperation in the solution of other regional disputes. The Bush administration was no more sympathetic than its predecessor to Moscow's regime in Kabul, and the U.S. arms flow continued unabated. When Shevardnadze had appealed to Baker on the arms issue in their get-acquainted meeting in Vienna, the secretary of state had responded bluntly, "Why didn't you accept a deal when we offered it to you last April?"

In early March 1989, only a few weeks after the withdrawal of the last Soviet troops, close to eight thousand Afghan guerrillas from several disparate tribal groups laid siege to the eastern city of Jalalabad in what became the biggest battle of the Afghan war. The siege was mounted under pressure from the Pakistani military intelligence agency, which distributed the U.S. and Arab aid to the *mujaheddin* tribesmen. The Pakistanis calculated that a sharp blow to the military position and morale of the Kabul army, such as the fall of Jalalabad, could bring the collapse of the Soviet-backed regime. It was a close call, but by the end of March the rebels had suffered heavy casualties and the prospect of a quick victory had faded. In the short run, at least, Jalalabad had been saved by emergency Soviet military aid, a resolute defense by Afghan government troops who were fighting for their lives, and the failure of the various guerrilla groups, who were unaccustomed to conventional warfare, to develop effective coordination or a competent battle plan.

In February Gorbachev had appealed to Bush privately by letter to assist in setting up an international conference to end the fighting, but Bush had refused. During March Gorbachev had presided over a special Politburo meeting to discuss the Afghan emergency, and personally instructed Ambassador to the United States Yuri Dubinin to use every possible means available to convince the United States to halt or reduce its support for the *mujaheddin*. By early April, the Soviet Embassy had launched an all-out campaign, with Dubinin and other diplomats calling on practically all the top foreign policy officials of the Bush administration as well as many members of Congress and journalists. I had been invited for coffee and a sales pitch on April 3 by Yevgeny Kutovoy, Dubinin's deputy, and Oleg Derkovsky, the Embassy's Middle East specialist, the only time in more than a decade of covering Soviet-American affairs that I had been summoned for an individual and personal appeal of this sort. On April 11, the Embassy even arranged a private meeting with the leading backers of the *mujaheddin* in Congress in an attempt to persuade them to drop their support for the insurgents. None of this had much effect in Washington, where the Soviet lobbying campaign was seen as a desperation effort before the inevitable fall of the Kabul regime.

By the time of the May meeting with Baker in Moscow, Shevardnadze had begun to feel more confident that his Afghan allies would be able to withstand the immediate military challenge. The victory at Jalalabad was being celebrated "like a Stalingrad victory," according to Yuli Vorontsov, who was the Foreign Ministry overseer of Afghan policy. Shevardnadze breathed a bit easier than before, and his main appeal to Baker in the Moscow meeting was for U.S. help in initiating a dialogue between the Kabul government and other Afghan factions, including representatives of the resistance. Baker responded that in Washington's view, the *mujaheddin* would never accept Najibullah, Moscow's man in Kabul, as part of a legitimate government.

Central America presented a more promising prospect for U.S.-Soviet cooperation, especially because of a secret letter from Gorbachev that had arrived in Washington on May 6, two days before Baker departed for Moscow. The letter, known only to a few top U.S. and Soviet officials during Baker's trip to the Soviet capital, conveyed the surprising news that Moscow's weapons shipments to Nicaragua's Sandinista government had ceased.

The breakthrough had been a long time coming. U.S.-Soviet diplomacy regarding Central America had a rocky start during the Reagan administration, and had only limited success before 1989. The conservatives who dominated Reagan's policy in Central America saw the struggle in that region as largely an unwarranted and dangerous extension of Soviet power in the back yard of the United States. They had little faith in political persuasion and mainly believed that the buildup of military muscle in the anticommunist cause, including support for the antigovernment Contra rebels in Nicaragua and government armies in El Salvador, Honduras and Guatemala, was the way to success.

When the series of U.S.-Soviet talks on regional issues in the Third World began in 1985, Elliott Abrams, the State Department's polemical assistant secretary for Latin America, was reluctant to engage with Moscow, and his bureau was the last one to schedule a meeting with its Soviet Foreign Ministry counterpart. In a planning meeting a day or two before the October 31–November 1, 1985, meeting with officials who had come from Moscow, Colonel Oliver North of the National Security Council staff vehemently objected that "the President has not approved this meeting with the Soviets. This is illegitimate." Abrams, who was presiding, calmed North and other officials who objected to meeting with the Soviets by making it clear that his opening remarks to the visitors would hardly be to their liking. Indeed, at the meeting, the ranking Soviet participant, Vladimir Kazimirov of the Foreign Ministry's First Latin American Department, declared that he was mightily insulted by Abrams's presentation and tempted to walk out. According to another State Department official who was present, the Soviet visitor declared, "It is clear you don't want to have a productive discussion of Central America, but we've come and I'm going to deliver my statement." That initial meeting was strained and unproductive, but the following year, when the U.S. conservatives began to see merit in the dialogue and Kazimirov was replaced by a more flexible Soviet expert on Central America, the discussions with Moscow began to make modest progress.

By early 1989, U.S. muscle in Nicaragua had drastically diminished. After the Iran-Contra scandal, Congress had reinforced its ban on U.S. military aid to the Contras, and it was unlikely that Bush would be able to obtain congressional approval to resume the aid. In this situation, Baker early in the new administration negotiated a pact with Democrats and Republicans in Congress that continued nonmilitary funding of the Contras for nearly a year while the administration intensified its efforts to reach a regional peace agreement. The appeal of the deal for the Democrats was the administration's pledge to turn from military force to negotiations as a way to resolve the conflicts in Central America.

Essential to the success of the new bipartisan accord, as the administration saw it, was persuading the Soviet Union to halt its military aid to Nicaragua, which was estimated by the State Department at $515 million in 1988, and its indirect support for Marxist guerrillas in El Salvador. In a private letter to Gorbachev on March 27, Bush said explicitly that continuation of the military aid "in this region of vital interest to the United States will . . . inevitably affect the nature of the [U.S.-Soviet] relationship." Bush wrote that a Soviet initiative to shut off the military assistance pipeline "would pay large dividends in American goodwill."

As Baker's trip to Moscow approached, the administration became increasingly outspoken in tying the entire future course of U.S.-Soviet relations to the Central American situation. A memo to Baker by his staff aides on Thursday, May 4, four days before his departure for Moscow, said, "We must convince the Soviets not that we are in trouble and desperately need them to throw us an anchor, but that it is they who risk being seen as a spoiler. The bottom line is this: Soviet reduction in aid and Soviet pressure on its clients are necessary to make up for the leverage we lost in Central America when military aid to the contras was ended."

In Moscow, the Soviet leadership sensed that support for Nicaragua was becoming *the* issue with Washington. "As a permanent problem, it was more and more unacceptable to us," said a senior Soviet official. Besides, the argument was made, the Nicaraguans already had such a large supply of Soviet weapons that they really did not need more. In addition to those in the country, according to this official, Nicaragua owned a large supply of Soviet arms that were stored in Cuban depots.

On Saturday night, barely thirty-six hours before Baker's departure from Washington, the Soviet Embassy delivered Gorbachev's reply to Bush's March 27 letter. Gorbachev wrote:

> We note the positive trends in Central America, including the intention of your administration and the U.S. Congress to "give diplomacy a chance." I agree that productive Soviet-U.S.

engagement on regional questions will lead to a growing potential of good will in Soviet-U.S. relations.

Then came Gorbachev's surprise declaration:

In order to promote a peaceful settlement of the conflict, and bearing in mind that the attacks by the Contras' troops against Nicaragua have stopped, the U.S.S.R. has not been sending weapons to [Nicaragua] since 1988.

While the action passage suggested a major change in the situation, it raised a host of questions, some of which have never been answered. If the arms flow had been stopped on January 1, why had nobody in Moscow or Managua said anything about it until May? Why had U.S. intelligence reported no substantial change in the pattern of Soviet deliveries? Did the word "weapons" in Gorbachev's letter apply to nonlethal war material? Did the cutoff apply to weapons that the Soviet Union was supplying to Cuba, but which Cuba could then redirect to Nicaragua? Was Gorbachev's letter a commitment to continue the arms halt into the future, or even make it permanent?

Baker raised some of these issues with Shevardnadze at the Foreign Ministry guest house on Wednesday, May 10. He also asked the Soviet Union to use its influence to convince Cuba and Nicaragua to halt their assistance to subversion within the region. Baker listed for Shevardnadze—and repeated to Gorbachev the following day in the Kremlin—some of the U.S. steps in return, most of which had been promised in negotiations of the bipartisan accords with Congress. If the forthcoming Nicaraguan elections scheduled for February were free and fair, Baker declared, the United States would accept a Sandinista victory. Subsequently the Soviets said they would accept the election returns as well and pressed the Sandinistas to permit election observers to assure fairness. With the prospect of a halt to Soviet military aid to Central America and the approach of real elections in Nicaragua, the conflict at the U.S. back door had taken a turn for the better, from Washington's point of view.

Baker's meeting with Shevardnadze in Moscow was also notable for the first U.S.-Soviet discussion of Eastern Europe in many years. Except for such emergencies as the imposition of martial law in Poland in 1981, Washington had avoided discussing the area with the Soviets on the grounds that this would legitimize the Soviet domination and that such a discussion was unlikely to be useful. In late January 1989, however, former Secretary of State Henry Kissinger had suggested to Bush in a White House meeting that it was time to explore with the Soviets an arrangement under which Eastern European countries would move toward self-rule and the West would provide security guarantees that NATO would not advance into Eastern Europe or use the present Soviet bloc nations as a threat to the Soviet Union. The State Department career professionals reacted in horror to Kissinger's ideas, but Baker told *New York Times* correspondent Thomas Friedman late in March that they were "worthy of consideration" and "a novel approach."

Baker broke the ice in the discussion with Shevardnadze on the subject of Eastern Europe by discussing the July trip that Bush planned to Poland and Hungary, a trip that had been announced five days earlier by the White House. "This isn't meant to create problems for you," said Baker. It wasn't intended to trigger any kind of instability but was seen by the new administration as consistent with its approach of working with the Soviet Union, he said. Baker made the point that Bush would be seeking to promote those who had invited him to come, notably including Polish President Wojciech Jaruzelski. Shevardnadze's reaction was immediate and positive. At Baker's suggestion, the Soviet minister went on to describe his view of the Eastern European scene. Though the discussion was brief, it was considered important, because Baker and his aides could see that a gathering tide of change in Eastern Europe would require steady communication with Moscow on the subject.

The morning after his meeting with Shevardnadze, Baker went to St. Catherine's Hall in the Kremlin for his first working session with Mikhail Gorbachev. In characteristic Baker style, he began it in intimacy with a conference with only himself, Gorbachev, Shevardnadze and two interpreters present at the long conference table. The rest of the two delegations waited in the next room until they were called in after an hour.

Gorbachev began by saying that the visit was a timely one. "I am sure the dialogue should be continued, should be brought to a new level," and out of the dialogue would grow increased cooperation. "The main thing is not to lose touch with reality." The discussions over several years showed that any other approach was ineffective and dangerous, Gorbachev said. But "realism and getting rid of delusions made for progress in many fields, and for achieving what earlier seemed impossible."

At Baker's invitation, and especially because the U.S. policy reviews were still in progress, Gorbachev went on to describe at length the status of *perestroika*. It used to be a policy, he said, but now is a reality; "it used to be a reflection of what we want to achieve, but now it's beyond that." Nevertheless, "in a big and complex country such as the Soviet Union, no one can expect the process to be easy, especially in a period of revolutionary change." Gorbachev added, in what turned out to be an overly optimistic estimate, "Perhaps we are now passing through the most difficult moment."

In his travels throughout the Soviet Union, Gorbachev said, he had observed great changes from what he had seen two years earlier. But the challenges were great, especially the task of arraying forces to make the bureaucracy change. The facile view was that this was a matter of simple arithmetic, said Gorbachev, but the reality was as complex as calculus.

Baker said that in the United States there were different views of *perestroika*, but that nobody wanted to see it fail. In their intimate session, Gorbachev had raised the subject of Defense Secretary Cheney's televised comments two weeks earlier that Gorbachev "would ultimately fail" to reform the Soviet economy and that he was likely to be replaced by a leader who would be "far more hostile" to the West. Bush and Baker had distanced themselves from Cheney's remarks, and Baker had gone out of his way to declare in a speech just before departing for Moscow that "the President has said and I have said that we have no wish to see *perestroika* fail. To the contrary: we would very much like it to succeed." Baker told Gorbachev that in the U.S. view *perestroika* brought big possibilities for stable and fruitful relations between the United States and the Soviet Union.

At dinner the previous night in Shevardnadze's apartment, Baker had counseled quick movement on price reform, while Gorbachev still possessed the political strength to take it on and while it was still possible to blame major problems on his predecessors. Referring to such comments from the U.S. visitor, Gorbachev said it had been difficult to tackle price reform in the early stages of *perestroika* because it "would have taken money out of the pockets of people" and "hurt the trust of the people." It is necessary to go forward in "a balanced way . . . a middle course," he said, with political reforms paving the way for new economic reforms. Baker concluded from these and other remarks, he said later, that price reform is "a gorilla in their minds and the longer they wait, the bigger a gorilla it will be."

Toward the end of the meeting in St. Catherine's Hall, Gorbachev and Baker turned to the subject of arms control. With the U.S. reviews still unfinished, Baker could only present a general reassurance that the United States would be ready to resume negotiations in June and take into consideration the tentative agreements that had been reached on many points during the Reagan administration.

Sitting at the negotiating table in full uniform, with eleven rows of military ribbons covering the left side of his tunic and the big star of a Soviet marshal on his shoulder, was Sergei Akhromeyev, who had retired as chief of staff of the armed forces the previous December but who remained the personal military adviser to Gorbachev. As Akhromeyev looked on, the Soviet leader disclosed the dimensions of the proposals that his negotiators would table in the East-West conventional arms talks, calling for cutbacks of more than a million men and large numbers of tanks, aircraft and artillery on each side. Then, saying he wanted to give Baker advance notice, Gorbachev announced that the Soviet Union had decided unilaterally to withdraw five hundred tactical nuclear warheads from Eastern Europe to give impetus to the drive for nuclear disarmament.

Gorbachev's unilateral reduction in tactical nuclear weapons was small compared to the ten thousand or more warheads the Americans estimated that the Soviet Union had in the European theater, but the move was a master stroke of timing.* NATO was at the high point of a passionate and unseemly dispute over the future of just such U.S. tactical nuclear weapons, with the West Germans and some others wanting to negotiate with Moscow to eliminate them from Europe and the United States and Britain pushing for a commitment to modernize and retain them in the NATO arsenal. The Atlantic alliance was committed to settling the long-running dispute by the time NATO heads of state met May 29–30 to celebrate the organization's fortieth anniversary, and the maneuvering on the issue was intense. Gorbachev's unilateral reduction of five hundred warheads would make headlines in Western Europe and the United States, putting Baker and the other supporters of retaining short-range nuclear weapons on the defensive.

Baker had been warned to expect a surprise of some sort from Gorbachev, who seemed to be seeking to counteract his slipping popularity

---

* Later and better information as Moscow withdrew its forces indicated that the Soviets had far fewer warheads in the area than had been estimated, and that Gorbachev's May cutback was therefore more substantial than described by Americans at the time.

at home with even greater acclaim abroad. The secretary of state asked if he could have a copy of the proposals that Gorbachev had just unveiled for him, and his request was granted. Baker said he planned to meet NATO foreign ministers in Brussels the following day and asked if it would be all right with Gorbachev for him to brief the allies on the Soviet plans. Gorbachev gave his permission, and left the impression that his initiatives would be announced in a short time. As it turned out, only the broad outline of the new Soviet plan was announced in Moscow that day. Baker, who helpfully provided the details he had been given to reporters on his airplane bound for Brussels, inadvertently contributed to the wallop of Moscow's latest arms cut story.

His first trip to Moscow had been a substantive success for Baker, especially on Central America, and he had reengaged the United States and Soviet Union across a broad front and laid the foundation for progress to come. He had gained a first impression of Gorbachev as a formidable figure who was well prepared and had his notes "in apple-pie order." In public relations terms, however, the trip had been a debacle, due to Gorbachev's surprise announcement of a cutback of short-range nuclear weapons in Europe. Columnist Robert Novak, who joined the press contingent that accompanied Baker to Moscow, wrote that "Baker is one of the foxiest of inside operators dealing with Congress and in American politics. But he is a new boy in the global high-stakes game, and Gorbachev left him sprawled in the dust." Novak's view was widely shared, to the dismay of the press-conscious secretary of state. On the flight home from Brussels to Washington, Baker invented reasons to come back to the press area of his plane three times, for over an hour in all, for off-the-record chats that seemed intended to improve his relations with the reporters. He did not complain about the PR pounding he had taken. He seemed determined, though, that the Soviets would not upstage him again.

• TO THE NATO SUMMIT

By the spring of 1989, the world was in flux. The Soviet Union in late March had held the freest elections in its seventy-year history, for a new Congress of People's Deputies—elections in which many Communist Party functionaries were defeated. There had been violent clashes be-

tween the army and nationalist demonstrators in Soviet Georgia, in which
twenty demonstrators were killed, and separatism was rising dramatically
in the Ukraine and the Baltic states. Soviet military forces were being
reduced in Eastern Europe, where it was becoming increasingly clear
they would not be used. Soviet troops were out of Afghanistan, and China
had agreed to a visit by Gorbachev to patch up the historic quarrel
between the two communist giants. The communist government of Poland
had legalized the Solidarity movement and agreed to free elections.
Hungary had begun dismantling the barbed-wire fence along its boundary
with Austria, making it the first Soviet bloc country to open a border
with Western Europe. Led by West Germany and France, the nations
of Western Europe were moving rapidly toward agreement on economic
and monetary union by 1992. Inside NATO, Germany was maneuvering
to avoid modernization of the U.S. nuclear weapons on its soil and to
have them eventually removed.

In the first week of May, just before Secretary Baker flew to Moscow,
I surveyed leading U.S. foreign policy figures outside of government,
nearly all of whom said that the changes underway were bringing an end
to the post–World War II era. "We are quite literally in the early phases
of what might be called the postcommunist era," said Zbigniew Brzezinski, who had been President Carter's national security adviser. "This
is a massive, monumental transformation. Communism shaped much of
this century. And now it is coming to an end." Robert McNamara, who
had been secretary of defense under Presidents Kennedy and Johnson,
said, "We face an opportunity—the greatest in 40 years—to bring an
end to the Cold War." Henry Kissinger, who had been secretary of state
under Presidents Nixon and Ford, told me, "International factors have
rarely been so fluid. The one thing that cannot occur is a continuation
of the status quo."

The most prescient comments came from William Hyland, the editor
of *Foreign Affairs*. "What's happening in Russia is spilling over into
Eastern Europe and affecting Western Europe," said Hyland, a former
CIA and NSC official. "If there is some kind of new order in Hungary,
Poland and perhaps Czechoslovakia, with less of a Soviet presence, a
substantial reduction of troops and liberalization inside the countries
with multiparties and so on, then the question is whether that can be
applied to East Germany. And if it is, aren't you just a step or so away
from the unification of Germany altogether?"

In the midst of all this, the fledgling Bush administration was settling in at a painfully slow pace. The outcome of its vaunted policy review toward the Soviet Union had been summed up by a State Department aide as "status quo plus," a set of unexciting, muddle-through suggestions that were universally recognized as inadequate to the times. In a cacophony of mixed messages and discordant voices, the administration seemed to be going back and forth about its policy toward the Soviet Union: "Keep your guard up." "It's a new day." "We want to see performance, not public relations." "Yes, Gorbachev is real and important." "But he won't succeed." "We don't want *perestroika* to fail." "But we can't determine his future." And so on.

President Bush had agreed to be the commencement speaker at Texas A&M University on May 12, and had planned this to be the first of several speeches announcing the administration's stance toward the Soviet Union at the end of the policy review. Attending one of the many discussions preceding that speech, the thirty-four-year-old Soviet expert on the National Security Council staff, Condoleezza Rice, found herself searching for ways to summarize the situation. Containment of the Soviet Union had worked; just as George Kennan had originally hoped, it had forced the Soviets to halt expansion and turn inward, reasoned Rice, who had been recruited from the Stanford University faculty by Brent Scowcroft for his NSC staff. The new era was "postcontainment," or in more exciting terms, "beyond containment," she decided. But beyond it to what? To the death of Soviet foreign policy? To the rollback of communism? The new era, it seemed to Rice, could move "beyond containment" to almost the reverse of containment, the encouragement of Soviet integration into the Western economic and political community.

Bush liked the idea and the phrase at once when it was presented to him by Scowcroft. It became the centerpiece of the speech at Texas A&M:

> Wise men—Truman and Eisenhower, Vandenberg and Rayburn—Marshall, Acheson and Kennan—crafted the strategy of containment. They believed that the Soviet Union, denied the easy course of expansion, would turn inward and address the contradictions of its inefficient, repressive and inhumane system. And they were right. The Soviet Union is now publicly facing this hard reality. Containment worked. . . .
>
> We are approaching the conclusion of an historic power struggle between two visions: one of tyranny and conflict, and one of

democracy and freedom. The review of U.S.-Soviet relations that my administration has just completed outlines a new path toward resolving this struggle. Our goal is bold, more ambitious than any of my predecessors would have thought possible. Our review indicates that 40 years of perseverance have brought us a precious opportunity. And now, it is time to move beyond containment to a new policy for the 1990s—one that recognizes the full scope of change taking place around the world and in the Soviet Union itself.

In sum, the United States now has as its goal much more than simply containing Soviet expansionism. We seek the integration of the Soviet Union into the community of nations. And as the Soviet Union itself moves toward greater openness and democratization, as they meet the challenge of responsible international behavior, we will match their steps with steps of our own. Ultimately, our objective is to welcome the Soviet Union back into the world order.

Bush's new concept made little impact at first because of the cautionary notes in the same speech and, especially, the absence of an operational program to make even a credible start on achieving his ambitious goals. The specific proposals in the speech were an "Open Skies" program, a throwback to an Eisenhower initiative of 1955, and a temporary and conditional waiver of Jackson-Vanik, the U.S. law tying normal trade relations to Soviet emigration policy. Bush's speech engendered as much skepticism about his intentions as Gorbachev's declarations and unilateral actions had engendered among some of the senior members of the Bush administration. The doubts that Bush was serious intensified after White House Press Secretary Marlin Fitzwater on May 16 described Gorbachev as a "drugstore cowboy," reflecting the administration's frustration at the Soviet President's skill—and its own ineptitude—at capturing the public imagination. The tone of the second commencement speech in Bush's series, at Boston University on May 21, was more positive, but still without specific new moves, although by this time Bush was working secretly on a new proposal to make deep cuts in conventional forces in Europe. The press and political criticism of Bush continued.

The day before the third and last commencement speech in the planned series, at the Coast Guard Academy on May 24, the Soviet

Union put its new conventional arms reduction proposals on the table in the East-West talks in Vienna, and they were very surprising. Even more positive and important than the huge scale of the proposed reductions, in the U.S. view, was acceptance of important basing limitations on Soviet forces in Europe that Moscow had previously rejected. Many elements of the proposal were so close to those of NATO that it was evident Gorbachev was driving for an early treaty on the best terms he could get.

With the news of the Soviet conventional arms proposal, Bush's determination to offer a bold new proposal of his own redoubled and his unhappiness with his speeches boiled over. The Coast Guard Academy speech draft, which had been planned to discuss military policy, had major contributions from the Pentagon, and Bush complained bitterly that it was "too nuclear, too military." He wanted a more positive approach. The White House staff worked on the speech until midnight the night before, and Bush made more changes on Air Force One on the way to New London, Connecticut, to deliver the speech. Due to the many last-minute revisions, the TelePrompTer, which scrolled the text in front of Bush as he delivered it, broke down in midspeech, causing the puzzled President to exclaim, "The text is going crazy in this machine here." In a passage that he inserted at the last minute, Bush declared, "Our policy is to seize every, and I mean every, opportunity to build a better, more stable relationship with the Soviet Union." He welcomed the unilateral arms cutbacks Gorbachev had announced in December at the United Nations and for the first time praised the Soviets for "being forthcoming" in the conventional arms talks. "Through negotiations, we can now transform the military landscape of Europe," Bush said.

In his campaign for the presidency, Bush had placed special emphasis on cuts in conventional armies in Europe, suggesting that reductions in Soviet ground-based power in Europe should come before big new cuts in nuclear weaponry. In Bush's early weeks in office the subject had come up in discussions among his inner circle, but initially Bush had felt locked into the proposal for East-West reductions in conventional forces that had been worked out in extensive consultations within NATO during the last year of the Reagan administration. NATO officially presented its proposal in early March 1989, at the opening of the new talks on conventional forces in Europe, with Baker and Shevardnadze participating. The Western proposal called for minimal NATO cutbacks of 5 to 10 percent in tanks, armored personnel carriers and artillery, to be matched by massive Warsaw Pact cuts of 50 percent or more in these categories. Surprisingly, the Soviet Union accepted the principle of such disproportionate reductions in its official counteroffer.

Baker had been impressed with Gorbachev's seriousness as well as his agile tactics on European arms cutbacks in his May 11 meeting in the Kremlin. Bush, after conferring with Baker on his return, put the top rank of his government into high gear to prepare a new and more sweeping conventional arms proposal that he could sell privately to key U.S. allies and unveil at the May 29–30 NATO summit meeting in Brussels. "I want this done. Don't keep telling me why it can't be done. Tell me how it can be done," Bush insisted in an Oval Office meeting at which Baker and others were present. The secretary of state was enthusiastic. He and Bush were being increasingly criticized in the press and Congress for passivity and lack of leadership in a time of rapid change, and Baker felt it was essential that Bush establish himself at the NATO summit as a strong leader of the alliance.

Bush's summer home at Kennebunkport, Maine, was the site for his first big decisions on U.S. policy toward Europe and the Soviet Union, hammered out in the intimate and secret fashion that would become characteristic of his foreign policy deliberations. In a series of meetings with his top advisers starting on Friday, May 19, Bush fashioned a much bolder NATO proposal on cuts in conventional forces in Europe. Abandoning the previous NATO position that cuts in numbers of troops were unverifiable and less important than reductions in weapons, Bush decided to propose big cuts in U.S. and Soviet manpower in Europe. At one stage the discussions envisioned cutting U.S. forces in Europe by 75,000 troops, nearly 25 percent of the existing force of 305,000, on condition that the Soviets cut their European forces to an equal number. Led by its chairman, Admiral William Crowe, the Joint Chiefs of Staff resisted, saying that such a big reduction would cause NATO to abandon its venerable "forward strategy" for defending Europe. Eventually Bush settled for a 30,000-troop cut, about 10 percent of the U.S. force committed to NATO. Reversing another longstanding NATO position, Bush also proposed specific cutbacks in warplanes and helicopters to match Soviet proposals. Another crucial innovation was in the timing of the cuts, to take place starting in 1992 rather than five years later as proposed by Gorbachev. This permitted Baker to paper over the dispute within NATO over the future of short-range nuclear weapons—a family quarrel that had threatened to dominate the NATO summit meeting. Bush got the advance approval of other NATO leaders by sending Deputy Secretary of State Lawrence Eagleburger and Deputy National Security Adviser Robert Gates on a secret two-day consultation trip to six European capitals and through other confidential communications.

The President unveiled his proposal in a press conference at NATO headquarters in Brussels on May 29, minutes after having discussed it in private and obtaining a resounding vote of confidence from his fellow NATO heads of government. "Here we go now, on the offensive with a proposal that is bold," proclaimed Bush, in a pivotal moment when he seemed to break out of the passivity that had characterized his first months in office. It suddenly seemed as if a wimpish, cautious George Bush, in Europe for his first NATO meeting as President, had stepped into a telephone booth like Clark Kent in the comic strip saga and emerged as a powerful and dashing figure, if not Superman himself. Shevardnadze called Bush's proposals "serious" and "a step in the right direction," and they won nearly universal praise in the West. The cheers were mixed with a sense of relief that the U.S. President had finally seized the initiative from Gorbachev and had taken the leadership for the West.

My sense of being present at a great historical event was heightened by the opportunity to interview Bush three days later, on the morning of his last full day in Europe, in the company of *Washington Post* White House correspondent Ann Devroy. I was struck by how calm and comfortable Bush was sitting over coffee, orange juice and rolls in the dining room at Winthrop House, the residence of the U.S. ambassador in London. "I'm the same guy I was four days ago," the President said when asked about his sudden rise from the target of widespread criticism to the recipient of nearly universal acclaim. He seemed to understand that the cheers were transitory and perhaps to suggest, from his vantage point, that they were as undeserved as the catcalls.

Several days before, *New York Times* columnist William Safire had called Bush "the first U.S. president since Richard Nixon to be in full intellectual command of his national security policy," and the comment seemed apt as I watched Bush answer questions about his new policies in almost perfect paragraphs, without looking at a note and only rarely asking for a detail from Scowcroft, who was at the other end of the dining-room table. Although Eastern Europe was then relatively quiet, certainly compared to what was to come, Bush referred to it as "the most exciting area for change in the world" and came back to it time and again in response to questions on other subjects. Asked to explain the thinking behind his "beyond containment" concept, Bush replied:

The Soviet Union might well be in a state of radical change. And as this change asserts itself, and as they genuinely change, our doctrine need no longer be containing a militarily aggressive Soviet Union. It means a united Europe. It means a Europe without as many artificial boundaries. It means much more freedom and democracy, not only in the Soviet Union, but in Europe. As those things happen, the role of NATO shifts, our own role shifts, from the main emphasis on deterrence to an emphasis on the economic side of things. . . . Beyond containment means a significant shift in the Soviet Union. A lightening up on the control in Eastern Europe and thus freeing them to move down the democratic path much more.

Reminded that he was the first President to propose bringing a large number of U.S. troops out of Europe since the end of World War II, Bush responded:

I think I'm the first President to deal with these demonstrable changes in the Soviet Union. Again, keep your eyes open. Don't make proposals that are naive or naive militarily. But think anew. We've got new conditions facing us. It's not just the Soviet Union. What's happening in Poland. In Hungary. Here we go again. In these countries there's this change, this ferment. I think I'm the first President who has faced a Soviet Union that is in the posture it's in. Now what we've got to do is through cautious contact and hopefully some other bold proposals, challenge the reality of all this. Or put this way, encourage change. We can't dictate change to any country, large or small. But we can say what we stand for. We can make clear that if others can meet those standards, relations with us will be better.

The whirlwind of change that was on Bush's mind would develop even more quickly than he anticipated. Before the year was out, Soviet control would be broken in all of Eastern Europe.

• THE REVOLUTION OF 1989

When 1989 began, Europe was divided from East to West along the lines that had been established in the aftermath of World War II and with few exceptions frozen ever since. On the eastern side of what Winston Churchill in 1946 had named the Iron Curtain, the nations of Poland, Hungary, Czechoslovakia, Bulgaria and Romania were dominated by communist parties beholden to Moscow and kept in power by the threat of Soviet military intervention, as they had been for four decades. Behind fortified barriers and watch towers snaking across the countryside and an ugly concrete and steel wall through the heart of Berlin, East Germany was a powerful half a nation, ruled by orthodox communists who had contempt for Gorbachev's reforms.

By the end of the year, the leaders of all those nations would either change their political orientation or be ousted by popular uprisings. In every case except for Romania, hardly a drop of blood would be spilled. The armored and reinforced borders between East and West Germany would be opened, to the joy of Germans from both sides dancing triumphantly on the Berlin Wall. With dizzying suddenness, the Soviet Union's European empire, its buffer zone between Soviet territory and the West, would collapse. Rarely in history has such a sweeping reorientation of political, economic and military power taken place so swiftly without military conquest or bloody revolution.

The downfall of the Soviet dominance over Eastern Europe, with no intervention or resistance from Moscow and even hints of prodding by Gorbachev in the direction of change, would demonstrate that the Soviet Union had fundamentally changed the policies it had applied with force and determination on its periphery since World War II. Beyond the massive shift in Soviet intentions, the revolutionary developments of 1989 would also signal a sharp decline in the Soviet Union's capability to use military power beyond its borders to mount an attack in Europe. Although Soviet troops would still be in Eastern Europe in large numbers at the end of 1989, their exodus would be underway. While the popular revolutions would be still incomplete in many cases and Germany not yet reunited, it would be clear by the end of the year that none of the nations of the former Soviet empire in Europe would seek or even accept Soviet domination in the future. All this would have powerful effect on the basic requirements and premises of U.S. policy toward the Soviet Union.

How the Revolution of 1989 happened—and happened so suddenly—will be the subject of historical study and analysis for decades to come. To a greater extent than is now generally acknowledged, the peoples of Eastern Europe and those who stepped forward to be their leaders are likely to be credited as the key protagonists. Nonetheless, Gorbachev and his associates in the Soviet Union, whether by calculation or miscalculation, played a crucial role in permitting it to happen so quickly and peacefully. The Bush administration played at least a significant role through the conduct of its dialogue with Moscow and with the nations involved.

For most of his official career, Mikhail Gorbachev had had little contact with the Soviet bloc in Eastern Europe. His earliest, and for a long time probably his most important, contact with the fraternal countries was his friendship in Moscow University's law school with Zdenek Mlynar, a Czech student, who later became one of the reformist leaders of the Czechoslovak communist party during the 1968 Prague Spring. Mlynar was expelled from the party and eventually fled to the West after Soviet military intervention ended this effort at constructing "socialism with a human face." Years later he described the 1968 showdown meeting in which Leonid Brezhnev bluntly told the Czech leaders they must yield to the Kremlin's wishes. Brezhnev's logic, Mlynar wrote, was simple:

> Your country lies on territory where the Soviet soldier trod in the Second World War. We bought that territory at the cost of enormous sacrifices, and we shall never leave it. The borders of that area are our borders as well. Because you do not listen to us, we feel threatened. In the name of the dead in World War II who laid down their lives for your freedom as well, we are therefore fully justified in sending our soldiers into your country, so that we may feel secure within our common borders. It is immaterial whether anyone is actually threatening us or not: it is a matter of principle, independent of external circumstances. And that is how it will be, from the Second World War to "eternity."

After the Czech reformers were ousted by Soviet tanks, Brezhnev issued a public justification for the action, which became known as the

"Brezhnev Doctrine." In essence, it stated that a threat to the political system in any socialist country was "a threat to the security of the socialist commonwealth as a whole." In other words, once a "socialist" country, forever a "socialist" country, as long as the Soviet Union had the military power to keep it in the fraternal camp.

Twenty-one years later, in October 1989, Soviet Foreign Ministry Spokesman Gennadi Gerasimov officially declared that "the Brezhnev Doctrine is dead" and in its place offered a new hands-off policy summed up in a witty reference to American popular culture. "You know the Frank Sinatra song 'My Way'? Hungary and Poland are doing it their way. We now have the Sinatra doctrine."

Even though he took power in 1985 as a reformist leader for the Soviet Union, Gorbachev did not initially suggest any change in the relationship between the Soviet Union and the Eastern European states. As noted earlier,* his first foreign policy statement gave highest priority to preserving and strengthening "fraternal friendship with our closest friends and allies, the countries of the great socialist community." He quickly extended the Warsaw Pact military alliance for twenty years in a meeting with Eastern European communist leaders in the Polish capital, and seemed to suggest modest internal reforms along with strengthened discipline as a way to deal with growing disaffection in Eastern Europe.

Many of the Soviet reformers who surrounded Gorbachev had experienced the Prague Spring or its aftermath while working in the Czech capital and were well-disposed to such reformist movements. This "Prague Club," as it came to be called, included Ivan Frolov, the editor of *Pravda*; Gerasimov, the Foreign Ministry press spokesman; Georgi Shakhnazarov, who became Gorbachev's personal adviser on Eastern Europe; Anatoly Chernyaev, Gorbachev's personal foreign policy assistant; and Fyodor Burlatsky, a journalist and policy adviser. Frolov told me in an interview in 1990 that he and others believed that Eastern European nations might be reformed along Prague Spring lines under the guidance of local communists. There is considerable evidence that it was also Gorbachev's working assumption that reformist communism would triumph in Eastern Europe if given a chance, and perhaps a push from Moscow. "The Soviets thought they were creating lots of little Gorbachevs," said a White House foreign policy aide later; "so did we." As it turned out, that was a historic miscalculation. True, reformist

* Chapter 4, p. 112.

communists were preferred over more doctrinaire alternatives, but in most cases they in turn were easily swept away by a powerful tide of anticommunist and anti-Soviet sentiments whenever people had a chance for self-expression.

The first major issue between Moscow and the bloc countries in the Gorbachev era was whether the others would be required to follow the Soviet leader's path as his reforms got underway in the USSR, according to Aleksandr Tsipko, an expert on Eastern Europe on the staff of the Soviet Communist Party Central Committee from late 1986 to 1990. Tsipko said that the issue was decided by a summit meeting of the "leaders of fraternal parties of Socialist countries," including Gorbachev, all six Warsaw Pact party leaders, Fidel Castro of Cuba, Truong Chinh of Vietnam and Jambyn Batmonh of Mongolia in Moscow in November of 1986. According to Tsipko, Gorbachev made public the essence of the results in his speech in Prague in April 1987, including this central point: "No one has a right to claim special status in the socialist world. The independence of every party, its responsibility to the people in its own country, the right to decide questions of the country's development are unconditional principles to us."

This decision had something in it for both sides of the political debate. Conservatives such as the elderly Warsaw Pact leaders at the time who had been in power for decades, and Gorbachev's conservative colleague, Yegor Ligachev, took heart that each fraternal party would not be required to implement a local version of *perestroika*. In Ligachev's words from April 1987, "Every country looks for solutions independently, not as in the past. It is not true that Moscow's conductor's baton, or Moscow's hand is in everything . . . every nation has a right to its own way." For progressives, the decision had another clearly implied and, in the end, more important meaning: that the Soviet Union should keep hands off the internal processes among its allies, whatever direction they might take, and would not bail them out if they failed to adjust rapidly enough to new realities. Just how far Soviet tolerance extended—whether to the bounds of socialism or even beyond—was an open question through the events of 1989. For many experienced outside observers, and insiders too, it was simply unthinkable that Gorbachev would permit the Eastern European states to break away from the Soviet embrace.

No one was thinking or talking in 1986 about the Eastern European nations' abandoning "socialism," according to Tsipko. But the reformers in Moscow, he said, were impressed by the relatively progressive and seemingly successful policies of the Polish head of state, General Wojciech Jaruzelski, the youngest (sixty-three) and most newly minted (1981) of the Warsaw Pact leaders. "It was believed that if Jaruzelski had managed to deal with his problems and the unrest and riots without any interference on our part, then we shouldn't interfere," Tsipko recalled.

In late 1986 the other Eastern European communist party leaders were conservative figures more in the mold of Leonid Brezhnev or, in some cases, even Joseph Stalin than in tune with Gorbachev. The leaders were:

- Todor Zhivkov of Bulgaria, age seventy-five, in power since 1954

- Gustav Husak of Czechoslovakia, age seventy-three, in power since 1968

- Erich Honecker of the German Democratic Republic (East Germany), age seventy-four, in power since 1971

- Janos Kadar of Hungary, age seventy-five, in power since 1956

- Nicolae Ceausescu of Romania, age sixty-eight, in power since 1965

U.S. Ambassador to Hungary Mark Palmer, a Soviet expert who was watching the slow unraveling of Eastern Europe from his post in Budapest starting in late 1986, realized "that Gorbachev's vibes with these guys were not right, that he had to pay deference to them because they were older, had more tenure in the communist system than he had, and yet they weren't really any of them willing to do anything very radical. They'd talk a little bit about it, but they weren't willing to do it. So I remember thinking that he must be very frustrated with these guys as partners." It also struck Palmer as he traveled periodically to Moscow that Soviet officials were so consumed with their own problems that developments in Eastern Europe seemed to them increasingly remote. Although Palmer was visiting Moscow from his post in Budapest, it seemed to him that the Soviets were uninterested in Hungary and wanted to talk instead about what was happening inside the USSR.

As seen from Eastern Europe, several developments in Moscow raised doubts about Soviet determination to use force (as Moscow had done in East Berlin in 1953, Hungary in 1956, and Czechoslovakia in 1968) or the threat of force (as in Poland in 1981) to keep its regional allies in the communist camp. In making a deal to remove U.S. missiles from Western Europe under the INF Treaty, Moscow had agreed to remove its missiles from Eastern Europe. Moreover, the decision to withdraw Soviet troops from Afghanistan suggested that Moscow was ready to pull back rather than hold on to troublesome military commitments, even on its own border, and that the people and government of the Soviet Union were hardly prepared to mount new military interventions.

Perhaps more than any other single event, however, Gorbachev's appearance at the United Nations in December 1988 set the stage for the revolutionary events that would follow. Gorbachev's declaration renouncing the threat or use of force and his commitment to "freedom of choice" for all nations, a principle that "knows no exceptions," suggested that Moscow would not again send its tanks and troops into action in Eastern Europe. And his dramatic announcement of unilateral withdrawal of fifty thousand Soviet troops and five thousand tanks from Eastern Europe was an unmistakable message that the capacity as well as the will to protect Warsaw Pact regimes from their own people was sharply declining. The "fear factor" that had held Moscow's empire together for four decades was abruptly disappearing, leaving the leaders of unpopular regimes to face their people without Soviet tanks to back them up.

The first internal crisis came in Poland, the most politically advanced of the six Warsaw Pact regimes. Jaruzelski's martial law regime had jailed Solidarity union activists and banned the popular anticommunist movement in 1981, but had not succeeded in destroying it. By January 1989 Solidarity was stronger than ever and Jaruzelski, amid growing economic crisis, was forced to deal with it. After a battle within the communist United Workers party, Jaruzelski moved toward opening "round table talks" intended to bring the opposition into a coalition firmly led by the communists, in return for restoring legal status to the communist world's first independent union. The Polish leader told U.S. Ambassador John Davis that he was in close touch with Gorbachev through frequent communications. There was no sign of objection or interference from Moscow.

In the negotiations with Solidarity, the communists surprisingly agreed to free elections for a new upper house of the Polish parliament, on condition that communists and their traditional parliamentary allies continue to control the more powerful lower house. The results of this unprecedented free choice, in June 1989, stunned everyone: Solidarity won ninety-nine of the one hundred seats in the new upper house; thirty-three of the thirty-five top party and government leaders lost their seats in the lower house, even though unopposed, when more than half the voters crossed out their names on the ballots.

At this juncture, President Bush paid a visit to Poland and Hungary July 9–13, his first presidential trip to the Soviet bloc. As vice president, he had made a memorable trip to Poland in September 1987, and he felt he had made a commitment to Jaruzelski that if the general would undertake serious internal reforms, the United States would respond quickly and imaginatively. Since early 1989 Bush had been watching the situation in Poland with growing fascination.

On April 17, 1989, the same day that a Warsaw court took the final step in legalizing Solidarity after a seven-year ban, Bush announced a new U.S. program for Poland in the heavily Polish-American Detroit suburb of Hamtramck, Michigan. Bush's plan contained little in the way of direct U.S. expenditures, relying mostly on rescheduling debts, lowering tariffs and encouraging loans from international institutions. Under the pressure of unfolding events and attacks from an impatient Congress for being too timid, Bush revised the Polish program upward in July and again in October, and in November finally put his signature on a Polish aid package costing nearly twice as much as his highest recommendation.

By the time of his July visit, Bush had worked out his basic orientation to the events of Eastern Europe. Poland and perhaps other nations had a good chance to win their freedom, he believed, but only with the acquiescence of the Soviet Union. An important U.S. role, he explained to aides, was to make it as easy as possible for Gorbachev to do what he had to do, and especially to avoid words or deeds that could inflame Soviet conservatives. There should be no gloating or triumphant declarations as Eastern European countries broke free of their old restraints, Bush decreed, and no insistence that the Eastern Europeans turn their backs on Moscow and join the West. He told Poles and Hungarians in private meetings during his visit, "We're not here to make you choose between East and West." While condemning the failure of the "Stalinist system" in his public statements, Bush quoted approvingly from Gorbachev on freedom of choice and told reporters he had informed Polish and Hungarian leaders that "we're not there to . . . poke a stick in the eye of Mr. Gorbachev; just the opposite—to encourage the very kind of reforms that he is championing, and more reforms."

Secretary Baker conveyed the same message to Foreign Minister Shevardnadze in Paris on July 29, where both were attending an international meeting on Cambodia. He and the President had been impressed with what they had seen in Poland and Hungary, Baker said, and were trying to support the reform process to the extent that they could. He emphasized that Bush had "made very clear throughout that in supporting that reform process we were not trying to create problems for the Soviet Union." He also told Shevardnadze that serious problems would arise in the U.S.-Soviet relationship if Moscow were to use force to stop the development of peaceful change.

For the Soviet Union to use force to stop the reforms in Eastern Europe, Shevardnadze said, "would be the end of *perestroika*." Rather than viewing the reforms in Poland and Hungary as a threat, he said, Moscow saw them as positive and consistent with *perestroika*. "The pace, the movement, the process" in those countries was up to them, Shevardnadze told Baker, and their decisions were "left up to them." It was not surprising, Shevardnadze added, that these countries were attracted to the West economically; if the Soviet Union were to be a good competitor, he said with what proved to be unrealistic hope, it had to make itself much more attractive.

In August the Polish situation came to a head when the Solidarity movement was struggling to form a coalition government with the defense and interior ministries reserved for the communists. At this point the Central Committee of the Polish communist party was split, with some leaders holding out for greater control of the new government and some ready to join. At the peak of the crisis on August 22, a celebrated forty-minute telephone conversation between Gorbachev and Polish General Secretary Mieczyslaw Rakowski appeared to turn the tide toward communist participation in the coalition government.

Gorbachev's telephone call has been often cited as the most tangible evidence available that he was actively pushing democratization in Eastern Europe, even at the risk to communist rule. It was reported in front page articles from Warsaw in *The Washington Post* and *The New York Times* quoting Polish communist spokesman Jan Bisztyga as saying shortly after the call that Gorbachev had encouraged communist participation in the Solidarity-led coalition. An account from Moscow by *The Los Angeles Times* based on Soviet sources said, "Gorbachev told Rakowski bluntly that the time had come to yield power." Bush publicly praised Gorbachev for helping persuade the Polish communists to join the coalition. A senior U.S. intelligence official, enunciating a widespread consensus on the historic nature of Gorbachev's intervention, told me later that "the Rubicon was crossed with the Gorbachev phone call to Rakowski. Its real meaning was that Soviet power would not be used to maintain communist power in Eastern Europe."

Rakowski, now retired from politics, responded to my pleas for more information by furnishing an excerpt from his forthcoming memoirs, which provide his version of the call. Rakowski relates that it was he rather than Gorbachev who initiated the exchange, because he thought it was a good idea to confer with Gorbachev in his new position as party secretary. In Rakowski's account, Gorbachev exerted no pressure on the Polish party to enter into compromises, but said he agreed that a line of national reconciliation should be followed and the opposition should be pressured to remain loyal to their earlier agreements during the "round table" talks. Gorbachev's most explicit statements, according to Rakowski, were that "the Soviet Union will not change its policy toward Poland and toward the [communist] party," and that "we grant our full support to both Jaruzelski and yourself." But Gorbachev went on to say, "Should the opposition move to attack the party or the achievements of the socialist system, the Soviet Union will change its policy toward Poland—do make it clear to the opposition."

Two days after the Gorbachev-Rakowski conversation, Solidarity adviser Tadeusz Mazowiecki was overwhelmingly elected Poland's prime minister with the communists agreeing to participate in the Solidarity-led government. He received a cordial telegram from the Soviet government.

The impossible had happened: the communists had given up power to a noncommunist government in a Warsaw Pact country, and the Soviet Union had let it happen. If it could happen in Poland it was no longer unthinkable in the rest of Eastern Europe. Communist governments were shaken, and noncommunists were emboldened everywhere. The drama in Warsaw was a precipitating event for the rest of Eastern Europe, proving the essential truth of the Czech dissident playwright (later Czech president) Vaclav Havel's observation in his book *The Power of the Powerless*:

> The moment someone breaks through in one place, when one person cries out, "The Emperor is naked!"—when a single person breaks the rules of the game, thus exposing it as a game—

everything suddenly appears in another light and the whole crust seems then to be made of a tissue on the point of tearing and disintegrating uncontrollably.

Just hours after Gorbachev's telephone call to the Polish communist party chief, Hungarian Foreign Minister Gyula Horn made a decision, after a sleepless night, that would initiate another historic change in the face of Europe. Earlier in the year, Hungary had dismantled its border fence with Austria, an act of only symbolic importance to Hungarian citizens, who already were free to travel to the West. It was more important to disenchanted East Germans, who began to make their way to Hungary in large numbers to flee through this back door to Austria and West Germany. Under a 1968 treaty with East Germany, Hungary was required to prevent such escapes, and Hungary had continued to stop Germans from leaving through its territory for the West. Now the number of East Germans, many of them young couples with small children, was building up, and Hungary was becoming a holding pen for East Germans on the run from their tyrannical government.

Horn had authorized his deputy minister, Laszlo Kovacs, to assess informally the reaction of the Soviet Union if Hungary should change its policy and let the East Germans go. "We didn't specify, but we hinted," said Kovacs. The Soviets did not object.

By the morning of August 23, Horn had decided to ignore the twenty-one-year-old treaty and open the gates to the West for the East Germans. "It was quite obvious to me that this would be the first step in a landslide-like series of events," he said later. After Horn officially informed the East German government, which strenuously objected, Hungary announced its decision on September 10. Within three days, more than thirteen thousand East Germans fled to the West through Hungary, the largest East German exodus since the Berlin Wall was built in 1961. East Germany enlisted the help of the Czech government to stop its citizens from reaching Hungary, with the result that tens of thousands of East German refugees sought refuge in the West German Embassy in the Czech capital of Prague; eventually they were permitted to travel to the West. Next East Germany cut off travel even to Czechoslovakia, but this generated mass protests at home and redoubled the sharply rising pressure on the East German borders.

Now the hurricane gathered even more force.

In Hungary on October 7, the Hungarian Socialist Workers (communist) party officially abandoned Leninism and reconstituted itself as the Hungarian Socialist party, the first time a ruling communist party had abandoned its fundamental ideology. Later in the month, on the anniversary of the 1956 uprising, Hungary declared itself a "republic," in which Western-style democracy and democratic socialism would be practiced, rather than a "people's republic." Over the coming months the reformist communist-turned-socialist party would try assiduously to gain public favor through democratic means, but it was able to win only 8 percent of the vote in national elections in April 1990.

In East Germany the visit by Gorbachev on October 6 and 7 to celebrate the fortieth anniversary of the German Democratic Republic added new force to the biggest nationwide wave of protest demonstrations in that regime's history. Gorbachev stood on a reviewing stand in East Berlin waving with an open palm to tens of thousands of East German youths; beside him the hard-pressed and ailing seventy-seven-year-old East German leader, Erich Honecker, pumped the night air with his clenched fist. In several cities Honecker's police attacked demonstrators who were chanting, "Gorby! Gorby! Gorby!" but the crowds of protesters became bigger each day. In East Berlin, a Western European diplomat observed a significant change in public behavior: "People are not afraid anymore to stand up and rally in masses, and proclaim their desires."

The turning point for East Germany came on October 9 in Leipzig, the second-largest city, when local communist party leaders refused Honecker's orders to attack the seventy thousand marchers who paraded through the streets. Honecker's security chief, Egon Krenz, embraced the Leipzig revolt and on October 18 led the battle within the Politburo that forced Honecker to resign. Krenz was named his successor.

The crowds of protestors only became bigger. In East Berlin on November 4, more than five hundred thousand people demonstrated, and another five hundred thousand turned out in other cities. Prime Minister Willi Stoph and his entire cabinet resigned; there was another big shakeup in the communist party Politburo. Nothing could stop or even slow the prodemocracy fever. According to several members of the GDR communist party Central Committee, Krenz called Gorbachev in Moscow to find out if the Soviets had any suggestions. These sources said Gorbachev replied that the border between the two Germanys had to be opened to provide an escape valve and prevent unrest that threatened to bring down communist control.

On the night of November 9, after a day of confusion, the crossing points in the Berlin Wall were flung open, never to close again. Jubilant East Germans thronged through the Wall's eight crossing points, to be met by West Berliners with champagne and fireworks. "The Wall is gone! The Wall is gone!" cried West Berliners, many of whom crossed over in the other direction. Near the Brandenburg Gate, scores of young East and West Berliners climbed to the top of the Wall to greet one another and celebrate. In high emotion, some in tears, people on both sides began to chip away at the ugly concrete and steel barrier with hammers and chisels.

Officially, the reaction in Moscow was muted. Tass said, "The pulling down of the Berlin Wall, which has symbolized the division of Europe for many years, is surely a positive and important fact." A *Pravda* correspondent in East Berlin called the move "a bold and wise political step" by the GDR government that "graphically confirms its will for renewal" along the lines of Gorbachev's "new thinking." Nonetheless, Tass and Soviet officials warned that Moscow would not tolerate the demise of the East German state, which was described as "our strategic ally," or East German departure from the Warsaw Pact alliance.

Inside the offices of Communist Party Central Committee in Moscow, according to staff member Aleksandr Tsipko, the reason for the low-key initial reaction was the mistaken belief that changes in the East German communist leadership "would lead to the setup of a truly democratic socialist state in Germany." The initial instructions to the veteran Soviet ambassador to the GDR, Vyachislav Kochemasov, were not to interfere, not to exert any pressure and in fact not to do anything, said Tsipko. He said it took about two weeks for Moscow to realize that the progressive weakening of the GDR and the opening of the Wall were likely to bring the collapse of the regime and its consolidation as part of the West.

The news that East Germany had decided to open its borders reached Washington in the early afternoon of November 9. At 3:30 P.M. Bush called reporters to the Oval Office for an on-camera reaction that was positive but so restrained in comparison to the almost delirious joy being seen on television that his questioners and viewers found it odd. With Gorbachev in mind, Bush said, "We are handling it [the East German move] in a way where we are not trying to give anybody a hard time." When a reporter commented that the President did not seem to be elated about this historic and unexpected victory for the West, Bush responded, "I am not an emotional kind of guy." Commented CBS anchorman Dan Rather about the President's performance, "He looked as relaxed as a pound of liver."

For nearly three decades, since its construction in 1961, the Berlin Wall had been the most visible and potent international symbol of communist tyranny. Its demise had a major effect on American opinion. Pollster Louis Harris found nearly unanimous (90 percent) public agreement that the event was "one of the most exciting and encouraging signs for peace in the world in years." Another survey, by NBC News/*Wall Street Journal*, reported that more than half the public (52 percent) saw the events in Germany and Eastern Europe as "the beginning of a long-term positive relationship" with the Soviet Union rather than "temporary and easily changed" (37 percent). The Public Agenda Foundation, which studies American opinion in depth, found a startling reversal in the views of a "focus group" of representative citizens who were interviewed in Edison, New Jersey, in mid-August (before the Wall was opened) and a similar group interviewed in San Francisco in mid-November (just after the breaching of the Wall). The consensus of the earlier group was that the changes in Eastern Europe were reversible, that the Soviet Union had control of events and would intervene if an "invisible line" was crossed, and that the reunification of Germany was impossible. The consensus of the second group three months later was that the changes in Europe were irreversible, the Soviets would not intervene and the reunification of Germany was likely.

The day after the Wall was breached, a worried Gorbachev dispatched a message to Bush and several Western European leaders expressing alarm about the breakneck speed at which events in Germany were taking place. Events in Germany should be handled slowly, Gorbachev insisted, and the interests of the Soviet Union should be taken into account. History had dictated that there be two Germanys, Gorbachev said in the message, implying that for the present era, at least, two Germanys should remain. Finally, the Soviet leader broached the possibility that events in Berlin could become violent or spin out of control; in view of this the Soviet Union suggested urgent consultations and insisted on being part of any forthcoming decision-making process. After consulting European allies, Bush sent back a vague reply, emphasizing the importance of German self-determination but not, at this point, accepting the Soviet demand for a role in decision making.

As the Wall was being opened on November 9, the Bulgarian communist party was holding a showdown Politburo meeting. Todor Zhivkov, Eastern Europe's longest-serving leader, planned to top off his thirty-five years in power by crushing the opposition of Foreign Minister Petar Mladenov, who had been in office nineteen years. But at the meeting, the tables were turned and the Politburo chose Mladenov rather than Zhivkov to lead the shaken party. Under Mladenov and several successors, the reform communists were able to hang on to power in Bulgaria for more than a year before finally being overtaken by democratic forces.

The events in Germany also ricocheted in Czechoslovakia, where on November 17 a student rally in Prague was attacked by nervous police. In response to police brutality and rumors that a student had been killed, demonstrations quickly escalated: 10,000 people on November 19; 200,000 on November 20; 250,000 on November 22; 350,000 on November 24. That night at an emergency communist party meeting, General Secretary Milos Jakes and his entire twelve-member Politburo resigned, and a new top party hierarchy was elected. Antigovernment forces denounced the move as a trick, bringing out even bigger crowds and a two-hour general strike that brought the capital and most of the rest of the country to a standstill.

Early in December, a reformist communist leadership promised to form a new cabinet, including a noncommunist majority. On December 10 long-time communist leader Gustav Husak, who had given up his party post to become president of the country two years before, resigned, and Czechs celebrated a new era. His eventual successor was Czechoslovakia's most renowned opposition leader, playwright Vaclav Havel.

With the triumph of the Velvet Revolution, as the Czech uprising was called, the leadership had been ousted in five of the six Warsaw Pact allies of the Soviet Union. Only Romania's Nicolae Ceausescu remained.

• HEADING TOWARD MALTA

In Paris on July 13, the day before the two-hundredth anniversary of the storming of the Bastille in the French revolution, Bush had taken a run in his jogging clothes outside the U.S. ambassador's residence and was resting on the porch steps facing the garden in the back of the house before dressing for colorful official ceremonies. As the President relaxed, he discussed with Baker and Scowcroft their impressions of their four-day trip to Poland and Hungary that had ended that morning. Bush had been impressed by Polish President Wojciech Jaruzelski's view, expressed in a long private conversation in Warsaw, that it would be "extraordinarily good for the Poles" for the U.S. President to meet Gorbachev at this critical period. In the opinion of Jaruzelski, who prided himself on being the closest Eastern European leader to Gorbachev, such a meeting could encourage Gorbachev to continue backing political change in Poland and elsewhere. Bush had heard similar sentiments in Hungary, and had the impression that Western European leaders, too, would view a meeting with Gorbachev as desirable and even important.

Bush, a devotee of personal relationships in diplomacy as well as politics, had been attracted to a meeting with Gorbachev since early in his presidency. However, National Security Adviser Brent Scowcroft, especially, was fearful that such a meeting could raise expectations in an unhelpful and perhaps dangerous fashion if there were no solid signs of U.S.-Soviet progress to justify it. It seemed unlikely that a strategic arms agreement would be ready in time to warrant a summit meeting before early 1990 at the earliest; the Bush team, in fact, was still cautious about moving to complete START quickly. While Bush had accepted the reason for postponing a Gorbachev meeting and even repeated it, he had not been completely comfortable with it. A meeting with Gorbachev kept coming up in conversation with Scowcroft and others in the White House inner circle in the spring and summer of 1989.

Talking over the issue again on that July day in Paris, Bush recalled later, "I just did about a 180 [degree reversal] on it and said, 'Wait a minute. Change is so fast, future change is so unpredictable that I don't want to pass in the night with this guy.' " Scowcroft was still reluctant because of the expectations problem, and Baker could see some risk in it, though he was inclined to believe a meeting with Gorbachev could be useful. After some discussion Bush made up his mind on the spot. "Well, let's do it," he said emphatically. "Hell, we're talking about it, let's just do it." Baker and Scowcroft said they would begin planning for what they called a "no agenda" meeting of an informal nature with Gorbachev, with as little pomp as possible to keep international expectations down. On Air Force One on the way home from Paris, Bush wrote Gorbachev a letter proposing the sort of interim informal meeting he had in mind.

Gorbachev replied promptly, accepting the idea in principle; however, the practical details proved to be much more difficult than anyone anticipated. Bush proposed that Gorbachev come to the United Nations in September and that the two leaders then go to the secluded presidential retreat at Camp David, Maryland, or Bush's vacation home at Kennebunkport, Maine, for informal discussions away from the public eye. Gorbachev responded that he had already addressed the United Nations the previous December and had nothing new to say and no reason to go to Camp David or Kennebunkport. At another point Bush suggested meeting on U.S. and Soviet ships off Alaska, which is only a few miles from the Soviet Far East, but Soviet experts checked and found the seas would be so rough at that time that a meeting would not be feasible. Bush proposed to meet on the shores of Alaska, but Gorbachev did not wish to come to U.S. territory. The Soviet leader proposed a rendezvous in Spain, but the White House feared that meeting in any third country would inevitably involve ceremonies and protocol involving the host country, as well as heavy television coverage and hordes of press—all giving rise to the sort of expectation-raising that Bush wished to avoid.

The lengthy negotiations with Moscow over the meeting took place in complete secrecy, which increasingly became a hallmark of Bush-Baker diplomacy. In August Gorbachev sent Deputy Foreign Minister Aleksandr Bessmertnykh to Washington as his emissary to discuss the meeting; even Baker's closest aide on Soviet affairs, Dennis Ross, did not know why Bessmertnykh had come or what was under discussion. Bessmertnykh speaks excellent English, which obviated the need for an interpreter in his two meetings with Bush at the White House. When Baker took up the issue with Shevardnadze in September, he did so on an intimate social occasion with no other U.S. officials present. At one point, he relied on Shevardnadze's interpreter so that even a U.S. interpreter would not be in on the secret.

Finally in early October, after learning that Gorbachev would be going to Italy and the Vatican on a state visit at the end of November, Bush proposed that the two leaders meet on U.S. and Soviet naval vessels in the Mediterranean. The White House initially suggested a site near Naples, but that would have required Gorbachev to stay in Italy after his state visit, which was awkward. Finally someone brought up Malta in a White House session, and the President was immediately enthusiastic because his brother, William, an international businessman, had been there and reported it was "a lovely place" in summertime. Malta was also neutral and thus a safe haven politically, but, as it turned out, a near disaster meteorologically. Bush and Gorbachev agreed to keep their planned meeting a secret until the very end of October, about a month before the December 2–3 meeting at sea.

While the meeting of the two leaders was being arranged, Baker and

Shevardnadze were beginning to forge closer personal and professional ties that would rival those that had developed between George Shultz and the Soviet foreign minister.

In mid-July Baker received a message from Shevardnadze inquiring whether the U.S. secretary of state planned to attend an international conference on the future of Cambodia, which was being sponsored late that month by the French Foreign Ministry in Paris. Baker had been uncertain about attending due to dubious prospects that the meeting could produce results—as it turned out, it did not—but in view of Shevardnadze's interest sent word back to Moscow that he was leaning toward going. Shortly thereafter, Shevardnadze announced he would attend, and Baker quickly followed suit.

For the U.S. and Soviet ministers, the most important event was not the formal conference with delegates in the French conference hall, but a meeting lasting more than three hours at the Soviet Embassy residence in Paris. Fully two hours was devoted to an intimate session with only an interpreter and a note-taker on each side joining the ministers.

At the outset, Baker reminded Shevardnadze that in Moscow in May he had suggested that they occasionally consider holding their full-scale ministerial meetings outside Washington or Moscow in order to change the environment and give the visiting minister a chance to see more of the other country. Baker then produced color photographs of the place he had in mind for his first visit from Shevardnadze planned for September: the magnificent mountains-and-plains country of Wyoming, where Baker had vacationed for years and the previous December had bought a rustic ranch. Before the translation of Baker's statement was completed, U.S. note-taker Dennis Ross noticed the face of his opposite number, Sergei Tarasenko, who understood English, brighten with approval. Shevardnadze was similarly pleased, taking the invitation as a symbol of change in a U.S.-Soviet relationship that, to that point, had been slow to develop in the new administration.

With little prompting from Baker, the Soviet foreign minister launched into an extensive discussion, which consumed the rest of the private meeting, of the crises taking place inside the USSR.

The Soviet Union is "in a crucial stage of its development . . . a revolutionary process," Shevardnadze began. The word, he conceded, might be audacious but it seemed to him that there was really no other term but "revolutionary" to describe what was happening. It was apparent to him, he told Baker, that "political renewal" was proceeding at a much faster pace than "economic renewal." And the people of the country, it seemed to him, were ready to move faster than were many officials.

Shevardnadze then turned to a detailed discussion of the wave of strikes that had beset the Soviet Union, especially the strike of nearly five hundred thousand miners, which had endangered the country's energy supply and had just been settled only by promising major wage increases and further political reforms. Gorbachev and other members of the Soviet leadership, including Shevardnadze, had been deeply involved in settling the unprecedented work stoppages. Shevardnadze said that in view of the working conditions for many of the miners, their demands were actually "quite reasonable." The miners were not challenging *perestroika*, he said, but were pushing the bureaucracy to implement it faster.

Finally Shevardnadze spoke of explosive regional problems, including some of a social and economic nature, that were facing the country, including his home republic of Georgia. It was difficult to manage the vast country's problems effectively, said Shevardnadze, but it had to be done. It gave him hope, he told Baker, that some regions of the country were doing better, taking on more local responsibility and avoiding shortages of food and housing. No matter what happens, according to Shevardnadze, "this whole process is irreversible."

Sitting across a small round table from Shevardnadze in a room where he could hear kitchen noises and smell the lunch being prepared by a Soviet cook, Baker was surprised at the intensity and frankness of the presentation. It struck him even more than it had in his Moscow meetings two months earlier that Gorbachev and Shevardnadze were "men in a hurry," racing against time with no inclination to keep up appearances about the depth of their problems in their private conversations. The discussion with Shevardnadze in Paris turned out to be only the first of many frank talks with Baker, as the Soviet Union sank deeper into trouble. At this stage, the secretary of state was able to respond only by offering U.S. technical advice on dealing with market economics, a gesture that had been recommended by an interagency administration task force organized in June to study the Soviet economy. Shevardnadze appeared interested, but no specific arrangements were made.

As the late September meeting in Wyoming approached, it seemed to many in the two capitals that the continued caution of the Bush administration in East-West matters was in jarring contrast to the growing urgency of the problems in the Soviet Union and the dramatic speed of revolutionary developments in Eastern Europe. In Moscow on September 12, Shevardnadze complained in an unusual interview in *Izvestia* about "the American administration's restrained, irresolute stand" on issues between the two countries, especially the absence of any progress in the Geneva arms negotiations. In Washington on September 18, Senate Democratic Leader George Mitchell fired a broadside against the administration for being "almost nostalgic about the Cold War" in the face of the unprecedented changes in the Soviet Union and Eastern Europe. He called on Bush to "reach behind the status-quo thinking that appears to dominate administration policy" and adopt "a more energetic and engaged policy" toward the Soviet bloc.

At the State Department the following day Baker, who nearly always preferred anonymity and behind-the-scenes maneuvering in contacts with the press, appeared at his first State Department press conference in his nine months as secretary to discuss the coming ministerial meeting with Shevardnadze. Asked repeatedly about Mitchell's criticism, Baker finally replied with perhaps the most self-damaging comment he had ever made. In a remark that was widely condemned as a throwback to his days as a partisan campaign manager, Baker said, "When the President of the United States is rocking along with a 70 percent approval rating on his handling of foreign policy and I were the leader of the opposition party, I might have something similar to say." Privately, Baker took the rising dissatisfaction with U.S. policy more seriously, arguing for compromises in U.S. positions that would move the arms negotiations with Moscow.

The U.S.-Soviet sessions at Jackson Lake in the Grand Tetons would be the end of the beginning of Bush administration policy toward the Soviet Union. In looking back on the event, Baker said nine months later, "We'd come to the conclusion they were for real; Wyoming is where they came to the conclusion we were for real." Shevardnadze's retrospective assessment was that the meetings under the western skies were "very important from the point of view of outlining the priorities, the main directions of our cooperation." He added, "That was the first time—and this was of fundamental importance—when we said that from mutual understanding we have to move to a new quality for the relationship, from understanding to interaction, and wherever possible to partnership."

The stage was set for a breakthrough in the personal relations of Baker and Shevardnadze during the four-and-a-half-hour flight from

Washington aboard Baker's U.S. Air Force executive jet. Following the usual Soviet procedure, Shevardnadze had brought his own Aeroflot jet and was reluctant to fly in Baker's plane. He quickly relented, however, when he was told that the secretary hoped to use the long flight west for a free-wheeling talk between just the two of them. It proved to be an even more candid discussion of even more sensitive Soviet domestic issues than had been covered in the meeting two months earlier in Paris.

Baker in his shirtsleeves and Shevardnadze in a white shirt and black vest sat across from each other at a small table in the front passenger cabin of the DC-9 with their interpreters beside them and their note-takers, Dennis Ross and Sergei Tarasenko, perched uncomfortably atop thick State Department attaché cases that had been pulled up to the table as temporary seats. The U.S. journalists sitting near the rear of the plane could hear nothing of the conversation but they could observe its intensity and seriousness from the body language of the two ministers, who gestured frequently and at times seemed to be talking almost nose to nose.

Just before leaving Moscow, Shevardnadze had participated in a two-day Central Committee plenum, which had addressed the increasingly vexing issues of separatism and ethnic conflict, and at which Gorbachev had engineered his largest shakeup of the Politburo, ousting five conservative members. Deeply immersed in the nationalities issues, Shevardnadze spoke to Baker without a single note for two hours with only occasional interruptions by the secretary of state. Shevardnadze spoke of the unjust and unhealthy policies of the central authority in Moscow that had been established in the Stalin era and that had generated powerful opposition in the Soviet republics, including his home republic of Georgia. The foreign minister advocated "total autonomy" for the constituent republics, but at the same time emphasized how interdependent they had become for power generation, industry and defense, among other essentials. After a break for dinner, the discussion resumed on another area of deepening crisis, the sagging economy. Shevardnadze had brought along one of the country's most radical economists, Nikolai Shmelev, to make an informal presentation to Baker on the growing crisis.

In years past, Soviet officials had rarely discussed with Americans the weaknesses of the USSR in realistic terms, for fear the United States would exploit any Soviet vulnerability. All that had changed dramatically, at least so far as Shevardnadze's private conversation was concerned. In an *Izvestia* interview before the trip, Shevardnadze said that his relationship with Shultz had been "without exaggeration, unique" and that this had become a factor in the diplomacy between the two nations. The Soviet minister said that he and Baker had "begun well" in their first four meetings and that he was confident they would be able to work "in a good atmosphere . . . to discuss and resolve the most difficult questions." It seemed to Dennis Ross, who was a witness to the airborne dialogue, that the two men had "crossed a threshold" of candor and confidence as they crossed the American continent to their fifth meeting and that this would have an effect on the diplomacy that followed.

Assisted by some key concessions that were hinted at or spelled out in a Gorbachev letter that Shevardnadze had brought from Moscow, the Wyoming talks ended with the signing of seven bilateral accords, major progress on solving several of the most important issues standing in the way of a START Treaty and the announcement that a summit meeting between Bush and Gorbachev would be held in the spring or summer of 1990.

One of the most significant Soviet shifts was Shevardnadze's declaration to Baker at Jackson Lake Lodge that the two nations could complete and sign a START Treaty slashing their offensive nuclear arms even if they had not agreed on limits on the U.S. SDI program. Gorbachev had suggested that he could accept such an arrangement during Oval Office discussions at the 1987 Washington summit, but the Reagan administration had not picked up the offer. Among other problems, the Joint Chiefs of Staff objected that the Soviet Union claimed the right to abandon the strategic arms reductions if it judged that U.S. SDI tests were violating Moscow's interpretation of the ABM Treaty limits. Such a Soviet right, if accepted by the United States, could damage the value of the strategic arms treaty by making its enforcement highly unpredictable.

At Jackson Lake, however, the Bush administration hailed the new Soviet position on space defense as a breakthrough and seemed willing to declare victory on the issue. Shevardnadze's new posture represented a further downgrading of the SDI issue from its high priority in the mid-1980s. The veteran Soviet arms negotiator, Viktor Karpov, said the shift in Wyoming represented an effort to move the issue toward a practical solution and away from the fruitless haggling in the space talks "resembling some medieval discussions of how many devils you can have on a needle."

A second Soviet shift of major significance in Wyoming concerned the giant phased array radar at Krasnoyarsk in Siberia, which the United States had long charged was a violation of the ABM Treaty. For years, the Soviet Union denied that construction of the radar was a violation, though its denials had been increasingly weak. Although some elements of the Soviet military still opposed giving in to U.S. protests, Shevard-nadze at Jackson Lake agreed to dismantle the big radar. Despite the military objections, Shevardnadze in a report to the Supreme Soviet a month after the Wyoming ministerial would condemn "this station on the scale of the Egyptian pyramids" as a misguided "breach of the ABM Treaty" and said it was being dismantled for legal and moral reasons.

When the Wyoming ministerial meeting concluded successfully, only a handful of top officials on both sides knew that Bush and Gorbachev were hoping to meet only a short time later. Their meeting would take place in storm-tossed waters off Malta in early December amid a flurry of revolutionary developments in Europe.

• THE SHIPBOARD SUMMIT

All the other sixteen U.S.-Soviet summit meetings since World War II had been based on the familiar Cold War framework of U.S.-Soviet relations. But at Malta for the first time, Bush and Gorbachev began to grapple with the sudden crumbling of that framework as the East-West lines in Europe were shifting almost daily, leaving the future highly uncertain.

Between July, when Bush had secretly proposed the meeting to Gorbachev, and December, when the two leaders met on the Soviet cruise ship *Maxim Gorky*, a political avalanche had changed the face of Europe: Poland had installed a noncommunist government; Hungary's communist regime had molted into an independent socialist state on the way to capitalism; East Germany had opened the Berlin Wall and was beginning a slide toward absorption in the more confident, powerful and affluent West German state; Bulgaria had ousted its long-time leader in an experiment with reformist communism; and Czechoslovakia had over-thrown its communist regime altogether in a bloodless revolution. Of the six Moscow-dominated governments that had been its Eastern European front line in the Cold War, only the corrupt regime of Nicolae Ceausescu in Romania was still clinging to power.

For all the high drama on its outer edges, the full impact had not yet been felt inside the Soviet Union, which was preoccupied with growing domestic turmoil. As the winter of 1989 arrived, the purchasing power of the Soviet ruble plummeted, stores had little to offer consumers and industrial production was far below the planned targets. "These are the tensest of times in the progress of *perestroika*," Gorbachev told a congress of Soviet students in November. There was little doubt by the time of Malta that Gorbachev's Soviet Communist Party and even his own authority had entered a zone of rough sailing, almost as perilous as the high winds and stormy seas that suddenly complicated the summit with Bush in the Mediterranean.

Ever since the meeting with Gorbachev had been conceived in July, Bush had insisted that, so far as possible, it be a private and casual affair without the pomp and protocol of a major international event, without hordes of government experts seeking to impose limitations on their chief and, especially, as insulated as possible from the press. The President told Deputy Foreign Minister Bessmertnykh in one of their secret White House discussions in August that he would like to duplicate the atmosphere of intimacy and informality he had enjoyed in meetings at his Kennebunkport summer home in July with French President François Mitterrand. In this way, Bush said, he and Gorbachev could get right to the basics of the U.S.-Soviet relationship.

The final agreement to hold the discussions on U.S. and Soviet warships anchored near each other in a Maltese bay, cut off from the prying eyes of the television cameras and the questions of reporters by miles of well-patrolled ocean, met Bush's demand for privacy in spectacular fashion. As planned, the two days of talks involving a very small group were to be held aboard the guided missile cruiser USS *Belknap*, the flagship of the U.S. Sixth Fleet, and the Soviet guided missile cruiser *Slava*, with the two leaders and a few advisers traveling between one another's naval craft by small motorized launches. Bush, who had been a naval aviator in the Pacific in World War II and who loved to skim the waves in a fast boat off his Kennebunkport home, was delighted with the arrangements. Unfortunately, Mother Nature had other ideas. Just as the meetings were to begin, gale force winds, heavy rains and powerful waves battered the area in one of Malta's most severe storms in years.

Bush convened his final summit planning session at midafternoon Friday, December 1, in the wardroom of the USS *Belknap*. Sitting at a table decorated with U.S. and Soviet flags in preparation for use as the site of talks with Gorbachev, Bush discussed and reviewed for two hours U.S. initiatives that had been prepared in Washington for the Malta meeting.

Bush and Baker had been saying since early in the year that the United States hoped *perestroika* would succeed and wished to move "beyond containment" but, in fact, nothing had been done to dismantle the panoply of Cold War economic restrictions intended to isolate and penalize the USSR. But now in the midst of the dramatic upheaval in Eastern Europe, with the difficult issue of German unification looming ahead and the Soviet champion of change under fire at home, Bush and Baker agreed that the time had come for visible gestures of U.S. support. It was increasingly difficult, according to a senior Bush adviser who was involved in the White House talks, to separate support for Gorbachev's policies from support for the Soviet leader himself. "The President said, 'Look, this guy *is perestroika*. Maybe somebody else would continue it, but there isn't any doubt that what's going on now is directly traceable to the policies he's been following.' " Bush told aides he wanted to take specific steps to assist Gorbachev and his reform drive.

Two National Security Council staff members, Robert Blackwill and Condoleezza Rice, and two State Department staff members, Dennis Ross and Robert Zoellick, were assigned by Bush and Baker to prepare U.S. initiatives that the President might present to Gorbachev at Malta. The aides kept their work secret from the government bureaucracy in order to avoid leaks and second guessing, which turned out to be abundant. When Bush presented the ideas to his senior economic team, including Treasury Secretary Nicholas Brady and Special Trade Representative Carla Hills, there were many objections. Bush heard them out in a White House meeting but decided to move ahead anyway.

In the wardroom of the *Belknap* Friday afternoon Bush went over each of the nearly twenty suggested initiatives, deciding just how far to go with each one and how he would explain each of them to Gorbachev. Aides were assigned to draw up the detailed "talking points" for Bush to use in his presentation. Bush decided in the course of the discussion to unveil all of his initiatives in one package at the very start of the meetings Saturday morning rather than present them piecemeal or at a later stage of the talks. This was a more important decision than it seemed at the time; by demonstrating his support for Gorbachev immediately, Bush established the framework for the meeting and changed the Soviet plan to introduce some contentious issues.

While the Americans finished their preparations, Gorbachev was completing a three-day visit to Italy with a remarkable audience with Pope John Paul II that ended seven decades of bitter ideological conflict between the Kremlin and the Vatican. Gorbachev, who was an atheist but who had revealed earlier in the year that he had been baptized as a child by a Russian Orthodox priest, announced the establishment of diplomatic relations between the Soviet Union and the Roman Catholic Church for the first time since the Bolshevik revolution of 1917. In a reversal of past policies of militant atheism, Gorbachev also proclaimed the right of all Soviet believers to "satisfy their spiritual needs" and said the Supreme Soviet would soon pass a law guaranteeing freedom of conscience. In a speech in Rome, one of his most memorable, Gorbachev declared that his country was ready and anxious to rejoin the Western civilization from which it had been alienated for many years.

> We have abandoned the claim to have a monopoly on the truth; we no longer think that we are the best and that we are always right, that those who disagree with us are our enemies. We have now decided, firmly and irrevocably, to base our policy on the principle of freedom of choice, to build our economy and technology on the principle of mutual advantage, and to develop our culture and ideology through dialogue and acceptance of all that is applicable in our conditions, and hence, all that should be digested and used for our own progress. . . . Briefly, this is the essence of *perestroika*'s philosophy: we are getting to know ourselves, revealing ourselves to the world, and discovering the world.

By the time Gorbachev landed at Malta Friday night, rain was pelting the island and the wind was rising. By Saturday morning when the meetings were scheduled to begin, the storm was so severe that Gorbachev was reluctant to venture out into the bay to the planned rendezvous on the Soviet cruiser *Slava*, suggesting to Bush that they meet instead on the Soviet cruise liner *Maxim Gorky*, which the Kremlin had brought to Malta and tied up at the dock as a floating hotel for the Soviet official party and accompanying Soviet journalists. After brief greetings as Bush and his advisers arrived by launch from the *Belknap*, the Soviet and U.S. teams of six and seven officials, respectively, took their places at a narrow table covered with a brown cloth in the Card Room on the promenade deck of the Soviet liner. While the photographers recorded the scene, Gorbachev joked about the improvised conference table, which was only three feet wide. "It's so narrow that if we don't have enough arguments, we will kick each other," he said through his interpreter.

When the journalists had been ushered out, Bush as the guest on the Soviet ship asked for the right to speak first. "As we follow events in Eastern Europe, we watch with admiration the *perestroika* process" in the Soviet Union, he told Gorbachev. "You are dealing with an administration that wants to see the success of what you are doing. . . . The world will be a better place if *perestroika* succeeds." For the next seventy minutes, with little interruption, he disclosed the initiatives and proposals he had brought from Washington to help *perestroika* along.

Of greatest interest to the Soviet leader were the measures in the economic field: the immediate start of negotiations on a U.S.-Soviet trade agreement, to be completed by the time of their summit meeting in Washington, which Bush proposed to hold in the last two weeks of June 1990; the setting of the June summit as the target date for lifting the Jackson-Vanik amendment barring most-favored-nation trade status for the Soviet Union; the start of discussions on a U.S.-Soviet investment treaty; expansion of U.S. technical economic advice; exploration with Congress of extending Export-Import Bank credits to the USSR; U.S. support for observer status for the Soviet Union in the General Agreement on Tariffs and Trade, the key organization of international trade, which the Soviets had been seeking and the United States opposing; and improved ties between the Soviet Union and other international economic organizations of which the United States was a member. The moves outlined by Bush were incremental and mostly procedural advances rather than bold steps that would have an early economic impact, but together they added up to an unmistakable reversal of U.S. attitudes. "It's the end of economic warfare," said an ebullient Georgi Arbatov, the Moscow expert on the United States.

In the arms control field, Bush proposed to put current negotiations on a fast track: accelerating the START negotiations with the aim of resolving all substantive issues by the June summit; completing work on protocols to the 1970s nuclear testing treaties so they could be signed at the June summit; a U.S.-Soviet agreement by June on destruction of most of their chemical weapons stocks; and completion by the end of 1990 of the East-West negotiations to reduce conventional forces in

Europe. Bush's proposals added up to a reversal of his administration's earlier caution and its refusal to set deadlines for arms control progress.

Gorbachev listened intently, taking copious notes in a little orange-bound notebook. The warming atmosphere in the book-lined room was in stark contrast with the raging storm outside. When Bush had finished, the Soviet leader began a long philosophical reply. The world was changing, he said. It was no longer bipolar, although the United States and Soviet Union continued to have special and heavy responsibilities. The Soviet Union was doing its best to preserve stability in a serious way amid change, and would continue to do so. As to Bush's presentation, he had taken note of the President's repeated statements of support for *perestroika* and had never questioned that. But until this morning, he said, he had been waiting for evidence that Bush was ready to move the relationship forward in tangible ways. It was no longer necessary for him to wonder whether Bush was ready, Gorbachev continued with a satisfied smile: "Now I know." To one of the Americans at the table, NSC aide Robert Blackwill, this seemed to be the transforming moment of the post–World War II era. In preparation for Malta, Blackwill had read the minutes, some of them still highly classified, of nearly all the previous U.S.-Soviet summits. This and the exchanges that followed at Malta marked the first time, he thought, that the drive for active cooperation was stronger than the mutual suspicions of the two sides.

The one difficult issue was communist activity in Central America, which Bush referred to as the single most disruptive factor in U.S.-Soviet relations; it was "like a gigantic thorn in your shoe as you try to walk smoothly along." Although the Soviets appeared to be keeping their word that they had ceased to supply weapons to Nicaragua, Cuban arms shipments to the Sandinista regime had risen substantially, evidently to make up for the Soviet cutoff. And on November 25, just a week before the Malta summit, the crash of a Nicaraguan light plane ferrying surface-to-air missiles from Nicaragua to the El Salvadoran rebels raised the arms issue anew. Shevardnadze had visited Nicaragua in October and had reported to Baker that the Sandinistas denied they were supplying arms to the Salvadoran rebels. Under fire from Bush, Gorbachev repeated that "firm assurances" had been received from Managua that no arms deliveries were being carried out. ("Notice the precise wording," the Soviet Foreign Ministry expert on Latin America, Yuri Pavlov, later cautioned. Gorbachev said, " 'We have assurances' from the Nicaraguans, which in fact we did. But he didn't say we believed them.")

After lunch on the *Maxim Gorky*, Bush was scheduled to return to the *Belknap* for three hours of staff work before returning to the Soviet cruise ship in midafternoon to continue the discussions. In view of the raging storm, Gorbachev suggested that Bush change plans and remain on board to assure that the talks could continue. Bush declined. Together with his secretary of state, national security adviser and chief of staff, the President got into a Navy launch in the howling winds and pelting rain and set off for the U.S. cruiser. Horrified viewers at home watching through long-range television cameras could see the small boat bobbing about in the violent ocean swells, from time to time being lost from sight amid the waves. It took half a dozen passes at the *Belknap* before the Navy crew was able to make a solid enough contact for the President and his party to climb aboard the swaying ship. On shore, dozens of U.S. and Soviet flags were being ripped from their staffs by gale force winds and roads were submerged under water from the heavy rains. Shortly after Bush returned to the *Belknap*, the Navy determined that it would be too hazardous for the commander in chief or anyone else to brave the storm again. Stranded on the U.S. warship, Bush was forced to cancel his afternoon meeting with Gorbachev and the dinner on the *Belknap* they had planned for that night. Instead of meeting the Soviet leader, the sea-loving U.S. President spent ninety minutes on the bridge of the U.S. warship observing the storm, and later took a walk on the aft deck in the heavy rain and wind.

Before leaving the *Gorky*, Baker had accepted Shevardnadze's request for a meeting of their aides to discuss proposals that the Soviet side had brought to the summit. After Bush and Baker left, State Department Counselor Robert Zoellick and Policy Planning Chief Dennis Ross remained on the Soviet cruise ship to meet arms negotiator Alexei Obukhov and Georgi Mamedov of the U.S.A. Department of the Foreign Ministry. The Soviets had an extensive draft of a joint statement to be issued by the leaders, including a proposed ban on antisatellite testing in space and other contentious space-related issues as well as principles of U.S.-Soviet relations of the sort that had created a last-minute dispute at the Moscow summit the previous year. Zoellick and Ross argued that such a detailed joint statement was not appropriate to this informal meeting, and they were opposed to some of the specific Soviet proposals. In the light of the Bush initiatives in the morning, Gorbachev and Shevardnadze decided not to argue. Nothing more was said about the proposed joint statement; it was simply dropped, and with it the only substantive consideration at Malta of the SDI issue that had dominated the Geneva, Reykjavik and Washington summits. Though the issue had not been settled, the two sides had just decided to put aside their differences and move on to more practical business.

The summit discussions were to have resumed on the *Belknap* Sunday morning but, although the storm was tapering off, Gorbachev declined to leave the docked Soviet cruise ship for even a short trip through the still-roiling waters of the Marsaxlokk Bay. Bush and his party consented to hold the remaining talks on the *Maxim Gorky*, which had not been prepared to be used for any of the discussions but turned out to be the sole venue for the Malta summit.

This time, it was Gorbachev's turn to lead off. After some preliminaries, he turned to the changes in Europe and their meaning for the Soviet-American relationship. "We want you in Europe. You need to be in Europe. It's important for the future of Europe that you are in Europe, so we don't want to see you out of there," Gorbachev volunteered in remarks that surprised the American team.

Shevardnadze would say publicly several months later that the Soviet aim until quite recently had been "to force the Americans out of Europe at any cost." Implicit in Gorbachev's reversal, some of Bush's aides thought, was the recognition that Germany was heading toward unification and that a United States role would be essential to balance and to some extent check a powerful Germany in the center of the continent.

Then Gorbachev went on. "We don't consider you an enemy any more. Things have changed. We don't think of you in those terms." He assured Bush that the Soviet Union would never start a war against the United States.

Gorbachev's words did not seem especially important at the moment they were spoken, but the Americans on the other side of the narrow table later came to believe that they were of fundamental significance. Shevardnadze said later Gorbachev's no-enemy statement at Malta was "an important milestone" on the path to better U.S.-Soviet relations. "Those were bold words, and it was very difficult to say them," according to the Soviet foreign minister. Shevardnadze told Baker that "we took some real heat" for that position internally, referring to conservatives at home who said that Moscow had given away Eastern Europe and given up its opposition to U.S. imperialism—and was still encircled by the Americans. Aleksandr Yakovlev, who was also at the conference table aboard the *Maxim Gorky*, considered Gorbachev's words a natural summation of how far the relationship had come in the four years since the summit meeting with Reagan at Geneva. "Psychologically, in Geneva, our leaders weren't sure that America would not attack us, and the Americans weren't sure that we wouldn't attack [them]; in Malta this idea will not occur to anyone."

Across the table on the *Maxim Gorky*, Gorbachev had one strong complaint to register: the statements by Bush, Baker and others that Eastern Europe and, especially, Germany were changing their political orientations "on the basis of Western values." Two weeks earlier, Shevardnadze had complained to a Supreme Soviet committee that "to think of democracy and freedom as Western values is complete arrogance, a Western delusion of grandeur" when in fact these were "universal human values," which the new Soviet Union observed. Now Gorbachev took up the refrain. "You always accuse us of seeking the export of revolution and asserting the primacy of socialism," the Soviet leader argued, and "now you are doing the same thing" by demanding changes on the basis of "Western values." Gorbachev protested, "Why do you have to say Western? We accept democratic values. That's what we're all about." Up to that point, Bush had thought that Western values and democratic values were the same thing. But in view of Gorbachev's sensitivity, Bush henceforth changed his terminology. He told NATO leaders the following day, for example, that the division of Europe and of Germany must be ended in accordance with "the values that are becoming universal ideals."

After the Sunday morning discussion was over, Bush stayed aboard the *Maxim Gorky* for a joint press conference with Gorbachev, the first such joint question-and-answer session U.S. and Soviet leaders had ever held. Gorbachev and Reagan had made joint appearances in public, beginning with the final day of the Geneva summit four years earlier, but they had never sat down to meet the world press—and the global television public—to answer questions together. This symbolic event had not been in the original plan, which called for the two leaders to have individual press conferences aboard their respective warships following a brief joint statement, but Gorbachev had suggested it at the outset of the talks Sunday. Having thought through its significance, he said in his opening statement that "it has never been in history that the leaders of our two countries hold a joint press conference" and that this was "an important symbol."

Sitting side by side in the hastily converted discotheque of the Soviet vacation cruise ship, Bush and Gorbachev personified the shift from open hostility to political and economic cooperation between the two leading nations. "We stand at the threshold of a brand new era of U.S.-Soviet relations," said Bush. In elaboration, Bush said:

> There is virtually no problem in the world—and certainly no problem in Europe—that improvement in the U.S.-Soviet relationship will not help to ameliorate. A better U.S.-Soviet relationship is to be valued in and of itself, but it also should be an instrument of positive change for the world.

Gorbachev was quick to agree with Bush's overall assessment:

> We stated, both of us, that the world leaves one epoch of Cold War and enters another epoch. This is just the beginning. We're just at the very beginning of our long road to a long-lasting peaceful period.

With the opening of the Berlin Wall four weeks earlier, the unification of Germany had become a real possibility for the first time since the Cold War began. With almost lightning speed, that possibility had become an immediate prospect with the collapse of the East German currency, the clamor of demonstrators for unity and, especially, with the prounity speech to the West German Bundestag by Chancellor Helmut Kohl on November 28, just four days before the first meeting at Malta. On December 3, while Bush and Gorbachev were meeting, the entire East German Politburo resigned, throwing the situation of that rigid communist regime into new uncertainty and confusion.

In answer to reporters, Gorbachev spoke of "the reality" of two German states, the Federal Republic and the German Democratic Republic, both members of the United Nations and sovereign states. In a statement that conspicuously did not rule out eventual unification, Gorbachev went on to describe the two Germanys as existing due to "the decision of history." He went on to express his concern about the startling pace of events: "Any artificial acceleration of the process would only exacerbate and make it more difficult to change. . . . Thus, we wouldn't serve that process by an artificial acceleration, or prompting of the processes that are going on in those two countries."

Bush got the point quickly and clearly. At NATO headquarters in

Brussels the following day, Bush declined to estimate how quickly a unified Germany might develop. He said: "I am not trying to accelerate that process. I don't think our allies are."

By the time the press conference on the *Maxim Gorky* was over, the rain had stopped and the wind had died down. When Bush and Gorbachev left Malta on their separate airplanes several hours later, the storm was over and the sun had come out for the first time since they had begun their Mediterranean rendezvous.

Bush flew out of Malta on Air Force One for Brussels, where he briefed the heads of government of the NATO countries on his meetings with Gorbachev and discussed the future of Europe, especially of Germany.

Gorbachev flew on his Aeroflot plane to Moscow where the following day he convened a meeting of the leaders of the Warsaw Pact at a guest house in the capital's Lenin Hills. It was a strange gathering that symbolized the drastic and dramatic shifts since the Warsaw Pact leaders had last met in Bucharest only five months earlier. The Soviet delegation led by Gorbachev was unchanged since July, but nearly all the others were different. The aged communist leaders were nearly all gone, replaced at the big hollow square table by transitional reformist figures or, in the case of Poland, a noncommunist prime minister, former Solidarity leader Tadeusz Mazowiecki. Only Nicolae Ceausescu of Romania remained from the group of like-minded communists who had met on such occasions for decades. Ceausescu seemed angry and upset, as if he knew his time was coming.

According to notes made at the time by a member of one of the Eastern European delegations, Gorbachev opened the meeting with a report on his discussions at Malta. "Bush had initiated the meeting in July," Gorbachev explained, and it had been important to confirm that there was "political continuity" in the leadership of the United States. In some respects, he went on, the situation was an improvement: Bush did not "lecture" him, he said, as Reagan sometimes had. "Bush is formulating his positions slowly, thoughtfully," Gorbachev reported.

Mentioning the emerging economic cooperation between Washington and Moscow, Gorbachev said that the former "enemy" has been changed into an "opponent" and a "competitor." This does not mean, he added, that the beliefs motivating the Warsaw Pact in the past have been discredited. By standing together, the members of the alliance had seen to it that the policy of intimidation by military might had not succeeded.

In the future as well, Gorbachev said, it was essential that the "confrontational policy" of the West be defeated.

Six months earlier, the Warsaw Pact leaders had issued a call for disbanding both the Warsaw Pact and NATO to rid Europe of military blocs. In December, however, the Soviet position had shifted. The Warsaw Pact seemed close to collapse and NATO seemed stronger than ever. Gorbachev told the others around the big table that "NATO and the Warsaw Pact should be maintained despite their shortcomings because they are elements of security."

As for the future of Germany, "The borders are inviolable," no matter what happens, declared Gorbachev. Chancellor Kohl's recent speech promoting unification had "gone too far ahead." Gorbachev explained that "there is an emotional side to this. The process should not be forced."

After completing his report, Gorbachev turned to the assembled group and asked for "your reflections." There was an uncomfortable and embarrassed silence, as nobody seemed to know what to say.

After some desultory discussion of economic relationships, finally Ceausescu spoke up in bitter tones, as the only leader at the table whose status or viewpoint had not changed. The resolutions that the Warsaw Pact had adopted at the last meeting in July still stood, but there were new problems to be faced, maintained the Romanian leader. "The anti-communist policies of the United States and Western Europe have become more intense. They want to liquidate socialism," he declared bluntly, contradicting Gorbachev's report of improved relationships.

NATO was becoming stronger than ever, Ceausescu declared, and therefore the Warsaw Pact must be stronger as well. On behalf of the workers' parties, which must strengthen their positions, Ceausescu said, he was ready to organize a conference in Bucharest to help meet the common danger.

Ceausescu's urgent plea seemed out of touch with reality and with the rest of the discussion. Everybody ignored his offer. Instead Gorbachev spoke of the need to eliminate the Cold War.

After the discussions around the table, the leaders of the Soviet Union, Bulgaria, East Germany, Hungary and Poland agreed to follow the Czech leadership in condemning the 1968 invasion of Czechoslovakia that put an end to the Prague Spring. These five parties to the Warsaw Pact declared:

The illegal disruption of the process of democratic renewal in Czechoslovakia had long-term negative consequences. History showed how important it is, even in the most complex international situations, to use political means for the solution of any problems, and to observe strictly the principles of sovereignty, independence and non-interference in internal affairs, which is in accordance with the tenets of the Warsaw Pact.

The statement effectively put an end to Warsaw Pact acceptance of the Brezhnev Doctrine that it was legitimate to intervene to save socialism, a doctrine developed in Moscow following the 1968 invasion.

Ceausescu did not agree to the statement about the 1968 Czech action although, ironically, he was the only Warsaw Pact leader to have denounced the invasion at the time it occurred. After what *Pravda* described as "a frank exchange of opinions" with Gorbachev—diplomatic parlance for lots of disagreement—the Romanian leader left Moscow for home. Within less than three weeks, Ceausescu was overthrown and executed, along with his wife, Elena. The last unreconstructed regime of the Warsaw Pact had been destroyed by the wrath of its people and by the new policies of the USSR.

9. A New Era

*On New Year's Day 1990, the bells of the ancient St. Basil's Ca-
thedral on Red Square rang out for the first time in many years,
floating over Moscow. The same day the second annual festival of
Russian Orthodox sacred music opened at the Hall of Columns of
the Central Council of Trade Unions a few blocks from the Kremlin. The Communist Party newspaper* Pravda *wrote of the festival
that sacred music "conquers with its fullness of feeling and depth
of thought, exalts the spirit, and makes one think about the most
important things of life. It is hard even to imagine how much all
of us have lost in our aesthetic and spiritual development—for a
long time most of us were deprived of the opportunity to listen
to this music." On January 6, the Russian Orthodox holy day
Epiphany, Soviet television for the very first time broadcast the
service from Moscow's Cathedral of the Epiphany.*

In Chicago the board of directors of the Bulletin of the Atomic
Scientists *voted to reset the famous "doomsday clock" on its cover
from six minutes to midnight to ten minutes to midnight, reflecting
the scientists' belief that the margin of safety for the endangered
human species had substantially improved. "The myth of mono-
lithic communism has been shattered for all to see, the ideological
conflict known as the Cold War is over, and the risk of global*

nuclear war being ignited in Europe is significantly lessened,"
explained the Bulletin *in an editorial.*

For all those hopeful signs, the predominant sentiment inside
the Soviet Union at the beginning of 1990 was a deep pessimism
about the condition of the country and about its future. The cause
was easy to identify: despite all the talk of reform and better days,
the economy was worsening rapidly. The old system of centralized
economic planning and operations was no longer working, and
the new system of decentralized decisions and "market socialism,"
as Gorbachev called it, was hardly a coherent theory, much less
a working reality. The result was a precipitous drop in national
output, a sharp rise in inflation, a more serious scarcity than ever
of consumer goods and an abiding sense of frustration and malaise.
The Atlantic Council of the United States, in a study completed in
January 1990, said Soviet society had entered a "general crisis."

In addition to the underlying economic crisis, Gorbachev in
only a few months had suffered the loss of the Eastern European
empire, civil strife between national and ethnic groups within the
Soviet Union, and the beginning of a constitutional crisis with
secessionist Lithuania. The question being asked abroad and in-
creasingly discussed within the Soviet Union was: How much more
could he withstand?

Gorbachev's answer, true to form, was to move anew to increase his
political authority. Early in February, he summoned the Communist
Party Central Committee to the Kremlin and asked for new power for
the presidential office that he already held, including greatly strengthened authority to issue emergency decrees. The party agreed to put the
creation of an "executive presidency" before the elected legislature, the
Congress of People's Deputies, which alone had the power to change
the governmental structure and the constitution. Gorbachev also asked
the Communist Party to give up its traditional monopoly of power and
permit the establishment of other political parties and popular political
organizations. In an atmosphere of national crisis, the Central Committee
accepted his plan.

Several months earlier, in the fall of 1989, surprisingly little had
been said in Moscow as the communist leaders of one after another of
the Soviet Union's allies were being ousted or were changing their stripes.

The political debate in the Soviet capital had turned inward, as had the focus of national attention. Somehow the startling developments in the former Soviet empire initially had a greater impact in the rest of the world than they did in the Soviet Union.

In the early weeks of 1990, however, Soviet conservatives began to use the debacle in Eastern Europe to attack Gorbachev and his policies. For the first time, Gorbachev's foreign policy began to be a political liability inside the Soviet Union, rather than the political asset it had been until that time. One of the most hard-hitting early attacks was by the conservative writer Aleksandr Prokhanov, who was reputed to have close ties to the General Staff of the Soviet armed forces. Under the headline of "Tragedy," Prokhanov wrote in *Literaturnaya Rossiya*:

> The entire geopolitical structure of Eastern Europe, the building of which cost our country dearly, tumbled down overnight. . . . The sentimental theory of "our common European home" has brought about the collapse of Eastern Europe's communist parties, a change in state structures, and imminent reunification of the two Germanys. . . . As the color and contours of Europe's political map are changing, the bones of Russian infantrymen stir in their unknown graves.

The February plenum of the Central Committee that accepted Gorbachev's proposal for a strengthened presidency and political pluralism witnessed a bitter attack on Soviet foreign policy by V. I. Brovikov, the Soviet ambassador to Poland who had been an eyewitness to the dramatic events of the previous year.

> Our country, the mother of us all, has been reduced to a sorry state. It has been turned from a power that was admired in the world into a state with a mistake-filled past, a joyless present and an uncertain future. All this is so much fun for the West which, while extolling us, lets out emotional whoops about the collapse of "the colossus with clay feet" and the downfall of communism and world socialism. Yet we are trying to present all this as a dizzying success for *perestroika* and the new thinking in international affairs.

A few days after Brovikov's blast, Eduard Shevardnadze fired back against those who bemoaned the world admiration that was lost. Said the foreign minister in the pages of *Izvestia*:

We know what they admired. We sent troops in Czechoslovakia and destroyed the progressive trends there. Do they think the world admired that? We "restored order" in Hungary in 1956. We went into Afghanistan. What was it called at the time, "internationalist duty"? The correct word is invasion. Did the world admire that too? At the UN, 128 countries voted against us, passing resolutions that condemned our Afghan policy. Such was their "admiration."

The touchiest foreign policy question was the future of Germany, which was held responsible for the deaths of 27 million Soviet citizens in World War II and the terrible suffering and privation that were all too real in the national memory. Close to a half-century later, Soviet children still fought against mythical and heinous Germans in their games of battle, and special homage was paid Soviet veterans of what still was called "the Great Patriotic War." As Gorbachev had remarked to the Warsaw Pact leaders when he briefed them after meeting Bush at Malta, there was "an emotional side" to the German question, and everyone was aware of it.

By the time of the February plenum, East Germany was on the verge of economic and political collapse, and its shaken communist regime had advanced the national elections to mid-March. There was every reason to believe that the communists would be soundly beaten, raising the prospect of a rapid drive for the incorporation of East Germany into the much stronger Federal (West German) Republic and perhaps even into the NATO military alliance that was arrayed against the Soviet Union.

The big gun among the conservatives, Yegor Ligachev, raised the warning cry at the February plenum. Ligachev had had his wings clipped in Gorbachev's sudden September 1988 Politburo reorganization, but he had remained a Politburo member. (He retired in July 1990.) Addressing the Central Committee meeting on its opening day, Ligachev warned of an "impending danger" that East Germany would be absorbed into the West.

It would be an unforgivable myopia and a mistake not to see that a Germany with immense economic and military potential has begun to loom on the world horizon. . . . I think the time has come to realize this new danger of our time and to tell the Party and the people about it at full voice. It's still not too late.

The answer to Ligachev from Politburo member Aleksandr Yakovlev highlighted the sensitivity of the issue across the political spectrum. The chairman of the party's foreign affairs commission and perhaps Gorbachev's most liberal adviser, Yakovlev still walked with a limp because of severe wounds suffered at German hands in the war. "The German question is especially complex . . . a matter for profound reflection" and had been before the Politburo several times, Yakovlev declared. He told a press conference called to report on the debate that, especially regarding Germany, "the Soviet people have not lost their memory." While a unified Germany might be foreseen "at a certain point in time," Yakovlev emphasized that "the security of our borders must be firmly guaranteed. We must avoid the emergence of any kind of a new threat from the well-known direction. We are in favor of a European Germany, not a German Europe. And this is a matter of great importance, a matter of principle for us."

• GERMAN ARITHMETIC: TWO PLUS FOUR

The Communist Party plenum, which had gone into a third day because of controversy over Gorbachev's proposals, was still in its final hours when Secretary of State James Baker arrived in Moscow on the evening of February 7 for his first meetings with Shevardnadze and Gorbachev since Malta three months earlier. In an unusual move for a Politburo member, Shevardnadze left the plenum before it was over to meet Baker. In their initial three-hour meeting that night, Shevardnadze spoke with concern about the outspoken criticism that had been aimed at Soviet foreign policy in the party meeting. Looking back on it later, Baker felt that this had been a more significant conversation than he realized at the time. Although it wasn't apparent until a few weeks later, the sentiments expressed at the party plenum and other attacks on Soviet foreign policy had begun to place Shevardnadze and the Foreign Ministry as well as Gorbachev on the defensive. As winter gave way to spring, they lost some of the flexibility that they had displayed in negotiations with the United States up to that point.

The early months of 1990 saw the dawn of a new age. The lines of East-West confrontation on the political and military map of Europe since World War II were suddenly dissolving, and as in the late 1940s when those lines had been drawn, there was a strong sense among policymakers of being "present at the creation." How to arrange the new Europe with a minimum of disorder and with guarantees for all became the highest priority of diplomats of the major nations. For Washington, this was a delicate job of multilateral diplomacy, especially with regard to Germany.

A dominant power in Europe for centuries, Germany had been the source of two world wars in the twentieth century. The prospect of a reunified and dominant Germany at the center of Europe was unsettling, to say the least, to many of its neighbors. Poland on its east worried that the new Germany would seek to reclaim territory given to the Poles after World War II. Britain, France and others on the west feared the economic power of a reunited Germany; some worried that eventually a resurgent German military could follow the deutsche mark. A Dutch official told *Time*, "Except for the Germans, no one in Europe wants reunification."

The deepest fears were those in the Soviet Union, not only because of the bloody history of World War II but also because of the unmistakable sense of Soviet decline as Germany was rising again. The German Democratic Republic had been the most vital front line for Soviet power since its creation in 1949 in the occupation zone manned by Soviet troops under the agreement with the wartime allies, the United States, Britain and France. As 1990 began, 380,000 Soviet troops were still stationed in East Germany; however, with the collapse of the East-West border in Germany and the disintegration of East Germany's government, currency and communist party, the Soviet troops seemed irrelevant and isolated. They were useless unless Moscow was prepared to intervene militarily in dubious battle against a popular and well-developed revolution on an open border with the West.

Since the Berlin Wall had been neutralized in November 1989, the Soviet Union had sent at least a half-dozen private diplomatic messages to Washington proposing that the World War II allies, which retained occupation rights in Germany, meet to assert their authority over Germany's future. Washington had agreed to a meeting of the ambassadors of the four powers in Berlin immediately after the collapse of the Wall to signal stability and assert a common interest in avoiding chaos. But for the West Germans, the reassertion of four-power authority over German affairs was anathema; the country had put World War II behind it and long outgrown the former military occupation. At the same time, both Bonn and Washington realized the necessity of giving the Soviet Union a role in the reunification process. Moscow probably could not stop the reestablishment of German unity, but it could make it much more difficult and dangerous through threats and obstructionist tactics. Moreover, failure to take Gorbachev's needs into account would be a serious blow to his position at home, endangering much that had been built in East-West relations since his coming to power.

Discussions within the Bush administration in January 1990 centered on how to involve the Soviets in the German question. "In our minds, going back to our assessments of Soviet actions over the course of the year and what we'd seen before we came into office, there were many things possible with the Soviets, things still untested," recalled State Department Counselor Robert Zoellick. In connection with Germany, the goal, as he saw it, was "to create a mechanism that would allow the Soviets to explain their actions at home, to show that they were participating, and indeed, to give them a role" in the deliberations over the German future. In private Baker referred to the aim more bluntly as "giving cover" to the Soviets on the subject of German unification.

The mechanism that Washington devised involved the four World War II allies—the United States, Soviet Union, Britain and France—in discussions on the external aspects of German unification, such as security arrangements, the confirmation of existing borders and the termination of postwar occupation rights. Crucial to the idea was that the two German states would make their own decisions on all domestic questions and have the leading role in the international discussions as well. In recognition of the German primacy, the arrangement was dubbed "Two Plus Four," with the "two" being clearly in the leading position to deal with the "four."

White House and State Department officials first broached the "Two Plus Four" arrangement during the visit of British Foreign Secretary Douglas Hurd to Washington on January 29. On February 2, there were more important soundings during the visit of West German Foreign Minister Hans-Dietrich Genscher, who had been thinking along similar lines. The German foreign minister had also conceived what was known as "the Genscher plan" for handling the most difficult subject for Moscow, the incorporation of a united Germany into NATO. Under the Genscher plan, Soviet troops would remain in the former territory of East Germany for a transitional period, and NATO would not extend its forces into that area.

Having touched base with the British and obtained a favorable response from Genscher, Baker discussed the "Two Plus Four" idea with French Foreign Minister Roland Dumas in a 5:00 A.M. meeting February 6 during a refueling stop at Shannon Airport on the first leg of Baker's trip to Eastern Europe and Moscow. Dumas, who seemed to welcome anything that could provide some structure to a chaotic situation, did not object.

When Baker met Gorbachev and Shevardnadze in the Kremlin, he found the Soviet leaders eager to discuss the looming issue of German unification. After initially opposing any talk of early unification, Gorbachev had recognized the inevitable, accepting a single Germany in theory January 30 during the visit to Moscow of East German Premier Hans Modrow. "Nobody casts any doubt upon it," Gorbachev said, in a remark that was widely hailed in German. But on the same occasion, Gorbachev also went out of his way to say that "four-power obligations still exist" regarding Germany and that these, together with the interests of the two German states and the all-European process established through the Helsinki accords, "must be combined in the common interest, with no infringement of the interests of any of the sides involved."

In St. Catherine's Hall on February 9, Gorbachev and Shevardnadze outlined for Baker four Soviet concerns about the drive for German unification: first, fear that it would create instability and uncertainty in Europe; second, concern about the depth of Germany's commitment to its present borders; next, unease about the future attitude of the West German leaders, because their present reassuring statements might mean little after Germany was unified; finally, determination that unification had to be "managed" on the grounds that "the lessons of history" required the Soviet Union to have an active part in the process.

Baker responded that the United States was sensitive to their concerns, but that no one except the Germans could decide the fate of Germany. Unification was inevitable and events were moving very rapidly, Baker said, with the internal aspects of unification expected to proceed quickly after the March 18 East German elections. The internal aspects were for the Germans alone, but external aspects of unification were "a different matter" because they involved the security of other nations.

This brought Baker to his suggestion for a mechanism to deal with the external aspects. A body made up of only the four World War II allies would be inappropriate because "the Germans would never accept it," Baker said. The Soviets had also suggested a major role for the thirty-five-nation Conference on Security and Cooperation in Europe (CSCE), which had grown out of the 1975 Helsinki Final Act, but Baker said that, aside from some help in validating borders, CSCE was "far too unwieldy and cumbersome" for practical decisions in a time of rapid change. Therefore it seemed to him, Baker proposed, that a "Two Plus Four" mechanism of the two Germanys and the four powers might be "the most realistic way to proceed."

Gorbachev expressed interest in this approach, commenting that it might be "suitable for the occasion." But as Baker was quick to say after the meeting, there was no commitment on the Soviet side.

The discussion then turned to the touchy issue of integrating the new Germany into the Atlantic alliance or, as Baker put it, "a united Germany remaining in NATO and not being neutral." The Federal Republic leadership strongly favored this idea and the United States agreed, the secretary explained; moreover, he believed that the Soviet Union should not reject this outcome. It was simply "unrealistic" to expect that a big and economically important country such as Germany could be neutral. Without explicitly offering U.S. or German security guarantees to the Soviet Union, Baker put his case across the Kremlin table in the form of a question that suggested such guarantees could be forthcoming: "Would you prefer to see a united Germany outside of NATO and with no U.S. forces, or would you prefer a unified Germany to be tied to NATO, with assurances that NATO's jurisdiction would not shift one inch eastward from its present position?"

"Certainly any extension of the zone of NATO would be unacceptable," Gorbachev responded, suggesting to Baker that, by implication, a NATO including Germany within its existing borders might be acceptable. The Soviet leadership was giving real thought to all such options, Gorbachev said, and would soon be holding "a kind of seminar" to discuss them further.

To the Americans sitting across the table, Gorbachev's discussion of this ticklish issue seemed rational and calm, as the Soviet leader could often be, although he acknowledged that part of his task would be to deal with the strong emotions that German questions always raised. There was a danger, he said, that rising German nationalism could stimulate a rising Russian nationalism that would be difficult to control. Both in Gorbachev's comments and in those of Shevardnadze, it was evident that the Soviet leaders were living under the shadow of the deep-seated feelings and outspoken views that had been expressed in the Communist Party plenum. This was the downside of democracy. Shevardnadze told Baker that opening up the Soviet political system had created a whole set of new foreign policy problems in Moscow. In earlier times, such attacks on official policy would not have been permitted.

The following day, as Baker prepared to leave Moscow, West German Chancellor Kohl arrived in the Soviet capital for his own meeting with Gorbachev. Shortly before he left Bonn, Kohl had received a letter from Bush describing his trip as the most important such mission since Chancellor Konrad Adenauer went to Moscow to establish diplomatic relations in 1955, and volunteering Bush's complete trust and confidence in his German ally. A grateful Kohl later told Bush his letter had been "a document of historical significance in the development of German-American friendship and partnership." Baker was anxious to coordinate with Kohl but could not meet him in Moscow due to the complications of their two schedules. Instead, Baker left a three-page letter recounting his discussions on Germany. In the key passage, Baker wrote:

> Gorbachev, at least, is not locked in. While he has real concerns about German unification—some of which may be related to the passions this issue evokes in the Soviet Union—he may be willing to go along with a sensible approach that gives him some cover or explanation of his actions.
>
> I suspect that the combination of a Two Plus Four mechanism and a broader CSCE framework might do that. But it is obviously too early to know, and we'll have to see how the Soviet position evolves.

As Baker had suggested, Kohl found a concerned but pragmatic Gorbachev in the Kremlin. The Soviet leader declared that "the question of unity of the German nation should be decided by the Germans themselves, and the Germans themselves should choose the forms of statehood, timetable, pace and terms on which they will realize this unity." At the same time, Gorbachev emphasized, the international community had a major stake in the developments, which must not damage East-West relations or "upset the European balance." The last phrase denoted Moscow's continuing resistance to a united Germany in NATO. "I said a long time ago that history would decide the German question. And now it has gone to work at an unexpected pace," Gorbachev declared. Kohl hailed Gorbachev's acceptance of a unified Germany, and at a Moscow press conference following the meeting, referred obliquely to the need for talks involving the two German states and the four principal World War II victors as part of the unification process.

Baker flew from Moscow to Bulgaria and Romania, and then on to Ottawa, where the foreign ministers of the sixteen NATO countries and the seven Warsaw Pact countries were meeting to discuss Open Skies proposals. Baker formally presented the "Two Plus Four" mechanism at a breakfast meeting with Genscher, Hurd and Dumas, on February 13; the U.S., West German, British and French foreign ministers drew up a proposed announcement of the international arrangement. They decided to try to obtain Soviet approval while all the ministers were still in Ottawa. Later that morning, as the Open Skies conference was preparing to open, Baker engaged Shevardnadze in a side conversation near the meeting table. Reading from a slip of paper in his own handwriting, Baker told the Soviet minister what he and the others proposed. Shevardnadze's translator copied it down in Russian, and Shevardnadze said he would speak to Gorbachev. Two hours later, he met Baker again in a private conference room and asked for small changes in the text. When everyone had approved, the foreign ministers of the two Germanys and the four World War II allies assembled for a photograph together and the issuance of a three-sentence press release announcing future talks among them on "external aspects of the establishment of German unity, including the issues of security of the neighboring states." It was the first step toward creating new international arrangements for a reunified Germany. "The process has been launched," said Soviet spokesman Vitaly Churkin minutes after the announcement was made.

• LITHUANIA: THE GAS-FILLED ROOM

While Baker was in Moscow in February, Lithuanians requested that he meet Vytautas Landsbergis, chairman of Sajudis, the Lithuanian political movement that advocated independence from the Soviet Union. Given the strong opposition by Gorbachev and others in Moscow to Lithuanian secession and the increasingly precarious domestic standing of the Soviet leader, Baker decided it was politically imprudent to see Landsbergis but arranged for the State Department's ranking Soviet expert, Deputy Assistant Secretary Curtis Kammen, to do so. When Baker appeared on February 10, his final day in Moscow, before the International Affairs Committee of the Supreme Soviet of the USSR, the first time a U.S. government official had ever done so, a Lithuanian delegate handed him a letter putting the United States on notice that the Baltic republic planned to move ahead toward declaring its independence. A few days later, the State Department sent back an oral message, a cautious form of diplomatic communication, restating the U.S. position that the fifty-year Soviet occupation of Lithuania had been illegal from the start, but urging the Lithuanians to pursue their goals through peaceful dialogue with the authorities in Moscow.

Although nationalities disputes had long plagued the Soviet Union, Lithuania's action in early 1990 was the first formal assertion of independence in many years. For the multinational Union of Soviet Socialist Republics, this was a dispute of great importance and political sensitivity, especially because of the precedents that might be set for other restive national groups. It was also an unusually touchy issue for the United States.

A very old though small state, Lithuania has had a checkered history of independence and varying degrees of domination by its neighborhood giants, Russia, Poland and Prussia. Along with the two other Baltic republics, Estonia and Latvia, Lithuania was forcibly incorporated into the Soviet Union in 1940 following the signing of a secret agreement between Hitler's Germany and Stalin's USSR. The existence of the secret protocol to the 1939 agreement had been denied by the Soviet Union for many years, but in the era of *glasnost* it was retrieved from the "special archives" (secret files) of the Soviet Foreign Ministry and officially exposed by a committee of the Congress of People's Deputies headed by Politburo member Aleksandr Yakovlev. In the eyes of Lithuanians, this action made the case for independence all the more persuasive and its continued denial all the more intolerable.

In theory, the Lithuanians had a sympathetic backer in the United States, which had never recognized the forced incorporation of the Baltic states into the USSR and continued officially to recognize Lithuania, Estonia and Latvia as independent states. At the height of the Cold War in the 1950s, U.S. demands for freedom for the Baltic nations were at the center of Washington's "captive nations" drive aimed at the Soviet Union. Refugees had flocked to the United States from the three Baltic states and acquired a significant voice in U.S. politics. In 1980 the U.S. Census Bureau identified 743,000 Americans of Lithuanian descent; nearly all were passionate advocates of Lithuanian independence from the Soviet Union.

In the late 1980s the demands for independence boiled up more fiercely than ever inside Lithuania as nationalists took advantage of *glasnost* and democracy, and as the growing economic failure of *perestroika* made Lithuanians even more discontented with the USSR. In June 1988 the proindependence Sajudis organization was founded in Lithuania and quickly became the most popular and important movement in the Soviet republic.

In October 1988 a fateful change took place in the Lithuanian communist party when an old-line leader loyal to Moscow was replaced by Algirdas Brazauskas, a politically astute Lithuanian sympathetic to popular sentiments. With the new leader's sponsorship or approval, there followed a series of highly symbolic and, to Lithuanians, exhilirating actions: the Roman Catholic Cathedral of Vilnius, the traditional center of religious life, was returned to the church after having been used as a Soviet museum of atheism for decades; the Lithuanian Statue of Freedom, a national symbol that had been hidden since 1940, was unveiled again in a state-sponsored event as thousands danced in the streets; the coffin of St. Casimir, the patron saint of Lithuania, was returned to the former royal castle in a procession through huge crowds in a patriotic event covered extensively on Lithuanian state television; a Soviet army plane at Lithuanian request brought back coffins of some of the tens of thousands of Lithuanians who had been deported to Siberia by Stalin after 1940. And on August 23, 1989, the fiftieth anniversary of the Nazi-Soviet Pact that had sealed the fate of the Baltics, more than a million people linked arms in an unbroken human chain stretching 430 miles through Lithuania, Latvia and Estonia in a dramatic appeal for independence and freedom.

Engrossed in their own political battles and in the dramatic events in Eastern Europe, Soviet authorities in Moscow issued a few warnings but took no action to stop these developments. But when the Lithuanian communist party voted on December 20, 1989, to declare itself an independent political organization no longer under the discipline or direction of the Soviet Communist Party, the alarm bells went off in Moscow. The Politburo met the next day to reject the Lithuanian action, and quickly convened a special meeting of the Communist Party Central Committee December 25 and 26 to deal with the Lithuanian crisis.

Gorbachev took a tough stand at the Central Committee plenum. While sympathizing with Lithuania's suffering under "decades of Stalinist tyranny" and calling for a continuation of reforms, he made clear the limits of his tolerance:

> The present Party and state leadership will not allow the breakup of the Union state. I want to state this at the plenary session of the Party Central Committee. I say this bluntly. The necessary actions to preserve the Union and ensure its unity are a hard necessity. There should be no illusions here regarding the center's intentions and capabilities.

The Soviet leader reminded the world that "there is also a very important international aspect to this problem," saying that a stable and powerful Soviet Union was a necessary component of world order. Undermining Soviet stability, he declared, could destabilize "the political situation in Europe and the world."

On January 11, shortly after the New Year's holiday, Gorbachev flew to Lithuania for three days of public appearances of a sort never before seen from a Soviet leader. In meetings with communist leaders and with intellectuals, factory workers, collective farmers and people on the streets, Gorbachev sought to persuade the Lithuanian people almost one by one that they should remain in the Soviet Union rather than seek their independence. *Vremya*, the main Soviet television evening news broadcast, showed ten to fifteen minutes every night of Gorbachev, "the man in the arena," in his fedora and topcoat in a circle of Lithuanians, arguing intensely, almost pleading, that they should "think a thousand times" before embarking on a risky independent course. Gorbachev reminded everyone that it was he who had launched the reforms that permitted this open debate in the first place, and at one point declared that "my own fate" was in the balance with their decisions.

The Lithuanians were respectful of Gorbachev's earnestness, his power and his mission, but they answered him with bluntness and a determination to rid themselves of Soviet control. "Our lives have been like in a dormitory," said a man on the street. "It's time we all had separate rooms." When Gorbachev asked sarcastically if anyone thought a complex and dangerous independence from the Soviet Union would solve all their problems, the crowd responded with proindependence shouts, although some voices said, "If not tomorrow, then step by step."

Two weeks after Gorbachev's dramatic but unsuccessful visit, I flew from Moscow to Vilnius to judge for myself what was happening there. Talks with communist and noncommunist leaders and others in the Lithuanian capital made it clear to me that the sentiment for declaring independence from the Soviet Union was overwhelming. There was no consensus, though, on how or when to arrange the break. Some wanted to make the break immediately after the February 24 local legislative elections, which Sajudis was certain to win easily. Landsbergis, the professor of music history who was the leader of Sajudis, was among the more cautious voices, telling me that simply proclaiming independence "would be a political step without a new reality" and that a better way would be to send representatives to Moscow to negotiate the separation. The Kremlin would resist at first, he said, but eventually would be forced to talk.

On the night of March 11, however, the Lithuanian independence forces moved suddenly and preemptively. In Moscow, Gorbachev had convened the Congress of People's Deputies to meet the following day to establish a strengthened presidency, which would give him powers he had lacked before. Fearful that an empowered Gorbachev would quickly decree emergency rule over Lithuania or otherwise forbid any breakaway actions, the newly installed Lithuanian Supreme Soviet elected Landsbergis its chairman or president, proclaimed itself the Republic of Lithuania instead of the Lithuanian Soviet Socialist Republic, and by unanimous vote just before midnight declared itself once again an independent nation.

In Washington, the White House quickly issued a statement that had been prepared earlier in extensive interagency discussions. It pointed out the United States "has never recognized the forcible incorporation" of Lithuania or the other Baltic states into the Soviet Union and urged the Soviet government to "respect the will" of the Lithuanian parliament, while urging Lithuania to "consider the rights" of its Russian inhabitants. The statement also called for a peaceful resolution of the independence issue through "immediate constructive negotiation" between Moscow and Vilnius.

The Soviet reaction to Lithuania's move was hostile. Gorbachev described the parliament's action as "alarming" and told the Congress of People's Deputies that the decisions in Lithuania "affect the fundamental interests and destiny of the republic itself, of the people and of our entire state."

Gorbachev and the Politburo decided from the first that they would not seek to put down the independence drive with military force, directly applied. The chosen alternative was a war of nerves and pressures to induce Lithuania to step back at least part of the way from its assertion of independence and to show the secessionist forces in the fourteen other Soviet republics that pulling out of the USSR would not be painless or easy.

A week after the declaration of independence, Soviet military airplanes and helicopters circled over Vilnius in unscheduled "maneuvers." Some dropped anti-independence leaflets. A few days later Gorbachev, in the first order of his new executive presidency, directed Lithuanians to turn in all weapons. Soviet authorities confiscated the weapons of the Lithuanian National Guard. In the next step, Soviet tanks and armored personnel carriers rumbled into Vilnius and paraded past the parliament building where legislators were working. Then Soviet troops raided a psychiatric hospital where several dozen Lithuanian deserters from the Soviet army were being sheltered, and Soviet forces took over the Lithuanian communist party headquarters. Except for a minor scuffle at the psychiatric hospital, there were no physical clashes during the war of nerves, but tension mounted day by day.

Each day's developments brought new headlines in the American press and new footage on television of a brave people being slowly squeezed by Soviet force. Lithuanian authorities voiced nearly daily protests and complaints through the international press, and in Washington the White House and State Department issued a stream of slowly escalating statements of disapproval. All of the assumptions of an improved relationship with Moscow, which had taken hold since the meeting at Malta, were called into question.

At the end of March, Bush suddenly reversed course and the administration lowered its rhetoric. Bush made the decision to back off after receiving a report of a seventy-five-minute meeting between Gorbachev and Senator Ted Kennedy on March 26, during which the Soviet leader had complained bitterly that U.S. criticism was undermining his attempts at moderation. With the secession bandwagon starting to gather momentum in Soviet Georgia, Azerbaijan and Armenia as well as the other

Baltic states, Gorbachev told Kennedy he was under intense domestic pressure to clamp down on Lithuania with an economic boycott that would bring the rebellious republic to heel. In the internal discussions in Washington, Bush expressed concern that the U.S. rhetoric was also encouraging Landsbergis to take an uncompromising position, which could lead to a violent showdown that the Lithuanians could only lose. In meetings with aides and with Baltic Americans, Bush recalled the abortive 1956 Hungarian uprising and said, "I am not going to be a president who gives subject peoples the false impression that if they rebel, they are going to get help."

Gorbachev brought the war of nerves to a head on Easter weekend by issuing an ultimatum that Lithuania annul its independence declaration within forty-eight hours or face economic retaliation. Predictably, Vilnius refused to act. On April 18, three days after the deadline, Moscow ordered the flow of oil stopped to Lithuania's only refinery and shut off 84 percent of its natural gas, leaving just enough to permit the most essential services to continue.

While the cutoff was being implemented, Bush announced he was considering "appropriate responses," and the White House began consultations with the Western European allies and with members of Congress on sanctions that could be adopted against the Soviet Union. At this point, the widespread assumption in Washington among officials as well as lawmakers and journalists was that Bush would act in the familiar pattern of imposing sanctions to penalize the Soviet Union and demonstrate U.S. displeasure, as Jimmy Carter had done after the invasion of Afghanistan and Ronald Reagan after the martial law crackdown in Poland. The main issue under discussion within the government was whether Bush would adopt largely symbolic sanctions such as interrupting pending trade, aviation or maritime negotiations, or more substantial measures.

To the surprise of nearly everyone, Bush announced on April 24 that he had decided not to retaliate against Moscow after all. Quoting baseball philosopher Yogi Berra's famous fractured grammar, Bush said, "I don't want to make the wrong mistake." For the first time in the postwar era, the political and international benefits of being tough with the Kremlin were balanced by an important U.S. interest in the continuation of existing Soviet policy. A major factor in Bush's thinking was the importance of Soviet acquiescence in the unification of Germany within the NATO alliance, one of the most important developments of the postwar era. A cooling of U.S.-Soviet relations or change in the shaky status quo in Moscow could severely complicate this highest-priority international effort. Bush told an aide in explaining his decision, "I don't want people to look back 20 or 40 years from now and say, 'That's where everything went off track. That's where progress stopped.' " Bush saw too much at stake and too much uncertainty, according to Condoleezza Rice, the ranking Soviet expert on the National Security Council staff. Bush was "afraid to light a match in a gas-filled room," she told me several weeks after he declined to order sanctions.

The aggrieved Lithuanian president reacted bitterly to the decision. "This is Munich," declared Landsbergis. "We feared that America might sell us. . . . I don't understand whether it is possible to sell the freedom of one group of people for the freedom of another. If that is so, then of what value is the idea of freedom itself?"

As congressional and public reaction continued to build against the Soviet economic embargo and Bush's failure to act, Bush on April 30 sent a letter to Gorbachev warning him not to expect the U.S.-Soviet trade agreement, which negotiators had virtually completed, to be signed at the coming summit if the Lithuania standoff continued. In view of his mounting economic difficulties at home, signing the trade pact was expected to be Gorbachev's highest priority at the forthcoming summit. Bush said in the letter that his inability to move forward with the trade agreement did not mean that he had abandoned his support for *perestroika*. Rather, he insisted, it reflected political reality in Congress, where outrage was running strong over the Soviet crackdown in Lithuania. The Bush letter set in motion a test of wills over the trade issue that would be a key element in the coming summit.

• THE RISE OF THE SOVIET MILITARY

The spring of 1990 was also notable for emergence of the Soviet military as a major independent player in negotiations between Moscow and Washington, especially on issues of strategic arms. It was early evidence of the reassertion of power by an important institution of Soviet life that had been beset by a host of troubles and was increasingly convinced its civilian overlords were making too many concessions at its expense, at home and abroad.

In a marathon meeting the last day of his trip to Moscow in February, Baker made surprising progress on key outstanding issues of strategic arms. However, some the deals tentatively struck did not sit well with Soviet military leaders, who strenuously complained about one-sided arrangements, and appear to have taken their case to Gorbachev. By April, Soviet negotiators were backtracking on the agreements that had been worked out two months earlier by imposing a host of new conditions and restrictions, all of them unwelcome and some of them unacceptable to the Americans. The future of the START Treaty on strategic arms, which had appeared so promising early in the year, suddenly was cast into doubt.

The weapon that brought the conflict to a head was the cruise missile: a winged, jet-powered drone that can deliver nuclear or conventional warheads with great accuracy by using advanced microelectronics to "read" a computerized map of the terrain on the way to the target. When the United States developed cruise missiles in the early 1970s, they were described as "a potential disaster" for strategic arms control because of their small size, the relative ease with which they could be hidden on aircraft, submarines and surface ships, and the difficulty of distinguishing a nuclear-armed cruise missile from a nonnuclear missile. Within a few years, the Soviet Union was developing its own cruise missiles as well, compounding the arms control problem. But the United States was well ahead in this high-technology weapons race, and it seemed to Moscow that U.S. negotiators were determined to preserve the U.S. advantage unfairly.

From the Soviet viewpoint, one of the most important achievements of the INF Treaty signed by Reagan and Gorbachev in December 1987 had been to remove the U.S. ground-launched cruise missiles that had been based in Western Europe and were considered a deadly threat by the Soviet military. As the bargaining on strategic arms proceeded in 1989 and 1990, the Soviet negotiators focused on eliminating the air-launched and sea-launched cruise missiles as well.

At the negotiating table in February, Shevardnadze and his team agreed on many previously disputed details of how to limit air-launched cruise missiles, essentially by limiting the permissible number of bombers on which they could be deployed. Even more important, the Soviets had agreed for the first time to accept the U.S. approach to the formidable issue of sea-launched cruise missiles. Instead of seeking verifiable limits on these weapons, the two sides agreed simply to declare to the other once a year the number of weapons it proposed to deploy, with no attempt at on-site inspection. U.S. arms adviser Paul Nitze had sought to convince the Soviets to accept such a nonbinding "declaratory approach" in the Reagan administration, but it had been consistently rejected as permitting the Americans virtual free rein.

In the crucial meetings on these issues, the lead negotiator on the Soviet side was Sergei Akhromeyev. This was the same Akhromeyev who had presided over deal making in the all-night session at Reykjavik and in later meetings with the Americans, but his role had changed. The Soviet marshal had resigned as chief of staff of the armed forces in December 1988 and was now taking part as an adviser to Gorbachev, not an active duty officer. The nature and origin of Akhromeyev's instructions in the February compromises are unclear; what is certain is that the active leadership of the armed forces strongly resisted the deals that were made. Afterward, Soviet military officers told American negotiators in Geneva and elsewhere that Akhromeyev no longer represented them.

The rebellion against the cruise missile accommodations was an early symptom of profound discontent in the Soviet military, which had previously occupied an enviable position in government and society but was suffering painful blows from many directions. Under Gorbachev, political accords had begun to displace military might as the basis for national security; military manpower and budgets were being cut; and Soviet armed forces were being forced out of Eastern Europe, returning to much worse conditions at home than those they had enjoyed abroad. Meanwhile, the army of East Germany, previously the Soviet Union's most reliable military ally, was evaporating and that country seemed headed for a merger with West Germany, perhaps even as part of NATO, the adversary alliance. At the same time, the hard-pressed Kremlin leadership was increasingly relying on Soviet troops to perform the dangerous and unpopular task of cracking down on nationalistic activities when they got out of hand. During the early months of 1990, Soviet troops were deployed in Azerbaijan, Armenia, Tajikistan and Lithuania. The previous year, the Kremlin had used troops to restore order in four other republics.

The Soviet leadership's internal discussions on arms control following Baker's February trip were shrouded in secrecy, but an official of the Communist Party Central Committee said that "the Soviet equivalent of the U.S. military-industrial complex" went into action in highly unusual fashion, telling the political leaders that some of the deals that had been made were "unacceptable." Confirmation of the intensity of the arguments came from Shevardnadze in a speech to the Communist Party organization at the Foreign Ministry after the Baker trip. Singling out the "complex" problems of air- and sea-launched cruise missiles, Shevardnadze declared:

> Some of our colleagues are demanding of us: "No compromises!" Their reasons are not those one rejects out of hand. But there is no mistaking the main question: "If there is no treaty, will this be to our benefit or not?" What will be the correlation of forces in several years unless we halt the arms race, particularly in the sphere of cruise missiles? Unless we succeed in establishing some inhibitors, some boundaries, how will we sustain all this? What is our real interest? . . . What could happen in 10 or 30 years time under the conditions of the growth of the scientific and technological revolution and our present backwardness in this sphere?

When Shevardnadze came to Washington in early April, it became apparent that the active duty military had moved to a front seat in policymaking. Akhromeyev was with him in the U.S. capital, but this time he was also accompanied by Major General Aleksandr Peresypkin of the General Staff of the Soviet armed forces. The newcomer, whom U.S. diplomats had not encountered before, wore civilian clothes and was on the Soviet delegation list as "Mr. Peresypkin," but the Americans quickly noticed that he was referred to as "General Peresypkin." At the meetings, cruise missile issues that had previously been resolved were reopened, or new conditions imposed that complicated the matter. When the Americans expressed surprise and dismay, Soviet civilian negotiators hinted broadly that the military was to blame. Two weeks after the ministerial meeting, Shevardnadze sent his veteran arms negotiator, Viktor Karpov, to Washington to continue discussions on the deadlocked issues. Karpov was accompanied for the first time by a deputy chief of the General Staff, Colonel General Branislav Omelichev. There was little give in the position of either side.

In earlier times, the U.S. administration would have made much of the Soviet backtracking. This time Baker swallowed hard and, understanding that Shevardnadze and perhaps Gorbachev were in a difficult spot, got approval for a package of U.S. compromises on cruise missiles to meet some of the Soviet military's objections. The secretary of state had scheduled a trip to Moscow May 15–19 to make the final preparations for the summit meeting in Washington set for May 30–June 3. To improve the chances for success, Baker had secretly given the new arms package to Shevardnadze ten days in advance, when they met in Bonn May 5 to begin at the ministerial level the "Two Plus Four" meetings on conditions for German unification.

By the time Baker prepared to fly to Moscow, the economic and political troubles of the Soviet Union had mounted to the point that Washington officials were uncertain whether Gorbachev was still capable of making major decisions or how long he would last. The dramatic changes in Soviet foreign policy could not have happened without Gorbachev's leadership, but increasingly he and his senior aides seemed so preoccupied with troubles at home that they could no longer play a dynamic role in world affairs. The Soviet Union now seemed to be in a highly unpredictable situation.

On the first leg of the mid-May trip to Moscow with Baker, strategic arms negotiator Richard Burt, who had watched Moscow's performance closely as assistant secretary of state for European affairs and ambassador to Bonn in the Reagan administration, told me that the Soviet Union, for so long a consistent if unyielding force in international politics, had become "a wild card" in the international game. Burt's pessimism about the Soviet internal situation reminded me of a conversation I had had with a senior CIA official in Washington a few days earlier. When I asked what he thought would happen in the Soviet Union, the official had startled me by answering bluntly, "I think they are going to have a revolution."

For all his troubles, Gorbachev quickly showed Baker he was still able to maneuver. The night before their meeting in the Kremlin, Gorbachev summoned Lithuanian Prime Minister Kazimiera Prunskiene to discuss ways to resolve the ten-week-old constitutional crisis. The Lithuanians had consistently been asking for negotiations, and Gorbachev had consistently refused until Lithuania recognized once more the primacy of the Soviet constitution. Prunskiene, who had been to Washington in early May and made a strong impression on Bush, Congress and the U.S. public, was from the communist wing of the Lithuanian independence movement and was more acceptable to Gorbachev than its chief, President Landsbergis. Gorbachev's May 17 meeting with Prunskiene during Baker's visit did not settle any issues, but it was the first break in the confrontation and brought an immediate easing of the international tension. Baker was pleased, though cautious. It seemed clear that the start of discussions, which the United States had been advocating, would be enough to permit Gorbachev to surmount criticism on the Lithuanian issue he was certain to face in his forthcoming visit to the United States.

In St. Catherine's Hall in the Kremlin on the morning of May 18, Baker found not only Gorbachev, Shevardnadze and Akhromeyev but two new people on the Soviet side of the table. One was Yevgeni Primakov, the foreign policy expert and member of Gorbachev's new Presidential Council. Shevardnadze had brought Primakov with him the night before when he had dined with Baker at the Moscow home of a noted Georgian artist. Rumors had been rife in Moscow for months that Primakov would replace Shevardnadze as foreign minister. Before the May meeting, Shevardnadze had acknowledged publicly that he had threatened to resign as foreign minister and as a Politburo member the previous December, when a military commander and military prosecutor had sought to cover up the truth regarding the killing of unarmed demonstrators in Shevardnadze's native Georgia eight months earlier. According to a Foreign Ministry aide, Shevardnadze had written his resignation letter and discussed it with his family. Only Gorbachev's persuasiveness and, apparently, the repudiation of the coverup at an emergency Politburo meeting had prevented him from quitting at that time.

The other new presence at the Kremlin table was Colonel General Omelichev of the General Staff. Americans at the table wondered if he would be inhibiting to Gorbachev, but as the meeting went on, this did not appear to be the case. With the military official looking on, Gorbachev and Baker engaged in old-fashioned horsetrading to settle cruise missile controversies that had suddenly reappeared since their last meeting in February.

The stickiest issue was a relatively new concern of Washington: a high-tech air-launched cruise missile known as Tacit Rainbow, which the Air Force hoped to purchase and deploy by the thousands in coming years. Although Tacit Rainbow as a long-range cruise missile would have been covered under the guidelines being negotiated, it was designed as a nonnuclear missile and the Air Force was adamant it should not be limited in a nuclear arms treaty. As part of a complex of compromises, Baker proposed and Gorbachev agreed that Tacit Rainbow be "grandfathered" under the START Treaty—in other words, excluded from coverage on the grounds that it already existed outside the treaty. Summarizing their agreement on all other points, Baker said across the table, "You've got a deal, and we close ALCMs (air-launched cruise missiles), provided that Tacit Rainbow is grandfathered." Gorbachev responded, "Yes, we've got a deal," and shook hands with the secretary of state.

When U.S. negotiators arrived at the Foreign Ministry guest house several hours later to draw up treaty language for the accord, however, they had two surprises. One was that the usual Foreign Ministry negotiators, Viktor Karpov and Yuri Nazarkin, were accompanied by General Omelichev plus two other Soviet military officers. The other was that the Soviet team now demanded new guarantees regarding Tacit Rainbow, including limitations on its future modernization and a requirement that it not be converted later to a nuclear weapon. The Americans erupted with charges of bad faith, but the Soviets stood their ground. The negotiations went on most of Friday night and into Saturday afternoon, delaying Baker's departure from Moscow. Eventually the dispute was settled with a letter from Baker to Shevardnadze describing the characteristics and limits of Tacit Rainbow without explicit promises about the future.

As Baker's Air Force plane finally flew out of Moscow headed for Andrews Air Force Base outside Washington, the secretary came back to chat with the fifteen reporters on board. He had changed from his conservative diplomatic garb into the light blue jogging suit he had come to prefer for the long airplane flights that were increasingly part of his life. He told us that Gorbachev was a man under heavy pressure, and at times it showed, but that he was still very much in charge. Paul Wolfowitz, the under secretary of defense, who had been involved in the key negotiations, told me that while Gorbachev was under tremendous strain, he remained amazingly confident. Wolfowitz thought Shevardnadze rather than Gorbachev was showing outward signs of strain and worry.

• GORBACHEV IN WASHINGTON: THE 1990 SUMMIT

The circumstances of Mikhail Gorbachev's second summit trip to Washington were very different from those of the first one twenty-nine months earlier. In December 1987 Gorbachev had still been a rising star on the world stage, full of hope and promise, and close to the high point of his popularity and unchallenged authority in the Soviet Union. By the end of May 1990 it was evident that Gorbachev's star had passed its apogee and was on its way down.

Whatever his troubles at home, however, Gorbachev continued to be admired and acclaimed by the American people. A *Washington Post*–ABC News poll taken two weeks before the 1990 summit reported that 73 percent of Americans had a favorable impression of Gorbachev, more than most presidents or other U.S. politicians can expect to enjoy, and close to the abnormally high 80 percent rating that George Bush enjoyed at that time. Perhaps more important, by mid-1990 the great mass of the American public had changed its view of the Soviet Union dramatically. In the five-year span from May 1984—near the beginning of the slow move toward improved relations—to the summer of 1989, the number of Americans who viewed the Soviet Union as "not friendly" or "an enemy" dropped from 89 percent to 49 percent, according to polls. At the same time, those who viewed the Soviet Union as "friendly" or even "a close ally" shot up from 3 to 47 percent. As Gorbachev arrived in Washington, public opinion polls indicated that three-fourths of Americans believed that the military power of the Soviet Union was a lesser threat to U.S. security than the economic power of Japan; an even greater proportion of Americans thought that the Soviet Union was a lesser threat to U.S. security than drug traffickers in South America. Many Americans, remembering the ups and downs of U.S.-Soviet relations in the past and not confident that the recent changes were permanent, continued to express a lack of trust in the Soviet Union; nevertheless, the U.S. public view was remarkably different from the deep-seated fear and antipathy of the early 1980s.

The sketchy data available from the Soviet Union strongly suggest that the public there had lost much of its fear of the United States. A scientific sample of households in two Soviet cities in 1988 reported that the Soviet public was almost equally divided between those who perceived an American threat to the USSR (46 percent) and those who believed there was no such threat (41 percent). But only one-fourth of the former group said the U.S. threat was a military one, and nearly all the rest who said there was a threat from the United States could not say what sort of threat it was.

As Gorbachev prepared for his second Washington summit, there was no mistaking the trouble he was in at home. On May 24, Prime

Minister Nikolai Ryzhkov announced details of the long-anticipated economic program intended to move the country toward a market economy, including a tripling of bread prices and increases in meat, milk and other food prices in stages beginning July 1. The public response was immediate panic buying and hoarding in Moscow and other major cities that swept the food markets bare. On May 27, the eve of his departure for a state visit to Canada en route to Washington, Gorbachev went on national television from his Kremlin office, a red Soviet flag at his side, to plead for calm. His rambling forty-eight-minute address did little to diminish the unrest. The economic program and price increases were rejected by the Supreme Soviet before they could take effect.

On May 29, the day before his arrival in Washington, Gorbachev suffered a serious political blow when the legislature of the Russian Republic, by far the Soviet Union's largest and most powerful, elected Boris Yeltsin as its president, despite strong opposition and extensive personal lobbying against him by Gorbachev. With the election of the popular and combative Yeltsin to a key post from which he could and clearly would challenge Gorbachev, the prospect of more formidable and open political opposition to the Soviet President increased dramatically.

When Gorbachev arrived, the U.S. news media was full of talk of decline and possible fall. *Newsweek*'s cover for the summit week depicted a worried Gorbachev hunkering down for shelter under a crumbling stone hammer and sickle and the big headline, "Why Gorbachev Is Failing." *The Boston Globe* carried a six-column front-page headline, "A Weakened Gorbachev Arrives in U.S."

Gorbachev's special Aeroflot plane landed at Andrews Air Force Base at 7:00 P.M. on Thursday, May 30. The U.S. welcoming party for Gorbachev and Raisa was led by Secretary of State Baker and his wife, Susan. After brief ceremonies, the two couples rode into Washington in the Soviet leader's armored Zil at the head of a forty-car motorcade. Gorbachev's troubles might have grown, but so had his entourage. He had brought 140 people to the Geneva summit, including an accompanying press corps, and close to 200 people to the first Washington summit. This time the official list provided to U.S. protocol included 360 people aboard eighteen aircraft, with eighty tons of supplies and equipment, including all the dishes, silverware and food for the Soviet Embassy dinner for Bush.

Bush welcomed Gorbachev the following day at 10:00 A.M. in a sun-drenched ceremony on the South Lawn of the White House, where

Gorbachev had said good-bye two-and-a-half years earlier to Ronald
Reagan in a December rain. The most important topics on Bush's agenda
were Germany, Lithuania and the domestic situation in the Soviet Union,
and he touched on all of them in his public welcome:

> We've seen a world of change this past year. Now on the
> horizon we see what, just one short year ago, seemed a distant
> dream: a continent cruelly divided East from West has begun to
> heal with the dawn of self-determination and democracy. In Ger-
> many, where the Wall once stood, a nation moves toward unity
> in peace and freedom. And in the other nations of the most
> heavily militarized continent on Earth, at last, we see the long
> era of confrontation giving way to the prospect of enduring co-
> operation in a Europe whole and free. Mr. President, you deserve
> great credit for your part in these transforming events. I salute
> you as well for the process of change you've brought to your own
> country. . . .
>
> Mr. President, I firmly believe, as you have said, that there
> is no turning back from the path you have chosen.
>
> Since our meeting in Malta, we've reached agreements in
> important areas—each one, proof that when mutual respect pre-
> vails, progress is possible. But the agreements reached cannot
> cause us to lose sight of some of the differences that remain.
> Lithuania is one such issue. We believe that good faith dialogue
> between the Soviet leaders and representatives of the Baltic peo-
> ples is the proper approach—and we hope to see that process
> go forward.
>
> Over the next four days, we're not going to solve all of the
> world's problems. We won't resolve all the outstanding issues
> that divide us. But we can and will take significant steps toward
> a new relationship.

For Gorbachev, who looked much older than in his last appearance
at the White House, the highest priority was a U.S.-Soviet trade agreement and U.S. help for the faltering Soviet economy. He managed to
touch on this obliquely as he responded to Bush's welcome:

> I remember well my first visit to the United States—and not
> only because I saw America for the first time then. During those

days in December, 1987, President Reagan and I signed the treaty on the elimination of INF missiles. That was truly a watershed, not only in our relations, but in the history of modern times. It was the first step taken together by two powerful countries on the road leading to a safe and sensible world..

Since then, our two great nations have traveled a long way toward each other. Thousands of American and Soviet citizens, dozens of agencies, private companies and public organizations are involved in political and business contacts, humanitarian exchanges, scientific and technological cooperation.

In the same years, the world around us has also changed beyond recognition. Mr. President, this generation of people on Earth may witness the advent of an irreversible period of peace in the history of civilization. The worlds, which for years separated the peoples, are collapsing. The trenches of the Cold War are disappearing. The fog of prejudice, mistrust and animosity is vanishing.

After the ceremony was over, Bush and Gorbachev went into the Oval Office for their first meeting, which had been planned as largely a "get reacquainted" session, but which became so intense that it went forty-five minutes over its planned ninety-minute duration. Scowcroft, who along with an interpreter was the only other U.S. participant, noticed that Bush didn't even glance at his watch until twenty minutes after the allotted time was up. In this meeting, and repeatedly in the next twenty-four hours, Gorbachev appealed to Bush to sign the U.S.-Soviet trade agreement, despite the political costs in the United States of doing so. "I need this," Gorbachev said bluntly.

Bush, in his April 30 letter, had told Gorbachev that it would be difficult to sign a trade agreement with the Soviet Union while the Soviet economic embargo of Lithuania continued. On May 1, as if to underscore the point, the Senate had asked Bush by a seventy-three to twenty-four vote not to send up the trade pact to Capitol Hill for approval as long as Lithuania was being blockaded. When Baker was in Moscow in mid-May, he had told Shevardnadze and Gorbachev not to expect signing of the trade agreement at the summit. On the eve of the summit the same message had been passed again from the State Department to Aleksandr Bessmertnykh, who had replaced Yuri Dubinin as Soviet ambassador to Washington. Nonetheless, Gorbachev persisted in appealing for the trade pact almost from the time he landed in Washington. It was the one thing under discussion that might make a substantial favorable impact at home. While he refused to promise that the embargo against Lithuania would be lifted, he did tell Bush, as he had told Baker in Moscow, that he did not intend to use force against the breakaway republic and that he hoped the crisis could be settled through dialogue.

Following the meeting with Bush, Gorbachev returned to the Soviet Embassy to host a luncheon meeting for what the Embassy described as "American intellectuals and opinion leaders," an eclectic group that included Gregory Peck, Douglas Fairbanks, Jr., and Jane Fonda, as well as Henry Kissinger, John Kenneth Galbraith and science fiction authors Ray Bradbury and Isaac Asimov. Movie stars had been invited because word had arrived from Moscow that Raisa would like to meet some. Bradbury and Asimov were there because they were the favorite writers of the Gorbachevs' daughter, Irina. As in 1987, Gorbachev sought through his meetings with Americans to promote his leadership and the cause of *perestroika*. This time a dark note of trouble mingled with bright promise in Gorbachev's passionate extemporaneous oratory, and he cautioned—as he had privately to Bush—against seeking to put pressure on "a weakened Soviet Union." He spoke at some length of his efforts to stem the panic of the previous week at home and of the agony of introducing a market economy. "Frankly speaking, everything now comes up against people's unpreparedness for great changes. A revolution in people's minds must take place," Gorbachev declared.

The summit's most extensive discussion of its most urgent subject, the future of Germany, took place late that afternoon in the Cabinet Room of the White House. Bush and his aides had carefully prepared for it, believing this to be a crucial moment in the drive to obtain Soviet acquiescence in the Western plan to anchor a unified Germany in the NATO security alliance. Expecting serious objections from Gorbachev, Bush had decided to raise the issue early, so that if progress seemed possible, there would be time for further discussion and, if not, the disagreement could be put aside as the summit moved on to more productive topics.

Since the "Two Plus Four" mechanism had been approved in Ottawa on February 13, German developments had raced ahead in quickstep. Bush and Chancellor Helmut Kohl had solidified their alliance in a late February weekend at Camp David, and on March 18 East Germans had given their votes overwhelmingly to Kohl's conservative Christian Democrats, who favored speedy unification. It was the first free election in that part of Germany since Adolf Hitler had come to power in 1933. The reformed communist party won only 16 percent of the vote. Armed with this mandate and alarmed by the collapsing economy, the new East German government had begun moving rapidly toward unification. Meanwhile, Bush had discussed international strategy regarding Germany in meetings with British Prime Minister Margaret Thatcher in Bermuda and French President François Mitterrand in Florida. In early May, the foreign ministers of the two Germanys and the four wartime allies, including the Soviets, had met in Bonn in the first "Two Plus Four" ministerial session to begin discussing the external aspects of unification. Kohl had visited Washington again in the middle of May, and Baker had discussed Germany with Shevardnadze and Gorbachev during his trip to Moscow.

Through all this activity, the Soviet position had seemed to be shifting with, and sometimes against, the wind. Gorbachev had moved by fits and starts to accept the inevitability of early unification, but the issue of a unified Germany in the NATO alliance was more difficult and much more painful. At various times Moscow said that a united Germany should be neutral, that unified German participation in NATO was "absolutely ruled out," that a unified Germany might be part of both NATO and the Warsaw Pact, or that the two Germanys could be united domestically but subject to external controls by the World War II allies for a lengthy transitional period. When Shevardnadze was in Washington in April, he had agreed in meetings with Baker that neutrality was not the answer, but had continued to resist incorporation of the new Germany in NATO. Conservatives in Moscow, who had started a drumfire of criticism against the loss of Eastern Europe and the potential threat of a new Germany, were clearly part of the problem.

In the Cabinet Room discussion, Bush and, in more detail, Baker presented Gorbachev with a list of nine commitments to the Soviet Union, intended to make Germany's inclusion in NATO easier for Moscow to accept. The "nine assurances," as they came to be known, were essentially restatements of existing policy that had already been adopted by the United States, West Germany or NATO. They ranged from commitments to leave Soviet forces in East Germany and not to extend NATO forces to that area during a transition period, to firm German commitments not to expand Germany's borders, and West German economic support for *perestroika*, an item of great importance to Moscow. The nine points had been drawn up at the suggestion of State Department Counselor Robert Zoellick, Baker's staff-level coordinator for the "Two Plus Four" diplomacy, on the theory that packaging these commitments and presenting them to Moscow would signal U.S. seriousness about meeting Soviet concerns. Baker had already presented them in sketchy fashion to Gorbachev and Shevardnadze in Moscow, and Zoellick had given them to midlevel Soviet diplomats, but it was hoped that a display of Bush's personal concern for Soviet fears—and an assurance that U.S. policy was not directed against the Soviet Union—would have an effect on Gorbachev.

In what was later described as a rambling and disjointed presentation, Gorbachev seemed to reject the U.S. position. NATO membership for a united Germany would "unbalance" Europe, and it was very important that Europe not be unbalanced, the Soviet leader said. One suggestion from Gorbachev was that a united Germany should be "anchored" in both NATO and the Warsaw Pact. "You are a sailor," he said to Bush. "You will understand that if one anchor is good, two anchors are better." Bush responded that it was precisely because he did not see how such a plan could work that he wanted to persuade Gorbachev that a united Germany should be in NATO. Another Gorbachev suggestion was that a political relationship between NATO and the Warsaw Pact might help resolve Germany's future. Baker agreed to follow up on that, but without optimism that it would make a major difference.

Gorbachev also said in a casual, jocular way that perhaps the Soviet Union would apply to join NATO, which had been its nemesis throughout the Cold War. Bush responded that the NATO supreme commander had always been an American, and wondered how Marshal Akhromeyev, who was sitting at the Cabinet Room table, would like serving under an American general.

The most significant exchange came when Bush said that under the CSCE (Helsinki Act) guidelines, nations had the right to choose their own external alliances. Gorbachev responded matter-of-factly that indeed this was so. This comment prompted questioning glances from some of the officials on the Soviet side of the table, and a note to Bush from Robert Blackwill, the senior aide for European affairs on the National Security Council staff, urging Bush to confirm Gorbachev's remark. "I'm gratified that you and I seem to agree that nations can choose their own alliances," Bush said. Surprisingly, Gorbachev not only agreed but sought to establish clearly that the United States was willing to abide by this principle. "It was a curious kind of anomaly, because on the one hand Gorbachev was seizing on it as if he'd discovered the Holy Grail," according to an American official who was present. "On the other hand, it was exactly what we thought was the pathway out" of the confrontation as a unified German state simply continued its alliance with NATO. An excited Bush telephoned Chancellor Kohl in Bonn immediately after the meeting with Gorbachev.

On his way back to the Soviet Embassy from the White House, Gorbachev stopped his Zil and the heavily guarded motorcade and plunged into a crowd of tourists and office workers for a spontaneous round of handshaking on the order of his 1987 crowd-pleasing stop. Despite all the talk that Washington was blasé this time around, the hundreds of people near Gorbachev jumped up and down, screamed and shoved to get close to him. Esther Koebler, a Salvadoran hair stylist, told Gorbachev, "You are a courageous man," and she hoped he would bring peace to El Salvador. Others just shook hands or shouted "Good luck." For his part, the Soviet President told the crowd through his interpreter, "I feel really at home here. I feel that people everywhere want the good life."

Gorbachev returned to the White House on a balmy evening for the most glittering state dinner of the year, given in his honor in the State Dining Room. In his dinner toast, he referred to the "long and difficult road, which led from Geneva, via Reykjavik, Washington, Moscow and New York to Malta, and now, once again to Washington."

> Today, I would like to repeat here what I said to the President six months ago at Malta: the Soviet Union does not regard the United States as its enemy. We have firmly adopted the policy of moving from mutual understanding, through cooperation, to joint action.
>
> Today, when I was meeting some American intellectuals at the Soviet Embassy, I said to them this: yes, indeed, we used to be enemies or almost enemies. Now we are, maybe, rivals, at least to some extent, and we want to become partners. We want to go all the way and become friends.

Friday, the second day of the summit, began for Gorbachev with a 9:30 A.M. breakfast for congressional leaders at the Soviet Embassy. After a welcome and brief introduction, the doors were closed and the pool of reporters was ushered out. Gorbachev suggested he would be more candid when the press departed; it was unclear whether he realized that the Soviet Embassy was permitting his remarks and those of his twelve guests during the entire meeting to be broadcast live by Cable News Network. Certainly the senators and representatives did not know that the meeting was being televised, and were startled to learn it later. The Soviet President was remarkably frank, telling the lawmakers that the Soviet Union felt "that we are being squeezed out" of Europe and that "pressure is being applied to us for a unilateral advantage of the other side." Should an imbalance develop in Europe—he clearly had in mind the adherence of a unified Germany to NATO—the Soviet Union would have to "reconsider" and "reassess" its arms control positions.

The Soviet President spent much time outlining the dismal economic situation at home, where he said subsidies kept the price of bread so low that children played ball with it and cattle were fed with it. Yet even the promise of price rises had caused a run on the markets and near riots. "We have dismantled the old system but we have not yet put in place a working system, a new system. Our ship has lost anchor and therefore we're all a little sick," Gorbachev admitted.

The American press, he observed, was saying, "Gorbachev compared to any other Soviet leader has come to Washington very weak and he will not get anything." After declaring he was not going to ask for anything, not to beg for anything, he nevertheless asked the lawmakers forthrightly for "a favorable gesture from the U.S. Congress on trade." Approval of the U.S.-Soviet trade agreement or even the granting of most-favored-nation trade benefits to the USSR would not bring tangible results quickly because "the trade relationship now between us is very primitive." But in an appeal that the congressional leaders could identify with, Gorbachev declared, "I think it is very important that you make this gesture mostly from a political standpoint."

Back at the White House, Bush, watching with fascination on CNN as Gorbachev made his trade appeal, was impressed with how much it meant to the Soviet leader. In addition to asking Bush for the trade agreement in their initial meeting Thursday morning, Gorbachev had also brought it up in a private conversation with Bush just before the State Dinner that night. Second- and third-level Soviet officials—but not Gorbachev—were beginning to tell Americans that if the trade pact were not signed, the Soviet Union might not go ahead with the scheduled signing Friday afternoon of the new Long-Term Grain Agreement authorizing expanded Soviet purchases of U.S. grain, an accord of great interest to U.S. farmers.

Publicly and privately, Bush had tied signing the trade agreement to the Soviet sanctions against Lithuania, while the most-favored-nation trade benefits that would flow from the pact were tied to a longstanding U.S. requirement that the Soviet Union enact into law the more lenient policies on emigration it had been following. In Lithuania, the economic blockade was still in place, and no assurances that it would be lifted had been provided by Gorbachev. The emigration legislation was stuck in the Supreme Soviet, which had unexpectedly postponed action on it shortly before Gorbachev's trip to Washington.

Nevertheless, Bush was concerned about the difficult spot Gorbachev was in domestically and impressed by the urgency of his plea for the trade agreement. Bush saw the force of the argument that Lithuania could obtain its independence only through the sufferance of Gorbachev and therefore it was in Lithuania's interest to support him.

When Gorbachev came to the White House at 11:00 A.M., Bush told him he was exploring the possibility of signing the trade agreement that afternoon, but he repeated that it would very difficult to obtain congressional approval without an easing of the Lithuanian crisis. Bush instructed aides to sound out the congressional leaders who had been at the Soviet Embassy about their probable reaction if the President went ahead to sign the trade agreement. Ten of the twelve lawmakers who had met Gorbachev were reached; some supported signing the trade deal, but others expressed reservations. Opinion inside the administration was also divided. Bush's key economic officials were in favor of moving ahead with the greatest speed possible to normalize U.S.-Soviet trade relations; other officials were concerned about the political impact, mindful of the overwhelming Senate vote tying the trade agreement to Lithuania. In midafternoon, after a telephone conversation with Baker, who favored signing the trade pact, Bush decided to go ahead with it. Negotiations with Gorbachev and Shevardnadze ensued, right down to almost the moment of signing, about the conditions that would be placed publicly by Bush on the trade agreement, with the Soviet leader strongly resisting any explicit link to the Lithuanian issue.

While Bush and Gorbachev were discussing trade and other issues, their wives were on their way to commencement exercises at Wellesley College near Boston, where Barbara Bush had agreed to speak. The event had been in the news for weeks because of a student petition at the predominantly female college protesting that the First Lady was chosen not for her own achievements, but because of her husband. Mrs. Bush, who had dropped out of Smith College at the end of her freshman year to get married, was undaunted by the bad publicity. With Raisa Gorbachev at her side, she won thunderous cheers at the campus appearance. Mrs. Bush spoke in a warm and affecting way of human values and the importance of family; Mrs. Gorbachev made a speech of her own on *perestroika* and the role of women. Unlike the chilly relationship between Raisa Gorbachev and Nancy Reagan, Mrs. Gorbachev and Mrs. Bush seemed at ease with each other from the first. The two held hands during the introductions at Wellesley and Mrs. Gorbachev leaned over several times during the ceremony to grasp Mrs. Bush's hand.

In the morning meetings at the White House, the two presidents had been unable to reach agreement on several outstanding nuclear arms provisions of the START Treaty or on the details of a joint statement aimed at setting the broad guidelines for a future START II Treaty. In an effort to salvage the strategic arms accords, Baker and Shevardnadze and their teams of arms control specialists began meeting at 2:30 P.M. in Baker's seventh-floor Conference Room at the State Department. The aim was to resolve the differences so that agreements could be announced at the scheduled 5:00 P.M. White House ceremony. But with the Soviet General Staff participating in the person of Colonel General Omelichev, the battle raged all afternoon, well past the designated time. The negotiators finally agreed to disagree on some START I issues and adopted vague wording regarding START II that left key issues essentially unresolved.

Suspense was high as the U.S. and Soviet delegations, members of Congress and other guests assembled in the East Room at 6:00 P.M., an hour after the originally scheduled time for the ceremony. At the last minute, Baker and several other officials were called from the room to join Bush, Gorbachev and Shevardnadze. "Are we going to sign the trade agreement?" Gorbachev wanted to know. Bush said, yes, the signing would take place. The U.S. President, in view of Gorbachev's strong feelings, had agreed to put no Lithuania-related conditions on signing the trade agreement, but said he would not send it to Congress for approval until the Supreme Soviet passed its emigration law. By then, it was hoped, the Lithuanian issue would be resolved. The trade agreement decisions were so hurried and so late that it was discovered only at the last minute that the U.S.-Soviet pact itself had never been brought to the White House for signing; an aide rushed over from the Commerce Department with the document just before the ceremony.

Finally at 6:13 P.M., Bush and Gorbachev walked into the East Room, where Reagan and Gorbachev had signed the INF Treaty twenty-nine months earlier. This time there was a profusion of accords to sign and statements to be formally adopted. None was as momentous as the treaty banning intermediate-range nuclear missiles, but taken together they represented further steps to advance U.S.-Soviet relations along a very broad front that could hardly have been imagined during the tense days of 1983 and 1984, before Gorbachev came to power.

. The two that were under negotiation down to the wire were the trade agreement and joint statements summing up the progress that had been made on the strategic arms treaty and promising deeper cuts in a successor treaty. The others, most of which had been prepared in advance, included:

- A U.S.-Soviet agreement to destroy 80 percent of their chemical weapons stocks and push toward a worldwide chemical weapons ban that would eliminate the rest.

- Protocols to the 1974 and 1976 nuclear testing treaties that would permit Senate ratification at last. (The Senate ratified the two treaties unanimously on September 25, 1990.)

- An agreement on expanded university student exchanges.

- An agreement on increased cooperation in exploring peaceful uses of atomic energy.

- A joint statement pledging to speed negotiations on a treaty reducing conventional land armies in Europe so that it could be signed by the end of the year. (The Conventional Forces in Europe Treaty was signed by twenty-two nations in Paris on November 19, 1990.)

- A joint statement declaring their intention to create a large international park on Alaskan and Siberian land along the Bering Strait, which separates the two nations.

Baker and Shevardnadze or other officials also signed eight more agreements: expanding civil aviation (and thus undoing the limited sanctions against Aeroflot adopted by Reagan after the shooting down of Korean Air Lines Flight 007); opening new cities to maritime transport between the two nations; resolving the longstanding dispute over the maritime boundary between the two nations; renewing programs of joint oceanographic studies; providing for increased cooperation of customs services to deter narcotics trafficking and fraud; expanding Soviet purchases of U.S. grain; establishing new cultural centers in each other's capital; and increasing the circulation of the official magazines permitted to circulate in each other's country.

After listing the agreements to be signed or issued with Gorbachev, Bush took the microphone:

> Not long ago, some believed that the weight of history condemned our two great countries, our two great peoples, to permanent confrontation. Well, you and I must challenge history, make new strides, build a relationship of enduring cooperation.
>
> We may not agree on everything, and indeed we don't agree on everything, but we believe in one great truth: the world has waited long enough; the Cold War must end. And so today with gratitude in my heart for all those on the Soviet side and on the United States side that worked so hard at all levels to bring these agreements to fruition, I say let's renew our pledge and build a more peaceful world.

Gorbachev, in turn, took note of the surroundings and U.S. history in his remarks:

> This room has seen many important events and many agreements signed, but I think that what is happening now and what you have listed as the results of our work together represents an event of momentous importance not only for our own countries, but for the world.
>
> President Franklin D. Roosevelt half a century ago spoke of a world in which four essential freedoms will triumph: freedom of speech, freedom of worship, freedom from want, and freedom from fear. And this ideal has not yet been attained in the world and it could not be attained in the world of animosity and confrontation. And therefore, while liberating the world from fear,

we are making steps towards a new world. And this is the important work of our two nations, of our two peoples.

With the major ceremonies of the summit at an end, the Americans were guests at Gorbachev's return dinner at the Soviet Embassy Friday night and prepared for the discussions Saturday at the presidential retreat at Camp David. Bush considered the Camp David talks to be potentially the most important aspect of the summit.

The President had previously hosted Kohl, Thatcher, Mitterrand and other Western leaders either at Camp David or at his Kennebunkport home. Such visits in unofficial and informal settings were Bush's way of creating personal relationships with other major heads of state, in the belief that such personal ties could be crucial at moments of decision. The President had been trying since his invitation to Gorbachev the previous July to create such a setting with the Soviet leader. Malta, due in part to the weather, was less than a success in this respect.

The first Soviet leader to be invited to Camp David, Nikita Khrushchev, was initially insulted by the invitation, not having heard of the place and fearing that it was a camp somewhere outside Washington where visitors who were not accorded full honors were quarantined. When Khrushchev learned that it was a mark of distinction to be received at the personal "dacha" of the President, where visitors were rarely admitted, he accepted President Eisenhower's 1959 invitation. However, there was still uncertainty about the helicopter ride from the White House to the Catoctin Mountain retreat, because Soviet security frowned on their General Secretary traveling in helicopters, which they considered of doubtful safety—especially American helicopters. But when Khrushchev learned that Eisenhower would be along on the ride, he accepted that too. He was so entranced with the chopper ride, according to a Soviet diplomat, that he later insisted on traveling by helicopter from his dacha outside Moscow to his office at Central Committee headquarters. After a single ride, the security officials stepped in to forbid it.

When the 1990 summit was being planned, the White House sent a proposed program to Gorbachev that included a stay at Camp David with Bush and helicopter rides to and from the presidential retreat. When the Soviet version of the program came back from Moscow, Camp David had been omitted. Bush, who was greatly disappointed, was uncertain about the reason, and there was speculation in the administration's inner circles that Gorbachev did not wish to take time out to relax or perhaps to be seen enjoying a degree of informality and intimacy with the U.S. President. It turned out, according to a Soviet official involved in setting up the program, that once more Soviet security had objected to the Kremlin leader flying in a helicopter to and from the presidential retreat. The authorities in Moscow suggested that perhaps Gorbachev could go by road, but relented after learning that the road trip would take more than two hours instead of the twenty-minute chopper ride and that, as with the case of Eisenhower and Khrushchev, the U.S. President would be in the helicopter with Gorbachev.

On Saturday morning, Gorbachev rode to the White House in his Zil and then accompanied Bush onto Marine One, the President's helicopter, which was waiting for them on the South Lawn of the White House. Barbara Bush and Raisa Gorbachev followed in a separate helicopter. As they flew over some of the pricey Washington suburbs en route to the nearby Catoctin Mountains, Gorbachev looked down at big houses with swimming pools, some with tennis courts, and he wondered how much such houses cost and who lived there. He quickly decided these were not homes at prices Soviet citizens could afford, and he understood from Bush there were not many of them. The look at wealthy suburbs was at least the partial fulfillment of a recurrent dream of Ronald Reagan: to take a Soviet leader on a helicopter tour over the great expanse of American neighborhoods. Reagan, who never managed the feat, felt certain that it would have proven to his guest beyond doubt the superiority of the capitalist system.

At Camp David the two wives went off hand-in-hand over the walking trails amid the stands of oak, chestnut and hickory trees. Bush and Gorbachev, with Baker and Shevardnadze as their seconds and Scowcroft and Akhromeyev as their note-takers, settled down around the glass-topped table on the outdoor deck of Aspen Lodge, the presidential living quarters, overlooking the woods and a putting green. The Americans were wearing blazers and slacks, the Soviets business suits, but at the President's suggestion everyone removed his tie and coat to enjoy the mountain air in the mid-seventies on a perfect day. The subject for discussion was the various bloody conflicts in the Third World, a topic that had been squeezed out for lack of time at the White House. It was an incongruous setting to speak of wars and revolutions, but the two leaders and their foreign ministers warmed to the task. Scowcroft felt he could almost see Bush and Gorbachev relax little by little in response to the atmosphere of Camp David and of the emerging feelings of trust and friendship between them.

The discussions were made easier by developments in Nicaragua.

Violeta Chamorro had unexpectedly beaten Daniel Ortega in the February 27 presidential election, and her conservative coalition had taken over the government from the Sandinistas. Both the United States and the Soviet Union had agreed in advance to accept the results of a fair election, and Moscow had kept its word. Soviet military supplies to Cuba continued to be a sore subject for Bush, but at Camp David Gorbachev went part of the way toward satisfying the U.S. President by saying that Moscow was going to reduce the subsidies that aided Fidel Castro's regime. In the months thereafter, the subsidies declined.

Gorbachev, for his part, was feeling less apprehensive about the future of Afghanistan fifteen months after the withdrawal of Soviet troops, but he was still eager to bring the civil war to an end. Neither side changed its position, but the focus on a transitional process suggested that hope was still alive for an eventual accord.

The relaxed and far-ranging regional discussions lasted all morning and then resumed for several hours after lunch. Dennis Ross, the State Department policy planning chief and right hand to Baker on Soviet affairs, was called in for expert information. It seemed to him the U.S. and Soviet leaders were really "schmoozing" in a way that he had never seen them do before and in a way that their predecessors had never been able to do. Reagan had not been conversant with the details of international affairs. Before him, even during the brief flowering of détente in the early 1970s, the relationships had been too tense and confrontational. Now Bush, Gorbachev, Baker and Shevardnadze seemed to Ross to be swapping ideas without inhibitions or pretense, a real leveling with one another, that he felt could lead in time to something close to partnership in the management of difficult problems.

After the discussions, Gorbachev and his wife, on a stroll around Camp David, came to a horseshoe pit where Bush often played one of his favorite games. The Soviet leader idly picked up one of Bush's horseshoes and, to everyone's amazement, tossed a ringer on his first try.

The neckties were still off for the informal dinner at 6:00 P.M. around a big E-shaped table in Laurel Lodge. George and Barbara Bush and fifteen Americans from the senior ranks of the U.S. government were hosts to Mikhail and Raisa Gorbachev and fourteen senior Soviets. During the social hour before the dinner, Gorbachev seemed in high spirits, going from group to group, chatting in an unusually animated way. To Scowcroft, he seemed almost serene about his problems at home, not at all preoccupied or defeated by them. Ordinarily, Gorbachev did not strike Scowcroft as a serene person. During this 1990 trip of Gorbachev to the United States, several other Americans who saw him at close range used the same word, *serene*, to describe him.

In his toast to Gorbachev in Laurel Lodge, Bush said the day at Camp David had been important to the relationship of the two men and their nations. But, Bush added, "This isn't going to be all sweetness and light. I am a sportsman, a real competitor. I like to win." Then, announcing Gorbachev's beginner's luck at horseshoes several hours earlier, the President said it had been hard to imagine that Mikhail, as he called him, could score ahead of him in one of his own favorite games. He reached under the dinner table and presented to Gorbachev a wooden plaque on which Navy personnel at Camp David had mounted the horseshoe that he had used to throw the ringer.

Gorbachev seemed moved by the day's intimacy and by Bush's presentation of the plaque. In an emotional toast, the Soviet President said that in his country, a horseshoe mounted over a door signified good luck. Raising his newly acquired trophy, Gorbachev declared, "May this one be over the door of your house and my house and over the door of the American people and give us good fortune."

Gorbachev had declined Bush's offer to stay at Camp David overnight, so the leaders flew back to Washington after dinner to prepare for the final event of the summit, a joint press conference at the White House Sunday morning. Gorbachev met with the Soviet traveling party at the Soviet Embassy and said he was very satisfied with the day.

The two difficult topics of Germany and Lithuania had hardly been mentioned at Camp David except for the briefest of conversations when White House Press Secretary Marlin Fitzwater had informed the leaders that those topics were likely to dominate their Sunday joint press conference. Bush's National Security Council staff had drawn up his opening statement for the press conference in advance, and gave a copy of it at Camp David to Soviet Ambassador Aleksandr Bessmertnykh as a courtesy to Gorbachev. Buried within it, and reflecting the White House conversation of Thursday afternoon, was the assertion by Bush that he and Gorbachev were "in full agreement that the matter of [German] alliance membership is, in accordance with the Helsinki Final Act, a matter for the Germans to decide." The Americans believed that such a position would lead inevitably to a united Germany in NATO, and they were not certain that on reflection Gorbachev would accept it.

Condoleezza Rice, the NSC's Soviet expert, anxiously waited late into the night Saturday to see if the Soviets would object to the statement. At 1:00 A.M. she called her boss, NSC European affairs chief Robert Blackwill, to say, "I haven't heard from them yet—have you?" Bessmertnykh called Blackwill early Sunday morning to say they had no objection to Bush's planned remarks.

The joint press conference in the East Room at 10:00 A.M. Sunday was the last event of the summit—an event that was far more notable for what was implied than for what was said. With the exception of Bush's opening remark about the nature of the decision on Germany's alliances—a remark that no questioner sought to amplify or explore— there was little that was new in the leaders' comments on Germany, Europe, the Baltic states or other international issues. Gorbachev, asked by a Soviet journalist, bristled at Boris Yeltsin's "destructive efforts" against him, but otherwise repeated known positions.

The new development arising from the summit was that the relationship of Bush and Gorbachev had become much more personal and much closer. The political and military walls had gone down between the East and West in Europe, and now it was evident that personal walls had come down between the leaders of the United States and the Soviet Union. Their enhanced rapport was on display in their remarks about each other and the obvious warmth that implied something much more than official relations.

"We spent many hours together and were able to come to know each other very well. . . . Now we have a good human relationship and, I think, a good human atmosphere between us," Gorbachev said. Neatly reversing what had been said about the Soviet leader as he came to power, Gorbachev observed he had decided during the 1987 Washington summit that Bush was "the kind of person to do business with, to build our relations with." He traced their subsequent meetings through Governors Island in New York Harbor in December 1988, and on board ship at Malta in December 1989, to the intimate gathering at Camp David the previous day—meetings that were "a great accomplishment in and by themselves." The rapport that developed between him and Bush, Gorbachev said, "will be very important."

"We've moved a long, long way from the depths of the Cold War," said Bush. "We could never have had the discussions at Camp David yesterday, or as we sat in the Oval Office a couple of days before with President Gorbachev, 20 years ago. . . . There's been [a] dramatic move."

Later that day I discussed the contrast between the greatly improved personal relations and disappointing lack of substantive accomplishment with several White House and State Department officials. The two most analytical officials, Brent Scowcroft and Assistant Secretary of State Raymond Seitz, both predicted that the personal understanding that had been created would be more important in the end than the substantive positions taken. This sort of closeness was not possible before, and it is "likely to pay off down the road," said Scowcroft, although he was unable to say just how or when. Seitz said that the most significant development of the summit had been the emergence of "an identity of purpose" between the two sides to work on issues constructively when they could agree and with the minimum damage possible when their positions clashed. Nobody I interviewed was able to say what Gorbachev would do next, but there was an expectation, even modest confidence, that his trust in Bush would make a difference.

A Soviet shift on German policy would come more quickly than anyone expected, on the evening of May 5, two days after Gorbachev left Washington. In a meeting with Baker in Copenhagen on the fringes of a CSCE foreign ministers' meeting, Shevardnadze said for the first time that the German issues could be solved by the end of the year if a limitation on the military forces of a united Germany could be worked out. Shevardnadze told Baker that, under these conditions, "A Germany in NATO would be a Germany that the Soviet Union could have good relations with, and would in fact have good relations with." A euphoric Baker telephoned Genscher at his hotel in Helsinki to tell him of Shevardnadze's remarks, but the West German foreign minister was asleep. Baker asked that his staff wake him up while he dashed over to Genscher's hotel to give him the news. Later there was hedging and some backtracking along with promising advances, but in the end the new Soviet position stuck. When Chancellor Kohl met Gorbachev in Moscow and the Soviet leader's home town of Stavropol on July 15, Gorbachev dropped his opposition to a united Germany's remaining in the NATO alliance. "Whether we like it or not, the time will come when a united Germany will be in NATO, if that is its choice. Then, if that is its choice, to some degree and in some form, it can work together with the Soviet Union," Gorbachev announced.

Movement on the Lithuanian issue, though less decisive in the long run, would also come within weeks of the Washington summit. On June 26, Gorbachev met Lithuanian President Landsbergis, and later that day outlined a compromise Kremlin position in the dispute. At Prunskiene's urging, the Lithuanian legislature voted on June 29 to suspend its declaration of independence for one hundred days after the start of negotiations with Moscow over its future. The following day, Gorbachev lifted the ten-week-old economic embargo against the breakaway republic.

None of this had been promised or outlined to Bush during the Washington and Camp David conversations, but the President and others were certain that Bush's new relationship with Gorbachev had played a role.

An hour after the end of the joint press conference in the East Room, Presidents Bush and Gorbachev emerged from the White House side by side, followed by their wives, who strolled arm-in-arm. The two couples walked on a red carpet with gold trim through the door of the North Portico, facing Pennsylvania Avenue, past a U.S. color guard drawn from the Army, Navy, Air Force and Marines, carrying fixed bayonets and U.S. and Soviet flags. The two presidents shook hands. Behind them, the two first ladies embraced and then kissed each other on both cheeks, followed by a long handshake. Raisa shook hands with the U.S. President, and Barbara with the Soviet President. Then the visitors descended the steps to their long black Zil. "Good-bye, good luck," Bush called out as the Soviet couple settled into the limousine. The President and Mrs. Bush waved from the edge of the red carpet on their front porch, leaning forward as if to prolong the visit for a few more seconds, as the big Soviet car rolled away.

The Zil took the Gorbachevs to the Washington Monument grounds behind the White House. There four U.S. Marine helicopters were waiting to take the Soviet party to Andrews Air Force Base, and on by Aeroflot to Minneapolis and San Francisco before leaving for home. Baker and Shevardnadze had arrived at the helicopter site shortly before Gorbachev. "I think they were good meetings," said Baker. "You have any doubts?" Shevardnadze responded. Susan Baker and the Bakers' thirteen-year-old daughter, Bonner, came along to say good-bye. Shevardnadze shook hands with the young girl and then, on impulse, embraced her and kissed her on the forehead.

After the twenty-one-gun salute from Army howitzers just beyond the Washington Monument on the Mall, Gorbachev crossed the street to wave at a cheering crowd being held behind police lines, many waving small Soviet flags. There were more handshakes and waves, and the big olive green helicopters lifted off.

10. The End of the Soviet Union

The second half of 1990 and the year 1991 saw sudden developments that brought an end to the Cold War and dramatically
altered the global landscape. Faced with Iraq's invasion of Kuwait
in August 1990, the United States and the Soviet Union acted in
concert to resolve a military crisis for the first time since they had
battled common foes in World War II. Their tacit alliance made
possible the formation of a wall-to-wall coalition to oppose Iraq
and eased the way for the United States to deploy half a million
troops close to Soviet borders and eventually reverse the invasion
by the application of massive force. These developments gave rise
to hopes for a New World Order in which the two nuclear
superpowers would stand together to face down international
troublemakers.

In Moscow, Mikhail Gorbachev was enmeshed in an increasingly intense domestic struggle that culminated in August 1991 in a
coup d'état planned and executed by the principal officials of his
own government, including some of those who had been close to
him for many years. The coup failed to depose Gorbachev, but the
dramatic struggle unexpectedly empowered democratic forces led
by Russian Republic President Boris Yeltsin and loosed anew the
centrifugal tendencies of the multinational Soviet state. A weakened Gorbachev fought tirelessly but unsuccessfully to reverse the

tide. He was left virtually a president without a country as the Union of Soviet Socialist Republics passed into history at the end of 1991.

On August 2, 1990, three months after Gorbachev had waved goodbye to Washington at the completion of a successful summit meeting, Iraqi troops and tanks invaded Kuwait. Although Iraqi President Saddam Hussein's audacious act caught most of the world by surprise, his badly chosen timing made U.S.-Soviet collaboration against him more likely. On the day of the invasion, Secretary of State James Baker was at Lake Baikol in Siberia in his eleventh meeting with Foreign Minister Eduard Shevardnadze, who was playing host to reciprocate for U.S. hospitality at the very successful Wyoming ministerial meeting the previous year. In the midst of the conversations, Baker received a CIA report that an invasion of Kuwait was imminent, and he asked Shevardnadze to intercede with the Iraqis to stop it. His counterpart communicated with Moscow and reported back, "We've checked with our intelligence sources; it would be completely irrational for Saddam Hussein to do this. It's not going to happen. Don't worry about it."

Two hours later, as their meetings were ending, Baker was handed a one-page message from Washington stating that the invasion had begun. "Shevardnadze was thunderstruck, embarrassed for being misled by his own intelligence services and enraged by the lunacy of the deed itself," Baker recalled. He became convinced that Shevardnadze's anger at being led astray contributed to his determination to work with the United States to reverse the invasion. Baker decided to continue with a long-planned trip from Siberia to newly democratic Mongolia—if only on a truncated basis. However, Baker aides Dennis Ross and Robert Zoellick flew to Moscow on Shevardnadze's aircraft and began working with the foreign minister and his top assistant, Sergei Tarasenko, on a possible joint statement to be issued by the United States and Soviet Union opposing the invasion.

For Moscow, the complications were enormous. Since the Iraqi revolution of 1958 that overthrew its monarchy, Iraq had been the Soviet Union's closest ally in the strategic Persian Gulf and one of its most important weapons customers. Since the early 1980s, Moscow had sold $25 billion in weapons to Iraq, including advanced warplanes, attack helicopters, SCUD missiles, tanks, and artillery. While independent-minded Iraq did not share Soviet ideology, it had a Soviet-style Peace and Friendship treaty making it an official ally of Moscow, and it had relied on the KGB to organize its secret police, on the Soviet military to advise its armed forces, and on Soviet technicians to help develop its civil infrastructure and small arms industry. At the time of the invasion, 8,000 Soviet citizens, including advisors and their families, were living in Iraq, which made them potential hostages if relations between the two countries suddenly turned sour. For Gorbachev and Shevardnadze, lining up with the West against Iraq was all the more difficult because they had acquiesced in the dramatic transformation of Eastern Europe and, just the month before, had accepted the reunified Germany's inclusion in NATO. As a result they were under strong pressure from military, diplomatic, and intelligence elites not to surrender additional alliances. At the same time, the Soviet Union had decisively opted for Western standards of international conduct and morality. And with his economy reeling and his policies under increasing attack, Gorbachev needed political support and economic assistance from the West more than ever.

The decline of Soviet power, ironically, helped to make possible Saddam Hussein's cross-border adventure. In the Cold War era, the Soviet Union would have been more diligent in discerning Iraqi intentions and would have exercised a greater degree of influence over Baghdad, if for no other reason than to avoid a risky conflict with the United States, which probably would have seen the invasion as an extension of Soviet hegemony in a highly sensitive area. Six months before Iraq's attack, Saddam told visiting U.S. Assistant Secretary of State John Kelly that Moscow was "finished as a world power," leaving Washington "a free hand" to maneuver in the Gulf. Saddam also increasingly believed that since neither the Soviet Union nor the United States seemed to be paying much attention, he also had a free hand to do as he pleased.

On vacation at Foros, his dacha on the Black Sea, Gorbachev uttered an unprintable epithet when informed of the Iraqi invasion but left details of the official Soviet reaction largely to Shevardnadze. Assembling a meeting of Foreign Ministry department heads, Shevardnadze found no support for the proposal to make a joint statement with the United States. After the meeting, the chief of the ministry's Middle East department seized Tarasenko by the lapels, shoved him into a corner, and demanded to know what he would do if a school bus full of Soviet children living in Iraq were attacked by a mob as a result of the Soviet-American statement, saying, "Sergei, tomorrow if that happens, I will give your telephone number (to Soviet families) and you will explain to parents what happened to their kids."

Ross, with Baker's approval, was pressing Shevardnadze for a statement with teeth in it, specifically the announcement of a joint arms embargo against Iraq, which would be a tangible symbol of alliance and could have a powerful effect on other nations. Throughout the day of August 3, as Baker was flying from Mongolia in hopes of making a dramatic joint appearance with Shevardnadze to announce the statement in Moscow, Soviet officials debated among themselves and repeatedly waffled in talks with the Americans on the substance. Shevardnadze and Tarasenko, who were determined to go ahead despite the extensive opposition, agreed between themselves that they would both resign if the statement precipitated an attack on Soviet citizens in Iraq. Shevardnadze, unable to obtain authorization from Gorbachev or support from anyone else for a joint announcement of an arms embargo, finally decided in a tense conversation with Baker at Vnukovo II, the airport for high-ranking officials and ceremonial visitors, just after Baker had arrived from Mongolia, to announce the arms embargo then and there on his own authority.

"Let me tell you that it was a rather difficult decision for us . . . because of the long-standing relations that we have with Iraq," Shevardnadze told reporters as he stood beside the U.S. secretary of state in making the toughly worded joint announcement. "But despite all this . . . we are being forced to take these steps. . . . Aggression is inconsistent with the principles of new political thinking and, in fact, with civilized relations between nations." Much later Shevardnadze was even more emphatic, calling it "one of the most difficult decisions I had ever had to make" but saying it was fully justified. "If the world community could not stop the aggression against Kuwait, then it would have gained nothing from the end of the Cold War, from the renunciation of confrontation, from the positive initiatives in the international arena," he reflected.

The joint declaration was the beginning of a cooperative relationship in time of crisis that was both unprecedented and essential. The accord with Moscow, President Bush and Secretary Baker quickly realized, was vital in pursuing their chosen strategy of "coercive diplomacy" aimed at pressuring Iraq to retreat from Kuwait, and massive military action if diplomacy failed. Baker considered Soviet support a prerequisite to a credible coalition against Iraq. Without it, the UN Security Council could not function effectively, and radical Arabs such as Syria and the Palestine Liberation Organization would be less inclined to cooperate. American military deployments close to Soviet borders, which would have been strongly and possibly forcefully resisted in earlier times, would be cast in doubt or disrupted if Moscow objected. Yet a quasi-alliance with the United States against the actions of a Soviet client in the Persian Gulf would have been unthinkable in earlier times. Baker later identified August 3, 1990, as, for him, "clearly the day the Cold War ended."

• SUMMIT IN HELSINKI

By the end of August, Bush had decided that it would require a personal meeting with Gorbachev to keep U.S.-Soviet cooperation intact on the Gulf issue. He proposed to travel in early September to Finland, on the very border of the Soviet Union, to cement this important alliance. Gorbachev, who needed Bush's support at home as much as Bush needed his in the international arena, readily agreed.

In preparation for the meeting, Gorbachev summoned Iraqi Foreign Minister Tariq Aziz to Moscow to explore the possibilities for a political settlement that could forestall the use of the powerful U.S. military force that was rapidly building up in and around the Gulf. The Soviet leader bluntly told Aziz that calls for "tough measures" were rapidly increasing internationally and, if unchecked, would bring a "cruel fate" to the Iraqi nation. "We do not want a military solution and we will speak in Helsinki to Bush and will tell him that it is dangerous. But in order to avoid a military solution, your own position has to be constructive and realistic. We need realistic steps on your part."

There was no sign of give in Aziz's position. Responding to Gorbachev's request for new proposals, he refused to contemplate withdrawing from Kuwait, insisting that all Iraqis believed that Kuwait was part of their territory. Complaining of a plot against Iraq, Azis declared, "I can say in full responsibility that the Iraqi leadership and the Iraqi people are not afraid of confrontation. The potential of hatred and anger that has accumulated for many years in Iraq and in the entire

Arab world against the United States, against the pro-Israeli policy of the United States, is at a boiling point. All Arabs are ready for confrontation. We understand that the confrontation can result in a head-on collision and the consequences of that collision will affect not only the Arab region but the entire world. . . . the Americans are mistaken if they think that they would be able to take us out by a surgical operation. If they try it, then it will be a long and bitter conflict that might turn things totally upside-down in this region of the world."

When Gorbachev expressed dismay at Aziz's rigid and "unrealistic" position, the feisty foreign minister accused him of "speaking American" about the crisis. "Frankly, you have not left us any other choice," responded the Soviet leader. He added that Aziz might "be receiving instructions direct from the Almighty, but I would still like to give you some advice. You should not reject the search for a political solution on a realistic and constructive basis. We get the feeling that you don't see it that way. You should bear in mind, though, that in the future the situation is only going to deteriorate."

The one-day summit of Bush and Gorbachev took place September 9 at the Presidential Palace in Helsinki. After the photographers took their pictures and were ushered out of the second-floor Yellow Salon, the two leaders immediately addressed the growing crisis in the Gulf. Bush began by discussing something that had been on his mind since August 23, when he and Brent Scowcroft had gone fishing for bluefish together at the president's vacation home at Kennebunkport, Maine. With the United States and the Soviet Union working together to thwart aggression and to put down, rather than fuel, a regional disorder, it seemed to Bush there was the prospect of a "New World Order" in which the two world powers could become guarantors of international security and the United Nations could finally assume the role designed for it at the end of World War II. It was an appealing phrase for a world striving to redefine international relations as the Cold War was coming to an end, and it caught on quickly after it surfaced in a Scowcroft background briefing for reporters.

Now in the opening minutes at Helsinki, Bush tried it out on Gorbachev: "I see the real opportunity for a new order in the world to appear. I see new possibilities out of this crisis and out of this tragedy. But at the basis of the new order in the world, quite a definite principle must lie: we can't have Saddam Hussein benefit by this aggression." Bush emphasized that Iraq must pull out of Kuwait. While he assured

Gorbachev he did not wish to see the conflict escalate to the use of military force, he stressed that Saddam must understand that force would be used if he did not leave voluntarily. Bush asked Gorbachev to join him in supporting the use of force if all else failed.

Gorbachev, who was most comfortable when dealing with sweeping concepts, acknowledged that "we stand before a global choice." Picking up Bush's mention of a New World Order, he added, "Really, we must live in a new way and we must try to build our relations in a new way." Reflecting on the developments of the turbulent year just past, the Soviet leader said, "If we hadn't had the Malta meeting, if we hadn't come to a new level of relations, processes which started developing in Eastern Europe and processes connected with the unification of Germany would have created a situation even tougher than we now have in the Persian Gulf." It took tremendous political will, he reminded Bush, to respond to the revolutionary events in Europe according to the changed reality rather than in the old ways. Now the United States was in a tough position in the Gulf, and Americans were expecting swift, decisive actions. In a plea for caution, Gorbachev declared that "the most important thing is to maintain the new system of relations, cooperation between our countries, which has already formed."

Gorbachev complained that he had been told of the U.S. military deployments to the Gulf only after Bush's decision had already been made, which "complicated the situation to some extent." Mentioning his still-fresh memories of the quagmires in Vietnam and Afghanistan, he went on to speak at length of his concerns about the use of force, which he feared could result in "thousands of thousands" of casualties, terrible economic losses perhaps in the trillions of dollars, and reorientation of the Arab world in more radical directions.

Coming to his main point, Gorbachev said it was important not to push Saddam into a corner but to permit him to save his reputation while withdrawing from Kuwait. "That is the reality. It is unpleasant in a moral sense. But we must act proceeding from the real situation and consider variants which are the best and which can be realized," he insisted. Gorbachev then outlined a plan, which he later dropped, for a parallel phased withdrawal by Iraq from Kuwait and by the United States from Saudi Arabia. He then pushed hard for the reconvening of the long-recessed international conference on the Middle East, led by the United States and Soviet Union, to take up the Israeli-Palestinian issue as well as Iraqi withdrawal from Kuwait.

Bush and Baker, who was conducting parallel talks with Shevardnadze in a separate room, had two serious objections to Gorbachev's proposal to link the Iraqi withdrawal from Kuwait with an international conference on the Middle East. The first was the likely impression that Saddam was being rewarded, obtaining something of value to the Arab world, through his illegal seizure of Kuwait. The other was the potentially strong reaction of Israel, its friends in the United States, and conservatives in general to a deal that appeared to enhance Soviet influence in the region. The U.S. leaders bore down on the first objection but not the second, which was the kind of residual Cold War thinking that Gorbachev had condemned in his private talk with Bush. On the other hand, Bush and Baker were inclined to accommodate Gorbachev when they could, keeping the Soviet Union in the anti-Saddam coalition as it moved more explicitly into a military phase, and obtaining its explicit endorsement for military steps if possible. After his initial talk with the Soviet leader, Bush was doubtful of securing Gorbachev's continuing approval of the U.S. position unless Bush endorsed convening the international conference to take up Israeli-Palestinian issues.

In the end the two sides made a subtle but workable deal. Gorbachev agreed to a joint statement declaring that the two nations preferred to roll back Saddam's aggression peacefully but that "we are determined to see this aggression end, and if the current steps fail to end it, we are prepared to consider additional ones." In return, Bush privately committed himself to work with the Soviets on a regional Mideast conference after Saddam had left Kuwait, but he did so with the understanding that this commitment would not be made public, so as not to reward Saddam. The joint statement only hinted at the understanding, and the two presidents refused to elaborate. Gorbachev referred to it later as "the invisible package." The commitment was not forgotten, however. More than a year later, after intensive and often tortuous diplomacy led by Baker, Bush and Gorbachev presided at Madrid on October 30, 1991, over the convening of the Middle East Peace Conference attended by Israel, Syria, Egypt, Jordan, Lebanon, and representatives of the Palestinians.

The Soviet economy was in dire shape. Just before the summit, another round of panic buying had erupted in Moscow, fueled by rumors of new price rises, and long lines had formed even to buy bread. Bush and Gorbachev extensively discussed the USSR's increasingly desperate need for external support, but Bush had little to offer. Three days later, when Baker was in Moscow to sign the documents sealing the reunification of Germany, Gorbachev took him aside to ask for emergency help: "I understand there's a limit to what you can do, but can you help get some money from the Saudis for us?" He mentioned a figure of $4–5 billion. After obtaining the approval of Bush, Baker put the request to Saudi Foreign Minister Saud al Faisal at the UN shortly thereafter. The stoutly anti-communist Arab kingdom provided a line of credit of $4 billion to the Soviet Union to help Gorbachev's economy through the winter.

• AUTHORIZING THE WAR

American diplomacy, immensely assisted by the intransigence of Iraq, had kept the Soviet Union in tune with U.S. policy in the first weeks after Iraq's invasion of Kuwait. As America's military buildup continued apace in the Gulf and the war clouds grew darker, the Soviet position became more difficult. Shevardnadze, who had become the most dedicated exponent of universal values, was strongly committed to reversing Iraq's aggression, no matter what the price. Gorbachev was committed in principle but uncomfortable with the prospect of the United States and its allies waging war against a longtime Soviet client state close to the borders of the USSR. According to his foreign policy aide Anatoli Chernyaev, Gorbachev also feared that the use of force would undermine the "new political thinking" in international affairs that he had been preaching—and practicing—for five years. Especially after having been awarded the Nobel Peace Prize in October, Gorbachev sought to play the role of mediator between Washington and Baghdad in an effort to avert the outbreak of military action and, after the bombing of Iraq began, to avert the ground war that followed.

The two old friends were beginning to grow apart for personal and political reasons. Shevardnadze felt that Gorbachev was not backing him sufficiently against the harsh criticisms of Soviet foreign policy from the right. Paval Palazchenko, the English language interpreter who served both men in important conversations with foreigners, noticed in September that Shevardnadze mentioned Gorbachev less frequently, and when he did there was no enthusiasm in his voice. Gorbachev was increasingly embattled at home, struggling to maintain his position of leadership amid the dwindling relevance and authority of the Communist Party, increasingly torn between the reformists urging him to go further, faster, and conservatives, who were appalled at the disintegration of the established Soviet system and wanted to retreat.

That fall Yevgeni Primakov, who was a friend of both men and was often rumored to be Shevardnadze's successor, intensified the subterranean struggle over Gulf policy by persuading Gorbachev to let him try mediating with Iraq. Early in his career Primakov had been a *Pravda* correspondent working in the Middle East, and he continued his interest and expertise during the three decades thereafter. He had known Saddam for more than twenty years and argued that he might be able to produce results that others, especially those in the straight-laced Foreign Ministry, could not. Primakov was also ambitious. He observed Gorbachev's yearning to play a peacemaker's role and avert a clash of arms in the Gulf and made himself the instrument of that desire. Shevardnadze was furious, privately fuming, "We can't have two foreign policies." He was unable to stop Primakov's maneuvering, however.

In early November, as Bush was preparing to announce a massive new increase in U.S. deployments in the Gulf, Baker arrived in Moscow to line up support for a new UN Security Council resolution authorizing the use of force. Unimpressed with the pale hints of flexibility that Primakov had reported finding on a trip to Baghdad, the U.S. leadership was more convinced than ever that it would probably require military action, not merely the threat of such action, to eject Iraq from Kuwait. In order to maximize support at home and abroad for the first large-scale use of U.S. force since the Vietnam War, it was crucial to obtain the clearest possible UN authorization and to gain the assent of the U.S. Congress. A strong UN resolution would help on Capitol Hill.

In a lengthy meeting with Shevardnadze, Baker found his counterpart wary about military action and insistent, in the light of the Soviet experience in Afghanistan, that "if you're going to use force, you have to know that you will succeed." In an action with little precedent, the conference room of the Soviet state guest house was cleared of everyone except principals and interpreters as Baker summoned the top military official in his delegation, General Howard Graves of the Joint Chiefs of Staff, to give a detailed briefing to Shevardnadze on the U.S. war plan. Baker reflected later, "In another era, it would have been the most far-fetched thing imaginable that a high-ranking U.S. military officer would be authorized to brief the Soviet foreign minister on our war plans against a Soviet client state." Shevardnadze was impressed with what he heard and agreed on the spot to give his personal backing to a tough new UN resolution.

Gorbachev, who saw Baker the next day, was more reluctant than his foreign minister. He suggested two UN resolutions, one authorizing the use of force but only after a six-week hiatus to allow Saddam to withdraw from Kuwait, the other authorizing an actual assault if Iraq still occupied its neighbor when the hiatus ran out. Baker argued that it would be too difficult to obtain approval of the second resolution. He proposed instead a single measure authorizing the use of force, but only after a substantial pause (as it turned out, six weeks) to give Saddam a final opportunity to withdraw peacefully. After the conversation, Baker reported in a cable to Bush that Gorbachev was close to supporting a new resolution but is "not there yet. . . . Gorbachev's image of the new international order is such that he has a hard time reconciling the fact that we might need to use force in this initial test."

In Paris ten days later, when the U.S. and Soviet leaderships were together at a summit meeting of the Conference on Security and Cooperation in Europe (CSCE), Shevardnadze persuaded Baker to soften the language of the UN resolution by having it authorize nations to employ "all necessary means" to eject Iraq from Kuwait rather than explicitly endorse "use of force." Gorbachev then approved the resolution on condition that it include a "pause of goodwill" to allow Iraq a last chance to withdraw. He asked that his approval of the war resolution be kept secret until he could arrange another attempt at mediation. The Soviet leader's subsequent meeting in Moscow with Iraqi Foreign Minister Aziz produced no results.

On November 28, the Soviet Union joined the United States, Britain, France, and most of the rest of the UN Security Council in voting for Resolution 678, which authorized the use of "all necessary means" if Iraq did not withdraw from Kuwait by January 15. Baker, who voted and spoke for the United States, made it abundantly clear that "all necessary means" included war. China abstained from the vote, despite heavy lobbying from Washington to vote yes. Only Cuba and Yemen, which had remained obdurate despite a personal visit by Baker to its capital, voted no. Afterward, Baker sent a message to the Yemenis: "That is the most expensive vote you ever cast." The U.S. foreign aid program of $70 million annually was subsequently withdrawn.

• SHEVARDNADZE RESIGNS

On December 20, three weeks after casting the crucial vote on the Gulf issue in the UN Security Council, a distraught Shevardnadze rose in the Congress of People's Deputies to deliver what he declared to be "perhaps the shortest and most difficult speech of my life." He began by rejecting criticisms of the Gulf policy that had been hurled by parliamentarians the previous day, saying that the policy "is serious, well considered, sensible, and in accordance with all standards, present standards, of civilized relations between states." Despite the friendly relations with Iraq that had been built up over years, he declared, "we have no moral right at all to reconcile ourselves to aggression and the annexation of a small, defenseless country. In that case we would have had to strike through everything that has been done in recent years by all of us, by the whole country, and by the whole of our people in the field of asserting the principles of the new political thinking." The attacks on this policy, he declared, "overfilled the cup of patience."

Shevardnadze went on to condemn attacks on him and his policies, personal slights, and insults in the struggle taking place between "reformers," in which camp he placed himself, and "reactionaries," as he acidly described the forces of the right. Then he reached his shocking peroration:

> Democrats, I will put it bluntly: comrade democrats, in the widest meaning of this word, you have scattered. The reformers have gone to seed. Dictatorship is coming; I state this with complete responsibility. No one knows what kind of dictatorship this will be and who will come—what kind of dictator—and what the regime will be like.
>
> I want to make the following statement: I am resigning. Let this be—and do not respond, do not curse me—let this be my contribution, if you like, my protest against the onset of dictatorship.
>
> I express profound gratitude to Mikhail Sergeyevich Gorbachev. I am his friend. I am a fellow thinker of his. I have always supported, and will support to the end of my days, the ideas of *perestroika*, the ideas of renewal, the ideas of democracy, of democratization. We have done great things in the international arena. But I think that it is my duty, as a man, as a citizen, as a Communist; I cannot

reconcile myself to the events taking place in our country and to the trials awaiting our people. I nevertheless believe; I believe that dictatorship will not succeed, and that the future belongs to democracy and freedom.

Sitting behind him on the dais of the Kremlin hall, Gorbachev appeared to be stunned, sitting motionless in his place. Shevardnadze had told him nothing in advance, fearing that Gorbachev would talk him out of resigning as he had done the previous December, when he had planned to leave over the killing of unarmed demonstrators in his native Georgia. When Gorbachev took the floor later in the day, he ridiculed the idea that a coup or any other move toward dictatorship was in the wind, saying he had was well informed and had no such information. Gorbachev angrily charged his friend with deserting him "at our most difficult time," saying this was "unforgivable." He revealed that, as rumored, he had planned to name Shevardnadze to the newly created post of vice president. Rather than a promotion, Shevardnadze considered this a means of getting him out of the way in foreign affairs and perhaps of making him responsible for failing domestic policies.

Shevardnadze's eruption had been building within him for months. He was furious at the entry of Primakov into policymaking toward the Gulf, which he had been powerless to stop (although at one point he undercut a Primakov mission to Washington by sending Baker a confidential message that he personally opposed the proposed deal with Iraq that Primakov was bringing). Shevardnadze was appalled and embarrassed when the Soviet military, with Gorbachev's acquiescence, unilaterally reinterpreted provisions of the Conventional Forces in Europe Treaty (CFE), which he had negotiated with the West in order to preserve large numbers of tanks that otherwise would have to be destroyed. A proud and sensitive man for whom self-esteem and personal rectitude were vitally important, he was deeply wounded by Gorbachev's growing failure to defend him and the policies they had jointly advanced.

Most of all, Shevardnadze was in despair because of Gorbachev's notable turn to the right politically. Under growing attack from Russian President Boris Yeltsin and his allies on the left, Gorbachev turned sharply to the right to gain support as public and political opposition to his policies mounted. On December 2, Gorbachev had fired his progressive minister of interior, Vadim Batakin, who had irritated conservatives by his restraint in the Baltics, and replaced him with Boris Pugo, a conspiracy-minded former KGB operative and party official in Latvia. General Boris Gromov, the last Soviet commander in Afghanistan and a vocal critic of Shevardnadze, was named deputy minister. Gorbachev's turn was the signal for rightist figures within the Soviet leadership to assert themselves. KGB chief Vladimir Kryuchkov, for example, warned publicly that the county was threatened by dissolution and charged that "foreign intelligence organizations" were seeking to "destabilize" the USSR.

When informed of Shevardnadze's resignation, Baker recalled that he had confided in a recent private conversation, "We have an absolute crisis. We could have a dictatorship very soon in our country." Baker tried to call the man on whom he had relied so extensively to craft Soviet policy but was told that Shevardnadze was too exhausted to come to the phone. Later the two men exchanged letters. Baker wrote, "We developed a special relationship that built the bonds of trust between our two nations. In doing so, we served not only the interests of our two nations, but the interests of the world."

It did not take long for Shevardnadze's foreboding to be borne out by events. In early January, Gorbachev began tightening his grip on independence-minded Lithuania, which had been such a troublesome problem for U.S.-Soviet relations the previous spring. On January 11, 1991, Soviet troops began occupying public buildings in Vilnius, the Lithuanian capital. When protesters gathered, the troops opened fire, hitting several people. Two days later, commandos of the KGB's elite Alpha unit, in the guise of members of the local Soviet Army garrison, attacked the television tower, which had been broadcasting news of the Soviet actions. With bravery reminiscent of that in Tiananmen Square in Beijing, several young men confronted Soviet tanks, some fatally. Within hours, several hundred Lithuanians were wounded and fifteen killed.

Boris Yeltsin and his Russian Republic legislature responded vigorously, saying such a crackdown could happen to them next. Yeltsin dramatically flew to Estonia, where he signed a "mutual support pact" with the three Baltic states, sharply increasing his challenge to Gorbachev. The Soviet president lamely claimed that he had not authorized the attack on the television tower and, more surprisingly, that he did not know who had given the order.

Documents that came to light many months later disclosed that the incidents in Vilnius had been conceived long in advance by high officials in Moscow, including Defense Minister Dmitri Yazov. The night of the attack on the television tower, it was revealed later, high-ranking plotters including KGB chief Kryuchkov, Gorbachev's chief of staff Valery Boldin, and Valentin Pavlov, soon to become Soviet prime minister, met secretly in the Kremlin before the action began to monitor events as they unfolded. This was the inner core of the group that would seek to depose Gorbachev eight months later. In a real sense, the Vilnius crackdown was a dress rehearsal for a historic coup d'état.

• DIPLOMACY AND WAR

Just before 3 A.M. on January 17, only twenty-seven hours after the expiration of the "pause of goodwill" that provided Iraq a last chance to remove its forces peacefully from Kuwait, the streets and buildings of Baghdad shook with the impact of laser-guided bombs and the skies lit up with the glow of antiaircraft fire. The powerful and almost entirely successful strike, calculated to cripple Iraq's command and communications systems, was the opening of the air war phase of Operation Desert Storm. Joining the more than 500,000 troops of the United States in combat operations were smaller contingents from Saudi Arabia, Kuwait, Britain, France, Egypt, and the United Arab Emirates. The Soviet Union, which had participated in shaping the UN ultimatum to Iraq, stood by but did not take part in combat against its erstwhile ally.

Keeping the turbulent Soviet Union part of the united front against Iraq while responding with disapproval to the eruption in the Baltics, and all without further weakening the swiftly eroding ability of Gorbachev to govern, posed a difficult set of problems for American diplomacy, the renewed trouble in the Baltics being the most immediate. Bush and Baker made public statements deploring the use of force and calling for peaceful dialogue. In diplomatic messages, Moscow was told that such incidents would have a negative effect on the willingness of the West to provide economic assistance. In a telephone call to Aleksandr Bessmertnykh, who had been summoned by Gorbachev from his post as ambassador to Washington to replace Shevardnadze as foreign minister, Baker said, "Our ability to pursue our new relationship depends on your government upholding the principles of *perestroika*." He added, "I hope what we've seen doesn't represent a return to old thinking and past practices."

As prodemocracy demonstrations spread and Moscow's crackdown continued, Bush informed the Soviet president by letter that he would have no alternative but to suspend a number of programs of U.S. aid if intimidation, pressure, and use of the armed forces continued in the Baltics. "Try to help your president understand," Gorbachev told Ambassador Jack Matlock, who presented him with the letter, "that we are on the brink of a civil war. As president, my main task is to prevent it." At times, he would have to do things that might seem inexplicable, he said. Ahead he saw a period of "zigs and zags." Many were demanding that he resign, Gorbachev noted. "Believe me, that would be very easy. But suppose I resign, what then? It would be a disaster for everybody, including for our relations with America." Ending the conversation, Gorbachev said, "Tell my friend George Bush: no matter what pressure I get over the Gulf War, the German question and ratification of the conventional forces [CFE] agreement, I'll act as we agreed. I will do everything." Bush, as before, refrained from ordering sanctions despite calls for such action at home. However, a U.S.-Soviet summit meeting that had been planned for February was put on hold.

The Gulf War was the overwhelming preoccupation of the Bush administration in early 1991, and Gorbachev's role in it a persistent problem. Before hostilities began, Gorbachev sought to avert the war with Primakov's travels to Baghdad and Western capitals and his own meetings with Aziz in search of a face-saving compromise. Although he had approved the UN resolutions permitting the use of force, Gorbachev remained determined to find political rather than military means to solve the crisis. However, the Bush administration's perspective was very different. Bush's unqualified objective was to force Iraq to reverse its aggression without receiving any rewards for its action. As Baker reflected later, having obtained UN Security Council resolutions requiring unconditional Iraqi withdrawal from Kuwait, "there really was no room for a negotiation." Although Baker himself had a lengthy meeting with Aziz in early January, it was essentially to present an ultimatum rather than to seek a compromise. It did nothing to avert the war.

Minutes before the start of the air war in the early hours of January 17, Baker telephoned Bessmertnykh, who had been confirmed as foreign minister two days earlier, to notify him that hostilities would begin within an hour. When Bessmertnykh awakened Gorbachev with the news, the Soviet president instructed him to appeal for a delay of at least twenty-four hours as "my one personal request of Bush" so that he might seek a political solution. When Bessmertnykh called Baker back, the attack had already begun. Undeterred, Gorbachev instructed the Soviet ambassador in Baghdad to request an emergency meeting with Saddam, but the Iraqi leader had already disappeared into an underground bunker.

On January 19, Gorbachev telephoned Bush to express his anxiety over the ferocity of the air attack. Saying that the coalition had made its point, Gorbachev called for a pause in the bombing during which he would seek to persuade Saddam to withdraw from Kuwait. Bush refused. A week later, Bessmertnykh flew to Washington to discuss the continuing crisis in the Baltics, where new violence had erupted due to the actions of Soviet troops, and to seek U.S. cooperation in arranging a political solution to the war in the Gulf. The result was continued U.S. forbearance on the Baltics and a joint Baker-Bessmertnykh statement on the Middle East that roiled diplomatic waters and touched off a political controversy by hinting that the attacks would stop if Saddam merely expressed an "unequivocal commitment" to withdraw. White House officials were furious at State Department fumbling.

As the air war continued, Gorbachev sent Primakov back to Baghdad in early February to seek a negotiated solution. The Soviet envoy proposed that Saddam announce his willingness to withdraw from Kuwait in a specified period of time in exchange for a cease-fire by the U.S.-led coalition. The plan, which had not been checked with Washington in advance, fell short of what the United States would accept. Saddam did not accept it either, though Primakov reported some unspecified "encouraging elements in Saddam's behavior." The Iraqi president decided to send Aziz to Moscow to discuss the plan further. Gorbachev then sent Bush a written summary of the proposal under discussion, with a request that the ground war not begin while the talks with Aziz were taking place. Bush's private reaction was slangy and succinct: "No way, Jose." Publicly, he rejected the plan as "a cruel hoax."

Gorbachev refused to give up. He worked on an elaboration of the Primakov plan with Aziz in Moscow and sent it to Bush, who rejected it and again declined to put off the start of the ground war while discussions continued. Aziz then traveled home to consult Saddam, and returned at midnight on February 21, as Washington was making final plans to launch the ground attacks. Bit by bit the Iraqis were moving closer to the U.S. position, but they still insisted on some conditions, while Washington would accept none. On February 22, Gorbachev telephoned Bush to say that the Iraqis had "reached a position that was quite realistic, which meant that the chances for finding a solution to the conflict were good." Bush, determined to go ahead with the war but also determined not to alienate Gorbachev, expressed appreciation for his efforts but added, "Time is running out, and running out very quickly." The White House then announced a twenty-four-hour deadline, ending at noon Washington time on February 23, for Iraq to begin full-scale withdrawal from Kuwait and agree to all UN resolutions, including payment of compensation and reparations. Final plans were made for the ground war to begin eight hours later.

On the deadline day, a Saturday, Bush went to Camp David with Baker to await the inception of the ground war. Meanwhile, the Iraqis finally accepted the latest Gorbachev plan, which called for immediate withdrawal but not for compliance with the other UN resolutions. In Moscow at 12:05 P.M. (4:05 A.M. in Washington) Aziz told a news conference that Iraq had agreed to withdraw immediately and unconditionally, but he also referred to the conditions that had been stipulated in the negotiations with Gorbachev. The Soviet president then proposed to convene the UN Security Council in emergency session to consider his accord with Iraq, and he spent the day on the telephone with world leaders including (in this order) British Prime Minister John Major, Italian Prime Minister Giulio Andreotti, French President Francois Mitterand, Egyptian President Hosni Mubarak, Syrian President Hafez Assad, German Chancellor Helmut Kohl, Japanese Prime Minister Toshiki Kaifu, and Iranian President Hashemi Rafsanjani. Finally, Gorbachev called Bush at 7:15 P.M. Moscow time (11:15 A.M. at Camp David) in a plea to postpone the noon deadline for another day or two to let diplomacy work.

Bush responded with indignation that Saddam was still setting oil wells ablaze in the Gulf in an effort to penalize his opponents and retard the invasion. "His line is to draw us into negotiations and have us abandon the UN mandate. I gave him a time in which he could have demonstrated his compliance. . . . I told him he must start pulling out his troops by midday. He keeps on burning oil wells. I can't have him get away with that." Bush told Gorbachev that after all his efforts there were still preconditions to Saddam's withdrawal offer. "I firmly believe Hussein is just trying to get more time. . . . That is why I can't see why we should be flexible."

Gorbachev, almost distraught, countered, "Let's try to be cool. We are talking about living people, about human beings. It's not Hussein we need. His fate is clear. We must use this chance to reach the aims that we together set in the UN Security Council—I mean, avoiding the tragedy and destruction." He pleaded again for "another day or two" to work out an acceptable accord under the aegis of the Security Council.

Bush was having none of it: "I appreciate what you say, but I don't want anybody to have the impression that we've got time. Of course, let Baker and Bessmertnykh talk. But the coalition doesn't have any wish to prolong the matter. I understand your concern about human casualties, but it's clear that Saddam Hussein is just trying to get more time, and at the same time he sets fire to oil wells and kills Kuwaitis. There's no reason we should trust him. That is why I don't think we could postpone our actions." With the clock ticking toward the noon deadline, if Saddam wanted to act, said Bush, he should do so "in the nearest minutes."

Gorbachev made one final stab: "I understand what you say. And still I think that one or two days are not going to be crucial, taking into account what we have already done. But these one or two days can provide an opportunity to have the result we both want."

Bush cut him off with as much politeness as he could muster: "Thank you for your call. Goodbye."

At the other end of the line, in the Kremlin, Gorbachev put down the telephone with resignation and disappointment. "They have decided," he told the aides, including Primakov and Bessmertnykh, who were gathered round him. A realist, he had no harsh words for his American interlocutors.

Eight hours later the coordinated, massive ground attacks began. Three days after that, with its troops routed, tens of thousands of them killed, and all resistance to the invasion crumbling, Iraq sued for peace, accepting through the Soviet ambassador in Baghdad a complete withdrawal from Kuwait and compliance with UN resolutions. Shortly thereafter, the United States and its coalition halted all military action. Gorbachev had failed to stop the war, but the cause and the coalition he joined at the outset had triumphed.

• THE UNRAVELING OF SOVIET POWER

The Gulf War dramatized and validated the leading role of the United States and the shift in the balance of power in the post–Cold War world.

No one else could have organized and led the international effort as Bush and his government did or have prosecuted the war to force Iraq out of Kuwait with such stunning impact and success. On the other hand, the secondary role of the Soviet Union, and Gorbachev's determined but ineffectual efforts to forestall Operation Desert Storm, emphasized the international weakness of Moscow's position. Shorn of its former European satellites, uncertain of its relations with many of its constituent republics, and in deep economic trouble and political uncertainty at home, the Soviet Union no longer seemed to merit the popular title of "superpower," although it still retained 3.5 million well-armed troops and a gigantic arsenal of 11,000 strategic nuclear weapons. The United States, it was repeatedly said, had emerged from the Gulf as the world's single superpower.

In April 1991, two months after the end of the Gulf War, the Central Intelligence Agency took a long look at the USSR's present and future in a highly classified report to senior policymakers under the title "The Soviet Cauldron." In its main conclusions and much of its detail, the CIA proved remarkably prescient. The report said:

- "Economic crisis, independence aspirations and anti-Communist forces are breaking down the Soviet empire and system of governance." The report cited the rise of Yeltsin; restiveness in the Baltics, the Ukraine, Belorussia, and Georgia; the irretrievable breakdown of the centrally planned economy without creation of a coherent market system; the growth of independent news media; and the disintegration of the Communist Party.

- "In the midst of this chaos, Gorbachev has gone from ardent reformer to consolidator. A stream of intelligence reporting and his public declarations indicate that Gorbachev has chosen this course both because of his political credo and because of pressures on him by other traditionalists, who would like him to use much tougher repressive measures. . . . As a result of his political and policy failures, Gorbachev's credibility has sunk to near zero."

- "Gorbachev has truly been faced with terrible choices in his effort to move the USSR away from the failed, rigid old system. . . . The economy is in a downward spiral with no end in sight. . . .

The continued preference given to reliance on a top-down approach to problems, particularly in regard to republics, has generated a war of laws between various levels of power and created a legal mess to match the economic mess."

- "In this situation of growing chaos, explosive events have become increasingly possible." The agency cited several potential explosions, including riots or massive strikes; new violence in the Baltics, the assassination of Gorbachev, Yeltsin or other leaders; and the emergence of a new popular hero. The fifth and last possibility cited was that "reactionary leaders, with or without Gorbachev, could judge that the last chance to act had come and move under the banner of law-and-order."

- "Of all these possible explosions, a premeditated, organized attempt to restore a full-fledged dictatorship would be the most fateful in that it would try to roll back newly acquired freedoms and be inherently destabilizing in the long term."

The report expressed special concern about this last possibility, pointing out that Gorbachev's recent personnel appointments, estrangement from reformers, and attempts to rule by decree seemed to the increase the chances for a rollback. "More ominously, military, MVD [Ministry of Internal Affairs] and KGB leaders are making preparations for a broad use of force in the political process," the CIA said. The report cited recent statements by KGB chief Kryuchkov; Marshal Sergei Akhromeyev, Gorbachev's military adviser; Defense Minister Yazov; and Ground Forces Commander Valentin Varennikov. All would play roles in the whirlwind to come.

As Gorbachev's popularity was plummeting, that of his old foe, Boris Yeltsin, was soaring. Initially Yeltsin was an ally of Gorbachev, but the two men had had a hostile relationship since Yeltsin's ground-breaking criticism of the slow pace of *perestroika* during the October 1987 Central Committee meeting (see p. 254). A few days later Gorbachev summoned Yeltsin, who was in a hospital bed suffering from nervous tension, chest pains, and severe headaches, to a Stalin-style meeting of the Moscow Central Committee of the Communist Party, which Yeltsin then headed, to be officially denounced and ousted from office. He was also ousted as a member of the Politburo and given a minor position at the state building conglomerate. But the politically astute Yeltsin, who was courageous and bold, eventually made Gorbachev's and the party elders' disapproval of him into a powerful political asset, positioning himself as leader of the people against the party bosses. Despite Gorbachev's efforts to oppose him, Yeltsin was elected chairman of the Russian Republic legislature in May 1990. Shortly thereafter he dramatically quit the Communist Party, walking out the central aisle of the Twenty-Eighth Party Congress on national television after criticizing Gorbachev and the party, and saying he could not serve both the party and the people.

In March 1991, a referendum backed by Yeltsin established the presidency of the Russian Republic as a post to be filled by popular vote. On June 12, Yeltsin was overwhelmingly elected president of Russia with 57 percent of the votes cast. The balloting gave Yeltsin a tremendous political boost as the elected leader of the Soviet Union's core republic and the first Russian leader in history to make popular election the basis for his legitimacy. Gorbachev had never been elected by popular vote but had gained his position by the decision of Communist Party elders and more recently by vote of the Congress of People's Deputies. With Gorbachev in attendance at his inauguration, Yeltsin declared, "Great Russia is rising from its knees. . . . Having passed through so many trials, with clear goals in mind, we can be absolutely certain of one thing: Russia will rise again!" To cap his popular appeal, he had himself blessed by the Russian Orthodox patriarch of Moscow. It was the first time since Tsar Nicholas II advanced to the throne in 1894 that a Russian leader had sought and obtained the blessing of the established church.

On June 17, in a very strange maneuver, Prime Minister Valentin Pavlov asked the Supreme Soviet to grant him extraordinary power to make decisions that until then had been Gorbachev's to make. His bid for power was endorsed by KGB Chairman Kryuchkov, Defense Minister Yazov, and Minister of Internal Affairs Pugo, all of whom accused Gorbachev of failing to defend the country against encroachment from the West. As all these officials had been put into office by Gorbachev, the maneuver was seen by some liberal deputies as a "constitutional coup," especially after Pavlov admitted that he had not discussed his plan with the president. Gorbachev rebuked Pavlov and eventually engineered the defeat of the proposal in the Supreme Soviet, but not before it raised new questions about the loyalty of Gorbachev's entourage.

Yeltsin was making a visit to Washington and was scheduled to see Bush on June 20. On that day Moscow's reformist mayor, Gavril Popov, rushed to Spaso House, the residence of the U.S. ambassador, on urgent business. Sitting down alone with Ambassador Matlock, Popov pointed silently to the ceiling, where he suspected hidden microphones. While the two carried on an unremarkable conversation, the mayor scribbled a note in Russian:

"A coup is being organized to remove Gorbachev. We must get word to Boris Nikolayevich [Yeltsin]."

Matlock kept the conversation going as if nothing had happened, but responded in his own hand:

"I'll send a message, but who is behind this?"

Popov wrote four names: Pavlov, Kryuchkov, Yazov, and Anatoly Lukyanov, chairman of the Supreme Soviet and a law school contemporary and longtime personal friend of Gorbachev. When Matlock had read the note, the mayor took back the paper, tore it into little bits and put them in his pocket. After further desultory conversation for the benefit of any hidden microphones, Popov left.

Matlock immediately dispatched a top priority message to the State Department, which several hours later instructed him to warn Gorbachev immediately. Baker, who was informed while in Berlin for a foreign ministers' meeting, warned Bessmertnykh, who was unable to communicate the substance of the report because his communication channels to Moscow were controlled by the KGB. Bush cabled Gorbachev and asked him to receive Matlock at once. Thus, before the day was out, the U.S. ambassador was ushered in to see the leader of the USSR to tell him the U.S. president wished him to know of a plot to remove him from office. Gorbachev seemed to make light of it, but then grew serious: "Tell President Bush I am touched. I have felt for some time that we are partners, and now he has proved it. Thank him for his concern. He has done just what a friend should do. But tell him not to worry. I have everything well in hand."

Back in Washington, Bush informed Yeltsin of the report when the Russian president came to the Oval Office. They tried to call Gorbachev, but could not reach him. As he left the White House, Yeltsin commented to an aide that Bush seemed still "under the illusion" that everything depended on the U.S. relationship with Gorbachev.

THE FINAL SUMMIT

George and Barbara Bush landed in Moscow aboard *Air Force One* on the evening of July 29 for the sixteenth, and final, full-fledged U.S.-Soviet summit meeting, nearly twenty years after Richard Nixon had met Leonid Brezhnev in the first of the series in Moscow in 1972. The Bushes were met on the tarmac by Vice President Gennadi Yanayev, a colorless, hard-drinking apparatchik who had been named to the newly created post of vice president the previous winter during Gorbachev's move to the right. Bush told aides later in the trip that Yanayev seemed a "friendly sort of guy" but definitely "not a heavy hitter."

The main purpose of the summit was to sign the Strategic Arms Reduction Treaty (START) which had been proposed by President Reagan in 1982 during the era of Leonid Brezhnev's leadership of the USSR and had been under negotiation ever since. In meantime, the world had changed. The United States and Soviet Union were no longer global enemies, and the overarching danger of nuclear war between them had diminished. The arsenals of intercontinental missiles and bombers and nuclear weapons were more imposing than ever, however, and the treaty was intended to begin finally reducing them by mutual accord. Because the military leaders of both countries sought to protect their weapons systems and were wary of permitting advantages to the other side, the nine years of negotiations had been a continual wrangle over mind-numbing details, which were difficult for the political leaders to resolve and in many cases even to grasp.

Two weeks earlier, Gorbachev had traveled to London to join Bush and other leaders of the Group of Seven (G-7) Industrialized Nations in search of a major injection of economic aid, which he needed desperately. Bush was noncommittal, partly because his government was under intense congressional pressure to cut expenses, and because large-scale assistance to the Soviet Union was still a controversial issue in American politics. Moreover, Gorbachev had consistently backed away from taking the painful steps needed to convert the USSR's deteriorating command economy to reliance on market forces.

Stanislav Shatalin, a prominent economist and Gorbachev advisor, had proposed a plan in mid-1990 to shift to a market economy in 500 days. Fearful of the political consequences, Gorbachev watered it down almost beyond recognition. In the spring of 1991, Grigori Yavlinsky, who had been a coauthor of the "500 Day Plan," worked with Harvard professor Graham Allison and former NSC aide Robert Blackwill, now also at Harvard, on a proposal for massive economic aid from the West in return for decisive shifts toward a free-market system. However, once again Gorbachev opted for only a watered-down version, and Yavlinsky refused to accompany Gorbachev to London to sell the G-7 leaders on what was left of his plan.

In the view of Bush and others, all the economic aid in the world would do little good without a far-reaching and fundamental reform program, which Gorbachev lacked. Consequently, the G-7 meeting produced only minimal assistance for Moscow and a decision to hand off the problem to the International Monetary Fund and World Bank, where the Soviet Union was to be granted a special "associate membership."

At a private luncheon with Bush in London before the climactic meeting, Gorbachev took a remarkably challenging stance, which dramatized both his intense frustration and his great need. As recorded in the notes of his aide Chernyaev, Gorbachev told Bush:

> As regards security policy, we have already accomplished a lot. . . . But at the same time I have the impression that my friend, the president of the United States, has not yet reached a final answer to one fundamental question: What does the United States want the Soviet Union to be like? Until we get an answer to this question, many issues in our relationship cannot be clarified. And time is running out.
>
> So I ask: What does George Bush want from me? If my colleagues among the 'Seven' tell me, when we meet later, that they like what I am doing and they want to support me but first I have to stew in my own soup for a while, I must tell them that we are all in that soup. Isn't it strange: a hundred billion dollars were scraped up to solve a regional conflict [the cost of the Gulf War]. Money can be found for other programs. But what we have here is a project to transform the Soviet Union, to give it a wholly new quality, to bring it into the world economy so that it will not be a disruptive force and the source of threats. There has never been a task so great and so important!

By the time Bush arrived in Moscow, Gorbachev understood that large-scale U.S. aid would not be forthcoming under existing circumstances, and he was determined to obtain any marginal gains possible. The meeting with Bush once again was in St. Catherine's Hall of the Great Kremlin Palace, the gilded room with malachite columns where the two had first met in 1985 after the funeral of Konstantin Chernenko. Across the polished table, Gorbachev assured Bush that he intended to make major changes in the Soviet economy as soon as it could be done practically. He also complained about lingering Cold War restrictions on U.S.-Soviet trade, saying, "You've got all these nice words about how you want us to succeed, but when it comes to specifics, you put up roadblocks." Bush countered with complaints about Soviet roadblocks in the way of U.S. firms prepared to do business in the USSR.

A difficult problem of protocol and policy arose from the assertive presence of Yeltsin, who was determined not to be cast as a subordinate of Gorbachev. Consequently, he declined to attend the arrival ceremony for Bush at the Kremlin or a working lunch hosted by Gorbachev, insisting on his own private meeting with Bush in another room of the Kremlin. The meeting was scheduled to take fifteen minutes, but Yeltsin stretched it to forty, throwing off the U.S. president's schedule. When time came for the state dinner after the first day, Yeltsin sent his wife, Naina, ahead and through the receiving line with Moscow Mayor Gavril Popov. He himself arrived in regal splendor after the receiving line had disbanded and sought unsuccessfully to escort Barbara Bush into the dining room. President Bush complained privately that Yeltsin was "really grandstanding."

The following day, Bush and Gorbachev met for their most significant discussion in the informal setting of the presidential dacha at Novo-Ogarevo, the Soviet equivalent of the U.S. presidential retreat at Camp David, Maryland. Gorbachev had just spent days and often nights at the dacha negotiating with leaders of Soviet republics, notably Yeltsin of Russia and Kazakhstan's President Nursultan Nazarbayev, on the Union Treaty intended to establish a new relationship between the republics and the center. Difficult negotiations over taxation had been successfully completed by those three leaders at 3 A.M. the morning after Bush's arrival. It was agreed that the treaty would be signed on August 20. In a confidential discussion, Gorbachev had promised that he would then reorganize his government and dismiss a number of the rightist officials he had placed in top jobs, including his KGB chief. Neither Gorbachev nor the others had been aware that Lieutenant General Yuri Plekhanov, the KGB officer in charge of presidential security, had bugged the dacha and alerted those who were about to be purged.

Dispensing with coats and ties as they had at Camp David the previous summer, Gorbachev and Bush, accompanied by only their closest aides, looked south on a sunny outdoor porch toward the Moscow River. The Soviet leader, who had prepared his ideas well in advance, proposed to extend into new dimensions the goal of strategic stability that the two nations had long been seeking.

"In former times this concept [of strategic stability] was just military parity, equality and the military aspect of security," Gorbachev began. "I think now we need a new approach, because a new situation has arisen when we abandon [the use of] force, the arms race, when new processes come to life in our economic relations.

"We have made the choice in favor of reforms, and no dogmas, stereotypes or old ideology are going to stop me. The chief priority for me today is solving the problem of our statehood [the Union arrangements] and moving toward a new economy. And I shall promote public accord by all means. American leaders are our constant judges in all this and we understand that. You want to have confidence in our intentions and to understand what we do. Obviously, this confidence of yours hasn't been formed yet."

Bush tried to be reassuring without making commitments. "I trust your intentions," he replied. "And after yesterday's conversation [in St. Catherine's Hall] I am more confident than before my visit here that you know where you are heading and how to achieve your goal. . . . We think you want to be a strong partner in international relations. And for that, you want to carry out changes, and avoid chaos within the framework of the [Union] law. We hail this approach of yours."

As they had at Camp David, the U.S. and Soviet leaders ranged the world in their discussion of current problems and prospects. They agreed to proceed with invitations to Israel, Arab nations, and the Palestinians to a Middle East peace conference to be jointly convened by Bush and Gorbachev in October. They discussed at length the disintegrating situation in the former Yugoslavia without coming to a conclusion about how to stop it. They discussed Europe, Africa, the Indian subcontinent, China, and Japan, among others. In nearly all those areas the two nations were no longer at cross-purposes.

It was a domestic matter rather than a foreign question that most immediately concerned Gorbachev: worry about Bush's postsummit stopover in Kiev, the capital of the restless Ukraine republic, where secessionist sentiment was high. Gorbachev's government had tried mightily but unsuccessfully to persuade the U.S. president to cancel the visit, fearing it would further stir anti-Soviet feeling. Bush assured Gorbachev he would not allow his appearance in Kiev to be interpreted as support for separatist tendencies.

The final afternoon of the summit saw the signing of the START treaty in St. Vladimir's Hall, the commodious chamber where Ronald Reagan and Gorbachev had signed the Intermediate Nuclear Forces (INF) Treaty in 1988. As a symbolic reminder, Bush and Gorbachev signed the 47-page treaty and 700-page protocols with pens made from the metal taken from missiles banned under the INF treaty. The new treaty mandated the first negotiated reductions in the vast strategic arsenals of the two nuclear superpowers, bringing the limits of authorized weapons down by about 25 percent for the United States and 35 percent for the Soviet Union, to approximately where they had been when the negotiations began in 1982. By the time the treaty was signed, however, the business of arms control was no longer a central concern of Washington and Moscow. The danger of war between them had receded, and the cutbacks seemed much less ambitious than the post–Cold War world required. The two sides agreed to begin work in the fall on further reductions.

After saying goodbye to Gorbachev, Bush flew to Kiev for the stopover intended to show U.S. interest in the increasingly independent republics of the USSR. Conscious of the importance of not encouraging separatism, Bush delivered a speech to the Ukrainian Parliament that offended the large and popular Ukrainian independence movement, Rukh. Bush referred to his listeners as "Soviet citizens" and praised Gorbachev, who was highly unpopular in Ukraine, for having achieved "astonishing things." In discussing the continuation of the union, which he endorsed, Bush declared that "freedom is not the same as independence. Americans will not support those who seek independence in order to replace a far-off tyranny with a local despotism. They will not aid those who promote a suicidal nationalism based on ethnic hatred." While all that was indisputably true, it seemed to be taking the side of Moscow against Ukraine. It was resented by some in Kiev and by more in the industrial cities of the U.S. Midwest with large Ukrainian-American populations, many of which were intensely anti-Soviet. *New York Times* columnist William Safire, in a biting description that stuck, called Bush's statement a "dismaying Chicken Kiev speech."

COUP AND COUNTER COUP

On Sunday afternoon, August 18, Mikhail Gorbachev was at the desk in the study of his vacation villa at Foros on the Black Sea when he was told that "a group of comrades" had arrived to see him. Gorbachev was startled and displeased, since well-established procedures and the three rings of security around the villa were designed to protect him against unplanned intrusions. Seeking more information, he picked up first one, then another of the telephones on his desk, only to find all of them dead. Finally he tried the heavily protected red phone that directly connected him to the defense minister and chief of the military General Staff in case of nuclear attack. It was also dead. He turned on the television set, but found it inoperative.

It did not take Gorbachev long to realize that a plot against him was under way. He rushed outside to his wife, Raisa. "If they think that they will get me to change my policies, they will not succeed. I will not give in to any blackmail of threats," he told her. Together they summoned their daughter and son-in-law, who were visiting with their two children. Remembering how Nikita Khrushchev, the last reformist General Secretary, had been deposed in a coup, and, even worse, recalling the grisly fate of the last tsar and his kin, the family understood that anything might happen.

Presently Gorbachev returned to his study to meet "the comrades," who had already come up to the second floor uninvited. They were Oleg Baklanov, secretary of the Communist Party Central Committee in charge of the military-industrial complex; Oleg Shenin, another party secretary; Valery Boldin, Gorbachev's chief of staff for the past fifteen years; General Valery Varennikov, commander of Soviet ground forces; and Yuri Plekhanov, KGB chief of security for the president. It was on Plekhanov's authority that the visitors had been able to pass the guards at Foros. Gorbachev summarily ordered the security chief out of his office, considering him a flunky who had no business dealing with political issues.

"Who sent you?" Gorbachev demanded.

"The Committee" was the reply.

"What committee?"

"Well, the Committee set up to deal with the emergency situation in the country."

"Who set it up? I didn't create it and the Supreme Soviet didn't create it. Who created it?"

Baklanov, who did most of the talking, named some of the members of "the Committee," the most powerful men remaining in Moscow, all of whom owed their prominence to Gorbachev, including Vice President Yanayev, Prime Minister Pavlov, KGB Chief Kryuchkov, Defense Minister Yazov, and, most shocking to Gorbachev, Supreme Soviet Chairman Lukyanov, a close friend and associate since they had attended Moscow University law school together forty years earlier.

Gorbachev was informed that the signing of the Union Treaty, scheduled for August 20, had been canceled. Baklanov said Yeltsin had been arrested, then corrected himself: "He will be arrested." Baklanov presented two documents and gave Gorbachev his choice: a decree declaring a state of emergency or a paper transferring his powers to the vice president.

Gorbachev angrily rejected the ultimatum, saying: "You and the people who sent you are irresponsible. You will destroy yourselves, but that's your business, and to hell with you. But you will also destroy the country and everything we have already done. Tell that to the committee that sent you."

Boldin, who had always been obsequious in his boss's presence, appealed, "Mikhail Sergeyevich, you don't understand what the situation in the country is." "Shut up, you prick," Gorbachev shot back to his staff chief. "How dare you give me lectures about the situation in the country."

Varennikov, a former commander of Soviet troops in Afghanistan, glared at Gorbachev as if he were a lowly subordinate and shouted "Resign!" Gorbachev pretended to have forgotten the general's name. "Valentin Ivanovich, is it? So just listen, Valentin Ivanovich. The people are not a battalion of soldiers to whom you can issue the command, 'right turn' or 'left turn, march' and they will do as you tell them. It won't be like that."

Calling his visitors "adventurers and criminals," Gorbachev swore that nothing would come of their plans. With some choice Russian curse words, he sent them on their way.

The idea of deposing Gorbachev had been brewing for a long time. According to the information now available, it came to a head when

Kryuchkov received the transcript of the bugged conversation of Gorbachev, Yeltsin, and Nazarbayev at Novo-Ogaryovo revealing that he and several others would be fired after the Union Treaty was signed on August 20. After learning of his likely ouster, the KGB chief ordered the preparation of contingency plans and emergency decrees for running the country without Gorbachev.

On August 17, Kryuchkov met with Pavlov, Yazov, Boldin, Baklanov, and Shenin at a KGB hotel-spa in Moscow, where they took steam baths, drank vodka and Scotch, and agreed to Kryuchkov's plan. They would form a committee to declare a state of emergency and demand Gorbachev's support. If he refused, they would isolate him at Foros and announce that he was incapacitated. In that case, Yanayev, who had not yet been approached, would become acting president and the Supreme Soviet, under Lukyanov's hand, could legalize the procedures after the fact. Kryuchkov had already arranged for technicians to cut off all Gorbachev's communications when he gave the signal. The group then decided to send five "comrades" to Foros to deal with Gorbachev.

The following day, while awaiting return of the five, the rest of the coup leadership met around a conference table in the prime minister's office in the Kremlin. Nobody was willing to take the place at the head of the table that would imply leadership. Several of the group, especially Vice President Yanayev and Prime Minister Pavlov, had been drinking. Parliament Speaker Lukyanov, while participating in the plot, insisted that on balance of power grounds his name be taken off the State Committee for the State of Emergency that was being formed.

Shortly after 10 P.M. the group from Foros returned and reported Gorbachev's belligerent attitude and actions. The discussion then proceeded on the fiction that the president was seriously ill. Yanayev, who had spoken to Gorbachev by telephone earlier in the day and knew that nothing was wrong with him, was reluctant to assume the acting presidency, saying he was not "morally or professionally ready" for such heavy responsibility. He was pressured by the others, who said a takeover was the only way to avert civil war and that he would merely have to sign a few decrees. Finally he put his signature in a shaky hand on the previously prepared paper saying he was assuming the office of president "in connection with the inability of Gorbachev, Mikhail Sergeyevich to fulfill his duties . . . due to his state of health." Others then signed an order declaring a six-month state of emergency.

Foreign Minister Bessmertnykh, who had been summoned to the

meeting from vacation, arrived shortly after the papers had been signed. After hearing the explanation, he struck his name off the list of emergency committee members, saying that no foreign leaders would deal with him if he were listed. In the next several days he did nothing to foster the coup, but he took no forceful action against it.

The following morning at 5:30 TASS announced Gorbachev's "illness" and the new regime. The Emergency Committee, it was announced, had taken over the government, suspended all political activity and demonstrations, and reintroduced censorship. Long columns of military units were already on the move into Moscow from its environs. While some democratic leaders were placed under surveillance, no large-scale arrests took place.

Yeltsin's youngest daughter, Tanya, who had heard the news on television, awakened her father, who was asleep in his house. At first he couldn't believe it. He tried to call Gorbachev, but was told the call could not be put through. He tried calling Yanayev but was told the "acting president" was resting after working all night. He called Nazarbayev and other republic leaders, but those whom he could reach were noncommittal, saying they lacked information. He decided to head for the White House, as the gleaming white nineteen-story headquarters of the Republic of Russia was known. There he and his senior aides began to organize resistance, composing an appeal to the people of Russia to oppose this "right-wing, reactionary, unconstitutional coup." The appeal was photocopied, faxed, and sent by e-mail throughout Moscow and around the world. It was broadcast in full by independent Moscow radio stations defying censorship.

With a burst of energy and bravery, Yeltsin walked purposefully down the building's front steps and climbed atop a tank that had taken up a threatening position. As television cameras recorded the scene, he pulled himself up to his full six-foot-four inches and defiantly read from the "Appeal to the Citizens of Russia" in a booming voice. The crowds around him cheered.

In Foros, the Gorbachev family, supposedly cut off from all contact with the outside, managed to hear news of the state of emergency and Gorbachev's "illness" on a small transistor the president had brought along to listen to while shaving. The outer guards around the estate had been replaced, but the inner group of presidential guards, who were still heavily armed, had pledged continued loyalty. The coup directors had placed a fire engine and a street cleaning vehicle on the helicopter pad to bar a possible rescue attempt. Trucks barred the road. Unusual patrol vessels appeared offshore. The family, fearful of poisoning, decided to eat only food that had been in the house before the coup. Worried that the house was bugged, they held all confidential conversations in open air outside.

The black briefcase containing the presidential nuclear codes that could authorize a nuclear weapons launch, known as the *chemodanchik,* or "little suitcase"—the Soviet equivalent of what the White House calls "the football," which constantly accompanies the U.S. president—was still being guarded by a Soviet colonel stationed in a guest house on the Foros estate. In fact, the briefcase had been useless since all communications had been cut off. Now the officers in charge of the codes were called back to Moscow, taking with them this ultimate symbol of presidential authority.

George Bush, at his vacation home at Kennebunkport, was informed by Scowcroft, who was staying at a nearby hotel, of the startling announcement from Moscow that Gorbachev had been replaced. Scowcroft had first received the news not from government channels but from CNN. "My God!" exclaimed Bush. Although both men were appalled, Scowcroft advised caution in wording an official reaction, on grounds that the coup might succeed and the United States would have to deal with its leaders. Rather than characterize it with such words as *illegal* or *illegitimate,* Bush and Scowcroft decided to use the milder term *extra-constitutional.* U.S. statements turned much more negative as the situation became clearer, but the coup group repeatedly broadcast the original U.S. reaction—but not the later ones—as a sign that the U.S. leadership did not seriously object to their maneuver.

The takeover had been planned on assumptions of popular passivity and universal conformity that had been hallmarks of an earlier era. But despite censorship orders, independent radios were still on the air and accurate foreign broadcasts could easily be heard. Yeltsin and other democratic leaders, nearly all of whom were still free, issued ever more challenging statements from the Russian White House. Tens of thousands of supporters responded by gathering outside the building and other public buildings, making a formidable barrier for Soviet troops who had been ordered to positions nearby. The troops and their commanders were reluctant to move with the massive lethal force that would be needed. After a half decade of increasing *glasnost* and democracy, much more information was available, and public sentiment had begun to count. The Russian people were not as easily cowed by authority and the threat of force as they had been in the pre-Gorbachev era. Yeltsin and his aides were cheered by increasingly hostile statements about the plot from abroad, including a well-publicized telephone call of encouragement to Yeltsin from Bush.

On the second day of the coup, Vice President Yanayev, Interior Minister Boris Pugo, Central Committee Secretary Baklanov, and two other leaders held a televised press conference to explain and justify their actions. Yanayev's hands shook with nervousness or the effects of a hangover, and the coup leaders appeared pitifully unsure of themselves. These factors contributed to the perception that the operation might not succeed, which in turn contributed to the growing boldness of its opponents.

By late that night, it was clear that the coup had failed. Defense Minister Yazov called a halt to all threatening movements and ordered Soviet forces back to their normal positions outside Moscow, but not before three young men had been killed in a clash with a tank. KGB chief Kryuchkov telephoned Yeltsin to tell him there would be no attack on the White House. Members of the coup group who were not hopelessly drunk—as Yanayev and Pavlov were found to be—flew to the Crimea in the presidential plane to make their peace with Gorbachev. He refused to see them, with the notable exception of his old friend Lukyanov, who claimed to have had nothing to do with the plot but was unable to convince Gorbachev. At Gorbachev's demand his communications were restored; he spoke to Yeltsin and other republican leaders and then called Bush to say that the coup was over and he was once more in power.

Gorbachev and his family flew back to Moscow in the early hours of August 22, immediately after being freed. Raisa had suffered a mild stroke under the pressure of events and had to be helped off the plane. Their daughter, Irina, was in the first phase of a nervous breakdown. Gorbachev was exhausted and also poorly informed about all that had happened while he was confined. As he came down the aircraft steps blinking against the television kleig lights, he looked uncertain and disoriented.

"I have come back from Foros to another country, and I myself am a different man now," Gorbachev told journalists at the Kremlin the following day, but in fact he did not grasp the fundamental change that had occurred in his absence. Yeltsin and democratic, mostly anticommunist, forces had faced down and vanquished the established leaders of the army, the KGB, the interior ministry, and other organs of physical force. They were in the saddle now, and they wanted no more of Gorbachev or the Communist Party, which he still led. Gorbachev, however, did little to recognize Yeltsin's increased authority and soaring popularity. He initially vowed to preserve and reform the party to make it "a living force of *perestroika*." The dominant political ethos of Moscow had gone far beyond that perhaps impossible aim. Yeltsin banned the publication of *Pravda* and other party newspapers in the Russian republic and suspended all activities of the Russian Communist Party. Huge crowds mobbed the KGB building and tore down the statue of the founder of the Soviet secret police, Felix Dzerzhinsky. More crowds surrounded the offices of the Central Committee. Gorbachev was persuaded by his aides to resign as general secretary, disband the Central Committee, and transfer party property to the parliament, which voted to ban all party activity. Thus, after three quarters of a century, the Communist Party, which had ruled the Soviet Union since the Russian Revolution of 1917, ceased to exist as a decisive force.

The members of the Emergency Committee were arrested, except for Interior Minister Pugo, who had committed suicide along with his wife. Sergei Akhromeyev, a hero of the seige of Leningrad and of arms control progress with the United States, hung himself in his Kremlin office, dressed in the full uniform of a marshal of the Soviet Union. Akhromeyev had heard about the coup attempt while on a holiday. Increasingly convinced that the Soviet motherland and its armed forces were being destroyed under existing policy, he rushed back to Moscow and volunteered to aid the Emergency Committee. Akhromeyev drew up plans, which were never implemented, for storming the White House. After the coup had failed, he left a suicide note on his desk: "I cannot live when my motherland is dying and everything that I ever believed in is being destroyed. My age and my previous life give me the right to leave this life."

On the political front, Yeltsin took his revenge for his 1987 humiliation by humiliating Gorbachev before the Russian parliament. When the Soviet president said he had not read minutes of a cabinet meeting dramatizing the disloyalty of his own associates, Yeltsin wagged his finger in Gorbachev's face and imperiously instructed him, "Well, read them!" Gorbachev did so.

Watching the scene on television in Kennebunkport, Scowcroft observed to Bush, "It's all over. . . . Yeltsin's telling him what to do. I don't think Gorbachev understands what's happening." Bush said sadly, "I'm afraid he may have had it."

THE FINAL DAYS

The results of the abortive coup speeded up history in a way that nobody had anticipated. Gorbachev, rather than being the victor, found himself increasingly embattled, struggling to keep his powers and those of the Kremlin. The defeat of the coup plotters destroyed the conservative forces seeking to block the union treaty, which had been expected to create a new Soviet Union of a more decentralized sort. Unexpectedly, one effect of the downfall of the army leadership, the KGB, and the Communist Party was to free Yeltsin and leaders of other constituent republics from the organs of coercion and oppression that had bound them to the central power in the Kremlin. With this realization came a rush to proclaim independence: first the three Baltic states, which had been acquired by Stalin after a secret deal with Hitler and had never fully accepted Soviet rule; next Ukraine, the most powerful non-Russian republic, subject to a popular referendum; then in quick succession Belorussia, Moldova, Azerbaijan, Uzbekistan, Kyrgystan, Tajikistan, and Armenia. Georgia, which had declared its independence several months earlier, announced that it was breaking all ties with the Soviet Union. Like Russia, which did not declare its formal independence but which increasingly practiced it, many of these states began to ignore Moscow's authority whenever they chose.

Gorbachev's fear that the Soviet Union would fall apart was rapidly being realized, step by step. "Although the state still had a president, the President himself no longer had a country," observed Andrei Grachev, a longtime official of the Central Committee who became Gorbachev's press secretary after the coup.

While Yeltsin and some others declared continuing support for the Union Treaty, everyone agreed it would have to be renegotiated with much greater concessions to the republics. On September 2, Gorbachev and the leaders of ten republics, including Russia, agreed to work out a new treaty to form a Union of Sovereign States to eventually replace the dying Union of Soviet Socialist Republics (USSR). They also decided on a radical overhaul of central bodies in the administrative, legislative, and economic fields. Gorbachev used his dwindling but still-viable clout, plus the promise of continuing salaries and personal perks, to persuade the Congress of People's Deputies to vote itself out of existence as part of the new arrangement.

Official Washington was observing the maneuvering and uncertainty with growing concern. "As the Soviet external empire collapsed in 1989, the Soviet internal empire seems to be collapsing now," said a memorandum to Baker from two senior aides. They foresaw the possibility that the drive toward independence would lead to territorial, economic, and even military disputes between the constituent parts of Moscow's previous domain. In an attempt to influence the process, Baker devised and announced "five principles" that in the U.S. view should be respected in the dissolution of the Soviet Union. They were peaceful self-determination, respect for existing borders, respect for democracy and the rule of law, human rights, and respect for international law and obligations. They were well received in Moscow, where Baker took them on September 10 when he arrived for a long-scheduled foreign ministers' meeting conference on human rights.

Baker's initial talks were with Boris Pankin, who was named Soviet foreign minister after Bessmertynkh had been fired by Gorbachev because of his flaccid conduct during the coup. In talks with Pankin and separate meetings with Gorbachev and Yeltsin, Baker was able to reach agreement on two outstanding issues that had long plagued U.S.-Soviet relations:

- The two nations finally agreed to stop military supplies to both sides in the war in Afghanistan, which still continued despite the withdrawal of Soviet troops in 1989. All previous U.S.-Soviet negotiations about an arms cutoff had failed.

- Gorbachev also agreed to begin withdrawing the Soviet brigade in Cuba, which had been stationed on the island since before the 1962 missile crisis and had caused a political flap when rediscovered by U.S. intelligence, to the embarrassment of the Carter administration, in 1979. More surprising, pressed by Yeltsin's stand on the matter, Gorbachev agreed to announce the decision at once in a joint press conference with Baker, even before the Cubans had been informed.

It was clear enough to Baker and the White House that the tenuous balance of power inside the Soviet Union was only temporary, while new arrangements were emerging. Hoping to encourage Gorbachev and the Soviet military to reduce their military arsenals before a process of disintegration resumed, Bush announced a dramatic set of unilateral U.S. arms reductions on September 27. These included elimination of most ground- and sea-based tactical nuclear weapons, cancellation of several new weapons programs, and removal of all strategic bombers and many missiles from alert status. He called on Moscow to follow suit, but did not make these actions dependent on Soviet approval.

Gorbachev responded on October 5 by announcing the Soviet Union would eliminate even more ground- and sea-based nuclear weapons than the United States, and like the United States would also take strategic bombers and missiles off alert and cancel planned weapons programs. He also announced that Moscow would reduce the number of its strategic nuclear warheads permitted under the START Treaty, which he and Bush had signed only two months earlier, from 6,000 to 5,000, and he called for new negotiations to cut remaining U.S. and Soviet strategic offensive weapons by half (this was done a few months later in START II). In late 1991, Gorbachev reveled in "racing downhill" with Bush to eliminate military forces. It accorded with his long-held desire to make radical arms cutbacks, and also gave him the ability to act as commander in chief of the shaky governmental structure that had been created since the abortive coup. At least temporarily, he strode back onto the national and international stage as leader of one of the two nuclear superpowers.

Another chance to return to the world spotlight came at the end of October, when Gorbachev joined Bush in Madrid for the opening of the long-awaited Middle East Peace Conference that would begin the formal process of negotiating an end to the Arab-Israeli conflict. Just before Gorbachev left home, however, Yeltsin announced that Russia would undertake radical economic reform on its own, including accelerated privatization and lifting of price controls, without regard to the Kremlin and without waiting for others. Ukraine had already declared that it would not join the new economic treaty being planned; others were also backing away from joint action. As part of his new economic package, Yeltsin also ceased financial support for most of Gorbachev's ministries. The Soviet Union's coffers were already so depleted that at Madrid, the United States paid many of the Soviet delegation's expenses.

At Madrid, Gorbachev struck Baker as being as "unfocused as I had ever seen him." His mind was as sharp as ever, the secretary felt, but the overwhelming complexity of the multiple challenges beating down on him seemed more than he could bear. Gorbachev would begin discussing the Mideast, then veer off to his domestic problems. He condemned republic leaders for taking a "disastrous course" and told Bush that further dissolution of the Soviet Union would destabilize the globe. At the same time, he sought to reassure the Americans and others, saying that despite appearances to the contrary, everything was under control and would work out all right. To Baker, "he seemed like a drowning man looking for a life preserver." A most important lifeline, in his view, would be major U.S. economic aid. Bush told him, however, that this could not be supplied until the fast-changing relationships between the center and the republics, and between him and Yeltsin, were clarified.

In mid-November, amid the continuing struggle with Yeltsin, Gorbachev reached, perhaps almost instinctively, for another means of support—the renewal of his long and close comradeship with Shevardnadze, who had been estranged from him since resigning as foreign minister the previous winter. Pankin, who had served in the job since the aftermath of the attempted coup, was sent to London as ambassador and Shevardnadze returned to try to reinvigorate the Foreign Ministry, which was by now demoralized by confusion and cutbacks. Rather than engage negotiating partners abroad, Shevardnadze's first efforts were inside the disintegrating union—visits to the capitals of wavering republics. As the former party leader of Georgia, Shevardnadze had credibility in his discussions of relations with central authority in Moscow.

As it turned out, his efforts were far from sufficient. Gorbachev's drive to win full agreement on the treaty setting up the proposed Union of Sovereign States was stymied by Yeltsin and others. On December 1, Ukraine, which had refused since the coup attempt to take part in the negotiations for a new union treaty, voted overwhelmingly for independence, as expected. This set in train the final act that doomed the Soviet Union: an agreement reached by Yeltsin with the presidents of Ukraine and Belarus, in great secrecy on December 8, to abandon Gorbachev's stillborn union and create instead a loose confederation titled the Commonwealth of Independent States. The joint declaration crafted by the three presidents at a Belorussian hunting lodge, a place where Nikita Khrushchev and Leonid Brezhnev had liked to hunt and relax, declared flatly that "the Union of Soviet Socialist Republics is ceasing its existence as a subject of international law and a geopolitical reality."

With their agreement concluded and their statement drafted, Yeltsin telephoned Bush to tell him the news. Calls were also made to the Soviet and Russian defenses ministers. Only after that did the Belarus president, Stanislav Shushkevich, inform Gorbachev in a telephone call that his country and his job had been abolished. Furious at what he considered an underhanded deal about which he had not been informed, Gorbachev erupted at his caller. "This is a disgrace. You've been speaking with the president of the United States, and you failed to speak with the president of your own country? This is shameful." In Washington the same day, before the news from the Belarus hunting lodge had been received, Baker was asked on the CBS Sunday program *Face the Nation*, whether Gorbachev would be able to hold the Soviet Union together. The secretary of state responded, "I think the Soviet Union, as we've known it, no longer exists."

One week later, Baker returned to Moscow on his final trip to the crumbling Soviet Union. In the Kremlin, he saw the transfer of power taking place before his own eyes. Yeltsin, who had the upper hand, met Baker in St. Catherine's Hall, where so many history-making Soviet-American meetings had taken place in the past. Sitting next to Yeltsin at the conference table, in another symbolic display of his authority, was the Soviet defense minister, General Yevgeni Shaposhnikov. "Welcome to this Russian building on Russian soil," boomed the ebullient Yeltsin. After explaining his version of how and why the Soviet Union had been junked and the Commonwealth of Independent States created, Yeltsin told Baker that most of the Soviet ministries and other organs would be disbanded, and the rest taken over by Russia. Moreover, Russia would take over all Soviet embassies and trade missions as well as the Soviet seat on the UN Security Council. He said Soviet nuclear weapons would be controlled by a single unified command structure in the new Commonwealth, with Russia ultimately becoming the sole possessor of the weapons.

A half-hour later, after the Kremlin staff had refurbished the room, Baker returned to meet Gorbachev. Snow was falling heavily outside, and the winter light had faded from the windows of the Great Kremlin Palace. Gorbachev's former ebullience had also ebbed. Flanked by his two original *perestroika* partners, Shevardnadze and Yakovlev, he called the meeting at the Belorussian hunting lodge "a kind of coup." Gorbachev said that despite all that had happened, he and his longtime colleagues wanted to help the Commonwealth succeed—"but I don't believe they will." Failure would jeopardize "all that we have worked so hard for over these years," he said with more resignation than anger. Gorbachev urged that the United States not recognize the new arrangement immediately but use recognition as leverage to achieve common goals.

Baker's throat was dry, and he took out one of the sugarless mints he habitually carried in his pocket. When he noticed Gorbachev's interest, he gave him one, and another to Shevardnadze. Tasting it, Gorbachev recalled that "that's the same thing you gave me at Camp David." It seemed to Baker that for the moment, Gorbachev was savoring the memory of better days.

Later that evening, Baker met Shevardnadze over dinner in another elegiac session. The white-maned foreign minister felt he had made a mistake to return to duty as the Soviet Union's top diplomat but said he had no regrets. "We made friends again with Gorbachev. In these, the last days of the Soviet Union, we are still here together." He and Baker then met the American and Soviet diplomatic press corps for one last time.

The Commonwealth of Independent States was officially established by Russia and ten other former republics at Alma Ata on December 21. It issued a statement declaring that with its formation, "the Union of Soviet Socialist Republics ceases to exist." The presidents of the Commonwealth composed a joint message to Gorbachev thanking him "for his great, positive contribution" and informing him formally of the cessation of the Soviet Union and of his presidency.

Gorbachev resigned his office on December 25. Two hours before his final address to the nation he had led into a new era, the Soviet president telephoned Bush, who was celebrating Christmas with his family at Camp David. Beginning with Christmas greetings, Gorbachev said that, although he had hoped and worked for a different outcome, he would do all he could to assist the new Commonwealth. He asked Bush to do the same: "We must promote cooperation rather than disintegration and destruction."

Turning to the issue of nuclear control, Gorbachev disclosed that he had already signed a decree transferring the "little suitcase" containing the nuclear launch codes to the "president of the Russian Republic," avoiding the use of Yeltsin's name. "You may therefore feel at ease as you celebrate Christmas, and sleep quietly tonight."

Bush responded with praise for the way in which the nuclear control issue had been handled, calling it a matter "of crucial international importance." On the broader issue of Gorbachev's accomplishments,

Bush said he had written a letter that Gorbachev should soon receive expressing "my conviction that what you have done will go down into history and that future historians will give you full credit for your accomplishments." Recalling the summer day in 1990 they had spent together at Camp David, Bush said, "The horseshoe pit where you threw that ringer is still in good shape. I hope our paths will cross soon again. You will be welcome to come and we will be glad to welcome you, once things settle down, perhaps here at Camp David."

In the meantime, the U.S. president said, he would deal "respectfully, openly, positively and I hope progressively with the leader of the Russian Republic and the other republics. . . . We will work with them on the whole range of issues as we have worked with you. . . . On this special day of the year, at this historic crossroads, I salute you and thank you for all that you have done for the world. And thank you for your friendship." After putting down the telephone, Bush was surprised to learn that Ted Koppel and a crew from ABC television's *Nightline,* which was recording the last days of the Soviet Union, had videotaped the conversation on Gorbachev's end.

Shortly before the broadcast hour of 7 P.M., Gorbachev left his office and walked down the hall to the room where he would give his farewell address. The room was filled with photographers, technicians, and journalists from three television networks, including Cable News Network from the United States. Before making his speech, Gorbachev planned to sign a decree resigning from the post of commander in chief of the armed forces, making him no longer eligible to wield the awesome nuclear destructive power that had belonged to the Soviet Union. He didn't care for the pen that was offered him and signed instead with the pen of a CNN crew member. Then all was still in the makeshift studio, and he began his speech.

At the outset, Gorbachev announced that, "due to the situation created by the formation of the Commonwealth of Independent States, I am terminating my duties as president of the Union of Soviet Socialist Republics." After lamenting the dismemberment of the country into separate states, he gave his own capsule review of the road he and the USSR had traveled since 1985:

> As fate would have it, at the time when I acceded to the highest office of the state it was already clear that something was wrong with the country. We have everything in abundance here: land, oil, gas, coal, precious metals, other natural resources—not to mention the

talents and intelligence that God has liberally bestowed on us. And yet we live under much poorer circumstances than the developed countries. We are always lagging behind them.

The reason for this was already obvious: Society was being strangled by the bureaucratic-command system. Condemned to serve the ideology and bear the terrible burden of the arms race, society had reached the limits of its endurance. All attempts at partial reform (and we have had many) failed, one after the other. The country's prospects were increasingly dim. We could not live this way any longer. Everything had to be radically changed.

Gorbachev realized, he went on, that far-reaching reforms would be "extremely difficult and even dangerous" but that there was no choice. The process proved to be more arduous than expected, but still he counted major accomplishments:

- The totalitarian system, which deprived our country of the opportunity for happiness and prosperity that it would otherwise have had long ago, has been liquidated.

- We have made a breakthrough toward democratic reforms. Open elections, freedom of the press, religious freedom, representative government and a multiparty system have become reality. Human rights have been recognized as the paramount principle.

- The move to a diversified economy has been initiated, and the equality of all forms of ownership has been established.

He then turned to the field of foreign affairs, where he had made so much of his mark on the history of his time:

We live in a new world: The Cold War is over, the threat of a world war has been averted; the arms race and the insane militarization that distorted our economy, our social consciousness and our morality have been halted . . .

- We have opened up to the world; we have renounced interference in the affairs of others and the use of armed forces outside this country. In response, we have obtained trust, solidarity and respect.

- We have become one of the mainstays of the restructuring of modern civilization on peaceful and democratic foundations.

- The peoples, the nations have gained real freedom to choose their own path to self-determination. Our efforts to democratically reconfigure the multinational state brought us very close to concluding a new union agreement.

All this, Gorbachev recounted, required tremendous effort against fierce opposition. Consequently, "the old system crumbled away before the new one could be set in motion. And the crisis that had befallen society became still worse." The August coup, he declared, pushed the general crisis to its farthest limits. Although he expressed concern about the resulting collapse of the state, he appealed to the people to preserve the democratic victories of recent years, to not give them up under any circumstances.

Finally, it was time for thanks and good-byes:

I want to express my gratitude to all the citizens who supported our policy for the country's renewal, and who played a part in the realization of democratic reforms.

I am grateful to the statesmen, to the leading figures in politics and society, to the millions of people in other countries who understood our plans, supported them, and came forward to meet us, offering their sincere cooperation.

I leave office with anxiety. But also with hope, and with faith in you, in your wisdom and your strength of mind. We are heirs to a great civilization, and it is now up to each and every one of us to ensure that this civilization is reborn to a modern, dignified new life.

I wish to thank from the bottom of my heart those who stood by me through all these years in a just and good cause. Certainly, some mistakes could have been avoided and many things could have been done better.

I am certain that, sooner or later, our joint efforts will bear fruit, and that our peoples will live in a democratic and prosperous society.

I wish you all the very best.

After a five-minute break, Gorbachev submitted to a CNN interview, which was broadcast live to most of the world and two hours later on Soviet central television. Then he walked back to his office for his final duty, the turning over of the nuclear launch codes. General Shaposhnikov was waiting for him, expecting that Yeltsin would join them for the official handover. Shortly word came that Yeltsin had been displeased with Gorbachev's speech and would refuse to appear in his office, suggesting the "neutral" site of St. Catherine's Hall for the handover. Gorbachev stiffened and rejected that plan. Instead, he simply told Shaposhikov to take charge of the *chemodanchik*. The defense minister left the room and headed down the hall in Yeltsin's direction, accompanied by two inconspicuous men in civilian clothes, carrying the small but powerful package that for more than six years had accompanied Gorbachev wherever he went.

While these events were taking place, the red hammer-and-sickle flag of the Soviet Union was being taken down from the dome of the Senate building in the Kremlin, the site of the presidential office, at Yeltsin's order. The blue, white, and red flag of Russia fluttered triumphantly in its stead.

The Soviet Union was no more.

AFTERWORD

The end of the Cold War and the collapse of the Soviet Union transformed the geopolitical map of the world almost beyond recognition, and more rapidly than at any time in the modern era except in the violence or immediate aftermath of war. The dramatic changes in the relations among the leading states were remarkably peaceful, having come about through dialogue, negotiation, and a radical reconsideration of the balances and uses of military power. The great turn in world affairs that is recorded here was grounded in shifting economic and political trends adverse to the existing structure of the Soviet Union.

One of the fundamental questions debated by historians is whether history is predominately fashioned by the human will of extraordinary people or largely determined by external forces more powerful than the individual actors. There is evidence in this chronicle for both theories.

Surely, great trends were evident in abundance: the ever more burdensome buildup of military forces, whose enormous costs devastated the economy of the Soviet Union and strained that of the United States; the spiraling growth and massive overkill of nuclear weapons and the growing speed and accuracy of missile systems that delivered them, putting the very survival of both nations at risk as never before; the rapid development of the global economy and global means of digital and mass communications, which were increasingly important to economically advanced nations and from which the Soviet Union and its Eastern European satellite states were virtually excluded because of their autarkic policies; the Soviet Union's crisis of confidence in communist ideology and its system of rigid political, economic, and social control, which gave rise to a widespread receptivity to reforms; the deepening opposition in Eastern European countries, East Germany, and some of the outlying Soviet republics to regimes that had been imposed and sustained by the Kremlin's power, and their growing thirst for independence and freedom.

Nevertheless, the way in which the underlying trends were applied in practice could have been very different had other leaders been in charge and other choices made. Aleksandr Bessmertnykh, a key figure on American affairs in the Soviet Foreign Ministry during most of the period covered and later Soviet ambassador to the United States and Soviet foreign minister, told me that the great shift in the relations of the two nations was "a rare case in history when a major change didn't just develop—it was willed to happen." I think he was right.

We are still too close to the events recorded here to reach ultimate judgment about who was primarily responsible for the reconciliation of the United States and the Soviet Union, or how the main protagonists will be regarded in the history of the twentieth century. Even now, however, some observations may be offered.

There is little doubt that Mikhail Gorbachev, flawed as he was and ultimately discarded as a result of the revolutionary changes he set in motion, will be a great historical figure. The Gorbachev found in these pages, especially the feisty, self-confident, and incisive figure of his early dialogues with American officials, made his mark on Soviet society and international relations in ways that were often surprising and nearly always dramatic. In these pages one can almost see Gorbachev grow in stature and maturity; at the same time, however, one can observe his failure to act decisively or with insight as his troubles multiplied.

From an early point in his leadership, Gorbachev captured the imagination of his American interlocutors—and of the world at large— more than did any of his predecessors. He grasped that change was essential if the Soviet Union was to remain a major power; while he hesitated fatally to take bold economic steps, he moved with strength and determination on the political and military fronts. As both apostle and victim of change, Gorbachev was the central figure in the transformation of his country and its relations with the outside world.

Eduard Shevardnadze, who resigned as Soviet foreign minister in December 1990 warning against the threat of dictatorship and who rejoined Gorbachev for the final days of the Soviet Union, is a remarkable figure meriting a place of his own in the annals of his time. A man without diplomatic ambitions or experience until tapped by Gorbachev, his longtime friend, Shevardnadze proved to be an able diplomat whose candor and authority won the respect of his peers abroad. The political and moral precepts he espoused within the Soviet system were little short of astounding, as in a meeting of the Foreign Ministry's Communist Party members in the spring of 1990 when he answered criticism that the Soviet Union had lost respect in the world:

> The belief that we are a great country and that we should be respected for this is deeply ingrained in me, as in everyone. But great in what? Territory? Population? Quantity of arms? Or the people's troubles? The individual's lack of rights? Life's disorderliness? In what do we, who have virtually the highest infant mortality rate on our planet, take pride? It is not easy answering the questions: Who are you and who do you wish to be? A country which is feared or a country which is respected? A country of power or a country of kindness?

Ronald Reagan, the U.S. president who seemed at first least likely to accomplish a rapprochement with the Soviet Union, made a crucial contribution to the developments of the late 1980s. Reagan's self-confidence and the confidence that he instilled in the American people, his surprising eagerness to negotiate with the leaders of the Soviet "evil empire," and his deep belief that nuclear weapons posed a deadly peril to his nation and to mankind—all played a major part in what took place. It is unlikely that an American president who was considered a moderate or liberal could have accomplished such a dramatic improvement in U.S.-Soviet relations so swiftly and with so little conservative opposition.

When I asked Reagan in early 1990 why the change in U.S.-Soviet relations had taken place, he responded that it was due to "mutual interest"—Gorbachev's interest in dealing with an economic "emergency" at home, caused in large measure by massive military expenditures, and his own belief that "it was a danger to have a world so heavily armed that one misstep could trigger a great war."

One of the most insightful tributes to Reagan's role came from the prominent Soviet journalist and later diplomat Aleksandr Bovin, who described the president as a major political figure comparable to Nikita Khrushchev in the Soviet Union, a man who "was not afraid of bold, extraordinary decisions." Bovin noted that Reagan was not a professional politician—the sort, as he put it, who slices off small bits of decisions, bit by bit—but a figure with a bold approach and keen intuition, even if he did not understand many of the important details.

The role of George Shultz as U.S. secretary of state was of central importance in Washington, given the paradoxes in Reagan's views and the endless disputes on Soviet policy within his administration until its final year. Reagan knew that he wanted a less dangerous relationship with the Soviet Union, but he did not know how to go about achieving it. Shultz provided two key ingredients that were otherwise lacking: a persistent and practical drive toward the goal of improved relations through the accomplishment of tangible objectives, whether they were arms control pacts, the settlement of regional conflicts, human rights advances, or bilateral accords; and organizational skills to mobilize at least parts of the fractious U.S. government to interact on a systematic basis with the Soviet government. Reagan wanted it to happen; Shultz was the key figure in his administration who made it happen.

Writing about the uses of history for decision-makers, Harvard Professors Richard E. Neustadt and Ernest R. May praised the rare policymaker who takes a long view, seeing and thinking in "time streams" beyond the horizon of the current day. In Soviet affairs, it seems to me, Shultz was such a figure. Perhaps due to his training and experience as an economist, Shultz worked patiently to apply steady inputs over time toward his long-range goal of improving U.S.-Soviet relations. As a former labor mediator and domestic affairs cabinet member accustomed to temporary ups and downs, Shultz was undeterred by the many obstacles, disappointments, and setbacks along the way. Like the tortoise in the race with the hare, he just kept coming, moving slowly but relentlessly toward his goal.

George Bush and James Baker brought to office a very different style of policymaking while retaining a large measure of continuity in the direction of U.S. policy. After a slow and overly cautious start, their interaction with Moscow took the relationship to a new stage of intimacy and cooperation. By the time the Bush presidency began, however, Gorbachev and his *perestroika* efforts at reforming the Soviet system were already on the downward slope. As Baker observed later, it was a critical paradox that "just as U.S.-Soviet cooperation was reaching its highest point, Gorbachev's domestic political position and the stability of the Soviet state were reaching their lowest levels."

Unlike Reagan, Bush was cautious as a domestic and international policymaker, with the dramatic exception of his immediate and unswerving determination to halt Iraq's advance in the Persian Gulf and reverse its invasion of Kuwait. His caution and forbearance averted crises in the Soviet-American relationship, notably over events in the Baltic states, but they also lessened the U.S. response to Moscow's growing economic distress. In retrospect, however, it is doubtful that anything Washington could have done would have saved the Soviet Union from the downfall that was dictated fundamentally by crises within. It is not clear that it would have been in the national interest of the United States to do so, even had it been within its power.

Baker, an extremely able negotiator who capitalized on an unusually strong relationship with his president, was ever alert to the political aspects, both domestically and internationally, of the U.S. relationship with Moscow. Alongside the efforts of Bush, his leadership of the drive to support German unification, his work to create and sustain the Gulf War coalition and, later, to restart the Middle East peace process—all of which required Soviet-American cooperation of unprecedented dimensions—showed great skill and agility in alliance diplomacy.

To depict these events of a world in transition while the shocks are still being felt is a hazardous enterprise, since still unknown developments can affect the perspective with which this drama and its main actors will some day be viewed. These pages seek to record what could be learned in the immediate aftermath of one of the great turning points of history, and to convey something of the excitement, vitality, and wonder with which it unfolded before our eyes.

ACKNOWLEDGMENTS

A journalist covering major events on a daily basis is able to observe and report only the tip of the iceberg. By returning later to interview those who were intimately involved, it was possible for me to go well below the water line to find out how and why the decisions were made that produced the events we had seen. For this book, scores of officials or former officials of the United States and the Soviet Union explained to me, often with great candor, what had happened beneath the surface. Without their assistance and that of other close observers, this book could not have been written. I am grateful to them all.

As mentioned in the introduction, I am particularly grateful to former Secretary of State George Shultz, who was generous with his time and recollections, even while working on his own memoirs. I also wish to acknowledge the assistance of his associates at Stanford, Charles Hill, Phyl Whiting, Grace Hawes, Juanita Nissley and Cynthia Gunn.

I am grateful for the help of the many officials or former officials of the United States government and private Americans who spent time with me for the purpose of this book, some of them in extensive interviews. These include President Ronald Reagan and President George Bush and (using their titles at the time of the action) Assistant Secretary of State Morton Abramowitz, Under Secretary of State Michael Armacost, White House Chief of Staff Howard Baker, Secretary of State James Baker, Confidence-and-Security-Building Negotiator Robert Barry, National Intelligence Officer for the Soviet Union Robert Blackwell, National Security Council Director of European Affairs Robert Blackwill, Assistant Secretary of State and Arms Negotiator Richard Burt and Moscow Embassy Political Counselor Shaun Byrnes.

Also, National Security Adviser and Secretary of Defense Frank Carlucci,

Secretary of Defense Richard Cheney, National Security Adviser William Clark, Chairman of the Joint Chiefs of Staff Admiral William Crowe, Nicholas Daniloff, White House Deputy Chief of Staff Michael Deaver, White House speechwriter Anthony Dolan, White House Chief of Staff Kenneth Duberstein, Under Secretary and Deputy Secretary of State Lawrence Eagleburger, Robert Einhorn of the State Department Policy Planning Staff, National Intelligence Officer for the Soviet Union Fritz Ermarth, Professor Murrey Feshbach of Georgetown University and Special Assistant to the Secretary of State Karen Galatz.

Also, Deputy CIA Director and Deputy National Security Adviser Robert Gates, Vice Presidential National Security Adviser Donald Gregg, U.S. Ambassador to the Soviet Union Arthur Hartman, David Hoffman of *The Washington Post*, Undersecretary of Defense Fred Ikle, Deputy Assistant Secretary of State Curtis Kammen, Arms Negotiator Max Kampelman, National Security Council Arms Control Director Colonel Robert Linhard, author Suzanne Massie, U.S. Ambassador to the Soviet Union Jack Matlock, National Security Adviser Robert McFarlane, Arms Adviser Paul Nitze and National Security Council Director of Middle East and South Asian Affairs Robert Oakley.

Also, Deputy Assistant Secretary of State Mark Palmer, State Department Director of Soviet Affairs Mark Parris, Assistant Secretary of Defense Richard Perle, National Security Adviser John Poindexter, National Security Adviser and Chairman of the Joint Chiefs of Staff General Colin Powell, Eleanor Randolph of *The Washington Post*, State Department Spokesman Charles Redman, National Security Council Director of Soviet Affairs Condoleezza Rice, Assistant Secretary of State Rozanne Ridgway and Hal Riney, author of the bear ad.

Also, State Department Director of Policy Planning Dennis Ross, Arms Adviser Edward Rowny, National Security Adviser Brent Scowcroft, Assistant Secretary of State Raymond Seitz, Peter Shultz, Director of Soviet Affairs and Deputy Assistant Secretary of State Thomas Simons, State Department Legal Adviser Abraham Sofaer, Arms Control Adviser to the Deputy Secretary of State James Timbie, State Department Director of Soviet Affairs Alexander Vershbow, Secretary of Defense Caspar Weinberger, pollster Richard Wirthlin and State Department Counselor Robert Zoellick.

Many Soviet officials and citizens made major contributions to this book, providing an unusual window on the developments as seen from Moscow. I wish to acknowledge the assistance of the Soviet Embassy in Washington, the International Department of the Central Committee of the Communist Party of the Soviet Union, the Soviet Foreign Ministry and the Novosti Press Agency Publishing Company, all of which helped in arranging interviews. The Moscow Bureau of *The Washington Post* was also of great help, as always.

I am particularly grateful to former Foreign Minister and Politburo member Eduard Shevardnadze for giving me the only book interview during his time in office, and to Yevgeni Primakov and Aleksandr Yakovlev, then members of the Politburo and Presidential Council, for their help. I am also grateful for the assistance of (using their titles at the time of the action) Chief of Staff of the Soviet Armed Forces and Military Adviser Marshal Sergei Akhromeyev,

General Secretary's Foreign Policy Assistant Andrei Aleksandrov-Agentov, Director Georgi Arbatov of the U.S.A. and Canada Institute, First Deputy Foreign Minister and Ambassador to the United States Aleksandr Bessmertnykh and Sergei Blagovolin of the Institute of World Economy and International Relations.

Also, *Izvestia* commentator Aleksandr Bovin, Supreme Soviet Delegate Fyodor Burlatsky, Foreign Ministry Spokesman Vitaly Churkin, Ambassador to the United States Yuri Dubinin, Chief of the CPSU International Department Valentin Falin, Yuri Gankovsky of the Institute of Oriental Studies, Foreign Ministry Spokesman Gennadi Gerasimov, Deputy Chief of the CPSU International Department Andrei Grachev, Conventional Arms Negotiator Oleg Grinevsky, Deputy Foreign Minister Viktor Karpov, Deputy Director Andrei Kokoshin of the U.S.A. and Canada Institute, First Deputy Foreign Minister Georgi Kornienko, Andrei Kortunov of the U.S.A. and Canada Institute and Special Ambassador for Afghan Negotiations Nikolai Kozorev.

Also, Chief of U.S.A. Section Dmitri Lisavolik of the CPSU International Department, Igor Maleschenko of the CPSU International Department, historian Roy Medvedev, Foreign Ministry Director of U.S.A. Affairs Alexei Obukhov, Deputy Foreign Minister Vladimir Petrovsky, Deputy Foreign Minister Igor Rogachev, Sergei Rogoff of the U.S.A. and Canada Institute, Aleksandr Tsipko of the CPSU International Department, Vice Chairman of the USSR Academy of Sciences Yevgeni Velikhov and First Deputy Foreign Minister and Ambassador to Afghanistan Yuli Vorontsov.

I would also like to thank Chargé d'Affaires Miagol of the Afghanistan Embassy in Washington and Ambassador Riaz Khan of Pakistan for their assistance in connection with Afghanistan, and Hans Henning-Horstmann of the Federal Republic of Germany Embassy for help regarding German reunification.

I am grateful to John Doble and Amy Richardson of the Public Agenda Foundation and Jonathan Halperin of Americans Talk Security for assistance in connection with U.S. public opinion.

My *Washington Post* colleague Lou Cannon, the biographer of Ronald Reagan, made available the manuscript of his book *President Reagan: The Role of a Lifetime* (Simon & Schuster, 1991). John Parker of the State Department and U.S. Embassy, Moscow, made available the manuscript of his two-volume work on Soviet foreign policy from Brezhnev to Gorbachev, *Kremlin in Transition* (HarperCollins, 1991). Tom Simons, now U.S. ambassador to Poland, provided the lectures that are the basis of his book, *The End of the Cold War?* (St. Martin's, 1990).

I wish to express special thanks to several Washington friends and experts who took time to read the manuscript while it was in preparation and who made numerous suggestions. These were Kenneth Adelman, former director of the Arms Control and Disarmament Agency; Charles Bailey, novelist and former editor of *The Minneapolis Tribune*; Raymond Garthoff, senior fellow of the Brookings Institution; Gary Lee, former *Washington Post* Moscow correspondent; and Strobe Talbott, editor-at-large of *Time*.

The very most important reader at every stage was my wife, Laura, whose support and help in this, as in everything else in the past thirty-five years, was essential.

Joy Harris, my literary agent, encouraged me from the very first and was invaluable in bringing the book to life. I also owe special thanks to Elaine Pfefferblit, my editor at Poseidon Press. Mary Drake, who produced the transcripts of my many interviews, and Cathy Wall, who provided research assistance, were vital to the project.

Finally, I wish to thank my editors at *The Washington Post*, who made possible my front seat at the most important diplomatic drama of our time, and who granted me a six-month leave of absence starting in mid-1990 to finish this book about it.

NOTES AND SOURCES

I began with my dispatches for *The Washington Post* of the period covered, with notes I had taken in preparation for those stories and with the stacks of spiral-bound theme books that I have kept as a journal since 1978. The journal, written in longhand on airplane flights, overseas trips and weekends, records personal encounters and my own impressions and speculations. It proved to be valuable in recalling the feel and atmosphere of key events.

In the fall of 1988 I began to think seriously about this book, and had my first discussion on the subject with Secretary of State George Shultz. I also consulted a number of friends and colleagues. Having decided to proceed, I conducted my first interviews in late November 1988. Altogether I conducted 122 interviews for this book, most of them before I began full-time writing in June 1990. These included 24 interviews during my book-related trip to Moscow in January–February 1990, nearly all on the record.

These extensive interviews, along with detailed U.S. accounts of the Shultz-Gorbachev discussions and key parts of the Geneva and Reykjavik summits that were made available to me, are the most important sources for the book. Even though much of the cited material is not available to others at this stage, I am providing these notes so that, to the greatest extent possible, students and historians will be able to identify the sources of what is reported here. I have not noted the source of material that is widely available and generally known to those working in the field. Sources of some other information, especially regarding the Bush administration, are not identified because of ground rules of not-for-attribution interviews.

In my recounting of conversations and events, I have tried to adhere closely to what I have learned from sources that journalists or scholars would consider highly reliable, preferably detailed recollections or records of firsthand participants or authoritative published accounts. I have used direct quotation only when I believed with confidence, based on my knowledge of the sources involved, that this is what was said.

The following abbreviations are used in the Notes:

AAL   Ronald Reagan, *An American Life,* Simon and Schuster, 1990.

AFPCD   *American Foreign Policy Current Documents*, Department of State, Office of the Historian. Volumes published annually. Dates are specified.

CD   *Current Digest of the Soviet Press.*

FBIS-SOV   *Foreign Broadcast Information Service, Soviet Union.*

GS   George Shultz interviews. Dates are given.

NYT   *New York Times.*

WP   *Washington Post.*

CHAPTER 1. A CANDLE IN THE COLD

REAGAN-SHULTZ DINNER   GS, 7/11/89 and 8/7/90, and other sources.

REAGAN-DOBRYNIN MEETING   GS, 7/11/89; GS log for 2/15/83; Simons interview, 11/29/88; Reagan, *AAL*, pp. 558, 572. Deaver's view: Deaver interview, 5/8/90. The Pentecostals: Jack Matlock interview, 1/10/90.

ANDROPOV'S HEALTH   Aleksandr Bovin, the prominent Soviet journalist and one of those who shed light on Andropov's health, interviewed 2/5/90, said that while Andropov was still chairman of the KGB, prior to mid-1982, he showed Bovin a catheter that had been implanted in his arm to make periodic kidney dialysis a more convenient procedure. The most authoritative source of information, which mentions the February 1983 episode, is the medical report on Andropov issued 2/10/84, the day after his death. See also "Putting the Rumors to Rest," *Time*, 2/20/84, p. 19.

REACTION TO DOBRYNIN'S CABLE   Kornienko interview, 1/19/90; Aleksandrov-Agentov interview, 1/15/90. Notification to State Department: Simons interview, 11/29/88.

GRAIN AGREEMENT   Reagan, *AAL*, pp. 558, 572. Shultz's view: GS, 7/11/89, and letters to me, 10/15/90 and 11/2/90.

Evil Empire and Star Wars

REAGAN'S DICHOTOMY ON THE SOVIETS   Deaver interview, 5/8/90. McFarlane on Reagan as a historic figure: McFarlane interview, 10/18/89. Others who contributed to this section preferred not to be named.

EVIL EMPIRE SPEECH   Dolan interview, 7/5/90. See also "An Interview with President Reagan," *Time*, 1/2/84. Reagan has maintained on several occasions, including an interview with me 3/27/90, that he spoke of the "evil empire" deliberately to put the Soviets on notice about his views in the context of negotiations. Nevertheless, what is known of the origin and delivery of the Orlando speech suggests no such grand intention behind Reagan's declaration.

ORIGINS OF STAR WARS   For the NORAD visit and other data, see Martin Anderson, *Revolution* (Harcourt Brace Jovanovich, 1988), esp. pp. 80–99. Weinberger on Reagan's anti–nuclear weapons views: Weinberger interview, 3/23/90. One hundred fifty million American dead: Reagan, *AAL*, p. 550. The Vessey and McFarlane quotations are from the most authoritative history of the Star Wars decision, Donald R. Baucom, "Hail to the Chiefs," *Policy Review*, Summer 1990, p. 72. Baucom was the official historian of SDI before his retirement from the Air Force in 1990. Reagan's remarks to Shultz: GS, 8/7/90. McFarlane's role and views on SDI were related to me in several interviews in October and November 1989. An excellent account of Perle's initial reaction and other maneuvering is in Hedrick Smith, *The Power Game* pp. 603–16. Shultz's initial qualms were discussed in GS, 7/11/89, 3/22/89 and 8/7/90, and in a 6/13/90 memorandum to me from his office.

MOSCOW'S REACTION TO SDI   Velikhov interview, 5/25/90; Aleksandrov-Agentov interview, 1/15/90. Effect of SDI on Soviet policy: Michael McGuire, *Perestroika and Soviet National Security* (Brookings, 1991), chap. V; also Allen Lynch, "Does Gorbachev Matter Anymore?" *Foreign Affairs*, Summer 1990, pp. 23–24.

A Golden Anniversary

DIRE STATE OF RELATIONS   Kennan quotes: George Kennan, speech to the American Committee on East-West Accord, Washington, D.C., 5/17/83. De Tocqueville quotes: Alexis de Tocqueville, *Democracy in America*, vol. I (Vintage Books, 1955), p. 452. U.S. and Soviet population, arms data: Ruth Leger Sivard, *World Military and Social Expenditures 1983* and *World Military and Social Expenditures 1986* (World Priorities, Washington, D.C.). Nuclear Warhead estimates: "U.S.-U.S.S.R. Strategic Nuclear Forces," *Defense Monitor*, vol. XII, no. 7, Center for Defense Information, Washington, D.C., 1983. Third World wars: "A World at War—1983," *Defense Monitor*, vol. XII, no. 1, Center for Defense Information, Washington, D.C., 1983. The Defense guidance data were from a reliable U.S. source.

Moving Toward a Thaw

SHULTZ ACTIONS, PLANS   Papers for Reagan: GS, 8/7/90; also, for a remarkably extensive report on Shultz's recommendations, see Leslie Gelb, "Expanding Contacts with Soviet: Shultz and Dobrynin Make a Start," *NYT*, 6/30/83,

p. A1. McFarlane on NSC "fly specking": GS, 8/7/90. McFarlane quotes to Matlock: Matlock interview, 1/10/90.

SHULTZ SENATE FOREIGN RELATIONS TESTIMONY   The *Times-Post* conflict in coverage was the subject of several journalistic postmortems—see, for example, Thomas Collins, "Deciphering Diplomatic Jargon," *Newsday*, 6/29/83, part II, p. 2. In retrospect, Taubman was right in his interpretation and I was wrong. Tom Simons was interviewed 11/29/88.

REAGAN'S LETTER TO ANDROPOV   The Reagan letter to Andropov was first made public by former Reagan aide Martin Anderson in the 1990 paperback edition of his book, *Revolution*, published by Hoover Institution Press, Stanford, Calif. I obtained copies of the letters and associated correspondence independently. Kornienko's reaction: Kornienko interview in Moscow, 1/19/90. Clark's maneuvering and memos: from a U.S. source.

Showdown for Shultz

SHULTZ RESIGNATION   Shultz problems from a confidential source; GS interviews (esp. 3/23/90) and GS letter to me, 11/2/90. See also Don Oberdorfer, "Disgrace: Shultz's Roar on Policy-Making Got Results," *WP*, 10/23/83, p. A1. Shultz's testimony to the Joint Senate-House Select Committee Investigating the Iran-Contra Affair, 7/23/87, made public the three attempted resignations in August 1983, December 1985 and August 1986. He also acknowledges November 1984, after the election.

CHARACTER OF SHULTZ   Family data: Peter Shultz (son of George) interview 8/8/90. Regan quote: Donald T. Regan, *For the Record* (Harcourt Brace Jovanovich, 1988), p. 123. Perle quote: Perle interview, 4/12/90. Nixon quote about Shultz in 1980: Lou Cannon, *President Reagan: The Role of a Lifetime* (Simon & Schuster, 1991), p. 79. Shultz's views of the Soviet Union before becoming secretary of state: see esp. his 4/9/81 lecture at Stanford, "Economic Policy Beyond Our Borders."

REAGAN'S AUGUST LETTER TO ANDROPOV   Reagan, *AAL*, pp. 579–82.

CHAPTER 2. THE EBB TIDE

SHULTZ ON MORNING OF SEPTEMBER 1   Breakfast quotes: Cynthia Gunn, one of the house guests, interview, 3/23/90. Details of Shultz's activities that day: GS interviews and "Record of Schedule" kept by his office for 9/1/83. For details of the shootdown and reports of the intelligence, see Seymour M. Hersh's well-researched book, *"The Target Is Destroyed"* (Vintage Books, 1987). Also helpful on this and other aspects of the crisis is Alexander Dallin, *Black Box* (University of California Press, 1985).

The KAL 007 Crisis

THE SHOOTDOWN   Reagan quote on cause of incident: Reagan, *AAL*, p. 583. Osipovich first told his story in an interview with the Soviet Novosti Press Agency's correspondent Yuri Zenyuk, published in *Armed Forces Journal International*, October 1989, p. 19. A more detailed interview with *Izvestia* in December 1990, translated in *Defense Week*, 2/19/91, pp. 17–20, produced more information on what Osipovich saw. The "trouble" quote and assertion that he saw lights and flashes are from the latter interview.

U.S. REACTION   Reagan quotes to Clark: from authoritative U.S. source. Shultz on letting the Soviets know the U.S. knew what happened: GS, 7/12/89. Eagleburger on getting the news out: Eagleburger interview, 9/16/89. Seitz's view: Seitz interview, 4/17/90.

Moscow Reacts

SOVIET REACTIONS   Akhromeyev on military decision-making: Akhromeyev interview, 1/10/90; Kornienko on decision-making: Kornienko interview, 1/19/90. Carlucci on the Yazov conversation: Carlucci interview, 3/5/90. Akhromeyev's continuing suspicions: Akhromeyev interviews, 1/10/90, 1/19/90. The 1978 Kola Peninsula incident: see Seymour Hersh, *"The Target Is Destroyed,"* esp. pp. 17–21.

ANDROPOV'S DECISION   This account is from an interview with Kornienko, 1/19/90. Bovin conversation with Gorbachev: Bovin interview, 2/5/90. Zhores Medvedev in his book *Gorbachev* (Norton, 1987), p. 130, reports that Gorbachev headed a crisis management group for the Politburo in the KAL 007 incident, but senior Soviet figures I interviewed in 1990 had no such recollection.

Meeting in Madrid

PRINCIPALS' CHARACTERIZATIONS   Shultz on "rock-and-sock meeting": GS, 4/8/89. Gromyko's comments: Andrei Gromyko, *Memoirs* (Doubleday, 1989), p. 301.

PREMEETING DECISIONS   Weinberger on "intolerable" action: Weinberger interview, 5/23/90. Shultz's view: GS, 4/8/89.

THE MADRID MEETING   The color and scene: from my dispatches and my journal describing the event. The substance of the Shultz-Gromyko meeting was recounted by Shultz and several other U.S. participants. Quotations from Gromyko's presentation: Gromyko, *Memoirs*.

Moscow's Season of Gloom

BUSH, SHULTZ ON ANDROPOV   Bush interview, 5/7/90; GS, 7/11/89.

ANDROPOV'S HEALTH   Some of the best reporting on Andropov's health and other aspects of his life was by former *WP* Moscow correspondent Dusko Doder. See his books *Shadows and Whispers* (Random House, 1986), and (with Louise Branson) *Gorbachev* (Viking, 1990). See also Mark Frankland, *The Sixth Continent* (Harper & Row, 1987), p. 97. Several of Andropov's former aides and associates confirmed the basic facts of his condition in interviews with me in January 1990, though they were not privy to medical details.

AIR OF CRISIS   "Soviets Prepare People for Crisis in U.S. Ties," *WP* 10/30/83, p. A34.

EXERCISE ABLE ARCHER   SIOP figures: see Desmond Ball and Robert C. Toth, "Revising the SIOP," *International Security*, Spring 1990. Reagan's quote: Reagan, *AAL*, pp. 585–86. Among the public sources for the Able Archer episode is Gordievsky's book, *KGB: The Inside Story* (HarperCollins, 1990) written with Christopher Andrew, esp. pp. 599–601. Gordon Brook-Shepherd, a British writer, interviewed Gordievsky in 1988 and reported the episode in the London *Sunday Telegraph*, 10/16/89, and in his book, *The Stormbirds* (Weidenfeld & Nicolson, 1989). One of the earliest reports of the Gordievsky revelations was by Murrey Marder in "Defector Told of Soviet Alert," *WP*, 8/8/86, p. A1. This section owes much to interviews with McFarlane on 10/18/89 and 12/28/90 and to interviews with current and former U.S. intelligence officials who declined to be quoted by name. Soviet officials interviewed by me in 1990, including Akhromeyev, who was deputy chief of the Soviet armed forces in 1983, had no recollection of a special alert in November of 1983. Aleksandr Bessmertnykh, who was chief of the American section of the Soviet Foreign Ministry in 1983, also said he had heard of no unusual alert.

REAGAN'S REACTION TO ABLE ARCHER   McFarlane's views and his discussion with Reagan: McFarlane interview, 12/28/90. Reagan on Soviet fears: Reagan, *AAL*, pp. 588–89.

SOVIET WAR SCARE   Tom Simons, 11/29/88. Laqueur quote: Walter Laqueur, "U.S.-Soviet Relations," in "America and the World, 1983," *Foreign Affairs*, vol. 63, no. 2, 1984.

Ivan and Anya Meet Jim and Sally

USTINOV'S SPEECH   *FBIS–SOV*, 12/15/83, pp. V1–V7.

ORIGINS OF JANUARY REAGAN SPEECH   McFarlane's discussion with Reagan: McFarlane interview, 10/10/89. Burt's plan, Shultz discussions: GS, 7/12/89; correspondence with Grace Hawes of GS staff, 6/13/90; Tom Simons interview, 11/29/88, Jack Matlock interview, 1/10/90; Mark Palmer interview, 3/30/90. For speech text see *CD*, 1984, p. 406ff.

SOVIET REACTION   Dusko Doder, "Times Are Tough for Jim and Sally, but They Can't Tell Ivan and Anya," *WP*, 1/22/84, p. A11. Gromyko's comments:

Strobe Talbott, *Deadly Gambits* (Knopf, 1984), p. 345; speech is from "Statement by Andrei A. Gromyko at the Conference on Confidence- and Security-Building Measures and Disarmament in Europe," Stockholm, 1/18/84.

SHULTZ-GROMYKO MEETING   "The ice was cracked": GS, 4/8/89.

The Death of Andropov

GROMYKO-ANDROPOV "GAP"   Georgi Kornienko interview, 1/19/90; see also "Yuri Andropov Answers Questions Submitted by the Newspaper *Pravda*," *News and Views from the USSR*, Soviet Embassy Information Department, Washington, 1/24/84. Andropov letter: Reagan, *AAL*, p. 591.

THE FAILING ANDROPOV   Aleksandrov-Agentov interview, 1/15/90; Bovin interview, 2/5/90. See also Doder, *Shadows and Whispers*.

CHAPTER 3. THE CHERNENKO INTERLUDE

CHERNENKO'S HEALTH AND CAPABILITIES   His initial health: John W. Parker, *Kremlin in Transition* (Unwin Hyman, 1991), vol. 1, pp. 339–40; Medvedev, *Gorbachev*, p. 139; see also "Russian Leader Lost for Words," London *Times*, 3/3/84, p. 1. Aleksandrov-Agentov quote: Aleksandrov-Agentov interview, 1/15/90. The Chernenko hat incident was reported in Celestine Bohlen's obituary on Chernenko, "Chernenko Rose Through Ranks as a Tenacious Apparatchik," *WP*, 3/12/85, p. A25. Hartman observations: Hartman interview, 12/21/90. For the initial Chernenko letter, dated February 23 by a State Department official: Reagan, *AAL*, p. 592–93.

INITIAL U.S. REACTIONS   Shultz-McFarlane preparations: GS, 8/7/90. Scowcroft channel: McFarlane interview, 10/18/89; Hartman interview, 12/21/89; GS, 7/12/89; see also Leslie Gelb, "U.S. Says Moscow Refused a Letter from President," *NYT*, 3/24/84, p. A1. Reagan-Chernenko correspondence: Reagan, *AAL*; my account is also based in part on data provided by a State Department official. Kornienko's comment: Kornienko interview, 1/19/90.

The Summer of Reengagement

EXCHANGE OF LETTERS, POSITIONS   This section is based on a chronological account by a State Department official; news accounts of the time; Reagan, *AAL*; and a variety of interviews, especially with Robert McFarlane, 10/10/89, and Jack Matlock, 1/10/90. Text of the Reagan "bombing Russia" gaffe and the Soviet and U.S. reactions can be found in *NYT*, 8/16/84, p. A4.

DECISION TO INVITE GROMYKO   GS, 4/8/89, 7/12/90, 7/13/90.

Gromyko Visits the White House

BACKGROUND OF GROMYKO   Contrary to widespread belief, Kennedy did not ask Gromyko point-blank about the missiles, not wishing to tip the U.S. hand, according to Raymond Garthoff. In a lengthy article in *Izvestia* on 4/15/89, shortly before his death, Gromyko wrote that Khrushchev confided in him about his intention to deploy the missiles in May 1962, about five months before they were discovered, and that Gromyko warned unsuccessfully that such a move "would cause a political explosion in the United States." See "Gromyko Rejoinder on 1962 Missile Crisis," *CD*, vol. XLI, no. 16, 1989, p. 15ff. There are several versions of the famous "cake of ice" quote; this one comes from former U.S. Ambassador to the Soviet Union Malcolm Toon, as reported by David Remnick in "Gromyko: The Man Behind the Mask," *WP*, 1/7/85, p. D1. Toon said he was present when Khrushchev made the remark. Kornienko's views: Kornienko interview, 1/19/90.

SOVIET PRELUDE TO THE MEETING   The Politburo's collective decision: Aleksandrov-Agentov interview, 1/15/90. Gromyko's statements to McGovern: Seth Mydans, "Gromyko Predicts Space Arms Talks Will Not Be Held," *NYT*, 7/30/84, p. A1. Gromyko's statement to Mondale: Don Oberdorfer, "Relations Appear Unaffected by Talk," *WP*, 9/29/84, p. A1; see also Gromyko, *Memoirs*, p. 306.

U.S. PREPARATIONS   Shultz's talk with Gromyko: Tom Simons interview, 7/6/89. Reagan's own "talking points": GS, 7/13/89.

WHITE HOUSE MEETING   Reagan's opening remarks are from several contemporaneous accounts, especially the near-verbatim summary published by *Time* in its 10/8/84 edition. Gromyko's quotes and the information about his monographs: Gromyko, *Memoirs*. The Reagan-Gromyko toilet episode: Palmer interview, 3/30/90; Gromyko's version of the "standing conversation": Gromyko, *Memoirs*, pp. 308–9. Nancy Reagan's views on Soviet policy: Nancy Reagan with William Novak, *My Turn* (Random House, 1989), esp. pp. 63–64 and 336–37. Deaver's recollections: Deaver interview, 5/8/89.

GROMYKO'S REACTION   Kornienko interview, 1/19/90; Gromyko, *Memoirs*, p. 308.

In Search of the Bear

THE BEAR AD   Riney interview, 8/7/90; see also Jack W. Germond and Jules Witcover, *Wake Us When It's Over* (Macmillan, 1985), pp. 517–19.

PUBLIC OPINION IN U.S.   The 1984 poll data are from *Americans Talk Security*, a compendium of poll findings on national security issues published in December 1987 by the Daniel Yankelovich Group; specific findings referred to in this section can be found on pp. 62, 121, 103, 185, 145, 211, 201. See also Daniel

Yankelovich and John Doble, "The Public Mood: Nuclear Weapons and the U.S.S.R.," *Foreign Affairs*, Fall 1984; *Voter Options on Nuclear Arms Policy* (Public Agenda Foundation, 1984).

SHULTZ'S LINKAGE SPEECH   *AFPCD, 1984*, pp. 451–57.

Coming of the Arms Talks

REAGAN'S POSTELECTION INTERVIEW   "An Interview with the President," *Time*, 11/19/84, p. 52.

SHULTZ APPEAL FOR UNIFIED POSTURE   GS, 7/13/89. The Reagan response to McFarlane: McFarlane interview, 11/7/89. See also the good reporting on this episode by Jane Mayer and Doyle McManus in *Landslide* (Houghton Mifflin, 1988), p. 55.

SHULTZ-WEINBERGER CONFLICT   This is based primarily on interviews with Shultz and Weinberger. Crowe quote: Crowe interview, 11/16/89.

SHULTZ PREPARATIONS FOR TALKS   GS, 7/13/89. Timbie quote: Timbie interview, 1/6/89. Adelman's view of big delegation: Kenneth L. Adelman, *The Great Universal Embrace* (Simon and Schuster, 1989), pp. 91–92.

ANNENBERG ESTATE MEETING   GS, 7/13/89; McFarlane interviews, 11/1/89 and 12/18/90; Weinberger interview, 5/23/90. Reagan decision quote: McFarlane interview, 12/18/90.

Negotiations in Geneva

SHIP OF FEUDS   From my journal, which I kept on this and other trips. Summoning of Perle: Perle interview, 4/12/90.

THE NEGOTIATIONS   Nitze's observation on lack of warmth: Paul H. Nitze, *From Hiroshima to Glasnost* (Grove Weidenfeld, 1989), p. 405. Adelman's observations: Adelman, *Great Universal Embrace*, pp. 93–94.

CHAPTER 4. GORBACHEV TAKES COMMAND

BACKGROUND OF GORBACHEV   Kennan's quote: interview of Robert MacNeil with George Kennan on *The MacNeil/Lehrer News Hour*, 12/21/88. Personal travails of Gorbachev's grandparents: "Gorbachev Defends USSR Unity to Cultural Group," *Pravda*, 12/1/90, reported in *FBIS-SOV*, 12/5/90, p. 43.

U.S. FIRST IMPRESSIONS   Shultz on Gorbachev having been in charge: GS, 4/9/89. The description and historical data on St. George's and St. Catherine's halls are from a tour of the Grand Kremlin Palace I was given 1/12/90 by Galina Kovshev, senior researcher/archivist there. Bush on "something different": Bush interview, 5/7/90. Notes on Shultz briefing: Adelman, *Great Universal Embrace*, pp. 121–22. Shultz comments to Mulroney: Mulroney address to Stanford alumni in Toronto, 3/9/90. Bush comments on meeting the challenge: interview with Donald Gregg, who accompanied Bush to Moscow as his national security aide, 9/8/89.

A Cautious Beginning

GORBACHEV'S BEGINNINGS   Raisa's interjection and "not living like that": *FBIS-SOV*, 6/4/90, p. 15. Aleksandrov-Agentov's initial observations on Gorbachev's views: Aleksandrov-Agentov interview, 1/15/90. Falin's observations on Gorbachev and the studies: Falin interview, 1/11/90. Grinevsky's meeting with Gorbachev: Grinevsky interview, 2/7/90. Smolny speech: *FBIS-SOV*, 5/22/85, pp. R1–12.

THE MINSK MEETING   Akhromeyev interviews, 1/10/90 and 1/18/90. For earlier reports on Minsk, see "Gorbachev: What Makes Him Run," *Newsweek*, 11/18/90, p. 18.

Stumbling Toward the Summit

GORBACHEV'S LETTER   Reagan, *AAL*, pp. 612–14.

SHULTZ-GROMYKO MEETING IN VIENNA   GS, 4/8/89 and 7/14/89; Nitze, *From Hiroshima to Glasnost*, pp. 409–10.

Enter Shevardnadze

GORBACHEV'S APPOINTMENT   "The greatest surprise of my life": Shevardnadze interview, 1/17/90; see also Shevardnadze's account of the conversation in *Ogonek* (Moscow), no. 11, March 1990. Shevardnadze's views toward other diplomats: Bessmertnykh interview, 6/28/90. Shevardnadze-Gorbachev lack of information about the invasion of Afghanistan: Cynthia Roberts, "Glasnost in Soviet Foreign Policy: Setting the Record Straight?" *Report on the USSR*, Radio Liberty, 11/15/89, pp. 4–5. Gorbachev's statement to Aleksandrov-Agentov: Aleksandrov-Agentov interview, 1/24/90.

SHEVARDNADZE'S BACKGROUND   Elizabeth Fuller, "A Portrait of Eduard Shevardnadze," *Radio Liberty Research*, 7/3/85. Story on collecting fancy watches: "The Boss of Smolensky Square," *Time*, May 15, 1989, p. 30.

INITIAL FOREIGN MINISTRY ACTIVITY   Meetings with Bessmertnykh and other top aides: Bessmertnykh interview, 12/26/90. "Higher mathematics": Shevardnadze interview, 1/17/90.

FIRST MEETING WITH SHULTZ   Shultz impatience with Gromyko: Hartman interview, 11/3/89. Shultz plans for meetings with Shevardnadzes: GS, 7/14/89.

Meeting in Finlandia Hall: Ridgway interview, 11/25/88. Dialogue between Shultz and Shevardnadze on speech: GS, 7/14/89. First business meeting at U.S. ambassador's residence: Shevardnadze interview, 1/17/90; Bessmertnykh interview, 12/26/90. Dumas and Howe quotes: Celestine Bohlen, "Soviet Impresses in Helsinki Debut," *WP*, 8/2/85, p. A1. Shultz's reaction: Reagan *AAL*, p. 623.

Reinterpreting the ABM Treaty

TREATY REINTERPRETATION EPISODE   I relied on the 1985 reporting that went into my retrospective piece at the time, "ABM Reinterpretation: A Quick Study," *WP*, 10/22/85, p. A1, as amplified by interviews with Shultz, Nitze, McFarlane, Perle and Sofaer. I also relied on Nitze's memoir, *From Hiroshima to Glasnost*, pp. 412–15, and on Strobe Talbott's book *The Master of the Game* (Knopf, 1988), pp. 237–49. Karpov quote: Karpov interview, 1/11/90.

Meeting in Moscow

FIRST SHULTZ-GORBACHEV NEGOTIATION   Unless otherwise noted, the section on the Gorbachev-Shultz meeting was based on a detailed account made available to me by a U.S. source, on interviews with Shultz, Shevardnadze, Robert McFarlane and Arthur Hartman and on my journal and news dispatches at the time. Quotations from the dialogue are principally from the detailed account. Origin of Gorbachev's "pornography lawyer" statement: "ABM Reinterpretation: A Quick Study," *WP*, 10/22/85, p. A1. Shultz's retrospective view: GS, 7/14/89. Shevardnadze's retrospective view: Shevardnadze interview, 1/17/90. Reagan diary entry: Reagan, *AAL*, p. 631.

Moments of Truth at the Geneva Summit

SETTING FOR GENEVA   Reagan's arrival: from my notes and journal. Gorbachev's quotes about the summit: Mikhail Gorbachev, *Perestroika* (Harper & Row, 1987), p. 227.

GORBACHEV ON THE EVE   See John W. Parker, *Kremlin in Transition* (Unwin Hyman, 1991), for an excellent account of Gorbachev's early views. See also Gorbachev's speech to the French parliament, 10/3/85. Gorbachev's nervousness and intentions: interview with a Soviet official, 5/27/90. Earthquake prediction: Adelman, *Great Universal Embrace*, p. 124.

REAGAN ON THE EVE   Massie's advice: Massie interview, 5/20/90. Reagan "in the year 1830": Palmer interview, 3/30/90. Nancy Reagan's comments: Nancy Reagan, *My Turn*, p. 338.

FIRST MORNING AT GENEVA   Reagan's view of "something likeable" about Gorbachev: Reagan, *AAL*, p. 635. Reagan's quotes about coming from small towns and being programmed: Palmer interview: 3/30/90. "Two men in a room . . . who could start World War III": Reagan interview, 3/27/90. Reagan on the invasion from outer space: see his remarks to students and faculty of Fallston High School in Fallston, Maryland, 12/4/85.

FIRST AFTERNOON AT GENEVA   Except for material otherwise attributed, the discussion on arms control is taken from a detailed account of the conversation made available to me by a U.S. source. Summerhouse arrangements, see Regan, *For the Record*, p. 308–9; Larry Speakes, *Speaking Out* (Avon Books, 1989), p. 166–67. "Guidelines": point three is quoted in Strobe Talbott, *Master of the Game*, p. 286; see also Don Oberdorfer, "Afghanistan, Arms Major Summit Themes," *WP*, 11/22/85, p. A9. U.S. balk at sharing SDI secrets with its allies: Michael Weisskopf, "U.S. Might Not Share All Its 'Star Wars' Secrets with Europeans," *WP*, 5/2/85, p. A32.

APPROVAL OF FUTURE SUMMITS   Reagan-Gorbachev discussion about future summits: Reagan interview, 3/27/90.

SECOND DAY ON ARMS CONTROL   Except as otherwise attributed, this is from a detailed account made available by a U.S. source. The dramatic turning point, with Gorbachev saying, "Mr. President, I don't agree with you, but I can see you really mean it," was not in the detailed account, but is based on Shultz's vivid recollection in GS, 7/11/89, confirmed by McFarlane interview, 12/28/90. "Like a coin dropping": GS, 7/11/89. McFarlane on Gorbachev's frustration: McFarlane interview, 11/7/89.

Wrapping Up the Summit

THE JOINT STATEMENT   Reagan-Gorbachev dialogue, "We'll have to tell people": from a detailed account made available by a U.S. source. Shultz's complaint to Reagan that Defense would throw up roadblocks: Reagan, *AAL*, p. 628. Weinberger's ire and the tangled history of the statement; GS letter, 10/15/90; McFarlane interview, 11/7/89; interviews with U.S. diplomats Mark Parris, 12/1/88, and Mark Palmer, 3/30/90. The quotation that Weinberger objected to is cited in Adelman, *Great Universal Embrace*, p. 150.

GORBACHEV'S INITIAL STATEMENT VIEWS   Proposals re: nuclear war not being inevitable: Bessmertnykh interview, 12/26/90; September proposal to Reagan: Reagan, *AAL*, p. 625.

SHULTZ ON JOINT APPEARANCE   "You have to get up and make statements": GS, 7/14/89.

FINAL RENDITION OF JOINT STATEMENT   Text of statement: *AFPCD, 1985*, p. 427. Soviet insistence there was no word for "human rights" in Russian: Ridgway interview, 11/25/88. Afghanistan byplay at Geneva: Don Oberdorfer. "Afghanistan, Arms Major Summit Themes," *WP*, 11/22/85, p. A9; Adelman, *Great Universal Embrace*, p. 141.

SOVIET POSTSUMMIT VIEWS OF REAGAN   Yakovlev interview, 1/12/90; Aleksandrov-Agentov interview, 1/15/90.

REAGAN'S POSTSUMMIT VIEWS   Reagan interview, 3/27/90.

SHEVARDNADZE'S IMPRESSION OF REAGAN   Shevardnadze interview, 1/17/90.

CHAPTER 5. HIGH STAKES AT REYKJAVIK

Gorbachev's New Program

PRESENTING THE JANUARY 15 PLAN   This is based in large part on Nitze, *From Hiroshima to Glasnost*, as amplified by others.

ORIGINS OF JANUARY 15 PLAN   Skepticism of Gorbachev after Geneva: Charles Bremner, Reuters dispatch from Moscow, 1/6/86. Re: Reagan proposal for June summit, Reagan, *AAL*, p. 649, says the invitation was issued early in the New Year, but I had already reported the U.S. proposal and Dobrynin's response on January 1; see Don Oberdorfer, "Soviets Suggests Summit Delay to September," *WP*, 1/1/86, p. A1. Falin timing of presentation of January 15 plan: Falin interview, 1/11/90.

27TH PARTY CONGRESS   Primakov on reaching the limit of nuclear danger: Primakov interview, 1/9/90. There are several translations of Gorbachev's Political Report to the Twenty-seventh Congress. I have relied prinicipally, though not exclusively, on the British Broadcasting Company translation from the BBC Summary of World Broadcasts, 2/26/86. Re: Gorbachev's one-world views, Gorbachev cites his debt to Palme in *Perestroika*, p. 207. Shevardnadze quotes on the revolutionary nature of the changes as seen at the Soviet Foreign Ministry: Shevardnadze interview, 1/17/90. Akhromeyev on the changes: Akhromeyev interview, 1/18/90. Change in "peaceful coexistence" and dropping of "bury inperialism" statement: Gorbachev, *Perestroika*, pp. 147–48.

GORBACHEV AT THE FOREIGN MINISTRY   The first publication of the gist of Gorbachev's remarks was in the initial Russian-language issue of the Foreign Ministry's new house organ, *Vestnik*, 8/8/87. This summary was republished in the first English-language edition of *Vestnik*, titled *Soviet Diplomacy Today*, published in 1989. I have used the English translation from the latter publication, which also is the source for my quotation from Shevardnadze's 7/25/88 speech to the Ministry of Foreign Affairs Scientific and Practical Conference regarding the military policy shift discussed by Gorbachev in his 1986 Foreign Ministry appearance. This Shevardnadze quote and much else in this section were first called to my attention by John Parker's well-documented two-volume work *Kremlin in Transition* (Unwin Hyman, 1991).

SOVIET DIPLOMATIC SHIFTS   Changes in diplomatic personnel: Daniel S. Papp, "The Impact of the Shevardnadze-Dobrynin Apparatus on Soviet Foreign Policy," a paper prepared for Georgia Institute of Technology, May 1988. See also John Van Odenaren's excellent account in "The Role of Shevardnadze and the Ministry of Foreign Affairs in the Making of Soviet Defense and Arms Control Policy," *Rand*, July 1990, p. 17. Dobrynin as "your Uncle Ralph": Hugh Sidey, "Barometer of Superpowers," *Time*, 3/17/86, p. 41.

A Case of the Blahs

EXPULSION OF SOVIET DIPLOMATS   Don Oberdorfer, "Order for Soviet Cuts at U.N. Had Been Delayed 6 Months," *WP*, 3/12/86, p. A1.

BLACK SEA NAVAL INTRUSIONS   Stoppage after Akhromeyev's plea: Crowe interview, 11/16/90.

CHERNOBYL DISASTER   Figures on evacuees and cleanup workers are from Michael Dobbs, "Chernobyl: Symbol of Soviet Failure," *WP*, 4/26/91, p. A1.

GORBACHEV COMPLAINTS TO REAGAN   Reagan, *AAL*, p. 663.

SALT II BATTLE   Adelman, *Great Universal Embrace*, especially p. 269.

Zero Ballistic Missiles

ORIGINS OF ZERO BALLISTIC MISSILES   This section was based on interviews with Weinberger, Shultz, Poindexter, Ikle, Perle, Nitze, Timbie, Linhard, Crowe, and others, and GS letter of 12/6/90. Nitze deals with the subject in his book *From Hiroshima to Glasnost*, as does Kenneth Adelman in *Great Universal Embrace* and Strobe Talbott in *Master of the Game*. The Reagan letter has never been published, but a close paraphrase of the July 25 proposal was made public by Reagan 9/22/86, in his address to the UN General Assembly. Reagan's statement to Gorbachev at Geneva about eliminating nuclear-armed missiles: McFarlane interview, 5/12/90; Reagan's quote from February letter: Reagan, *AAL*, p. 657. Ballistic missile proliferation data: "Ballistic Missile Proliferation Potential in the Third World," Congressional Research Service report 86-29 SPR, 4/24/86. Ikle's ideas: Fred Charles Ikle, "Can Nuclear Deterrence Last Out the Century?" *Foreign Affairs*, January 1973, p. 283. Ikle's discussions with Fortier and Kampelman: Ikle interview, 5/4/90, and subsequent correspondence; Kampelman interview, 5/9/90. Shultz's views on ballistic missiles: GS, 7/17/89. Shultz's view on Weinberger's proposal: GS letter, 12/6/90. Nitze on the proposal as "ridiculous": contemporaneous memo by a White House staff member. Linhard, Poindexter and Crowe views: Linhard interview, 12/2/88; Poindexter interview, 11/1/90; Crowe interview, 11/16/90.

The Daniloff Case

ZAKHAROV-DANILOFF ARRESTS   Principal sources for Daniloff materials are his book, *Two Lives, One Russia* (Houghton Mifflin, 1988), and an article by

Daniloff, "The 'Zakharov-Daniloff Affair,' " *Northeastern University Alumni Magazine*, February 1990; also, news accounts and interviews as noted. For Simons quote on doing "the right thing": Simons interview, 6/17/89. Decision to choose Daniloff for retaliation: Dimitri Simes, "Gorbachev's Game in the Daniloff Case," *WP*, 9/14/86, p. D1; also telephone interview with Simes, 9/19/90. The "Father Roman" episode: Daniloff, *Two Lives, One Russia*, pp. 215–20, 254–59.

REAGAN'S DECISION   Diary entry asserting that this was not a trade: Reagan, *AAL*, p. 668. Sofaer's investigation: Sofaer interview, 8/17/89. The Shultz-Sofaer meeting with Reagan: Sofaer interview, 8/17/89, and GS, 7/17/89.

SHULTZ-SHEVARDNADZE MEETING   Shultz's views, statements to Shevardnadze on 9/19/86: GS, 7/17/89. Shevardnadze's charge that Daniloff was a spy: Daniloff interview, 3/16/90.

REAGAN MEETING WITH SHEVARDNADZE   GS, 7/17/89; Reagan, *AAL*. "I enjoyed being angry": Reagan, *AAL*, p. 669.

SHULTZ-SHEVARDNADZE NEGOTIATIONS   According to logs kept by Shultz's office, his private meetings with Shevardnadze 9/19/86 through 9/28/86 totaled ten hours, forty-five minutes. Ridgway quote ("The two sides"), the byplay with Bessmertnykh and evaluation of importance of the negotiations: Ridgway interview, 11/25/88.

Reykjavik: How It Happened

VIEWS OF REYKJAVIK   Schlesinger's quote: James Schlesinger, "Reykjavik and Revelations: A Turn of the Tide?" *Foreign Affairs*, vol. 65, no. 3, 1987, p. 429. Nixon quote: Richard Nixon, *1999*, as quoted in Schlesinger "Reykjavik and Revelations." Gorbachev on "turning point": Gorbachev, *Perestroika*, p. 240. Reagan on "turning point": Reagan, *AAL*, p. 683.

PRELUDE TO REYKJAVIK   Adamishin rejecting "an empty summit": John Goshko, "Soviets Still Pessimistic on Summit After Talks: 'It Has to Have Some Results,' " *WP*, 8/20/86, p. A23. Shevardnadze perceiving "no movement at all": Shevardnadze interview, 1/19/90. Preparation of invitation letter: Bessmertnykh interview, 12/26/90. For text of letter: Reagan, *AAL*, p. 672.

PREPARATIONS IN MOSCOW   Teams, "group of five" and "breakthrough" quote: Bessmertnykh interview, 12/26/90. Yakovlev quotes: Yakovlev interview, 1/12/90. Gorbachev on showing up SDI as "main obstacle": Gorbachev, *Perestroika*, p. 243. Importance of secrecy: interview with a Soviet official, 5/27/90. Akhromeyev's statement on surprise: Akhromeyev interview, 1/10/90.

WASHINGTON PREPARATIONS   Dobrynin tip: Nitze, *From Hiroshima to Glasnost*, p. 429. Nitze also spoke to me about his going-in views when I was preparing my retrospective article, "At Reykjavik, Soviets Were Prepared and U.S. Improvised," *WP*, 2/16/87, p. A1. State "concept paper": Simons interview, 6/17/89. Adelman on no "tough negotiations": Adelman, *Great Universal Embrace*, pp. 26, 35. Reagan's "curious" quote: Hugh Sidey, "I Think I Have Some Room to Maneuver," *Time*, 10/20/86, p. 31. Adelman on "urinal diplomacy": Adelman, *Great Universal Embrace*, p. 103.

The Reykjavik Summit

IMPROVISED PREPARATIONS Ruwe's account: Ruwe interview in Reykjavik, June 1987. Haunted house: Robert McCartney, "In the Spirit of Diplomacy," *WP*, 10/3/86, p. A1; Robert McCartney, "A Supernatural Summit," WP, 10/4/86, p. A33.

FIRST DAY AT REYKJAVIK Except where otherwise noted, my account is from my earlier reconstruction, "At Reykjavik, Soviets Were Prepared and U.S. Improvised," *WP*, 2/16/87. p. A1, plus additional interviews with participants. The Soviet text of Gorbachev's opening proposals in the form of proposed "directives" was published in its English-language form in *Reykjavik: Documents and Materials* (Novosti Press Agency Publishing House, Moscow, 1987). Reagan statement "He's brought a whole lot of proposals": Talbott, *Master of the Game*, p. 316. Shultz on proposals "coming our way": GS, 7/17/89. Nitze's excitement: Talbott, *Master of the Game*, p. 316.

UNOFFICIAL DISCUSSIONS Poindexter's impressions: Poindexter interview, 11/1/90; Hill's: Hill interview, 7/20/89.

AFTERNOON, EVENING TALKS Gorbachev on "moth-balled proposals": Gorbachev's press conference in Reykjavik, 10/13/86. Reagan's medication: GS, 7/17/89. Reagan on pills: Reagan interview, 3/27/90. Akhromeyev on the Leningrad battle: GS, 7/17/89. Akhromeyev's opening remarks at evening meeting and the incident with Karpov: Adelman, *Great Universal Embrace*, pp. 49–50. Timbie's comments: Timbie interview, 6/13/90.

SECOND MORNING TALKS "Literally a miracle": Reagan interview, 3/27/90.

SECOND AFTERNOON Especially for the bargaining session that brought forth the U.S. proposal, I have drawn on my 2/16/87 report in *WP*, "At Reykjavik, Soviets Were Prepared and U.S. Improvised," p. A1. Linhard on "tools" at hand: Linhard interview, 12/2/88. Poindexter's surprise: Poindexter interview, 11/1/90. Initial U.S. proposal was made public by Shultz before the National Press Club, 10/17/86. U.S. caucus: my 2/16/87 piece and interviews with several participants. "He gets his precious ABM Treaty": Talbott, *Master of the Game*, p. 324.

LAST AFTERNOON AT REYKJAVIK Adelman on the differences in weapons and "He wants to have a summit. Right here": Adelman, *Great Universal Embrace*, pp. 72–74. "Look, here's what we're prepared to do" and the discussion that followed: unless otherwise noted, from a detailed account provided by a U.S.

source, augmented in a few places by a second detailed account from the U.S. side.

SHULTZ'S RETROSPECTIVE VIEWS   GS, 7/17/89.

REAGAN'S RETROSPECTIVE VIEWS   Reagan interview, 3/27/90.

SECOND AFTERNOON CONTINUED   Final bargaining: as above, from a detailed account from a U.S. source, augmented by a second detailed U.S. account. "I don't know what else I could have done": Reagan, *AAL*, p. 679.

The Aftermath of Reykjavik

SOVIET REACTIONS   Shevardnadze interview, 1/17/90; Bessmertnykh interview, 12/26/90; see also "Shevardnadze Views Current Foreign Policy Issues," *Argumenty i Fakty*, Moscow, no. 18, May 6–12, 1989, in *FBIS-SOV*, 5/15/89, p. 90.

U.S. REACTIONS   "We sure tried" and Perle's view: Perle interview, 5/1/90. Shultz comments in dining room: Adelman, *Great Universal Embrace*, p. 76. Ottaway on Shultz grief: David Ottaway, "The Rise of George Shultz," *WP*, 10/17/86, p. A1.

WASHINGTON AFTERMATH   October 27 meeting: Adelman, *Great Universal Embrace*, p. 85; Crowe interview, 11/16/89.

SOVIETS ON REAGAN   Yakovlev interview, 1/12/90; Akhromeyev interview, 1/10/90.

CHAPTER 6. TO THE WASHINGTON SUMMIT

Marking Time

CHANGE IN USSR   The demographic and economic data are primarily from Murray Feshbach, research professor of demography, Georgetown University. Diphtheria and hepatitis figures are from Feshbach. Other health data: Anders Aslund, *Gorbachev's Struggle for Economic Reform* (Cornell University Press, 1989), p. 19. Microcomputers comparison: Aslund, *Gorbachev's Struggle*, p. 16.

JANUARY PLENUM   Elizabeth Teague, "Conflict of Interests and Ideas: The January Plenum" and "Experiment with Contested Elections," *Soviet–East European Survey, 1986–1987* (Westview Press, 1988), pp. 24–33 and 42–46.

Shultz in Moscow: The Second Zero

EMBASSY SPY SCARE   This account is based primarily on my retrospective report, "A Spy Scandal That Melted," *WP*, January 17, 1988, p. A1. Impact in Moscow: Don Oberdorfer, "Moscow Views Shultz Trip as Crucial," *WP*, 4/12/87, p. A23.

SHULTZ-GORBACHEV MEETING   Except as noted, exchanges in the Kremlin discussion were based on a detailed account from a U.S. source. I have also used some material from the remarkably detailed Soviet account of the meeting published at the time by Tass. The Shultz presentation on the Information Age was reconstructed from GS, 3/22/90, and the State Department Global Trends Presentation that was prepared by Richard Solomon, director of policy planning, at Shultz's direction. Ridgway's comments on Shultz "trying to get inside of Gorbachev's mind": Ridgway interview, 12/28/88. Gorbachev's remarks in *Perestroika*: from p. 135. Shultz's offer to take out *refusniks* on his plane: GS, 7/19/89. Quotes from broadcast (and unbroadcast) Shultz comments on Soviet television re: Afghanistan: Bohdan Nahaylo, "Criticism of the Afghanistan War," *Soviet–East European Survey, 1986–1987*, p. 72.

Opportunity Lands in Red Square

FLIGHT OF MATHIAS RUST   Akhromeyev's comments: Akhromeyev interview, 1/18/90. Koldunov's ignorance of the flight was revealed by his successor, General Ivan Tretyak, in *Moscow News*, and was cited in Parker, *Kremlin in Transition*, vol. II, p. 180.

CIVIL-MILITARY RELATIONS   The military warnings that Gorbachev was moving too fast: Akhromeyev interview, 1/10/90. Akhromeyev essentially confirmed a report by Paul Quinn-Judge, "Gorbachev Hints at Troubles in Military," *Christian Science Monitor*, 7/12/89, p. 1, though he said the complaint did not come from "marshals" as reported.

NEW MILITARY DOCTRINE   Akhromeyev on military leadership discussions: Akhromeyev interview, 1/18/90. Grechko's comments and a good discussion of the changing doctrine are in Raymond L. Garthoff, "New Thinking in Soviet Military Doctrine," *Washington Quarterly*, Summer 1988.

SHIFT TOWARD OPENNESS   Primakov's comments: Primakov interview, 1/11/90. Burlatsky's comments: Burlatsky interview, 1/25/90. Grinevsky on the discussions leading to the policy change at CDE: Grinevsky interview, 2/7/90. His comment to Barry, "You watch": Barry interview, 4/2/90. Gorbachev's comment that Reagan "will be *astounded*" at Soviet position: Tom Simons, letter to author, 1/3/91. Yakovlev's story: Yakovlev interview, 1/12/90.

Afghanistan: Toward the Exit

The account of the Soviet decision to withdraw is taken primarily from my lengthy report "A Diplomatic Solution to Stalemate," *WP*, 4/17/88, p. A1. Other sources are as noted below:

SHULTZ-SHEVARDNADZE MEETING   GS, 7/19/89; also interview with Michael Armacost, 4/20/89.

DECISION TO INVADE   The report on the crucial meeting comes from a well-placed Soviet expert who asked not to be named but who had access to an eyewitness account.

GORBACHEV ON "MISTAKE"   *Mikhail S. Gorbachev: An Intimate Biography*, by the editors of *Time* magazine (NAL, 1988), p. 126.

DENG ON SINO-SOVIET SUMMIT   Interview with Deputy Foreign Minister Igor Rogachev, 1/8/90.

GORBACHEV'S MANEUVERS   Cordovez quotes: see my 4/17/88 *WP* retrospective, "A Diplomatic Solution to Stalemate." Shevardnadze's dating of "political decision": "The Foreign Policy and Diplomatic Activity of the USSR," presented by Shevardnadze to the Supreme Soviet 10/23/89, and published in the January 1990 edition of *International Affairs*; the statement on Afghanistan is on p. 12. Vorontsov on Gorbachev remarks to Karmal: Vorontsov interview, 1/18/90. Karmal quote, "If you leave now": Boris Pyadyshev, "The Way It Was, as Told by Afghan President Najibullah," *Pravda*, 11/28/89, as quoted in *CD*, vol. XLI, no. 50, 1989, pp. 16–17.

WITHDRAWAL DECISIONS   Vorontsov-Sattar talks: interview with Pakistan Ambassador Riaz Khan, 4/18/90. Gorbachev-Najibullah meeting on 12/12/86: Vorontsov interview, 1/18/90; Pyadyshev, "The Way It Was," *Pravda*, 11/28/89. The PDPA meeting was reported by Olivier Roy, a leading French expert on Afghanistan, who interviewed the defector shortly after he fled. The quotes from Akhromeyev and Vorontsov on military attitudes toward the war are from Akhromeyev interview, 1/10/90 and Vorontsov interview, 1/18/90.

A Treaty Takes Shape

HOWARD BAKER ON REAGAN'S INTENTIONS   Baker interview, 6/26/90.

HOAGLAND ON "RUNAWAY HORSES"   Jim Hoagland, "Reagan's Nuclear U-Turn," *WP*, 4/24/87, p. A2.

Gorbachev Balks

THE SPECIAL TRAIN   From my jounal.

SHULTZ-GORBACHEV MEETING   Unless otherwise attributed, the report on the Gorbachev-Shultz meeting is based on a detailed account provided by a U.S. source. *Soviet Influence Activities*, the report to which Gorbachev objected, is Department of State Publication 9627, released October 1987.

U.S. EVALUATION   GS, 7/19/89 and 8/7/90, and letter of 12/6/90. Ridgway, Matlock, Simons and others told essentially the same story. For Yeltsin's speech and other details, see Boris Yeltsin, *Against the Grain* (Summit, 1990). Celestine Bohlen's news analysis is "SDI Issue Dashes Expectations Again," *WP*, 10/24/87, p. A30. Shultz's report to Reagan, "I think we should just pass": GS, 7/19/89. Reagan comment, "The Soviets blinked": Reagan, *AAL*, p. 696.

The Washington Summit

WHITE HOUSE MEETING   Gorbachev's "you're not a prosecutor" remark is from his recounting of conversation in his meeting with U.S. publishers at the Soviet Embassy, 12/9/87; see also Reagan, *AAL*, p. 698. Nancy Reagan's astrologer and the summit signing: Selwa Roosevelt, *Keeper of the Gate* (Simon and Schuster, 1990), p. 245. Shultz missing SS-20 photograph: GS letter to author, 12/6/90. "Christmas, Hanukah, the Fourth of July": Tom Shales, "The Pageant on a Day of Grace," *WP*, 12/9/87, p. B1.

REAGAN'S INAPPROPRIATE JOKE   The story, one of Reagan's old faithful, was told in Reagan, *AAL*, p. 715. U.S. reactions: GS, 3/22/90; Baker interview, 6/26/90.

GORBACHEV'S CHARM   Oates, Graham, Newman comments: Bernard Weinraub, "The Gorbachev Effect: Charming, Very Tough," *NYT*, 12/13/87, p. 22. Nancy and Raisa: *Mikhail S. Gorbachev: An Intimate Biography*, p. 207; also Nancy Reagan, *My Turn*, p. 346. Bush's description of the Gorbachev stop on Connecticut Avenue is from a breakfast with reporters, which I attended, on 12/11/87, the day after the end of the summit.

SDI DISCUSSION   Reagan's exchange with Gorbachev, "We are going forward" and "Mr. President, do what you have to do": Talbott, *Master of the Game*, pp. 363–64. Gorbachev's change of position on laboratory testing and possible Soviet withdrawal from the START Treaty: Carlucci interview, 3/5/90; see also David Shipler, "Reagan Aide Says Moscow Opposes 'Star Wars' Tests," *NYT*, 12/30/87, p. A1.

THE NICARAGUA DISCUSSION   Reagan's version is in Reagan *AAL*, p. 701. A more nuanced and, I believe, more accurate version can be found in the wrap-up piece on the Washington summit written by David Hoffman and myself, "Leaders' Central Compromise: Missile Defense Tests 'as Required,' " *WP*, 12/13/87, p. A1.

FINAL ARMS NEGOTIATION COMPROMISE   U.S. discussion in the White House Library: Hoffman and Oberdorfer, "Leaders' Central Compromise," *WP*, 12/13/87. Soviet discussion: Talbott, *Master of the Game*, p. 368.

CHAPTER 7. REAGAN IN RED SQUARE

Endgame in Afghanistan

ARMACOST'S BET   Armacost interview, 4/20/89.

SHULTZ-GORBACHEV MEETING   The report on the meeting is based on a detailed account provided by a U.S. source.

SHEVARDNADZE ON AFGHANISTAN   Shevardnadze's views as chairman of Politburo commission on Afghanistan: Shevardnadze interview in *Ogonek*, no. 11, March 14–17, 1990. Vorontsov on "totally and absolutely unacceptable" nature of a Soviet arms cutoff for the Kabul government: Vorontsov interview, 1/18/90. Shevardnadze quote on his mixed emotions after signing Afghan accords: Shevardnadze speech at the Twenty-first Party Conference of the Ministry of Foreign Affairs, *FBIS-SOV*, 4/26/90, p. 9. Shevardnadze and Kryuchkov offer to family of Najibullah: see Pyadyshev, "The Way It Was," *Pravda*, 11/28/89.

April in Moscow: Rhetoric and Realism

U.S.-SOVIET ECONOMIC COMPARISON   Henry S. Rowen and Charles Wolf, Jr., *The Impoverished Superpower* (Institute for Contemporary Studies, 1990), especially p. 4; also Hobert Rowen, "Capitalism Called Only Soviet Hope," *WP*, 11/22/90, p. A12.

GORBACHEV-SHULTZ MEETING   Except as otherwise attributed, the report on the Gorbachev-Shultz meeting is from a detailed account from a U.S. source. State Department clearance of the Springfield speech: from a senior State Department official. Controversy in Moscow about inviting Reagan: from Gary Lee, former *WP* Moscow correspondent, 1/19/91. Status of START discussions within the administration: Carlucci interview 3/5/90; Crowe interview, 11/16/89; Powell interview, 2/9/89; see also Talbott, *Master of the Game*, chap. 14, and Lou Cannon, "Reagan: No Pact by Moscow Summit," *WP* 2/25/88, p. A1. Nitze on Gorbachev's intelligence penetration of the NATO meeting: Nitze interview, 3/5/90.

The Moscow Summit

STATE OF U.S. PUBLIC OPINION   Public opinion data: from *Americans Talk Security Compendium*, October 1987–December 1988 (Marttila and Kiley Inc.), esp. pp. 65, 80, 111.

REAGAN'S "GRAND HISTORICAL MOMENT"   Lou Cannon and Don Oberdorfer, "The Scripting of the Moscow Summit," *WP*, 6/9/88, p. A29.

SUMMIT FIRST DAY   Reagan on human rights and Berlin Wall: Reagan, *AAL*, p. 705–7. Canceled trip to Ziemans' apartment: Nancy Reagan, *My Turn*, p.

353–54; Ridgway telephone interview, 12/21/90. Arbat incident: Reagan, *AAL*, p. 709; Duberstein interview, 12/27/89; Lou Cannon and Don Oberdorfer, "The Superpowers' Struggle Over 'Peaceful Coexistence,' " *WP*, 6/3/88, p. A26.

RED SQUARE VISIT   Shultz's role in decision to visit Red Square: GS, 7/20/89. Details of Red Square walk: primarily from the report by White House spokesman Marlin Fitzwater released shortly thereafter and a pool report by Karen Gilmore of AP. Suzanne Massie's suggestion on recognizing Soviet women: Massie interview, 5/20/90. Tom Shales on the politicians and babies: Tom Shales, "Media Glasnost, Soviet Savvy," *WP* 6/1/88, p. B1. Evil empire being "another time, another era": quoted by Lou Cannon, in "Russians, Reagan: A Sizing Up," *WP*, 6/1/88 p. A1; Gorbachev cited it at his June 1 press conference. "*Da da*": White House pool report, Kremlin Pool B—Signing Ceremony, 5/31/88.

MOSCOW STATE UNVERSITY   Student comments: Gary Lee, "Students Find Reagan a Pleasant Surprise," *WP*, 6/1/88, p. A30; Gary Lee, "Public Impressed," *WP* 6/1/88/, p. A1.

STRUGGLE OVER "PRINCIPLES"   Powell's view: Cannon, *President Reagan*, p. 788. Simons's view: Simons interview, 7/6/89. Gorbachev's final argument and discussion: Cannon and Oberdorfer, "The Superpowers' Struggle," *WP*, 6/3/88; also GS, 7/20/89.

President Gorbachev

NINETEENTH PARTY CONFERENCE   History of party conferences: Eric F. Green, "The 19th Conference of the CPSU: Politics and Policy," American Committee on U.S.-Soviet Relations, Washington, November 1988.

FOREIGN MINISTRY "SCIENTIFIC AND PRACTICAL" CONFERENCE   Vorontsov quote: Vorontsov interview, 1/18/90. "In-house 'dissident' ": John Kohan, "The Boss of Smolensky Square," *Time*, 5/15/89, p. 32. Shevardnadze's speech can be found in *Soviet Diplomacy Today*, selections in English from *Vestnik* (USSR Ministry of Foreign Affairs, 1989), pp. 73–91. At some points I have used the FBIS translation as published in the *FBIS-SOV Annex*, 11/22/88. For a discussion of Shevardnadze and the military, see Van Oudenaren, "The Role of Shevardnadze," *Rand*, August 1990. Shevardnadze's closing speech was printed in the Foreign Ministry's publication *International Affairs*, October 1988, pp. 58–64.

POSTCONFERENCE POLICY STRUGGLE   Ligachev's and Yakovlev's speeches are quoted in Baruch A. Hazen, *Gorbachev's Gamble* (Westview Press, 1990), pp. 52–53.

GROMYKO'S RETIREMENT   Gromyko, *Memoirs*. For his intention, pp. xiii–xiv. His farewell speech is quoted on pp. 346–47.

In the Shadow of Lady Liberty

INVITATION TO GORBACHEV   This section is based on interviews with Shultz, Powell, and Ridgway.

GORBACHEV AT UNITED NATIONS   Khrushchev quotes and performance: Michael Beschloss, *Mayday* (Perennial Library, 1986), p. 338. Quotes from the Gorbachev speech are based on the English version provided by the Soviet Mission, as published in abridged form in *WP*, 11/8/88, plus additional quotes from Novosti Press Agency's English-language text, issued later. *NYT* editorial on Gorbachev and Wilson: *NYT*, 12/8/88, p. A34. Goodpaster quote: R. Jeffrey Smith and George C. Wilson, "Decision Welcomed in U.S.," *WP*, 12/8/88, p. A29. *Newsweek*'s comment: "Bush Gropes for a New Grand Strategy," *Newsweek*, 12/19/88, p. 29.

THE UNILATERAL CUTS   A report on the Soviet proposal for a unilateral Warsaw Pact troop cut appeared in Kay Withers, "Warsaw Pact Reportedly Cool to Gorbachev's Ideas," *Baltimore Sun*, 7/17/88, p. 4A. Statements on the start of planning in July 1988 were made on several occasions by Marshal Akhromeyev. On Shevardnadze's role and other aspects of the cutback, see Harry Gelman, "The Soviet Turn Toward Conventional Force Reduction," *Rand*, December 1989. The quote on the importance of tanks to the Soviet military officers was from a senior Soviet Foreign Ministry official, December 1990. The same source described Gorbachev's successful persuasion of Akhromeyev. For the influence of the economic and other political factors, see Gelman, "The Soviet Turn," *Rand*, December 1989.

GOVERNORS ISLAND MEETING   Preliminary quotes from Reagan, Bush, and Gorbachev: White House pool reports. Luncheon table quotes from Gorbachev about his purposes are from a 2/9/89 interview with Colin Powell, who attended as national security adviser. Shultz on Bush's reluctance and Gorbachev's "Jesus Christ" answer: GS, 7/20/89. Powell's "no surprises" admonition to Soviets: Powell interview 2/9/89. Luncheon toast quotes: "Last, and First," *Time*, 12/19/88, p. 22; Lou Cannon and Don Oberdorfer, "Good Feeling All Around at Gorbachev-Reagan-Bush Luncheon," *WP*, 12/8/88, p. A29. Bush's private statement to Gorbachev: Bush interview, 5/7/90. Reagan's diary entry: Reagan, *AAL*, p. 720. Telephone call from Ryzhkov on the ferry: see Gorbachev's interview with a correspondent of the *Journal News* of the Soviet Communist Party Central Committee, as distributed by the Soviet Embassy in Washington, 5/19/89.

The End of the Reagan Administration

U.S. PUBLIC OPINION   Data from *Americans Talk Security Compendium*, October 1987–December 1988, pp. 94, 109.

REAGAN'S FINAL BRIEFING   Cannon, *President Reagan*, p. 18.

THE SHULTZES ON INAUGURATION DAY   GS, 7/20/89.

CHAPTER 8: THE REVOLUTION OF 1989

Early Bush: A Cautious Consensus

BUSH'S CALL TO GORBACHEV   Bush discussed the telephone call in his first press conference, 1/27/89; see also White House Notice to the Press, 1/23/89. Duration of the call: from White House official, January 1991.

BACKGROUND OF BUSH   Scowcroft quote about Bush as a Rockefeller Republican and other data: Don Oberdorfer, "A Bush Foreign Policy," *WP*, 10/21/88, p. A1. Bush on "unrealistic" nature of Reykjavik: Bush interview 5/7/90. Dialogue with Craig Fuller on end of Cold War: Alessandra Stanley, "More Worldly Than Wise," *Time*, 8/15/88, p. 18. Bush's meeting with Shevardnadze before election: GS, 7/20/89. Quotes from campaign vs. Dukakis: remarks at University of Michigan, Dearborn, Michigan, 10/19/88. Dennis Ross on "hopeful but cautious" Bush: Ross interview, 9/30/88.

INITIAL POLICY REVIEW   Soviet-related section of review: *WP* and *NYT*, 4/9/89; also Patrick Tyler and R. Jeffrey Smith, "Bush Alerted in May to Soviet Military Cuts," *WP*, 12/11/89, p. A1. Bush on "a prudent review": David Hoffman, "Bush Dismisses Gorbachev Complaint," *WP*, 4/8/89, p. A14.

The Greening of Baker

AFGHAN CASUALTY FIGURES   Telephone interview with Thomas Gouttiere, director of the Center for Afghanistan Studies of University of Nebraska at Omaha, 1/7/91. Official Soviet figures: Col. V. Izgarshev, "Afghan Pain," *Pravda*, 8/17/89, quoted in *CD*, vol. XLI, no. 33, 1989, pp. 32–33. Unofficial estimate of Soviet losses: Gouttiere, on the basis of his Soviet contacts.

CENTRAL AMERICAN DIPLOMACY   An authoriative and useful source on Bush administration diplomacy with Moscow on this subject is Michael Kramer's long piece in *Time*, 6/4/90, p. 38, "Anger, Bluff—and Cooperation." This is the source of my quotations from the Bush letter to Gorbachev, the aides' memo to Baker and the Gorbachev letter to Bush.

BAKER-SHEVARDNADZE ON EASTERN EUROPE   Baker's quote to Friedman: Thomas L. Friedman, "Baker, Outlining World View, Assesses Plan for Soviet Bloc," *NYT*, 3/28/89, p. A1. Baker-Shevardnadze discussion on Eastern Europe: background briefing by State Department official on Baker's plane, en route from Moscow to Brussels, 5/11/89; also Ross interview, 10/30/90.

BAKER-GORBACHEV MEETING   This account of the Gorbachev-Baker meeting is drawn principally from a background briefing by an administration official on the flight from Shannon to Andrews Air Force Base, 5/12/89, and from the official Soviet account in *Pravda*, 2/12/89. Cheney's prediction: Molly Moore, "Cheney Predicts Gorbachev Will Fail, Be Replaced," *WP*, 4/29/89, p. A17. The Baker speech was to the Center for Strategic and International Studies, Washington, D.C., 5/4/89.

To the NATO Summit

WORLD IN FLUX My story on the future: Don Oberdorfer, "Eased East-West Tension Offers Chances, Dangers," *WP*, 5/7/89, p. A1.

BEYOND CONTAINMENT Rice interview, 11/6/90.

COAST GUARD SPEECH Bush's reaction and changes: based on a memorandum to me from David Hoffman, 6/8/89.

ORIGINS OF FORCE REDUCTION PROPOSAL Bush quotes from Oval Office, "I want this done": background interview with a participant in the meeting, 6/5/89. The 75,000-troop-cut plan and Crowe's role: George Wilson. "Bush Halved Proposal to Cut Forces," *WP*, 6/11/89, p. A1.

The Revolution of 1989

BREZHNEV DOCTRINE Mylynar on Brezhnev's thinking: Zdenek Mylynar, *Nightfrost in Prague* (Karz Publishers, 1980), p. 240. Brezhnev doctrine: Charles Gati, *The Bloc That Failed* (Indiana University Press, 1990), p. 73.

GORBACHEV'S "SINATRA DOCTRINE" Gerasimov quote: "Ol' Bushy Brows vs. Ol' Blue eyes," *Time*, 11/6/89, p. 42. Prague Club: William Luers, "Czechoslovakia: Road to Revolution," *Foreign Affairs*, Spring 1990, pp. 79–80; also interview with Aleksandr Tsipko, 11/16/90. "Little Gorbachevs": interview with a senior U.S. official, November 1990.

ORIGINS OF BLOC SELF-DETERMINATION See the remarks of Aleksandr Kapto of the Central Committee staff to the Foreign Ministry's Scientific and Practical Conference, as published in *International Affairs*, November 1988, p. 29. He refers to the November 1986 meeting and also to a memorandum drawn up by Gorbachev for the Politburo, apparently at that time. Ronald Asmus of the Rand Corporation, who has written extensively on the Soviet Union and Eastern Europe, believes there were two meetings with Eastern Europeans dealing with key aspects of their relationship and a Politburo meeting between the two at which major decisions were made. This possibly could have been the meeting of CEMA heads of government, including Soviet Prime Minister Ryzhkov, in Bucharest on 11/3/86, and the meeting of the Communist Party leaders of the CEMA countries in Moscow 11/11–12/86. Ligachev quote: Karen Dawisha, *Eastern Europe, Gorbachev and Reform* 2d edition (Cambridge University Press, 1990), p. 214. Ligachev told David Remnick after being ousted from the leadership that the Kremlin's "noninterference" stance in Eastern Europe had been decided in late 1985 and 1986; see David Remnick, "A Soviet Conservative Looks Back in Despair," *WP*, 10/15/90, p. A1.; Tsipko on Jaruzelski as model: Tsipko interview, 11/16/90.

UNRAVELING IN EASTERN EUROPE   Palmer observations: Palmer interview, 3/30/90.

CRISIS IN POLAND   Jaruzelski to Amb. Davis: Davis telephone interview 11/29/90; see also Gati, *The Bloc That Failed*, and the *WP* series "The Turning Points," published 1/14/90.

BUSH'S EASTERN EUROPE POLICIES   No gloating, no insistence on turning their backs: interview with a senior U.S. official, 11/6/90. Bush on not being there to "poke a stick": David Broder, "Bush to Push E. Europe Aid," *WP*, 7/14/89, p. A1.

BAKER-SHEVARDNADZE PARIS MEETING   Baker's comments and Shevardnadze's responses: background briefing by senior State Department officials, 7/29/89, amplified by Baker interview, 11/10/89.

GORBACHEV-RAKOWSKI CALL   A. D. Horne, "Gorbachev Urges Communists to Join Solidarity Government," *WP*, 8/23/89, p. A1; Francis X. Clines, "Gorbachev Calls, Then Polish Party Drops Its Demands," *NYT*, 8/23/89, A1. The *Los Angeles Times* account was written by Michael Parks for the issue of 12/17/89. Bush's comments: David Hoffman, "Bush Lauds Gorbachev Stand on Polish Government," *WP*, 8/24/89, p. A26. Rakowski's version was furnished by him in Polish-language galleys of his memoirs provided to me in March 1991.

HAVEL ON RULES OF THE GAME   William Echikson, *Lighting the Night* (William Morrow, 1990), p. 69.

HUNGARY'S DECISIONS   Blaine Harden, "Refugees Force a Fateful Choice," *WP*, 1/14/90; Kovacs interview in Budapest, 1/3/90.

EAST GERMANY DEVELOPMENTS   Krenz's call to Gorbachev: Marc Fisher, "One Year Later, World Is Learning How Berlin Wall Opened," *WP*, 11/10/90, p. A23. Moscow reaction at fall of Wall as seen by Tsipko: Tsipko interview, 11/16/90.

U.S. PUBLIC OPINION   Poll data: Daniel Yankelovich, *Coming to Public Judgment* (Syracuse University Press, 1991), pp. 146–47. "Focus group" data: Public Agenda Foundation, New York.

GORBACHEV'S MESSAGE TO BUSH   From a U.S. official source, 12/17/90, and background interviews with two other U.S. officials in December 1990.

Heading Toward Malta

BUSH'S DECISION TO MEET GORBACHEV   Bush interview, 5/7/90; conversations with Baker and Scowcroft.

BAKER-SHEVARDNADZE MEETING IN PARIS   From a background briefing by senior State Department officials, 7/29/89, plus additional interviews with U.S. officials in 1990.

IMPORTANCE OF JACKSON LAKE MEETING   Baker comment: Baker interview, 6/27/90; Shevardnadze comment: Shevardnadze interview, 1/17/90.

ARMS CONTROL ISSUES   Karpov on "fruitless haggling": Karpov interview, 1/9/90. The military resistance to the dismantling of Krasnoyarsk: interview with a Central Committee staff member, April 1990.

The Shipboard Summit

BUSH VIEW OF GORBACHEV   "This guy *is perestroika*": interview with a senior Bush adviser, 4/23/90.

SHIPBOARD MEETING   "As we follow events": from a U.S. source at the table, quoted in Don Oberdorfer and Ann Devroy, "Bush Offers Soviets Concessions on Arms, Trade," *WP*, 12/2/89, p. A1. Gorbachev's responses to Bush: interviews with a White House official, 12/5/89 and 12/27/90. On Central America, "thorn in your shoe" quote: from a U.S. participant, quoted in Oberdorfer and Devroy, "Bush Offers Soviets Concessions," *WP*, 12/2/89. Yuri Pavlov's quote: Kramer, "Anger, Bluff," *Time*, 6/4/90.

SOVIET VIEW OF U.S. "ENEMY"   Shevardnadze on the previous aim of forcing out U.S. from Europe and "milestone" and "bold words" quotes of Shevardnadze: *Izvestia*, 2/19/90, as reprinted in *CD*, vol. XLII, no. 7, 1990, p. 16. "Milestone" and discussion of U.S. as enemy: interviews with State and NSC participants at Malta, Yakovlev interview, 1/12/90; see also Hugh Sidey, "A Game of One-on-One," *Time*, 12/18/89, and Michael Dobbs, "Summit Goal Said to Set U.S.-Soviet Timetable," *WP*, 11/18/89, p. A17.

WARSAW PACT SUMMIT MEETING   Description of the meeting is principally based on notes taken at the time by an Eastern European participant and made available to me in early 1990.

CHAPTER 9. A NEW ERA

SIGNS OF CHANGE   Description of New Year's Day observances in Moscow: *CD*, vol. XLII, no. 1, 1990, p. 31. The Atlantic Council study is Lewis W. Bowden and James A. Duran Jr., *Perestroika Update* (The Atlantic Council of the United States, January 1990). Prokhanov's attack: quoted in Van Oudenaren, "The Role of Shevardnadze," *Rand*, July 1990. Brovikov's statement: *CD*, vol. XLII, no. 6, 1990, p. 8; and Van Oudenaren, "The Role of Shevardnadze," *Rand*, August 1990. Shevardnadze's response: Eduard Shevardnadze, "Everything in the World Is Changing at Dizzying Speed," *Izvestia*, 2/19/90, quoted in *CD*, vol. XLII, no. 7, 1990, p. 36. Ligachev quote: from the transcript of the plenum issued in Moscow at the time. Yakovlev quotes: press conference, 2/7/90, which I attended.

German Arithmetic: Two Plus Four

EUROPEAN CONCERNS   Dutch quote to *Time*: Bruce W. Nelan, "East Meets West at Last," *Time*, 2/26/90, p. 15.

U.S. VIEW OF SOVIET ROLE   Zoellick on need for a mechanism: Zoellick interview, 12/4/90.

BAKER-GORBACHEV MEETING   The description of the 2/9/90 meeting is derived from background interviews with Baker party officials at the time and later, and from Baker's description in his letter to Kohl, 2/10/90. Gorbachev's statements to Kohl: "M. S. Gorbachev Meets with H. Kohl," *Pravda*, 2/11/90, as published in *CD*, vol. XLI, no. 6, 1990, p. 23.

Lithuania: The Gas-Filled Room

LITHUANIAN SITUATION   My impressions are based in large part on my trip to Vilnius, 1/27-29/90. The recounting of the exciting events since October 1988 owes much to a 1/28/90 talk in Vilnius with Arvydas Zygas, a visiting Fulbright exchange professor from the University of Illinois.

WASHINGTON REACTIONS   I have relied heavily on the *WP* coverage of the Lithuania crisis. See esp. David Hoffman and Don Oberdorfer, "Bush Heeds Visitors to Moscow," *WP*, 3/30/90, p. A1, from which the Hungary analogy is taken. Condolleeza Rice quote on "gas-filled room": Rice interview.

The Rise of the Soviet Military

MILITARY ARGUMENTS AGAINST COMPROMISE   The "military-industrial complex" revolt against "unacceptable" compromises: interview with a Central Committee official, April 1990. Shevardnadze's remarks about resistance to compromises: "Shevardnadze Addresses Foreign Ministry on Policy," *Literaturnaya Gazeta*, 4/18/90, as translated and published in *FBIS-SOV*, 4/26/90, p. 10.

SHEVARDNADZE'S RESIGNATION THREAT   See Shevardnadze interviews in *Ogonek*, no. 11, 3/14–17/90, and on Moscow television's *View* program, 4/13/90 (*FBIS-SOV*, 4/16/90, pp. 51–53); also Julia Wishnevsky, "Shevardnadze Said to Have Threatened to Resign in Dispute Over Tbilisi Commission," *Radio Liberty Research*, 2/2/90, pp. 1–3.

BAKER-GORBACHEV MEETING   This is based primarily on my reporting at the time, amplified by interviews with U.S. officials during book research.

Gorbachev in Washington: The 1990 Summit

CHANGING U.S. PUBLIC OPINION   U.S. opinion: T. R. Reid, "Giving Gorbachev Credit," *WP*, 5/27/90, p. A1. "Enemy" and "friendly" poll data: Yankelovich, *Coming to Public Judgment*, p. 146.

SOVIET PUBLIC OPINION   Andrei Melvil and Aleksandr Nikitin, "The End of the Consensus That Never Was: The Future of Soviet-American Relations as Viewed by the Soviet Public," in *Mutual Security*, edited by Richard Smoke and Andrei Kortunov (St. Martin's Press, 1991).

GORBACHEV'S SWOLLEN ENTOURAGE   Geneva and Washington 1987 figures: *Mikhail S. Gorbachev, An Intimate Biography*, pp. 175–76. Figures in 1990: from a senior State Department official, 6/15/90.

DISCUSSIONS OF GERMANY   Shifting Soviet views: Suzanne Crow, "The Changing Soviet View of German Unification," *Report on the USSR*, Radio Liberty, vol. 2, no. 31, 1990.

WHITE HOUSE DISCUSSIONS OF BUSH AND GORBACHEV   This section is based on interviews with White House and State Department officials immediately after the summit and later in 1990, and on Jim Hoagland, "Bush-Gorbachev Talks: A View to the Future," *WP*, 6/3/90, p. A24. See also the summit wrap-up by myself and David Hoffman, "Behind the Scenes at Summit," *WP*, 6/5/90, p. A1.

GORBACHEV'S EXCHANGE WITH WASHINGTON CROWD   Dana Priest and Brooke A. Masters, " 'I Feel Really at Home Here,' " *WP*, 6/1/90, p. A1.

MEETING AT CAMP DAVID   Gorbachev's impressions of the helicopter ride: "Gorbachev Answers Deputies' Questions 12 June," *FBIS-SOV* 6/13/90, p. 46. The Camp David discussions were described in detail by several U.S. participants, who asked not to be quoted by name.

POSTSUMMIT SHIFT ON GERMAN POLICY   Interviews with administration officials, December 1990; see also Marc Fisher and David Hoffman, "Behind German Unity Pact," *WP*, 7/22/90, p. A1.

DEPARTURE FROM WASHINGTON   White House press pool reports of 6/3/90.

CHAPTER 10. THE END OF THE SOVIET UNION

INITIAL MEETINGS ON THE GULF WAR   Baker and Shevardnadze quotes are
from Baker's remarks at the Princeton University–Baker Institute Conference
on "Cold War Endgame," Princeton, N.J., 3/30/96 and from Baker's memoir,
The Politics of Diplomacy (Putnam, 1995). Soviet-Iraq data are from Elaine
Sciolino, *The Outlaw State* (Wiley, 1991), pp. 141, 144–47. Saddam quotes to
Kelly are from Don Oberdorfer, "Missed Signals in the Middle East," *WP
Magazine*, 3/17/91. Tarasenko and endangered Soviet children, from Tarasenko
remarks at Princeton Cold War Endgame conference.

SUMMIT IN HELSINKI   Gorbachev-Aziz quotes are from Anatoly Chernyaev's
remarks at the Princeton Cold War Endgame conference and from Gorbachev's
Memoirs (Doubleday, 1996), pp. 552–53. Bush-Gorbachev summit quotes are
from the Soviet transcript of the meeting (in Russian), to which my translator
and I were given access at the Gorbachev Foundation, Moscow, 10/4/96.
Gorbachev appeal for Saudi funds: Baker memoir, pp. 294–95.

AUTHORIZING THE WAR   Palazchenko observation on Shevardnadze:
Palazchenko, *My Years with Gorbachev and Shevardnadze* (Penn State Univ.
Press), 1997, p. 218. Shevardnadze on "two foreign policies" Michael Beschloss
and Strobe Talbott, *At the Highest Levels* (Little Brown, 1993), p. 271. Baker on
Graves briefing: Baker memoir, p. 310. Baker cable to Bush, from his memoir,
p. 313.

SHEVARDNADZE RESIGNS   Baker recollection of Shevardnadze on "absolute
crisis": Beschloss and Talbott, p. 296. Quotes from Baker letter to Shevardnadze
from letter dated 2/20/91, released at the Princeton Endgame conference.
Revelation on Moscow meeting on Vilnius crackdown: Michael Dobbs, *Down
with Big Brother* (Knopf, 1997), pp. 346–47.

DIPLOMACY AND WAR   Baker quote to Bessmertnykh: Baker memoir, p. 380.
Gorbachev to Matlock: Jack F. Matlock Jr., *Autopsy on an Empire* (Random
House, 1995), p. 471. Additional quotes are from Russian excerpts of
Chernayev's memoir, *Six Years with Gorbachev* (in Russian), translated for the
Princeton Cold War Endgame conference. Baker on "no room for negotiation":
his comments at Princeton conference. Bush to Gorbachev, "time is running
out": Gorbachev memoir, p. 561. Bush-Gorbachev final telephone conversation,
from Russian transcript made available at Gorbachev Foundation, 10/4/96.

UNRAVELING OF SOVIET POWER   CIA document, *The Soviet Cauldron*, 4/25/91,
was declassified and released for the Princeton Cold War Endgame conference.
Quote from Yeltsin inauguration: Matlock memoir, p. 522. On the United States
alerting Gorbachev on coup threat, see Matlock, Baker, Beschloss-Talbott, and
Princeton Cold War Endgame transcript.

FINAL SUMMIT   Bush on Yanayev: Beschloss and Talbott, p. 416. Quotes from
Chernyaev notes on Gorbachev-Bush in London: Matlock memoir, p. 553.
Gorbachev to Bush on "strategic stability" in Moscow, from Russian transcript

made available at Gorbachev Foundation, 10/4/96. START reductions: Raymond L. Garthoff, *The Great Transition* (Brookings, 1994), p. 466.

COUP AND COUNTER COUP   Most useful sources were Dobbs, *Down with Big Brother;* Matlock, *Autopsy on an Empire;* Beschloss-Talbott, *At the Highest Levels;* Gorbachev's *Memoirs,* and his earlier book, *The August Coup* (Harper-Collins, 1991), from which quotes and details were taken.

THE FINAL DAYS   Grachev quote is from his *Final Days* (Westview, 1995), p. 50. Baker on Gorbachev being "unfocused": Baker memoir, p. 559. Gorbachev quotes to Shushkevich: Dobbs, p. 445. Yeltsin on "Welcome to this Russian Building": Baker memoir, p. 570. Baker meeting with Gorbachev: Baker memoir, pp. 474–77. Gorbachev telephone call to Bush on 12/25/71, Beschloss-Talbott, pp. 461–63.

INDEX